The Indians' New World

The Indians' New World

Catawbas and Their Neighbors
from European Contact through
the Era of Removal

James H. Merrell

WITHDRAWN

Published for the Institute of
Early American History and Culture,
Williamsburg, Virginia
By the University of North Carolina Press,
Chapel Hill and London

Publication of this book has been supported, in part, by a donation from FIGGIE INTERNATIONAL, INC. in memory of the former Governor of Virginia, JOHN N. DALTON.

The Institute of Early American History and Culture is sponsored jointly by the College of William and Mary and the Colonial Williamsburg Foundation.

Library of Congress Cataloging-in-Publication Data

Merrell, James Hart, 1953–
    The Indians' new world: Catawbas and their neighbors from European contact through the era of removal / James H. Merrell.
        p. cm.
    Bibliography: p.
    Includes index.
    ISBN 0-8078-1832-1
    1. Catawba Indians—History. 2. Catawba Indians—Social conditions. 3. Indians of North America—South Carolina—History. 4. Indians of North America—North Carolina—History. 5. Indians of North America—South Carolina—Social conditions. 6. Indians of North America—North Carolina—Social conditions. I. Institute of Early American History and Culture (Williamsburg, Va.) II. Title.
E99.C24I53   1989   88-22658
975.6'00497—dc19   CIP

This volume received indirect support from an unrestricted book publications grant awarded to the Institute by the L. J. Skaggs and Mary C. Skaggs Foundation of Oakland, California.

Figure 1. Colonist. 1771. *Courtesy of South Caroliniana Library*
Figure 2. Catawba Warrior (Captain Redhead?). 1771. *Courtesy of South Caroliniana Library*

To My Parents
Jessie Clark Merrell
David John Merrell

Permissions

Portions of this manuscript have appeared or will soon appear in print. I am grateful to the editors or publishers for permission to reproduce those portions here:

"Reading 'An Almost Erased Page': A Reassessment of Frank G. Speck's Catawba Studies," American Philosophical Society, *Proceedings*, CXXVII (1983).

"The Brafferton Experiment," *William and Mary: The Alumni Gazette Magazine*, LII (1984).

"The Indians' New World: The Catawba Experience," *William and Mary Quarterly*, 3d Ser., XLI (1984).

"'Minding the Business of the Nation': Hagler as Catawba Leader," *Ethnohistory*, XXXIII (1986).

"'This Western World': The Evolution of the Piedmont, 1525–1725," in Roy S. Dickens, Jr., *et al.*, eds., *The Siouan Project: Seasons I and II*, Research Laboratories of Anthropology, University of North Carolina Monograph Series, no. 1 (Chapel Hill, N.C., 1987).

"'Their Very Bones Shall Fight': The Catawba-Iroquois Wars," in Daniel K. Richter and James H. Merrell, eds., *Beyond the Covenant Chain: The Iroquois and Their Neighbors in Indian North America, 1600–1800* (Syracuse, N.Y., 1987).

"'Our Bond of Peace': Patterns of Intercultural Exchange in the Southern Piedmont, 1650–1750," in Peter H. Wood *et al.*, eds., *Powhatan's Mantle: Southeastern Indians in the Colonial Era* (Lincoln, Nebr., 1989).

Preface

In tracing the origin of a people, where there are
no records of any kind, either written, or engraved,
who rely solely on oral tradition for the support of
their antient usages, and have lost great part of them—
though the undertaking be difficult, yet. . . . where
we have not the light of history, or records, to guide
us through the dark maze of antiquity, we must
endeavour to find it out by probable arguments.

—James Adair

ON HEARING that I am working on a study of the Catawba Indians and their neighbors in early America, people often ask whether this is Indian history or colonial American history. My glib, stock answer—"Yes"—started out as a defensive measure; in the initial stages of my research I was by no means certain of the correct reply, and the question was fostering something of a professional identity crisis. With time, however, as I heard the same query again and again, I began to think that maybe something was wrong, not with my answer, but with the question. It presumed a barrier between Indians and everyone else in early America that my reading of the sources did not turn up.

The question has come up so often, I suspect, because the notion that Indians are somehow separate from the history of colonial America—indeed, of all America—is so common. Too accustomed to picturing native Americans in our own day as a tiny minority inhabiting remote lands under federal supervision, we are prone to think that it has always been this way. The Indians' story seems so distinct from America's, set off as sharply as a reservation's boundary on a map, that it is hard to make the imaginative leap necessary to envision them in an earlier age, when most of the continent was Indian country. In order to restore natives to their proper place in our historical consciousness, it might help to consider certain instructive similarities in the lives of all peoples occupying eastern North America during the colonial era. Exploring the Indians' new world is one way to begin that task.

The concept is useful in part because it already holds an exalted place in our historical vocabulary. The idea that Americans lived in a New World has always been the foundation of efforts to interpret this country's development. From Frederick Jackson Turner to David Grayson Allen, from Melville J. Herskovits to Daniel C. Littlefield, scholars have analyzed encounters between people from the Old World and conditions in the New, studying the interplay between European or African cultures and the American environment.

It seems logical to ignore Indians when examining these issues; after all, they did not cross an ocean to inhabit some faraway land. But modern research suggests that a lengthy sea voyage was not always what separated one world from another. Many settlers in New England recreated familiar forms with such success that they did not really face an alien environment until long after their arrival. Africans, on the other hand, were struck by the shock of the new at the moment of their enslavement, well before they stepped on board ship or set foot on American soil. If the Atlantic was not a barrier between one world and another, if what happened to people was more a matter of subtle cultural process than mere physical displacement, perhaps we should set aside the maps for a moment and think instead of a "world" as the physical and cultural milieu within which people live and a "new world" as a dramatically different milieu, demanding basic changes in that way of life. Considered in these terms, the experience of natives more closely resembled that of immigrants and slaves, and the idea of an encounter between worlds can—indeed, must—include the aboriginal inhabitants of America.

For American Indians a new order emerged in several overlapping stages. First, alien microbes killed untold numbers of natives, sometimes before the victims had seen a white or a black face. Next came traders who exchanged European technology for Indian products and brought native groups into the Atlantic market. In time traders gave way to colonial settlers eager to develop the land according to their own lights. And amid these intrusions— here carrying the first diseases, there arriving with the traders, elsewhere not showing up until after the settlers—were missionaries bent on winning souls for Christ. These invasions combined to transform native American existence after 1492, disrupting established cultural forms and requiring creative responses to drastically altered surroundings. Like their new neighbors, then, Indians had to blend old and new in ways that would permit them to survive in the present and prepare for the future without utterly forsaking their past. By the close of the colonial era, native peoples as well as whites and blacks had created new societies, each similar to, yet very different from, its parent culture.

Indians coped with changed circumstances in as many different ways as Africans or Europeans did, and by singling out Catawbas for scrutiny I hold no brief for their typicality. These people represent only a narrow band in the broad spectrum of native responses; nonetheless, the Catawbas' response is revealing. Neither distant from the intruders nor destroyed by them, Catawbas experienced —and survived—a wide variety of European contacts, from lethal diseases, pushy traders, and exotic goods to government officials, colonial settlers, and enthusiastic preachers. Hence their history can illustrate the consequences of the invasion of America and illuminate one way natives learned to live in their own new world.

While the Indians' new world forms the larger context for my study, those who look for detailed comparisons with other inhabitants of early America will search in vain. I have resisted the temptation to call attention to every similarity or point out every difference in the experiences of Catawbas and colonists, Catawbas and blacks, Catawbas and other Indians. My task here is more modest: to tell how this particular people dealt with dramatically different conditions from its first contact with Europeans and Africans until the adjustment was largely complete some three hundred years later. The idea that these circumstances constituted a new world, that everyone else in America at the time faced comparable (albeit not identical) challenges will, I hope, resonate through the pages to follow and set the reader thinking about connections hitherto obscure. But the story itself is my primary concern.

In its general outlines this story conforms to the course of native development plotted by Robert Berkhofer in a 1971 article, "The Political Context of a New Indian History." Lamenting "the simple decline and death theme so prevalent in the writing of Indian history," Berkhofer asked scholars to be more sensitive to "multiple declines and renascences," and he cited Anthony Wallace's classic study, *The Death and Rebirth of the Seneca*, to show how "the history of a tribe can be seen as a series of renascences according to varying forms of activity which revitalize and reorient Indian life." No Catawba version of the Seneca prophet Handsome Lake has come to light. Nonetheless, Catawbas, too, etched an uneven trail across the generations, as survivors of epidemics sought to cope with the arrival of eager traders, the demands of distant officials, the pressures of nearby planters, and the blandishments of devout Christians. Following that trail, I take a topical approach within a chronological format, probing how each intrusion threatened old ways and forced Indians to rearrange their lives in accordance with new imperatives. If the ebb and flow of challenge and response, crisis and calm, disintegration and reformation gives Catawba history something of a rollercoaster rhythm, it is, I think, more attuned to the pattern of the past than the tragically plummeting trajectory so commonly charted.

In tracing the ups and downs of Catawba history I emphasize both Catawbas and their neighbors. Besides permitting me to include Europeans and Africans, a wider angle of vision adheres more closely to native realities. The Indians colonists in the eighteenth century came to call "the Catawba Nation" actually included not only Catawbas (a term that was itself rarely used before 1700) but many smaller communities that once had been scattered through the southern piedmont. To understand the Catawba story we must also understand theirs, and I have adopted a regional approach that aims to transcend narrow (and still poorly understood) ethnic or tribal boundaries. These piedmont Indians shared a cultural tradition and a history; they responded to European contact in similar fashion and, ultimately, moved to the Catawba

River valley to become part of the Catawba Nation we know today. A broader perspective, which gradually moves in to focus on the Catawba Nation as it became in turn the focus of life in the region, is part of my attempt to abandon hindsight and adopt the actors' point of view.

In fact, of course, the only task more difficult than abandoning hindsight is adopting the actors' point of view. All historians face this problem, few more than students of native America, and perhaps none more than those studying Catawbas and other piedmont communities. Little of what might be called the mind or inner life of these Indians survives. How they worshipped their gods, how they reckoned kinship, how they chose names for their children— these and many other aspects of native life have been all but erased from memory. Not one of the missionaries who visited the upcountry bothered to map the realm of thought and behavior he sought to replace, and most traders, officials, and settlers had no interest in keeping a record of Indian ways. Moreover, those few outsiders curious enough to ask the natives questions often ran head-on into a wall of silence. In 1709 the explorer John Lawson complained that "many other Customs they have, for which they will render no Reason or Account; . . . there are a great many of their Absurdities, which, for some Reason, they reserve as a Secret amongst themselves." The trader James Adair, after living for several decades among Catawbas and other southeastern peoples, also grumbled about "the secrecy and closeness of the Indians as to their own affairs."

By necessity, then, what follows is only part of the story. Though I do not always insert the requisite (and cumbersome) qualifiers, it should be said at the outset that even the story I have managed to piece together is at times speculative. Where I felt lost in Adair's "dark maze of antiquity" without clear evidence to guide me, I have tried to find my way out by the light of his "probable arguments." Like him, like Lawson, I have poked around, asked questions, tried to find out as much as I can about Catawbas and their neighbors in hopes of penetrating the silence. But silence remains.

Contents

Illustrations

Maps

Figures

The Indians' New World

Prologue

The Flower of Carolina:
John Lawson's Journey

The Savages do, indeed, still possess the Flower
of *Carolina*, the *English* enjoying
only the Fag-end of that fine Country.
                                    —John Lawson

IN THE spring of 1700 an Englishman named John Lawson decided to see the world. No set itinerary cluttered up his plans; he
later recalled that his "Intention, at that Time," was simply "to
travel." A chance meeting with one more experienced in such
things turned Lawson's thoughts away from Rome and convinced
him "that *Carolina* was the best Country I could go to." The rest was
easy. A ship stood ready in the Thames, Lawson booked passage,
and by the end of the summer he was sightseeing in Charleston.
Neither the South Carolina capital's charms nor the hospitality of
its citizenry could hold Lawson for long, however. Before the year
was out, the restless traveler set off again, this time on an overland
journey to North Carolina in the company of five colonists and
four Indians.[1]

During the next two months Lawson and his companions canoed
or walked more than five hundred miles through the heart of what
would later be known as Catawba Country. The rigors of travel in
the middle of winter did nothing to dampen Lawson's enthusiasm,
for in the Carolina interior he at last found a feast to satisfy his
appetite for adventure. "Every Step present[s] some new Object,"
he wrote a month after leaving Charleston, "which still adds Invitation to the Traveller in these Parts." The landscape itself was literally wonderful. In the coastal plain the travelers slogged through

vast pine barrens and swamps of cane or cypress, all of it covered by the worst flooding in local memory. Wet and weary, they were only too glad to leave the Santee Valley and head into the piedmont along the east side of the Wateree River. There savannas replaced swamps, the path hugged the ridges rather than the valleys, and the monotony of sand and pine gave way to rich soil with oak trees so tall that a turkey roosting in their upper branches was safe from the hunters' guns.[2]

Besides "great gangs" of these enormous birds, both lowcountry and uplands were populated by enough animals to occupy a naturalist for several lifetimes. "Panthers, Tygers, Wolves, and other Beasts of Prey" crossed Lawson's path and sometimes shared his campsite, piercing the dark with their cries. Most species were less threatening but no less interesting. Swarms of ravenous insects, several peculiar-looking ducks, passenger pigeons in flocks so large that they broke off branches of trees at night and blocked the sun by day—these were but a small sample of the creatures Lawson became acquainted with in the course of his journey.[3]

Fascinated as he was by the land and wildlife, Lawson's attention was drawn again and again to the human inhabitants of the interior. He came upon Indians everywhere—from hunting quarters in the woods to clusters of bark houses scattered along upland streams to large towns, many palisaded, some with impressive thatched council houses that could hold dozens of people—and everywhere they were the object of his scrutiny. With their tawny color embellished by paint or tattoos, their long fingernails, their dark eyes "marbled with red Streaks," their hair coated with grease and fixed into assorted shapes, Carolina natives appeared strange, even fantastic, to one more accustomed to the citizenry of London or Charleston.[4]

Lawson soon learned that these people were every bit as different from him as they looked. All were friendly, offering food and lodging (and sometimes female companions) for the night; but native hospitality had its drawbacks. While the exploring party found many Indian dishes delicious, the mere sight of other delicacies— fawns "taken out of the Doe's Bellies, and boil'd in the same slimy Bags Nature had plac'd them in" or "one of the Country-Hares, stew'd with the Guts in her Belly, and her Skin with the Hair on"—

could kill the appetite of the hungriest guest. After a meal the travelers might bed down on comfortable cane benches in the best dwelling a village could boast; some nights, however, the quarters were so cramped, smoky, and flea-infested that Lawson yearned for a breath of the frigid January air. Even the "trading girls" that a village leader placed at the disposal of an honored visitor proved a mixed blessing. Among the Waxhaws one of Lawson's companions was only too happy to abide by local custom until he discovered the next morning that his "dear Spouse" had made off with all of his belongings. Twice shy, the travelers found that the consequences of ignoring native etiquette could be as unpleasant as observing it. When, three days later, they declined a Catawba chief's offer of a girl, "his Majesty flew into a violent Passion, to be thus slighted, telling the *Englishmen*, they were good for nothing."[5] Every new settlement held out the prospect of delight—or disaster.

Once Lawson had been properly welcomed and Indians returned to their own affairs, they behaved even more oddly. For two hours he peered over the shoulders of some Congaree women "very busily engag'd in Gaming," and still he could not figure out the rules. Several days later the travelers entered a Waxhaw town on the day of an important ceremony to celebrate the harvest and pray for success with the next planting. Lawson sat through the night in the hot, dark "State-House," ate his fill, gaped at the "frightful Postures" of masked Indian dancers, and listened while two old men filled the thick air with songs and stories. Experiences like these did nothing to diminish Lawson's capacity for astonishment. When a violent wind struck the Saponi town one night toward the end of the trip, he staggered from his bed to watch in amazement as the village chief calmed the storm.[6]

Local variety added dazzling colors and bizarre shapes to the Indian life Lawson saw. Though the fifteen groups his party visited shared certain fundamental similarities, no two peoples were alike. Keyauwee men grew beards. Most of the inhabitants of "the Lower Quarter" were for some reason missing an eye. Lawson judged Congaree women among the prettiest, Waxhaws—"call'd by their Neighbours flat Heads" because they practiced head deformation —the ugliest. And differences, like beauty, could be more than skin-deep. "Dispositions" varied from place to place, as did lan-

Map 1. Carolina and Virginia, circa 1700. *Colonial settlement distribution adapted from Herman R. Friis,* A Series of Population Maps of the Colonies and the United States, 1625–1790, *rev. ed. (New York, 1968). Drawn by Linda Merrell*

guages, which tended to change every few miles. It was impossible to become bored.[7]

Taken aback by the natives' diversity, Lawson was also surprised by the extent to which Indians traveled about Carolina. He met a Congaree living with the Keyauwees, an Indian trader from south of Charleston heading toward Esaw territory, Tutelos among the Saponis, and a Saponi ambassador at the Waxhaw town. These and others were the lifeblood of a communication system that apprised people of events both near and far. Catawbas had heard of Lawson's approach three weeks before his men finally marched into their settlement, and once he arrived they were able to warn him about Iroquois war parties then on the Virginia frontier. Lawson soon learned that these enemy warriors already had taken their toll in the upcountry. In the Yadkin River valley he met Saponis about to join Tutelos and Keyauwees for protection against the raiders sweeping down from the north. Farther along the trail Shakoris and Enos had moved into a single town some time before, dimming the colors and blunting the shapes spawned by localism.[8]

Like enemy war parties, colonial traders were exerting a profound influence on native life when Lawson passed through the interior. Apart from one of the men in his company, who had been among the Sewees and Santees, traders were surprisingly scarce in the winter of 1701. The visitor from Charleston met a Virginian named John Stewart among the Catawbas and later crossed paths with four more men from the James River leading a packhorse train into the uplands.[9] But if fellow colonists were rare, signs of their presence were not. Every village bore the imprint of European contact, whether it be the mixed-blood children running about or the rum Lawson's Indian guides drank too much of. Even more obvious than offspring or alcohol was the evidence of the new diseases that traders had unwittingly carried into native communities. Indians near the coast were the most severely afflicted, but all of the nations trading with the English had recently been visited by smallpox.[10]

It did not take Lawson long to recognize that the trade had shaped native existence in more subtle ways. Nearby nations were not only "well-humour'd and affable" but also "very tractable" because their proximity to Anglo-America had left them dependent on English goods. South Carolina officials, well aware of trade's power, were seeking to include more distant villages within its magic circle. Among the Esaws a war captain told Lawson that the colony's governor, James Moore, had demanded ten skins from each town in the area, a ploy designed to open diplomatic relations, bring Esaws into Charleston's orbit, and eventually make them as "tractable" as Santees.[11]

While Moore talked of tribute, Lawson lost himself in dreams of a time when Indians would be gone and colonists could take over. Almost daily, the explorer assessed the land's prospects. Could this soil be tilled? Would these rocks make sturdy fences, or those over there good millstones? Was this creek navigable? Can these narrow valleys, sheltered from the wind, support grapes or other fruit? Could this savanna, those canebrakes, that upland field be turned into range for cattle, hogs, sheep, goats, horses? The answer was usually an excited yes, "provided the *English* were seated thereon." Lawson's enthusiasm knew no bounds; he even considered buying the Saponi town on the Yadkin, which the Indians had offered to sell him because he talked so much about settling there.[12]

In the end the explorer turned the Saponis down. Lawson was an optimist, not a fool; he knew that his grand schemes were years, even decades, from fulfillment. The plans he drew up, talked over, and jotted down were not just promotional gimmicks, however. They helped him render an exotic place less strange and less frightening. By picturing the region shorn of its aboriginal inhabitants and tamed by men like himself, he could escape for a moment the hard fact that both the land and its people—fascinating though they were—appeared savage indeed.

Lawson strove to make himself (and his reader) more comfortable still by comparing "this new world" with "the *European* world" he had left behind. Bushes yielded berries "much like to our Blues, or Huckle-berries, that grows on Heaths in *England*." Rivers were the size of the Derwent in Yorkshire or the Thames near Kingston. Bags of sand Waxhaws used to flatten an infant's head were "such as Engravers use to rest their Plates upon," and dancers there made a "stamping Motion, much like the treading upon Founders Bellows."[13]

But neither comparisons between Old World and New nor dreams of Carolina without the Indians succeeded in making Lawson feel at home. His travels taught him that nothing—not traders, not viruses, not imperious messages from the capital—had put an end to native control of Carolina. Colonists might visit upland towns for a day, a week, a month or two; but as the frontier folk along the Santee warned Lawson when he stopped there on his way upriver, the land ahead was still "a Country inhabited by none but Savages." Relying on a far-flung web of contacts that kept them informed of events from Virginia to the Savannah River and from the coast to the mountains, Indians were masters of the piedmont. Hunters and traders, ambassadors and priests, dancers and warriors, gamblers and lovers peopled the stage Lawson crossed, living out their lives according to their own customs. Hanging onto the "Fag-end" of Carolina in a geographical sense, he and his contemporaries were marginal men in a cultural sense as well.[14] Along the coast the English ruled; when colonists ventured beyond the European settlements, native ways prevailed.

Lawson's journey, while offering a glimpse into the Carolina interior, also brought to light the elements that would shape piedmont life over the next century. The infiltration of alien traders, alien goods, and alien diseases; the threat of Iroquois attack; the disintegration and reformation of native identities; the simultaneous contact with Virginia and South Carolina; the spread of colonial settlement; the Catawba chief's inability to make the new men conform to local customs, and his angry condemnation of the foreigners' ignorance—all of these themes, played out during Lawson's brief visit in the winter of 1701, would recur again and again in the seasons to come. While coping with his own transition from a European to an Indian world, Lawson witnessed the stirrings of a more general movement in precisely the opposite direction.

1

A People from under the World: Europeans and Other Intruders

We demanded why they came in that manner
to betray us, that came to them in peace, and to
seeke their loves; he answered, they heard we were a
people come from under the world, to take their
world from them.

—Conversation between John Smith
and Amoroleck, a Mannahoac Indian

ONE hundred sixty years before John Lawson took ship for America, the Spanish explorer Hernando de Soto plunged into what is now central South Carolina in search of the Cofitachiques, a powerful Indian nation he had been hearing about for months. De Soto, who had served in South America under Francisco Pizarro, was now driven ever deeper into the unknown by rumors that the Cofitachiques' riches rivaled those of the Incan city Cuzco.[1] On May 1, 1540, after weeks of grueling travel, he and his army stood gazing over a river at the Cofitachique capital. Summoned by the shouts of the expedition's guides, six headmen crossed over and cautiously approached the Spaniards. The explorer called for the "rest seat" he carried with him specifically to "receive the curacas and emissaries with a gravity and embellishment befitting the grandeur of his station." Then, bowing once to the east, once to the west, and once to the seated explorer, the Indians inquired, according to custom: "My Lord, do you seek peace or war?" He sought peace; the six returned to inform their ruler, and within minutes the "mistress of the town" set out with her attendants to greet de Soto and his men. Like him, the Cofitachique leader brought her own chair. Stepping from a large canopied canoe, she seated herself and formally welcomed the strangers.[2]

Two chairs, two people surrounded by their followers: thus began the first known encounter between Europeans and the aboriginal inhabitants of the Carolina interior. The scene on the riverbank, which took place generations before John Lawson was even born, reveals the limits of the Englishman's vision. His notes resemble a single frame lifted from a film: they bring native societies at the turn of the eighteenth century into sharp focus, but offer only hints of what came before. Everything was new and fascinating to Lawson; to natives he met, however, his arrival was fairly routine. They had seen men like him already, men at once timid and arrogant, men who, intentionally and unintentionally, changed the piedmont forever. Lawson's sojourn was his, and our own, first intimate acquaintance with the upcountry. But his visit was only one point on a long line of contact, a line reaching back almost two hundred years.

I

The native peoples that early European explorers found in the area called "the Upper Country," "the hilly Parts," "Hill-Country," or "the Highlands" were politically independent but culturally related.[3] From Esaws along the Catawba River to Mannahoacs on the Rappahannock, all were descended from Siouan-speaking migrants who had drifted over the mountains centuries before Columbus. As they fanned out along the rivers slicing through the upcountry, some of their cultural uniformity dissolved. A "people" became one village or a cluster of settlements. Contact with different neighbors fostered diverse pottery styles and arrowhead shapes and may also have touched other, less visible, modes of existence. In the more southern villages a warmer climate and perhaps also richer soils encouraged heavier reliance upon agriculture. And everywhere the passage of time encouraged the growth of a babel of languages from the Siouan root.[4] Still, these societies were variations on a common theme. A fundamental unity underlay piedmont life, a unity grounded in a shared cultural heritage and physical environment. All spoke Siouan. All built towns on terraces above the rivers and creeks.[5] All followed a seasonal routine that balanced farming the rich alluvial soils in the bottomlands, fishing the nearby waterways, hunting in the hills or canebrakes, and gathering wild plants at selected spots.

Some may even have retained a vague sense of kinship despite time and distance. While upcountry warriors launched raids on outsiders in every direction, conflict within the piedmont itself apparently was rare or nonexistent. Monacans are our "neighbours and friends," said the Mannahoac Amoroleck in 1608, "and did dwell as [we] in the hilly Countries by small rivers."[6] Neighbors and friends leading similar lives in the hill country—this was the southern piedmont in the centuries before European contact.

After people arrived from across the sea, these Indians also shared a common destiny. They were far enough away from the coast to be spared the shock of having colonists land in their midst, but not far enough away to avoid men toting foreign bacterial and technological baggage. Weakened by the bacteria, attracted by the technology, perhaps sobered by the fate of coastal groups that fought European intrusions, upcountry Indians would choose cooperation and survival rather than resistance and ruin. After 1700, many of them drew upon their cultural affinities and their common plight, migrated to the Catawba River valley, and became part of the Catawba Nation, thereby reuniting fragments of the ancient Siouan migration. First, however, each group had to confront, on its own, men seeking fame and fortune in the upcountry.

On the surface, initial encounters with Europeans varied widely. Indians along the Catawba and Yadkin rivers met de Soto's Spanish army in 1540 and two more, both commanded by Juan Pardo, a quarter of a century later. Settlements to the north first saw the strangers when Ralph Lane, governor of the English colony at Roanoke, led forty men up the Roanoke River in 1586. Those Indians in the James and Rappahannock valleys knew only rumor and hearsay until Christopher Newport and John Smith embarked from Jamestown on separate expeditions in the late summer of 1608.[7] But the differences between 1540 and 1608, between the

Catawba and the Rappahannock, between Spaniards and Englishmen, between large armies and tiny bands were dwarfed by the
similarities in the natives' first fleeting exposure to Europeans.

Members of these expeditions were cut from the same coarse
cloth as de Soto, described by one follower as "an inflexible man,
and dry of word, who . . . after he once said a thing he did not like
to be opposed, and . . . all bent to his will." Intoxicated with a sense
of their superiority, toughened by service against Incas, Irishmen,
Turks, and other alien peoples, soldier-adventurers wasted little
time with the delicate art of diplomacy. Promises of peace could
abruptly give way to threats if a village proved uncooperative. All
would have understood Lane's men when they swore to head inland "till they had seene the Mangoaks, either as friends or foes."[8]
Explorers were more inclined to compel than cajole to get what
they wanted.

What they wanted was gold. Silver, pearls, gems, or a passage to
China would do; anything else was a bitter disappointment. Spanish soldiers and English colonists alike were lured into the uplands
by rumors of a "minerall country" said to be there.[9] De Soto and
his men broke into native temples to hunt for pearls and waded
into the rivers to search for gold. Pardo brought along a silver-
smith, Andres Xuarez, who checked for mines near the Catawba
River, and William Callicutt did the same for Newport along the
James. Lane's adventurers nearly starved looking for a town where,
it was said, huge plates of copper covered the houses. Even Smith,
prevented by Indians from peering past the falls, pestered his informants to tell him what lay beyond the mountains. All came back
empty-handed yet totally convinced, as only true believers can be,
that one day more, one turn to the right rather than the left, would
have brought them to the promised land.[10]

A man so "inflexible" and determined was not likely to care
much about those who might be sitting on a fortune, and his behavior reflected this dangerous blend of indifference and desperation. De Soto thought nothing of setting dogs on Indians or burning them alive to extract information. Others he simply carried
off in chains to accompany his pilgrimage to a nonexistent mecca.
Pardo initially tried a different strategy, preaching obedience to the
Spanish crown and the Christian god at each town he visited and

backing up his words with several forts, each manned by a handful of soldiers and a priest. When disputes arose, however, Pardo's people also chose weapons over words and were driven back to the sea by angry warriors. The English explorers lacked the manpower for such open displays of force. But they, too, followed the example of de Soto, routinely holding a local headman hostage to ensure their safety.[11]

Indians meeting men with gold on their minds and harsh words on their tongues regarded the newcomers with attitudes ranging from thinly veiled suspicion to outright hostility. Tales of the European slave raids and other skirmishes along the coast must have drifted into the uplands well before Europeans themselves did, alerting natives there to the unpleasant outcome of a visit. Still, headmen greeting de Soto and Pardo were helpful at first; they became unhappy only when the explorers' response to hospitality turned out to be so impolite. The welcome accorded the English latecomers was even less enthusiastic. Lane came no closer to Mangoaks than finding their cold campfires. Monacans stayed put but only tolerated Newport's intrusion, "neither using us well nor ill." Newport might have considered himself fortunate: a hail of arrows from Mannahoac bows greeted John Smith when he reached the falls of the Rappahannock. Only the capture of Amoroleck, brother of a headman, enabled Smith to persuade the natives to put down their weapons.[12]

Colonists could not have known, of course, but when Newport retraced his steps to the falls and Smith left his new Mannahoac friends "singing, dauncing, and making merry" on the riverbank, they were lowering the curtain on the first act of the intercultural drama in the piedmont.[13] Priests replaced Spanish explorers and had enough lost souls along the coast to keep them busy. Virginians found their first taste of the interior unappetizing and had little immediate interest in a second. Why bother? The people there were at best suspicious, and there were plenty of Powhatan's Indians close at hand to worry about. Besides, tobacco promised to make a man wealthy here and now, not in some remote land at some future time. And, in any case, thicker furs and better deerskins could be had up Chesapeake Bay than up the James. So people set aside thoughts of the "minerall country," and an important era in the history of the piedmont came to an end.

Fleeting as they were, these initial encounters with Europeans must have created quite a stir in native villages. It was one thing to hear tales about strange men astride enormous animals and carrying mysterious weapons; it was another to come face to face with pasty complexions, curly hair, and beards, to stand near a horse and sense its frightening power, to hear the roar and see the flash of a musket. In 1540 one southeastern Indian leader voiced what must have been a more general reaction when he told de Soto: "The things that seldom happen bring astonishment. Think, then, what must be the effect on me and mine, the sight of you and your people, whom we have at no time seen . . . things so altogether new, as to strike awe and terror to our hearts." Mannahoacs, who had heard a great deal more about Europeans before they shook hands with John Smith, were no less impressed. Once Amoroleck convinced them that "to doe us any hurt it was impossible," Smith wrote, they let the English land and crowded around the party, "wondering at every thing we had, and heard we had done."[14]

The wonder was genuine. Yet vivid images of native societies stunned by their first contact with Europeans cannot do justice to the era of initial engagement. Indians were indeed impressed, frightened, fascinated, perhaps even awestruck. But like anyone else, piedmont natives responded by drawing upon what they knew to comprehend what they did not know. They had never met anyone quite like these men. They did, however, have experience with aggressive and complex societies, experience that helped in coping with the first Europeans to visit the high country.[15]

De Soto, like the Europeans who came after him, had neither the time nor the temperament to listen to natives recite tales about their past. Had he listened, and had his hosts chosen to tell him, he would have learned that the Cofitachiques were themselves intruders from the southwest. They came for land, not gold, and they came to stay. A branch of the Mississippian culture then spreading throughout the Southeast, ancestors of the people de Soto met had migrated to the Wateree Valley before A.D. 1400, displaced the indigenous population, and settled the extensive floodplain near the falls. Later some of these migrants drifted northeast through the pine barrens in search of similar bottomland. They found it along the Pee Dee–Yadkin River and there established the settlement known today as Town Creek. The people later called Waxhaws—the "flat Heads" Lawson met—may have been a second, smaller branch that settled upriver from the Cofitachiques.[16]

Other upcountry settlements saw nothing like these Mississippian intruders until the second half of the sixteenth century, when Indians below the falls of the rivers flowing into Chesapeake Bay developed a centralized political organization. By the time the English founded Jamestown, Powhatan, head of this new order, received tribute from some thirty different peoples. Thus within a generation or two, Monacans and Mannahoacs, like their counterparts farther south, confronted powerful societies on the piedmont's frontiers.[17]

Neither Powhatan nor the Mississippians had a John Smith to set down their adventures for us. But these developments must have come as quite a shock to upland communities, for important cultural differences separated upcountry from coast. Piedmont polities tended to be small, homogeneous, and egalitarian; their new neighbors boasted an extensive domain dotted with large towns, accented by impressive temple mounds, and ruled by a hierarchy of leaders who received tribute from distant and often culturally distinct peoples. Moreover, the words spoken by Muskogean Mississippians and Algonquian Powhatans sounded as odd to Siouan ears as Spanish or English did.[18] Finally, tidewater groups, like the intruders along the Pee Dee and Wateree, relied heavily on agriculture. Hence they considered the inhabitants of the highlands, where hunting may have remained more important, to be inferior. Monacans and Mannahoacs were "very barbarous," Powhatans told John Smith, "living for most part of wild beasts and fruits." Powhatan names for their western neighbors—"people who dig ground-nuts," "those who gather fruit," "people of roots or tubers"—underscore their contempt.[19]

Cultural differences led to conflict. The Mississippian colonists along the banks of the Wateree and the Pee Dee were preoccupied with defense, settling in loops of meandering streams and everywhere erecting palisades or digging ditches to secure their towns.

Powhatans met equally fierce hostility, and clashes with their western neighbors were routine when the first English colonists arrived.[20] On the James as on the Pee Dee, the failure to advance much beyond the falls in large numbers points to determined resistance by inhabitants upriver. Survivors of the forts Juan Pardo erected in the hill country could have sympathized with the opposition that these other foreigners faced.

Eventually the powerful native cultures arrayed along the edge of the piedmont recognized the limits beyond which they could not hope to advance, and more peaceful forms of intercourse emerged. The first step was to establish some means of communicating. Sign language or knotted strings were followed by a facility with one another's language that permitted more extensive conversation. Europeans slipped smoothly into these forms of discourse, exchanging grains of maize, small stones, or knotted cords with upland villages and finally relying upon interpreters to convey messages back and forth.[21]

Whether they bore strings in their hands or speeches in their heads, some of these messengers, Indian and European alike, were agents of conquest even if they came to talk rather than fight. Powhatans and Mississippians, like Europeans who followed them, were intent on domination one way or another. Powhatan was still consolidating his authority over the tidewater and not yet in a position to conquer his western neighbors. Mississippians were, and Waxhaws may have been the vanguard. Those making their way up the Wateree Valley were accustomed to ruling and filled with the glory of the Cofitachiques; they expected others to recognize this glory by contributing deerskins, copper, or other products to their coffers. Thus when Pardo called on piedmont headmen to swear obedience to the Spanish king, when English authorities demanded that tribute—a few arrows, a pack of furs—be sent to the coast, they were giving speeches heard in the upcountry before.[22]

Whether in English, Spanish, or Muskogean, the words of the would-be conquerors had little impact. During the sixteenth century, Cofitachiques apparently exercised some authority over settlements upriver, but anyone with pretensions to ruling had to contend with the powerful political, economic, and ethnic localism dominating native existence. At best, the alien society's power was highly unstable. The Waxhaw settlement, if indeed it was related to the society downriver, remained more isolated outpost than agent of domination, and the resistance was chronic. When de Soto passed through in 1540, local village headmen were challenging the Cofitachiques by seizing the tribute in an attempt to end this tax on their people. A generation later, chiefs in the upcountry were shipping food to the Cofitachiques to meet the demands of Pardo's army while going out of their way to assure the Spanish commander that he would find storehouses filled with maize for him in their own territories. The Cofitachiques' influence beyond their immediate environs ebbed and flowed; even at high tide, however, it must have had only a limited impact on the everyday lives of piedmont communities, communities which, of course, paid even less heed to Pardo's speeches and Anglo-American calls for tribute.[23]

The inability of Indian or European intruders to control the hill country stood in sharp contrast to the more subtle, indirect effects of their presence. Upcountry inhabitants busy repulsing explorers and would-be colonists or resisting demands for tribute were equally busy embracing, in their own time and their own fashion, elements of these nearby alien cultures. The Cofitachiques and the people at Town Creek were better farmers than their neighbors upriver and may have introduced improved strains of corn to the area. Certainly, settlements in the piedmont were not averse to agricultural experiments, for they readily adopted European plants once these became available. By the time Lawson arrived in Carolina, the peach—dried or cooked, as food or medicine—had become so much a part of native life that both he and the Indians were convinced it was indigenous to America.[24]

Other consequences of contact with the aliens on the piedmont's borders were less obvious but no less important. Odd as the foreigners appeared, reluctant as local villages were to welcome them, Powhatans, Mississippians, and Europeans clearly possessed enormous cultural energy that others sought to acquire for themselves.[25] Some invested the physical relics left behind by visitors—a cross, a stone or iron axe, a shell gorget, a gun—with special meaning, giving them an honored place in the community or burying them with important leaders. Did others without access to a relic

Figure 3. Potsherd, Upper Saratown Site. *Courtesy of Research Laboratories of Anthropology, University of North Carolina at Chapel Hill*

tap its magic by capturing its image? A potsherd found at a piedmont site with the outline of a musket etched into it, done in the days before the town's inhabitants had acquired firearms, suggests something of the excitement generated by first encounters with another world.[26]

Pottery can also indicate the direction cultural power might flow. After 1400, characteristic Mississippian styles spread northward until, three centuries later, natives as far away as the upper reaches of Roanoke River were shaping some of their vessels in that fashion. Similarly, colono-Indian pottery, made by natives copying European models, began to turn up at village sites soon after English settlement began, hinting at incorporation of alien form if not alien function.[27] Tracing the diffusion of new shapes and decorative patterns is far easier than interpreting its significance. But if imitation is indeed the sincerest form of flattery, these trends may have been part of an effort to siphon off the cultural power of the Indian and European coastal plain peoples.

Perhaps intercourse with these neighbors changed more than

pots or plants; it may well have encouraged loosely structured communities in the highlands to develop more complex polities. Confrontation with powerful societies often compels those on the defensive to organize some means of meeting this new challenge. It is possible that the Monacan and Mannahoac confederacies John Smith heard about had arisen in response to the growing threat from below the falls.[28] Perhaps, too, the peoples that came to be known as the Catawba Nation owed something to lessons learned over years of contact with Mississippian neighbors downriver. The eighteenth-century Catawba Nation could not match the size or scope of the sixteenth-century Cofitachiques. Yet the willingness to incorporate many groups into a single entity is reminiscent of Mississippian practices, and it may be the Cofitachiques' greatest legacy.[29] In any event, dealing with Indian foreigners, unpleasant as it could be, had helped prepare communities in the uplands for the likes of de Soto and Newport.

II

If it is important to recognize that piedmont peoples were accustomed to alien neighbors, it is no less essential to see that the European intrusion was not just one more in a series of encounters with strangers. Amoroleck, John Smith's Mannahoac prisoner, understood this when he informed his captors that the English were said to be "a people come from under the world." The rumor's meaning is obscure. Mannahoacs may literally have considered Smith's company to be creatures from what Indians called the Under World, a realm inhabited by powerful, dangerous beings whose behavior was unpredictable and mysterious.[30] In any case, it was clear that the intruders were not from the Indians' own world.

Amoroleck's neighbors to the south in the Carolina interior were confronted with this harsh fact before they ever faced Spanish adventurers. Among the Cofitachiques in 1540 de Soto's army saw "large vacant towns, grown up in grass" because, the Indians explained, "there had been a pest in the land" two years before, a "pest" probably carried from distant Spanish outposts by other natives. Was it smallpox? Measles? Influenza? We do not know. Neither did the Indians who had been infected. But we do know (and perhaps the afflicted did, too) that bringing these invisible invaders to America marked Europeans as different from the Cofitachiques, the Town Creek people, or the Powhatans. Here upcountry communities faced a truly unprecedented challenge as diseases returned again and again.[31] By the time Lawson visited the interior, the Indians there must have been veterans of many battles against deadly germs. Congarees were "a small People," he wrote, "having lost much of their former Numbers . . . by the Small-pox, which hath often visited them." And Congarees did not suffer alone. "Neither do I know any Savages that have traded with the *English*," Lawson continued, "but what have been great Losers by this Distemper."[32]

Piedmont populations were devastated. According to Lawson, so "many thousands of these Natives" succumbed that "there is not the sixth Savage living within two hundred Miles of all our Settlements, as there were fifty Years ago." It "destroy'd whole Towns," he went on, "without leaving one *Indian* alive in the Village." A Cheraw settlement on the Dan River was awful confirmation of Lawson's claim. Occupied for a single generation in the late seventeenth century, the village contained so many bodies that every family, every dwelling must have been touched by the scourge.[33]

Counting burials helps suggest the dimensions of demographic disaster. But it cannot begin to convey what Cheraws and others endured when a strange malady struck their community. Perhaps rumors of sickness elsewhere reached the village, brought by people who themselves could be carrying the virus. The alarming news would be especially disturbing if memories of earlier epidemics were still fresh in people's minds, kept there by folklore or massive burials near the town. Concern became fear when someone in the village sickened, suffered, and died; fear turned to terror as others followed the same path to the grave. Perhaps the healthy tended the sick, doing what they could to relieve the pain. Perhaps they simply fled to the woods or to other settlements, spreading the word—and the infection—still farther. Those left behind tried everything to stop the horrible course of events, offering prayers or purging themselves in sweat lodges and plunging into nearby streams, an ancient cure for various ailments that generally hastened the end among those afflicted by a new disease. Meanwhile, the community came to a standstill. Water was not drawn, fires were not tended, deer were not hunted, weapons were not repaired. Crops were not planted, or if planted not weeded, or if weeded not harvested. Nothing stirred. Death reigned.[34]

After weeks or months the scourge left as mysteriously as it had come, and survivors faced a situation every bit as alien as the one confronting a colonist or a slave. After an epidemic the barrier between past ways and present conditions was as vast as the ocean separating America from Europe or Africa. Yet, like transplanted Europeans or Africans, Indians crossed the barrier; they constructed societies that enabled them to carry on. Life could never be the same again, but survivors of epidemics managed to restore some semblance of order.

At the most fundamental level, disease played havoc with the relations that defined a person's identity. Everyone born in a piedmont town had automatically become part of a network of real or fictive kin. Houses, fields, food storage and preparation—all were divided on this basis. Kin taught children the ways of the world, from the secrets of making pots or arrows to the enemies of their people, from proper behavior toward one's fellow villagers to the mysterious forces controlling the universe. Kin punished with teasing, shaming, and ostracism those who forgot these lessons. Kin met to celebrate a young hunter's first kill or decide on the propriety of a marriage offer. Kin avenged one when one was harmed, took care of one in sickness, and mourned one after death. Small wonder that the most enduring memory among Indians taken out of the Carolina interior by Pardo's men was of a life surrounded by "children, grandchildren, and great-grandchildren."[35]

An epidemic tore apart this fabric. Who would bury the dead? Who mourn? Whom could one turn to in time of need? Whom should one marry? The answers to these and other questions, once simply assumed, were no longer clear. We do not know how Indians found new answers in the aftermath of illness; we know only that they did. They mended the gaping holes disease left, and kinship remained central to Indian existence. "Uncles, Brothers, Sisters, Cousins, Sons, and Daughters" were still the most significant people in one's life, at once a bridge to the wider world and a shelter from it.[36]

People patching up kinship networks often did so without the guidance of those most knowledgeable in such things, for disease might sweep away many of the elderly. The shock of losing these people went well beyond kinship to touch every corner of native life. As repositories of ancient secrets and special skills, the aged were a vital part of the community: they offered knowledge derived from long experience, tutored the young in the ways of their people, and linked past to present. Generations of collected wisdom could vanish in a matter of days if large numbers of old people succumbed to illness. "They have forgot most of their traditions since the Establishment of this Colony," Etiwan Indians living near Charleston informed a South Carolinian in 1710. "They keep their Festivals and can tell but little of the reasons: their Old Men are dead."[37]

But, like the importance of kinship, the position of the elderly endured. Their ranks were depleted; their authority remained. "Old Age [is] held in as great Veneration amongst these Heathens, as amongst any People you shall meet withal in any Part of the World," Lawson wrote. Society set off old from young by different titles, secret languages, and special access to temples or other sacred places. They took precedence in welcoming strangers, speaking in council, and making decisions. And they still enlightened "the younger Fry" with "a Traditional Relation" "in Remembrance of . . . the famous Exploits of their Renowned Ancestors, and all Actions of Moment that had (in former Days) been perform'd by their Forefathers."[38]

Other forms of authority underwent similar permutations. Native "priests" or "conjurers" had always stood above the people by virtue of their ability to interpret and manipulate the invisible forces ruling a community's existence. Here, too, disease weakened the hold of customary ways, not merely by killing these men (and with them their secrets) but also by rendering them impotent in the face of mysterious illnesses. None could do anything to combat a disease like smallpox, "which is a contrary Fever to what they ever knew." Yet this impotence did not wipe out all of their expertise. In fact, the priests Lawson met still prided themselves on their ability to heal wounds and treat illnesses. Some carried medicinal plants on a string about their necks, ready to hand and symbols of their power. Others delighted in showing a visitor the collection of medicines that they kept in the house. All had the answer to a whole host of different problems at their fingertips, "not often going above 100 Yards from their Abode for their Remedies."[39]

Most important, priests lived up to their promises. Among the Santees, Lawson listened as a trader told him of seeing one old man conduct an elaborate ritual to predict, correctly, the fate of a war party. Later the traveler watched another conjurer cure wounds that Lawson claimed would have baffled the best English physician. The explorer, refusing to believe his own eyes and ears, insisted that these men were nothing more than "cunning Knaves[s]," "Impostor[s]" who duped "an easy, credulous People." But the priests' continued success, based on "Years and the Experience of repeated Services," better explains their enduring hold on the community.[40] Though disease struck again and again, the magic still worked; the "Knave" had not lost his touch.

Priests also had a hand in making sure that a person still received proper burial despite the alarming climb in the number of deaths. Cheraws living along the Dan River during the years between de Soto and Lawson created a cemetery by arranging graves around a circular mound or building. Each corpse destined for that sacred ground was placed in a flexed position, wrapped in cane matting, and set, facing the sunrise, in a grave lined with logs, bark, or mats. Beside the body, to accompany the departed on its journey, the mourners laid precious goods, tobacco pipes, and clay pots filled with food and drink. Then the grave was covered, and the survivors commemorated their deed, and their dead, with a funeral feast held around a fire kindled over the spot. With time the Cheraws' careful attention to proper placement of graves in the cemetery broke down, until interments became almost random in the settlement. Yet still the graves were dug, the bodies placed just so, the fires kindled, and the feasts held. Whatever the toll taken by sickness, among the Cheraws, at least, the gods lived.[41]

Neither priests nor gods proved able to order the diseases to go away or save those afflicted. Eventually epidemics left Cheraws and everyone else in the upcountry too few and too weak to sustain an independent existence, forcing survivors to combine with others who found themselves in similar straits. The result was a kaleidoscopic array of mergers, an ordeal already under way when de Soto and his men arrived on the borders of the upcountry. The Spanish, curious about those ghost towns among the Cofitachiques, were told that survivors of the "pest" had moved in with their neighbors.[42] Thereafter the details of mergers are hazy, but it is clear that no one in the piedmont was immune. The various peoples of the Mannahoac constellation Smith met melted into a single remnant group, and Monacans apparently did the same, becoming one village by the end of the seventeenth century. Eventually the only recourse was to look beyond one's own people. Saponis, for example, lived with Nahyssans in 1670, Occaneechees a decade later, and Tutelos and Keyauwees shortly after 1700. The Keyauwees soon left this last arrangement and tried to live on their own for a time before joining Cheraws.[43] And so it went, with characters changing but the plot much the same.

Like counting Cheraw burials, listing mergers can only begin to capture how profoundly unsettling this experience was for those involved. They were heirs to a cultural tradition in which the center of activity, the focus of loyalty, and the source of identity was tightly circumscribed. Whatever the connections of trade or tribute linking one group with another, life revolved around the local community or cluster of settlements that defined a people. Self-sufficient in subsistence, every group was also independent in virtually every other way, as Cofitachiques and others learned. Each possessed its own council house, where decisions could be made and ceremonies conducted. Within sight of the council house stood the sweat lodge, a social and curative center attended by a priest.[44]

Natural boundaries—rivers, swamps, upland ridges, or simply areas of poorer soil—served to reinforce localism. Buffer zones (often called "deserts") clearly divided piedmont from coastal plain, and within the upcountry itself other deserts separated peoples. Tales of the evils awaiting those who ventured beyond a people's boundaries strengthened these environmental barriers. Coastal Indians informed early English explorers that natives to the north "were noughts, [their] land Sandy and barren, their Country sickly."[45] A story about a fierce creature inhabiting the headwaters of Neuse River frightened hunters away and may have been designed to keep contending groups out of another border region. Explorers who traveled through uninhabited areas and had to live off the land rather than off the natives were unwittingly charting these boundaries for us.[46]

Piedmont Indians did cross these zones to trade, hunt, or simply meet with others to discuss matters of common interest. Yet a traveler was always aware that he was in foreign territory. A glance at his new surroundings immediately made him feel out of place. His hosts dressed oddly; their welcoming speeches sounded strange; they might tower over him, since some peoples were of "mean stature" while their neighbors could be "Gigantick." If the visitor spent any time there, he would quickly discover many more hints of an existence somewhat at variance with his own. Was the chief with whom he stayed an absolute ruler or merely a figurehead? It varied from time to time and place to place. Did these people eat snakes? He had been taught never to touch them. Did his hosts play games? Some were new to him. Did he promise to return in the Strawberry Month? His announcement might draw blank looks, for some peoples named the months after trees that blossomed.[47]

However warm the welcome, however long he remained, the visitor would have trouble shedding the status of outsider. Indians everywhere in the highlands were devoted to their "Country-Folks" or "Nation," and relationships with these people differed significantly from those with strangers. Natives were "very kind, and charitable to one another," Lawson remarked, "but more especially to those of their own Nation." Foreigners desiring a liaison with a local woman had to approach her parents and the village chief. On the other hand, "if it be an *Indian* of their own Town or Neighbourhood, that wants a Mistress, he comes to none but the Girl." Even standards of honesty varied. Lawson discovered, to his dismay, that a "Thief [is] held in Disgrace, that steals from any of his Country-Folks," "but to steal from the *English* [or other strangers] they reckon no Harm."[48]

When different piedmont peoples came together, then, they had to redefine the meaning of "stranger." The necessary stages of exchanging messages and discussing proposals had passed; now the outsiders had arrived, eyeing their new home and their new "Country-Folk" with a mixture of wariness and curiosity. Many questions demanded immediate answers. What language would be spoken?[49] Where would they sleep? Plant? Hunt? How would decisions be reached, offenders punished, ceremonies performed? With time such matters were sorted out, but not without some sacrifices. "There is nothing more coveted amongst them, than to marry a Woman of their own Nation," Lawson wrote. Disease and the mergers that followed quashed many hopes, for "when the Nation consists of a very few People (as now adays it often happens) so that they are all of them related to one another, then they look out for Husbands and Wives amongst Strangers."[50] "Amongst Strangers"—this was life in the piedmont after European contact. The difficulty of harmonizing discordant peoples, of turning outsiders into insiders, may explain the many temporary alliances.

Refugees, in order to soften the impact of disease and depopulation, followed the "principle of least effort" to coalesce with others most like themselves.[51] Hence Saponis sought out Siouan-speaking, piedmont-dwelling Tutelos or Occaneechees but shunned Iroquoian Nottoways and Algonquian Nansemonds of the coastal plain.[52] Peoples in the hill country shared an environment and a common cultural tradition that had been kept alive by generations of peaceful contact. These affinities combined to ease the way toward closer ties and make a merger less disruptive.

Remnant groups made their transition easier still by clinging to their former identity as long as possible. When Saponis, Stuckanocks (probably descendants of Mannahoacs), Occaneechees, and Tutelos agreed to settle together on Virginia's southwestern frontier in 1714, the colony's treaty proclaimed that they would "hereafter be deemed as incorporated into one Nation." The Indians had other ideas. Leaders from each group placed their marks on the document, and a year later Virginia's lieutenant governor Alexander Spotswood described the village as "a people speaking much the same language, and therefore confederated together, tho' still preserving their different Rules."[53]

"Rules" could extend from this life to the next. In earlier times some piedmont folk buried their dead at random in the village, making the community itself, in effect, a cemetery, and suggesting that all in the settlement shared an identity. During the historic era, on the other hand, Indians made interments in clusters, creating a handful of separate graveyards. The evidence hints that several different groups now occupied one town, remained conscious of their differences, and expressed that consciousness through distinct burial grounds. Using such devices, people thrown together by circumstances lived as one but remained in some ways apart.[54]

The difficulty of being Occaneechee when the people next door were Tutelos, of speaking Cheraw when one's spouse spoke Eno, was of course compounded by the migrations that were the prelude to any merger. One move often led to another. Between 1670 and 1710, for example, Saponis went from the Staunton River to the Roanoke to the Appomattox to the Yadkin and back toward Virginia, and other Indians scratched equally convoluted patterns into the piedmont's surface. Whatever course each chose, the very act of leaving was traumatic. A people's village and the surrounding area were vital elements of native identity. Here the past lived. Buried beneath the house, in a nearby temple or cemetery, alongside the palisade, the dead still occupied the land and demanded continual consecration.[55] Elsewhere in the village or its neighborhood were ceremonial circles of reeds left in place as a reminder of the rituals there performed. Piles of stones commemorating important events in the life of the people served a similar function. Built by a community, these structures were maintained by passersby, who added a stone as a personal means of keeping in touch with bygone days. Indians extended those attachments into the future by teaching children about the special sites and the accompanying rituals.[56]

Natural formations were also important to residents of the upcountry. "In our way," wrote Lawson on leaving one piedmont town, "there stood a great Stone about the Size of a large Oven, and hollow; this the *Indians* took great Notice of, putting some Tobacco into the Concavity, and spitting after it. I ask'd them the Reason of their so doing, but they made me no Answer." Villages throughout the interior treasured similar places—a rock near the falls of the James imprinted with "the trac[k] of their god," a stone "where at certain times they held religious services"—places that could not be left behind without some cost.[57]

The toll could be physical as well as spiritual, for even the most uneventful of moves interrupted subsistence routines. Belongings had to be packed and unpacked, dwellings constructed, palisades raised. Once migrants had settled in, the still more arduous task of exploiting new terrain awaited them. Living in one place season after season endowed a community with intimate knowledge of the surrounding environment. The richest soils, the best hunting grounds, the choicest sites for gathering nuts and berries—none could be learned without years of experience, tested by time and passed down from one generation to the next. No wonder Carolina natives worried about being "driven to some unknown Country, to live, hunt, and get our Bread in."[58]

Some uprooted groups tried to leave "unknown Country" behind and make their way back to more familiar territories. In 1716, Enos asked Virginia's permission to resettle "Enoe Town" on the North Carolina frontier, their home in Lawson's day. Seventeen years later, William Byrd II came upon an abandoned Cheraw village on a tributary of the upper Roanoke River and remarked how "it must have been a great misfortune to them to be obliged to abandon so beautiful a dwelling." Cheraws apparently agreed, for in 1717 the Virginia Council received "Divers applications . . . by the Saraw [Cheraw] Indians and others incorporated with them [then living along the Pee Dee River] for Liberty to Seat themselves on the head of Roanoke River." Few were lucky enough to return to their old homes. But their efforts to retrace their steps hint at a profound sense of loss and testify to the powerful hold of ancient sites.[59]

III

Enos, Cheraws, and the other uprooted peoples invite pity: before 1700, many died, many fled, cures failed, older voices fell silent. Yet life, for the survivors, went on. A bewildering round of mergers and migrations had not robbed piedmont Indians of their past—or their future—for they had undertaken a reformation that healed or hid the scars left by sickness. A similar process of reformation occurred when colonial traders followed lethal microbes and belligerent explorers into the interior.[60]

Every adventurer since de Soto had brought along some European merchandise to hand out to important natives in order to smooth his way. But trade did not begin in earnest until the middle of the seventeenth century, when Virginia colonists had reason to think again of the country past the falls. Tobacco's fluctuating prices and heavy labor demands made it a harsh mistress, prompting men to consider other roads to riches. Some had pursued the fur trade with Indians up Chesapeake Bay, but after 1634 the newly arrived Marylanders put a stop to that. Meanwhile, the destruction of Powhatan's empire in the aftermath of the 1622 and 1644 uprisings offered colonists easier access to the interior than Smith or Newport would have thought possible. Together these developments rekindled interest in the southwest. The construction of Fort Henry at the falls of the Appomattox River in 1646 officially sanctioned this fresh attention and provided a headquarters for tentative forays into the lands beyond.[61]

Gold, gems, and China still preyed on the minds of men coming and going at the fort. In June 1670 a party returned from the western mountains determined to go back and "try for mines, being yet very confident that the bowels of those barren hills are not without silver or gold."[62] By then, however, such talk was laced with more realistic assessments of the piedmont's possibilities. John Lederer, a member of the expedition, had pressed on to make further discoveries after his companions headed home. He came back torn between old exotic dreams and new, mundane (yet profitable) schemes, alert to signs of the Indian Ocean yet careful to offer instructions on how to succeed in the deerskin trade. The next year young William Byrd took over his late uncle's trading post on the James and heeded Lederer's advice. Byrd's hunt for crystal in 1688 was only a sideline to his lucrative trade for peltry. One disappointment after another—even the crystal Byrd found was judged "foul, and full of flaws"—finally forced transplanted Europeans to lower their sights from the grandiose visions of the conquistadors.[63]

Fortified by devout faith in a combination of "gods blessing and our Endeav[o]rs" but spurred on now more by profits and pelts than glory and gold, traders replaced adventurers and pushed themselves, their packhorses, and their luck in order to penetrate the piedmont. Up and down across the rolling hills they went, to the Roanoke River and then beyond, marking their progress by carving notches or their initials into trees. Rivers forded became like old friends (or enemies), with new names· added to the list as the years passed: the Tar, Flat, Little, and Eno, then across the Haw Old Fields to the Saxapahaw, Aramanchy, Deep, and Yadkin, where traders rested their horses before pressing on to the Catawba.[64] At the end of the century fifty or sixty Virginians annually embarked on this "tradeing Voyage," peddling their wares in the far corners of the southern piedmont.[65]

European merchandise and colonial traders were novelties to piedmont natives; traders and exchange were not. For ages Indians in the interior had traded with coastal peoples for a variety of different goods, and some of this commerce was untouched by the new intercultural exchange. Even after 1700, coastal natives still gathered the yaupon leaves used to brew the ceremonial "black drink" and collected seashells for fashioning ornaments, carried these items upcountry, and bartered them for scarlet roots growing near the mountains that could be made into paint.[66]

Eventually Indians located closer to Anglo-America began to toss a string of glass beads or a strip of cloth into their packs before heading west. In 1670, Cheraw traders were visiting villages deep in the interior, and the Cheraws' proximity to Virginia makes it likely that they were swapping as many iron hatchets as pieces of native copper. A generation later Lawson crossed paths with several Indian traders who were selling everything from stolen horses to jugs of rum in upcountry towns. The flow of European merchandise began as the tiniest of streams and followed well-worn channels.[67]

Indian middlemen were an endangered species, however. William Byrd and his contemporaries were not the sort to allow natives to collect the profits middlemen commonly enjoy, and colonists took trade into their own hands as soon as they dared. Still, men flushed with their success in gaining direct access to precious furs and hides discovered that it was easier to replace native traders than native trade forms. Someday soon the new men and their new merchandise would transform Indian life, but in the trade's infancy colonial adventurers, far from being revolutionaries, observed local rules.

From the beginning to the end of his journey the trader was bound to Indian ways. In fact, native habits took command before the colonist even got started, for he had to bide his time until Indians sent word "when they will come in, when they shall have any truck for us to go out, or the like." Once permission was granted, the newcomers continued to obey, relying heavily on Indian advice and sticking close to Indian trails. Only Lederer neglected to hire a local guide, only Lederer ignored native directions—and only Lederer became hopelessly lost, wandering for days "over steep and craggy Cliffs," in "a continued Marish over-grown with Reeds," and across "a barren Sandy desert." Upon his return he warned anyone trying to retrace his route that "the way . . . [is] thorow a vast Forest, where you seldom fall into any Road or Path." Those who did come after him, aware that one did not in fact "fall into" a trail, consulted the locals, hired competent native guides, and remained on the beaten path.[68]

After following the trail to a piedmont community, the trader became the lead player in a drama directed by the townspeople. The plot, developed long before, made no distinction among visitors, hosts "always entertaining Travellers, either *English*, or *Indian*." First a band of warriors came out to welcome the visitor and escort him into the settlement. Safely inside, the wise guest did as he was told. Even John Lederer, who was so rash as to ignore Indian directions, knew enough to adopt a submissive attitude when he stumbled upon a village. "Being arrived at a Town," he advised his readers, "enter no house until you are invited; and then seem not afraid to be led in pinion'd like a prisoner: for that is a Ceremony they use to friend and enemies without distinction." "You must accept of an invitation from the Seniors, before that of young men," Lederer continued; "and refuse nothing that is offered or set afore you: for they are very jealous, and sensible of the least slighting or neglect from strangers, and mindful of Revenge."[69]

If their guest behaved himself, the Indians might offer to make him a member of their community. This was a frightening prospect to a novice like Lederer, and he fled the Saponis when they declared their intention to marry him to a headman's daughter. But most colonists, recognizing the social (not to mention sexual) benefits of such an arrangement, were less reluctant. In Lawson's day a trader generally lived with an Indian woman while in the interior.[70]

Here again, upcountry communities were treating a colonist like any other visitor. Native travelers had long been accorded the same privilege, and Europeans or Africans who ran away to the highlands probably married into local communities.[71] Colonial traders accepting Indian wives were therefore part of a system of dealing with outsiders. Adoption or marriage brought one into a kinship network that carried duties and rights understood by all in a village. Saponis and others, unfamiliar with a relationship based strictly on economics, enticed traders into the traditional forms governing social intercourse. By taking an Indian companion the colonist, to native eyes, signaled his acceptance of local rules.

Even a trader embraced by the native community would not get ahead in business unless he followed certain time-honored trade customs. Among Indians reciprocal gift giving was an essential grease in the wheels of exchange. William Byrd, who apparently learned this from experience, had to warn his English suppliers that, while Indians traded for tools and cloth, "the want of beads, or some other trifles [is] often times a great prejudice" to success.[72] Once these preliminaries were out of the way, a colonist had to take one more step outside his own frame of reference and discard his standards of measurement. In the native world a string of roanoke beads was not a foot or a yard but an arm's length; rum came, not by the quart or gallon, but by the mouthful.[73]

Plodding along Indian trails, pushed and pulled about Indian towns, sleeping with an Indian woman, doling out beads Indian-fashion—the colonial trader of the late seventeenth century had to know the tricks of the trade. How did he learn them? Simply following the natives' lead, as Lederer suggested, one could pick up a great deal. Indian wives were also important teachers, "instructing 'em in the Affairs and Customs of the Country." If the outsider was particularly slow or stubborn, Indians might resort to teasing or shaming to compel conformity. Another tactic was simply to avoid anyone who refused to respect native customs. "They never frequent a Christian's House that is given to Passion," Lawson remarked, "nor will they ever buy or sell with him, if they can get the same Commodities of any other Person; for they say, such Men are mad Wolves, and no more Men." When subtle rebukes failed, harsher measures might teach a man proper manners. Indians apparently overlooked Lederer's bungling breaches of etiquette;

other colonists were less fortunate. During the 1680s Byrd lost eight traders in the space of two years, and they were neither the first nor the last to be killed somewhere in the interior.[74]

Colonists also learned from one another. At Fort Henry, at plantations, at taverns, those just returned and those about to depart must have gathered to swap information. There, amid the drink, the smoke, and the tall tales, they taught a curriculum of towns and peoples, habits and customs, which Indians to seek out and which to avoid. Others benefited when someone like Lederer made mistakes and lived to tell about them. His chapter of "Instructions to Such as Shall March upon Discoveries into the North-*American* Continent" and another "Touching Trade with Indians" were more formal versions of the schooling every trader received.[75]

By the time Lawson passed through, thirty years after Lederer, the elementary lessons had been learned. While among the Santees the party stopped overnight at a hunter's empty hut and "made our selves welcome to what his Cabin afforded, (which is a Thing common) the *Indians* allowing it practicable to the *English* Traders, to take out of their Houses what they need in their Absence, in Lieu whereof they most commonly leave some small Gratuity of Tobacco, Paint, Beads, *etc.*" Ten days later a Waxhaw Indian came to invite the travelers to his village, and they "receiv'd the Messenger with a great many Ceremonies, acceptable to those sort of Creatures."[76]

European merchandise had to be as "acceptable" as European behavior during these early years of exchange. Piedmont Indians were discriminating shoppers: if cloth was the wrong color, beads were too large, or hoes too small, natives refused them.[77] A trader could make a profit bartering large blue and red beads to customers living west of the falls; the same items found no market among those to the south, where small black and white ones were preferred.[78]

Indians further smoothed the transition to an alien technology by reshaping what commodities they did accept to fit familiar forms or functions. An Occaneechee punched a design into the bowl of a metal spoon to make it resemble the shell gorgets that were common ornaments. Waxhaws tied metal bells instead of tortoise-shell rattles about their ankles or necks at ceremonial dances,

Figure 4. Spoon and Gorget, Occaneechee Town. Late Seventeenth Century. *Courtesy of Research Laboratories of Anthropology, University of North Carolina at Chapel Hill*

and a few of the stone pipes passed among the spectators at these ceremonies had been shaped by metal files. Kinfolk burying one of their own first dressed the deceased in garments decorated with glass beads and brass bells, next wrapped the body in a cane mat and pointed it toward the rising sun, then placed a musket, an axe, or a wine bottle in the grave to accompany the soul on its journey.[79] Some hunters fashioned arrows out of glass from broken bottles; others busied themselves with their new muskets, aiming the weapon as they would a bow, with the left hand as far forward as possible, and taking great pains to "set it streight, sometimes shooting away above 100 Loads of Ammunition, before they bring the Gun to shoot according to their Mind."[80]

Indians were eager customers, not slaves to imported fashion. The native did not relentlessly pursue European commodities once he first donned a matchcoat, raised a musket to his shoulder, or drew a metal knife from its sheath. Men glad to acquire firearms still made bows from locust or mulberry, shafts from "arrow wood," and arrowheads from stone. Women valuing the durability of copper kettles still produced clay pots. People recognizing the advantages of cloth reserved strouds and duffles for special occasions and wore deerskin mantles or loincloths much of the time. Natives offered glass beads of every imaginable size and color nonetheless wanted roanoke and wampum peake.[81]

The persistence of Indian manufactures limited dependence upon European goods and baffled colonial traders, whose products, carried hundreds of miles along hard trails at considerable cost in time, toil, and sweat, ended up in storage in some village. "This yeere the Indyans will have Roanoake," one frustrated trader reported in 1682, "not with standing all other comodities be p[re]sented. . . . I having at this time a considerable parcell of other goods amongst them unsold." Occasionally William Byrd also grumbled that there was "a dull trade of itt here," in part because "English goods [are] plenty amongst those Indians."[82]

Ironically, natives conversant with the skills of their ancestors were best equipped to participate in the new trade, for they gave colonists aboriginal products in return. Supplying merchandise for the English, like greeting English traders or using English goods, marked no radical departure from earlier patterns of existence or exchange. The cane baskets Byrd's traders brought back from distant towns were products of a long craft tradition among women there, a tradition flourishing in de Soto's time. Similarly, the Indians Byrd sent up the James to hack samples from an outcrop of crystal probably had already been doing the same thing at the same place to make arrowheads.[83]

Neither rocks nor baskets made up much of a packhorse's load on its return trip to Virginia, however. Most of the burden consisted of hides and furs, particularly deerskins.[84] Here, too, there was no reversal of customary ways. Deer were already a vital part of upcountry life, and Indians were adept at killing them. Piedmont communities, like natives throughout the Southeast, had developed sophisticated hunting strategies that yielded the most animals with the least effort.[85] That a good hunter was a hero among his people encouraged men to perfect their skills. One of the first lessons they learned was the importance of careful timing. Hunters focused their energies in the fall and winter months when, freed of agricultural tasks, a community could move en masse to the upland areas where deer were then congregating to feed on acorns and hickory nuts. Within this seasonal rhythm lay a daily routine. "The men goe a hunting mornings and evenings," one colonist observed scornfully; "other times they eat and sleep like Hoggs." There was method in this apparent laziness: at dawn and dusk deer were most likely to be feeding and were therefore easiest to find.[86]

Once they found the target, piedmont hunters had a variety of techniques for taking their prey. Individual stalking that relied upon stealth or a deerskin disguise may have been most common, but settlements also engaged in communal fire-hunting, in which natives set a large circle ablaze and drove the quarry to the center, where it could easily be dispatched. Controlled fires were useful hunting tools in less direct ways, too, for by burning selected sites Indians cleared underbrush and encouraged the grasses and forest edge that deer favored.[87]

Efforts to manipulate the environment to concentrate game in certain spots worked so well that at least one European believed tales about domesticated deer in the Southeast. Others, less gullible, were nonetheless struck by the many open meadows in the hill country, meadows that supported vast "herds" of these animals. But herds or no, only a fool or a novice thought it easy to hunt them. Those who tried their luck learned that timing, patience, and experience lay behind the natives' success. "The Indians never lacked meat," one of de Soto's companions admitted, "being very skilful in killing game, which the Christians were not."[88]

Natives were, of course, equally adept at processing the animals taken. Deer supplied as much as 90 percent of their meat, and hungry Europeans were impressed by the savory venison stews laid before them. Visitors with business in mind were less interested in dinner than in the knack women had for turning skins into fine leather. Better yet, Indians were in the habit of storing surplus deerskins for future use or for trade with peoples near the coast, where the quality of skins was poorer.[89] In the 1620s a Virginia trader was astonished that Indians along the Potomac River routinely burned the pelts of animals they took and had to be taught the value of these items.[90] No such surprises awaited a trader in the piedmont; Indians there were accustomed not only to take and eat deer but also to stow and swap deerskins. In short, they were, quite without planning it, prepared to meet the demands of the European market.

Deerskins were certainly the bulkiest but not always the most valuable commodities Englishmen extracted from the piedmont. Trudging alongside the horses or perched atop the packs of peltry were children—some only three years old, yet already worth more than their weight in deerskins—destined for a life of servitude on a tobacco plantation. The attention focused upon South Carolina's trade in Indian slaves has obscured Virginia's version. It is clear, however, that this branch of the trade peaked in the latter half of the seventeenth century, coinciding closely with the expansion of colonial commerce into the highlands. Virginia laws marched right in step, making it progressively easier to convert free natives into unfree laborers until, in 1682, any Indian brought into the colony could be legally enslaved.[91]

By then the slave trade was well established. In 1673 William Byrd sold a four-year-old Indian boy, Taythea, to Thomas Harris; he may have acquired Taythea from Indians along the Savannah River, who were trading animal pelts and young Indian slaves to Virginia at this time. When Cadwallader Jones summarized his business with native towns four hundred miles south-southwest of his Rappahannock River plantation in 1682, "indyan children Prisoners" came first, followed by "most Deereskines and some Furs." At almost the same moment, his competitors along the James, Edward Hatcher, Thomas Shippy, and John Dubis, were sealing a formal agreement to split the profits from "what goods and slaves shall . . . be purchased" in the interior, and Hatcher headed south carrying an order from a customer to buy an Indian boy in the villages along the Catawba River.[92]

Like methods for trading deerskins, the procedures for taking human beings were refined long before Hatcher arrived in a piedmont settlement clutching an order for an Indian slave. A century earlier, Spanish explorers in the area "found many natives of other provinces who had been enslaved" after being "captured in ambushes made while hunting and fishing" along a people's borders. The fates of these prisoners varied. Some were tortured to atone for the death of a relative; others were adopted and took that relative's place. Between death and adoption lay a vague status Europeans termed "slavery," in which persons lived on the margins of the community and performed menial tasks for their captors.[93]

Thus piedmont peoples already had candidates for tobacco planters seeking slaves. When this supply ran out, the natives could turn to an array of old enemies to replenish it. Warfare was part of the natural order in aboriginal times, just as palisaded villages were a natural part of the landscape. Men fought to gain status and revenge and to ease the pain of souls killed by enemies; captives, like scalps, had always been a prize of conflict. Anglo-American traders did indeed, as one colonist charged, "excite [Indians] to make War amongst themselves to get Slaves which they give for our European Goods." But excitement was in the air already; natives simply grafted the traders' demands onto traditional reasons for going off to war, and it is difficult at this remove to untangle a man's motives. When Westos from the Savannah River valley captured Indians, did they drag them off to Byrd, or "sacrifice [them] to their Idols," as Lederer believed? When a Santee war party set out against enemies near the mouth of the Winyaw River, was it bent on settling old scores, acquiring slaves for men like Hatcher, both, or neither?[94] All that can be said for certain is that Virginia's demand for slaves built upon an existing framework of conflict and capture.

Piedmont Indians had slipped easily into the Atlantic trade system, already manufacturing goods that were in demand, making foreign traders behave, choosing carefully from among the new products. But they did not let participation in the market take them away from the everyday pursuits that had long sustained them. Hunters were not so absorbed in stalking deer that they gave up killing bears, turkeys, and other game to feed kinfolk. Young men still took time from the chase and the warpath "to labour stoutly, in planting their Maiz and Pulse." Women still tended these fields in summer, in winter gathering wild plant foods. Moreover, all of these activities remained thoroughly rooted in ceremonies without which, natives believed, life was unthinkable. Rituals to celebrate the harvest and pray for future bounty continued to occupy the piedmont winter. Hunters were no less careful to propitiate the unseen yet powerful forces governing their fortunes. "All the *Indians* hereabouts carefully preserve the Bones of the Flesh they eat," Lawson noted while among the Keyauwees, "and burn them, as being of Opinion, that if they omitted that Custom, the Game would leave their Country, and they should not be able to maintain themselves by their Hunting."[95]

That Indians set the general tenor and tempo of intercultural exchange cannot obscure another, darker side to the trading story, a side less obvious at that early date but ultimately no less important to piedmont life. In retrospect, it is clear that the peoples there, caught up in the excitement of obtaining new and wonderful things, did not pause to consider the hidden costs. "Guns, and Ammunition, besides a great many other Necessaries, . . . are helpful to Man," they told colonists.[96] Seeking more and more help, they lost sight of, or perhaps never even saw, the price they paid, a price more difficult for them (and for us) to calculate.

Although production for the colonial market did emerge from established forms of belief and behavior, trade slowly and subtly altered those forms. More was involved than a simple increase in the quantity of skins, slaves, or baskets produced; the meaning of these commodities also changed. Indians once had gone to war, hunted, and made baskets strictly for their own practical or symbolic reasons. Each activity had been couched in ritual terms, infused by private and public ceremony that governed the process from start to finish. With the opening of the colonial trade, goods crossed cultural boundaries, and old habits took on new definitions. Natives able to put traditional skills to use in the Atlantic economy were nonetheless unable to prevent production from being, to some degree, divorced from its ancient context. Slaves formerly adopted or killed to atone for other deaths were now sold; hides or baskets that one day were used locally now disappeared from native society.[97]

The products obtained in return for this merchandise also changed native existence. A cloth shirt, a copper kettle, or a trading gun by itself posed little threat, and an Indian who acquired one did not give up its aboriginal equivalent. Nonetheless, clothes, kettles, and firearms undermined traditional modes of production in ways difficult to discern yet vitally important. Bows and arrows, for example, used to have symbolic significance. Men would "stake their whole happiness upon the beauty and polish of their weapons," Spaniards reported. "Those that they make for ornament and daily use, they fashion with all the skill they possess, each striving to outdo the other with some new invention or a finer polish, so that there is generally a very gallant and honest rivalry and emulation going on among them." When an Indian transferred this devotion to a musket made by other hands, he lost something valuable, though difficult to measure. The manufacture of native goods did not die out, but the time, effort, and skill invested in making them declined sharply. Pottery became simpler in design and cruder in construction, and arrowheads followed the same descending course as craftsmen, instead of going out to find fresh material, chipped new points from the old flakes or broken pieces that past generations had discarded.[98]

The consequences of incorporating most alien products were gradual and all but invisible. Liquor had more immediate and more obvious effects. Natives were by no means innocents plied with rum by a conniving trader; they eagerly sought alcohol and, occasionally, outright demanded it. Nor were its effects wholly destructive. Piedmont Indians fitted drinking into their ceremonial life as a ritual means of achieving an altered state and communing with spiritual powers. They went "as solemnly about it," wrote one colonist, "as if it were part of their Religion," preferring to drink only at night and only in amounts sufficient to stupefy them. Once stupefaction was achieved, an intoxicated person's behavior was, like dream states or spirit possession, a level of existence not bound by ordinary rules of behavior. According to Lawson, "They never call any Man to account for what he did, when he was drunk; but say, it was the Drink that caused his Misbehaviour, therefore he ought to be forgiven."[99]

Despite efforts to tame liquor, its destructive tendencies were clear and at times overwhelming. Intoxicated Indians stumbled over a cliff or fell headlong into a campfire. Those who did not hurt themselves were liable to hurt others, for alcohol, overcoming inhibitions that prevented individual confrontations, ignited battles among townspeople. To natives, rum was like a "poisonous Plant" that could "make People sick," but still they could not abstain. "They have no Power to refrain this Enemy," "though sensible how many of them (are by it) hurry'd into the other World before their Time, as themselves oftentimes will confess."[100]

While the liquor trade created new tensions within a piedmont town, the colonial trade itself disrupted relations between settlements. Aboriginal communities, largely self-sufficient, had traded nonessential items which, changing hands with appropriate ceremony, created or maintained amicable relations among villages.[101] As European materials filtered into the piedmont, the equation of exchange acquired new variables. Trade no longer involved intercourse between two self-sufficient parties, and in the scramble for precious cargoes competition replaced comity at the foundation of every encounter. Some groups were better able to profit than others. In the early 1670s Occaneechees enjoyed power out of all proportion to their numbers by virtue of their location astride the main trading path into the piedmont, and they used threats, even force, to remain middlemen. Their privileged status as "the Mart for all the Indians for att least 500 miles" was obliterated by the Virginia rebel leader Nathaniel Bacon's army in 1676, but the jockeying for position went on.[102] In Lawson's day Tuscaroras occupied a similarly exalted place in the trade regime, "hating that any of these Westward *Indians* should have any Commerce with the *English*, which would prove a Hinderance to their Gains."[103]

The firearms gained through access to Anglo-America warped relations among Indian peoples even further. Some piedmont villages may have taken advantage of their newfound friendship with Virginia to turn on others that were not so well connected. Sometime in the seventeenth century the Cofitachiques and the Town Creek people disappeared, and Indians from the hills occupied some of the abandoned towns. Why the sudden reversal of fortunes? One possible explanation is that these intruders were driven out by upcountry war parties carrying muskets—weapons that Mississippians, denied direct contacts with the James River men, still lacked.[104]

Any celebrations of triumph over these old foes were probably short-lived, for in this native American arms race others enjoyed even better connections to European suppliers. From their base on the Savannah River, Westos (the term meant, ominously, "enemies") traveled across much of the Southeast in search of captives and plunder. These natives were, as one colonist put it, "another sorte of Indians." A loose collection of uprooted peoples from as far away as Virginia and Florida, they had lost the self-sufficiency and attachment to a particular homeland characteristic of aboriginal life and replaced it with a society based strictly on warfare and trade.[105]

Already well stocked with muskets from Virginia at a time when most piedmont Indians were still scratching pictures of firearms into pottery, Westos found those less fortunate than themselves an easy target. When the English established Charleston in 1670, natives along the coast were "Affraid of the very foot step of a Westoe," and those in the Carolina interior lived "in a continual fear of the *Oustack*-Indians [Westos]."[106] South Carolina authorities, quickly realizing that Westos made better friends than enemies, began to ship them arms, which only made an unfair fight even more lopsided. Within a decade, however, Westos fell out with their Charleston friends and were hunted down by the colony's newest friends, the Savannahs, another migrant group similar in character to their defeated foes. By 1683 the Savannahs were ensconced along the river that would bear their name and lobbying for continuation of the slave trade.[107]

Piedmont peoples facing aggressive and well-armed intruders from the south also had to cope with similar pressures from the opposite direction. Unidentified northern Indians had been preying upon Virginia natives since John Smith's day. But the very presence of the many Indian settlements Smith found along the rivers that drain into Chesapeake Bay, and the Iroquois Five Nations' preoccupation with peoples elsewhere, limited penetration of the southern piedmont until much later. Only after 1660 did word of northern visitors to frontier settlements begin to reach Jamestown officials. At first a nuisance, these outsiders did not begin to be a genuine threat until the late 1670s, when Susquehannocks— driven from Maryland by colonists in 1675, attacked in 1676 by Occaneechees and other piedmont Indians, and in 1677 incorporated with the Five Nations—returned southward with their new friends to settle old scores.[108] Thereafter, war parties from the Iroquois and their confederates "infested" the Virginia frontier almost annually, and some headed farther south to more distant towns located "und[e]r the mountaines."[109] By the time John Lawson visited the upcountry, Iroquois warriors menaced every piedmont town. "These [Iroquois] are fear'd by all the savage Nations I ever was among," he wrote, "the Westward *Indians* dreading their Approach."[110]

The Iroquois were not driven by the same forces that impelled Westos or Savannahs. They came south in search of glory, to quiet the cries of those mourning lost relatives, and to bring distant nations under the *"pax Iroquois."*[111] But the Five Nations' deep involvement in the fur trade also lay behind their incursions—and their success. Many were obviously searching for new sources of furs. Virginians worried that these frightening outsiders might "gett the whole trade from our neighbouring and tributary Indians," and indeed what colonists termed war parties were often bands of hunters come to slay deer and trap beaver. Whether they hunted animals or people, Iroquoians, like Westos and Savannahs, were heavily armed by their French and English allies. When Seneca warriors returned from the southwest with fifty prisoners in 1677, an observer noted that the victims had been outgunned. Senecas had muskets aplenty; these captives "were of two nations, some whereof have few guns; the other none at all."[112]

Westos or Savannahs, Iroquois or Susquehannocks—ultimately it did not matter much to communities in the piedmont. They found these raids different from earlier times, when most battles were border skirmishes confined to the spring and summer months.[113] Once European traders armed warriors and spurred them on with the promise of a ready market for captives or furs, enemies penetrated to the heart of the upcountry. A day's walk north of Sugar Creek, John Lawson passed by seven stone piles marking the graves of Indians slain by the Iroquois. A few days farther north, Saponis, Keyauwees, and others were huddled in forts, and everywhere Indians altered ancient rhythms to deal with the threat of foreign attack, which now seemed to fit no seasonal pattern. People spent more time constructing palisades, setting watches, and storing food. Some had no food to store, for enemies preyed upon anyone who ventured into the fields to farm.[114]

Beneath the disruptions of communal life lay countless personal misfortunes, painful memories of a cousin killed, a child taken, a season's hunt wiped out. Among the Keyauwees, Lawson met an Indian who had escaped from his Iroquois captors despite having half of each foot cut off to prevent such attempts. Though he "got clear of them," the Englishman observed, he "had little Heart to go far from home, and carry'd always a Case of Pistols in his Girdle, besides a Cutlass, and a Fuzee." Physically crippled, emotionally scarred, the Keyauwee, like the graves Lawson saw, was a constant reminder of how precarious life in the piedmont had become now that the colonial traders spanned half a continent.[115]

IV

The traumas of disease, trade, and warfare combined to redraw the outlines of piedmont experience in the generations prior to Lawson's journey, loosening people from their aboriginal moorings and setting them adrift in the gray area between old and new, native and European. Two Indian leaders illustrate what had changed and what had not.

Enoe Will was John Lawson's guide during the final leg of the journey from South to North Carolina. Chief of the Eno-Shakori Indians, Will was widely known among colonial traders. He could handle horses, knew the land and its peoples, and spoke more than one language (including, probably, English)—skills indispensable on the Carolina frontier. Better still, Enoe Will could be trusted; he had a "real Affection" for colonists and had always proved "a very faithful *Indian*" with "the best and most agreeable Temper." Lawson found him fascinated with everything English and eager to have his son brought up by colonists. The English adventurer and the Indian headman became friends.[116]

During their travels together, Lawson discovered that his companion was deeply troubled. Will was "apprehensive of being poison'd by some wicked *Indians*," he confided to Lawson one day, and he begged the explorer "to promise him to revenge his Death, if it should so happen."[117] Apparently the Chief's "real Affection" for colonists had alienated some of his own people. Now he was ostracized, bereft of the protection that kinfolk afforded most natives, and reduced to pleading with outsiders to take on the traditional obligations he feared his own relatives had disavowed.

Will survived the threats on his life by leaving his people and drifting into the backwaters of colonial society. Some thirty years later he lived, apparently alone, between the Nottoway and Meherrin rivers, his loyalty to Anglo-America unshaken, his eagerness to please colonists intact.[118] He had fallen into the limbo between two cultures, no longer fully a part of native society yet only a marginal member of colonial life. His career suggests something of the dilemma faced by Indians exposed to another world.

Equally instructive, however, was Will's reaction when Lawson urged him to take the next logical step and convert to Christianity. The friendly demeanor quickly darkened. "He made me a very sharp Reply," the surprised Englishman wrote, "assuring me, That he lov'd the *English* extraordinary well, and did believe their Ways to be very good for those that had already practis'd them, and had been brought up therein; But as for himself, he was too much in Years to think of a Change, esteeming it not proper for Old People to admit of such an Alteration."[119] Devoted to the English, abandoned by his own people, Will nonetheless remained bound to the old ways by threads that Lawson could not see.

A Santee "chief Doctor" Lawson had met earlier in his travels might have understood Enoe Will better than Lawson ever could. This priest had recently fallen ill with "the Pox" and retired to the woods with another who had been similarly afflicted. The two survived the ordeal, an amused Lawson reported, "at no easier Rate than the Expence of both their Noses."[120] What more obvious evidence of his failure to command access to the powers of the universe? How could this be explained in a way that would sustain his authority?

Like Enoe Will, the "Nonos'd Doctor" looked to the colonists for support without fully embracing Anglo-America. Upon the patients' return to the Santee town "the *Indians* admir'd to see them metamorphos'd after that manner; enquir'd of them where they had been all that Time, and what were become of their Noses? They made Answer, That they had been conversing with the white Man above, (meaning God Almighty) . . . he being much pleas'd with their Ways, and had promis'd to make their Capacities equal with the white People in making Guns, Ammunition, *etc.* in Retalliation of which, they had given him their Noses."[121] The explanation was one man's attempt to fuse elements of two cultures. The Santee had not converted to alien ways or shed his own; the foundation of priestly prestige still lay in special access to the mysteries of the cosmos. But now those mysteries included European as well as native secrets, a blend that at once acknowledged important changes yet left Indians firmly grounded in their own cultural traditions.

V

Enoe Will and the Santee priest personified larger forces at work in the piedmont before 1700. Contacts with Europeans were clearly transforming the face of the upcountry. Abandoned towns—their houses caving in, their palisades collapsing, their fields returning to grass—dotted the landscape, mute testimony to the ravages of disease. Among survivors, trade left more subtle but still obvious signs of change. The jangling bells of a packhorse, the crack of a whip, the shout of a trader now filled the air. The sound of flint-knapping gave way to the sharp report of a musket. The texture of cloth replaced the feel of furs against one's skin. The white, blue, and red stripes of duffles contrasted sharply with the natural hues of fox, bear, and deer.

Important as these changes were, Amoroleck's fears about losing his world had not been fully realized even a century after he and John Smith talked aboard the ship anchored near Rappahannock Falls. Though diseases decimated them, the compass points—kin, village, hunting, planting, celebrating, mourning—around which people oriented their existence remained. The deep pools of memory had become shallow, but few had evaporated completely, and a colonist's prediction that Indians would be "ambitious of subjection" to the intruder had not yet come to pass.[122] All had been touched by contacts with the European world. But for every Enoe Will perched precariously on the cultural fence, there were many more with scarcely a trace of doubt. For every priest scrambling to explain his inability to cure new diseases, there were others who were never asked the embarrassing questions.

Despite generations of contact and decades of exchange, the limits to the European presence in the hill country were striking. In

1679 the clergyman and naturalist John Banister, newly arrived in Virginia, boasted: "The Indian Trade. . . . is . . . our Vinculum Pacis [bond of peace]. For since there has been a way layd open for Trade, . . . many Things which they wanted not before because they never had them are by that means become necessary both for their use and ornament." Banister was only half-right. Exchange was indeed a "bond of peace," but only because colonists who entered the uplands abided by native rules. His friend and mentor William Byrd had a clearer view of reality. Well versed in Indian ways, fearless and (at times) ruthless in dealing with natives, Byrd nonetheless sensed that he lived at the edge of an alien universe. "Wee are here att the end of the world," he wrote his English father-in-law in 1690. Others felt the same way. In the frontier county of Henrico was a plantation dubbed "the worlds end"; beyond, according to one trader, lay "the Indain Contry."[123]

The barrier Byrd and many of his contemporaries ran up against was as much cultural as physical. Over the years, Indians and colonists had learned enough to get along in the marketplace, yet deeper understanding eluded them. On the one hand, Indians were amused by these bumbling foreigners. They laughed when a colonist ate his stew with a little spoon, clipped his fingernails, lost his belongings to a clever trading girl, or captured, cleaned, and cooked a bird that natives had "design'd for another Use."[124] On the other hand, however, a deeper and more dangerous befuddlement, almost an annoyance, lurked beneath the laughter. "They say, the *Europeans* are always rangling and uneasy," Lawson remarked, "and wonder why they do not go out of this World, since they are so uneasy and discontented in it." Not even the conjurers could make sense of these intruders. "They say," wrote a colonist of the Virginia Indians in 1689, "that though their God can tell them when their neighbouring Indians have any design upon them, yet he cannot acquaint them with the designs of the English."[125]

Colonists were no better equipped to cross the cultural gulf and understand the world they helped destroy. "Their language is very wonderful," wrote one recent arrival from Europe after overhearing Indians in Virginia talk, "so that I cannot describe how it sounds and how they change their voice." The simultaneous capacity for wonder and incapacity to describe (much less comprehend) what one saw or heard characterized encounters with Indians during these years. Lawson, who time and again witnessed the priests' successful cures or accurate predictions, still dismissed them as frauds. He was impressed by the ceremony inside the Waxhaw council house, but considered the natives' dance nothing more than "strange Gestures" made by "a confused Rabble."[126]

Nowhere was Anglo-American blindness to the realities of native life more evident than in the names colonists came up with to identify piedmont Indians. A dozen or more terms crop up in the records, but a few generic ones were the most common, and the most bewildering. South Carolina, preoccupied with Westos, Savannahs, and other groups west of Charleston, could perhaps be forgiven for labeling all those living toward Virginia as "Northern" and denizens of the Wateree-Catawba Valley as "Esaws" (a term meaning "river" in the local Siouan language). Virginia, which supposedly knew better, was no more specific, calling them all "Western" Indians or adding the suffix *-ri* to "Esaw" to form "Usheree."[127] Neither colony used a single term or said exactly what any of the names meant.

Accompanying the vague nomenclature common at the close of the seventeenth century was a profound ignorance of Indian polities. The first South Carolina settlers, perhaps influenced by Spanish accounts of the natives a century before, wrote excitedly of an "Emperour" among the Cofitachique remnants in the interior.[128] Such inflated talk—along with any reference to Cofitachiques— soon disappeared from the records, yet Anglo-Americans, still unable to wake from the old dreams or discard their own political notions, failed to see the limited character of native authority.[129] "Emperours" there were none, but colonists insisted that the piedmont had "kings" aplenty, in spite of the evidence that most of these figures had little power beyond greeting visitors, organizing ceremonies, and offering advice. Moreover, along with the Indian kings and emperors peopling colonial minds were kingdoms and empires; as late as 1697, for example, South Carolina officials were convinced that Esaws ruled several other piedmont groups, though events proved otherwise.[130]

John Lawson's journey revealed the limits to colonial comprehension. Esaws were there, a populous "nation"; but nearby were other "nations," each with its own territory, its own villages, its own "king." Lawson introduced *Catawbas* to Anglo-America, the term that, in time, would replace all others. For now, however, the word was only one of many; like Western and Northern, Usheree and Esaw, it was neither consistently used nor clearly defined.

The continuing confusion over nations and names hinted at a deeper ignorance of the lands and peoples beyond the colonial settlements along the coast. Trade had permitted amicable relations to develop between colonists and Indians. But it masked profound differences in interest, motivation, and behavior, differences that could bring disaster if they ever surfaced, differences that Lawson sensed. Indians "are an odd sort of People," he concluded, "for their way of Living is so contrary to ours, that neither we nor they can fathom one anothers Designs and Methods."[131] A decade after completing his circuit through the interior, he and many others, both colonist and Indian, would pay for this ignorance with their lives.

The Power of the Steelyard:
The Triumph of Trade

An instance of their resolute stupidity and obstinacy
in receiving a new custom, I have seen in the prodigious trouble of bringing them to sell their skins,
and buy gunpowder by weight; for they could not
apprehend the power and justice of the stilliard.

—Hugh Jones

AROUND 1700 a band of Sewee Indians pushed its canoes
into the water near the mouth of the Santee River and headed east.
The Indians' cargo was deerskins, their destination England. The
journey climaxed years of careful observation and months of feverish activity. From their coastal homes Sewees had watched English
ships filled with supplies—including trade goods—sail past them to
dock in Charleston. Disgusted with the "Cheats" who then carried
these commodities to them, Sewees decided to bypass the middleman and take their deerskins directly to England, where, they were
certain, "a better Sort of People" lived. The scheme met with general approval, and the entire community set to work: some built
large canoes equipped with sails made of reed mats, others hunted
deer and tanned the hides, the rest gathered provisions for the
voyage. At last all was ready, and the fleet disappeared over the
eastern horizon. It was hardly out of sight when a sudden storm
came up, overturned the fragile vessels, and sent most of the Indian sailors to their graves. One of the English ships Sewees had

sought to emulate picked up the rest and sold them as slaves in the West Indies.[1]

John Lawson heard this story from a Carolina trader and retold it with great relish as a bizarre example of Indian stupidity. Bizarre it may have been. But in a larger sense the pathetic tale was a common experience among Carolina natives during these years. Peoples living in the interior between the Santee River and the James were, like Sewees, thoroughly entangled in the web of exchange. They, too, would search for some way to rid themselves of unscrupulous traders without forsaking the precious goods these "Cheats" brought. And piedmont Indians also settled on a bold solution drawn from study of the alien society. Before 1700 a Sewee noticed ships sailing by and looked to his canoe, convinced that the English would be different. After 1700 an upcountry Indian watched Virginians fight South Carolinians for the privilege of purchasing deerskins and, when South Carolinians misbehaved, looked to his musket, certain that an attack on one province would not harm relations with the other. Both decisions combined a serene confidence in the natives' continuing ability to shape events with a profound misunderstanding of the physical and cultural dimensions of the Anglo-American world. England turned out to be much farther away, and her squabbling colonies much closer together, than Indians expected. Inspired by their miscalculations, Sewees set sail and foundered; piedmont warriors invaded South Carolina in the Yamasee War of 1715 and fared little better.

Neither would make the same mistake again. Lawson found Sewees angry with a trader for telling of their ill-fated voyage but also "better satisfy'd with their Imbecilities in such an Undertaking."[2] Similarly cowed, after the Yamasee War upcountry natives were forced to admit that "they cannot live without the assistance of the English."[3] Thereafter, Indians would learn to live with them.

Beneath the frightening lurch from peace to war and back to peace lay the trade. Trade was the lens through which Indians viewed Anglo-America, a lens that provided a distorted image of colonial society and encouraged natives to risk war. It was the loss of trade that then forced them to give up the fight, and the promise of trade's return that helped restore amicable relations. But even as Indian and colonist hammered out a new framework of exchange, it became clear that native independence was a thing of the past; the days when Indians could take trade or leave it were over. Trade was king.

I

Before 1700 no one could have predicted that South Carolina ultimately would rule the southern piedmont. While Iroquois, Westo, or Savannah warriors hovered near upland settlements waiting for the moment to strike, while Virginians loaded their packhorses for another voyage beyond the falls, South Carolinians themselves displayed little interest in the area. From its founding in 1670 the colony had looked south and west. There, large Indian nations presented the greatest economic opportunity and the gravest military threat. There, England's European rivals had footholds from which they could turn the natives against Anglo-America. Before 1700, South Carolinians probably knew as much about Indians on the Mississippi River as about those beyond the Santee. A tentative foray or two into the upcountry, here and there a little trade—this was the extent of contact. When natives from the Wateree River valley arrived at a lowcountry plantation in 1692, startled Charleston officials considered the delegation "strange Indians."[4]

South Carolinians learned the price of their indifference in October 1697 when a band of Sugaree, Keyauwee, and Saxapahaw warriors killed the adventurous son of a prominent planter somewhere in the piedmont. In Charleston a furious Commons House of Assembly demanded that the culprits be delivered up within the month. Winter came and went, then spring, then summer—no answer. In the fall the legislature, still waiting, called on the governor to declare the offending groups to be enemies of the province. These were empty threats. Charleston had no sure means of contacting, much less coercing, anyone in the area.[5]

The episode taught South Carolina that it had little knowledge of and still less influence over powerful, obviously dangerous Indians located practically in its own backyard. To remedy the situation the colony looked to trade, a sure means of getting native neighbors to pay attention. Overseeing their colony's affairs from England, the True and Absolute Lords Proprietors of Carolina had recognized as early as 1681 that "furnishing a bold and warlike people with Armes and Ammunition and other things usefull to them . . . tyed them to soe strict a dependance upon us . . . that whenever that nation that we sett up shall misbehave themselves towards us, we shall be able whenever we please by abstaineing from supplying them with Ammunition . . . to ruine them."[6] Trade, in other words, was a weapon, one the province already had turned against Westos with deadly effect. Charleston officials now aimed at towns to the north.

South Carolina was well aware that in order to be effective the colony must be the sole supplier of essential goods that Indians "could not fetch from Virginia New England New Yorke or Canider without great labour and hazard."[7] Here was the problem: as matters now stood, piedmont natives did not have to "fetch" anything. Men from the James River were happy to bring merchandise to each settlement, even settlements within easy striking distance of Charleston. If South Carolina was ever to establish what it termed a "Reputation" in these villages, it would have to treat Virginians as it did Frenchmen or Spaniards and drive them out.[8]

Only days before asking the governor to outlaw Sugarees, Keyauwees, and Saxapahaws, the Commons House fired the opening salvo in an intercolonial trade war with a resolution "that the Virginians be Prohibitted from Tradeing in This Province."[9] Over the next decade officials experimented with several different measures to achieve this end, issuing demands for tribute and passing a law against bringing horses into the colony, a roundabout attempt to abolish the Virginia traders' packhorse trains.[10] At last, in July 1707, Charleston lawmakers drew up a comprehensive act regulating trade with Indians—complete with a licensing requirement and a board of commissioners to enforce it—and slipped in a seemingly innocuous clause that "any person whatsoever" trading in its territories had to obey South Carolina's rules.[11]

That fall the colony sent James Moore upcountry looking for Virginians. He found none, but—even better—in a Shuteree village he stumbled upon a cache of fifteen hundred deerskins and some English goods that Robert Hix and several other James River traders had stored there before going off to other settlements. Here was an opportunity to make a point without confrontation: when Hix returned to the Shuterees, he found the storehouse empty. To add to his consternation, he learned that his Indian friends were mulling over Moore's suggestion that they strip the Virginia men of clothes and valuables, then invite them to go home.[12] The old trader dissuaded the natives; getting his deerskins back was not so easy. After spending ten weeks in Charleston petitioning the Commons House, posting a bond for good behavior, and bribing various officials, he returned to Virginia with a parcel of skins worth half as much as those Moore had confiscated.[13]

Meanwhile, as part of its campaign to get rid of Hix and his companions, South Carolina offered itself as a suitable replacement for the departed Virginians by sending traders into Indian country with Moore in order to fill the void he expected to create there. These interlopers quickly realized that trade was not the only way to acquire influence in the piedmont. Within a month the new men sent word to Charleston that Indians in the area were being harassed by the same Savannah raiding parties that had been attacking colonial plantations all year.[14] The news created quite a stir in official circles. How convenient that South Carolina's enemies were also enemies of the very Indians the colony was trying to wean from Virginia! The Commons House could not let this chance to win friends slip away; in February 1708, without being asked, it rushed arms and ammunition to the Northern villages, along with encouragement "to Attack the Said [Savannah] Indians our Enemies."[15]

Ousting Hix and enlisting fresh troops against Savannahs was a start, but not much more. The following September, writing of the "Nations of Indians that Inhabit to the Northward of Us," the South Carolina governor and Council admitted, "Our Trade as yett with them is not much." But, they added, "wee are in hopes to improve it very shortly." The road to improvement was paved with alliances, and South Carolina kept trying. In 1709 the Assembly talked of inviting Waxhaws and Esaws down to help defend the colony from a Spanish threat. Nothing came of the rumors of invasion, and the plan was shelved, but soon thereafter officials had reason to retrieve it. In September 1711, Tuscaroras—alarmed by the expansion of North Carolina settlements, disgusted by the severe punishment the colony had meted out to an Indian, goaded by Iroquois who "advised them that they were fools to slave and hunt to furnish themselves with the white people's food"—captured and killed John Lawson before falling upon the colonial plantations along the Neuse and Pamlico rivers. Survivors of the initial onslaught cried for help, and South Carolina responded with two expeditions, the first commanded by John Barnwell, the second by James Moore, Jr. Together the rescue parties killed hundreds of Tuscaroras, enslaved hundreds more, and drove most of the rest to New York to seek refuge with the Five Nations.[16]

Each army of reinforcements was made up primarily of Indians from South Carolina's trading partners. Each contained large contingents from Shuterees, Sugarees, Cheraws (who by then had moved south from their Staunton River home), and other peoples in the Catawba-Wateree and Pee Dee valleys. These settlements, more or less in the line of march, were logical places to recruit an army. Better yet, the warriors' participation would strengthen Charleston's connections to the piedmont. On their part, the natives probably were attracted by the promise of plunder and the chance to go after a traditional enemy like the Tuscaroras. Equally important was reluctance to disappoint a friend. To the Indian mind, an alliance, like trading, was a means of cementing amicable relations. Upcountry warriors who marched off with Barnwell and Moore were expressing, in symbolic language, their newfound friendship.

Despite the colony's harassment of Virginia traders and the attention it lavished on the Northern Indians, South Carolina's hopes for monopoly remained unfulfilled. In fact, William Byrd II and other James River planters shipped more deerskins to England in the five years after South Carolina's 1707 trade act than in the five years before.[17] The secret of their success? It was certainly not the Virginians' political counterattack, though Hix and his partners, angry and well-connected, did their best to see that South Carolina was punished. Upon returning home they had enlisted the aid of Virginia officials, who rebuked Charleston and petitioned London. The case eventually reached the Privy Council, which found against South Carolina. Word of the ruling no doubt pleased Hix and company. But Charleston ignored it, went on seizing men and merchandise, and in 1711 passed another law, this time specifically excluding Virginia.[18]

More important to the Virginia trade's continuing health was the benefit of seniority. As one Williamsburg official boasted, Virginians had been in the upcountry "long before Carolina was reduced into a Governm[en]t" and were therefore deeply entrenched.[19] Add to this Virginia's ability to offer wares at better rates, owing to its more favorable location for English shipping, and more than an occasional alliance or a few presents would be needed to unseat the colony's men.[20] Most important of all may have been native custom, which protected Byrd's men while also encouraging South Carolina. No community rejected overtures from Charleston *or* ousted men from Virginia, because habits of avoiding confrontations within the village dictated neutrality in the growing trade war. Perhaps Robert Hix did talk Shuterees out of robbing him, but the Indians were reluctant to take Moore's advice anyway. They were, by tradition and probably also by choice, noncombatants in the battles raging in their midst.[21]

The piedmont Indians' rare visits to South Carolina suggest that some of them were learning to capitalize on their position between two Anglo-American spheres of influence. The first occurred in the summer of 1692, when a delegation of Congarees, Waxhaws, and Esaws—those "strange Indians" who had surprised Charleston officials—turned up at Andrew Percival's Ashley River plantation. This may have been more than a trade encounter that happened to find its way into the records. A year before and hundreds of miles away, the Virginia Council had worried that proposed high taxes on deerskins and furs would ruin the Indian trade.[22] William Byrd agreed. "The Indian trade [had] been prohibited (all last winter)," he complained in June 1691. "Now the Assembly have laid itt open, but with so great an imposition on all commoditys of that sort, that I fear itt can never bee worth while." Meanwhile, South Carolina officials, for reasons of their own, were slowly tightening the circle of trade until in the spring of 1692 the colony called off the Indian trade altogether.[23]

These events give added significance to the visit "divers Northern Indians" made to Percival's. During the 1670s Percival had

been an important figure in the Indian trade, and while his reach
never extended very far north, he was probably in contact with
Santees or Congarees, who could in turn have carried his goods
farther upstream.[24] It is possible, then, to connect the decisions
made in Williamsburg and Charleston with the Indians' journey to
Percival's house. Catawba-Wateree Valley peoples, their trade from
the north inexplicably reduced, may have been looking to open
more direct contacts with the south.

The only other recorded visit piedmont Indians made to South
Carolina during the colony's early years occurred under similar
circumstances. Sometime between November 1708 and June 1709,
a delegation of Catawbas arrived in Charleston to pay a call on
Governor Edward Tynte. Gifts changed hands, and the Indians
returned home. Why had they come? Once again the explanation
may be found in Virginia. In October 1708, Williamsburg had cut
off trade with all Indians south of the James River in an attempt to
force Tuscaroras to turn over natives suspected of killing a colonist.
The following spring officials lifted the ban, but the embargo elic-
ited protests from William Byrd II similar to those his father had
voiced against high tariffs years before. An embargo that pinched
Byrd could well have pinched those awaiting the arrival of his em-
ployees. If so, the Indians' journey to Charleston may have been
designed to establish closer trade relations so that their people
would not run short of goods again.[25]

No direct link between colonial action and Indian reaction can be
drawn in either instance. But the timing of the visits suggests an
ability to tap diverse sources of European merchandise, thereby
ensuring a more reliable, more abundant supply. This strategy was
also important to Indian survival, for it stymied South Carolina's
plan to crush piedmont natives in the vise of trade.

II

Well placed to approach both Virginia and South Carolina and
profit from being neutrals in a widening trade war, upcountry
towns were also able to observe events among native neighbors
that illustrated the consequences of relying too much on any one
colony. To the south, Savannahs were learning the hidden costs

of such dependence. After they replaced the ill-fated Westos as Charleston's principal trading partner in the early 1680s, Savannahs had enjoyed the rewards of being "good Friends and useful Neighbours to the English." Around 1700, however, the relationship began to sour. Some Savannahs headed north, eventually settling in Pennsylvania.[26] Others stayed on but, for reasons that remain unclear, commenced the raids on colonial plantations and Indian towns that had brought South Carolina capital and piedmont village together in the winter of 1707–1708. Charleston officials finally ended this conflict by driving more Savannahs from the colony and patching up relations with the rest. The province also persuaded Savannahs and the Northern groups to set aside their differences in exchange for colonial guarantees of protection. But Savannah warriors would not be stopped, and they continued to slip across South Carolina to surprise Indians north of Charleston.[27]

That was a mistake. In the spring of 1711, piedmont headmen taught Savannahs a lesson about the benefits of befriending two colonies. Charleston officials received word from upcountry Indians "that they have had divers of their people lately killed by Savannah's, threatning that if they cant live in safety and quiet or have Liberty from us to take their Own revenge, they'l fall on the Savannah's and white men of this Province, and then fly to the Virginians who are ready to receive and protect them."[28] By threatening to attack and warning of a move to Virginia, the piedmont peoples touched on two very sensitive issues that had arisen in the fierce intercolonial competition of the past few years.

Their message had the desired effect. South Carolina authorities hastily arranged a parley between Savannahs and a delegation from the Catawba-Wateree River settlements. The meeting's immediate outcome is unknown, but there can be no doubt that over the long run Savannahs lost. In 1712 more of them left the colony to join their kinfolk in Pennsylvania, and by 1725 only a handful lingered along the Savannah River, as proof that two colonies were better than one.[29]

While the once-feared Savannahs straggled north to escape the honor of being Charleston's best friends, on the other edge of the piedmont Saponis and their confederates were learning a similar lesson in a different way. Soon after John Lawson visited them along the Yadkin River in 1701, Saponis were again huddled under the Virginia umbrella they had forsaken some twenty years before. Williamsburg, considering them "Stout fellows" who were "verry friendly," welcomed the prodigals' return, applauded their decision to settle along the Meherrin River, and agreed when Occanee-chees, Tutelos, and others asked to join them there.[30] In a treaty with these groups in February 1714, Lieutenant Governor Alexander Spotswood gave these developments his official approval and added his own missionary zeal to the relationship. Saponis and their friends, now numbering some three hundred in all, would move to a reservation on the Meherrin beyond the limits of colonial settlement, where they could continue as border guards. In return, Spotswood would build a fort to protect them and a schoolhouse to educate them. After moving several times in the space of a generation, their sojourn was over for a time.[31]

The agreement had obvious advantages for the Indians. Just up the hill from their village was a garrison bristling with five cannons, and trade fairs held there every other month guaranteed a steady supply of merchandise.[32] If in the meantime a gun broke, a blacksmith shop stood in the fort for immediate repairs. And while the Indians were obliged to permit the schoolmaster, Charles Griffin, to instruct their children, Griffin was either unable or unwilling to tread very far beyond the classroom. One day boys from the Saponi town would recite prayers under Griffin's approving gaze; the next they might perform a war dance outside the fort, with "antic motions" and loud shrieks. A deal had been struck that both sides could accept. In 1717 Griffin was pleased to report that the Saponi leaders "express much Satisfaction with their present habitation."[33]

But satisfaction had a price. While Saponi peoples enjoyed use of a tract of land six miles square, they needed permission to travel elsewhere to trade, hunt, fish, or fight. When the Iroquois attacked them or a colonist cheated them, they had to rely on Spotswood rather than their own devices. Moreover, certain clauses the colony put in the treaty were ominous. One would reduce the size of the reservation should native numbers fall. Another permitted the province to push the Indians farther west if settlers coveted the lands at Christanna.[34]

Living at opposite ends of the piedmont and following opposite courses in their relations with Anglo-America, Savannahs and Saponis nonetheless exemplified the same sad moral. One had gambled on South Carolina and lost; the other had fallen into the sheltering yet suffocating arms of Virginia. We are left to wonder whether, as other Indians picked through the ruins of a Savannah town or gazed up at the fort looming over the Saponi settlement, they paused to draw any lessons from what they saw.

III

While skirting the traps that caught Savannahs and Saponis, piedmont peoples were stepping into another. Avoiding dependence on a single colony, they drifted into a less obvious but no less dangerous dependence on colonial society as a whole. The same visits to Percival and Tynte that demonstrated the Indians' ability to manipulate Anglo-America also pointed to a growing need for European manufactures. Natives now could be touched by decisions made in distant capitals by men they did not know and for reasons they could not fathom. This was more serious, and more subtle, than the erosion of craft skills or the heightened competition among towns seeking trade. A foreign technology had blanketed the region, and people were not just accustomed to it: they were addicted.

The process by which dominance or parity gave way to dependence was gradual, even imperceptible to those caught up in it, but in retrospect its outlines are unmistakable. As early as 1670 John Lederer had detected a difference in levels of native participation in the trade. "Neighbour-Indians" bartered with Virginia colonists for cloth, metal tools, and weapons; less experienced "remoter Indians" were content with mirrors, beads, bracelets, knives, scissors, "and all manner of gaudy toys and knacks for children."[35] Only two decades later, piedmont Indians had become so thoroughly familiar with firearms that, according to one colonist, "they think themselves undrest and not fit to walk abroad, unless they have their gun on their shoulder, and their shot-bag by their side." Soon more distant towns would follow, their initiation speeded up by South Carolina's entry into the trade. In 1701 John Lawson considered Wateree Chickanees, a small group settled on the east side of the Wateree River, "very poor in *English* Effects" because a few of the men lacked muskets.[36]

Indians near and far adapted traditional skills to limit their dependence on fresh supplies of goods. A broken ramrod could be replaced with one fashioned from the same wood once used to make arrow shafts. If a musket's stock cracked, its owner mended it or found another Indian who could. Native fletchers learned to chip new gunflints, and there are hints that some people were learning to make their own lead shot.[37] But no native could repair a broken hammer, fix a rusted barrel, or fill an empty powder horn; the Santee "Nonos'd Doctor" had not yet divulged these secrets of manufacture. In time even those Indians between two provinces came to rely heavily on the colonial traders.

As European goods became necessities instead of luxuries, those traders changed from the timid observers of John Lederer's day to confident participants in piedmont life. William Byrd II, who knew many of the Virginia traders and occasionally went with them into the uplands, discovered that these men had made themselves at home in a place Byrd's own father had considered foreign. Experience had provided the trading community with knowledge to combat the perils of the interior. The trader knew which plants cured a rattlesnake bite, where to rest his tired horses, how an enemy warrior's signal whistle sounded, what color sky predicted violent storms.[38] From the Indians he had learned the best way to keep warm at night, the tastiest recipe for cooking a bear hide, the most intoxicating natural substitutes for rum.[39] He had even successfully (if reluctantly) adjusted his eating habits to the natives' fast-and-feast cycle, stuffing himself when food was available and doing without the rest of the time.[40]

Traders also developed a code of conduct. Selfishness and an aggressive, quarrelsome independence—traits some scholars have found at the heart of colonial Virginia society—could lead to disaster in the interior. Hence what Byrd called "the laws of traveling" or "the discipline of the woods" aimed to foster cooperation and sustain morale. All were enjoined to bear up stoically under the rigors of travel. Impassable swamps were a challenge, heavy packs a mere nuisance, injuries not worth mentioning, and rain, cold, or bad food routine.[41] Those who complained or questioned these rules met with public rebuke if not physical punishment. In sum, the traders "made sport of what others would have made a calamity."[42]

It was essential that travelers not only endure but do so cheerfully, for laughter drove fatigue and fear farther from the door. "Innocent jokes" helped lighten burdens and smooth rough terrain. If food ran short, thoughts about the next meal could be laid aside by telling a novice, "who looked very plump and wholesome, that he must expect to go first to pot if matters should come to extremity." When night fell, the adventurers might sing "trading songs" or tell funny stories about their adventures and narrow escapes. Besides passing the time, the entertainment "put . . . all into a good humor," turning danger into the stuff of harmless tunes and tales.[43]

Stories and secrets, recipes and signs—traders had created a culture that blended native customs with personal experience and common sense to render the uplands more manageable. The intruders also felt more at home because they were slowly remaking the patterns of exchange, becoming as much teachers as pupils. Indians watched, listened, perhaps were pushed, and slowly came to trade by colonial rules. In John Lederer's day only "neighbour-Indians" had understood European concepts of value and the accepted means of obtaining that value. These groups "greedily barter for" goods, Lederer remarked, and "will spend time in higgling for further abatements" in price. "Remoter Indians," on the other hand, would happily "purchase them at any rate." As these more distant peoples caught on, however, a trader had to badger his English agents to ship cheaper goods.[44]

Indians transposed lessons picked up from the traders and began "higgling" with one another. When Tuscaroras carried rum to upcountry towns, for example, market day became exciting. Natives measured liquor by the mouthful: "The Buyer always makes Choice of his Man, which is one that has the greatest Mouth, whom he brings to the Market with a Bowl to put it in. The Seller looks narrowly to the Man's Mouth that measures it, and if he happens to swallow any down . . . the Merchant or some of his Party, does not scruple to knock the Fellow down, exclaiming against him for false Measure. . . . This Trading is very agreeable to the Spectators, to see such a deal of Quarrelling and Controversy, as often happens, about it, and is very diverting." Such incidents more resemble what Carolina's proprietors once termed the "Jealousys and heart-burnings" of colonial competition than they do the passive stance of "remoter" groups still operating within the restraints of aboriginal exchange.[45] Native behavior was coming to be shaped by Anglo-American example.

While learning the colonists' noisy art of confrontation, Indians were also introduced to new methods of communication. Natives who watched colonists busily scribbling in a journal or carried letters from one trader to another came to appreciate the power contained in marks on paper. Some, hoping to capture that power for themselves, carefully copied the letters or pestered a visitor to teach them to "make Paper speak." Few if any Indians found their voice at this early date, but many more must have learned from necessity to read the brands that traders placed on deerskins stored in a piedmont hut.[46]

Near the branded packs of skins stood kegs of powder with notches indicating weight, marks that an Indian would also learn to decipher, for traders were bringing natives to measure merchandise in new ways. A mouthful of rum or an arm's length of beads remained common units, but alongside these forms colonists placed pounds, yards, and other unfamiliar standards. Persuading their Indian customers to accept these was not easy. One particular point of contention was the steelyards traders used to weigh the skins and powder. Anyone venturing to set up this gadget had "prodigious trouble" at first, one colonist reported, because of the natives' "resolute stupidity and obstinacy in receiving a new custom . . . for they could not apprehend the power and justice of the stilliard." Nowhere was the tug-of-war for control of the trade more apparent. Piedmont natives could tell whether the person measuring an arm's length of wampum was tall or short. They knew when the "Mouthpiece" stole a swallow of rum. They could not understand a contraption designed, manufactured, controlled—and often rigged—by outsiders.[47] Colonists exaggerated the justice of the steelyard; they did not exaggerate its power.

IV

The trader's ability to introduce to the piedmont foreign elements like steelyards or quarrels grew out of his own burgeoning confidence and the natives' increasing dependence on merchandise he carried inland from the coast. With this influence came a greater readiness to stray from the cultural paths laid out by Indians; and when traders went astray, trouble followed. The transgressions seemed minor at first. Sometime around the turn of the eighteenth century, traders stopped waiting for a summons from the interior and began setting forth when they pleased. Colonists formerly had entered the piedmont for a month or two in late winter and early spring to rendezvous with Indians recently returned from their winter hunts; the rest of the year natives had the place virtually to themselves. After 1700, the traders came at any time and remained as long as they chose. When John Stewart hastened up the path to Virginia in January 1701 after four months among the Catawbas, he met a party of traders heading in the opposite direction, bound for distant towns. An exchange of pleasantries, and they went their separate ways, one more brief encounter that marked an important change in the cadence of the upcountry.[48]

Once in the village, even men who abided by local custom did so more out of deference to their hosts than from any deep commitment to piedmont life. Natives and strangers still interpreted hospitality quite differently. People feeding and housing a visiting trader acted out values governing treatment of visitors and the need to develop a personal relationship with potential trading partners. Colonists viewed the arrangement in their own way. After staying with Shuterees and other piedmont groups in the early eighteenth century, for example, the Virginia trader John Evans pulled out his notebook and entered payments made to his "Landlord" and "Landlady."[49]

An Indian who went further and accepted Evans or some other colonist into the native kinship network through marriage expected him to behave as custom required. It seems unlikely, however, that even the most experienced trader ever fully understood, or really cared, that this union involved obligations as well as rights.

According to John Lawson, colonists saw only the practical advantages of the arrangement. "They find these *Indian* Girls very serviceable to them," he observed. Such "Familiarity . . . preserves their Friendship with the Heathens," "makes them learn the *Indian* Tongue much the sooner," and offers them "the Satisfaction of a She-Bed-Fellow." "Moreover," Lawson concluded, "such a Man gets a great Trade with the Savages."[50]

On top of their failure to grasp a custom's meaning, traders were also shucking outward conformity. Some built a trading hut near but not in the native community, which took them out of the chief's dwelling and placed them both figuratively and literally beyond Indian control. Others mingled careful attention to local etiquette with callous breaches of the rules. During his overnight stay in the vacant Santee hut, for example, John Lawson left the requisite gift, but merely shrugged when he accidentally burned down part of the building while cooking his dinner.[51] Lederer would have fled in panic; Lawson sauntered away the next morning, unconcerned. His nonchalance offered a glimpse of the future. As late as 1692, Virginia officials had been complaining of "the Indians when Our Trad[e]rs are in their Towns[,] useing them very basely . . . often times killing some of them, and takeing their goods away."[52] Increasingly, however, the roles were reversed, and it was the host, not the guest, who had grounds for complaint.

The line between impolite and abusive is blurred; but, once South Carolinians shoved their way into piedmont villages, more and more men clearly stepped across it. These newcomers made up in arrogance for what they lacked in experience. Indeed, David Crawley, a Virginia trader, maintained that by the early eighteenth century his South Carolina competitors had inaugurated a reign of terror in the native Southeast. "When [they] have had ocasion for anything the Indians had," Crawley reported, traders simply took it. To carry goods to or from Charleston, colonists "would Demand Somany men as was able to Doe it . . . and pay very Little for it." Some made up reasons to torment their hosts, drafting an Indian to carry a letter to another trader hundreds of miles away "that hath had Little in it only to Call one another names and full of Debauchery." While these messengers were away, Crawley heard the Carolinians "brag to each other of Debauching their [wives]

Sumtime force them and ons see it my self in the Day time Don." If any Indians "Grumbled or Seem Discontented" with such behavior, traders "threten to beat and verry often did beat them verry Cruelly."[53]

Crawley was by no means an impartial judge. He had lost his wares to Charleston's men more than once, and comparable bad manners of Virginians are conspicuously absent from his indictment.[54] But there was truth in his one-sided account. Virginia traders apparently tended to manipulate natives more often than abuse them (at least the records are almost silent on abuses). South Carolina's own documents, on the other hand, vividly confirm Crawley's charges and spin their own tale of the Carolina traders' theft, extortion, enslavement, and murder.[55]

Why did Indians let them get away with it? The basis calculus of contact remained unchanged: colonists were still a long way from home and vastly outnumbered. Perhaps the same customs limiting a town's control of visitors, customs that kept natives on the sidelines when trader fought trader, also precluded a firm response when trader abused Indian. But what of those who married a local woman and were, whether fully aware of it or not, subject to certain rules of conduct? Perhaps these men behaved, or perhaps they were punished. But native reliance on shame and ostracism as penalties for misbehavior was probably too subtle to hurt the uncomprehending Anglo-Americans. Finally, and most important, the sterner methods of correction that may have cost several of Byrd's men their lives in the 1680s became less common after 1700, for Indians now feared that chastising an unruly colonist risked the loss of trade. John Lawson exaggerated when he claimed that native dependence on European goods had become so complete that South Carolinians were "absolute Masters over the *Indians* . . . within the Circle of their Trade."[56] But his claim was not without foundation.

Indians could also eschew direct confrontation because colonial officials encouraged them to seek redress of their grievances through diplomatic channels. Many natives took up the offer, and in the years prior to 1715, complaints about trade abuses rained down upon Charleston. Most came from Yamasees, who had moved to the coast near Port Royal in 1685 to become important trading

partners and staunch allies against Spaniards in Florida and Tuscaroras in North Carolina. Colonists repaid this friendship by taking
Yamasee lands, stealing Yamasee goods, and abusing Yamasee people. Alarm over the situation to the south had been one of the
forces impelling Charleston to pass the 1707 act regulating trade.
But tough laws passed in the capital were feeble in Indian country.
The commissioners of the Indian trade issued orders, launched
investigations, and demanded punishment. In the end, however, as
they admitted, they were "but a bare Board" which found it "impossible att this Distance" even to stop traders from carrying rum
to the Indians.[57]

To reduce the distance between assembly hall and native village,
the commissioners' agent was to spend much of his time among the
Indians, investigating charges and carrying out instructions. Unfortunately, the man best qualified to serve as agent to the Indians
was—who else?—a trader. The first appointee, Thomas Nairne,
was a success. The second, John Wright, was not. David Crawley
met him and came away unimpressed. Wright, Crawley asserted,
"would when out amongst the Indians have a Great numbers only
to wait on and Carry his Lugage and packs of Skins from one town
to another puerly out of Ostentation." At one stop Crawley over-
heard the agent boast that "hee would make them Honour him as
their Governour," and "often" Wright would be "threatning them
one purpos to make them present him with Skins."[58]

Trade, once a "bond of peace," now provoked bitter conflict.
Soon after the Yamasees returned from helping the Carolinas
in the Tuscarora War, the situation in their homeland south of
Charleston became desperate. Native hunters had fallen deeply
into debt, and hopes of easing their burden were eroded by the
encroachment of cattle ranches that destroyed deer habitat and,
with it, the deer. At the same time, years of warfare were closing
off an alternative means of paying debts by selling Indian captives
as slaves; there simply were not enough candidates for bondage.
Colonial traders, an impatient lot, would respond by nabbing a free
Indian and selling him to cover his debts.[59]

When South Carolina sent several men to conduct a census of
native towns in early 1715, wary Indians interpreted it as part of an
official plan to enslave them all. On April 12 the commissioners of

Indian trade convened to discuss frightening rumors brought by two frantic traders: Creeks, with Apalachee and Yamasee support, were planning to kill the colonists among them and then attack the province. The commissioners sent one of the two back to calm native fears and arrange a meeting with Governor Charles Craven, but by then it was too late.[60] At dawn on Good Friday, April 15, Yamasees who had welcomed the messenger from Charleston killed him and the other traders among them, then fell upon colonial settlements around Port Royal. Sixty colonists died there; one hundred more fell to a second war party between the Combahee and Edisto rivers; the rest fled in canoes or scrambled aboard a ship in Port Royal harbor that lay at anchor just beyond the range of the Indians' guns. Meanwhile, Governor Craven gathered a force together and at the end of the month beat back the initial onslaught.[61]

Despite the victory, the colony's situation was grim. South of the capital, Indians were putting plantations to the torch and killing the livestock they found. By early May stunned survivors were pouring into Charleston, preferring the risk of disease or famine in the overcrowded city to the fate awaiting them on the frontier. "The Consternation is very great everywhere," the Anglican clergyman Francis Le Jau wrote. In the streets "the cries and lamentations of women and children" filled the air.[62]

When it met on May 6, the Assembly did its own share of lamenting. While Governor Craven stressed that "we are still almost naked and defenceless" and "have but little time to deliberate," parliamentary procedure was abandoned as members tried to outshout each other in their eagerness to offer plans for defense or escape. Eventually order was restored, and the Assembly set about collecting supplies, stringing forts along the colony's frontier, and issuing calls for help to everyone from Cherokees to fellow colonists to the crown.[63]

The Assembly's deliberations became more urgent when news arrived on May 8 that "a mixture of Catabaws, Sarraws [Cheraws] Waterees etc." had killed the South Carolina traders among them and were at that very moment advancing through the plantations on the south side of the Santee River.[64] The news was a shock, for the colony had been counting on these Northern Indians to come to its rescue. Now that they had joined the attack on the province, Le Jau observed, enemies "Surround us on Every Side but the Sea Side . . . from the Borders of St Augustin to Cape fear. [W]e have not one Nation for us."[65]

Trapped and outnumbered, some colonists were plunged into despair. At the end of May the Anglican minister Benjamin Dennis considered the situation from Captain George Chicken's fortified plantation on Goose Creek northwest of the capital, one of a handful of outposts still standing between the Indians and Charleston. Confined to the garrison and forced to keep watch half the night, Dennis had had enough. For himself he requested a transfer; for those poor souls with him in the colony he was "afraid [we] must (unless we have timely Assistance) be forct to give up our pretentions to Carolina and be content if we Escape barely w[i]th our Lives." Le Jau, driven from his Goose Creek parish by the enemy's approach, was making plans to sail to Virginia. "If this Torrent of Indians continue to fall Upon us," he wrote his superiors in England, "there is no resisting them. . . . The Time to come is in God Almighty's Hands."[66]

V

Colonists peering into the night for signs of danger or foraging for food in a city already flooded with refugees had little time to write about the causes of their misery. Those who did offered a wide range of reasons, from divine punishment for the colony's sins to the Indian's savage nature, from French or Spanish intrigues to trade abuses.[67] Abuses topped most lists and account for the attack by Yamasees and their neighbors south of Charleston.

The invasion from the colony's northern frontier was more difficult to explain. The surviving evidence contains few hints that these Indians suffered anything like the oppression Yamasees endured. The native complaints from the colony's southern flank had no counterparts in villages to the north.[68] Traders there shaped the trade as they saw fit and bent Indian rules whenever possible. But the presence of Virginia competitors in the piedmont villages may have checked the worst excesses prevalent elsewhere. In any case, it seems unlikely, given the silence of the historical record, that violence had yet reached the Yamasee level or that many of Crawley's tales came from Northern towns. Nor were Indians beyond the Santee River hemmed in by colonial plantations like those crowding the Port Royal area. Hence they did not have to cope with settlers in their towns or with livestock in their hunting grounds.

If these peoples were not driven to war by abusive traders or aggressive settlers, why did they enter the fray? The answer can be found in the piedmont Indians' experiences since John Lawson passed through their towns. During these years "Catabaws, Sarraws Waterees etc." drew upon their contacts with Anglo-America to fashion an image of colonial society that contained a good deal of truth but even more falsehood. To understand their attack in May 1715, we must examine their education.

The intercolonial trade war was a crucial classroom. Indians knew nothing of the flurry of charges and countercharges that flew between Williamsburg and Charleston before scattering across the Atlantic to London. They did, however, witness firsthand the spirited (not to say vicious) competition among colonial traders. Confiscations and confrontations became routine, and a war of words probably accompanied this war of nerves as each tried to persuade Indians of his own virtues and his competitor's vices. Piedmont peoples learned a great deal merely by keeping their eyes and ears open. Colonists looked and acted much alike, they all called themselves children of the great English king, they all pulled wonderful things out of their packs. But there were deep divisions among them, and they quarreled with one another like the "mad Wolves" Indians found so repulsive.[69]

The Tuscarora War also taught Indians important lessons about British America. During the Barnwell and Moore campaigns natives saw more of colonial society than ever before. They encountered not only traders but settlers and officials, not only men but women and children, not only the artifacts of an alien world that could be found in a trader's pack but plantations and towns. It was an education of enormous significance, not least because it only confirmed the impressions natives had gleaned from trade.

Hints of divisions akin to those among the traders cropped up as soon as the colonial reinforcements arrived in a piedmont village to recruit warriors. Indians listening politely to Barnwell or Moore must have wondered why, if North Carolina's rescue was so vital, the Charleston people had been able to rally only a handful of men to the cause. In native society, an important warrior would have gone from town to town explaining his mission and harvesting young men.[70] Considered in these terms, Barnwell's thirty-three soldiers and Moore's thirty made a poor showing. Were South Carolinians unwilling to save their fellow colonists to the north? Indians in the Catawba-Wateree and Pee Dee valleys listened, pondered, and went. But doubts about these strange men and their expedition must have lingered.

The doubts were confirmed when the armies arrived in North Carolina to find Virginia conspicuously absent. Negotiations with Spotswood had brought the beleaguered colony more broken promises and charges of bad faith than blankets or muskets.[71] Even worse, it appeared that, while Virginia officials balked at helping North Carolina's friends, Virginia traders had few qualms about aiding North Carolina's enemies. A Tuscarora captured by Barnwell's Indian allies reported that what little powder his people still possessed they had bought from colonists, and settlers later released from Tuscarora captivity confirmed that Virginians had sold the Indians four hundred buckskins worth of ammunition. On making a tenuous peace in April 1712, Barnwell demanded that the Tuscaroras turn over to him their horses, deerskins, and plunder, only to be told that they had already traded it all to Virginia.[72]

Lieutenant Governor Spotswood had done his best, slapping an embargo on trade as soon as he learned of the Tuscarora attack. It was not enough, and he was forced to order the arrest of several men for trading with Tuscaroras, "even for powder and shott to the manifest endangering the peace of this Colony."[73] Once the war ended, he admitted that he could do little to dam the river of goods. "Notwithstanding the repeated Orders of the Government against furnishing these Indians with Stores of War," he explained, "it is but too certain they had Supplys, both from the people of Carolina and of Virginia." In fact, he went on angrily, "some of them [Virginia traders] were so open as to tell me they could [not] Submit to have their Trade restrain'd . . . whenever a Governor thought fitt to declare an Indian War." Piedmont warriors accompanying Barnwell or Moore did not have to be told any of this. After joining an army composed of nine Indians for every colonist and finding "a world of plunder" (including trade goods) in deserted Tuscarora towns, they knew as well as officials who read Barnwell's dispatches or Spotswood's letters that colonists had failed to unite.[74]

At the same time, visits to North Carolina planted in native minds the notion that Anglo-America was as weak as it was divided. Even at its best, North Carolina was an unimpressive example of English colonization; in the midst of a war it was a sorry sight indeed. On the way to Bath, Barnwell's Indian allies passed through one ruined plantation after another. The town itself was not much better, filled with "poor distressed wretches," including some three hundred "miserable" women and children, most of them without food or clothes in the dead of winter.[75]

This was the first glimpse many natives had of Anglo-American settlements, the source of traders and their wonderful goods. No doubt Indians knew that they were seeing a society in extremis. Nonetheless, nothing they saw would overturn their growing convictions about colonial America. Spotswood, for one, knew the danger of letting natives see too much. It was essential to prevent "all Indians from coming near the dwellings of any of the English," he declared. "They have naturally an opinion of the power of the English, but when they are permitted to come frequently among the Inhab[itan]ts, to see the weakness and scattering manner of living of many Familys on the frontier plantations, these Impressions wear off." If a visit to any colony might "wear off" Indians' awe, a tour of North Carolina in 1712 or 1713 must have obliterated any remaining doubts about British America.[76]

Sugarees, Waterees, Cheraws, and other piedmont warriors who went with Barnwell or Moore carried the information they picked up back to their villages with the slaves and other plunder, related it to their kinfolk, and discussed it in the seasons to come. The knowledge they acquired supplemented rather than supplanted what they had learned from exchange. The "Jealousys and heart-burnings" of the traders now seemed only a sample of the bitter feelings dividing colonists. Moreover, a trip to North Carolina contradicted any boasts about the power of the English; Indians had seen with their own eyes that it was not so. Courted by two colonies, controlled by none, their confidence soared. "Our Indian Allyes are grown haughty of late," a colonist observed in 1712.[77]

The Tuscarora War taught Indians as much about each other as about colonial America, and this, too, helped bring on the uprising in 1715. Both Barnwell and Moore recruited warriors from distant and culturally distinct communities. While almost nothing is known about contacts among Catawbas, Yamasees, Apalachees, Creeks, Cherokees, and the others during the expeditions into North Carolina, it is not hard to imagine their discussing the colonists they were helping as well as the Tuscaroras they were fighting. Traveling, camping, and foraging together, Carolina's Indian allies had an opportunity to discover common problems and common grievances that might, ultimately, find a common solution.

Once again, Spotswood recognized the danger. Soon after hearing of the Indians' attack on South Carolina in 1715, he suggested that the fault lay with Charleston officials, who "whenever their necessitys required, (as . . . in reducing the Tuscaroros after the massacre of No. Carolina,) Called to their Assistance great numbers of different Nations, and by this means [have] given them an opportunity to forme a general Conspiracy against that Province." Certainly for the natives involved, attachments formed during the North Carolina campaigns lasted long after the war was over. "If you have aney Eneyme the[y] Shall Be owers to[o]," Catawbas promised Creeks in 1751, "for we Do not forget Sence Your Naiton and owers went with the white Pepol to Cut of[f] the thuskeroros."[78]

The Yamasee War was not planned around campfires in Tuscarora country. But it *was* planned, and events in 1712 made the planning easier by making piedmont towns more receptive to a Yamasee ambassador when he did arrive to recruit allies. The message that these men carried around the fringes of English Carolina in the months before that fatal Good Friday must have included gruesome tales of the desperate situation south of Charleston along with assurances that Creeks, Cherokees, and even Spaniards had joined the conspiracy. In addition, threats about the fate of those who decided to sit out the coming conflict left villagers in the country north of the Santee River to contemplate the costs of neutrality.[79]

Virginia traders may well have helped overcome any hesitation. Certainly the besieged South Carolinians thought they had. Some in Charleston issued blanket condemnations of all Virginians operating in the area; others named names. All asserted that these men had "encouraged our Indians to do what they have done and promised to supply them at a much easier rate than our Indian Traders did and that they would give them much better treatment."[80]

Officials in Williamsburg vehemently denied the charge, but they were far removed from the smoky townhouses where piedmont warriors and colonial traders talked through the long winter nights. One scrap of evidence belies those stout denials. The Virginia trader John Evans carried an account book with him on his journeys into the interior. In it he scribbled—haphazardly, cryptically, often illegibly—some of his dealings with Indians. Between 1702 and 1705 Evans recorded several voyages into the upcountry, in the course of which he exchanged the usual array of merchandise—cloth, kettles, shirts, tomahawks, powder, rum—for deerskins and a few furs. Then the notebook is silent until March 1715, the month before the outbreak of the Yamasee War, when Evans jotted down a trading spree with unidentified Indians. Again he acquired peltry. But this time the array of merchandise he traded in return had narrowed considerably. A few knives, a pair of tobacco tongs, a little paint, a "flap" or two of cloth: the rest—twenty-three of thirty-six recorded transactions—was powder or shot. The striking shift in the wares Evans apparently sold is hardly sufficient evidence to convict him of fomenting war. But if he recognized the change, if he suspected that his native trading partners were stocking up for something more than hunting, he did nothing to spread the alarm.[81]

At the very least, Virginia traders, merely by their rivalry with Charleston, helped Indians reach a decision. For years men from the north had been doing everything they could to poison the minds of their piedmont customers against South Carolina, to assure Indians that rough treatment of these newcomers would not affect friendship with Virginia. The fingerprints of Virginia traders were all over the threat upcountry chiefs had sent South Carolina in 1711. No Williamsburg official would have harbored Indians guilty of attacks on fellow colonists, but at the time piedmont natives could not know that, because direct contacts between village headmen and colonial officials were rare if not nonexistent. Traders served as go-betweens, and the role gave them enormous influence. William Byrd I, for example, was known to "all the *Indians* round about, who, without knowing the Name of any Governour, have ever been kept in order by Him." After Byrd's death in 1704, others took his place. Even a colonial official as interested in Indian affairs as Alexander Spotswood had to confess that the bulk of the colony's trade was with distant native groups whose "names [are] scarce known to any but the Traders."[82]

Thus the information about colonial society that traders dispensed was every bit as important as the guns or axes they sold. Little of what natives learned can be recovered, but it seems clear that the traders were painting a false portrait of the world developing along the coast, and natives apparently believed them. The 1711 message was an example; in 1715 came a second. When it was time to kill the men from South Carolina, upcountry warriors robbed and detained—but did not dispatch—the Virginians among them. By sparing these men, Indians were, according to their understanding of the rules of war, keeping alive the crucial connection to Virginia.[83]

Piedmont peoples did not have to accept the word of Yamasees or Virginians on faith, of course. Events gave substance to the promises and the rumors. Was there indeed a widespread conspiracy? Seventy Cherokees arrived to accompany the upcountry bands on their march downriver.[84] If the Indians did attack, could South Carolina destroy them as it had the Tuscaroras? Success in that conflict had been due largely to Indian allies, and those warriors now were arrayed against the province. Would Virginia rush help to the stricken colony? For years traders from the two provinces had been squabbling in the natives' midst, and during North Carolina's troubles Williamsburg helped Tuscaroras more than colonists. Perhaps North Carolina would come to the rescue? Experience suggested that this colony was unable to defend itself, much less anyone else.

Still, doubts remained, and the Northern Indians hesitated. Perhaps the decision pitted old against young, as it had among the

Tuscaroras a few years before when "the old men and chiefs wept bitterly and told them the ill consequences would follow." If Virginia traders who were in the area at the time can be believed, upcountry peoples were actually preparing to aid South Carolina against the Yamasees. But the atmosphere was so charged with tension and uncertainty that the smallest spark could ignite a conflagration. The spark took the form of a rumor that colonists had killed a party of piedmont Indian traders making its way through the lowcountry to Charleston.[85] Whether the story was true is unknown and unimportant. Indians recalled past incidents, knew colonists were capable of such things, and believed it. The doubters fell silent, and the South Carolina traders were doomed.

By itself, neither a rumor nor a generation of intercultural contact would have brought war. Together, however, they were explosive. According to the Indians' calculations, war's potential benefits outweighed its risks. They could gain revenge for real or imagined wrongs, placate powerful Indian neighbors, perhaps get out from under their debts—all without jeopardizing the flow of precious goods from Virginia. With horror stories of traders' crimes against the Yamasees still ringing in their ears (and perhaps a few of their own to tell), with native support guaranteed, with confidence that the Virginia men would not desert them, in early May piedmont warriors killed the South Carolina traders and headed for the lowcountry.

VI

During the next month a string of successes seemed to confirm the wisdom of the Indians' decision. Except for a handful of fortified farmsteads manned by colonists and their slaves, the lands between the Santee River and Charleston were empty, and even those forts posed little threat to the invaders.[86] Colonists were reluctant to venture out of their makeshift bastions in search of Indians, and warriors who chose to pay a call found that the defenders could be easily duped. On May 14 a war party arrived at John Hearn's outpost on the banks of the Santee, Hearn gave the Indians food "according to our Usual friendly manner"—and they killed him. Three weeks later the commander of another Santee

River garrison, Schenkingh's Cowpen, believing the natives' talk of peace, disarmed his men and opened the door to Indian emissaries, who promptly drew weapons from beneath their cloaks and killed twenty-two of the defenders.[87]

Colonial reinforcements fared no better. On May 15 the Assembly, as yet unaware of the recent setbacks on its northern frontier, sent Captain Thomas Barker with a band of twelve blacks and ninety colonists to Hearn's plantation. By then Hearn was dead and his fort smoldering rubble, but it made no difference to Barker; he never got there. The relief force was only two days out of Charleston when piedmont warriors ambushed it at a place known henceforth as Barker's Savannah. The army, strung out along the path and tangled up in trees toppled by a recent hurricane, was an easy target for Indians hidden among the fallen trunks. In short order Barker and thirty of his men were down, the Indians had vanished, and what was left of the militia withdrew.[88]

Stealth and surprise had combined with a deadly mixture of words and deeds to give piedmont Indians striking victories. The colonists' plantations were vulnerable, their forts few and easily taken, their forces inexperienced in native combat. Soon after capturing Schenkingh's Cowpen, however, the invaders' luck ran out. On hearing the news from a slave fleeing the slaughter on the Santee, Captain George Chicken set out in pursuit at the head of seventy colonists and forty blacks and Indians. Chicken was not a man to trifle with; it was he who had calmed the panicked Assembly in early May and forced members to attend to business. He now took the uncharacteristic step of carrying the fight to the Indians instead of waiting for them to find him.

The bold tactics worked. Late in the afternoon of June 13 he came upon the warriors, along with some of their women and children, celebrating their victories at a deserted plantation near Schenkingh's. Chicken had caught the Indians in precisely the kind of situation they sought most to avoid, a pitched battle in open field at a time and place they had not chosen. The conflict lasted until night, when, under cover of darkness, the natives slipped into a nearby swamp, taking their women, children, and wounded with them but leaving behind their plunder and sixty corpses.[89]

Piedmont war parties never returned, either to that or any other lowcountry battlefield. Little more than a month after George Chicken's victory, four Cheraw Indians suddenly materialized on the Virginia frontier with two bedraggled Virginia traders and six packhorses of deerskins in tow. He had come, the Cheraw chief announced, to arrange a peace with South Carolina on behalf of his people and the Catawbas. Formal treaties were months away, but with this visit upcountry Indians were on the road to submission.[90]

A delighted Lieutenant Governor Spotswood greeted the chief, listened to his proposals, and considered "the Overtures of Accommodation made by the Indians as a particular favour of Providence."[91] The real inspiration for the "Overtures" was at once more mundane and more complex. The stunning defeat in June must have made many Indians reconsider the path they had chosen, especially when some apparently had harbored serious doubts about choosing that path in the first place. Natives unaccustomed to heavy casualties may have feared that, if colonists had succeeded once, they might easily do so again, perhaps even pressing their advantage into the upcountry. Moreover, Indians were prone to consider defeat a sign that their aims were misguided and they should give up the fight.[92]

Doubts mounted as South Carolina's unexpectedly vigorous efforts to defend itself began to pay off. The night before Chicken's attack, Cherokee warriors accompanying the invasion from the north abruptly headed home upon hearing that Charleston had invited their headmen to peace talks.[93] A month later Maurice Moore marched south along the coastal path from North Carolina with some sixty colonists and an equal number of Indian allies, destroying the towns of the Cape Fear Indians and taking eighty prisoners along the way. Natives in his path must have spread the news that South Carolina no longer stood alone.[94]

The four Cheraws then visiting Virginia were learning the same lesson. They had brought the deerskins and traders along, apparently in hopes of reopening trade immediately. Their reception was chilly. Spotswood, who had just shipped weapons and troops to South Carolina, was in no mood to placate Indians. Hiding his delight at the prospect for peace behind a stern demeanor, he ordered the deerskins impounded and the Indians taken under guard from Fort Christanna to the capital. Once there, the chief received only encouragement, a passport, and a blanket.[95]

Further proof of Virginia's unexpected stance came in October, when the Cheraw chief returned to Williamsburg with a Catawba headman to resume peace talks. Upon entering the Council chamber they came face to face with George Evans and Robert Fenwicke, commissioners from South Carolina, who proceeded to interrogate the Indians about the war.[96] By this time the colonies were falling out again over South Carolina's promises to pay the Virginia troops, but the piedmont ambassadors saw only that men from the two provinces were sitting in the same room. The scene must have come as a shock to an Indian accustomed to nothing but bitter contention between these old rivals.

As the Cheraw and Catawba ambassadors made their way home from Williamsburg, they found still more evidence of the support South Carolina had mustered. Iroquois war parties had destroyed a Cheraw town in September and remained in the area hunting for other victims.[97] Raids by the Five Nations were nothing new, of course. But these attacks had been explicitly encouraged by New York's governor Robert Hunter, acting on a request from Charleston. By July South Carolina's pleas reached Iroquois towns, so that by fall Hunter could report that warriors had gone out, "and [I] doubt not but they will put an end to the Carolina War by putting an end to the enemies of that Colony." Hunter was not far wrong. The following June, Le Jau surveyed the situation among the Catawba River Indians and reported that "the Mohacks have been very hard upon them of late, and they are almost starved."[98]

Piedmont peoples might have been able to absorb all of these blows had Virginia not placed an embargo on trade. In the past, as towns in the upcountry well knew, embargos had been roundly ignored. But what Indians could not know was that conditions in Virginia were different from the days when traders sold arms to rebellious Tuscaroras and laughed at efforts to stop them. In 1714 the Virginia Assembly passed a law that gave the executive more control over the trade in wartime; Spotswood, for one, was thrilled.[99]

The colony's Indian customers were not. While South Carolina bitterly disputed the effectiveness of Virginia's embargo, in villages north of Charleston the absence of traders and their goods was quickly and keenly felt.[100] Natives fleeing from George Chicken had dropped all of the weapons and other goods they had plundered and most of what they had brought with them.[101] Any caches stored at home were soon exhausted, and by summer's end the situation was becoming desperate. Even colonists in Charleston began to sense that their enemies "want ammunition and are not able to mend their Arms."[102]

The Indians' need for European merchandise was obvious in their negotiations with Virginia. Piedmont headmen visiting Williamsburg invariably spoke of "a Peace and a free Trade" in the same breath. Spotswood distributed a blanket here, a coat there, and even a little ammunition to safeguard their homeward journey. But he recognized that these were only tokens, "their necessity of all manner of goods being very great."[103]

It was not the absence of Cherokees, the presence of Iroquois, the courage of George Chicken, or the arrival of troops from North Carolina and Virginia that ultimately brought piedmont Indians to submit. It was the loss of trade, a loss no upcountry native could have anticipated. Spotswood saw its central role as few others did. "The Liberty of Trade was constantly denied to those Indians," he noted in February 1716, "and to this firmness may be chiefly attributed that the Province of Carolina has obtain'd a Peace upon such easy Terms, seeing the Indians would never have apply'd to that Government, if they might have been allowed the liberty of trading with this." "The principal Inducement" to peace, he said again two months later, was "the promise of goods at cheap rates."[104]

The transition from war back to peace was far less abrupt than the leap from peace into war. Headmen from the Catawba River towns did not arrive in Charleston to sign a formal treaty until the summer of 1716. Virginia, perhaps because it was never directly involved in the conflict, had to wait even longer; piedmont chiefs visited Spotswood at Fort Christanna only the following spring.[105] Even with a treaty in hand, however, colonists were in no position to gloat, for aftershocks of the 1715 earthquake rattled the En-

glish for years. North of Charleston, Waxhaws, Santees, Congarees, Cheraws, and Waccamaws peppered South Carolina as late as
1720, and Yamasees continued to strike British America's southern
flank from their new base at Saint Augustine.[106]

VII

While stamping out these brushfires, colonists had a chance to
reflect more deeply on events of the years past, thanking God
for their salvation, affixing responsibility, and searching for ways
to prevent war's return. As always, some blamed Indians, those
"Cruel and Barbarous" people, "monsters of mankind" with "nothing but the shape of Men to distinguish them from Wolves and
Tygers." Others, however, realized that since natives "Seldom give
the first offence," the trading regime must lie at the foundation
of the recent calamity.[107] Trade had brought war, trade's absence
forced peace; if peace was to endure, something would have to be
done to fix intercultural exchange on a safer footing.

Indians in the interior could only agree. They, too, had been
severely shaken by the war. In the spring of 1717, rumors that
colonists "had a Design to destroy them" panicked villagers along
the Catawba-Wateree River. "All the Towns thereabouts are gathered together," a visitor reported, "building and erecting Forts to
defend themselves." Even as they prepared to repel an attack, they
showed no inclination to resume the war. Their hope, as they told
Spotswood, was simply "a Peace with the English and a Trade with
this Colony as formerly."[108]

Colonial officials were eager to reopen trade, but they did not
want it conducted "as formerly." Virginia had already set up a new
system in 1714 that placed trade in the hands of a group of inves-
tors called the Virginia Indian Company. This outfit would have a
monopoly of the colony's commerce with Indians south of the
James River. In return for this privilege, it was to build and maintain the fort and the Indian school to be placed on the Meherrin
River and stocked with Saponis. Company affairs would be handled by a board of directors empowered to set rates and hire trust-
worthy personnel. Designed to restore commerce and ensure harmony by putting a stop to "the evil practises of some persons

concerned in the Said Trade," the experiment was given twenty years to prove itself.[109]

On June 30, 1716, when Northern headmen were in Charleston suing for peace, South Carolina followed Virginia's lead. Convinced that Indians "are no longer to be kept in Subjection th[an] Necessity or Interest obliges them which may be accomplished by ... making them Dependent for necessaries of all kinds, and in these keep[in]g them bare and unstored," planters in the Commons House overcame the objections of merchants in the Council and passed a new trade act. Instead of a joint-stock company, Charleston lawmakers created a public monopoly to be run by a board of commissioners the Commons House would appoint. The board was instructed to erect trade factories at Savannah Town, the Congarees, the Winyaw River, and anywhere else it saw fit. Using public funds, the commissioners were to purchase trade goods from local merchants and send these commodities to the factories. There, at prices set by the board, men on the government payroll would trade with Indians who brought in their skins and furs. The pelts would then be shipped to the South Carolina capital and sold at public auction, and the native traders would return home with their goods.[110]

Like Virginia, South Carolina aimed to clear the debris of the past all at once. The private traders, those "People of the vilest sort," were eliminated, and with them went the price wars and the burdensome debts.[111] All unchaperoned contacts between colonist and Indian were also forbidden: no more traders in native villages, abusing their hosts; no more Indians straggling into the settlements to trade, stirring up trouble, or, worse, learning the lay of the land. South Carolinians had suffered more, and they made more radical changes, placing trade in the public's hands and dreaming of a day when all Indians traded at a few colonial outposts. But both monopolies addressed similar problems in similar ways.

Both monopolies also angered the merchant community and, as a result, did not last long. The Privy Council struck down the Virginia Indian Company in July 1717; South Carolina's law followed it into oblivion within a year.[112] The Virginia House of Burgesses was quick to get out of the business of umpiring the trade. "Wee are not apprized of any abuses in the Indian Trade," it blandly announced, "and therefore cannot lay it under any regulations." South Carolina, still stung by Indian raids, was not as ready to invite back the disaster a laissez-faire approach could bring. The monopoly was gone, but the lessons learned during the war were not forgotten. Trade laws passed by the legislature over the next few years still sought to limit contacts with Indians and to control those that did take place. No Indian was to enter the settlements unless summoned; no colonist could venture inland without first purchasing a license and posting a bond to be forfeited if he misbehaved. The license restricted a trader to one nation of Indians and forbade him to extend credit. These and other clauses were designed to keep the spirit of the public monopoly alive in a private trading system.[113]

All of these political and legal maneuvers had to contend with conditions in the interior, where traders met and commodities changed hands. The frontier was not a blank canvas onto which officials in Charleston, Williamsburg, and London could paint their vision of a trading utopia. Traders, colonial and native alike, had their own way of doing things. This is not to say that the tinkering going on in assembly halls was wasted; legislators did put together a framework for conducting trade. But within that structure, the defeated Indians managed to shape things to suit themselves. The result was a system in some ways answering Indian hopes that trade be "as formerly."[114]

Natives, though long deprived of essential goods, remained selective about the quality of the powder, the size of the hoes, or the shape of the beads. If the merchandise fell short of the mark, Indians complained. They would also protest if the price was too high. To silence the critics, the commissioners of the Indian trade instructed William Waties, director of the factory on the Winyaw, to barter at prewar rates of exchange. The old trader Eleazar Wigan, appointed to run the outpost built along the Catawba, was given a free hand to sell goods at whatever prices he "shall see best and most proper." Even with favorable rates, some Indians tried to take advantage of the system. In the fall of 1717 the board welcomed the arrival of fourteen Catawba burdeners and three packhorses bearing 570 deerskins. An impressive haul, but according to the accompanying inventory they were 150 short. Investigation revealed that the burdeners had scraped off Wigan's brand and sold the skins separately. The outraged officials, "for good Reasons," said nothing.[115]

Why so lenient? These Indians had just surrendered; now the victors, far from dictating the terms of trade, were not only bending over backward to offer quality merchandise at good prices; they were also overlooking attempts to take advantage of their generosity. The explanation can be found in the piedmont towns, where Virginians had returned in force and a trade war raged once more. Williamsburg officially reopened trade to the piedmont Indians shortly before the peace emissaries arrived at Fort Christanna in April 1717, and forty traders with two hundred packhorses and three thousand pounds worth of merchandise were poised to head down the trading path. By fall Eleazar Wigan reported from his Catawba River trading house that "the Virginians [are] daily encroaching the Trade," and rumor had them among the Cheraws as well.[116]

"So soon as the Catawba Indians are informed of the approach of the Virginia caravans," William Byrd II observed, "they send a detachment of their warriors to bid them welcome and escort them safe to their town, where they are received with great marks of distinction." South Carolinians also noticed a marked change in the "Behaviour" of natives upon the Virginians' arrival. It is easy to see why: the James River men still offered better merchandise at lower prices. They also won the Indians' hearts by relying on packhorses to carry goods to and from the interior. The Charleston commissioners, to save the public money, preferred to hire native burdeners, a risky job with few rewards that the Indians came to despise.[117]

It was just like the old days, with colonists battling to acquire deerskins and vend their wares. Disgusted by "those Interlopers" and their "insinuations," the board in Charleston launched a counteroffensive with all of the weapons at its disposal. It harassed Virginia traders. It pestered Wigan to send detailed reports on the types and prices of his competitors' wares. It ordered him to keep trading "even if you should be obliged by the Virginians' Dealing to abate considerable of[f] your usual Price." It tried to match the samples of beads Indians preferred. It promised more goods, and more packhorses to carry them.[118]

None of these efforts blunted the Virginia offensive as effectively as the Privy Council's decisions to break up the monopolies dominating the southeastern Indian trade. Stripped of official encouragement, their enthusiasm dampened by low prices in England, their efforts restricted by South Carolina laws (which, like those of 1707 and 1711, required licenses), fewer Virginia traders visited the piedmont after 1720.[119] In the 1730s Byrd estimated that the trading caravans, once composed of one hundred horses and fifteen men, now were barely half as large. Nonetheless, Virginia remained important, for it offered piedmont Indians an alternative outlet for the products of their labors. As significant as any material benefit was the Virginia trader's role in continuing the standoff between colonies, keeping natives out of South Carolina's control. Catawbas, noted one unhappy Charleston trader in 1728, "are devided some to the interest of Virginia and others to Carolina so that wee cant properly call any of them ours."[120]

Thus the Catawba River communities were busy places after the war. Salesmen from South Carolina and Virginia paid regular calls, filling native towns with so many goods that the area became a magnet for other Indians. Cherokees volunteered to carry merchandise there from Charleston simply to have an excuse to stop on their way home. Other Cherokee burdeners heading in the opposite direction with deerskins on their backs occasionally took the liberty to sneak off to Catawba River settlements and gamble away the public's profits. Business was so good that the end of the public trade system had little impact. After South Carolina's trade factory disbanded around 1720, private traders quickly moved in and built stores of their own.[121]

Catering to the Indians in their own towns was not what the board had had in mind when it first sent Wigan off to construct that market along the banks of the Catawba in February 1717. The store there was to be temporary, a stopgap measure to placate Indians in the vicinity until a trading center could be built at the Congarees. The natives were then to be enticed to settle near the new fort and trade there happily ever after.[122]

It did not work out that way. Funding problems and recalcitrant workers delayed construction of the garrison at the Congarees until the summer of 1718.[123] By then the Indians, accustomed to being waited on in their own villages, resisted efforts to draw them farther afield. South Carolina did its best: once the Congarees Fort was built and manned by twenty soldiers, natives who came downriver were given a hearty welcome. On one occasion Cherokee traders arrived to find the garrison's gates closed to them and provisions denied. While they fumed outside, several Catawbas arrived and "before the Charikees Faces these Cattawbas was admitted into the Fort and had Regress and Freegress when they pleas'd as their own familier, and at their coming in orders was given to get them some victuals to eat, while the Charikees was allmost starv'd for want of it."[124]

Special treatment did not persuade the Catawba River peoples to abandon their towns and move downstream. It did, however, alert them to the advantages of trading at the Congarees, and, when the garrison there disbanded in the early 1720s, private traders took up the slack. Besides his store in the piedmont, Thomas Brown, the most prominent of these newcomers, established a second one on the site of the old trade factory. Native hunters grew so accustomed to swapping their pelts at the Congarees that in the late 1730s Brown feared that plans to close the store would start another Indian war (see Map 4).[125]

South Carolina officials thought that the freedom to trade at home or at the Congarees would satisfy the Indians. South Carolina officials were wrong, for natives continued to come into the lowcountry to hawk their peltry. Some visited Charleston; a few paid calls at the Winyaw River trade factory. Many others simply dropped in on plantations in search of a fair deal. During the public monopoly the low prices set for trade with the Indians who were still living among the English attracted uninvited traders from farther inland.[126] Terminating the monopoly did not end these visits; neither did proclamations forbidding the practice, nor a law passed in 1733 that raised the penalty for trading with "foreign" Indians in the settlements from one hundred pounds to five hundred pounds. Less than two months after this new act passed, two hundred Catawbas visited the lowcountry to trade with planters named Butler and St. Julien. The colony took steps to stop them, but no amount of diligence could maintain a barrier between piedmont and coastal plain.[127] Old habits were hard to break, whatever a treaty or a law might say.

Butler and St. Julien were only two names in a whole roster of illegal traders who further helped Indians avoid colonial regulations. The problem was not, of course, a new one, but South Carolina officials discovered that it would not go away. Eleazar Wigan himself traded illegally in the piedmont during the fall of 1716, and the colony was busy prosecuting him until it realized he was more use to the public in the upcountry than in prison. Lewis John, a trader among the Pedee Indians, was another who refused to observe the public monopoly yet who, because of his expertise, avoided colonial disfavor.[128] Many others siphoned customers both from the public factories and, later, from licensed private traders like Brown. Petitions to Charleston and surprise visits to native villages to check licenses left these smugglers unfazed.[129]

Whether or not they happened to obey Charleston's laws, the colonists who engaged in trade between the Santee and the James did abide by native rules. It is not that traders before 1715 were hardened criminals and their successors model citizens. But after the war there was a discernible shift back toward minding one's manners. The events of 1715 remained fresh to those who had escaped death during that spring, and survivors of the trade wars passed their memories along to the next generation. Thomas Brown, just arrived from Ireland, got his start in the mid-1720s with stock purchased from John Thompson and William Marr, and the two veterans of many seasons among Indians probably threw in some free advice as well. Brown's competitor John Evans, who established himself along the Santee at about the same time, may have been related to the Virginia trader of the same name. If not, he probably learned his craft while serving in the Congarees Fort.[130]

Entering the upcountry with eyes open, ears cocked, and minds filled with tales of what had happened there in 1715, few traders wanted to cause trouble.[131] Where John Lederer's contemporaries had been ignorant and frightened and John Lawson's experienced and arrogant, Thomas Brown's were experienced and frightened. Their very different relations with native women help to illuminate the change in behavior. Lederer ran from the prospect of an arranged marriage. Lawson's companion leaped at the chance without for a moment considering his hosts' expectations. Thomas Brown, John Evans, and others married native women and formed deep attachments to the offspring of these marriages, attachments suggesting an understanding of Indian ways that was unheard of before 1715.[132] Evans and perhaps some of his fellow traders went even farther, taking on the physical risks, and the social rewards, of heading out with native war parties.[133] The contrast with John Lawson's day could hardly have been greater.

That traders changed their ways reflected a more general reversal of their role in the Southeast. Instead of fomenting war, they now became indispensable to peace. Brown and Evans carried the governor's letters as well as European merchandise into piedmont villages, and they sent back messages with the peltry to Charleston. If communications broke down and a crisis developed, both sides called on the trader. Native leaders habitually visited Brown's plantation at the Congarees "to form their Councils" when trouble with the colony arose. Provincial officials were no less quick to send a trader into the upcountry to assuage upset natives or demand an explanation. When Indians called Evans "our old Freind and Linguister" or officials in Charleston pronounced one of Brown's partners, George Haig, "upon many occasions useful, and serviceable to his Country," they attested to the important role these men had come to play.[134]

In the 1730s William Byrd charged that the South Carolina traders were "petty rulers" or "little tyrants" who "pretend to exercise a dictatorial authority over" Catawbas "and use them with all kinds of oppression."[135] Byrd was either jealous of the Carolinians' success or out of date. Brown and Evans knew too well the fate of tyrants. They acquired influence by behaving correctly—as kinsman, warrior, or counselor—and then they exerted that influence through persuasion, not force. Only in this way could they advance their own interests as well as serve both Indians and colonists. Brown never would have survived two decades' trading among the Indians, and Evans twice that, had they been the "petty rulers" their detractors claimed they were.

VIII

Indians and colonists resurrected trade so quickly that it was almost possible to consider 1715 little more than a bad memory, a brief and unfortunate interruption in the regular rhythms of exchange. Men from Virginia and South Carolina rushed back to the piedmont, bickered over licenses and prices, and preached the gospel of commerce with renewed fervor. Indians there were easily converted once again, and by 1725, towns were brimming with merchandise. Natives were duly appreciative of the traders' return and keenly aware of the difference trade had made in their lives. In the past, the Catawba chief Hagler (Nopkehe) told a colonial audience in 1754, his people "had no Instruments To support our living but Bows which we Compleated with stones, knives we had none, . . . our Axes we made of stone we bled our selves with fish Teeth our Cloathing were Skins and Furr, instead of which we Enjoy those Cloaths which we got from the white people and Ever since they first Came among us we have Enjoyed all those things that we were then destitute of for which we thank the white people."[136]

Yet behind Hagler's gratitude, and indeed behind every encounter after 1715, lurked the fact that the revival of exchange could not hide: while piedmont Indians could still choose with whom they would trade, they could no longer choose not to trade at all. Hagler himself succinctly explained why when he observed that the English "could make Cloaths to supply those they wore out . . . and the Indians could not do so."[137] Carolina natives had learned this simple lesson during a decade of conflict, a decade that changed them forever. Many groups simply disappeared; others were whittled down to a handful of families. Those villages along the Catawba River—Esaw, Sugaree, Shuteree, and the others—survived the turmoil relatively intact, but even there the wounds inflicted by Chicken's troops and Spotswood's embargo were slow to heal.

The shift could be detected in a series of insults, some petty, some not, that Indians suffered after the war. A chief visiting Charleston left empty-handed when the Commons House refused to authorize a gift of three blankets. Another delegation was hustled out of town to make room for a party of Creeks said to be on its way. Still other ambassadors made their way to Williamsburg, only to be kept waiting for days while colonial officials combed the province for an interpreter.[138]

The true index of things to come occurred on the Virginia frontier in April 1717, when one hundred Indians from the piedmont towns arrived at Fort Christanna to turn eleven children over to Lieutenant Governor Spotswood. The youngsters, offspring of headmen, were to be hostages to peace, a practice that at once conformed to native custom and satisfied Spotswood's urge to recruit more students for Charles Griffin's school.

All went well at first. The Indians visited the fort, turned their weapons over to the soldiers as Virginia required, and made camp nearby. Spotswood, who came out to gauge the natives' mood on the evening of his arrival, found the ambassadors well disposed toward the colony and eager for peace. At dawn the next day the whole scheme almost collapsed when a band of Iroquois warriors swept through the sleeping Indian camp. In a matter of minutes the raiders killed five, wounded two more, carried away several others, and melted back into the woods.[139]

Colonists were incredulous. How dare the enemy attack "even under the mouths of our great guns, and whilst we were there?" The Indians, more than surprised, "were highly enraged at this Insult, and perswaded themselves that the English must have been privy to it." A few years earlier, as Spotswood admitted, the result would have been war, and the fort probably would have been overrun. But things had changed. Piedmont peoples had discovered that their destiny was no longer in their hands alone. While priests tended the wounded and buried the dead, while the cries of mourning women and the talk of angry warriors filled the air, the natives' fury subsided enough that Spotswood, with "abundant difficulty," was able to persuade them to go ahead and leave the children as planned.[140]

Adding to the injury, Virginia quickly tired of keeping the hostages. The Virginia Indian Company had maintained the experiment at Christanna, and after English authorities ordered the company disbanded, the House of Burgesses saw no reason to take on the responsibility. On May 20, 1718, the House ignored pleas from

Spotswood and the Council and decided that the hostages "are no advantage or Security to this Government and that therefore they be returned." In such casual fashion was a solemn commitment broken, a commitment arrived at after months of negotiations and one natives invested with great significance as a keeper of the peace.[141]

Such snubs became an accepted part of intercultural discourse, as provincial authorities emphasized the message of the Indians' utter dependence on trade. In a 1727 meeting with the Virginia councillor and trader Nathaniel Harrison, a Sugaree headman reiterated the traditional native understanding of trade as an arm of diplomacy, a means of confirming friendship. "To shew the kindness we have for [the Virginia people]," the Indian said, "we make it our business to kill deer and get skins, for their Traders." A set speech, one probably heard by every colonist since Lederer. Once upon a time the response would probably have been a simple nod of assent. No more. Harrison scoffed and replied, "We don't look on that as a particular freindship in you, for . . . I know you are oblig'd to kill deer for the Support of your Women and Children; and without our freindship in supplying you with Guns, and Amunition you must all starve, and what is as bad, become a prey to your Enemies so that the Freindship is from us in trading with and supplying you with these Necessarie Goods, for your support, and Defence."[142]

Insults like this easily turned into threats during a crisis. When Indians killed several colonists along the lower Wateree River during the winter of 1737–1738, Charleston rushed an agent to the piedmont armed with instructions to demand satisfaction. If the Indians proved unfriendly, he was ordered to remind them "that when they differed with us and applied to the People of Virginia for a free Trade with them, the People of Virginia knowing in what Manner they had used us, . . . refused to trade with them while they were at Enmity with us; . . . and as the same good Understanding remains between us and Virginia, as at that Time so they may expect in Case they disoblige us to be made sensible of the Resentment of both Provinces."[143] Before 1715 the Indians could have considered this sort of talk mere bluff and bluster, as Esaws did in 1697. They knew better now. Virginia and South Carolina might squabble, but in a crisis the differences between them evaporated, leaving Anglo-Americans on one side and Indians on the other.

Thus trade had become a potent weapon for coercing even those Indians living between two colonies. In 1733 William Byrd's exploring party came across the remains of a recent Indian encampment in the piedmont, a discovery that was "a little shocking to some of the company." Byrd was unperturbed. "In case they were Catawbas," he observed drily, "the danger would be . . . little from them, because they are too fond of our trade to lose it for the pleasure of shedding a little English blood."[144] At last, John Banister's dream had come true. As he had predicted in 1679, commerce had become a "bond of peace" tying Indians firmly to Anglo-Americans by a chain of trade.

The shift in the balance of power was real, but it was also incomplete. Because both sides wanted peace and trade, the chain of commerce rested lightly on Indian shoulders. For a generation after the Yamasee War the deer herds still browsed the forest edge or upland stands of hickory and oak, and small armies of traders still made their way into the piedmont. Peoples stunned by the war's dramatic proof that they could not live without the English made a place for themselves within the colonial regime, remodeling that framework but never again attempting to dismantle it. If that meant accepting insults and slights, it also enabled natives to live with a minimum of outside interference. The extent of the Indians' commitment to colonial ways was clear when Spotswood pressed the headmen assembled at Fort Christanna in April 1717 to join their children in embracing the culture of the English. Like Enoe Will, the natives politely but firmly refused. They "asked leave to be excused from becoming as we are," one colonist reported, "for they thought it hard, that we should desire them to change their manners and customs, since they did not desire us to turn Indians."[145] European trade had triumphed; European civilization had not.

3

Many Nations under That Name: A New Society Takes Shape

The Catawbas were a people of Great Extent,
and there were many Nations under that name.
—Shawnee Headman

IN THE spring of 1721, Francis Nicholson arrived in Charleston to take over as the first royal governor of South Carolina. An old hand at colonial administration—since 1686 he had seen service as governor or acting governor of New York, Virginia, Maryland, and Nova Scotia—Nicholson was new to Carolina, and he had much to learn.[1] To further his education, a piedmont Indian headman visited him soon after his arrival and painted a map on a deerskin to show the Indians living northwest of the colony's capital.[2]

Nicholson must have been puzzled as he spread out the unusual gift and pored over its details. Cherokees, Chickasaws, Virginia, and Charleston were all there, familiar enough even to a newcomer. But what of these circles—Succa, Suttirie, Charra, Nassaw, and the rest—that crowded the center and pushed the others aside? Probably few were known to Nicholson or, for that matter, to many in his government. Northwest of Charleston were the Catawbas; it was as simple as that.

Such simplicity was a recent invention. Only during the past decade or so had "Catawbas" become the standard colonial shorthand for the communities—Esaw, Sugaree, Shuteree, and others—at the confluence of the Catawba River and Sugar Creek. The term *Catawba*, mentioned once in the Juan Pardo chronicles and once by

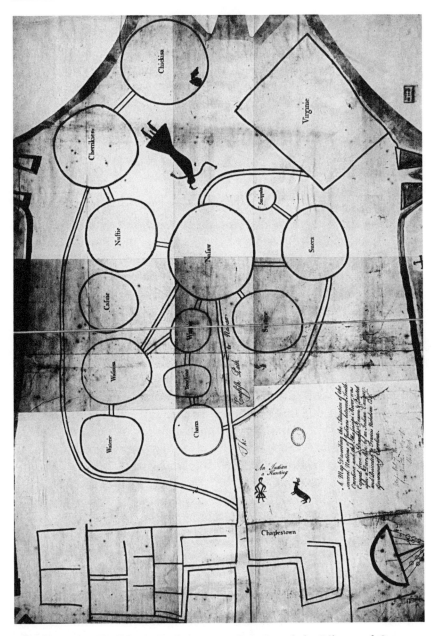

Map 2. Deerskin Map. Early 1720s. *Courtesy of the Library of Congress (original in the Public Record Office, London)*

John Lawson to denote a particular Indian group, began to take on
a whole new meaning after 1701. By some formula long since lost,
it was distilled from the many names for Indians on South Carolina's northwestern frontier until by 1715 it had replaced *Esaw* as the
colony's catchall term for the peoples of the area. During the same
year, perhaps instructed by the Charleston agents visiting Williamsburg to plead for help against Yamasees, Virginians went along,
dropping *Usheree* in favor of *Catawba*. This was the word Nicholson
would have known.[3]

He would not find it on the deerskin, for the headman saw
things differently. "Catawba" was missing from his map because
the word was not an important part of his vocabulary. Where
Anglo-Americans envisioned one people with one name, the mapmaker pictured a collection of independent nations. Some were
more significant than others: "Esaw," transposed to "Nassaw," remained central as it had been when Pardo and Lawson passed
through; at the other extreme were Saxapahaws, a tiny satellite
orbiting Succa (Sugarees). Large or small, each retained a distinct
identity with clearly defined boundaries and, in some cases, its own
paths to peoples beyond the upcountry.

The map failed to enlighten Nicholson (or anyone else). He took
a copy home to England, where it sank into the vast sea of curios
shipped from America. The original vanished; perhaps it rotted
away on some shelf in Charleston. In any case, the colonists' habit
of using "Catawba" to refer to the congeries of communities in
the Catawba River valley was already too deeply ingrained to be
broken by one headman or one deerskin full of odd circles and
strange names. As time went on, "Nassaw," "Shuteree," and the
other terms would crop up even less in the body of records detail-
ing England's relations with the natives there. When South Carolina governor James Glen informed his superiors in 1751 "that
those Nations called by us Catawbaas, Creeks, [and] Chickasaws,
are sometimes called by other names," he did not even list the alternatives to "Catawbaas."[4]

By then it no longer mattered much what the other words were,
for the Indians had begun to accept colonial nomenclature. Within
a generation of Nicholson's arrival the lands beyond the Santee
River had come to resemble his mental map more closely than they

did the headman's. Indeed, by midcentury *Catawba* had undergone yet another definitional mutation, a further broadening of its meaning into something now commonly called "Catawba Nation," to reflect changes in the piedmont. To Glen the new label signified not merely the settlements that had long lived on the banks of the Catawba River; it also embraced more than a score of refugee peoples that had sought sanctuary in the valley. Old or new, all of the Indians there now thought of themselves less as Esaw or Eno than as Catawba, spoke of their home as "the Nation," and in general conformed to the picture colonists had arrived at during the 1710s. The collapse of these many circles into one helped make the difference between life and death for those Indians still in the Carolina interior. Its importance cannot be overstated, nor should the tortuous route natives took to reach this destination be forgotten.

I

A map drawn on a larger scale shortly after the outbreak of the Yamasee War would show, not circles, but discrete clusters of Indian communities scattered through the interior, each battling to hold its own against wars, epidemics, and colonial traders. At Fort Christanna were Saponis, Tutelos, Occaneechees, and Stuckanocks. To the south along the Pee Dee River were Cheraws, Keyauwees, and some Enos, who had found a hiding place from the Iroquois and a trade outlet in Charleston. Due west of this group the Santees, Congarees, and Waterees lived in South Carolina's shadow, and upriver from them, still out of Charleston's reach, lay the Shuteree, Esaw, and Sugaree peoples. Even this more detailed map would soon be out of date, however, for events were plunging Indians into another round of mergers and migrations.

The Yamasee War itself destroyed some groups and diminished others. Santees and Congarees paid a heavy price when they carried on the fight and attacked colonial plantations in the fall of 1716. During the winter many were captured and sold into slavery; the rest fled. Waccamaws, Siouan-speakers from the lowcountry, suffered a similar fate in 1720, losing sixty people to the soldiers and slavers during "a small war" with South Carolina. In the same year, a satisfied South Carolina governor Robert Johnson could

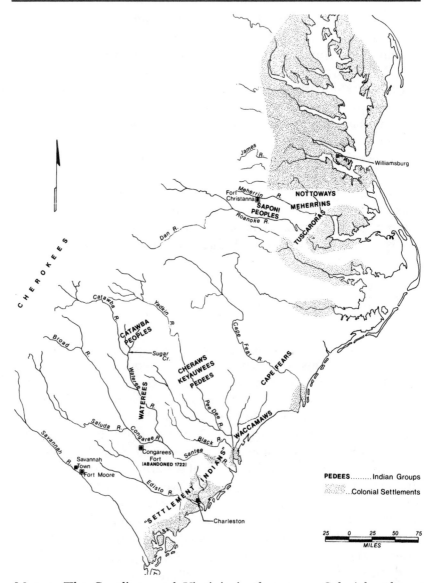

Map 3. The Carolinas and Virginia in the 1720s. *Colonial settlement distribution adapted from Herman R. Friis,* A Series of Population Maps of the Colonies and the United States, 1625–1790, *rev. ed. (New York, 1968). Drawn by Linda Merrell*

boast of "the Northward Indians": "Severall Slaughters and Blood Sheddings . . . has Lessened their Numbers and utterly Extirpating some little Tribes."[5]

While eager to give most of the credit to colonial forces, Johnson granted "Pestilence" a role in the continuing battle against the natives.[6] In fact, disease probably killed more Indians than colonists ever did. In 1718 another colonial executive, Alexander Spotswood, had detected a similar drop in native numbers. "Those Indian Nations that inhabit among or near the British Settlements are of small account, by reason of their daily Decrease," Spotswood wrote. Unlike his counterpart to the south, Spotswood recognized that the loss of population was due more to illness than to the militia. Catawbas in particular "are of late become much lessen'd, by a remarkable dispensation of Providence in rendring their women for the most part barren."[7]

It is difficult to translate official talk into reliable population estimates. On the eve of the Yamasee War, Catawbas (in this instance probably including Sugarees, Shuterees, and Esaws) were said to number 1,470 people, Waccamaws 610, Cheraws 100 fewer, and Santees and Congarees combined a mere 125. Five years later all of the Indians between Charleston and Virginia were put at only 2,500. These totals are low (5,000 would be closer to the mark), but it is clear that none could afford to lose any more people.[8] When a Tutelo headman spoke to Virginia officials on behalf of "the remains of that Nation," his greeting could have been shared by many others.[9] They, too, were mere shadows of their former selves.

Towns already crippled by disease found it increasingly difficult to withstand visits by another old nemesis, enemy Indians. At Fort Christanna, Saponis carried on their battles with the nearby Nottoways, Meherrins, and those Tuscaroras remaining in North Carolina. These groups retaliated by allying with the Iroquois (after 1722 called the Six Nations, with the formal adoption of Tuscarora refugees) and offering a northern war party their own settlements as a base for raids on the Indians at Christanna. Spotswood negotiated a treaty with the Iroquois in 1722 to curtail these attacks, but throughout the 1720s Saponis lost more people in skirmishes.[10]

Farther south the situation was even worse. Iroquois and Cherokee warriors lurked near a Cheraw trading outpost on the Pee Dee

River in the 1720s, ready to attack Indians who came there to barter their peltry. Another band of Iroquois fell upon the Waccamaws, carried off several, and was said to be "very busy in those parts." "The very name of a *Seneka* is terrible to them," a traveler wrote of the "small Remains" of the Cape Fear people, "as indeed it is to most of these southern Indians."[11]

People fighting losing battles against native enemies, diseases, and colonial troops also had to confront Anglo-American settlers for the first time. Soon after the Yamasee War, South Carolina planters began to move into the lands beyond the Santee River. By the end of the 1720s, as the treaty of 1714 had predicted, Virginians had pushed up the Meherrin River to Fort Christanna, and during the following decade Cheraws, Pedees, and Waterees also faced an invasion by colonial farmers.[12] Everywhere native met planter, trouble arose. Settlers sold Saponis rum, then wondered why intoxicated Indians became violent or abusive. More often, natives were the victims. In 1727 a Saponi attending a horse race along the Meherrin died when one John Prowse got him drunk and set his clothes on fire. Five years later William Kemp, an overseer or cowkeeper on a Black River plantation in South Carolina, killed a Pedee Indian named Corn White Johnney.[13]

These were only the more explosive sparks generated by constant friction. From Saponis to Pedees, familiarity spawned contempt, and the prospect of ruin loomed again. The Christanna peoples had been pushed beyond the frontier in 1714; the frontier soon caught up with them. Cheraws had left the upper Roanoke River to hide from the Iroquois; the Iroquois had found them again. And everywhere—even in the Catawba Valley, where colonial troops had never invaded and colonial planters had not yet ventured—everywhere people were tending the sick, burying the dead, and wondering when it would end. The recent past had been bleak; the immediate future looked little brighter.

Piedmont peoples had to search once again for shelter. Where could they turn? There seemed to be few choices left. Tuscaroras, Nottoways, Meherrins, and other nearby groups were culturally different, traditionally antagonistic, and in any case too small to offer much protection.[14] Creeks, Cherokees, the Six Nations, and the Spanish were more powerful, and some refugees did eventually join them.[15] But these people were far away and largely unknown, or if known, greatly feared. That left English colonists or the Indians along the Catawba, the only piedmont population still large enough to provide real sanctuary.

At first it might appear that this was no choice at all. Why would Indians already fighting planters decide to cast their lot with such unpleasant neighbors? Joining colonists offered certain advantages, however, and several coastal groups (generically termed "Settlement Indians" by South Carolinians) had already learned to get by, if not thrive, in this hostile environment. Some continued to hunt deer and trade the skins with nearby planters. Others worked in the South Carolina trading industry, driving packhorse trains to the Creeks, rowing a boat to Savannah Town, or tanning deerskins brought from more distant groups. Still others made a living by capturing runaway slaves, marching against the colony's foes, or accompanying colonial rangers on patrol.[16]

In exchange for a place among the planters, Settlement Indians had to surrender most of their privacy and virtually all control over their destiny. Whether they lived at Fort Christanna or on the outskirts of Charleston, these peoples were within easy reach of armchair missionaries, men devout enough to buttonhole a passing Indian but not zealous enough to venture away from the comforts of home to harvest souls. Each pestered local natives about beliefs and customs, plying them with liquor to loosen their tongues, breaking into their burial houses, sneaking into their ceremonies, asking questions, questions, questions, always condemning their ignorance and criticizing their culture. Why do they do this? Why do they not do that? Do they know of the great flood? Are any of the men circumcised? The interrogation went on and on.[17]

Indians generally met the barrage of questions with silence, saying as little as possible and resisting efforts to make them change. The encounters left both would-be missionary and potential convert angry. "The Indians who have lived many Years among the Europeans are so intractable and unwilling to be Civiliz'd that they will not 'emselves nor let their Children learn to wear decent apparrel to be instructed in anything of Literature or be either taught Arts or Industry," wrote the South Carolina clergyman Richard Ludlam in 1725. "They are wholy addicted to their own barbarous and Sloathful Customs and will only give a laugh w[he]n pleased or grin w[he]n displeas'd for an Answer. It must be the work of time and power that must have any happy Influence upon em."[18]

Settlers pestered Indians in a different way. There was a fine line between the traditional hospitality of the trading girls Lawson met and outright sexual attacks on native women in the neighborhood. As an Indian group's population fell, it became easier for nearby colonists to cross that line, to assume that the Indians' relatively liberal attitudes toward sex invited outsiders to take what liberties they pleased. A visitor to the Saponi town in 1716 recorded a short native vocabulary of useful terms that included—amid "the Sun," "snake," "water," and a list of numbers—the following suggestive exchange: "How d'ye do?" "Will you kiss me?" "Yes." "Come to Bed." "What you please." The same colonist may have tried out his new linguistic skills; he reported (presumably from experience) that the native women "are mighty shy of an Englishman and will not let you touch them." Some Virginians were less willing to take no for an answer. When Nottoway women did not offer themselves to William Byrd's surveying party in 1728, the men "were hunting after them all night" and, uninvited, visited their cabins the next morning.[19]

However attractive the women, however useful the men, planters generally considered native neighbors to be trouble. Indian hunters seemed to kill as many livestock as they did deer, and if their fire-hunting did not burn down a farmer's fences, they made a nuisance of themselves merely by "runing among . . . [colonial] Settlements under pretence of Hunting." A planter who tried to divert this energy to his own ends by encouraging Indians to hunt down runaways found that they killed the innocent African or Indian slaves as often as the guilty.[20] Some natives were no happier with this arrangement. In 1716, Winyaws, who had moved into the colonial settlements along the Santee River, announced that they "were resolved to return to their old Habitation [on the Winyaw River], this Fall; complaining of the Hardship they have met with, in living among the White People."[21]

Natives harassed by farmers and ministers found little help from colonial authorities. True, on occasion an official might distribute corn to hungry Settlement Indians, reward allies with a musket and a blanket, or discuss their need for protection from their enemies. And in 1714 the Virginia Council even went so far as to declare that leaders of the tributary groups no longer be called "king" or "queen" but would "be Treated only with the same denomination which is given them in their own proper Language."[22] But the "hoonskeys" (chiefs) of the Saponi peoples probably cared less about use of their titles than about the tendency among colonial officials to share settlers' doubts regarding Indian neighbors. As early as 1697 Virginia's governor Edmund Andros had argued that tributaries "are or can be of little use by any means yet known." They could hunt, of course, but beyond that Indians were "very impatient and . . . Jealous of liberty and not likely now to be made more Usefull." Even the solicitous Spotswood expressed satisfaction with the natives' declining population. It was, he proclaimed, "as if Heaven designed by the Diminution of these Indian Neighbours, to make room for our growing Settlements."[23]

If Settlement Indians refused to die or disappear, colonial authorities firmly believed that they should earn their keep. Fort Christanna was one example of the potential use of such natives, and in South Carolina the legislature also set out "to Render our neighbouring Indians more usefull to this Province." The first step was to move the Indians about like chess pieces, finding them "proper places" that got them out of the planters' way and stationed them in strategic spots. Once the natives were relocated, the colony drew up a plan to limit their hunting territory, referee their internal squabbles, cut off their supply of liquor, and end their fraternization with slaves. To ensure obedience, spies were sent out to keep an eye on any group thought to be sneaking a drink, visiting slaves, or trespassing on a colonist's land.[24]

Thus Anglo-American officials combined a missionary's fervor with a planter's disdain. In seeking to manipulate Settlement Indians, the authorities time and again demonstrated an insensitivity to native custom that the use of "hoonskey" could not offset. Virginia's relations with the Saponis, for example, exposed a strain of ignorance (or indifference) reminiscent of de Soto. In 1728 the province tried to stop Saponis from taking revenge on Nottoway raiders, even though colonial intervention had failed to obtain

redress for earlier wrongs. "They [and the Nottoways] seem'd resolved to take satisfaction their own way," wrote Lieutenant Governor William Gooch, "expressing great resentment against the English for not concurring with them therein." Resentment deepened
a few months later when Williamsburg officials hanged a Saponi
headman who had committed a crime while intoxicated. In a single
stroke the colony violated two fundamental tenets of native law:
the first against hanging, the second against punishing a person
for something done while under the influence of alcohol.[25] By
year's end Saponis, surfeited with colonial friendship, were on
their way from Fort Christanna to the Catawba River.[26]

The forces pulling Saponis and others in that direction were as
powerful as those pushing refugees out of the colonial sphere. Men
and women weary of angry settlers, nosy missionaries, and arrogant officials must have found the peoples that colonists were now
calling Catawbas a welcome relief. Different as this Catawba population might be in appearance, language, and custom, the cultural
variation here was as nothing compared to the chasm dividing Indians from tobacco farmers, rice planters, and Anglican clergy-
men. No less important, for most remnant groups the exodus to
the Catawba River valley was more an extension of established relationships than a forging of wholly new ties. Since the dawn of
memory, peoples in the region had been trading with one another
and forming alliances to meet outside threats. The arrival of English colonists added more links to the chain of shared experiences,
as Indians traded more and met to fight alongside or against the
newcomers.

The Yamasee War further expanded contacts. For one thing,
planning the war brought headmen from different towns together.
Cheraws were at various times among Enos, Pedees, Waccamaws,
and Saxapahaws, and Keyauwees were also said to be stirring up
trouble in the villages north of Charleston.[27] When the tide turned
in the colonists' favor, making peace united towns as much as making war had. Delegations to Charleston included people from the
Waccamaws, Cape Fears, Keyauwees, Pedees, and Winyaws; to Williamsburg went a party of ambassadors from the Catawbas, Waxhaws, Cheraws, Pedees, Saxapahaws, Sugarees, Shuterees, Keyau-

wees, and Enos.[28] These joint missions, like the joint war parties that had preceded them, were only the most prominent of the contacts stretching across several months and hundreds of miles, contacts where headmen talked of peace as they once had debated war, making common cause even while acting on behalf of their own people.

It was during the protracted negotiations with Virginia that Catawbas, now in common parlance embracing the towns where Sugar Creek emptied into the Catawba River, began to stand out from the rest of the piedmont peoples. At first they worked through intermediaries. That Cheraw chief who arrived in Virginia in July 1715 to make peace for his own people was also "impowered by the Chiefman of the Catabaw Indians" to ask the same for them. Since Cheraws had lived in Virginia until recently, this chief was the obvious candidate for the initial overtures. Once channels were open, however, Catawba leaders superseded him, so that by April 1717, Cheraws were last in a list of eight groups represented at Fort Christanna, Catawbas first. Whitmannetaughehee, "the Chief Man of all the Cattabaw Nation," dominated the proceedings at the fort. He alone had his name recorded by the Virginia scribe; he alone met with Spotswood on the governor's arrival. The peace talks that culminated in their encounter had increased interaction between independent towns and, for the first time, placed Catawbas at the center of those contacts, the hub around which others revolved.[29]

At the same time, Catawbas added to their growing prestige when they eliminated their greatest rivals, the Waxhaws. In August 1716, gleeful South Carolinians reported: "The Wascaws refus'd to make peace with us which obliged the Cattawbaws to fall on them, They have kill'd the Major part of them[;] the rest are fled." Colonists, of course, thought that the natives were living up to their promise to make peace and kill those who refused to follow suit.[30] Colonial encouragement may have been more an excuse than a cause, however; Catawbas had plenty of other reasons to hate Waxhaws. If these "flat Heads" were indeed an offshoot of the Cofitachiques with a culture substantially different from that of natives nearby, their presence may have been deeply resented. Their position astride the South Carolina path would only increase any hard feelings, for it made them competitors of Indians upstream. Catawbas may also have blamed Waxhaws for bringing on the war with South Carolina; it was a Waxhaw who had spread the word about an attack on piedmont traders, the rumor that had banished all doubts about joining the Yamasees. To compound their crimes, Waxhaws apparently abandoned the peace negotiations sometime after their headmen accompanied a delegation to Williamsburg in February 1716.

Thus this powerful group may well have been considered alien trade rivals who first drew others into a disastrous war and then sought to sabotage efforts to make peace. Catawbas needed little excuse to turn on them. The ensuing conflict, besides clearing the path to South Carolina and to undisputed pride of place in the upcountry, apparently had a profound effect on the victors; a century later the Waxhaw War lived on in Catawba memory.[31]

Whatever the Indians' motives for attacking Waxhaws, a delighted South Carolina soon rewarded Catawba loyalty with a trade factory, an outpost that further enhanced their stature in the native world. The store Eleazar Wigan built in early 1717 must have attracted Indian traders into the Catawba Valley, especially when access to European goods was still restricted everywhere else. The arrival of Wigan's Virginia competitors only added to the area's renown as a trade center. And this continued after Wigan left, the public factory closed, and fewer Virginians came down the path, for private traders like Thomas Brown still made the trek to Sugar Creek to sell their wares. The importance of a marketplace for products of the hunt must have weighed heavily in the mind of an Indian group, especially if colonial traders now bypassed that group because they considered it too small to be worth a visit.

This continual round of contacts—begun in the distant past and recently expanded by war, peace, and trade—built up a fund of knowledge that natives could draw on when the time came to discuss a relationship more intimate than exchange or alliance. The Saponi ambassador, the Cheraw trader, the Keyauwee warrior who visited Catawba River towns returned to his home village with information that one day could pave the way to incorporation. He knew which paths to take, which village to approach, which headman to address. He may also have known the local language, taught him by an Esaw warrior in the course of an expedition against Tuscaroras or perhaps picked up from a Shuteree woman during an extended stay in her dwelling.

The Catawba peoples drew on the same pool of knowledge and followed the same paths to approach a band of refugees about joining them. While happily remote from farmers, clerics, and legislators, these towns were sufficiently familiar with diseases and enemy raids; to bolster defenses and replenish a declining population, they began to recruit Indians. The best lure was protection from harm, and Catawbas went out of their way to offer shelter. During the winter of 1716–1717, Catawbas making peace with colonists and war with Waxhaws ignored Charleston's orders to join the hunt for Santees and Congarees; the renegades were welcomed upstream instead.[32] The following spring two Wateree women escaped enslavement in the lowcountry and made their way to Sugar Creek, their owners in pursuit; Indians there announced that the two belonged to them, and the colonists retreated.[33] A decade later, Saponis who fell afoul of Virginia boasted that Catawbas had promised them sanctuary and even had sworn to help them attack the colony. Nor were Catawba efforts limited to protecting people from colonists. Tuscaroras, Nottoways, and Meherrins also learned that raids on Saponis brought reprisals from Catawba war parties acting on behalf of their Saponi "Brothers and Freinds." Similarly, Cherokees who killed a Cheraw found that they had to answer to the Catawbas.[34]

It helped Catawba recruiters that every offer of assistance carried with it an implicit threat, the uneasy feeling that among the benefits of moving to the Catawbas was protection not only from colonists or Cherokees but from Catawbas themselves. Some Saponis were reluctant recipients of aid from their "Brothers and Freinds." "They did not desire their Company," headmen at Christanna informed a Virginia colonist in 1727, "but were affraid to tell them so, because it would make them angry and they were too powerful to pretend to quarrel with." Saponis were not alone in their fears; from time to time Catawba warriors attacked natives living among the Carolina colonists and killed or carried off the inhabitants.[35] Whether or not the harassment was a calculated policy, it was an effective means of persuading people to join the exodus to the upcountry.

Indians caught between colonist and Catawba had a real decision before them: which was the lesser evil? The splintering that occurred within each group forced to make the choice hinted at how hard it was to come up with an answer. Waterees, Pedees, Cheraws, and Waccamaws all broke into pieces, some making their way to the Catawbas in the 1710s and 1720s, some in the 1730s, some not at all.[36] Despite their reluctance to offend Catawbas and their urge to escape colonists, despite the invitations from native headmen and the crimes of provincial leaders, all paths did not lead to the Sugar Creek–Catawba River junction.

II

Those who chose to remain with colonists embarked on a long, slow slide into obscurity. Many joined like-minded groups and for a time maintained a collective identity. Pedees in the lowcountry, for example, divided in half, some living with Winyaws beyond the Santee River, the rest closer to Charleston with some stray Natchez from Louisiana and a few Cape Fears.[37] With "kings" and "war captains," each of these enclaves could boast some semblance of a political organization.[38] Well before the end of the century, however, kings and captains were gone, Pedee, Cape Fear, and other names were replaced by the nondescript terms Settlement Indians or "Parched-corn-Indians," and virtually all had broken down into their constituent parts, the extended family. The clergyman who in 1723 reported seeing "a few familys of Heathen Indians called Ittawacks [Etiwans] scattered up and down" captured the fate in store for every group.[39]

For many, survival hinged upon an ability to cultivate a powerful friend among the colonists. The Pedees near Charleston lived on or near the land of James Coachman, a prominent planter, and became known as "Captain Coachman's Indians." Coachman acted as their advocate, writing letters on their behalf and defending them in the capital. In return the Indians served him faithfully as slavecatchers and perhaps also as traders. Coachman was so pleased with the arrangement that in 1738 he sold the colony one hundred acres of land to set up a small reservation for the Natchez refugees wishing to join the Pedees.[40] Soon these Natchez left Coachman and attached themselves to a Mr. Everson nearby.[41]

Not every Indian was fortunate enough to find a Coachman or an Everson. For every Pedee or Natchez sheltered by a colonist, there were many more natives who drifted from one isolated backwater to another, following maps and schedules they alone knew. Thomas Hasell, minister of a parish near Charleston in the 1720s, reported annually on the five or six families of "Free Indians" in his neighborhood. They are "a moving People," he wrote in 1724, "often changing their place of habitation so that I can give no account of their Number."[42] Other natives must have had a similar itinerary, shadows flitting about the edges of colonial settlement, camping here and there for a few months before moving on. The routine enabled them to exploit a wide range of resources while ensuring that they would not wear out their welcome.

No amount of drifting from this spot to that would have saved Settlement Indians had they not learned how to behave. The rules were many, but survival demanded that they be memorized, and quickly. Where to camp, hunt, and plant, what to say when meeting a colonist on the road, the risks of befriending slaves—all required a crash course in etiquette, and the penalty for failure could be severe. Natives apparently mastered their lessons. After the mid-1730s, reports of conflicts with settlers over hunting, over innocent slaves' being killed, and over land dropped precipitously as Indians adopted a more submissive posture and took up the range of services—ally and slavecatcher, hunter and fisherman, hired help at planting time—performed by such groups since the colony's founding.[43] By midcentury Governor Glen considered them "a quiet and inofensive People and who upon many occasions are of great use to us," hardly what colonists were saying a few years earlier.[44]

Even a secure niche in the lowcountry could not fully shield Indians from the dangerous effects of prolonged exposure to European colonists and African slaves. Natives did not abruptly detach themselves from the ways of their ancestors, and colonists still condemned some of them for "living wild, and besides being a headstrong, idle, Stupid People . . . incapable of instruction."[45] Still, these islands in a sea of whites and blacks could not, without suffering casualties, withstand the cultural pounding they endured year after year. The boundaries between peoples eroded as Indians mastered a new language and adopted new customs; colonists even came to consider some of them "civilized."[46] Eventually the small size of these groups forced them to look for mates among their neighbors, diluting the natives' distinctive cultural tradition and physical appearance until the distinguishing marks became all but invisible.[47]

The capture of one Simon Flowers in the fall of 1766 sheds light on these shadowy peoples. "Brought to the Work-House," announced an advertisement in the *South-Carolina Gazette; and Country Journal*:

> October 26. An Indian or Mustee fellow, about 36 years of age, named SIMON FLOWERS, has a small beard, and born at Santee, says he is free, (but has nothing to prove it) that his father and mother were Indians, named Tom and Betty Flowers, his father dead, but his mother alive has two brothers named Ben and Will, they all live on Santee. He says that when he was little his father bound him to one John Thomas, who lives six miles over the Santee River (near John Morrice and Stephen Willes, planters) and that all his relations live close by; he says his master has used him very ill, and would not let him go when his time was out, but intended to keep him as a slave.—He is marked on the right cheek W, on his left with a single stroke thus 1, which he says his father did to all his children when they were small, with a needle and gunpowder: He has on an old negro cloth jacket, dyed yellow, blue breeches, osnaburgh shirt, and has been whipped very much about his back. Taken up at Mr. George Marshall's up the path.[48]

As far as one individual can be said to represent an entire people, the unfortunate Simon Flowers embodies the history of all Settlement Indians. His identity was at once abundantly clear and perilously ambiguous. The tattoos on his face were the most obvious reminders of his father's attempt to pass on Indian ways, an effort supported by the network of relatives setting Simon apart from his black and white neighbors.[49] At the same time, however, while marked by tattoos and perhaps also in less visible ways by his father's teachings, Simon had apparently lost any recollection of his particular heritage. Was he a Pedee? Sewee? A combination of many? Tom Flowers may have known; Simon did not.

The son knew less than the father because he grew up in a different environment, learning English, wearing non-Indian costume, and, through his apprenticeship, developing new skills. No one taught him enough about the surrounding society to save him from its perils, however. He was not aware that colonists now required proof of freedom; merely knowing one was free, and saying so, was no longer sufficient. Nor was he able to latch onto a powerful colonist who might have protected him from the John Thomases of his world.

Without patron or papers, Simon Flowers stood, with many others in early America, on the brink of the widening chasm that separated Europeans from everyone else.[50] As if by magic, a colonist's glance and the stroke of a pen transformed him from a free Indian into a person of uncertain race and status, and the door to enslavement lay open. Did Thomas or someone else shove Flowers through it? We do not know. In a final irony that again could stand for the Settlement Indians, Flowers's fate is unknown. He remained in the workhouse through the winter; the newspaper announcement abruptly ceased in April; and Simon Flowers, like his family, like so many of those Indians who cast their lot with colonists, simply vanished.

III

Simon's life would have been very different had he, or his father before him, torn himself away from his Santee River home sometime after the Yamasee War and headed into the upcountry. Following the same trails John Lawson once had walked, the Indian would pass the temple mounds of the Cofitachiques, covered now with dense brush, and skirt the silent ruins of the Waxhaw towns, in Lawson's day so full of life. Beyond these lay the current focus of Carolina Indian existence, the cluster of villages coming to be called the Catawba Nation but still known to the local inhabitants as Nassaw (also called Nauvasa, or "Catawba Town"), Newstee, Sugaree, Shuteree, Weyapee, and Weyaline (Weyanne, or "King's Town").[51] Each had its own character, its own fields, its own headmen, yet all were knit together by a shared culture and generations of coexistence.

Though its origins are obscure, a formal political organization was coming to express this larger sense of unity. Without forgetting their town loyalties, headmen, "war captains," and "wise old men" from every community met to discuss matters of common concern. The most prominent figure at these intervillage councils was the "eractasswa," whom colonists called "chief man" or "king." Chosen by the Indian councillors from among those who were kin to former rulers, the eractasswa hosted the council and spoke to the outside world on its behalf. If words failed, a war leader, or "head warrior," stepped forward to organize raiding parties, a division of authority familiar to every southeastern Indian.[52]

While learning their way around, the newcomers came across many others like themselves, people born in some faraway and now abandoned (if not forgotten) town, people who looked, acted, spoke, and dressed differently from their hosts. The Shawnee headman who observed in 1717 that "there were many Nations under that [Catawba] name" would have found many more two or three decades later.[53] James Adair heard more than twenty different languages spoken by the Indians in the Catawba River settlements when he traded there between 1736 and 1743. Adair listed only Eno, Cheraw, Congaree, Natchez, Yamasee, Wateree, and Coosah (probably Creek), but to these he could have added Saponi, Waccamaw, Pedee, Santee, Saxapahaw, Keyauwee, and many others.[54]

More confusing than the number of new groups was their variation in population and culture. Natchez and Yamasees were a mere handful of families, perhaps a score of people in all, while Waterees and Cheraws each numbered one hundred or more. The latter, Siouan-speakers and piedmont-dwellers, adapted to the Catawba River region and their Catawba hosts more readily than did the stray Natchez or Yamasees, remote both culturally and geographically. Between these two extremes lay Waccamaws, a Siouan-speaking people from the lowcountry, and Congarees, probably non-Siouans, who were intimately acquainted with the upcountry from years spent living at the Wateree River fall line.

Siouan or not, small or large, all migrant groups had to rear-

range their lives. Many were by now masters of the art of uprooting
and resettling, and they could draw on experience to smooth the
transition to yet another new home. Those with enough people
kept their distance from the Sugaree, Esaw, and Shuteree peoples
at the Catawba core. Waccamaws, Cheraws, Waterees, and Pedees
built their own towns nearby, each village choosing its own leaders,
sending out its own war parties, scattering to its own hunting
camps in winter, and in spring probably heading to its own fields.[55]
A young Wateree looked to Doueaint for leadership, not to the
eractasswa; a young Pedee followed Captain Twenty into battle, not
the Catawba head warrior. This physical segregation nurtured cultural persistence. A people with its own headmen in all likelihood
also conducted ceremonies, told stories, tended the sick, and buried the dead without interference from Nassaw or Weyaline. Well
past midcentury, Cheraws, Pedees, and probably others kept their
language, that badge of independence, distinct from "Kátahba,"
the Nation's "standard, or court-dialect."[56]

Independent villages were nothing new to Catawbas. Cheraw
Town or Wateree Town simply joined Weyapee, Newstee, and the
other communities already there. Despite the influence of the
council and the eractasswa, the loose collection of peoples depicted
on the deerskin map in the early 1720s continued to characterize
native life for some time to come. Like Cheraws or Pedees, the
towns in the Catawba nucleus—Nassaw, Weyaline, Sugaree, and the
others—selected their own leaders, raised their own war parties,
competed for the attention of colonial authorities, and squabbled
over various issues.[57] Such a flexible political and social order permitted alien groups to join this society without fuss and, once
there, to conduct their affairs much as they had in the past.

This deeply rooted localism had its costs, however. The same
habit of mind that permitted each town to go its own way precluded control over a community that went astray and endangered
the rest. An eractasswa might be able to bring Nassaw or Sugaree
into line through persuasion in the council; culturally related and
like-minded, these towns at the heart of the Catawba Nation had
worked out forms of political discourse for resolving problems.
The new peoples were another matter. Even though the core of
villages probably constituted a majority of the population, in the

complex, diverse entity developing in the piedmont this charter group of older settlements had no mechanisms for controlling its new neighbors, and these newcomers began to land everyone in trouble.

In 1726 Waccamaws and Cheraws "living amongst" the Catawbas committed a series of crimes against colonists and Settlement Indians. At Charleston's request, the Catawba chief and eight others visited the capital in September 1727 to discuss what had happened. Arthur Middleton, president of the Council, was astonished to learn that the Waccamaw town was only half a mile from the chief's own village. "Doe you look upon the Waccumaw's as your People?" the bewildered Middleton asked. Apparently not: "I have Talked to theire King," the Indian replied, "but he regards not." In an attempt to clarify things, the chief went on to explain that "the Wacumaws and Sarraw's [Cheraws] does not live along w[i]th me, And some are one way and some another." He probably meant that they were not under his authority and that some were friendly and some not; it lost something in the translation. Certainly Middleton was lost. "What makes you let The Wacumaw's live soe neare you When they are such Rogues," he inquired. There was no direct answer. "I will Tell them to doe soe noe more," the eractasswa promised.[58]

According to one report, the confusion Middleton had found grew worse. In 1745 Conrad Weiser, the Pennsylvania agent and interpreter, claimed that "the Catawbaws are . . . known to be an Irregular people; they have no Counsel; the richest or greatest amongst them Calles him self a King with the Consent of his Brothers, [C]ousins or wifes, and proofes often the greatest full [fool], acts all what he does as an arbitrator, the rest dont mind him, and after all sends him to the grave with a Broken head. This is what those that were prisoners amongst them all agree."[59] Spiteful gossip by the Catawbas' enemies? Perhaps. Yet there was probably truth beneath the hyperbole. With established lines of chiefly succession broken by disease, with more foreigners arriving almost annually, Catawba society was in turmoil. Hosts and guests alike were reordering their lives during these years, a virtual revolution in which the relatively homogeneous cluster of communities that

Lawson had wandered through became a polyglot "nation." A period of contention, conflict, and even chaos was almost inevitable.

The Iroquois claims may have been outdated or distorted by ignorance and prejudice, but the fuzzy picture the Catawba chief himself drew Middleton in 1727 points toward the same conclusion, a society that was in trouble. The confusion of these years only makes the Catawba peoples' ultimate recovery all the more remarkable. For recover they did, righting themselves after the wave of contagion swept over them in 1718 and somehow accommodating the new groups that moved into the neighborhood. Amid the reports of anarchy were hints of order, as Indians began to sort out rules and responsibilities.

Outside pressures helped the many peoples become one nation. The Iroquois were particularly important, for the same raids that had driven Indians to the Catawbas in the first place continued, forcing them to develop an effective response. The core Catawba villages extended channels of communication to include their new neighbors so that word of an approaching enemy could spread quickly. Waccamaw or Cheraw war captains consulted with their counterparts at Nassaw or Weyaline to plot strategy, check supplies of arms, and compare experiences. The war parties that went out introduced young men from one group to those from another and united them in the risks of a common enterprise.[60] On their return, peoples celebrated victory or mourned defeat together, and in the years to come all would tell stories of battles and heroes. The eractasswa's capture by Iroquois raiders at Fort Christanna and his dramatic escape; the woman who, taken prisoner in the same raid, broke free and made her way home, only to be recaptured a year later and escape once more; the young Cheraw who bested an Iroquois warrior in 1748—these and many more, living and dead, gave independent communities the stock of memories essential to any society.[61]

Anglo-Americans also helped Indians forge a united Catawba Nation. On top of the pressures of obnoxious settlers, Charleston adopted a policy of solving two problems at once by ridding the colony of troublesome Indians and dumping them on its northern frontier to create a sturdier defense there. In 1731 the colony unwittingly revealed its plan to sweep the lowcountry clean of natives when it discussed what to do with the "Ittewans Winyaws and w[ha]t other scattering Indians who have not *yet* joined themselves with the Catabaws." Governor Glen would later boast to a Catawba delegation, "We persuaded the Charraws the Waccumaws and some of the Pedees to Joyn you," and these efforts did indeed help some natives make up their minds. Thereafter, wishful thinking took over, as the colonists' conviction that these Indians all lived "as one People" tended to encourage the very unification outsiders assumed had occurred already.[62] In the Nation itself, the need to cope with British America brought headmen together to receive emissaries and send replies.

Nation building took time, as poor Middleton could attest. Yet a decade after his bewildering conversation with the Catawba chief, a similar dispute brought very different results, suggesting that, whatever the Iroquois prisoners might tell Weiser, natives were beginning to unite. Once again new arrivals (Cheraws and Waterees) had raided the settlements. Once again colonial officials made Catawbas responsible, arguing that since "the Charraws . . . live under their Protection" and Waterees "are also sheltered by the Catawbas, this Government expects that they shall take Care that ample Satisfaction be given." This time, instead of excuses or evasive answers, the official record is silent, a silence that points to an amicable resolution. Apparently the various native groups involved were able to come to an agreement, in part perhaps because they had by now expanded their council to include "all the Indian Chiefs and Head Men of the Nation *and* the several Tribes amongst them together."[63]

While the Catawba Nation appeared to owe its origins to Iroquois harassment and colonial pressure, in fact provincial authorities and enemy warriors only set up the experiment; they did not determine how that experiment would turn out.[64] Iroquois war parties could as easily destroy as unite a foe; it all depended on how that foe responded. Moreover, colonists had a spotty record when it came to putting together a new society from the pieces of several others. Just as Spotswood could not persuade Nansemonds to live at Fort Christanna with their Saponi enemies, so South Carolina's plans to drive Etiwans and other Settlement Indians to the Catawbas never succeeded. The Indians remaining in the lowcountry testified to the limits of colonial influence.

A coherent Catawba Nation could not be created by legislative fiat or provincial decree; it had to develop from within. It could not be manufactured to meet this enemy war party or that colonial agent; it had to be crafted slowly, over the course of many years. Like the hegemony Anglo-America had come to exercise through trade, the Indians' acceptance of the terms "Catawba" and "Nation," with the emergence of a native entity conforming to colonial expectations, points to expanding English control over the interior. Yet, as with trade, the accommodations were more complex. Colonial Americans could draw up plans and try to cajole Indians to follow those plans, but no colony was prepared to force unwilling natives to obey. Many refused to move to the Nation, and those who did modified it to fit their needs. Carolina Indians, as much as colonists, were the architects of the Catawba Nation.

Much of the groundwork for the Nation already had been laid before foreigners made their way to the Catawba Valley. The years, decades, even generations of contact that had brought people to consider joining Catawbas in the first place and made it easier for Catawbas to recruit new members now helped the newcomers settle in after the decision had finally been reached and the difficult move made. Once refugees arrived, time favored the Catawbas. Among the immigrants the old ones who remembered another home, another language, another life began to die out. The next generation might listen respectfully to its elders, but to the young people Enoe Town and Christanna were just names. They knew only the Catawba River and its environs; this was home.

The passage of time also brought depopulation, forcing even the largest migrant group to look beyond its own borders for basic needs. Men came together not only to fight Iroquois but to hunt. Headmen met in council to discuss affairs even if there was no crisis. Women forged ties of their own while tending crops or gathering wild plants. Young men looked for mates in the next village, blurring ethnic distinctions and tangling lines of kinship. And, of course, the need to talk about the war and the hunt, the planting and gathering, the love and marriage slowly silenced the babel of tongues Adair had heard, allowing one language to come through clearly.

Not all natives found life in the Catawba Nation to their taste. In May 1732, Saponis and a few Cheraws visited Lieutenant Governor Gooch to ask permission to return to Virginia. Permission granted, they erected a fort somewhere along the Appomattox or Roanoke river and settled back into familiar territory. The problems that had driven Saponis from Virginia three years before soon returned to plague them: Nottoway and Iroquois warriors picked up where they had left off, and planters hauled them into court for destruction of property.[65] Saponis under this pressure soon broke into fragments, some moving in with the North Carolina Tuscaroras, others seeking out a powerful friend like the trader William Eaton or the former Virginia executive Alexander Spotswood, the rest accepting the invitation of their Iroquois foes to move north and join the Six Nations.[66]

Saponis never told Spotswood, Tuscaroras, or the Iroquois why they left the Catawbas, and it is impossible at this remove to pinpoint the source of their unhappiness.[67] The doubts raised about these friends and brothers in 1727 apparently were confirmed once in the Nation. One Tutelo woman, daughter of a headman, took poison soon after moving south, "fearing she should not be treated according to her rank."[68] Her decision suggests a more general uneasiness, even a foreboding, that many of her people could not shake.

The Saponi experience helps to locate the limits of the Catawbas' ability to absorb outsiders. Though Siouan-speakers and piedmont peoples, Saponis were descended from the Monacan and Mannahoac stock, branches quite distinct in speech and custom from their southern cousins.[69] It would appear, then, that Catawbas could incorporate small and culturally variant peoples, a Natchez or Yamasee band, or sizable groups that were close relatives, like Cheraws and Waterees, but that large and foreign populations proved more difficult. Precisely how Saponis discovered this incompatibility is unclear; but they learned very quickly, and took steps to correct their mistake.

Among those who remained, a traditional, narrow ethnic allegiance slowly faded, to be replaced by a broader, Catawba identity. Out of proximity, common concerns, and shared hopes and fears, people developed ceremonies and myths that made up for those lost to disease and time. Some natives clung to that older ethnic identity.[70] But long before the American Revolution, most peoples in the Nation had begun to speak to one another and to the world with a single voice.

IV

Whatever burdens it placed on host and guest, the influx of refugees prevented demographic disaster. The 570 warriors South Carolina had counted in 1715 might have terrified colonists expecting an invasion, yet that number gave the Indians little chance of surviving the epidemics that struck in 1718 and again in 1738. By welcoming a handful of people here, a few families there, Catawbas prevented a precipitous and fatal drop in numbers. Warrior counts ranged between 300 and 500 through the mid-1750s.[71] Not very impressive when set alongside the 3,000 Cherokee men or the 1,500 Creeks, but enough to sustain a native society in the piedmont and earn the Catawba Nation a place as one of the four "most considerable" Indian peoples in the Southeast.[72] Most important, it protected upcountry Indians from their many native enemies. Between 1715 and 1740, Catawbas deflected the enmity of their Cherokee neighbors, dominated smaller groups nearby, and held their own against more distant, more dangerous nations.

With Cherokees, Catawbas maintained an uneasy truce, quickly settling any disputes that did occur so that no incident led to war. Both peoples faced challenges from other nations and could not risk adding another enemy, especially one so close. Moreover, Virginia traders en route to the Cherokees had to pass through two Catawba towns, and war would jeopardize this lifeline of commerce. It helped that the two sides knew each other well; an isolated outbreak of violence between hunting parties or headstrong warriors could not undermine good will created by trade contacts and a continual round of visits between piedmont and mountains.[73]

With their western border more or less secure, Catawbas were free to turn their attention elsewhere, and they roamed the lands between the Savannah and the James almost at will. Even Indians tucked away amid the South Carolina rice plantations were uneasy when a party of Catawbas turned up. The visitors may only have been stopping by on their way to Charleston or coming to confirm the peace, as good friends should.[74] On the other hand, they came to bully, kidnap, or kill often enough that no native could predict where a Catawba greeting would lead.

Settlement Indians nervously entertaining these guests could take no solace from the fate of other small enclaves farther north. Meherrins, Nottoways, and those Tuscaroras still in North Carolina anticipated a Catawba warrior behind every bush, and they were often right.[75] William Byrd's contacts with Indians during his travels illuminated the plight of remnant groups that had the misfortune to be on the Catawbas' bad side. In April 1728, three Meherrins who visited his surveying party's encampment at the mouth of the Nottoway River told him that their people, recently driven from their village by Catawba warriors, had taken refuge among the colonists in hopes of preventing another attack. A few days later Byrd's company stopped at the Nottoway town, a new and impressive fortress that had been built with Catawbas in mind. Tuscaroras were even more cowed. "Now there remain so few" of these Indians, Byrd remarked the following November, "that they are in danger of being quite exterminated by the Catawbas, their mortal enemies." Extermination never came to pass, but neither did peace. When he set out to explore the Roanoke five years later, Byrd hired three Tuscaroras to supply his party with game. They "were so fearful of falling into the hands of the Catawbas that they durst not lose sight of us all day," he complained, "so they killed nothing and we were forced to make a temperate supper upon bread and cheese."[76]

Raids on these helpless remnant peoples sharpened Catawba skills for more important battles against the Iroquois. The Five Nations became more dangerous after 1715 with the incorporation of Savannah-Shawnee and Tuscarora warriors who knew the Carolinas and could guide war parties to Catawba towns. These migrants were happy to oblige their Iroquois kinfolk: Catawbas had had a hand in driving both from the Southeast, and the transplanted southerners were eager to retaliate. Tuscaroras and Savannah-Shawnees were in on the dawn attack on the Indian camp at Fort Christanna in 1717, and several Savannah-Shawnee towns in Pennsylvania lay on the main Iroquois path south. Thus many men could join war parties passing through on their way to the Catawbas.[77]

Despite such reinforcements, for at least two decades after the Yamasee War the Catawbas were a match for northern raiders. Indeed, Catawbas were so successful that they made a name for themselves throughout the East. Governor Glen was convinced they were "the bravest Fellows on the Continent of America." Edmond Atkin, a member of the South Carolina Council during the 1740s and later crown superintendent of Indian affairs, agreed that "in War, they are inferior [to] no Indians whatever." Even James Adair gave Catawbas equal rank with his beloved Chickasaws for a "warlike . . . disposition." Indians in the Nation were, of course, quick to concur. "The Catawbaws are known to be a very [p]roud People," one colonist noted, "and have at several treaty's they had with the Cherokees used high Expressions, and thought them self stout warriors." "We are a small Nation but our Name is high," a Catawba chief boasted.[78]

Many commented on the Nation's fierce reputation; few sought to explain it. Why were Catawbas feared and their Cherokee neighbors scorned?[79] The answer may lie in their piedmont location. Cherokees could rely on their mountainous terrain for protection. Indians along the coast enjoyed the advantage of swamps that impeded an enemy's progress or, in an emergency, served as a refuge. Ancestors of the Catawbas lacked such natural defenses and may have compensated by developing superior martial skills.

The pattern of conflict that emerged in the early eighteenth century could only enhance any reputation Catawbas had already acquired. War parties from the Iroquois were generally the aggressors, penetrating deep into the upcountry to attack hunting camps, solitary travelers, or villages when the men were absent; Catawba warriors would then pursue and strike back. The Nation's settlement pattern facilitated a rapid, effective response. As Glen observed, "The Situation of their Towns makes them stronger than any Indian Nation of double their Number, for they are very compact, all their Gun Men . . . can be called together in two hours time" (see Map 5).[80]

Swift pursuit by furious Catawba warriors determined to avenge dead kinfolk or rescue captured ones caught many a retreating enemy war party off guard. Catawbas were often able to inflict heavy losses or, as the *South-Carolina Gazette* phrased it, to "repay [their foes] in their own Coin, and with Interest." The interest, and the Catawbas' fame, may well have been compounded because the attacking of enemy warriors carried more prestige than the killing or capturing of women and children. Moreover, losses in enemy territory were especially hard for a people to bear. Those killed far from home fell in what Adair called "unsanctified ground . . . distant from their holy places and holy things," and therefore did not receive proper burial. Some Indians went to great lengths even years later to recover the remains of their dead, but inevitably many were left behind.[81]

Catawbas were also famous (or infamous) for taunting their foes, who were shocked by such "spitefull and Offensive" behavior.[82] One Iroquois told South Carolina that "some Time ago we desired to have a Peace with the Catawbas Nation, who sent us Word that they had two Conveniencies, one for their Women, and one for us, and that they were Men and Warriours since which Time we are at War." Catawbas rebuffed similar peace feelers by sending "word that we [Iroquois] were but Women; that they were men and double men for they had two P———s." Adair reported that northern Indians "were fully resolved to prosecute it [war with Catawbas] . . . while there was one of that hateful name alive; because in the time of battle, they had given them the ugly name of short-tailed eunuchs." Such talk, combined with Catawba success in battle, guaranteed that the Nation's enemies would fight on. One disgusted headman promised that the conflict "will last to the End of the world, for they molest Us and speak Contemptuously of Us, which our Warriours will not bear."[83]

The Catawba penchant for what their foes considered treachery drove thoughts of peace still further from Iroquois minds. Cessation of hostilities was impossible, the Six Nations argued, for Catawbas could not be trusted. They were a "disorderly people," an "Irregular people," a "false People," "a deceitful People" who talked of peace and then made war, welcomed ambassadors and then butchered them.[84] The best-known episode occurred in 1729. In the spring of that year one hundred Oneidas had attacked a Catawba town while the men were absent. Two hundred Catawbas gave chase, caught up with their foes, and the battle began. During the second day Catawbas invited the Oneidas to a peace parley, then killed those who came out to meet them, including the renowned war captain Currundawawnah. At that the Iroquois surrendered, with a loss of fifty-nine killed and many more taken captive. For years neither side forgot the episode, Catawbas boasting of their triumph and Oneidas refusing to consider peace with the killers of Currundawawnah.[85]

The treachery, the insults, the tight cluster of settlements, the formidable skills—all combined to protect Catawbas in the first half of the eighteenth century. Yet more than mere protection or simple survival was involved here. These Indians did not cower in their villages, parrying Iroquois thrusts and hoping that the enemy would go away. War parties from the Nation ranged far and wide, actively seeking someone to fight. Warfare was part of life, and Catawbas shared with Indians throughout eastern North America a culture of conflict, with its own rules and symbols, sorrows and satisfactions. Like their Iroquois enemies and their southeastern Indian neighbors, Catawbas operated within a mourning-war complex that demanded vengeance for a community's dead. Indians fight "to satisfy the supposed craving ghosts of their deceased relations," James Adair reported. "They firmly believe," he went on, "that the spirits of those who are killed by the enemy, without equal revenge of blood, find no rest, and at night haunt the houses of the tribe to which they belonged. . . . Then they must go abroad to spill the enemy's blood, and to revenge crying blood."[86]

A powerful desire to prove oneself a warrior was also in the forefront of a Catawba's thoughts. "Our Warriors delight in War," one headman told colonists, "and our young Men are equally pleased that they have an Opportunity of going to Battle." A Catawba named Prenchee Uraw voiced the concerns central to one on the edge of adulthood. "I am a young Man," he asserted, "and have not yet distinguished myself in War but I am not a little pleased, that I have an Opportunity of doing it." The importance of war to a Catawba can hardly be exaggerated. They "think its as good as A Ballplay," one Cherokee visitor to the Nation observed, and "wont Leave off till [they] know who is the best."[87]

V

Fighting battles and collecting refugees gave Catawba Indians the latitude necessary to remain faithful to their past even as they lived within the larger confines of the Atlantic world. Unlike Simon Flowers or Saponis, they were not in the shadow of Cherokee or Iroquois, Carolina or Virginia. Feared by their native foes, beyond the grasp of prying Christians and meddling officials, Catawbas and their confederates developed a syncretic culture which included much that was new but much, too, that was not.

In 1728 William Byrd announced that the Saponi Indians settled at Fort Christanna "have no other lights but what they receive from purblind tradition."[88] Byrd should have known better. By this time Saponis and their Catawba relatives were in fact being exposed as never before to another world. The same Indian headmen who at Christanna in 1717 had refused wholesale cultural conversion would find, in the decades to come, that changes crept in nonetheless, touching not only material culture but the intangible realms of attitudes, tastes, and values.

To the disease and trade that continued to shape native existence were now added certain individuals who crossed the divide between Indian and colonist better than any who had come before. Some were colonial traders like Thomas Brown and John Evans, but more important were natives well acquainted with foreign ways. Indians fleeing from the Anglo-American settlements brought with them knowledge and skills acquired through contacts with planters, knowledge that could be passed on to their Catawba hosts. Further, eleven children from piedmont towns had spent more than a year with Charles Griffin at Christanna, and, as offspring of headmen and repositories of arcane knowledge, they may have been an important influence. Saponis, of course, had spent even more time under Griffin's tutelage and could instruct others in turn. Finally, the children of colonial traders and Indian women straddled the boundary between cultures and could explain each to the other. Soon after 1740 many mixed-bloods—the Pedee Lewis John, the Cheraw John Evans, the Catawbas Billy Brown and James Bullen, to name a few—came of age. According to Indian matrilineal rules, they were full members of native society; by colonial custom, they were their father's children. Thus mixed-bloods were equipped as few others before them to move easily from one society to the other. Whether they rose to prominence (John became a Pedee chief, Bullen and Evans important warriors) or merely lived out their lives in obscurity, all were well placed to introduce colonial ways.[89]

The most important skill these mediators possessed was language. Language was the key to another world, expanding cultural exchange from goods and people to ideas. It was especially important that Indians now knew English, for they alone possessed the intimate acquaintance with native society one needed fully to explain an alien world. Bilingual colonial traders could translate words and get the sense across; bilingual Indians—especially those (like Saponis and mixed-bloods) better versed in Anglo-America's ways—could translate the meaning, could pass on the message behind the words. Ironically, those engaged in this revolutionary endeavor were only adhering to the aboriginal custom that a few inhabitants in each village learn a neighbor's speech as a way of smoothing the path between peoples. What had once been a tool for coexistence became a force for change.

In the decades following the Yamasee War, Indians demonstrated a growing facility with English. In 1727, Catawbas for the first time spoke to colonial America through their own interpreter, and from then on the number of those capable of doing this job steadily increased.[90] A visitor who arrived in the Nation after 1750 would have no trouble finding someone to translate for him at each of the villages he entered. When two Catawbas had a fight with a colonist in 1756 and "some Words . . . passed between them and him," these words could have been English as easily as Catawba, a possibility unlikely a generation earlier and unthinkable before that.[91]

The arrival of English-speaking Indians well acquainted with colonial society accelerated the transformation already under way in the upcountry. As they had before, Indians interpreted what they did not know in terms of what they knew, rejecting some things and filtering others through a cultural screen. The result was a way of life at once firmly grounded in the past and open to the future. Had John Lawson survived his run-in with the Tuscaroras, lived to old age, and decided—some three, four, or five decades later—to retrace his steps through the Carolina interior, he would have found drastic changes as well as familiar sights.

The most obvious difference was simply the number of Indians he would meet. A land that had seemed crowded with natives at the turn of the century was, by comparison, practically empty. Towns that had been important way stations on the road to the interior were gone. Those remaining were concentrated where Sugar Creek met the Catawba, the only spot that even remotely resembled the "very thick" settlements of 1701. Within this narrowed compass the hub of activity was still Nassaw (Catawba Town). Other settlements radiated out from it, the most distant (still only a morning's walk away) haughtily called "out towns" by those at the center.[92]

The number of villages in this area remained a fairly stable six or seven despite depopulation, though the Indians' habit of moving settlements about led to confusion. During the 1740s Shuterees built "New Town," and Sugarees left their old homes along Sugar Creek for lands beside the Catawba River that Waxhaws had vacated some years before.[93] The need to replace worn-out soils and depleted timber supplies still prompted most migrations. But Sugarees had reasons of their own that earlier generations would not have considered. Besides the rich and extensive fields once tilled by Waxhaw women, the location permitted its new residents to escape their position as the Catawba village most exposed to Iroquois raiders. At the same time, while becoming the last stop for northern warriors, Sugarees also became the first stop for South Carolina traders making their way up the path from the Congarees.[94]

In appearance, these Catawba settlements blended two traditions. If enemy incursions discouraged the hamlets that once had stretched for miles along a river valley, natives still were not huddled in palisaded towns, peering out between gaps in the logs in anticipation of an onslaught. In 1717 and again in 1746 they were reported building forts to meet impending invasions, the implication being that the rest of the time such strongholds were either nonexistent or neglected. When they did bestir themselves to erect bastions, the Indians relied on concepts derived from both aboriginal and colonial models. Cheraws, Sugarees, and most others still "built circular" by raising palisades of vertical logs, arranging houses around the inside of this wall, and leaving a central area open for community gatherings. Waterees and Esaws apparently had developed different tastes, erecting square forts with dwellings scattered throughout.[95]

The buildings inside these villages were equally diverse. At Fort Christanna, Saponis had begun to fashion houses that were neither aboriginal nor European but a peculiar marriage of the two. While squared logs and rafters replaced bent saplings, natives still placed the logs vertically, as if they were building a palisade, and covered the entire structure with bark. The absence of windows and furniture and the presence of a smokehole rather than a chimney also harked back to ancient ways.[96] Most natives had not even gone as far as the Saponis, preferring instead the traditional round or oval structures made of saplings and bark.

A peek inside a house would have settled any doubts about the residents' identity. True, some Indians were new men, transformed from head to toe by a wardrobe that included shoes, stockings, and garters, ruffled shirts, suits of scarlet or blue, hats trimmed with gold and silver lace, and an occasional wig to top it all off.[97] A person dressed in such finery must have been something to behold. Yet the sight was a spectacle in part because it was so uncommon. Headmen alone acquired the more elaborate outfits, and they donned the costume only when paying a formal call on colonists. The rest of the time—and for most Indians, all of the time—less outlandish dress was the rule. Women wore a cloth blanket about their waist and draped a deerskin mantle around their shoulders. Men might put on an old coat or a shirt underneath a blanket wrap, but they shunned hats altogether and wore leggings, flaps, and moccasins instead of pants and shoes.[98]

Even those who did wear the more outlandish costumes would hardly be mistaken for colonists. The women greased their bodies with bear oil to fend off insects or the cold, giving their skin what one fastidious colonist considered "an ugly hue." Nor did the tattoos, the silver ornaments dangling from ears or nose, and the hair cut into various shapes do much to improve native appearance as far as Anglo-Americans were concerned. Colonists deemed such Indian fashions odd and unattractive; others they considered downright frightening. A visitor to Fort Christanna forgot all about the school, the blankets, and the other European trappings when fifty young men showed up dressed for war. Feathers stuck through their ears, heads shaved so that the hair on top stood up "like a cock's comb," faces painted blue and red—the warriors' appearance was "really . . . very terrible . . . like so many furies."[99]

Indians dressing up in English clothes were also trying on English names. Mixed-bloods generally took the names of their fathers; even George Chicken, South Carolina's Yamasee War hero, had a namesake among his old foes. Other Catawbas were named by colonists tired of trying to pronounce Indian names. It was much easier for a Carolinian to call Pickahassakehe "Sugar Jemey," Thus Saw Wontree "Captain Peter," and Top Con Sahagreea "Captain Weator." Indians, of course, preferred Handeku to "the Otter" and Chuckchuckhe to "New Comer." Still, a precedent was being set. There now was a choice of two terms, and the way was clear for the eventual obliteration of native names.[100]

Whether they wore maroon suits or deerskin cloaks, built dwellings of logs or saplings, called themselves by English or Catawba names, all Indians continued to follow a seasonal routine that had dominated the native calendar since beyond memory. From September to March virtually everyone—men, women, and children—went out on the hunt. The habit was so deeply embedded that most towns stood all but empty for months. John Evans arrived in the Nation in October 1755 to find "very few of the People at Home and those most of them Old Men and unable to go out to Hunt, there might be about twenty five Men on the whole."[101] The rest had broken into smaller groups of about six or eight families and scattered in all directions in pursuit of game. Once they set up camp, the Indians divided again, the women and children remaining behind to prepare food and dress the skins the men brought in.[102]

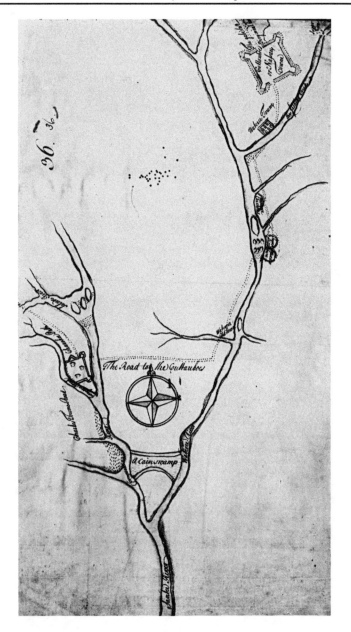

Map 4. "The Road to the Cuttauboes." Circa 1750. *Courtesy of the Library of Congress (original in the Public Record Office, London)*

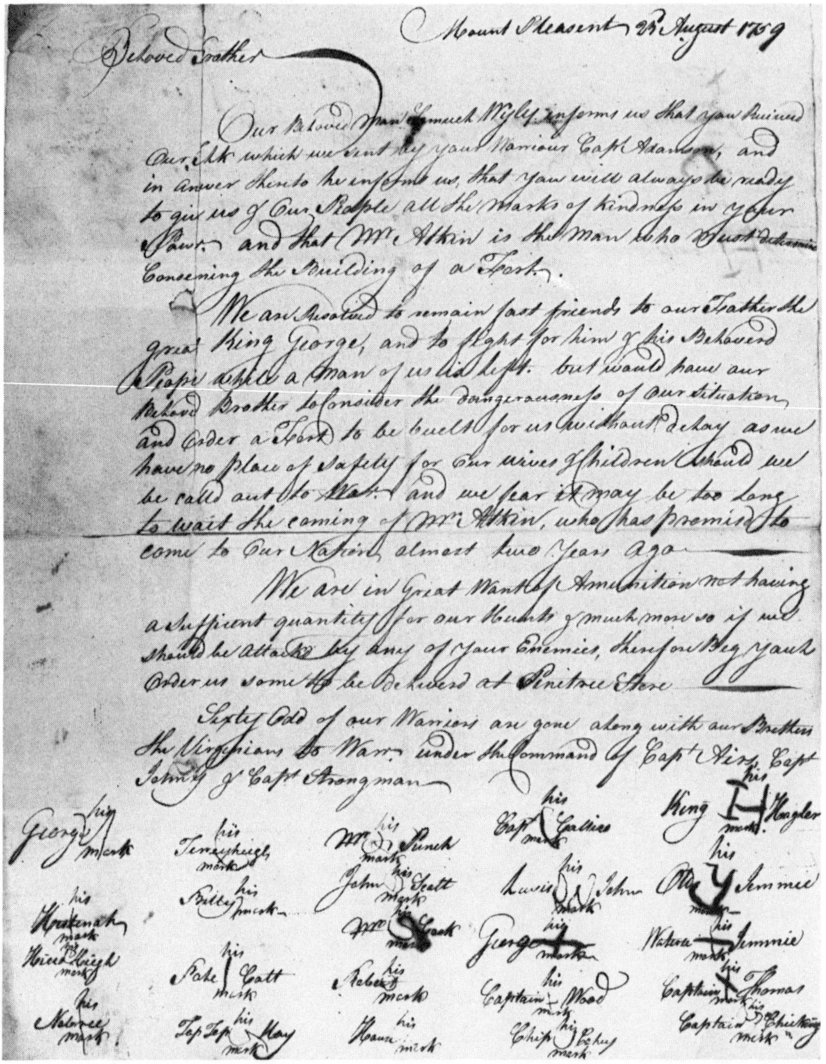

Figure 5. Catawba Letter to Governor Lyttelton. The Nation's letter to South Carolina governor William Henry Lyttelton illustrates the variety of English and Indian names among Catawbas during the mid-eighteenth century. *Courtesy of William L. Clements Library*

And yet while native families still followed an ancient rhythm, intercultural exchange now set a faster tempo. Involvement in the peltry trade increased the number of animals each Indian hunter killed, cutting the deer population drastically and forcing people to venture farther afield in search of game. Between 1730 and 1760, hunting parties from the Nation ranged from the upper Cape Fear to the Edisto, from the Pee Dee to the Broad.[103] To many observers it seemed that they were everywhere. During the 1730s Indian hunters turned up "in great numbers in all places like the Egyptian locusts," one early settler along the Black River recalled. A generation later, Governor Arthur Dobbs of North Carolina grumbled that Catawbas "hunt down to the Sea coast."[104]

The exigencies of exchange even determined the direction a hunter chose. Before 1720 most probably stayed close to home. By 1740, the Nation's principal hunting grounds lay in the vast cane swamp between the Congaree and Wateree rivers. Deer abounded there, and settlers were slow to penetrate it. Equally important, it was close to the plantations of Thomas Brown and his partners, who ensured the successful hunter a handy market for his peltry.[105]

Other developments made it easier for peoples in the Nation to shift the scope and focus of the hunt. Refugees brought with them knowledge of distant canebrakes and upland groves of oak and hickory. Did they return to their old grounds with their new Catawba friends? We do not know. But it is not hard to imagine Waterees and Congarees acquainting hunters from Nassaw or Sugaree Town with the best campsites in the Wateree Swamp, Pedees and Cheraws heading joint expeditions to their favorite spots east of the Nation, or Waccamaws leading the pursuit of game right down to Dobbs's seacoast.

Expansion of the hunting range was also facilitated by other recent migrants into the upcountry: horses. Indians in the area had these animals as early as 1670.[106] Thereafter natives bought or stole them until the beasts were common in and around upcountry villages. For a time they were strictly ornamental; headmen prized the animals but did not put them to use in ways an Englishman considered proper. "These Creatures they continually cram, and feed with Maiz, and what the Horse will eat," John Lawson had remarked in disgust, "till he is as fat as a Hog." Lawson did note that the Indians, appreciating the creatures' potential as beasts of burden, were using them to haul a deer home if it had been slain nearby. With time the animals carried their master's game farther and farther until the horse was almost as much a part of the hunter's equipment as the musket.[107]

Learning to use horses was one thing; learning to ride them, quite another. Even as Indians made fun of Virginians "who can't stir to a next neighbor without a horse, and say that two legs are too much for such lazy people, who can't visit their next neighbor without six," natives were learning to imitate the butt of their jokes. Now it was the colonists' turn to laugh. In 1716 Lieutenant Governor Spotswood gave a Saponi leader a horse to ride as the Indians accompanied Spotswood's party homeward from the frontier. After being thrown, the shaken chief returned the gift, to the colonists' amusement, saying he "could not imagine what good they were for, if it was not to cripple the Indians."[108] Byrd's surveying party found the natives somewhat more adept in 1728. "The most uncommon circumstance in this Indian visit," he wrote of a conference with Saponis, "was that they all come on horseback, which was certainly intended for a piece of state, because the distance was but three miles and 'tis likely they had walk'd afoot twice as far to catch their horses." They still needed practice: "The men rode more awkwardly than any Dutch sailor, and the ladies bestrode their palfreys *à la mode de France* [astraddle] but were so bashful about it that there was no persuading them to mount till they were quite out of our sight." But within another decade or two, Indians on horseback were unremarkable even in Charleston, where in 1739 Catawbas and Cheraws received saddles as gifts.[109] In 1762 a Catawba headman refused to make the trip to the South Carolina capital because he could not find his horse. Like so many other trade goods, the animals had become necessities.[110]

Hunting, for all the new equipment and greater attention devoted to it, never completely overshadowed the planting, tending, and harvesting of crops. Indians in the Nation still divided their year, as they divided their landscape, into halves, hunting and planting, "the Woods" and the fields. In neither calendar nor environment was the division absolute: men hunted in spring and summer, just as the boundary between forest and field was everywhere blurred. Yet each activity dominated its own season; each made quite different demands upon individual and community. The hunting bands that left in early fall made their way home in time for the April planting.[111] Men and deerskins, the focus of attention during the winter, retired and let women and their crops come to the fore.

The agricultural regimen remained so central to native life that colonists learned to peruse Indian fields in order to read Indian minds. In April 1729, William Gooch correctly predicted that the Saponis at Christanna were planning to leave. How did he know? They had planted no corn that spring. Later the Virginia Council would again attest to corn's importance by permitting those Saponis who had returned from the Catawba Nation (significantly, they had arrived early enough to get crops in the ground) to remain where they were until after the harvest.[112]

Anglo-Americans were reduced to using cornfields as tea leaves because native thought was still unfathomable; entry into the realm of belief that lay behind the planting and hunting, the tattooing and painting was still by permission only—and permission was rarely given. Yet since patterns of thought generally remain more resistant to change than their outward expressions, it seems likely that the Catawba Nation's peoples occupied a mental universe more akin to that of their ancestors than was the physical world of horses and ruffled shirts. Unfortunately, during these years only William Byrd II was able to explore this forbidden territory in even the most cursory way. During a conversation with a Saponi Indian named Ned Bearskin, Byrd caught a glimpse of "the religion of his country."[113]

Bearskin's people had spent several years attending classes at Christanna, and he may have known more of Christian teachings than most piedmont Indians did. Certainly hints of the schoolroom can be detected in his words. The belief in a single supreme being who punishes the bad and rewards the good, the road taken by "departed souls" after death, the "venerable old man" and the crystal gate at the entrance to the "land of delight"—these and other examples suggest a people in the process of developing a syncretic religion.[114] Beyond this, Bearskin's colorful portrait took on hues that were utterly foreign to the colonists who listened to his account.

Rewards and punishments for one's behavior began in this world. Evil people could expect sickness, poverty, hunger, and death at the hands of their enemies. After death the chastisements continued. The road to "the region of misery" was rocky and uneven, the place itself dark, cold, and barren, its inhabitants old and hungry, their days spent in hard work under the eye of ugly old women with claws like a panther's, shrill voices, and insatiable sexual appetites. The "regions of bliss," by contrast, were blessed with never-ending spring, perpetual youth, beautiful women, corn that grew by itself, game that was fat and plentiful, and trees heavy with fruit. Bliss or misery, Bearskin's afterlife was clearly a man's world. At the same time, the contrasting fates he laid out and his choice of subjects reflect immediate concerns—rocky paths, bad weather, lurking enemies, scarce game—fears all too real among the Indian peoples still living in the piedmont.

Beyond warning against those who "tell lies and cheat those they have dealings with," Bearskin's descriptions of the next world contain little clue how one's fate was determined in this. But alongside their vivid picture of the afterlife, Indians must have set equally detailed behavioral codes that helped a person propitiate the gods and control fate. Bearskin's taboo against mixing venison and turkey, a common southeastern stricture designed to separate elements of the terrestrial world from denizens of the Upper World, was only one in a panoply of similar rules governing thought and action.[115]

Buttressing the individual rituals were communal ceremonies linking people to the invisible world, to one another, and to their common past. If the ravages of time and disease simplified the annual round of ceremony, there is no reason to conclude that events charting the changing seasons, celebrating triumphs in hunting or war, commemorating the summer's first harvest, and marking the stages on life's course had disappeared completely. Catawbas wrapped their dead in cloth rather than cane mats before burial, but the priests and mourners still knew their duties.[116] Saponis at Christanna had modified their dwellings and their town, but nearby they built the communal sweathouses that had always stood near piedmont villages, visual reminders of the power of ancient curative practices and the importance of those who administered them. And war dances similar to the one at Christanna in 1716 remained an integral part of every Indian man's existence; like a hunter treating his kill with proper respect, a warrior knew that success was impossible without careful preparation and appropriate conduct.[117] It seems fair to conclude that the drums and dancers, the chants and tales, the songs of old men and the shouts of young warriors went on, unseen by colonists, or if seen unrecorded, or if recorded lost forever.

VI

Out of the chaos of war piedmont Indians had put together a society that gave them something of a respite, a life free from trade embargos, enemy attacks, and cantankerous colonists. The deer were still to be found, the corn still grew, and if every house bore marks of another way, the pulse of older times remained steady and strong.

At the center of this recovery lay the amalgamation of many native groups, groups that brought to the Catawba Valley warriors and women, knowledge of distant hunting grounds and familiarity with Anglo-America—all precious commodities in the eighteenth-century Southeast. Those who came to the Catawba River and those who greeted them there were characters in the closing chapter of the sad story begun two centuries before when some of the Cofitachiques surrendered their villages to the new disease and sought refuge with neighbors. At last, the swirling eddies slowed and finally stopped as peoples made a final choice—some with colonists, some with the Iroquois, many more with the Catawbas. The birth of a polyglot society called the Catawba Nation was, for Anglo-American and Indian alike, a necessary antidote to the poisons brewed after 1700 and served up in 1715. But the future of this fledgling nation was far from secure.

Modern Indian Politics: Catawba Diplomacy

We do not pretend to be well skill'd
in *modern* Indian politicks.
                    —*South-Carolina Gazette*

IN THE middle of the eighteenth century, informed Anglo-Americans thought the Catawba Indians to be approaching extinction. Governor James Glen, surveying the situation from Charleston in December 1749, feared "the Total destruction of that poor Nation." The governor's eyes and ears in the piedmont agreed. The trader Matthew Toole toured the Catawba villages in July 1754 and came away "perswaided that the Catawba Nation will be no more in one Year's Time." Toole was wrong: a year later it was still there, but in the fall of 1755 John Evans would return from the upcountry to report, again, the impending "ruin of that Nation."[1]

The verdict was not the product of wishful thinking. If Catawba society was indeed on the edge of the abyss that already had swallowed so many native groups, Glen (who needed allies) and the others (who profited from trade) were more interested in snatching it back than shoving it over. Nor could their words be written off as the rantings of ignorant men. Glen was an avid student of Indians in general and Catawbas in particular. He learned his lessons not only from what he termed "attentive and intimate observation, by occular inspection" of visiting Indians but also from Evans, tutor of every South Carolina governor since Francis Nicholson, and from Toole, another old Catawba hand.[2] Each of the men singing over the Catawbas' grave was an expert in the affairs of the Nation.

As it turned out, the grave sat empty. Where had the doomsayers gone wrong? The problem lay less in their understanding of the Catawba present than in their vision of the Catawba future. During the mid-eighteenth century the Indians did face a crisis, a crisis as serious as smallpox or the Yamasee War. As clearly as colonial observers saw the dangers facing the Nation, however, they underestimated the natives' ability to adjust once again to new circumstances. Glen, Evans, and Toole had no hope for the Nation because they failed to see that they themselves were the Nation's hope. *They* were the answer to the Catawbas' problems; the Nation, recognizing this, came to rely as never before on the very men writing its obituary.

I

The Catawba predicament looked so hopeless because the Nation confronted several different crises at once, and each, feeding off the others, became that much more difficult to master. The first signs of trouble cropped up in the Indian wars. Sometime after the Nation's victory over the Oneidas in 1729, Catawbas began to lose more battles than they won. The source of the change can be traced to decisions made in distant villages and councils. During the early 1730s Savannah-Shawnees left Pennsylvania for the Ohio country, where they could more easily ignore pleas from Philadelphia to stop their forays south. A decade later, Cherokees made peace with the Six Nations, providing northern war parties with an excellent staging area for raids on the piedmont. Meanwhile, the French stepped up their campaign to win Indians throughout eastern North America; when Catawbas spurned these overtures, Canadian officials retaliated by encouraging other natives to attack the Nation. Soon Catawbas had more enemies than they could handle, but not more than they could count. "I have heard them reckon up Eleven different Nations, as well in the English as the French Interest, who were at War with them at one time," wrote Edmond Atkin.[3]

Outnumbered, the Catawbas were not always outfought, as many a beaten and bloodied enemy war party could attest.[4] Still, the increase in conflict exacted a terrible toll, even when the defenders managed to hold their own. The four forts that the Nation erected in the spring of 1746 were symptomatic of the constricting circle drawn by native foes. Closer and closer crept the enemy, striking "a small mile" away from a Catawba town, 150 yards, 70 yards, even at its "very Doors."[5] In the spring of 1748 John Evans, recently roughed up and relieved of his trade goods by a northern war party, sent word to Charleston that "the Catawba Nation is so infested with the Enemy that neither the White People nor Indians dare go no where without being in a Body." Before long the natives could not find safety even in numbers. "Our Enemies are so thick about us we cannot go from Home," they informed Glen.[6]

Evans's offhand remark that Catawbas were not the only ones besieged points to a second important change in the piedmont: colonists were moving into the area. Once again, decisions made in faraway councils were responsible. In 1729 Governor Robert Johnson of South Carolina had unveiled a plan laying out townships in the interior for immigrants from Europe or the northern colonies, and over the next two decades the province established several settlements that impinged on Catawba territory.[7] The first to take Johnson up on his offer were colonial hunters, the "Skin People" eager to harvest the pelts of the upcountry.[8] But farmers were never far behind. The Congaree and Wateree valleys were soon thick with plantations, and in 1751 one old-timer along the Wateree River (he had been there for a decade) pronounced his neighborhood "pretty well settled."[9]

Disease, the Nation's "greatest Enemie," hampered the Catawbas' ability to fend off colonists and warriors. The smallpox epidemic that struck the Southeast in 1738 killed one of every two Cherokees, and it may have been equally lethal among Catawbas, whose tightly clustered settlements made it impossible to prevent the spread of the scourge.[10] Indeed, the Nation's susceptibility may have been greater, and recovery more difficult, because the inhabitants were already debilitated by one illness or another. Hardly a year passed without some "national Distemper" (often labeled "the Flux") striking Catawbas, afflicting nearly everyone and killing many. A visit by one or more ailments, usually in late summer or early fall, was now almost routine; it sapped morale, sent the sick to their beds or their graves, and forced the well to devote their energy to nursing and mourning instead of subsistence, trade, or defense.[11]

Diseases, enemy raids, and colonial invasions combined to threaten the triad of hunting, trade, and agriculture undergirding Catawba life. Among the first casualties was hunting. "They could not hunt, [because of] the Enemy," a disappointed Carolina trader reported in 1753. Some parties that did set out in search of game were interrupted by Iroquois raiders; others were stopped short by messages calling them home to meet real or imagined threats.[12] Even those who managed to devote themselves to the task found it much more difficult, thanks to competition from colonial hunters and the settlers' invasion of prime hunting grounds. "All the rest [of the men] and most of their Women and Children, were forced to go to a great distance to Hunt for Food[,] the White People having taken their Lands from them," complained Hagler (Nopkehe) in 1755.[13] Catawba hunters who were pushed to remote and perhaps unknown territories probably had to work harder for less return.

By the time Hagler expressed his concern, it was too late to reverse the trend. With game scarce and hunting risky, Catawba production of deerskins fell off, and trade all but ceased. No figures survive to chart its decline, but the signs were everywhere. After Virginians discovered a more direct route to the Cherokees in the late 1730s, few men from the north chose to make the long trek across the piedmont just to trade in the Catawba Valley, and what was once a center of commerce now became a virtual backwater. South Carolinians, too, were looking for better markets. Soon after 1740, Patrick Brown and James Adair left the Congarees outpost in hope of fame and fortune farther west. Thomas Brown, who stayed on at the old post, could no longer make a go of it; he died in 1747 burdened with "desperate debts."[14]

Northern war parties and Catawba anger drove out most of the rest of the traders. John Evans lost only his dignity and his goods when enemy warriors stopped him near the Nation; barely a month later, George Haig lost his life when another party waylaid him on the traders' path from the Congarees. And only months after that, the Catawba chief Yanabe Yatengway (Young Warrior) took the unprecedented step of cutting between two squabbling Carolina traders and forcing them to settle their differences. Men like these were loath to take orders from anyone, least of all an Indian. Word of Haig's fate and Yanabe Yatengway's meddling must have been broadcast over the trader grapevine, giving pause to those still pondering the Catawba market. Fewer skins, greater risks, haughty chiefs—was it worth it? While exchange never stopped altogether, the era of the great piedmont deerskin trade was over.[15] With it went the European commodities on which the Nation depended.

The forces destroying Catawba hunting and trade also helped bring on a crisis in Catawba agriculture. Illness must have reduced the labor force available to plant, tend, or harvest crops, and enemy warriors picked off anyone brave enough or desperate enough to venture into the fields.[16] Those fields would look even worse when drought struck the piedmont in the 1750s. In July 1753, the very time Catawbas should have been harvesting their first corn, a colonist sent word to Glen that "they have been in a very parishable Condition all this Summer. . . . and were obliged to give away what Cloathing they had for Corn, and since that was gone, they have lived entirely upon Blackberries." Three years later, Hagler informed Glen's successor William Henry Lyttelton that "our Corn is again this Year burnt up," a message that was to be repeated through the end of the decade. Catawbas continued to farm—"Our suffering in this respect is not owing to want of Labour," they assured colonists—but year after year the crops perished in the stifling heat.[17]

The simultaneous crisis in hunting and agriculture undermined a reliable and flexible subsistence system. In the past, Indians combining these two activities with gathering could turn to the other food supplies if one failed. When two collapsed, starvation was imminent. As they explained to Glen, and he in turn to his Council: "A bad Crop was not so great a Calamity to them in former Times: For then they had a wide Range to hunt in, and Venison, Bear and Buffalo, in some sort, supplied the want of Grain, and other Provisions; but the near Neighborhood of the English, they say, drives away their Game; and deprives them of the means of subsisting [i]n such Emergencies."[18] Only gathering was left, and they could not hope to live on blackberries for long.

Besides stripping Catawbas of corn and clothing, the pounding from several directions nearly destroyed the social order Indians had pieced together after the Yamasee War. As the Nation became less shield than target, some peoples reconsidered their decision to seek shelter in the Catawba Valley. As early as 1737 a party of Indians from the Nation, "not able longer to support themselves against the continual Incursions of the Senecas who had killed and destroyed great Numbers of their People," talked of moving closer to the colonists for protection.[19] South Carolina authorities urged them to stay where they were, and stay they did. But the problem would not go away. In the spring of 1746, Catawbas had to head to the Santee River valley to retrieve "some of their Straggling Friends who were there for Fear of the Enemy." Meantime, Cheraws and Pedees made plans to flee the Nation "and to retire to some place of greater safety, where they might have fewer Enemies."[20]

Internal divisions further weakened the Catawbas. In 1755 John Evans returned from the Nation convinced that civil war was near. "There was at present, and had subsisted for some time past," he told the South Carolina Council, "a very Dangerous Division among the Catawbaw Indians." James Bullen (Spanau), the son of a colonial trader and a Catawba woman, had won a following among the Nation's inhabitants and adopted the presumptuous title "Prince of Wales." North Carolina's governor, Arthur Dobbs, even claimed that the Indians "want to make [him] King, as they despise Haglar."[21] Though Bullen died in 1758, opposition to Hagler continued. A year after Bullen's death another important warrior, Colonel Ayers, stayed away from a meeting of the Nation's council, "the Hagler and He Being at varience."[22]

These threats to the eractasswa were related to the general malaise besetting the Nation. Sickness snapped established lines of succession, undermining one of the most important sources of a leader's authority. In the aftermath of the 1738 smallpox epidemic, for example, three different men were chief in as many years.[23] Hagler himself became eractasswa only after Yanabe Yatengway and fifteen headmen were killed by disease and enemy attack during a trip to Charleston. The Nation's new leader might be "the nearest of Blood" to the former ruler; he was also the only candidate left.[24] Thus Hagler may have come to the position by default, and his tenuous ties to earlier rulers would make it all the more difficult for him to command the respect granted his predecessors.

No less important in creating trouble for Indian leaders were the simultaneous failures of defense and subsistence. These fundamental and seemingly insoluble problems may have encouraged widespread discontent, discontent that could easily be directed at established authority. And who better to lead dissenters than mixed-bloods, many of whom came of age during these years? While possessing the traditional prerequisites of Catawba leaders such as proven valor in war, these men had advantages that could help catapult them into influential positions. In some cases a trader like John Evans tried to use his connections with provincial authorities to advance his children in native society.[25] But even if the direct approach failed, mixed-bloods enjoyed access to European goods as well as to the colonial world. These attributes were particularly useful at a time when contacts with British America were increasing and trade, once the principal source of essential products, was not. Ambitious or unhappy men like Bullen could become competing centers of knowledge, wealth, and authority, lightning rods for disappointment and frustration.

Beset by crippling illnesses, bitter enemies, grasping colonists, inclement weather, and internal disputes, the Nation's days did indeed appear to be numbered. Perhaps most serious of all, cultural tradition limited the choices available to Catawbas trying to grapple with these problems. Nowhere was this constraint more obvious than in efforts to recoup the losses from sickness. In all likelihood Catawbas, like most southeastern Indians, had limited population growth in a variety of ways, including abortion and infanticide; such customs could not simply be abandoned to compensate for a drop in population.[26] Nor were the more accepted means so ready to hand by midcentury. In the past, Catawbas could capture and adopt enemy women and children, filling the ranks of kinfolk lost to smallpox or raids. Increasingly, however, Catawba warriors were too busy defending their own people against foreign incursions to get near a distant enemy's town. Occasionally an Iroquois or Shawnee warrior might be captured, but here again tradition came into play, making it more likely that Catawbas would torture this prisoner than incorporate him into their society. That left recruiting refugees, which had served Catawbas well. The problem was that few candidates applied anymore. Those remaining in the lowcountry were accustomed to life there and reluctant to leave it for the dubious honor of being attacked by eleven different nations. Others—Tuscaroras or Nottoways, for example—carried too many unpleasant memories and too many alien ways to be seriously considered. The reservoir used to replenish a dwindling population had all but dried up.

The chances of checking the decline of either agriculture or exchange were equally remote. Colonists survived the drought by relying more on wheat than corn, but Catawbas, wedded to practices that had had generations of success, could not easily imitate them.[27] It was no easier to lure colonial traders back to the Nation by taking more deerskins, for hunting was also conditioned by certain cultural imperatives that Catawbas found hard to abandon. Some Carolina Indians stepped up their production of pelts by stripping the skin from a slain animal and leaving the carcass to rot. Apparently Catawbas resisted the temptation to do the same; they still took both hide and meat from what game they could find, a more laborious process that, while providing much-needed food, limited the harvest of skins and therefore did nothing to encourage the traders' return. In both the fields and the woods, then, Catawbas could no more forsake traditional ways than they could command settlers to turn back or the skies to bring rain.[28]

Other cultural constraints hampered the Nation's ability to heal its internal divisions. In crises, charismatic leaders sometimes step forward to save their people, and colonists were convinced that this was happening among the Catawbas during these years, that Yanabe Yatengway, eractasswa from 1741 to 1749, and his successor, Hagler, chief until 1763, wielded extraordinary influence over their society. Yanabe Yatengway "was very absolute among his People," Glen observed, "w[hi]ch is unusual with Indians." Hagler, too, colonists considered "a very great Man." The two leaders said nothing to contradict such assessments. After forcing the two colonial traders to settle their differences, Yanabe Yatengway boasted to Glen "that never such a thing had been done in our Nation before." "I am informed," he told the governor, "that you have been told that I have a Prison house in my Nation but I am Willing to let you know the Prison that I have is only the Words that I speak."[29]

In fact, however, these leaders remained strictly tied to traditional forms. For all the talk about absolute power, the Nation's council of headmen, important warriors, and "beloved men" from each town remained the true fountain of authority, where eractasswas were selected and decisions made. Both the "very absolute" Yanabe Yatengway and the "very great" Hagler called these men together whenever a message arrived or a dispute arose. At the bottom of the same letter in which Yanabe Yatengway proclaimed his power were the marks of five headmen signifying their approval of its contents. And the limits to Hagler's greatness became clear in 1757 when he tried to meet South Carolina officials on his own. The headmen "taxed him with it" and publicly rebuked him for acting without first consulting them.[30] So much for a Catawba Moses who might lead the Nation out of the wilderness.

One possible course of action still open was to pick up and leave. Perhaps Creeks, or Cherokees, or Iroquois had a panacea for what ailed the Nation. After all, Catawbas would hardly be the first Indians to seek safety in numbers, to leave home and wend their way toward ancient antagonists or distant friends. Catawbas considered it. "They daily Talk of moving somewhere," Evans wrote in April 1748. To investigate the possibilities, the Nation dispatched ambassadors to a band of Chickasaws living along the Savannah River, with instructions to push on to the Creeks "if things were Easie."[31]

If this delegation was to prepare the way for a general exodus, it failed. The talk of migration that reached Charleston every so often never came to anything. Did others refuse to adopt a people that needed more than the fingers on two hands to count all of its enemies? Perhaps. But it is at least as likely that the Catawbas' attachment to their homeland was stronger than the voices arguing for removal. Shortly after Yanabe Yatengway and the other leaders died during that journey to Charleston, Glen reported that "the Catawbaws notwithstanding their losses are determined still to remain in their own Country."[32] These Indians were going to stay. The only question was, How?

II

Stubbornness was no substitute for corn, guns, and men. If the Catawba Nation could not reverse its decline in population, force colonial traders and the rain to return, persuade enemy warriors to hunt glory somewhere else, or silence dissent among its own people, it was going to need help. In searching for that help Catawbas were drawn toward Anglo-America, and they came to rely as never before on a formal relationship with His Majesty's colonial governments, especially South Carolina. There, it seemed, lay the answers that Catawbas could no longer find within themselves, answers to the refractory questions posed by trade and drought, Iroquois raids and civil war.

The biggest obstacle in the Catawbas' way was the mistrust that colored their relations with Anglo-America. Governor Glen, who counted himself among the Nation's friends, argued privately that Indians, "whatever is said of them and of their native Simplicity and honesty, are a savage, cruel, perfidious, revengefull sett of Men." The Commons House of Assembly, which agreed with this governor on very little, concurred that "all Indians are of a Nature . . . inconstant and slippery." The feeling was reciprocal. Though natives as a rule were polite enough to a colonial official's face, traders who knew them best were aware "that they think as meanly of the whites, as we possibly can do of them," and that they "despised the English, as a swarm of tame fowls, and termed the[m] so, in their set speeches" to each other.[33]

Catawba headmen had to lay such feelings aside in order to approach British America and ask for assistance. But they knew that colonists were not in the habit of offering Indians something for nothing. What could Catawbas give in return? Perhaps most important, the Anglo-Americans prized Indian allies "as a Natural Fortification thrown around us, a Bulwark at our Backs" that fended off incursions by French and Indian enemies who might otherwise strike settlers. The Nation's villages were particularly valuable, sitting as they did astride the Catawba River corridor. "An excellent Barrier to this Province," "our Northern Barrier," "a good Barrier to us"—so colonists kept reminding themselves of the Catawbas' importance.[34]

While keeping enemies out of the province, the Nation could also help keep runaway slaves in. After a major slave uprising (the Stono Rebellion) in the fall of 1739, the South Carolina Council had called in Catawba headmen to go over plans for deploying Indian warriors as slavecatchers. Nothing came of the scheme, but colonial authorities kept it in mind. Meanwhile, the mere presence of Catawbas in the piedmont discouraged slaves' thoughts of escape. "It is necessary to keep up that nation as a distinct People to be a Check upon the runaway Slaves who might otherwise get to a head in the Woods," argued one official in 1754, "and prove as mischevious a thorn in our sides as the fugitive Slaves in Jamaica did in theirs."[35]

The very location and ferocious reputation that made Catawbas valuable friends also made them potentially dangerous enemies. Carolinians had not forgotten the lessons of the Yamasee War; thirty or forty years later, colonists were still talking about the attack in 1715 and fretting about the possibility of another Indian war.[36] In retrospect it is clear that by 1750 the southern colonies were safe from the destruction caused by Tuscaroras and Yamasees. But to people at the time the dangers were real. In a 1750 speech to the Assembly, James Glen summed up "our Situation with regard to Indians." While the governor may have exaggerated somewhat to heighten the effect, he was not being paranoid when he argued:

> We are a handful of People thinly spread over a widely extended Country, We are Surrounded with Indians much more Numerous than us, much more Accustomed to the use of Arms, . . . better able to indure the Severitys of the Winter and the Scorching Heat of the Summer, more patient of want, of hunger and thirst, and who can better endure Toil and fatigue. . . . I make no doubt we should get the better of them in a fair Field, but where are they to be met with, who can trace or follow them in their Marches, in-

deed they may be said more properly to transport themselves upon Wings then to March, they are here to Night spilling of Blood, burning and destroying, in the morning they are fifty Miles off at the Same Cruel Sport.[37]

The ghosts that had haunted the colonists' sleep in 1715 were still abroad more than a generation later. Catawbas were part of the nightmare, for they could, if they chose, plunge the Carolinas into a general war. Even without help from other Indians, one of the Nation's neighbors pointed out, if Catawbas ever turned against the English, "the[y] would be worse than twice the Number of other Indians the[y] being so well aquainted with the Country."[38]

Thus Anglo-Americans had almost as many reasons to befriend Catawbas as the Indians had to approach colonists. The Nation's headmen, with the full measure "of Natural Sence or the knowledge of their own Interests" that South Carolina's lieutenant governor William Bull attributed to all Indians, and "sensible of the importance they are to the Europeans," now set out "to make their advantage of all those who they know will court their Friendship."[39] To accomplish their goals, Catawba leaders had to work with their colonial counterparts to develop a body of ritual that enabled them to converse. Through trial and error over the course of many encounters—beginning, perhaps, with the visit to Andrew Percival in 1692 or the parley with Governor Tynte in 1708–1709—the two peoples formulated ceremonies permitting them to meet on common ground.[40] In 1739 diplomatic protocol was so well established that Bull could simply inform the Assembly, without spelling out the details, that Catawba and Cheraw headmen on their way to the capital "will doubtless expect at their Arrival to meet with the usual Reception and Entertainment."[41]

With the structure of diplomacy in place, contacts could expand dramatically. From only two recorded sessions in the 1720s and five in the 1730s, the number of meetings jumped to eleven in the 1740s and then to seventeen in the next decade. Colonial efforts to regulate native traffic into Charleston failed as Indians came pretty much when they pleased. Though officials had to be ready for a visit any time of the year, Catawbas were most likely to arrive in late spring just after planting or late summer following the harvest.[42] These were days of leisure and celebration in the Nation; the inhabitants, gathered in their towns, could hold councils, reach decisions, and organize expeditions to the coast. That provincial leaders might prefer another day troubled natives not at all. At other times of the year they had better things to do.

Anglo-Americans had as little success dictating the size of a delegation as they did scheduling its arrival. Legislators greeting nine Catawba leaders in 1727 and the eleven Catawbas and Cheraws in 1739 probably thought that those were about the right number, perhaps even a little high. Imagine their dismay, then, when in 1749 the number of headmen swelled to fourteen and they were accompanied by twenty-one young warriors, ten women, and two children.[43] This was no delegation; it was practically a whole town, and everyone had to be housed, fed, and clothed, not to mention have their illnesses treated, their horses pastured, their guns repaired. During the 1750s the rate of inflation worsened. The governor would invite six headmen, and twenty-five people would show up, or fifty, or more.[44] With this many Indians, it was expensive to "talk and feed them into a good humor," but if some budget-conscious official summoned the courage to ask for an explanation, Catawbas usually cited the danger of enemy attack on the path from the interior. The importance of making an impression on their hosts, a desire to obtain gifts, and curiosity about Anglo-America may also have swelled a delegation's ranks.[45]

Natives would have preferred not to meet in Charleston at all. The Congarees or, better still, the Nation itself would have been more in keeping with Indian customs, in which the location of a conference reflected the relative importance of the parties involved. On a more mundane level, Catawbas were beginning to appreciate that heading into the lowcountry was risky. Indian diplomats often fell ill in Charleston, and many a Catawba ambassador never made it home. When a Cherokee told a colonist "that before he went to Town, he heard it was a good place, but now said he, I don't know," he might have been referring to the diplomatic climate or his health. ("His meaning I can't Learn," the colonist had concluded.) Others made their point less elliptically, telling Glen "that if they stay'd here they should get sick, for . . . our Water was bad and our Air was stinking."[46] But because the Board of Trade discouraged tours like Glen's journey through the interior in 1746, Indians had to visit Charleston whether they liked it or not.[47]

Some delegations simply showed up at the Council's door. But colonists, if they had the time to prepare and the inclination to put on a show, could stage an elaborate welcome. When twenty Catawbas and a large party of Cherokees arrived in the spring of 1745, for example, Governor Glen went to great lengths to impress them. Several troops of horse met the natives on the road and escorted them into the capital along a route lined by two columns of the Charleston militia. At the city limits, colonial officials received the leaders of the delegations and accompanied them to the Council house in the governor's coach. The rest of the entourage followed, marching two by two down Broad Street to the accompaniment of beating drums, flying colors, and booming cannons. Afterward the Indians "thanked me for the great respect and civilitys that had been shown to them," Glen boasted, "and their reception and entertainment had been much greater than they expected or had any Idea of, and they wanted words to express their Sense of it." Lavish the reception may have been, but it is hard to imagine the Indians being at a loss for words. The pageant Glen had put on resembled native greetings, in which warriors went out to accompany a visitor into town in formal fashion.[48]

Once the Indians were settled in the provincial capital, the meetings could get under way. Each session opened and closed with what bored scribes termed "the usual Salutation of Shaking of hands." A mere formality to a colonist, the handshake was essential to Indians. They had long considered it a sign of friendship and endowed it with great symbolic power in relations with other peoples; now they transferred the gesture to a new forum by insisting that governors and councillors go along.[49] Colonists even got used to the Indian variation, more shaking arms than shaking hands, with one person grabbing the other's upper arm and "Locking his own Arm in his, at full Length."[50]

The negotiations that followed closely observed Indian ritual. Discussions were invariably conducted in Catawba, a practice of special significance to native delegations. John Lawson had noticed that "the most powerful Nation of these Savages scorns to treat or trade with any others (of fewer Numbers and less Power) in any other Tongue but their own," and headmen transferred the practice to their diplomatic parleys with colonists. A visitor to the Indians at Fort Christanna in 1716 remarked, "Notwithstanding some of them could speak good English, yet when they treat of any thing that concerns their nation, they will not treat but in their own language, . . . nor will not answer to any question made to them without it be in their own language." Catawbas meeting with South Carolina officials carried on the tradition. In 1744 at least one headman in a party visiting Charleston spoke English, but he was silent, and Thomas Brown acted as interpreter. Hagler, too, kept his English a secret from colonial authorities, forcing them to follow native custom.[51]

To the participants what counted was not just which language one spoke or what one said but how one said it. Here again colonists tended to heed Indian wishes, and native modes of discourse dominated every diplomatic occasion. These forms of expression, part of a rhetoric common throughout eastern North America, were dominated by metaphors.[52] Since so much of native life centered around kinfolk, Catawbas often described their relations with outside groups in kinship terms. At various times North and South Carolina officials, the Cherokees, and Hendrick (a Mohawk sachem) were the Nation's elder or eldest brothers; and besides King George, two men—James Glen and the Virginia trader and agent Christopher Gist—earned the right to be called father.[53] Other metaphors drew their power from everyday life or the human body, linking physical objects to ideas and relationships. Thus ears were closed, doors opened, and hatchets taken up or buried.[54] Friends came from one womb, ate from one spoon, smoked from one pipe, and slept by one fire. Perhaps the most pervasive symbol of all was the path. Representing the actual trails connecting Catawbas to the world outside, it also characterized the Nation's relationship with the inhabitants of that world. A path could be clean or bloody, white or dark, clear or obstructed, straight or crooked.[55]

Governors and councillors began sprinkling their speeches with kin terms and other Indian metaphors, but few colonists mastered the idiom. When Catawbas told William Bull in 1739 "that they looked upon the English as their fathers and Brothers," Bull missed the point, replying lamely "that he looked upon them as friends." Officials further confused Indians by tossing terms of their own devising into the pool of discourse. Some of the confusion resulted from simple inexperience: when Arthur Dobbs addressed Hagler as "Sir" instead of the standard "Friend and Brother" and talked of the ocean as the "Great River" rather than the "Great Water," the North Carolina governor had been in America only two years.[56] Other colonial leaders, accustomed to dealing with the Six Nations, offered to "wipe away [the Catawbas'] Tears," a practice common in Iroquois condolence ceremonies but apparently unknown in the Southeast. Still others, with years of experience, were not so much ignorant or mixed up as creative. James Glen and William Bull equated the Nation's enemies with "a Herd of [n]umerous Deer" that Catawbas should hunt and "make . . . fly before you," using "deer" in a way Indian speakers did not.[57] Similarly, Glen and a North Carolina official who assured Hagler that "we and our Bretheren the brave Catawbas shall stand firm together like a large mountain which cannot be moved" were employing a metaphor unknown in the surviving samples of Catawba speeches. Glen, determined to master Indian rhetoric, began using "fire" to denote destruction, as in "the devouring flame of war," which must have left his listeners bewildered, since among Catawbas the term called up images of peace or council, of a tool for hunting or warming a dwelling.[58] By giving an old metaphor new meaning, Glen revealed his rudimentary grasp of native speech. Like his colleagues, he was saying the same words without speaking the same language.

Fortunately, words were not the only way for Indians and colonists to converse. Presents, another form of communication, also allowed the two peoples to narrow the gap between them. As usual, colonists followed the native practice without fully accepting it or understanding its significance. To Indians, gifts were a sign of friendship and a means of establishing relations between equals. "We have seen the Goods," Hagler told Virginia officials, "and accept them as a Token of your Affection." Colonists accustomed to thinking of a present's monetary worth felt cheated when an Indian handed over a few deerskins or a clay pipe and took away muskets or clothing. To the Anglo-American mind, gifts became little more than a means of purchasing native loyalty. As a disgusted militia captain put it: "Indians are a Comodity that are to be bought and sold. . . . The highest Bidder carries them off."[59]

Most colonists shared the officer's sentiments, and we must remember that the hearty handshakes, the friendly words, and the piles of presents concealed contempt and a manipulative, even exploitative, instinct. Indians approached colonists because they wanted help. Colonists went along because they wanted control. Glen hoped to put "a bridle in the Mouths of our Indians" so that "instead of finding them chargeable by presents they might easily in a little time be made Tributaries." On their side, many Catawbas must have felt as one Cherokee did when he confided to a colonist, "If they were going to the English they would mind then what was said to them, because they would be then in hopes of having some Cloath given them, but at their return home would soon forgett what the English said to them or what they were to do."[60] This was the strained and strange alliance that set about rescuing the Catawba Nation.

III

The diplomatic dance of Catawba and colonist was awkward. Indians hated Charleston. Colonial officials grumbled about the cost. Yet for all its flaws, the ceremony served its purpose, and, after 1740, Catawbas came to depend ever more heavily on it to sustain themselves.

Support for traditional authority was among the most important functions of diplomatic relations. Military commissions issued over the governor's signature and the colony's seal came to bolster a leader's sagging prestige. Few, if any, Catawbas could actually read these precious pieces of paper, but the markings and seal, proof of the bearer's connections to Anglo-America, contained great power. First issued shortly after the Yamasee War, by midcentury the documents were a necessary part of any Catawba's credentials, so necessary in fact that Indians wore them out and had to request replacements.[61] A commission "gives [a Catawba] a distinction in his Nation without which they dont readily elect their King," Dobbs observed.[62]

A Catawba leader acquired prestige not only by the power vested in his own commission but also by controlling access to these prized commodities. When Hagler arrived in Charleston in 1750 to receive his first commission as chief, Glen asked him who his war captains were and then issued five more to the men the new eractasswa named. A few years later, Hagler was back to request still more. Glen, while handing the documents to captains Harris and Thompson, took the opportunity to remind the two men that they had Hagler to thank for their good fortune. "The King gave them a very good Character," Glen informed them, "and said that they had always behaved well in their own Nation and to the White People. Therefore he wished them Long Life and good health to enjoy their Commissions."[63]

By granting the priceless paper only to those tapped by an eractasswa, Charleston confirmed a ruler's legitimacy and frustrated those who tried to acquire authority in some other way. John Evans urged the Council to grant his mixed-blood son a commission to rule the Cheraws, but Glen would initiate no action until he had Yanabe Yatengway's approval, "being determined," he assured the chief, "to do nothing in those matters unless you approve of them." Glen already knew the etiquette; others had to be taught. Soon after William Henry Lyttelton replaced Glen as governor, what a disgusted Hagler called "straggling Fellows" took advantage of the new man's ignorance to come to him, pretend they were important leaders, and demand commissions. They succeeded—until Hagler found out. In no time the eractasswa protested, and an embarrassed Lyttelton hastened to reply that "none of them for the future should have Commissions or Presents but such as should be recommended by King Hagler." Similarly, when James Bullen evaded the chief's monopoly by acquiring a commission from Dobbs rather than from South Carolina, Charleston's agent persuaded the pretender not to exercise the power contained in his document, buying him off with a more potent one from Glen that would rank him second only to the eractasswa.[64]

Commissions were just one of many kinds of gifts to polish an eractasswa's tarnished image. Glen called Yanabe Yatengway "extremely vain" because he expected so many goods and, according to Matthew Toole, Hagler was "a Fellow that loved Presents." Neither colonist recognized that, although a Catawba leader might seek some things for their practical value, even the most utilitarian items had a significance far above any ordinary use. Like a commission, a silver armband or a fancy gun was a highly visible means of distinguishing a leader from his people, confirming his position in the Nation as well as his relationship with colonists. Thus a flag and drum were much sought after, not because a chief really needed them (there were already drums and probably a chief's standard, too), but because they were important symbols of status. A man who called his people together by beating a British drum and, once they were assembled, raised a British flag over the council's proceedings was announcing, in language none could misconstrue, his close friendship with a powerful people.[65]

Occasionally the support a Catawba leader received from his connections in the South Carolina capital was less tangible. Among Indians it was important to meet the English king's men face to face; simply by bringing his people before the South Carolina Council, then, a chief reaffirmed his standing among his people. It may have been particularly crucial to introduce young men. "I . . . have now brought some of the young Warriours to see you," a Cheraw chief told the Council in 1759. Three years later Hagler showed up with seven more young men in tow and informed Governor Thomas Boone that he had "brought some of my warriors with me, who never saw you before."[66] Besides sightseeing, the initiates could watch as their leader met with crown representatives and discussed affairs in the Nation. The elaborate ceremony, the formal speeches—and the gifts handed out—could not help leaving a deep impression on an adolescent warrior, an impression that helped sustain his loyalty to the chief.

A Catawba leader with the key to the South Carolina Council chamber did not, in fact, draw on this source of prestige to profit himself or consolidate authority; he exploited it to look out for his people. Indians expected their leaders to set a high standard for generosity by not only acquiring presents but distributing them through the Nation, and Catawba headmen did not disappoint them. Hagler and his fellows contrived to pry an enormous amount of merchandise from tightfisted officials. Besides the laced hats, British flags, and other personal gifts more useful as symbols than anything else, an impressive quantity of everyday commodities also flowed from coastal warehouses to Catawba villages. A single shipment delivered to the Indians in February 1752 contained large amounts of cloth, clothing, paint, kettles, pots, leather belts, wire, scissors, knives, saddles, buttons, needles, thread, combs, and mirrors—a haul worth perhaps one thousand pounds.[67] Windfalls like these were the Catawbas' only hope of replenishing the stock of merchandise depleted by the colonial traders' departure.

Paint and pots were nice to have, but arms and ammunition were even better, and Catawbas obtained gifts of powder, lead, and bullets almost annually. The amount might be as small as twenty-five pounds of powder, fifty pounds of bullets, and a few flints handed out to a visiting delegation; at other times Charleston would ship a small arsenal's worth of supplies to the Nation. In small batches and large, between 1740 and 1760 Indians acquired almost two thousand pounds of powder, twice that of bullets, and 2,750 flints.[68] Whether the ammunition and other wares received as presents compensated for what Indians lost from the trade's decline cannot be known. But it is clear that without them the natives would have been far worse off.

The same devices for funneling European commodities into the Nation were also capable of supplying food for Indians during the drought of the 1750s. In the winter of 1755–1756 South Carolina sent seven hundred bushels of corn to Catawba towns, followed barely a year later by another nine hundred, and by the end of the decade still more.[69] Once again it is impossible to measure the impact of this manna from Charleston. But, again, it was better than nothing, and indeed several hundred bushels of grain distributed among perhaps two thousand Indians may have made the difference between life and death. Certainly Hagler thought it did. After the first consignment arrived, he sent Glen "Thanks for the Corn as he believes that a great deal of his People's Children would [have] parished for Want but for your Bounty."[70]

When the time came, the diplomatic machinery so admirably suited for shipments of goods could be put to other uses. Catawba leaders began to deliver complaints to Charleston about colonial crimes, and settlers sometimes went the same roundabout route to seek redress for grievances against Indians. The chances of receiving satisfaction were usually as remote as Charleston was from the scene of the crime. Still, the very existence of diplomatic relations encouraged people to seek a resolution through peaceful rather than violent means. And South Carolina officials did what they could, conducting inquiries, writing letters, and issuing orders. Proclamations might not stop a crime wave, but, like the food and ammunition, they were better than nothing at all.[71]

Official support of the Catawbas extended well beyond the gifts and investigations to reach into the shadowy realm of relations among Indian peoples. The priority, if Catawbas were to be effective guardians of the frontier, was to keep the Nation intact. Thus when Pedees and Cheraws announced in 1746 that they were leaving and neither Yanabe Yatengway nor Thomas Brown could convince them they should stay, both men asked Governor Glen to step in. During his meeting with the Nation at the Congarees, Glen called the headmen of the two peoples forward, conveyed to them the disastrous consequences of disunity, and persuaded them to change their minds. Catawbas were so pleased that they later enlisted his aid in their campaign to add to the Nation's strength, asking that he counsel the Pedee Indians still living near the coast to move upcountry.[72]

A man like Glen could be as useful to Catawbas bent on defeating enemies as he was in helping them keep old friends or make new ones. The Nation used much of the powder and lead it received against the war parties circling its villages. At the same time, predicting when and where these foes might strike became simpler because diplomacy tied Catawbas into the intercolonial communication network, providing them with early warning of enemy attacks. After Glen helped put the Nation back together at the Congarees, for example, the headmen excused themselves by telling him: "We have received Intelligence from the Governor of *Virginia* that 600 *Northern Indians* are coming this Way . . . we therefore intend to go back, and lay in Wait for them." Warnings like this were routine. "I had intelligence that the Six Nations with some French Indians were forming a design to extirpate the Catawbas," wrote a Virginia official four years later. "As usual in such cases, I sent them notice of it."[73]

Anglo-American authorities were happy to alert their Catawba friends to an impending attack. But colonists worked even harder during these years to stop the fighting altogether. Glen made the first successful move in 1744, when a band of Natchez living in the settlements got several Catawbas drunk and proceeded to butcher them. On hearing the news, the governor set out to break the cycle of reprisal that was about to swing into action. First he persuaded the Nation to postpone its planned counterattack for three months; then he pressured Natchez leaders to surrender the perpetrators. The gamble paid off: the frightened Natchez delivered the heads of the killers to Glen, who pickled them, packed them in barrels, and rushed them to the Nation, where the headmen took a look and declared themselves satisfied. This success paved the way for similar efforts, and Catawbas came to expect Glen to mediate their quarrels with neighboring Chickasaws and Cherokees. "We leave it to your Excellency," they told him after Cherokees carried off some of their people, "as we have nobody to see us Rightified but you."[74]

Calming angry southeastern Indians was easy compared to making peace between Catawbas and their old enemies, the Six Nations. Yet here, too, diplomacy finally triumphed. Glen took the lead, with his colleagues in three other colonies joining in at one time or another. After endless false starts and dashed hopes in what the *South-Carolina Gazette*, commenting on the negotiations, called "*modern* Indian politicks," at last Hagler and five other Catawbas traveled to Albany by ship in 1751 to conclude a formal peace. "I have been at great pains to convince the Catawbaws how necessary a Peace was for them," Glen wrote proudly after the Indians returned. "Yet at length by my persuasion they consented."[75]

IV

Glen's pride in his ability to manipulate Indians raises the question of whether the Catawba Nation, in coming to rely so heavily on men like him, was only creating more problems for itself. Were the lines of communication connecting native headman to provincial official more like a web in which Catawbas became trapped? Colonists certainly thought so. When Glen boasted that South Carolina's Indian neighbors "come when we send for them, they go when they are bid and they do whatever is desired of them," Catawbas were his best evidence. Edmond Atkin, equally familiar with the Nation's affairs, was equally convinced that these people were "directed intirely by the Government of So. Carolina." Nor was there much doubt whether the investment in presents yielded a good return. A Catawba entertaining thoughts of turning against Anglo-America would be reminded that "the Difference between the Indians who are in friendship with the English and those who are not plainly appears from their Cloathing and plentiful Supplies of all other Necessaries." As one colonial agent put it when he doled out bushels of grain to the Catawbas, "The Corn was Given to them on Condition of their Good beheavour."[76]

There can be no doubt that the frequent calls on colonial cities had a profound effect on Catawba life. The paper commissions, scarlet coats, and other trappings of authority made it obvious that native leaders no longer fully controlled their own or their society's destiny. Moreover, receiving food and other presents must have hurt people who once had supplied their own needs or acquired European goods through their hunting prowess. Trade had helped Indians maintain some semblance of independence, some parity with colonists. When the crops withered and deer were scarce, the facade collapsed, leaving Catawbas exposed in their literal and figurative nakedness. A warrior who warned colonists against "Treating him like a Little Boy" spoke volumes about the personal costs of accepting handouts.[77]

New methods of settling disputes must have cut Catawbas no less deeply. The ancient explosion of violence set off by an enemy raid was defused when talk came to replace combat as the accepted response. Even if a negotiated settlement was reached, were all parties happy? Did women mourning their dead consider it the same when Glen shipped the offenders' heads to the Nation in barrels instead of allowing warriors to bring home scalps? Did young men deprived of that chance to prove themselves by hunting down the culprits feel the governor's way was better? "We all think it a very great Hardship upon us to see our People Stole away without some Revenge," they told Glen.[78] Nonetheless, they swallowed the hardship, and much else besides, in order to placate Anglo-America.

It is possible to read too much into official claims of control and the Catawbas' undeniable accommodation to colonial expectations, however. The Indians' dependence was not surrender, and while Catawbas were no longer masters of their own destiny, neither were they mere pawns in the hands of Machiavellian officials. A closer look suggests that the Nation was not as thoroughly controlled by colonists as Glen and other observers thought. Catawba headmen worked with crown authorities to establish a via media between base dependence and suicidal independence, a via media that secured protection and assured regular supplies of European goods yet left Indian society with some freedom to chart its own course.

The commission that chiefs carried is a good example of how deceptive appearances could be. Far from fabricating eractasswas out of mere paper, the document supplemented the traditional attributes essential to a leader in Catawba society. Yanabe Yatengway, Hagler, Hagler's successors Ayers and Frow—all were chosen by the Nation's council, which only then sent word to the colonial capital so that the governor could issue a commission signifying his approval. No governor ever challenged a council's decision. Even Glen, who in moments of enthusiasm would boast that "when I first made you King, I knew that you well deserved it," was fully aware of the actual procedure. As he told a delegation of Cherokees and Catawbas, "These Offices belong to you by Birth, you likewise hold them by a better Tenure, the Desires and Wishes of a willing People, and *lastly* they will be *confirmed* to you by the Commission which I shall give you."[79] A colonial blessing was certainly a significant addition to Catawba authority, but it was not a complete break with the past.

The formal relationship buttressing a chief's status also left him considerable leeway to settle intercultural conflicts as he saw fit. If a colonist was killed or his property stolen, Catawbas were sometimes left alone to investigate the crime and determine whether one of their people was responsible. Should a suspect be found, it was still up to the Indians to deal with him. "When your people do any of these things [crimes]," North Carolina agents told Hagler, "we have no remedy but are obliged to apply our selves to you, that the Offenders may be punished according to . . . your manner and Customs."[80] If the situation were reversed and a Catawba had been wronged, Governor Dobbs for one was willing to hand the culprit over to the Indians to do with as they saw fit. Other officials might not go so far, but they did agree to a request that an injured Catawba "receive something to make him Satisfaction for the sore pains he felt," a practice in accord with Catawba notions of justice.[81]

Catawba leaders could demand and receive satisfaction on their terms because they followed Anglo-American rules often enough to earn the trust of the men in provincial capitals. Rather than going after a colonial offender themselves, they went through formal channels, occasionally even naming names and suggesting appropriate sentences. They were also willing to forsake their own customs if need be. In 1754, for example, Catawbas executed a young warrior who, while drunk, had killed a colonist's child, a punishment that violated the rules excusing acts committed under the influence of alcohol.[82] Such a dramatic departure from traditional practice helped Indians accumulate the stock of good will that, on other occasions, permitted them to have their own way in tracking down and punishing Catawba offenders.

Catawbas had more latitude still in their relations with Indian peoples. Enemy warriors continued to sneak up on Catawba towns in spite of colonial efforts to stop them, for conflict was too deeply entrenched, and the arm of colonial power too short, to be halted by a treaty.[83] For every success in breaking up the cycle of reprisal, there were others where the cycle continued uninterrupted by outsiders. In 1759, Cherokees killed a Catawba woman visiting their towns, a reprisal for one of their own people recently murdered in the Nation. A colonist who ventured to interfere in such matters was likely to be told that he "had no concern with what they had to do there, their Business was with red and not white People."[84]

Peaceful contacts among Indians were, if anything, even further beyond colonial control. Only occasional glimpses survive of an entire round of diplomatic relations among natives that few colonists saw and fewer still understood. Throughout these years Catawba emissaries crisscrossed the Southeast, visiting various groups to settle disputes and make plans. In 1757 Governor Lyttelton heard from Fort Augusta on the Savannah River that the Chickasaws there intended to meet with Cherokees, Creeks, and Catawbas in the near future. The purpose of this congress? The informant knew only that it would involve "some affairs of Consequence that Concern'd those different nations."[85]

Officials who did enter the world of native American diplomacy did so more in the traditional role of mediators than in their own self-proclaimed role of master strategists. They were there because the Indians wanted them there. Catawbas faced with raids from the north could ill afford to add neighbors like Natchez, Chickasaws, or Cherokees to their long list of enemies, and they saw the wisdom in letting a governor do what he could to keep peace.[86] As attacks by French-inspired Indians increased, a treaty with the Iroquois also became more attractive, and Anglo-American mediation suited Catawbas as well as colonists. Only then, when both agreed, was there any hope of working together for a common goal. Only then could Glen persuade them.[87]

In fact, far from proving Glen's claims to mastery, the campaign for an end to the Catawba-Iroquois wars left little doubt about the limited control exercised from the coast. It was one thing for colonists to decide that peace had to be made, quite another to bring Catawbas and Iroquois together. A very detailed (and to Anglo-American minds pointless) procedure had to be followed before a cease-fire could be formally discussed. Indians, the South Carolina Council reported, are "jealous of their Honours, and very attentive to all Punctilios of Form[;] we apprehend they will decline sending any of their Head Men . . . unless they previously receive some Token . . . to serve as an Invitation to them." How could the Council be so certain? "We look upon this not to be a mere conjectural Opinion, but are induced to form it from the Behaviour of the Catawbas, who insisted on such a Preliminary from the Six Nations, before they would send Deputies thither."[88] One person's "Punctilios of Form" were the very essence of peace to another, and a colonist's worthless "Token" was priceless to a native looking for a sign of good will. Because they did not consider such things truly important, colonial officials repeatedly failed to heed native pleas that customary rules be observed. The result was a seemingly endless string of postponements, as governors pushed for peace and headmen refused to budge.

Debates over the location of peace talks caused still more delays. The Iroquois maintained that Albany was the "Antient and fixt

Place for all People to treat with them," and Catawbas insisted on meeting in "their own Towns or Country." Colonists suggested Philadelphia or Williamsburg as alternatives, but the former was "too remote a Place" for Catawbas, the latter "too far off" to suit the Six Nations. Crown officials might grow weary of the haggling over a proper site; the Indians never did. The Six Nations had formal ties to Philadelphia, the Catawbas to Virginia. Thus if the Iroquois went to Williamsburg, it would be the same as going all the way to Nassaw Town, and "would," they argued, "be dishonorable to Us."[89] Similarly, Catawbas knew that, as Glen wrote, "it was best to meet them there [Williamsburg.] Otherwise it would look like following them to Beg for Peace."[90]

Ultimately it was less Glen's powers of persuasion than the Catawbas' straits that put Hagler and the others on board the ship bound for New York in May 1751, more than a decade after the first peace overtures had been sent out. While the governor was quick to claim credit for the shaky truce that ensued, the real lesson here was how little direct influence he or any other colonist wielded in Catawba councils. Diplomacy benefited both sides and enabled distant officials to assume a larger role in native affairs. Catawbas would have to listen when Glen and Atkin spoke now, and in a general sense they would have to follow British policy. But a Glen or an Atkin could never be certain that the Nation would obey every command.

V

The Indians' effort to preserve independence was aided considerably by their ability to approach more than one colony. Catawbas never forgot the lessons of the years before the Yamasee War, when colonist fought colonist in their midst, and they kept up their friendship with Virginia long after the trade from that direction had all but ceased. The strategy was effective. When rumors reached Charleston that Catawbas were considering a move to Virginia, the Commons House fretted about "the bad Consequences that may attend this Province by the Removal of those People" and authorized Glen to send a large supply of ammunition to the Nation.[91] The Indians stayed where they were—they may even have started the rumor to extract the desired goods—but they stepped up their visits to Williamsburg, to the delight of the Virginians and the dismay of Glen and his Council.[92] With Virginia as a patron, Catawbas felt assured that the men in Charleston would never take them for granted.

To reinforce that feeling, Catawbas during these years befriended North Carolina. In 1750 Matthew Toole sent Glen "a treaty" between the Nation and agents from North Carolina that laid the groundwork for a formal relationship and provided Indians with yet another means of acquiring supplies.[93] Thus three colonies courted one small Indian nation, each suitor convinced that the headmen would favor it alone. Catawbas remained most closely tied to Charleston, but they encouraged everyone, and everyone responded. The result was a cacophony of flattery. South Carolina reminded Catawbas, "We have been your constant Protectors and have always treated you like the Children of the same Household, with ourselves." North Carolina considered them "our particular friends." Not to be outdone, Virginia promised that it would "on every Occasion endeavour to shew you the Respect due to great Warriours and faithful Friends."[94]

The wooing among these rivals jumped from ardent to feverish once North America became a battleground in the Seven Years' War that, beginning in 1754, pitted Britain against France. In retrospect it is hard to fathom why colonists wanted Catawba allies so badly, for the men who tried to command them considered these Indians more trouble than they were worth. George Washington complained of "their unmeaning promises and capricious humors," and he quoted with approval another officer who reported that one Catawba war party "behav'd in the most shamefull manner, and run away as a parcell of thieves rather than Warriors." "An avaricious, greedy Set of People," agreed Virginia's Lieutenant Governor Robert Dinwiddie when he, too, discovered that Indians came when it suited them, fought not for King George but for gifts and plunder, and stayed only as long as they wished.[95] Nonetheless, like John Barnwell, James Moore, and other predecessors who at once condemned and recruited native allies, military strategists were convinced that the Indian warrior was necessary, and they traveled throughout the East collecting war parties for the king's service.

Desperation made the diplomatic competition for Catawba favor anything but diplomatic. Spokesmen for each province, not content to boast about their own colony, denigrated the others. According to Glen, a Virginia agent "has spoken very disrespectfully of this Province to the Indians, telling them that they will not be treated *there* with old Cloaths." North Carolina officials tried the same approach, asking Catawbas "what they Look'd to this Province [South Carolina] for, it was now four season's since they had, had any goods here—and that this Governor had not goods; but that they of No. Carolina had goods Plenty of all Sorts and wou'd Supply them with Every thing." South Carolinians responded in kind, warning Catawbas "that the Intentions of the North Carolina people . . . would be to take their Lands from them and in a short time they might expect to become Slaves to those people, . . . [who] had never done any thing for them."[96]

Catawbas, sensing the desperation creeping into colonial speeches, made the most of the situation, acquiring clothing, ammunition, food, and other essential goods in return for service as allies. Often the trade-off was explicit, as Indians informed colonists that they would gladly fight for the English, but without some powder they "must sit over the Fire without any other Action."[97] In 1759 Lyttelton reported that Hagler "lately offered me their Service . . . provided I would cause [a fort] to be raised for the Security of their Wives and Children."[98] This stronghold had been an enticement for several years. Both Carolinas wanted the honor of building it (and establishing a permanent foothold in the Nation), and the Indians negotiated with each, receiving gifts but always putting off a final decision. Edmond Atkin, surveying the steady stream of promises and presents, concluded glumly that "the People of both Provinces . . . have I beleive tampered too much on both sides with those Indians, who seem to understand well how to make their Advantage of it."[99]

Running through all of these discussions was a new tone, suggesting that Catawbas were well aware of the good fortune the war had brought them. In the late 1750s the Nation's leaders often

Distance of the Towns In the Cuttahbaw Nation

from Sucah To Noostee Town 3 mile

from Noostee to Weyapee & Nassaw ¾ of a mile

from Sucah To Weyanne ~ 7 mile

from Weyanne To Charraw Town 1¼ mile

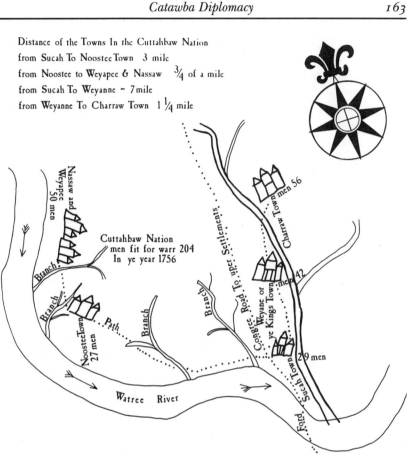

Map 5. "Cuttahbaw Nation: Men Fit for Warr . . . 1756." [By John Evans.] The large tributary stream at right is Sugar Creek; the estimate of "7 Mile" separating the two towns on the west side of that creek should probably be "1 Mile." *Redrawn by Linda Merrell from a microfilm copy in the South Carolina Department of Archives and History (original in Scottish Record Office, Edinburgh)*

delivered what Hagler termed "strong" speeches, in which the Indians were not afraid to approach the limits of polite discourse in order to get their point across. "We have waited a long Time for your Powder you promised to send us," they might say.[100] The slow-moving Atkin was a particularly easy target for gibes. "Squire Atkin promised me a long while ago that he would send us some goods and would do many things for us," Hagler told Lyttelton sarcastically. "I have long hunted for those goods but never could find them nor has he done any one thing for us." Occasionally the eractasswa's anger embraced all of British America. After one conference a surprised John Evans sent word that Hagler "with much Assurance demanded of me if the Governor had sent them any Powder and Ball. I told him I knew of none. He said the White People spoke much and performed but little."[101] The talk of having "no one to see us Rightified but you" had been abandoned.

VI

Great Britain's need for allies temporarily gave Catawbas the advantage again in their dealings with colonial America. To capitalize on the demand for their services required a keen understanding of the way colonial society worked, an ability to translate needs into requests that would bring results. The secret of the Catawbas' successful diplomacy was intimate knowledge, acquired through long experience, of what made Anglo-America tick. To appreciate the Indians' expertise, consider a journey Hagler made in the spring of 1759. Governor Dobbs had promised the Indians some beef and sent money to his agent in the area, one Major McClanahan, with orders to purchase and distribute the livestock. McClanahan had a better idea: he bought cheaper meat, handed that over to the Catawbas, and pocketed the difference. In other words, as one observer put it, "he gives them nothing But ould Bulls." In response, the report went on, "Hagler Cut the Cod of[f] one and tuck it tide to his Sadle all the way to Salsbury [North Carolina] Cort, and tould the Cort McClanaughan gave him nothing But Stallion Cows and Charged the Contery a great price."[102]

Hagler's trip proved that Catawbas had mastered the details of intercultural diplomacy. The chief turned to North Carolina because, cognizant of colonial jurisdictions and their meaning, he was aware that his grievance would be heard only in Dobbs's colony. He rode to Salisbury, and to the courthouse, because he knew that town, and that building, to be the nearest center of provincial authority. He planned his arrival to coincide with court day, the only time local officials would gather there. Finally, once he had their attention with his dramatic entrance, Hagler couched his argument in terms best calculated to persuade his listeners: he said nothing about justice to the Indians, emphasizing instead the cost to colonial taxpayers. His visit reveals a sophisticated understanding of an alien world, an understanding that enabled Catawbas to profit from their position in the colonial Southeast.

Hagler's day in court was but one example of a trend in Catawba society that saw Indians' using Anglo-America to solve their problems. While this habit forced natives to make certain sacrifices, it did not mark a repudiation of the past or a surrender to colonial whims. The Indians remained interested only in some of what colonial America had to offer. Just as Catawbas once had selectively incorporated trade goods, so they now accepted commissions, gifts, and mediation; beyond that they would not go. Though in 1757 the headmen asked Dobbs to teach their children to "fear and love God as you do," William Richardson, a Presbyterian clergyman who tried to take Catawbas up on their offer, quickly discovered that they were not eager for conversion.[103] At Cheraw Town one Captain Hamy told Richardson that "old Indian make no Sabbath and young Indian make no Sabbath," and then, according to the minister, Hamy decided "he was averse to talk to the Rev. so off he went." Undaunted, Richardson pushed on to Hagler's town. The eractasswa, while more polite, was hardly more encouraging, saying only that he would speak to his people about the matter when they returned from hunting. As Richardson was leaving, the chief extracted a promise of some corn, and when they met again, Richardson supplied money for the corn—along with a sermon. The limits of the Indian's interest were all too evident. "We had a good deal of Talk with him," the disappointed visitor confided to his diary. "When the Discourse was about Corn etc. he seemed to understand, but any thing else he seemed at a Loss."[104]

Far from embracing colonial culture, at times Catawbas seemed actually to be trying to distance themselves from it, to confirm and even strengthen barriers being breached by more frequent contacts, both formal and informal, with British America. The Indians asked Dobbs "to send us Smiths and other Tradesmen to teach our Children," a plea designed to reduce native dependence on outsiders' skills.[105] At other times the Catawbas stated more directly their determination to remain as far as possible beyond the colonists' reach. In 1754 Hagler stressed that "when the Great man above made us he . . . made our forefathers and [us] of this Colour and Hue (Showing his hands and Breast) he also fixed our forefathers and us here . . . and Ever since we Lived after our manner and fashion." Five years later the chief wondered aloud whether "may be the white people would go away and leave us to our Selves."[106] Catawbas were willing to live with the assistance of the English; they were not willing to become English themselves. The cultural frontier remained intact, despite—or, perhaps, because of—the growing presence of colonists in the natives' midst.

5

His Land Was Spoiled:
The Settlers' Invasion

His Land was spoiled . . . , they have
spoiled him 100 Miles every way.
—Colonel Ayers, Catawba Headman

IN THE FALL OF 1749 there was unrest in "the Catawbas Country."[1] According to North Carolina colonists living nearby, "several wicked and evil disposed Persons . . . had by divers suggestions and Artifices endeavoured to disturb the Peace." Led by one John Ellis, the troublemakers had been telling Catawba Indians that colonists settling the area "had no right to the Lands by them possessed and that even his Majesty had no right to those Lands," a line of argument quite naturally "tending to breed and foment a misunderstanding between his Majesty's said Subjects and the said Catawba Indians." Alarmed settlers sent word to the governor, who promptly ordered that anyone making such suggestions be arrested.[2]

Ellis was known as "a silly bragging fellow," but his incendiary speeches may have had a serious purpose.[3] Since he was a trader from Virginia, his words were probably designed to protect his livelihood against people threatening his Catawba partners. It might even be said that he was defending an entire way of life, a traders' way embracing both Indians and colonists and one that stretched back in the Ellis family half a century or more. His father (also named John) had used the piedmont trade as a vehicle to advance from digging cellars and guarding prisoners into the ranks of respectable landowners. Ellises were intimately connected with the trading community centered on the James and Appomattox: the elder sat on a grand jury with Henry Hatcher (whose namesake had been among the Cheraws in 1673) and John Stewart (whom John Lawson had met at the Catawbas); the younger witnessed deeds for the Colemans, another family of traders. And in 1728 both father and son accompanied William Byrd on his survey of the dividing line between Virginia and North Carolina, fighting for the honor of slogging through swamps and regaling the party with a story about battling a bear.[4]

Sometime after returning from Byrd's expedition, things began to go wrong. John Ellis, Sr., died, and his son apparently found the trade harder to keep up. Perhaps he lacked his father's knack for the business. Perhaps too many of the Catawbas' northern enemies waited beside the path to attack packhorse trains. Perhaps too many Catawbas were making their way downriver to Thomas Brown's place or some other South Carolina trading post. Whatever the reason, before his 1749 outburst Ellis was already uneasy. In 1746 he dropped by Brown's store at the Congarees, claimed that the Catawbas were on the verge of moving to Virginia, "and swore that he would at least carry away three Towns with him now." The trader George Haig, who heard about Ellis's antics, was the one who dismissed the Virginian as "silly" and then went on about his business, convinced (correctly) that Catawbas were not going anywhere. But within three years Ellis would become even more shrill when he had to add encroachment by settlers to his list of woes—even the Virginia traders' old way station on the Yadkin River was in danger of being overrun. This time his audience took steps to silence him.[5]

It might have comforted Ellis to know that his South Carolina competitors were in the same predicament, all but overcome by the newcomers moving into the interior. In 1735, settlers at the Congarees complained that Thomas Brown's post, a popular gathering place for Indians, was a public nuisance, and authorities in Charleston ordered Brown to move. He managed to stay, but his mentor, John Thompson, was not so lucky—or so well connected in the provincial capital. Two years after the challenge to Brown, farmers along the Pee Dee River accused Thompson of buying land from the Cheraw and Pedee Indians without official permission and, worse, turning the natives against the new immigrants. Charleston authorities believed Thompson's stout denial of the latter charge; nonetheless, they made him hand over the land. As compensation Thompson received a sum equal to what he had paid the Indians, and 560 acres among the very people who had brought charges against him. We may wonder whether the old trader felt that justice had been done.[6]

By themselves the tribulations of Ellis, Brown, and Thompson do not add up to much. The colonial interior always had its share of silly braggarts and petty disputes. Taken together, however, their falling fortunes herald the beginning of a shift from a world where trade was king to one where cotton would be. The boundary between the two was by no means clear-cut. After all, Thomas Brown was a settler as well as a trader, and Indians bound for his store picked their way past wheat fields, cattle pens, and slave quarters. Nor did the transformation take place overnight. John Ellis would continue to lead packhorses across the piedmont as he always had, and his father before him.[7]

But although Brown shipped wheat as well as deerskins to the coast and Ellis did not abruptly retire, they were the last of their kind. No John Ellis III would follow in his father's footsteps; Thomas Brown would never instruct some young man on the rise as Thompson once had tutored him. It was the end of an era, an era whose passing Catawbas might well mourn. For all their faults, traders generally had shown a willingness to abide by the rules native society laid down. They slept with Catawba women, fought alongside Catawba men, and sat in council with Catawba leaders. Moreover, a trader valued Indians as hunters and was uninterested in trying to change them or get rid of them. While he remained more colonist than Catawba, he at least made an effort to approach Indians on their own terms.[8]

Settlers hardly tried. Where a trader saw profits and a crown official saw allies, a planter tended to see nothing but trouble. To his mind, native neighbors were good only for obstructing settlement, threatening life and property, and attracting other Indians to the area. Settlers came, not to befriend the natives, but to avoid them—or bury them. These emigrants to the upcountry had little patience with the time-honored customs governing contact between Indian and colonist. To the farmer's way of thinking, a present placed in Catawba hands was worse than useless; far from purchasing friendship, it bought only trouble, "for the more gifts they get the more proud and deveilish they are."[9] Even the natives' acknowledged skill at woodcraft, commonly cited as a good reason to keep them around, came under fire from the new occupants of the interior. In 1748, one militia captain ranging the upcountry objected to the brace of Indian warriors Governor James Glen had appointed to accompany his troops, preferring "much rather to have two [more] of our own Colour." Were natives not better hunters? "[I] do Assure you Sir," the officer argued, "it is of no Purpose for I Question whether sir an Indian on the Main can compare with some of the men inlisted, not only in killing Provisions or the like but any other Property tha[t] an Indian is adapted to."[10]

The arrival of people with little understanding of and less use for Catawbas wrenched intercultural relations out of the safe confines of exchange or diplomacy. Contact once again was unpredictable and, therefore, explosive. But it was not only the newcomers' view of the Indian that caused problems; it was their view of the land. Traders like the men William Byrd rode with had learned to make their way in the alien environment of the interior; planters headed into the upcountry intent on changing the landscape rather than themselves. They, like John Lawson, dreamed of making the piedmont into a place of plowed fields and wooden fences, of millponds and wagon roads.

To Catawbas such plans were as provocative as anything John Ellis told them. Indians were not, despite Byrd's claims, "a people that are contented with Nature as they find her." Far from a tabula rasa on which newcomers could make their mark, the uplands bore native American signatures that colonists erased before scrawling in their own, leaving a palimpsest in which an earlier, Indian landscape was only faintly legible. Traders like Brown could easily adapt to a physical setting shaped by colonial needs and tastes. For Catawbas, it would be more difficult.[11]

I

Planters and plantations were, of course, nothing new to Catawbas. Since at least 1692, natives from the interior had visited colonial farms along the coast. By 1750, however, instead of Indians going to settlements, those settlements came to them. The township scheme launched in 1729 by South Carolina governor Robert Johnson continued, and new arrivals pushed steadily up the Wateree River past the frontier settlement at Pine Tree Hill. Farmers from the north moved in even faster, for they were unchecked by any plan controlling development of the interior. Together these streams flowed swiftly toward the very heart of the Nation. In 1750, North Carolina agents promised Catawbas that "in a year or two this Country will be . . . thick Settled Round you," and colonists quickly set about living up to that promise, undeterred by Indian complaints that they were getting too close.[12] By 1755 the Nation was almost surrounded: some five hundred families lived within thirty miles, and a few North Carolina surveyors were dragging their chains right through Catawba villages.[13] Twelve years later an itinerant Anglican minister, Charles Woodmason, reported that the Waxhaws, a Scotch-Irish community near the Catawbas, was "most surprisingly thick settled beyond any Spot in England of its Extent." And this was only one corner of a region now populated by more than ten thousand nonnative inhabitants (see Map 6).[14]

The crucial word in Woodmason's description was not "thick," but "settled," for it was less the number of newcomers than their definition of "settled" that posed the gravest threat to the Nation. To the Indian, the upcountry already was settled. Upon its surface generations of natives had inscribed their own version of an ordered landscape—the paths and fords, the villages and hunting camps, the fields and sacred sites that gave the place its distinctive appearance. Order to the Catawbas was chaos to the colonial planter, however; one person's wilderness was another's home, and in taming *their* wilderness, Carolinians rendered the piedmont alien and unfamiliar—in short, a wilderness—in the eyes of those already there. Without issuing a challenge to the native proprietors of the region, without necessarily even seeing an Indian, people straightening out the land according to their own notions were overturning a carefully established order.[15]

The first sign of trouble was the surveying parties that fanned out across the piedmont. Initially the surveyor himself may have aroused little suspicion, for traders like Evans and Haig, already familiar to Indians, often took on the job.[16] Once he set to work, however, the threat was clear. The surveyor, under orders to lay out everything in squares, attempted to impose an artificial geometric precision onto terrain customarily divided along the natural lines of watercourses or hills.[17] His methods were equally strange to a native watching him work. The chain and compass, along with the initials carved into trees and the stakes driven into the ground to mark claims, were symbols of the new age dawning, akin to the steelyards that once had announced the trader's dominance.[18] Ironically, the surveyor also recorded for posterity the features of the native landscape even as he helped replace them. Indian fields and cabins, hunting camps and peach orchards, ancient ditches and mounds—all went onto the colonial plats. Like the stakes or initials, they signaled the demise of an older environment and ushered in the new.[19]

Close behind the surveyor, or sometimes well ahead of him, came the farmer. In an age of interstates it is difficult to imagine what the first stragglers felt as they headed into a vast and (to them) uncharted territory. The task of mastering that exotic land must have seemed daunting, even overwhelming. Robert Witherspoon, who entered the area southeast of the Catawba Nation during the 1730s, suggests something of the vanguard's combination of despair and hope. Witherspoon moved to Williamsburg Township on the Black River as a child and, many years later, recalled, "My mother and us children were still in expectation that we were comeing to an agreeable place, but when we arrived and saw nothing but a wilderness and instead of a fine timbered house, nothing but a very mean dirt house, our spirits quite sunk." Even after living there some time, the Witherspoons "were still opprest with fears on divers accounts, especially of being massacred by the Indians or bit by the snakes or being lost or perished in the woods." Nor were these childish fantasies; the family knew firsthand of at least three neighbors who never came back from a trip into the forest. But the Witherspoons endured, buoyed by the dreams that Robert's father kept alive for them. "My father gave us all the comfort he [could]," Witherspoon remembered, "by telling us we would get all these trees cut down and in a short time they would be plenty of inhabitants, that we could see from house to house." Out of such promises and their fulfillment was the Catawbas' homeland transformed.[20]

The immediate task, as one upcountry settler put it, was constructing "proper Conveniencys for his Family." The first dwelling was invariably a temporary hut, a "bark tent" or "dirt house" consisting of poles covered with earth, branches, and pine needles, in its materials and general outline perhaps not wholly foreign to a native who happened to see it. Most colonists soon erected log cabins, and some eventually graduated to frame houses covered with planks.[21]

The Reverend Mr. Woodmason was appalled by most of the dwellings he saw on his travels through the interior. Drafty, dirty, smoky, in his view they made better stables than homes.[22] Yet to a Catawba, even to one acquainted with the hybrid buildings the Saponis had erected at Christanna, the crudest of log cabins represented a radical departure from the piedmont norm. Unlike the saplings, bark, and reeds Indians knew, the materials used in a colonist's dwelling had been removed from nature by a laborious process that transformed tree trunks into logs.[23] Moreover, the logs were used to create a structure that was square, not circular like most native houses. With time the addition of other features, from squat chimneys and wooden floors to door locks and window glass, heightened the contrast with earlier piedmont buildings.[24]

Once the basic need for shelter had been met, most farmers picked up hammer, saw, and nails and went about erecting other buildings such as kitchens, barns, stables, even slave quarters.[25] Some also constructed smokehouses, sawmills, gristmills, stills, and indigo vats to process the products of the interior, further adding to the inventory of objects cluttering Catawba Country.[26] Cowpens to keep livestock in and fences to keep them out added to one's control over a patch of land.[27] All of these structures, following the surveyor's lead, broke the landscape into parcels that every settler understood, separating one man's property from his neighbor's. If what people build is a statement, colonists were speaking in a whole new language.[28]

The mills, vats, and pens leave no doubt that use of the land changed as much as did the structures placed upon it. Corn remained the dominant crop, but colonial farmers proceeded well beyond Indian conventions. Before long, fields of wheat, barley, oats, rye, hemp, flax, indigo, and other plants dotted the upcountry.[29] And while many colonists still relied on methods that were akin to native practices—clearing fields by girdling trees, planting seeds in hillocks several feet apart, hoeing throughout the summer months—some came equipped with the knowledge and tools needed to introduce new techniques. Plows were becoming common on piedmont farms, and by 1766 at least one hill along the west side of the Wateree River was plowed to the very top.[30]

New crops and new methods must have had a profound effect on the Catawbas, for, like every society heavily dependent upon agriculture, they had come to orient their very existence to that pursuit. The daily routine, the ceremonial round, the land's appearance, the topic of conversation—all are shaped by the plants on which a people relies for its survival. Hence when a colonist moved onto an Indian old field and began sowing different seeds using novel techniques, he ushered in not just another way of doing things but another way of thinking. At the most fundamental level, a plowed field or a plot of wheat simply looked strange to those accustomed to seeing hillocks of corn, beans, and squash. In addition, colonists' crops required schedules and practices unfamiliar to Catawba cultivators. Indians in the habit of planting in April must have found it strange to see their neighbors sowing barley in February and plowing another field in March. In the past, natives could claim intimate knowledge of the mysteries of seed, soil, and season; now they found themselves at a loss to comprehend the new things being grown all around them. Coming at a time when the Catawbas' own plants were failing, the Anglo-American agricultural regime must have been especially disturbing.[31]

Another crop that flourished in the uplands and touched native life was livestock. Before settlers arrived, Catawbas had owned horses and tasted the occasional beef stew.[32] Still, the Nation was unprepared for the horde of cattle, hogs, sheep, and horses that colonists drove before them into the interior. Some herds numbered in the hundreds; but whether a particular herd was large or small, the cumulative effect on the Nation was profound.[33] A colonist routinely let these animals roam free to forage in order to save the trouble of penning and feeding them.[34] Left to themselves, the beasts headed straight for the same grassy areas and canebrakes that deer favored. A 1733 mapmaker who decorated his work by drawing a bull, a hog, and a deer in the Carolina piedmont proved prophetic: early settlers recalled seeing deer among the livestock grazing in upland fields.[35] As time went on, however, domesticated animals would push game out and take over more completely.

In an effort further to improve the lot of their animals, colonists were in the habit of burning the forests to build up the supply of grass. Ranchers with firebrands were like farmers with plows: both sought to increase their yield and conform the landscape to colonial practice, and both alienated Indians. The use of fire to modify the environment was nothing new to Catawbas, who employed controlled burning to direct deer into specific areas or eliminate undergrowth that could hide an enemy war party.[36] But planters now fired the woods for very different reasons: they established or maintained pastures, created clearings around their farms, and even used fire as a weapon against a rival. The technique was familiar to Catawbas; its purpose, and therefore its effect, was not.[37]

As colonists trekked into the piedmont, then, they grabbed any tool they could find, from a torch to an axe, to carve their surroundings into some semblance of home. The work on a particular farmstead was only part of the invasion, however. Individual settlers were also busy forging ties with one another, and these, too, hastened the transition from an aboriginal to a European universe. At first, colonists simply used Indian trails to reach their neighbors. But few were satisfied following in native footsteps, and they immediately talked of changing things to suit colonial needs. Among those needs were routes wide enough—ten feet wide, according to one plan—for wagons.[38] During the 1750s the inhabitants of the upcountry, often with public support, built thoroughfares that they designated "Cut Road," "Broad Road," "Great Road," and "Wagon Road." Along the east side of the Wateree River, for example, enterprising settlers began widening the old route John Lawson had taken, until by 1760 the road reached as far as the Waxhaws.[39]

The engineering program was so successful that wagons became an everyday part of the piedmont. A servant of Matthew Toole's was using one to haul corn near the Nation during the mid-1750s, before the end of the decade they were reported "Constantly going" from Pine Tree Hill to Charleston, and five years later the way was cleared for trips from deep in the interior to the coast in vehicles drawn by teams of four horses. Before long, a field near Sugar Creek would become a popular campground for wagoners going to and from the lowcountry.[40]

Similar things were happening on the region's waterways. Indeed, the two modes of transportation were so intimately connected in the colonial mind that settlers occasionally spoke of clearing rivers and cutting roads in the same breath. Colonial travelers initially used native fords across streams just as they had stayed on native paths; "the Waggon Ford at the Cataba Nation" and other shallows probably were located at the same spot where explorers' armies and traders' packhorses once had crossed. But the same urge that carved wagon roads out of Indian paths also impelled settlers to replace fords with bridges or ferries capable of transporting animals and carts as well as people.[41] It is unlikely that a Catawba traveler considered all of these internal improvements truly an improvement. While a 1766 law required a ferry operator to give free passage to the colony's Indian friends, this clause was later dropped and may never have had much force at landings along the Wateree or Congaree.[42]

For every colonist figuring out ways to get across upland streams, there were others tackling the problem of getting up and down them. Just as Indian trails were not proper roads because they could not accommodate wagons, so waterways were no use if a boat could not get through. Clear passage was so important that it affected colonial nomenclature. "Wateree above the falls," noted one South Carolina surveyor laying out lands along its banks, "therefore does not deserve the name of River." Carolinians would not do anything about those falls until the nineteenth century, but they wasted no time clearing the way farther downstream. In 1753 the South Carolina Assembly passed a bill to rid the Wateree of the trees blocking its lower course, and before the decade was out, the

Pine Tree Hill storekeeper Joseph Kershaw was shipping boatloads of grain to Charleston.[43]

Together with the rice dams and millponds that colonial intruders were building, removing debris from rivers and creeks modified the aquatic environment.[44] Blocking or clearing watercourses altered the habits of the fish, waterfowl, and other creatures on which Catawbas depended. Beavers could be flooded out, fish traps and marshlands either submerged or drained. Indians who frequented a hunting camp near the Wateree raft of trees and others at a camp across the river on the outskirts of Pine Tree Hill must have found their routines disrupted by manipulation of the streams.[45]

Colonists making paths into roads and the Wateree into a river were still more or less adhering to the same contours of the land that natives had known. Soon, however, the newcomers began to direct their steps toward different destinations, scratching out new trails on the surface of the interior. Once again Robert Witherspoon offers a glimpse of the experience of countless Carolinians. When his family first came to the Black River valley, Witherspoon remembered:

> There was few or no roads, every family had to travel the best way they could, which was here double distance to some, for they had to follow swamps and branches for their guides, for some time. And after some time some men got such a knowledge of the woods as to blaze paths, so the people soon found out to follow blazes from place to place.[46]

Throughout the interior, people who were tired of going "double distance" began to carve paths that bypassed or branched out from existing thoroughfares.[47] In so doing they were creating highways that were, for them, more sensible, and marking trails in a manner understood by their fellow colonists.

The extent to which they succeeded may be gauged by certain subtle changes in the traveler's routine. Lawson's route, commonly known as the "Path to the Catawba Nation" during the first years of colonial intrusion, gradually came to be called the "Road . . . to the Upper Settlements" instead.[48] Moreover, those following this and

other roads relied on colonial instead of Catawba guides, for settlers now knew the way better than Indians did. Natives had once
possessed the secret knowledge of routes; as colonists became familiar with these old routes and forged many more of their own,
the Indian pathfinders that John Lawson had hired became super-
fluous.[49]

Each fresh trail was the physical manifestation of the new cultural paths colonists were blazing as they went about the business of
remaking the land. A particular route might be born for any number of reasons. Thomas Howell, who lived between the Congaree
and Wateree rivers, had "an Avenue" to join his house to his brother's. Soon after 1750 Howell also managed to redirect traffic from
the old Catawba path, which headed straight for the trading posts
along the upper Congaree, to his own road leading to the ferry he
operated some ten or twenty miles downstream. Closer to the Nation, inhabitants of the Waxhaws hacked out a thoroughfare heading west from their farms to a Catawba River ford in order to reach
settlements on the other side.[50]

At the heart of this expanding road network lay social and economic centers where people could gather to swap goods and gossip. Mills were one locus of piedmont life, as the frequency of
names like "Mill Path" and "Mill Road" attests. "Meetinghouse
Road" was less common, but that should not be taken as a sign that
churches ranked lower on the settlers' scale of values.[51] Quite the
contrary: these buildings were so central to the life of the piedmont
that people grabbed every scrap of soil in the church's shadow and
therefore needed no road. Others who were not so early or so
lucky still found a way to get to church. A single plat of land along
Fishing Creek contained no fewer than two paths and a road, all
leading to the Fishing Creek Meetinghouse. Farther west a tract
depicting a church between the Broad and Saluda rivers resembles
a cartwheel, with the meetinghouse the hub and the paths to it
spokes.[52]

As popular as the church was, at least some people were convinced that among settlers it took a distant second to the tavern. In
numbers alone, taverns won handily. Salisbury consisted of seven
or eight houses in 1755, four of them taverns or inns. At the same
time, it seemed as if everyone too far away to pay a regular call

on these establishments was bombarding the county court with requests "to keep Ordinary Att his Plantation."[53] Petitions were common because business was good. Woodmason, who knew a rival
when he saw one, complained "that at these Rendezvous there is
more Company of a Saturday, than in the Church on Sunday." To
the tavern, people came to warm themselves at a fire and have a
glass with a friend. Here they could conduct business with merchants or magistrates, discuss the weather or politics, complain
about crops or Indians, and gamble at cards or dice. These establishments might be as large as Joseph Kershaw's and Samuel Wyly's
at Pine Tree Hill or as small as William Mitchell's near the Wateree
River, one of countless "Neighbours Houses . . . where there was
Lickuar to sell."[54] Size did not matter: all were powerful magnets,
and the colonist beat a path to their doors.

Such crossroads did more than etch another template of travel
and settlement onto the face of the land. They also helped to set
the very different rhythm that was coming to rule the piedmont.
The week took on a regular tempo, with Saturdays devoted to business and Sundays to worship. Even Woodmason's unceasing condemnation of the heathen people in the interior cannot hide the
fact that they turned out in large numbers—on one occasion a
thousand strong—to hear his sermons. Moreover, though they
may not have behaved as he deemed proper, they nonetheless followed a set of their own rules, worshipping, and getting drunk, "according to Custom." Nor was drinking confined to Sunday after
church; settlers celebrated the King's Birthday with a glass or two
and, no doubt, looked forward to other holidays to break up the
monotony of rural life.[55]

Between the weekly round of activities and the annual events
were new seasonal routines. At set times of the year livestock were
rounded up for branding. In August wagons left the interior
loaded with products for the Charleston market, and the stills
were hard at work to keep up with demand during this "Season of
Festivity and Drunkenness."[56] Stock rounded up, wagons hauling
goods, whiskey dripping into vats—these were now the signs of the
seasons, signs understandable only in a code colonists had devised.
The annual cycle itself remained the same (not even colonists could
control the climate), but the manner in which inhabitants marked

its passing did not. Almost without realizing it, almost out of necessity, natives began cracking the code, becoming so attuned to the
new routine that they called a minister who dropped in on them
the "Sunday man."[57]

While Carolina settlers paced off different seasonal, social, and
physical boundaries, they also stamped their imprint on the land
by renaming its features. Gent's Ford, Dutchman Creek, Barkly's
Branch, Webb's Mill Road—these and other local landmarks took
on new names and therefore new, nonnative identities. Even the
Indian place-names settlers used—Sugar and Cheraw creeks, Wateree and Catawba rivers, Hagler's Hill, and Johnney's Town Branch
—buried the aboriginal conceptual map, for Catawbas had identified these places by different terms. How one replaced another has
been lost. It is not hard to imagine a war of words, with each side
condemning the stupidity and stubbornness of the other, until
Broad River won out over Eswaw Huppeday through attrition or
the sheer weight of superior numbers speaking the new name.
However the battle was fought, the victor was clear: natives were
using alien labels to identify familiar spots, and colonial domination became that much more complete.[58]

The transformation of the Indians' homeland involved more
than different buildings, crops, paths, and names; it also involved
different people. In their contacts with traders Catawbas had encountered only a very small sample of the intruding population.
But since settlers generally came in family groups, Catawbas were
brought face to face with large numbers of colonial women and
children for the first time. It must have seemed as if the land were
being overrun by children. Governor Dobbs visited a settlement
east of the Nation and found that virtually every farm boasted
between five and ten children; Woodmason set the figure at ten or
twelve. A Catawba's reaction to these new arrivals is unclear, but
at least some Indians considered them easy targets for abuse or
amusement. In 1750, North Carolina officials accused the natives
of "disturbing or frightening Women and children in their Houses
when their Husbands are abroad." "If they enter a house and the
man is not at home," the Moravian bishop August Spangenburg
agreed after a tour of the region, "they become insolent and the
poor woman must do as they command."[59]

To compound the Catawbas' problem of adjustment, farmers often brought not only their families but their slaves. By 1768, blacks constituted almost 20 percent of the non-Indian population of the region, an influx that made the racial realities of the intruding society more evident. In the past, natives could remain ignorant of the color barrier developing in colonial America. Indians from the Nation had encountered Africans and Europeans in much the same context—as explorers with de Soto, as traders accompanying Virginians, as soldiers helping George Chicken defend the low-country in 1715, as enemies of the colony to be hunted down for pay like the French or Spanish—and had no reason to draw any sharp distinctions between black and white. After 1750, however, the spread of farms worked by slaves marked the beginning of very different contacts between Catawbas and blacks, contacts that eventually would reverse Catawba views and separate Indian from Afro-American as never before.[60]

From names to crops, from roads to children, Carolinians sculpted a landscape that, while by no means thoroughly tame by colonial standards, was taking on what the newcomers considered a more settled appearance. "Roads are making, Boats building—Bridges framing . . . as will . . . make the Country side wear a New face," Woodmason proudly proclaimed. People could now lift their eyes from the plow or the cattle or the road long enough to look around and discover that they felt at home. In drawing up a remonstrance on behalf of the area's inhabitants the Anglican clergy-man captured this growing sense of contentment: "Our Soil is not only fruitful, but capable of producing any Grain whatever. Our Vales and Woods are delightful Our Hills Healthful and Pleasant."[61] *Our* Soil, *Our* Vales and Woods, *Our* Hills—colonists had made the land their own.

II

Colonial Americans were taming the Carolina piedmont; taming the Indians there would take a bit longer. Natives in the Nation were well aware of what was going on all around them. Throughout these years Catawba hunters, warriors, and diplomats continued to pass to and fro across the Carolinas, stopping at bustling market towns or isolated plantations. Others went to church, dropped by mills, visited stores, and camped on nearby farms.[62] Still others were traveling among the colonists on errands that will be forever unknown. What brought a man and woman from the Nation to Gent's Ford on the Wateree River in October 1755? Where were a Catawba woman and her child headed when they walked past a Waxhaws tavern in the spring of 1760? Clearly, many Indians, like Hagler, went "very much among the White people." They walked wagon roads and crossed bridges, passed farmers plowing and slaves harvesting, entered log cabins and fenced fields, watched women gardening and children playing—and they did not like what they saw. Speaking for the Nation in the fall of 1763, the chief, Colonel Ayers, captured his people's reaction to what colonists had done to the Catawbas' homeland. "His Land was spoiled," Ayers informed British officials, "they have spoiled him 100 Miles every way."[63] A log cabin, a gristmill, a slave or two, a few cows: it all seemed innocent enough. But together these additions to the piedmont scene formed a powerful acid that ate away the Indians' world.

Inhabitants of the Nation confronted with this invasion had three choices: they could flee, they could submit, or they could resist. Flight was considered from time to time but rejected.[64] Submission lay in the future. Most elected to resist, and in the 1750s a choking cloud of contention settled over the piedmont as natives wrestled colonists for control of the land.

The contest was made especially bitter by the uncertainty. Since conflict often arose from deeply rooted and only dimly perceived differences in ways of arranging the landscape, it was impossible for anyone to predict when trouble might strike. Andrew Clewer could so testify. In 1753 he was apparently minding his own business at his farm along Fishing Creek some sixteen miles from the Nation's villages when a band of Catawbas showed up. The visitors handed him all of his "Effects," sent him on his way, and burned his house to the ground. The unfortunate Clewer was not alone. Six years later, inhabitants in the Waxhaws suffered a similar fate, though this time it was fences that Catawbas set on fire rather than a house.[65] Why did Indians single out that house and those fences? Perhaps Clewer was living on a sacred site or planting prime hunting grounds; perhaps the fences blocked a Catawba path. Whatever the reason, Indians found these structures offensive, and, in protest, they wiped the stain from the face of the earth.

Colonists could be equally unpredictable. For every upcountry farmer fretting about the prospect of Indians coming across the clearing there was a Catawba concerned that settlers might suddenly march into his hunting camp. Now and then they did. At one camp colonists barged in, "fired off their [the Indians'] Guns, and then threw them away." At another on the Catawba hunters' "old Grounds" along the Black River the Indians Isaac, Walker, and Lewis John were visited by twenty-six men, who destroyed the deerskins they found and assaulted the natives.[66] Neither of these gangs was thieves—thieves do not generally burn skins and destroy guns. Rather, they seemed to be making a protest of their own against the Indians' behavior, a protest that originated in sharply conflicting attitudes toward proper use of the land.

Such incidents left their victims not only scared and angry but bewildered, for in each case no one had intended anything provocative. A hunter on his "old Grounds" antagonized settlers; a planter insulted Indians merely by constructing "Proper Conveniencys." Little wonder that each concluded that the crime was senseless, its perpetrator vicious. Catawbas considered farmers "very bad and quarrelsome," and colonists repaid the compliment. A "haughty" people who made "ill neighbours," Indians acted as they did from "mere Wantonness," "for mischief sake."[67] Edmond Atkin, formulating his views in Charleston and London free from the fury and fear that obscured people's vision in the piedmont, came closer to the mark when he observed that Catawba and colonist were at odds "on account of the difference of manners and way of life."[68] Neither was evil or insane. They were just different, in ways both fundamental and hard to fathom. From those differences came conflict; from the conflict, more of the same.

Ironically, it was not only differences that caused trouble. Similarities also sparked many outbreaks of violence. First and most obvious, the two sides shared a single environment and, therefore, were often competing for resources. Hunters trekked through the same canebrakes on the trail of the same wild animals, farmers looked for the same fields alongside the same streams, and even the same stands of timber were points of contention.[69] Conflict worsened during the drought of the 1750s, which struck both peoples and left Catawbas more likely to ask for food and colonists more reluctant to oblige. In the autumn of 1756 Indians were reported "begging from the neighbouring Planters and thereby . . . oppress the Planters who are themselves scarce of Corn yet Dare not Deny them."[70] If a colonist took the dare and stashed food when he saw Catawbas coming, he might still lose it. The hungry and suspicious Indians, repeatedly rebuffed by people who obviously lacked proper manners, stopped taking no for an answer and began ransacking the settler's house in search of the cache they assumed was there. There was no victor here: the planter had been pillaged by "plundering and beging" ruffians, and the Catawbas had been insulted by "Churlish and ungreatfull" neighbors.[71]

Livestock was another sore point. Colonial animals and Catawba horses wandered freely across the upcountry, temptations to someone in search of a meal, a ride, or easy money. Catawbas short of food found the cows and hogs roaming around hard to resist; even horsemeat might find its way into the Nation's cooking pots.[72] More often, however, a native finding a horse sold it to a customer who asked no questions about the creature's history; one enterprising band of thieves went all the way to Charleston to unload its equine merchandise. These promising apprentices in rustling probably had learned everything they knew from colonists, who were masters. Indians began missing horses as early as 1752, and by the end of the decade Catawba leaders complained that settlers had stolen most of the Nation's stock.[73]

Efforts to stop the rash of thefts or settle any other disputes were doomed, for Catawba and Carolinian alike possessed a streak of independence that made them hard to rein in. Among colonists, those charged with keeping order were handcuffed by distance, border wars, and subjects who were at best sullen and indifferent, at worst downright hostile. The crown's authority—in London, Charleston, even Pine Tree Hill—was too far away and too easily ignored. Officials who betook themselves from their chambers to impose their personal authority on the populace at close range soon retreated, frustrated but wiser. For one thing, the boundary dispute between the Carolinas (which dragged on until 1772) meant that some people pledged allegiance to one colony, some to the other. "The[y] say the[y] will not Be Subject to our Laws," wrote Charleston's dejected agent after a visit to the North Carolina people near the Catawbas.[74] For another, many refused to obey *any-one's* laws. Woodmason's campaign to teach the denizens of the uplands some manners utterly failed to impress his would-be pupils, who "commit the grossest Enormities, before my face, and laugh at all Admonition." Even Governor Arthur Dobbs, the king's own representative, returned from a visit to the upcountry a shaken man, having been subjected to "Insult and abuse." "No officer of Justice from either Province dare meddle with them," North Carolina officials concluded, for these folk were "people of desperate fortune." "We are without any Law, or Order," Woodmason wailed during his sojourn among the "wild Peoples" of the interior.[75]

Catawba leaders faced the same problem for different reasons. By no means remote, faceless authority figures, they nonetheless lacked the coercive powers (except in extreme cases) that might keep restless Catawbas in line. Hagler explained again and again that while the headmen "oftentimes Cautioned" their people from causing trouble, "we Cannot be present at all times to Look after them." "What they have done I could not prevent," he would reply lamely when pressed by angry Carolinians.[76] Young Indian men were the hardest to control. Perhaps Catawba youths had to find new ways to prove their manhood now that the Iroquois wars were winding down and deer were scarce. Raiding slave quarters and ransacking farmhouses may have been poor substitutes for an enemy scalp or a fine buck, but they were better than nothing, and Indians approaching adulthood chose this avenue of achievement with what settlers considered alarming frequency. "The Insolence of the young Fellows here is unsufferable," wrote Matthew Toole from the Nation in 1752, "a going into the Settlements, robbing and stealing where ever they get an Oppertunity." It was impossible to reason with them, Toole went on, for "if I talke to these very Fellows that did the Fact, they laugh and makes their Game of it, and says it is what they will." Complaints to their elders generally drew nothing more than a nod of agreement that, yes, "some of our young fellows will do those tricks."[77]

A common fondness for liquor often loosened what few re-

straints there were. Alcohol had been a problem in the Nation long
before colonial settlers arrived, of course; after 1750 the Catawbas'
consumption of rum and whiskey showed no signs of diminishing,
despite efforts by leaders on both sides to curtail the Indians' access
to it.[78] Among nearby colonists the habit of getting drunk was also
deeply ingrained in the culture. "People continually drunk," a disgusted Woodmason noted, and the taverns blanketing the landscape suggest that he did not exaggerate.[79] With alcohol a staple of
everyone's diet, troublemakers from both camps easily lowered
their inhibitions and bolstered their courage with a bellyful of liquor. Hagler singled it out as "the Very Cause" of the crimes his
young men committed, and while colonial leaders made no such
admissions, it is clear that at least some of the settlers harassing the
Nation found their bravery in a bottle. In 1760 a Catawba woman
was murdered and her child wounded when they happened by a
tavern in the Waxhaws where four customers had just sworn that
"they would kill the first Indian they should meet with."[80]

If corn was not the problem, it was livestock; if not livestock,
liquor. Or perhaps the source of the trouble could not even be
pinpointed, but lay in that vague "difference of manners and way
of life" Atkin had cited. Whatever its cause, there seemed no end
to the strife, especially since there was little chance of catching the
culprits and less of punishing them. With old wounds still fester-
ing and new ones inflicted regularly, tempers grew short. Colonists wearied of reciting the litany of the Indians' "Insults," "gross
abuses," and "increasing Insolence." For their part Catawbas struggled to understand why "the White p[e]ople about us is very Cross
to us." Try as they might, they had to admit that they still "cannot
concieve the meaning of it."[81]

A conference at Matthew Toole's house in August 1754 called to
resolve disputes only revealed the depths of mistrust.[82] After the
Catawba delegation and two North Carolina commissioners had
assembled and Toole had been sworn in as interpreter, a settler
named William Morrison came forward to recount "the Indians
Insults to him at his own house." According to Morrison, a band of
Catawbas that visited his mill began to pour a pail of water into his
meal trough, and when he stepped in to stop them, they had tried
to brain him with their muskets. Right behind the irate Morrison

came James Armstrong, William Young, and William McNight to charge the Indians with several crimes, among them the attempted kidnapping of a colonist's child.

The Catawbas could not believe these people were serious. "What they Intended to do with the water," they explained, "was only to put a handful or Two of the meal into it to make a kind of a Drink which is their way and Custom." The alleged kidnapping was, if anything, still more absurd. "I hope you will not harbour this Thought of us so as to Imagine it was done in Earnest," Hagler replied, "for I am Informed it was Only done by way of a joke by one of our wild Young men in Order to Surprize the People, that were the parents of the Child, to have a Laugh at the Joke."

That Catawbas dismissed each incident as harmless and colonists considered it threatening, even terrifying, suggests how far the two sides were from understanding one another. Catawbas approaching Morrison's mill or grabbing a child never stopped to think how settlers might react. Among those jittery colonists a handful of meal and a bucket of water was a personal insult, and a prank was a provocation. Intercultural relations, like the scorched upcountry terrain, had become so dry and brittle that it seemed the tiniest spark would set off a wider conflagration.

III

Angry men facing off across a meal trough, frenzied parents trying to pull their offspring out of the grasp of a laughing Catawba, drunken farmers piling out of a tavern to fall upon a native woman and child—almost at random, deeper feelings of mistrust and fear led to confrontations, and sometimes to bloodshed. The next logical step was war, but war never came. Why not? Why was there no Catawba War to take its place alongside the Tuscarora and Yamasee wars in the history of colonial Carolina? Maybe it was still too early; perhaps settlers, despite all they had done to tame the piedmont, did not yet feel that it was truly theirs, that natives, not they, were the intruders. Or perhaps there was, in the minds of some, a vision of another, happier ending to the story.

Such a view was not sheer fantasy. Visible through the haze of hatred that enveloped the piedmont was the faintest glimmer of hope, the possibility that the course of contact need not spiral inevitably downward to destruction. For one thing, there were signs that Catawbas were grudgingly coming to accept, if not embrace, some features of the alien world being imposed upon them. Thanks to South Carolina, in the spring of 1759 Hagler was the proud owner of a log cabin, complete with chimney, and before the end of the century other Catawbas would copy him.[83] In the meantime they walked colonial roads, visited Morrison's mill to mix a favorite dish, even suggested to provincial authorities that "the Waggons . . . now a going down" to the capital should be used to haul powder to the Nation.[84] If no Catawbas were building mills, widening roads, or driving those wagons themselves, at least they displayed a readiness to make use of what the intruders had brought.

No less important than a willingness to live in another landscape was the enduring influence of older forms of contact, which on occasion brought some Indians and some settlers together in a spirit of cooperation. As they had since the Tuscarora War, common enemies pushed Indian and colonist into uneasy alliance. War parties from Cherokee, Iroquois, or Shawnee villages were as frightening to a farmer living near the Nation as they were to the Nation itself, for Indian foes did not always distinguish colonist from Catawba. Word of approaching enemies made neighborhood squabbles seem unimportant, and everyone was inclined to band together for protection. In 1754 Catawbas went out after a war party that had killed sixteen settlers, and occasionally there were joint expeditions against marauders.[85]

Trade proved even more cohesive. As men like Thomas Brown became little more than memories, Catawbas made do by trading for what they termed "the Nessecaries of life" with their new neighbors. Many nearby colonists peddled liquor in the Nation's villages. Meanwhile, some Indians began scouring the area for alternative sources of goods, calling at stores and taverns forty miles down the Wateree River, east as far as the Pee Dee, "and all over the Country."[86]

A few Indians worked out novel arrangements with colonial planters that brought in more merchandise with less work. In 1755, one "McClenhorn" (probably Robert McClanahan, the same man who would supply Hagler with "ould Bulls") informed the Catawbas that he was the official "Stray Master" for the area; natives who turned over to him horses that they found would receive a shirt or some other compensation for their trouble. How they actually got the beast was their business. The Catawbas were happy to oblige, and before long McClanahan's corral held no fewer than fifteen strays, waiting for their rightful owners to reclaim them— for a fee, of course. The scheme infuriated many settlers, but they directed their wrath at the self-appointed stray master, not his Indian accomplices.[87]

The stray masters, the liquor dealers, the joint war parties were unusual; they were not unique. Hagler told colonists more than once that "there are many in those Settlements that are very kind and Curtious to us," and some of his people received more than simple courtesy. In the fall of 1749 Archibald Campbell, a storekeeper at the Congarees, buried several Catawbas who had died en route from Charleston to the Nation. Nine years later the Indians had a chance to return the favor, burying colonists who had perished in an Indian raid.[88] Isolated incidents almost a decade apart: not much to get excited about. After all, neither Indians nor Anglo-Americans could have received what they would have considered proper burial. Yet the act, however hastily and clumsily performed, suggests the possibility of cooperation beyond the demands of common enemies or common interest. Amid the clamor over horses and rum, it whispers of peace.

IV

Despite hints that the Nation might make peace with settlers and remain in its homeland, history was against it. Edmond Atkin, aware of the road to disappearance that so many Indian groups in similar straits already had walked, could state with confidence that "Indians generally chuse to withdraw, as white People draw near to them." James Adair, another familiar of the Catawbas, counseled pushing them out if they did not "chuse" to budge. "We may observe of them [Indians] as of the fire," Adair wrote after considering the Catawbas' precarious situation, "'it is safe and useful, cherished at proper distance; but if too near us, it becomes dangerous, and will scorch if not consume us.' "[89] And these were the Nation's friends.

Against such sentiments Catawbas wielded a fierce determination to stay. "We Expect to live on those Lands we now possess During our Time here," Hagler informed those gathered at Toole's house that August day in 1754, "for when the Great man above made us he also . . . fixed our forefathers and us here and to Inherit this Land." The resolve to remain in their "little Bed of land" survived the great eractasswa's death in 1763. Seven years later, one of his successors, Frow, reminded the king's representatives that "the Ground they live on was their Fathers, and they will live there to[o]."[90] Speeches were poor weapons for mounting a defense of one's homeland, however. Catawbas were surrounded and outnumbered; their land was spoiled; they and their neighbors were at each other's throats. Could words and the occasional friendly gesture sustain them?

In the spring of 1759, that seemed unlikely. Even as Catawbas buried settlers and builders put the finishing touches on Hagler's chimney, the shouting and shoving went on. In April, colonists sent word to the South Carolina capital that the natives' "behav[i]or has been very bad almost Every Where." The Waxhaws settlement just downriver from the Nation had been especially hard hit. In recent months first one "Company" of Indians and then another had swept through the area, killing cattle, stealing horses, and robbing houses. The climax (or nadir) came when a Catawba stormed into a widow's house and beat her senseless with a shovel. Outraged inhabitants warned Governor Lyttelton that "if there be no means used to put a stop to such proceedings . . . we will be obliged to Com[e] to blows."[91]

Some colonists did not wait to see whether Lyttelton would respond. When the governor's agent, James Adamson, arrived at the Nation in early June, he was furious to learn that settlers were stirring up trouble. They "has the Con[science]" to take advantage of the Indians' food shortage, swapping corn at exorbitant rates for the presents Lyttelton had sent to the Nation, "a New gun for a Bushill of Corn and a match Coat for a Bushill." Extortion, though, was the least of the Catawbas' problems; they were being invaded by colonists with mischief on their minds and hatred in their hearts. "The white men [who] Lives Near the Neation is Contenuely asembleing and goes In the [Catawba] towns In Bodys," Adamson reported. At the head of the ragged army strode the Indians' former partner, McClanahan, as if he, personally, would ruin any hope that a little profitable cooperation might save the Catawbas. "The Indians is a frade that the[y] will Cut them of[f] Sum time or other," Adamson went on, and the natives could well be right, for "the[y] tretton the[y] will Kill all the Cattabues." Adamson looked into matters, "tuck a great deal of pains to make things Easey Between the white people and the Indians," and went home.[92]

John Evans, who had accompanied Adamson as his interpreter, left the Nation and headed downcountry worried that the agent, though "very Dilligent," had labored in vain. Evans, the Catawbas' beloved "old Freind and Linguister," had known these Indians since the end of the Yamasee War. He had seen them survive smallpox, Iroquois, and James Bullen. Now he saw for himself the threat his fellow colonists posed, and it must in some ways have been sadder than the cries of the women after disease struck, more chilling than the sound of an Iroquois war whoop, more dangerous than the whispers of the Prince of Wales. "The white People . . . and the Cuttahbaws, are Continually at varience," Evans wrote to Lyttelton, "and Dayly New Animositys Doth a rise Between them, which In my Humble oppion will be of Bad Consequence In a Short time, Both Partys Being obstinate."[93] Old as he was, it looked as if Evans might outlive the Nation.

6

Harmless and Friendly:
The Catawba Trail of Tears

[Catawbas] have now lived in the midst of a dense
white population for more than half a century and
your Commissioners all concur in testimony, that
they never have known or heard a dishonest charge
made against a Catawba, or their meddling with any
thing that did not belong to them, and have always
been harmless and friendly.
                    —South Carolina Treaty Commissioners, 1840

FOR THE REST of the summer of 1759, the approaching
storm that had alarmed John Evans and James Adamson held off.
By July more than sixty Catawba warriors—probably 20 percent of
the total number the Nation could muster—were on their way
north to help His Majesty's forces fight the French.[1] Closer to
home, Hagler and twenty-three others traveled through South
Carolina on something of a goodwill tour, lobbying their friends
for supplies and protection. During the first week in August they
stopped to see Adamson at his plantation on the Wateree River;
later in the month they dined with Samuel Wyly near Pine Tree
Hill; in early September they stayed for several days with their old
confidant Evans along the Santee. From each stop they sent run-
ners to Charleston bearing friendly greetings and requests for everything from a fort to a keg of rum.[2] Governor William Henry
Lyttelton was obliging; there were rumors of a Cherokee-Creek

conspiracy against the colony, and he needed every ally he could get.[3]

Despite the signs of friendship, the shadow of conflict remained. In September complaints again began to reach Governor Arthur Dobbs from his North Carolina frontier folk: Hagler was threatening some planters near the Nation and driving out others.[4] Apparently Adamson's diplomacy had been only a palliative, not a cure. What would happen when that war party, buoyed by gifts and victories, came home and spread out across the upcountry for the fall hunt?

The return of captains Strongman, Ayers, and Jemy and their men toward the end of September brought, not trouble for settlers, but death for Indians. Smallpox had been among the king's forces at the front all summer, and, despite efforts to keep the Catawba warriors away from it, they carried it home along with the shirts, moccasins, and leggings handed out by British officers.[5] The consequences were at once predictable and catastrophic. Almost immediately, what the Indians called "a Bad Desorder" killed several of the Nation's best men and afflicted several more. Through the winter the sickness lingered, "making a terrible Havack among them" and wiping out many of the warriors and headmen.[6] During the height of the scourge twenty-five corpses were being pulled from the Catawba River every day, sad evidence of the failure of traditional water cures to do more than hasten the end.[7] One settler heard that "the woods were offensive with the dead bodies of the Indians; and dogs, wolves, and vultures were so busy, for months, in banqueting on them, that they would scarcely retreat from their prey, when approached by any one."[8]

The Nation's initial reaction to the horror was "to Keep our people to Geather as much as possable," tending the sick and burying the dead. This resolve evaporated as the death toll climbed; by early November, Catawbas still able to walk began to flee into the woods and backwaters, leaving the rest to their fate. Hagler, who surfaced near Pine Tree Hill at the end of February with a band of survivors, admitted that he had not been in the Nation for months and had no idea how many of his people were still alive.[9]

Colonists did not share the eractasswa's reluctance to guess Ca-

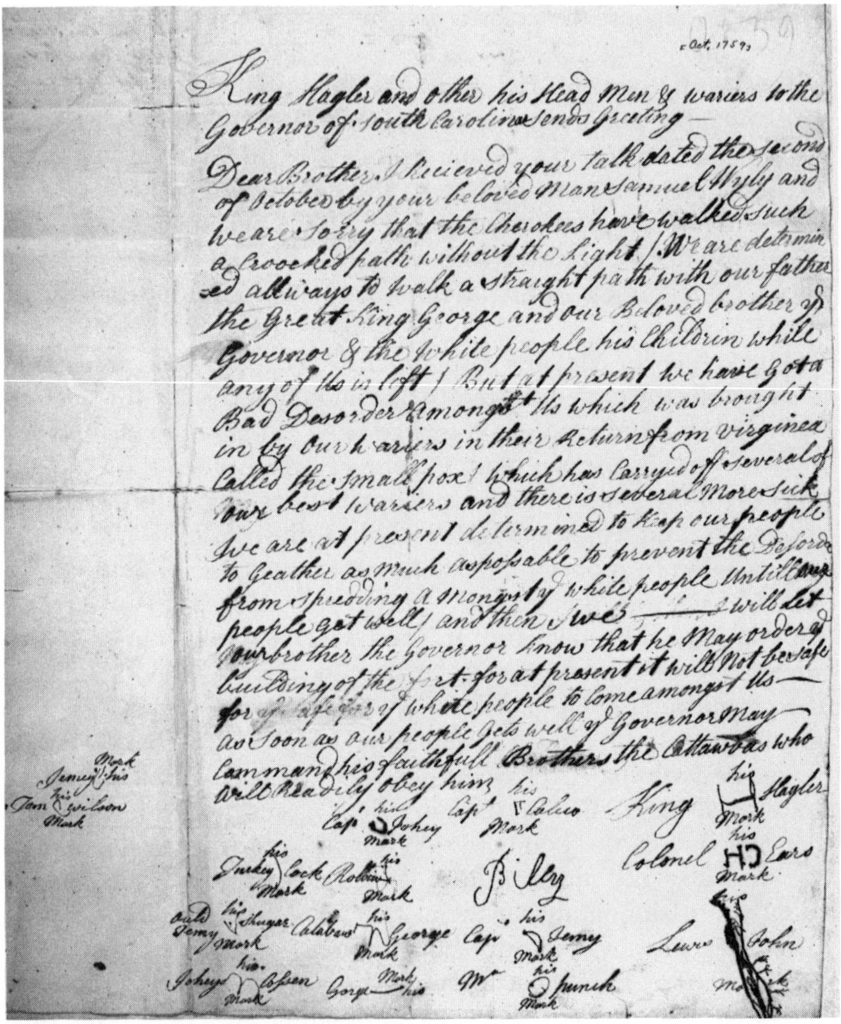

Figure 6. Catawba Letter Reporting the 1759 Smallpox Epidemic.
Courtesy of William L. Clements Library

tawba numbers. In December the *South-Carolina Gazette* reported that almost half of the Nation had perished; by spring Governor Dobbs put the casualties at 60 percent. For the rest of the century estimates of Catawba population varied widely, but when all of the totals are collected, the impact of the smallpox stands out starkly from the guesswork. Between 1740 and 1759, colonists had placed the number of Catawba warriors anywhere from 200 to 500, with most assessments falling around 300. After 1759 the comparable figures ranged from a mere 50 to 150, and the count was generally less than 100. In other words, in a single season the Nation's total population dropped from perhaps 1,500 people to 500 or so. Dobbs's 60 percent, appalling as it was, may have been too conservative.[10]

The specter of another outbreak of disease had long haunted the Nation—"We have no reason to be affraid of any thing but Sickness," they had said after making peace with the Iroquois—and now that the Catawbas' fears had been realized, the survivors huddled with Hagler on the outskirts of Pine Tree Hill did not know what they should do.[11] Some talked of joining the Creeks. Hagler opposed that idea, but he displayed no great eagerness to go back to the Nation's villages. Eventually they compromised: Catawbas would return to their homeland, but not to their homes. They would settle instead along Twelve Mile Creek, downstream from Weyaline, Newstee, and the other towns at the junction of Sugar Creek and the Catawba River.[12]

Why not go back to Sugar Creek? They did not say, and no one asked. Perhaps colonial planters had already marched into the area—the smallpox having accomplished what McClanahan's gang could not do—and now refused to leave. Perhaps Catawbas feared contamination or had no desire to pick through the rotting timbers and rotting corpses in order to learn what the scavengers had spared. To the Indians these villages, the heart of the Nation, were now ghost towns, inhabited by the spirits of people never properly mourned and buried.[13]

In abandoning its dead and its settlements, the Nation left behind part of its past, and there are hints that the scars never healed. For generations, Catawba elders would recount: "Long ago the people along the river caught smallpox and many died. The medicine man said that if anyone were to run far away during the night that the sickness might not be able to catch them, and so many people left." Even into the 1940s Catawbas, still awaiting the return of all who had fled, hoped that "some day the lost people may come back home."[14]

Physically and perhaps also emotionally, then, Catawbas were, as Governor Dobbs put it, "almost destroyed by the Small pox."[15] Almost, but not quite. Impossible as it seemed at the time, and unlikely as it might appear even in retrospect, the epidemic of 1759, by killing so many, may have saved the rest. A fall from some three hundred warriors to one hundred, and fifteen hundred people to five hundred, left Indians too few and too shaken to risk war by challenging planters. At the same time, and for the same reasons, official interest in what was now an "inconsiderable handfull" of Catawbas waned, leaving the Indians to cope with colonial settlement as best they could. Settlers themselves, however, now proved less ready to fight. Almost overnight the number of Indian villages had dropped from six to one, and that one was well away from the rich lands around Sugar Creek.[16] Why bother to drive Indians from some place nobody wanted? Defenseless natives, indifferent officials, less belligerent settlers—a new calculus of contact was emerging in the aftermath of disease. "Harmless and friendly" Indians were replacing "proud and deveilish" ones, "inoffensive" natives now lived where once an "unsufferable" people had resided, a gang of thieves was becoming a nation that "may beg, but . . . will not steal."[17] A planter looking back from the middle of the nineteenth century on the metamorphosis could pronounce the Indians' change from "crusty" to "pacified" something "soon and easily" accomplished.[18] For Catawbas, it was both painful and prolonged. The epidemic, important as it was in signaling a new direction in Catawba history, was no more than the first step on a long, hard road, the Nation's own Trail of Tears.

I

The smallpox marked the beginning of the end of the Catawbas' prominence in the colonial Southeast. It took some time, however, for the epidemic to tear down what Indians had built with the men in Charleston. Many of these officials agreed with the *South-Carolina Gazette* that, despite the smallpox, the Nation was "still important to the welfare and security of our Back-Settlements." When Touksecay (Red Tick) and forty-seven other Catawbas arrived in Charleston in May 1760 for the first formal meeting in a year, then, colonists welcomed them as usual. And his delegation was only the first of many in the early 1760s that followed well-worn trails en route to a rendezvous with the Council; over the next two years no fewer than seven more arrived for talks with South Carolina leaders.[19]

The reason for the stream of visitors was no secret: the rumors of Cherokee unrest that Lyttelton heard had proved true, and for two years the province was embroiled in a bitter war in the western mountains. The colony's desperate need for Indian scouts in the rugged terrain once again made the Catawbas sellers in a seller's market. Natives repeatedly announced that, while the Nation's numbers were depleted, its bravery was undiminished, its loyalty was intact, its men were "able and determined to strike our Hatchets into the Heads of the Cherokees." Such talk was music to frazzled South Carolina officials, and they continued their pursuit of the Nation's favor. As first one colonial force and then another marched into Cherokee country, anywhere from a handful to forty or more Catawbas went along.[20]

The Indians, who had lost so much to the smallpox, had not lost their knack for capitalizing on opportunity. During July 1760 what was left of the Nation met with Crown Superintendent of Indian Affairs Edmond Atkin at Pine Tree Hill for a general discussion of the Catawbas' relations with Anglo-America. The long-awaited meeting with Atkin could hardly have come at a better time for the Indians. Hagler and forty warriors had just returned from service against the Cherokees in what was the colony's first campaign but clearly not its last. Hence, as they sat down together, everyone knew that Catawbas, having just proved their loyalty, would have the chance to prove it again, and this was no time to irritate one of South Carolina's best friends. In short order a deal was struck: Catawbas relinquished their claims to a circular tract of land sixty miles across for clear title to one fifteen miles square and the promise of a fort to be built in the Nation.[21]

The Catawba fort had been a troublesome issue for several years already, with the Carolinas fighting for the privilege of securing this foothold in the Nation and the Indians agreeing to one plan, then changing their minds and sending the builders home. After the smallpox, however, the need for a refuge to protect the Nation's women and children was more pressing than ever, and it overcame any qualms about inviting colonists to break ground. "But do not forget the Fort," Ayers told Lieutenant Governor William Bull II as one Catawba delegation took its leave in October 1760, and Bull did not. Within a year the stronghold stood along the banks of Twelve Mile Creek, a symbol of the Nation's continuing influence in the centers of Anglo-American power.[22]

Alas, the fort remained more symbol than sanctuary. The colony had agreed to construct it, not to man or maintain it. Neither troops nor traders ever moved in, and Catawbas who requested that something more be done with the empty shell were invited to build houses in it themselves. Before the end of the decade the structure had fallen into such disrepair that Catawbas concerned about enemy raids asked for a fort, as if the first one no longer existed. This time the colony was less obliging: the Council put off the request until the Assembly's next meeting, and the Assembly did nothing.[23]

The reservation, which was slower to materialize, proved more durable. Once again Catawbas took the initiative, asking as early as 1757 that "their lands . . . be Measurd out for them." When the colony procrastinated after the Nation's agreement with Atkin, Indians reminded Charleston that they still awaited the surveyor.[24] At last, in February 1764, Samuel Wyly completed his survey of a tract of 144,000 acres that encompassed the Nation's traditional homeland.[25]

Those accustomed to reading about Indians' being herded onto reservations may well wonder why Catawbas would accept, even demand, such a fate. The Nation had little choice: if it was to inter-

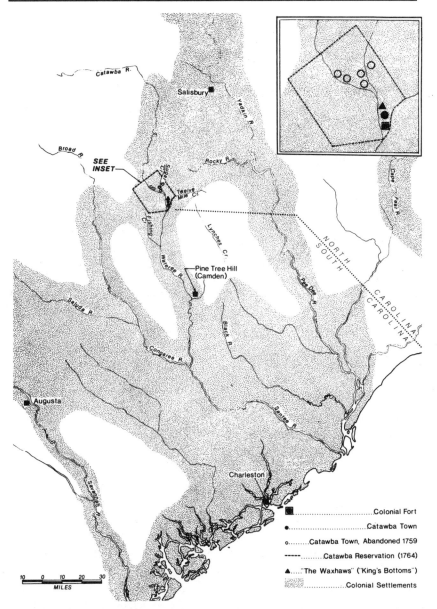

Map 6. The Catawbas and Their Neighbors in the 1760s. *Colonial settlement distribution adapted from Herman R. Friis*, A Series of Population Maps of the Colonies and the United States, 1625–1790, *rev. ed. (New York, 1968). Drawn by Linda Merrell*

rupt the sequence of dependence, decline, and dispersal that had already extinguished so many eastern Indian peoples, it had to erect a barrier against colonial Americans. Just as military commissions from governors had become essential to the political life of the Nation, so now deeds made by a surveyor were powerful weapons in the war for the upcountry. Planters pushing onto the Nation's territory "will not be stopped," Hagler observed, "for they say they will continue to do so unless we show them a paper to restrain them."[26] Thus Wyly's arrival with sextant and chain—and paper—marked a victory for the Nation, not a defeat.

The lines Wyly drew turned out to be better protection than the log stockade on Twelve Mile Creek. When settlers crept onto Catawba lands, the Indians now could do more than complain; they could unfold a piece of paper and point to the line the offender had crossed. If that did not work, a headman could inform South Carolina that "notwithstanding our land is run all round and Marked there is several people . . . Settled within our line," stating his case according to rules Anglo-Americans had laid down and obliging his listeners to take notice.[27] As usual, the crown's claims to authority exceeded its actual power, and many trespassers escaped punishment. Nonetheless, colonial officials were bound to continue trying, for now the Nation had the king's law on its side. With that law the Indians would not so easily be pushed out by the likes of McClanahan.

While helping to stop Catawba lands from being nibbled away by farmers, the reservation also blocked any attempt by prominent men to consume the Nation's territory in one huge bite. Late in 1772 William Henry Drayton, a member of the South Carolina Council, obtained a twenty-one-year lease of the entire reservation from his fellow councillors and the governor. Drayton offered himself as the solution to the Catawbas' problems with encroachment, the panacea for all that ailed the Nation. The plan was simple: he would "Be a father to them," dropping by now and then to make sure no one was abusing the Indians and to give each warrior a set amount of goods every year. In return, Catawbas would allow him to rent tracts on the reservation to colonists. Shortly after the new year, Drayton headed for the Nation with a letter from the gover-

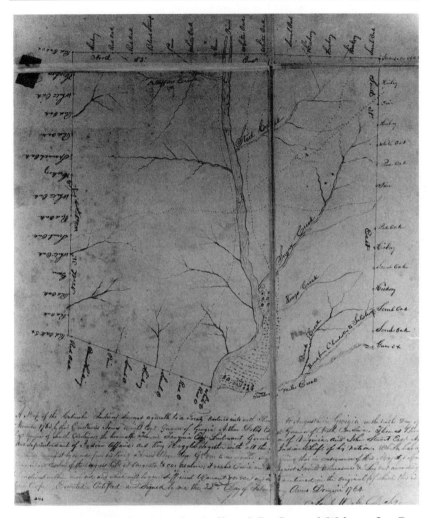

Map 7. "A Map of the Catawba Indians." By Samuel Wyly, 1764. *Records of the Secretary of State, Miscellaneous Records, Columbia Series, 1776–1875, vol. H, p. 461a. Courtesy of the South Carolina Department of Archives and History*

nor and Council advising the Indians "that they think this offer . . . is the best method by which your lands can be preserved."[28]

Drayton's arrival at the Catawba village on January 8 caught the Indians off guard, and in his haste to get back to Charleston he gave the Nation's leaders little time to think. Some liked the idea; others did not. Most apparently did not grasp the full implications of his proposal. According to one witness to the proceedings, "They did not understand that he was to Settle the whole of their Land." Despite their misgivings, the headmen, after reminding Drayton that the "Land should belong to them as long as ther[e] was one Catawba Indian left," agreed to the scheme. One colonist who learned what Drayton was up to was glad that he had missed the meeting, "as he did not want to have any thing to do with it."[29]

Fortunately for the Nation, another colonist—John Stuart, Atkin's successor as crown superintendent—did want to have something to do with this affair; on learning of Drayton's plan, Stuart took steps to defeat it. Drayton, he argued, needed not only the approval of the Catawbas but also of the superintendent and the crown, and such approval was highly unlikely. After Drayton returned from the Nation, the two men presented their arguments to the Council. That body, which initially had given its blessing only "Provided that . . . no Treaty nor instruction from the King forbid such a Lease," reversed itself and withdrew its support of the plan as "an improper and impolitic measure." Drayton gave up, and for the time being Catawbas were safe.[30]

If the Drayton affair proved that Catawbas still had powerful connections, it also hinted at a certain loss of enthusiasm among the Nation's old friends in the South Carolina Council. This body of men had once been central to the colony's Indian affairs. Here Catawba and colonist had worked out the ceremonies allowing conversation across the cultural divide. Here the Indians had come to assert their allegiance and complain about their neighbors. Here they had listened to the province's promises and picked up its gifts. Now the Council seemed all too willing to abandon its custodial role to Drayton, to carry out as he saw fit.

Shrewd observers of Catawba affairs might have foreseen that outcome. For more than a decade before 1773, South Carolina had been trying to distance itself from the Nation, a shift largely hidden by the fort, the reservation, and the continuing talks with Catawba ambassadors. A closer look at those meetings reveals unmistakable changes in tone, clues that the demise of Catawba diplomacy was at hand.

The first sign that something was amiss had come in September 1761, when Hagler and forty Catawbas arrived for talks with the governor.[31] Councillor Othniel Beale, standing in for the ailing Governor Thomas Boone, opened the session "in the Usual Manner," but the talk he delivered was anything but customary. The Indians were "heartily welcome," Beale began, and the colony was grateful for their services in the Cherokee War during the past summer. He could not help pointing out, however, "that this Province, has been at a Considerable expence for presents and Provisions . . . for . . . the Catabaws." Of course, Beale went on, the Indians deserved these tokens of friendship, so "the Province does not think much of the Expence." Still, Beale could not get "all this Expence" out of his mind. After all, Catawba friendship "has cost the Province a Considerable Sum." Then Beale, going from past sums to present ones, conveyed the governor's surprise that "so great a number" of Catawbas had come that day. "When the Indians came without Invitation," he informed Hagler, "unless on real Business, they could not expect Presents." In the space of a few minutes Beale had managed to suggest that Catawba friendship was not worth the price and that the headmen before him had no right to be there.

Catawba visits the following year confirmed that Beale's speech was formal policy, not personal pique.[32] In May, Governor Boone himself greeted Hagler and several young men with a brusque "Glad to see you . . . , but as you have been lately here, I presume you are now come upon some particular business." Hagler had—the Cherokees were still a threat, North Carolinians still encroached on the Nation's territory—but Boone, while polite enough, was skeptical, telling the Assembly that the Indians came "as well to Complain of some Encroachments on their Lands as in Expectation of presents from this Government." The Assembly committee assigned to consider the matter was more skeptical still, concluding "that these Indians have come often to Town on pretext to complain of pretended encroachments on their Lands when . . .

their real and only design has been to obtain presents." By the time
Captain Ayers led a party of eleven to the capital in early July,
Boone dropped the polite facade. "Why did you not come with
King Hagler and the other warriors of your Nation who were here
lately," he demanded. "You have been often told that when Indians
come hither having no particular business nor no message from
their Nation, and without invitation from the Governor, that they
are to expect no presents."[33]

Though Boone claimed that the Indians had heard this sort of
talk "often," in fact the record of diplomatic proceedings shows
that no one had ever spoken to Catawba headmen in quite such
terms before.[34] Not that earlier colonial officials had any real love
for Indians. One remembers that James Glen, the Nation's friend
and advocate, argued privately that Indians were "a savage, cruel,
perfidious, revengefull sett of Men." His successor William Henry
Lyttelton moaned, "No man is more sensible than I am how unpleasant a task it is to manage Indians." And Thomas Boone
echoed Glen in labeling natives "to a man, cruel, fearfull, perfidious, and revengefull, if any have proved otherwise, it may be ac-
counted for by some incidental circumstance."[35] The difference
was that Glen and Lyttelton kept their thoughts to themselves, hiding their feelings behind a pile of gifts and a torrent of flattery.
During Boone's tenure the smiling stopped. Certainly the death of
so many Catawba warriors had something to do with it; one could
now offend Catawbas without worrying so much about inviting a
repeat of the Yamasee War. More important was the end of the
Cherokee conflict. It was no coincidence that Beale had closed his
disdainful speech in September 1761 with the news that he expected a visit any day from Cherokees come to sue for peace.[36]
With the Cherokee threat subsiding, coddling every Catawba who
arrived in Charleston dropped far down on the provincial agenda.

Events during 1763 magnified this growing disdain and erased
any remaining illusions about the Catawbas' place in the larger
scheme. First, the peace with France in February, by removing one
more threat to Anglo-America, gave colonial authorities one reason fewer to call upon Catawba allies. Then Hagler's death in late
August robbed the Nation of a leader with formidable diplomatic
skills.[37] Finally, a conference held at Augusta in November both

symbolized and secured Catawba insignificance in the Southeast. The meeting, called to lay to rest Indian fears about British rule now that the Spanish and French were gone, brought John Stuart and the governors of Britain's southern colonies together with almost one thousand Indians from the Cherokee, Creek, Chickasaw, Choctaw, and Catawba nations. The sixty-nine Catawbas there were invariably last to be introduced, last to be addressed, and last to speak. In his report on the proceedings, John Stuart again placed Catawbas last and dismissed them in a few lines, a mere drop compared to the ink he spilled analyzing the affairs of the other nations. "The Catawbas," he wrote, "I consider as Inhabitants of this Province [South Carolina] who have an absolute dependance upon it and are inseparably connected with its Interests."[38]

After Augusta those South Carolina leaders on whom the Nation was so dependent, convinced of the Catawbas' insignificance and freed from constant worries about powerful enemies, became careless about their ceremonial deportment. In 1766, for example, the colony's new executive, Lord Charles Greville Montagu, received a visit from forty Catawbas shortly after his arrival from England. The bewildered Montagu, apparently unaware that a delegation always came to Charleston to welcome a new governor, inquired "what they came down for as he did not send for them." The Catawba chief, Frow—perhaps also a bit confused by now—made it clear that he was conforming to custom. "He heard there was a new fine governor come in," Frow said, "and he was very glad to come to see him and had brought him a present of some deer Skins," which the Indians proceeded to place under Montagu's feet. The governor promised an answer "another day," but if that day came, his words never found their way into the records. A week later the *South-Carolina Gazette* may have spoken for him; certainly it captured the failure to grasp the purpose of Frow's visit. An established ritual, with roots deep in the province's past? No: Catawbas were "on a visit to his Excellency the Governor, for presents."[39]

Montagu could be forgiven his befuddlement; he was, after all, a novice. More ominous was the reluctance of other officials to abide by rules they knew from long experience. Frow and twelve other Catawbas who visited the Council in 1768 must have been alarmed to find that their old friend William Bull had grown forgetful over the years. Every formal encounter customarily began with the acknowledged superior, the colonists, speaking first. This time, however, Bull, for reasons of his own, decided to break with custom. Confusion ensued. After shaking hands all around, "His Honor asked Him [Frow] what he had to say King Frow said he wanted to hear what the Governor had to say to which his Honor replied as he did not send for them so he had no talk to give them but his ears are Open to what they had to say." Only after this clumsy opening was the familiar diplomatic protocol followed.[40]

Such confusion was only a symptom of the more serious ailment that had come to afflict formal relations. South Carolina officials not only forgot the rules; they tried to change them, to do away with the gifts that kept the diplomatic machinery running smoothly. The complaints Beale had voiced to Hagler became a continual refrain heard by virtually every Catawba delegation. "Indians must not expect presents unless they were sent for." "When ever Indians come down without being sent for they are not to expect presents." "They never gave Indians presents unless they sent for them." "When Indians came down without being sent for he gave them nothing." And so on. The speech had become part of the ritual.[41]

To the Nation's relief, colonial officials for a time proved incapable of living up to their tough talk. Again and again the Council sternly told delegations that uninvited Indians received no presents; again and again the colony's spokesman then proceeded to distribute gifts. In 1762 Ayers listened to the lecture before accepting a new commission, repair of his gun and saddle, and an order for more weapons. Six years later Frow heard the same sermon, then hauled away powder and shot, rum, and paint as well as a saddle for himself. He was back the next year, placidly listening to the usual warning, then heading home richer by four muskets, twenty-five pounds of powder, and fifty pounds of lead, not to mention five gallons of rum. Some Indians left the capital with more than they had requested. When Frow asked for shirts in 1771, "his Honor thereupon told them, that whenever Indians came to Town without being sent for, they were not to expect presents, . . . but as they were all Brothers, he would for this Time give them a Shirt each *and* some Powder and Shott and a little Paint, but the Indians must remember, that when they came to

Town without being sent for, they must not expect any Presents."[42] The words may have been loud, the actions spoke louder, and the Catawbas kept showing up.

Thus the traditional diplomatic rituals were still persuasive enough to make stingy officials dig into the provincial pocket for gifts. The formulas worked in part at least because Catawbas remained masters at invoking them. Delegations were going to arrive at the door of the Council chamber whether the men inside liked it or not. Those deerskins were going to be placed under Lord Montagu's feet whether he understood what was happening or not. And whether or not provincial leaders wanted to listen, Catawbas were going to remind them of the Nation's services to the crown. "When he and his People are dead," Frow told the assembled councillors in 1768, "they will never see Indians so friendly Attach[e]d or so Steady friends to the English." Three years later another ambassador pointedly reminded the colony that few, if any, native peoples could match the Catawbas' record of loyalty, "that his Nation had always had the English by the Hand but it was not all the Nations of Indians that has done so."[43]

It helped that the Nation did not have to depend on former achievements. For if the French and Cherokee threats to South Carolina had subsided, a danger closer to home remained: runaway slaves. The colony had long talked of asking Catawba warriors to track down blacks, but nothing more developed until the end of 1765, when one hundred slaves took refuge in the swamps and backwaters near the capital. Lieutenant Governor Bull, convinced that "Indians strike terrour into the Negroes" and were "more sagacious in tracking" than colonists were, sent word to the Nation that the province needed help. Before the winter was out, almost fifty warriors came down, captured seven runaways, and drove the rest back to their masters. This time officials distributed gifts without the stern speeches.[44]

Delegations marching out of Charleston loaded down with presents, a war party again hunting the colony's enemies and being amply rewarded for its efforts—it might seem that all the discouraging talk was just that, mere talk. In fact, however, the lectures marked the first stage of a transition from fawning attention to total neglect. South Carolina was trying to let Catawbas down slowly, but let them down it did. Headmen in the 1760s and early 1770s had received conflicting signals from their South Carolina friends, but in 1774 a single clear message began to issue from the colony. In March of that year the Commons House of Assembly refused to spend another shilling to provision or placate natives who came to town of their own accord, and it stood by the resolution when suppliers submitted accounts for food and liquor dispensed to Indian ambassadors.[45] The Assembly's decision effectively put a stop to the old diplomatic round. Not only would Catawbas be turned away empty-handed by provincial leaders; a delegation would have a difficult time even reaching the capital, for planters and tavernkeepers on the way would be less hospitable once word got around that they would not be reimbursed for their trouble. The final stones in the wall South Carolina leaders erected between the capital and the Nation were added in 1781, when Joseph Kershaw informed them: "It is the desire of the Governor and House[?] that . . . rule in Charleston that none of your People would go down there unless sent for on business. . . . [W]henever you have anything to say get some one to write for you."[46] Thereafter South Carolina kept the Nation at arm's length, conducting business primarily through middlemen.

Meanwhile, Catawbas, perhaps foreseeing Charleston's new policy, had stepped up their diplomatic campaign to make as many friends as possible. In 1769, one delegation opened relations with Georgia, others continued to visit North Carolina into the 1770s, and the last recorded formal call on Virginia would come in the autumn of 1782. That same autumn two Catawba deputies went all the way to Philadelphia to meet with members of the United States Congress in an attempt to establish relations with the federal government. In both Williamsburg and Philadelphia they were to be disappointed. At their meeting with the Virginia governor the Indians "were informed the Executive of this State have no concern" with the "Matters" the Nation's representatives had raised.[47] In Philadelphia a congressional committee heard them out, then recommended that South Carolina "take such Measures for the Satisfaction and security of the said Tribe as the said Legis[lature] shall in their wisdom think fit."[48] Distant governments were returning the Indians to South Carolina's care; the problem was that South Carolina no longer cared very much. For all their efforts to keep up and even extend the diplomatic art developed by their ancestors, after 1760 the Catawbas found it more difficult to attract the attention of the authorities. The end of these formal encounters left Indians alone with their intimate enemies, the upcountry planters.

II

Catawbas stripped of diplomatic immunity had to make their peace with the people pressing in on them from all sides. Like the change in formal relations, this took time; the fear and anger Evans and Adamson had found would not dissipate overnight, and skirmishing went on. When North Carolina surveyors tramped across Catawba burial grounds during the summer of 1762, the Indians, who until that time "had contented themselves with complaining only," chased them out and "pursued with an intention to murder them." Five years later, Catawbas got into a brawl with colonists during a church service.[49] More common than battles at sacred sites were squabbles over land and hunting. Wyly's map carried little weight in some circles, and official passes permitting Catawbas to hunt were likely to be torn up or burned.[50] If the Indians were to escape the extinction that many predicted for them, such hostility could not continue.

The reservation was an important step on the road to salvation. Catawba efforts to defend their boundaries rankled squatters, but many planters decided that it was easier to rent than to steal land from the Indians. Legend has it that Thomas Spratt was the Nation's first tenant. According to his grandson, Spratt and his family, en route from North Carolina to the Savannah River valley, stopped overnight near the Catawba River. A band of Indians from the Nation came to the camp, invited Spratt to stay, and offered to rent him land. The story is more colorful than credible (it seems unlikely, for example, that Catawbas "almost forced him to set his stakes" down on the spot), and the 1761 lease that might substantiate it has disappeared.[51] Nonetheless, sometime before the Revolution the Spratts and two other families did obtain large grants on the reservation, setting up homesteads several miles apart and living "much in the Indian fashion."[52]

After the war, renting lands became routine. The original tenants began parceling out acreage among family and friends, and the Indians invited still more planters onto the reservation. A formal document signed by four or five headmen set the terms of each agreement, which generally included a ninety-nine year lease in return for an annual rent.[53] Settlers were so pleased with the arrangement that before long there was a land rush in the Catawba Valley. In 1791, three hundred "good citizens" lived on the Indian land; and while they reported the reservation "thickly settled," they were confident that it "will in a short time be much more so as there is a quantity yet to Lease." The "good citizens" were right: by the end of the century Catawbas had rented almost every acre of the reservation.[54]

That Catawbas "found it to our advantage to rent" stemmed less from any change of heart about planters than from the recognition that land was one of the only marketable commodities the Nation had left. "We were necessi[t]ated to Rent out our land," they noted in 1792, "for the Suply of our Wants." The bonanza brought less tangible rewards as well. Instead of a nuisance to settlers and wards of the state, Indians became landlords upon whom hundreds of men and women depended. This upset some settlers—we "are Tributaries to them," tenants wrote in 1787—but while they did not like the idea, they learned to live with it. The Indians, who were probably no happier about the circumstances that drove them to invite an invasion of their homeland, did the same. The complaints they made about the system were designed to make it work better, not to dismantle it.[55]

Land was not the only commodity Catawbas started trading to settlers. Many Indians took to the road as peddlers, their packs bulging with moccasins, baskets, table mats, and especially pottery.[56] The potter's art was an ancient one; after 1760, Catawbas simply put old skills to new uses and began manufacturing pans and vessels for sale. Judgments on Indians' skill varied sharply. One traveler called the pottery "an ill-formed kind of a half-baked earthen ware," and another labeled it "peculiar." Those who actually bought it tended to be more impressed, judging "some very neatly made and prettily colored," "not ill made, nor unseemly to the eye." Even the harshest critics were inclined to agree that Catawba pottery made up in durability whatever it might lack in beauty, and some people went so far as to claim that certain dishes should be cooked only in pots fashioned by Indian hands. Though tastes differed, the demand for inexpensive household goods was high, and, as early as 1772, Catawba women were going from house to house bartering their wares.[57] Over time the Indians' trade grew, until by the early nineteenth century Catawbas regularly headed into the lowcountry to dig clay and make pots, which they then swapped at plantations and on the streets of Charleston.[58]

One observer was quick to dismiss Catawba manufactures as "insignificant trifles" whose sale brought Indians only "the most worthless invaluable considerations."[59] Before condemning it, however, it would be wise to ask what choice Catawbas had. The old means of acquiring goods—presents, deerskins, perhaps plunder—were dead or dying, and pots, baskets, or land were the only substitutes that were at once available to the Nation and acceptable to its neighbors. A planter who chased Indian hunters out of his fields was unlikely to make a fuss when another party dug a little clay or cut a few canes. Even more important, marketing these commodities brought Catawba and settler together in a new, less confrontational arena. Through countless repetitions of the same simple exchange, a different form of intercourse emerged, a form based, not on suspicion and the expectation of conflict, but on consensus and a modicum of trust. When a farmer looked out his window and saw Catawbas approaching, he was now more likely to grab a few coins or a jug of whiskey than a musket or an axe. Indians now came, the planter knew, not to plunder or terrorize, but to collect rents or peddle pots. Certainly for beleaguered Catawbas, and for upcountry settlers, the trade was anything but insignificant.

As contact expanded after 1760, Catawbas tried to structure these new encounters by distinguishing "the good men that have rented Lands from us" and "the bad people [who] has frequently imposed upon us." This was an old habit: in John Lawson's day Indians, demanding conformity to their etiquette, had separated colonial traders into wheat and chaff and then rejected the chaff.

Catawbas did the same to planters, winnowing out those who were "exceeding Cross" and "did not behave well" from others the Indians considered "very good to Us."[60]

Once it had separated saint from sinner, the Nation recruited "good men" to protect Indians from "the bad people." Qualifications for the job varied: Thomas Spratt earned the Catawbas' trust by going off to war with them, as John Evans had before him; John Drinnon lived only two miles from the Nation and developed schemes to make money for Indians, as well as for himself; Joseph Kershaw, farther away, welcomed Indians at his store in Camden (formerly Pine Tree Hill) and supplied them on their way to and from Charleston; Robert Patton was simply a man "with whom we have been long acquainted."[61] All could slip easily across the cultural divide, and Catawbas, appreciating the value of that skill, accorded them greater stature as time went on. In 1770 the Nation's leaders noted only that Drinnon "writes and reads all our letters." A year later they approached Kershaw, asked that he "represent us when [we are] a grieved," and turned over to him for safekeeping the official crown land grant.[62] After the Revolutionary war the position became more formal. In 1784 Catawbas informed South Carolina that, after being "destitute of a man to take care of, and assist us in our affairs," they had selected Patton "to take charge of our affairs, and to act and do for us." The state, endorsing the plan, in 1786 invited the Nation to choose a few men who, as Catawba agents, could "cause Justice to be done them." Settlers, too, favored the idea. Some went to Spratt when a dispute with Indians arose; forty-three more signed beneath the fourteen Catawbas on the 1784 petition proposing Patton.[63]

A few Indians developed particularly close ties with the Nation's trusted advisers. Peter Harris, for example, a Catawba orphaned by the smallpox epidemic of 1759, was brought up by Thomas Spratt. Harris eventually returned to the Nation, but he never forgot Spratt's kindness. He paid frequent calls on the family, and in his old age he returned to the Spratt farm, put himself under the care of Thomas Spratt's son, and asked to be buried in the family graveyard. In the course of his visits Harris must have crossed paths with Sally New River, descendant of Hagler and wife of a later Catawba chief named New River, who was also close to the Spratts. Thomas Spratt's grandson, T. D. Spratt, knew her as "Old aunt Sally" and recalled that from her husband's death in 1804 until her own almost twenty years later she was something of a fixture around the Spratt farm, often residing there "for months at a time."[64]

If Peter Harris and Sally New River were unusual in their devotion to a settler's family, they were not alone in enjoying friendly relations with their neighbors. Other Catawbas, and other farmers, must have met regularly, if not daily. Because these encounters were so routine, few bothered to remark upon them. But when the documents mention that Sally New River visited a local grogshop; that her husband saved Thomas Spratt's son after a rattlesnake struck the boy; that another Catawba, Lewis Canty, regularly dropped by the Spratts'; that Peter Harris regaled settlers' children with tales of his travels and exploits; that these same children, decades later, remembered many Catawbas by name and spoke of overhearing the Indians' conversations with planters—when all of these fleeting glimpses of everyday encounters can be retrieved from the sparse record, it seems clear that they represent only a small fraction of the friendly exchanges that had become a fundamental part of Catawba life.[65]

One spring day in 1760 a Catawba woman is set upon by men spilling out of a tavern; one winter's day some decades later another is enjoying a friendly glass with the patrons of a similar establishment. The sharply contrasting images suggest how far Catawba-settler relations had come, but they do not reveal how Catawbas managed to travel that distance. It is not enough simply to say that they became landlords or began to swap pots and stories with settlers. In order to do such things without causing a stir, Indians had to learn certain lessons, lessons already mastered by Settlement Indians in the lowcountry. A Catawba had to know how to approach a tenant about the rent, what the going rate for a large pot was, when to tell tales and when to remain silent, how to act once the tavern door closed behind her. There was no "strategy for survival" here, no policy concocted by the Nation's leaders in response to the danger settlers posed.[66] Instead, the path from the unfortunate woman in 1760 to "Old aunt Sally" was blazed by countless now-forgotten individual decisions: to trade pots rather than plunder farmhouses, to complain rather than retaliate, to avoid confrontation rather than seek it out.

Planters did their best to help educate Indians. Catawbas who made little or no effort to accept the Nation's subordinate place in the piedmont world and behave accordingly were dismissed as having "C[h]aracter not good" and relegated to a category containing what one settler called the less "respectable" elements of the Nation. Those more willing to conform were rewarded, becoming akin to mascots to their neighbors. The role had certain benefits. Someone like Sally New River acquired such a reputation as a local character that even her inability (or unwillingness) to follow some of the new rules met with amusement rather than rebuke. Settlers made fun of her English and laughed because her "friends could not prevail on her to ride her horse like her white neighbors do[;] she persisted riding her own way (straddle)."[67]

The line between character and clown was never clearly drawn, and some Catawbas may have stepped, or been pushed, across it. Yet mastering the new rules, difficult as it may have been for Indians, gradually softened the hearts of Anglo-Americans, and before long the Nation began to enjoy a better reputation. One visitor in 1772 pronounced the Indians an "inoffensive, insignificant people" who were "simple, submissive, and obliging." A little more than a decade later another traveler "found among them a degree of civil hospitality and submissive kindness, which would have done no discredit to their white neighbors." Eventually those living among Catawbas year after year agreed with these assessments. In 1840, men who had resided on or near the reservation all their lives reported that the Indians "have now lived in the midst of a dense white population for more than half a century and . . . [we] never have known or heard a dishonest charge made against a Catawba or their meddling with any thing that did not belong to them, and have always been harmless and friendly."[68]

III

The substitution of molded clay, woven canes, and cheap soil for dressed deerskins and fighting prowess, the metamorphosis from mischief-makers to amusing characters—these changes helped Catawbas compensate for the loss of official protection and made the Indians more acceptable to neighbors whose ways differed sharply from their own. The changes were certainly necessary if the Nation was to survive; were they sufficient? Were dying rituals in distant capitals, memories of service in forgotten battles, a modest trade in crafts or acreage, and a reputation as "harmless and friendly" enough to mollify settlers? Fortunately, the question never had to be asked, much less answered, because the American Revolution rendered it moot. The Catawbas' service in that conflict was both the capstone of their adjustment to the new American world and the cornerstone of their ability to endure in that world for the next two centuries. It was, in many ways, the Nation's finest performance.

It was also, in some ways, a command performance. Unlike most Indian groups, which tried to stay out of the conflict between England and her colonies, the Nation's place amid Carolina settlers gave it little choice.[69] As Superintendent John Stuart observed in September 1775, since "they are domiciliated and dispersed thro' the Settlements of north and South Carolina, it is no wonder that they should be practised upon and seduced by the Inhabitants with whom they live." By the time Stuart wrote, "this ingratefull Little Tribe" was already lost to the king. Besides surrounding settlers, "good men" such as Joseph Kershaw and William Henry Drayton had been pressing the Nation to join the patriot ranks.[70] In early July two Catawbas had arrived in Charleston to learn more about the dispute between crown and colonists; the rebels' Council of Safety was glad to give them its version of events, and it sent them home with a letter to explain things to the Nation. The talk summarized the colonists' grievances, reminded Catawbas of their long friendship with South Carolina, argued that "your case and our case is just the same," promised trade and pay for Indians who served, and, finally, warned, "If you do not mind what we say, you will be sorry for it by and by." Before the month was out, Kershaw sent word that the Nation was "hearty in our interest."[71]

Over the next eight years Catawbas would live up to their pledge of allegiance.[72] By the fall of 1775, forty of them were scouring the lowcountry for tories and runaway slaves. The following spring a score of Catawba warriors headed in the opposite direction to join the campaign against the Cherokees.[73] Catawbas were with the rebel forces at engagements throughout the state, from Rocky Mount and Hanging Rock to Ninety Six and Stono. Before the war's end they had ventured into Georgia and over the border into North Carolina, where they traded fire along the Yadkin River with General Cornwallis's troops and served under Nathanael Greene at the battles of Guilford Courthouse and Haw River.[74]

Even when Catawbas did not go off to war, the war came to them. After the British captured Charleston in May 1780, the reservation became a center of rebel resistance. By early July some five hundred men had regrouped under the command of General Thomas Sumter at "the Catawba Old Town."[75] In the fall Cornwallis, with six or seven hundred regulars and perhaps half that many loyalists, was at Waxhaw Creek near "Camp Catawba Old Nation."[76] Within that beleaguered bivouac, provisions were so scarce that the soldiers dubbed it "Starve belley or poor hill." Catawbas, who for two or three years had been supplying corn to hard-pressed settlers, again did their best to help, driving their cattle to Sumter's men and camping nearby.[77]

The Indians paid heavily for their loyalty to the Americans. In June, before Sumter had even moved to the Nation, the approach of British forces from the south drove the frightened natives from their homes. Lieutenant Colonel Francis Rawdon, the commander of those forces, tried to entice the Catawbas back from their refuge in North Carolina by promising protection if they returned and destruction of their houses and crops if they did not. The Indians kept going, taking with them only what they could carry, and eventually ended up somewhere in Virginia.[78] When they at last returned home in 1781, they found that Rawdon was as good as his word: their village lay in ashes, and "all was gone; cattle, hogs, fowls, etc., all gone."[79]

The Catawbas' role in the war has been termed "rather negligible," and with so few men to commit to the cause, it does seem unlikely that the Nation ever determined the outcome of a battle.[80] But the significance of the Indians' contribution lay, not in the size of the Catawba company or the number of cattle they herded into Sumter's camp, but in their active and visible participation in the cause. The Catawba warriors' travels all over the South and Sumter's decision to make the reservation his headquarters acquainted hundreds, even thousands, of settlers and soldiers with the Indians' devotion to the United States. Like other patriots, Catawbas had sacrificed their fortunes and sometimes their lives; they, too, had been ousted from their homes by redcoats. Long after the fighting ceased, Americans celebrated what had been the most significant experience in their lives. Serving alongside and suffering with the American forces made Catawbas part of that experience and part of its celebration.

The most tangible rewards came immediately after the fighting subsided, when memories were fresh and gratitude therefore deepest. In February 1782, only months after the Indians returned to South Carolina, the state legislature agreed to send five hundred bushels of corn to tide them over until summer.[81] Two years later the same body, with Joseph Kershaw and Thomas Sumter leading the way in the House of Representatives, paid the Nation goods worth £299 sterling for its services in the conflict and reimbursed it another £125 for livestock it had supplied the army. The legislature could also help the Indians by doing nothing. When in 1785 Governor William Moultrie talked of renting the Catawba reservation and using the proceeds to raise the Indians from "their present Ignorant uncivilized manner" to "an enlightened Civilized People and usefull Inhabitants to the State," the House, noting that the Indians had not requested any such favors, refused to go along.[82] The corn, the goods, the protection—it seemed like old times.

Times truly had changed, however. One remembers that in 1781 Kershaw had warned Catawbas not to visit the capital, and before the end of the decade even the number of petitions from Indians began to decline. Thereafter Catawbas were less on the minds and in the pages of official South Carolina.[83] Nonetheless, the Indians were not wholly forgotten in influential circles. Men no longer interested in looking after the Nation were still more than willing to praise its loyalty to the glorious cause. Catawbas got a glimpse of the future before the war ended. Soon after the Indians' return home, their old friend Joseph Kershaw came to see them. "I . . . am happy to have it in my power," Kershaw told them, "to welcome you in peace to your native Land . . . after this Long and Bloody war in which you have taken so noble a part and have fought and Bled with your white Brothers of America." Kershaw's sentiments would persist among powerful South Carolinians into the nineteenth century. A 1786 petition, sent by the Nation's headmen but probably drafted by Kershaw, began by reminding South Carolina, "During the late War we have Exerted our selves as good Soldiers in behalf of this State."[84] More than thirty years later, Senator William Crafts requested a pension on behalf of Peter Harris, friend of the Spratts and veteran of the Revolutionary war. The language, clearly the senator's, shows how Catawba service in the conflict still gripped the imagination of prominent men. "I am one of the few stalks, that still remain in the field, where the tempest of the Revolution passed," the petition read. "I fought against the British for your sake, the British have disappeared, and you are free, yet from me the British took nothing nor have I gained any thing by their defeat." Even those who did not mention the Revolution by name clearly had it in mind when they insisted that Catawbas "were the best friends and allies South Carolina ever had" or recounted how these Indians "have always attached themselves to the Government of the State, and have fought for it in conjunction with its Armies."[85]

Memories of the Nation's role in the Revolutionary war also lived on outside legislative chambers and the speeches of powerful men. A historian prospecting among the Nation's neighbors shortly after the Civil War struck a rich vein of stories about Catawba patriots, stories that had been transmitted from father to son. A. Q. Madley, born and raised in South Carolina in the early nineteenth century before moving to Alabama, had not forgotten the Catawbas across the miles and the years. "I have heard in my youth stated," he recalled, "that many of them served under Sumter and other leaders." Another elderly Alabaman whose father joined Sumter in 1780 remembered that "his father never communicated much to him [about the Indians] except that all the tribe . . . served the entire war under Sumpter and fought most heroically."[86] Ezekiel

Fewell, a Catawba neighbor all his life, had "often heard it said" that Catawbas "were good Soldiers," and for decades after the Revolution Peter Harris and other Catawba warriors were "all called Revolutionary soldiers." Despite a few skeptics who recalled that Indian soldiers sometimes "hid like partridges," the majority had nothing but praise for Catawba valor.[87] One was so enthusiastic that he doubled the number of Indians who had actually joined the fight.[88]

Catawbas, not content simply to savor the glory being showered on them, worked to remind people of the Nation's service. Indian veterans were certainly not shy about their part; even settlers born after 1800 remembered listening to them. "I . . . knew a great many of the old ones of them that said they served in the revolutionary war," Ezekiel Fewell reported. One of Fewell's neighbors was certain that several Catawbas had served, for "he heard them say so." Peter Harris and perhaps other Catawba veterans offered details of that service. T. D. Spratt, Thomas Spratt's grandson, "heard when a boy from the mouth of old Peter Harris" of the Indian's exploits at Stono, and Harris told young Joseph White about killing a loyalist at a spring downriver from the Nation.[89]

More tangible reminders reinforced the tales spun by Catawba warriors. To the end of his days Peter Harris carried a gun that he had captured at Stono, and a Catawba colonel was no less devoted to his uniform. When guests arrived in the Nation unexpectedly one day in 1798, the man scurried off to don "an old Greencloth Coat, with gold binding, which buttoned very imperfectly over his naked body."[90] The outfit, ludicrous to the visitors, was probably a relic of the Revolution and therefore a priceless memento of the headman's attachment to the cause. Some Indians may have worn ruffled shirts and "very showy" suits for the same reason, and perhaps others carried weapons, medals, or wounds that reminded all who saw them of the Nation's sacrifice.[91]

Lest people tire of the stories or miss the symbolism of an old coat, Catawbas made their point more bluntly. Sometime after the Revolution the Nation, upon discovering that a few of its tenants were tories, tore down the offenders' houses and ushered these old foes off the reservation. Indians paid visits of another sort to patriots. One Catawba, after saving Captain Robert Craighead's life at the Battle of Hanging Rock, made a point of dropping by Craighead's Sugar Creek farm once each year, apparently to collect interest on the debt of gratitude.[92] Thomas Sumter's greater distance from the Nation—he lived south of Camden—did not shield him from frequent calls by his old Catawba soldiers.[93] Whether Craighead and Sumter sighed or smiled when they saw these guests coming is unknown. In either case, they were not likely to forget the Indian soldier.

Militia musters provided Indians with a public stage for relaying the same message. Well after 1800, warriors from the Nation were joining the local regiment every time it turned out, thereby assuring themselves a prominent place at these important social occasions. At one muster Major John Nettles, a Catawba wounded in the war, was "dressed as the whites were" to accompany the South Carolina leader Major General Thomas Carr, another wounded veteran, in a review of the troops. These officers, riding side by side across the muster field, embodied the enduring attachment between the two peoples, an attachment forged in war and now strengthened in a host of different ways.[94]

Together soldiers and warriors had marched, camped, fought, and died; together they kept alive the memory of those times. It is easy to imagine Indians and settlers who later crossed paths somewhere in the piedmont pausing to talk over old times at Hanging Rock, Rocky Mount, or "Camp Catawba" in the dark days after the fall of Charleston. "I have heard them talking often," Fewell remarked of his father and several Catawbas, veterans all.[95] And as Fewell's memory reveals, the friendship endured even after the old soldiers passed from the scene, because the stories guaranteed Catawbas a colorful chapter in the upcountry's Revolutionary annals.

The same people celebrating Catawba patriots were also saluting Catawba republicans, for during the Revolution Indians, like colonists, got rid of their king. When Rawdon and his troops marched into the Catawba village in June 1780, the story goes, he found the place deserted—except for old King Frow, only "nominally" the Nation's leader before, now "nearly imbecile" and abandoned by his people. Whether the two men actually met is unclear; other accounts have Frow wisely abdicating or conveniently dying. Whatever actually happened, Frow was gone, and with him went Catawba monarchy. The Indians entered the Revolution under King Frow and came out of it under General New River, who was, they said, elected by his people.[96]

The change from king to general and from hereditary succession to election was more public relations than political ideology.[97] But the new nation, intent on exporting its republican principles, was too delighted to inquire whether rhetoric matched reality. "What a pity," the Charleston *City Gazette* crowed in 1794, "certain people on a certain island have not as good optics as the Catawbas!" That same year the citizens of Camden, celebrating the anniversary of the fall of the Bastille, raised their glasses to toast "King [F]row—may all kings who will not follow his example follow that of Louis XVI."[98]

After 1800 the praise for Catawba republicans grew louder. During the Revolution, wrote a settler in the 1840s, "the Indians[,] having become so attached to republican principles, refused to live any longer under a monarchical Government. They therefore proceeded to elect a chief, under the title of General." On and on it went—"so Republican that they would not bear a King," "emulating the examples of their white brethren," "imbibed the prejudices of their white compeers to monarchy"—until Catawbas earned the ultimate accolade of "true Whigs." The Indians have added their voices to the chorus. Well into the twentieth century, one assured his audience that "the Catawba have always been a Democratic tribe," and a chief "always stressed that he had been elected and had not *inherited* this office."[99]

IV

The American Revolution was vital to Catawbas because in one stroke it reinforced their crumbling connection to distant capitals and warmed their uneasy friendship with nearby settlers. Before 1775, diplomatic rituals were losing their force, memories of past Catawba assistance were fading, and the chances of South Carolina's needing Catawbas in the future seemed remote. The Revolutionary war changed all that, giving Indians a permanent (if small) place in the pantheon of heroes honoring the nation's birth. If

South Carolina often neglected Catawbas after the Revolution, at least it was usually a benign neglect, a far cry from the policies of other states toward their original inhabitants. At the same time, patriotism became one more tool—along with pottery, land leases, and a less threatening countenance—Indians could use to carve a niche for themselves in the social landscape of the Carolina piedmont.

The Catawba achievement can be better appreciated by a glance at the Savannah River Chickasaws in the eighteenth century. Shortly after the Yamasee War this band had left the Chickasaw Nation proper and headed east to settle along the Savannah River; the emigrants were there at the invitation of Charleston officials hoping to establish new border guards where once Savannahs (and, before them, Westos) had lived.[100] These Chickasaws lasted longer as South Carolina's client than their two predecessors combined, and in their staying power they resembled Catawbas.[101] Both Chickasaws and Catawbas served the colony against Spaniards, Cherokees, and slaves, and both received title to lands as one reward for their loyalty.[102] Like Catawbas, Savannah River Chickasaws battled colonists who crossed these reservation boundaries or made away with the Indians' livestock, and like Catawbas, Chickasaws, too, went to Charleston to complain. Chickasaw headmen who visited the provincial capital after the Cherokee War even detected the same change of mood that their Catawba counterparts did, as officials shooed them away with one hand and passed out gifts with the other.[103] When Catawbas met Chickasaws in Charleston, along the Savannah, or in the Cherokee campaigns, it is not presumptuous to conjecture that they compared their common position in the Southeast.[104]

We may also wonder whether Catawbas recognized the differences setting them apart from their friends, differences that ultimately were the Chickasaws' doom and the Catawbas' salvation. For one thing, as recent emigrants who had left "that Spot of Ground, where their fore Fathers, had kindled their Fires and laid their Bones for so many Generations," Chickasaws could not lay claim to their Savannah River lands as ancient inhabitants of the soil, the sort of claim that sat well with Anglo-American authorities. The newcomers tried to get around this problem by acquiring a twenty-thousand-acre tract of land from the colony, but they jeopardized that grant by selling pieces of it, trying to exchange it for one or two smaller parcels nearby, and forgetting its boundaries.[105] The band still might have escaped the consequences of its carelessness —the colony blocked land sales and in 1765 promised another survey—had it not joined the wrong side in the Revolutionary war. South Carolina promptly confiscated the Indians' land and refused to give it back. Not only were these Indians traitors to the cause, the legislature argued, but there was no evidence that they had ever been anything more than tenants at will of the colony. Now the will to retain them as tenants was gone, and so, soon enough, were the Savannah River Chickasaws.[106] There but for their patriotism, and a homeland with clear title, went Catawbas.

Celebrating the Catawba Nation's good fortune in avoiding the Chickasaws' fate cannot obscure how close to oblivion Catawbas came. Nor can it devalue the true cost of survival. Despite all of their efforts to accommodate the conquerors of the piedmont, Catawbas could never feel wholly secure in the young Republic. Indeed, the Nation's leaders were so terrified of losing their lands that they tried to get laws passed prohibiting its sale "even with their own consent." They had good reason to be afraid. Though the state had taken control of the reservation from the crown and ceded it back to the Indians, after the Revolution people unconsciously whittled away at the Indians' land rights.[107] Instead of the 225 square miles (144,000 acres) that Samuel Wyly had laid out for them, the reservation shrank in some minds to a mere 62 (40,000 acres) or even 12 (7,500 acres). Instead of the free passage throughout the state guaranteed them, Catawbas were, according to some people, restricted to the reservation and prohibited from hunting beyond its borders.[108]

Even those willing to become tenants soon began circumventing the terms of their leases. So many sold or sublet the tracts granted them by the Nation that Indians found it impossible to penetrate the thicket of claims in order to collect rent.[109] While agents helped keep track of who owed what to whom, tenants, objecting that the men chosen by the Indians lived too far away or were "not so well Qualified" for the task, lobbied to get some of their own people appointed. On their part Catawbas fretted that the trustees lacked the authority to do the job properly.[110] For all the benefits leases conferred on the Nation, they remained more a marriage of convenience than affection.

Sometimes the agent was even worse than the tenants. Around 1800, one trustee, making a mockery of his title, persuaded Catawbas to lease him a shoal in the river used for shad fishing, ostensibly on a trial basis. Only after the Catawba headmen had made their marks on the document did the agent reveal that they had just signed it away for ninety-nine years. To mollify the unhappy Indians, he agreed to let them draw his seine two nights a week and keep the catch. The arrangement went on for some time until the trustee, claiming that the Indian fishermen tore the net, refused to let them use it anymore, proposing instead to give them a share of the fish he caught. Every night and every morning Catawbas showed up at the shoal: sometimes they got their fish, sometimes not. When Indians again complained, settlers began to "Raise Quarrells with our people and commits little Slye crimes," taking anyone who tried to retaliate to court. At the hearings, Indians, legally forbidden to testify and in any event "not heard when we speak the truth on our trials," were forced to pay fines in order to stay out of jail. In such slow but steady fashion were Catawba rights and freedoms chipped away by "Sharp witted and designing Christians," until the Indians were paying people who should have been paying them.[111]

"Slye crimes" and land frauds barely begin to total up the cost of survival. More often the records offer only hints of a more serious malaise. In the fall of 1786, women and children "fled in every direction" when a solitary stranger rode into the village unannounced.[112] Five years later another traveler heard a story that a young Catawba woman

> with whom a Gentleman not far distant had been criminally intimate, carried her child to him, informing him he was the father. The Gentleman would by no means allow he had ever seen her; on which she took her child by the heels, and dashed its brains out before his face, and left it on the ground.[113]

The stories generate more questions than answers. What were the women and children afraid of? Could the story of the young woman be true? If so, what did it mean? Why would she break the tradition that children were the responsibility of the mother's family and uphold another that permitted infanticide?[114] The records are mute, leaving only the questions along with lingering images of terror and tragedy.

The stench of contempt on one side and humiliation on the other spared no one, not even the Nation's most respected men and its best friends. Thomas Spratt's grandson remembered hearing how General New River had once borrowed a horse from Spratt. When the Indian chief accidentally injured his mount, a furious Spratt began "banging 'Old New River' with a pole all over the yard."[115] The episode gave the Spratts a colorful tale to pass on to children and grandchildren; its effect on New River and his descendants can only be imagined.

Catawbas had clearly paid an exorbitant price for admission into the new American nation. Once proprietors of the piedmont, they now existed only on the sufferance of people inclined to cheat them as often as protect them, mock them as readily as befriend them. It was a sad state, requiring more quiet resignation than open resistance, smiles in place of frowns, submission to the humiliations dished out by a swaggering Spratt or a local judge. Yet compared with the scores of other Indian peoples that entered the eighteenth century with Catawbas but did not live to see the nineteenth, the Nation's fate does not seem so bad: witness the Savannah River Chickasaws. Had Catawbas chosen another path, had they opted for something other than a life as potters and patriots, they would not have survived the century. And survive it they did, far better than their conquerors knew.

7

Indians Still:
The Nation Endures

These wretched Indians, though they live in the
midst of an industrious people, and in an improved
state of society, will be Indians still.
—Robert Mills

OBSERVERS of the Catawba Nation in the late eighteenth century saw only a wasteland. Just before the Revolution a traveler had reported the Indians "sinking fast into degeneracy and a state of servility and dependence." Thereafter the descent continued, with followers of the Catawbas' fortunes closely charting it. Shortly after 1800, the Nation touched bottom, "a state of degradation" marked by "depraved practices, and immoral habits."[1]

In the eyes of the outside world the denizens of these depths could hardly have been worse off. On the eve of the Revolution they were already said to "live perhaps the meanest of any Indians belonging to the British American empire," and fifty years later they remained "in a state of abject poverty."[2] Visitors were appalled. A traveler named John Smyth stayed overnight in 1772 and found his hosts "enveloped in filth and nastiness of person." Though he liked the Indians and judged them happy enough, he had to confess that "their habitual nastiness, coarse fare, and rude accommodations" were "disgustful to me." In 1786 another wayfarer, Elkanah Watson, could not bear to spend even one night among these people (perhaps because, as his choice of words suggests, he had read Smyth's book); they "were extremely nasty, wal-

226

lowing in dirt and filth, having coarse fare and rude accommodations." According to William Henry Drayton's son John, amnesia was poverty's companion. "They have forgotten their antient rites, ceremonies, and manufactures," he remarked in 1803. Some said the Indians' downfall was their own fault. John Drayton blamed liquor: "Caught by the allurements of ardent spirits," the Catawba "dwindles into a state of insignificance and drunkenness."[3]

The Indians, said to be drunk and dirty, inspired both pity and scorn in their conquerors. Many people felt that "these poor deserted sons of the forest" presented "a melancholy picture" and "excited no other feeling than that of commiseration for their fallen condition." To others they were "objects of contempt," neglected by most and despised by the rest.[4] Drayton optimistically argued that the natives stood to gain more than they had lost. "By their connexions with the whites," he wrote, Catawbas "assume much of their manner and mode of living; and by easy progression, are altering the very colour of their persons." Whether the Nation was loved or hated, whether it was destined for extinction or civilization, the underlying message was the same: these Indians were suffering a cultural collapse.[5]

There is no denying that Catawba life during these years was marked by poverty and oppression. It is a mistake, however, to deduce from these harsh facts that the Indians had committed cultural suicide. The problem with this conclusion is that the people reaching it were poorly equipped to judge. Most of those reporting the Catawbas' decay were only casual acquaintances of the Indians. The news about the Nation was largely secondhand, and what eyewitness accounts there were generally derived from visits of a day or two.[6] Even men who lived near the Indians for a lifetime lacked extensive knowledge of native ways. Despite proximity and regular contact, the lives of most Catawbas and most settlers intersected at no more than a few points (none of them on the Indians' own ground), and planters had other things to do than get to know their native neighbors better.[7]

The information outsiders did pick up could be as distorted as it was limited. All of them held what they saw or heard of Catawbas up against any number of inaccurate yardsticks and, of course, found these Indians wanting. The most common standard was European culture or its American offspring, though few were so honest as Watson, who came ready to "contrast them [Catawbas] with the polish and refinement of France." John Smyth preferred to set these people alongside "the native, uncivilized, wild, western Indians." Catawbas, he concluded, "would excite the derision and contempt of the more western savages, for these [Catawbas] are in a kind of state of civilization, which the Indians consider as enervating effeminacy, and hold it in the utmost abhorrence."[8] Another handy measure was a rosy picture of the Nation's own past. Whether John Lawson would have found the food and lodging any worse or the liquor flowing any more freely in 1800 than he did in 1701 is open to debate. But he was not around, and his successors had no doubts. "How different" Catawbas today are "from their ancestors of former times," Drayton sighed in 1802, though his knowledge of those ancestors was rudimentary at best.[9]

One of Drayton's correspondents, the Philadelphia naturalist Benjamin Smith Barton, illustrated how this sort of ancestor worship could be used to denigrate Catawbas. "I am informed," Barton wrote in 1797, "that the Katahba have an anniversary meeting, intended to commemorate their former greatness. This must, indeed, be a melancholy task." Whether the ritual really was a sad affair is unknown. It sounds much like the evening Lawson had spent with the Waxhaws a century earlier, listening to old men sing "in Remembrance of their former Greatness." But Barton would draw his own conclusions. Catawbas were "fast passing to destruction"; therefore, the ceremony must be the Nation's death rattle.[10]

The Catawba Nation contributed to the narrow and distorted field of vision outsiders imposed on themselves. A "very long, tedious and disagreeable ride" to the Nation on paths winding through dense woods discouraged curiosity-seekers, and the hardy souls who did follow one of these trails to a village were often disappointed.[11] At one house an Indian woman hid her infant under a blanket the moment visitors barged in because, they were told, "she was afraid lest the eyes of a Stranger should be *evil*." A similar reticence welcomed every sightseer, leading each to conclude from the natives' silence that Indians had nothing to say. Drayton's claims about the Catawbas' faulty memory, for example, were based on his failure to learn much about their religion. That Indians were notoriously unwilling to divulge such secrets does not seem to have occurred to him. Disposed to look for signs of disintegration, he took the news (or the lack of it) as further proof of Catawba decline.[12]

To say that Drayton and company were myopic is not to say that they were blind. Catawbas were easy to pity, in part at least because they were now so few. For some reason the Nation's numbers, which had remained fairly steady at around four or five hundred from 1760 to the end of the century, began to drop after 1800, until by 1826 only thirty families were said to be living on the reservation.[13] Given the routine injustices large and small committed against these few, observers of the Nation had indeed captured a central theme of Catawba life. But that theme was not the only one. The exclamations about the Indians' poverty and ignorance obscure another side of Catawba existence. We need to follow Smyth and Watson down those paths into the Nation and, once there, to look more carefully for signs of life.

I

A glimpse of any Catawba would have contradicted John Drayton's claims about these people's becoming white. They certainly did not look white. Quite apart from the "wild sparkling" in their "brilliant black eyes," many still went around "half nakid," exposing their "fine clear dark olive" skin to public view. Those who put on clothes displayed their own tastes. A woman donned a woolen petticoat and draped a blanket over her shoulder; her daughter might add decorative paint and feathers to this outfit; her husband, if he was an important man, sported a fancy cotton suit accented by a silver breastplate. And everyone, man or woman, young or old, wore a silver nose ring, often with a tiny silver heart dangling from it. Even after scalp locks and facial tattoos went out of style, no one was likely to mistake a Catawba for a planter or slave.[14]

Following one of these bejeweled and bedaubed Indians home would have confirmed the initial impression of their distinctive ways. Home might well be a traditional bark dwelling with the family sprawled on deerskins around a central fire, but a visitor might be taken to one of the Catawbas' log cabins, complete with

chimney and chairs. Any resemblance to a settler's house ended
there, however, for Indians had their own customs governing design and furnishings. None divided the log cabin into rooms or
deemed it necessary to acquire a table to go with the chairs. Chair
or no, a traveler invited in to share a meal was going to eat from a
tub placed on the floor.[15]

The dishes served—hoecake, smoked venison, turkey—indicated
that Catawbas still ate pretty much what their ancestors had eaten.
Outsiders' claims that the Indians were usually too lazy or too
drunk to grow food were contradicted by the patches of corn and
other vegetables near native towns.[16] While women tended these
crops, men carried on their task of killing game for food and skins.
Visitors to the Nation in the fall or winter were likely to find that
the men were off on a hunt, and a traveler many miles away occasionally met one of these hunting parties camped beside the road
or peddling deerskins. Well into the nineteenth century, men carrying hides accompanied women lugging pottery into Charleston,
where both set up shop and sold the products of these ancient
crafts.[17]

To their traditional occupations Catawba farmers, potters, and
hunters added another: landlord. Just how much Indians earned
from rent is difficult to judge, but it was nowhere near what tenants claimed. To hear these people tell it, the standard agreement involved a substantial bounty when the lease was signed and
then ninety-nine years of stiff rent payments, for "Indians never
thought of taking less than ten dollars [a year] for any land, however small." The leases tell a different story. Fewer than ten tracts
in a hundred went for as much as $10.00; most were around
$2.50–$3.50, and one fell as low as $.12½.[18] The settlers' version
of the bounty business was equally misleading. A new tenant might
hand over a dollar when the deal was struck; anything more was an
advance, not a bonus, and it guaranteed that for a certain number
of years (the average was twelve) rent would be a token payment of
$.50 or so before jumping to the fee originally set.[19] The arrange-
ment left Indians in a dilemma: pick up the sum due every year,
which they knew usually meant "Some Small trifle that is Easily
Squandered away or of but little use to us," or ask for more and

mortgage the future.[20] Either way, it was not easy to get rich from rent.

Perhaps the most that can be said for the land system was that it supplemented what Catawbas took in from their other pursuits. Tenants paid Indians an array of merchandise, from tobacco or bacon to a bridle or a blanket. Horses were a popular advance against future rent, and some Indians chose small amounts of food or clothing each year. Occasionally a leaseholder would establish a credit line for his landlords at a local store and let them buy what they liked.[21] The favorite means of payment, however, was neither goods nor credit, but cash, for money gave natives the freedom to spend when, where, and how they chose. This independence was so important to them that one lease stipulating an annual rent of three dollars worth of goods noted that the Indian would accept two dollars in cash instead. In sums large and small, money was continually changing hands on the reservation.[22]

The amount of currency or merchandise an Indian obtained depended in part on who that Indian was. The Nation's headmen, abiding by rules long since lost, were responsible for deciding who was entitled to the rent from each farm, and they took pains to spread the wealth around: close to 50 different Indians were assigned tracts on the east side of the Catawba River, and between 1810 and 1830 no fewer than 114 people collected rent. Still, some collected more than others. Billy Canty and Rebecca Marsh, with one lease each, stood well below the likes of Sally New River and Jesse Ayers, who owned or shared rights to almost ten.[23] In her old age Sally New River almost made a career of her leases. In twelve transactions with tenants during 1815, for example, she earned $18.05 in cash, along with almost twelve yards of cloth, one-half a bushel of salt and two bushels of wheat, a pound of coffee, and two pairs of horseshoes. The next year fifteen different calls netted her a nickel less in cash, but she more than made up for it with fourteen yards of cloth and the same quantity of wheat as the year before, not to mention meat, corn, salt, and a bridle.[24] Others probably depended less on their tenants to make ends meet. No Indian, however, relied solely on the bounty of fields and woods any more.

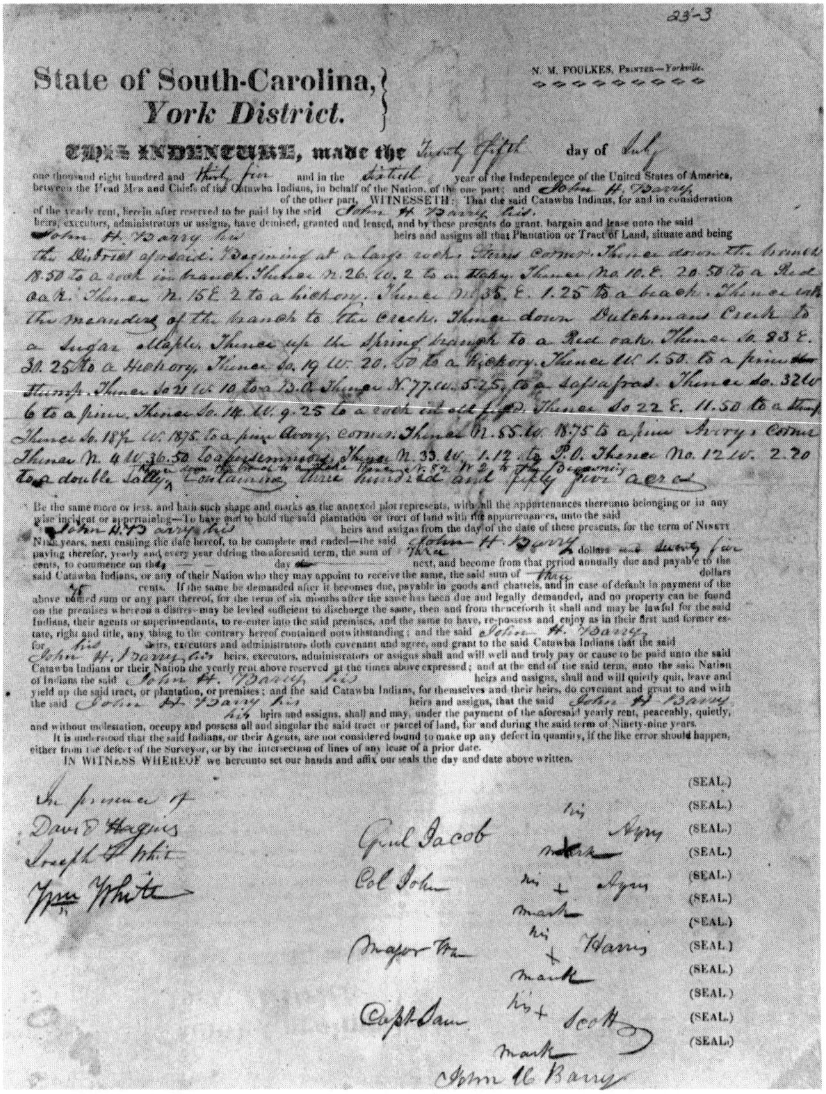
23-3

State of South-Carolina, York District.

N. M. FOULKES, Printer—Yorkville.

THIS INDENTURE, made the Twenty fifth day of July one thousand eight hundred and thirty five and in the sixtieth year of the Independence of the United States of America, between the Head Men and Chiefs of the Catawba Indians, in behalf of the Nation, of the one part; and John H. Barry of the other part, WITNESSETH: That the said Catawba Indians, for and in consideration of the yearly rent, herein after reserved to be paid by the said John H Barry his heirs, executors, administrators or assigns, have demised, granted and leased, and by these presents do grant, bargain and lease unto the said John H. Barry his heirs and assigns all that Plantation or Tract of Land, situate and being the District aforsaid. Beginning at a large rock ... corner. Thence down the branch 18.50 to a rock in branch. Thence N. 26. W. 2 to a stake. Thence No. 10. E. 20.50 to a Red oak. Thence N. 15 E. 2 to a hickory. Thence N. 35. E. 1.25 to a beech. Thence with the meanders of the branch to the creek. Thence down Dutchmans Creek to a Sugar Maple. Thence up the Spring branch to a Red oak. Thence So. 83 E. 30. 25 to a Hickory. Thence So. 19 W. 20. 50 to a Hickory. Thence W. 1.50. to a pine stump. Thence So 21 W. 10 to a B.O. Thence N. 77. W. 5.25 to a sasafras. Thence So. 32 W 6 to a pine. Thence So. 14. W. 9.25 to a rock ... Thence So 22 E. 11.50 to a stump Thence So. 18½ W. 18.75 to a pine Avery's corner. Thence N. 55. W. 18.75 to a pine Avery's corner Thence N. 4 W. 36.50 to a persimmon. Thence N. 33. W. 1.12 to P.O. Thence No. 12 W. 2.20 to a double sally ... Thence N. 82 W 2 to the Beginning Containing three hundred and fifty five acres

Be the same more or less, and hath such shape and marks as the annexed plot represents, with all the appurtenances thereunto belonging or in any wise incident or appertaining—To have and to hold the said plantation or tract of land with the appurtenances, unto the said John H. Barry his heirs and assigns from the day of the date of these presents, for the term of Ninety Nine years, next ensuing the date hereof, to be complete and ended—the said John H. Barry paying therefor, yearly and every year during the aforesaid term, the sum of Three dollars and twenty five cents, to commence on the — — day — next, and become from that period annually due and payable to the said Catawba Indians, or any of their Nation who they may appoint to receive the same, the said sum of three dollars 25 cents. If the same be demanded after it becomes due, payable in goods and chattels, and in case of default in payment of the above named sum or any part thereof, for the term of six months after the same has been due and legally demanded, and no property can be found on the premises whereon a distress may be levied sufficient to discharge the same, then and from thenceforth it shall and may be lawful for the said Indians, their agents or superintendants, to re-enter into the said premises, and the same to have, re-possess and enjoy as in their first and former estate, right and title, any thing to the contrary hereof contained notwithstanding; and the said John H. Barry for his heirs, executors and administrators doth covenant and agree, and grant to the said Catawba Indians that the said John H. Barry his heirs, executors, administrators or assigns shall and will well and truly pay or cause to be paid unto the said Catawba Indians or their Nation the yearly rent above reserved at the times above expressed; and at the end of the said term, unto the said Nation of Indians the said John H. Barry his heirs and assigns, shall and will quietly quit, leave and yield up the said tract, or plantation, or premises; and the said Catawba Indians, for themselves and their heirs, do covenant and grant to and with the said John H Barry his heirs and assigns, that the said John H Barry his heirs and assigns, shall and may, under the payment of the aforesaid yearly rent, peaceably, quietly, and without molestation, occupy and possess all and singular the said tract or parcel of land, for and during the said term of Ninety-nine years.

It is understood that the said Indians, or their Agents, are not considered bound to make up any defect in quantity, if the like error should happen, either from the defect of the Surveyor, or by the intersection of lines of any lease of a prior date.

IN WITNESS WHEREOF we hereunto set our hands and affix our seals the day and date above written.

In presence of
David Hagins
Joseph White
Wm White

Genl Jacob his mark Ayres (SEAL.)
Col John his + mark Ayres (SEAL.)
Major Wm his + mark Harris (SEAL.)
Capt Sam his + mark Scott (SEAL.)
John H Barry

(SEAL.) (SEAL.) (SEAL.) (SEAL.) (SEAL.) (SEAL.) (SEAL.) (SEAL.) (SEAL.) (SEAL.) (SEAL.) (SEAL.)

Figure 7. Catawba Land Lease. *Records of the Secretary of State, Catawba Indian Land Leases, 1809–1841, box 1, bundle 23, p. 3. Courtesy of South Carolina Department of Archives and History*

Sally New River's advanced age and her heavy involvement in the land business may have combined to keep her close to home throughout the year, but she was an exception. Most Catawbas did not let new responsibilities squeeze out the old or alter the calendar. Scarcely one rent payment in seven was made during the winter months; hunters and potters were abroad then, and few Indians were around to collect. From May through August, on the other hand, when these other tasks could be set aside, nearly half of all the transactions took place, with almost 20 percent of them in July alone.[25] The old rule—home in summer, away in winter—still applied to the annual schedule of activities in the early nineteenth century, a cycle as predictable as the seasons themselves.[26]

Catawbas making those seasonal rounds—from the Nation to the clay pits and cane swamps near Camden to the streets of Charleston to the tenant's door, and back again—did so as families, not as individuals.[27] On the road or at home, kin groups remained the basic units of Catawba society. As if to underline this point, a visitor in 1798 reported finding an elderly leader "surrounded with Sons Daughters and grand Children," a scene reminiscent of descriptions of native life in the Carolina interior some two centuries before. Everyone belonged, even those another society might exclude. In that Catawba leader's house the same visitor was shocked to see "an Ideot" squatting in the corner, "in form figure and posture a *large ape*, blind, and playing on his teeth with his fingers." Far from shunning this person, the Indians embraced him, for "these unfortunate objects are not only held sacred, . . . but it is esteemed *fortunate* to have one in your family."[28]

Parceling out reservation lands strengthened kinship ties. The bulk of the leases went to individuals, but at least two were assigned to entire families, and others might designate the intended recipients as a husband and wife, two sisters, or a mother and her daughter.[29] The families receiving a tract divided up the collecting chores as well as the profits; so, apparently, did people with sole claim to a lease. General Jacob Scott, New River's successor, took turns with his daughter Sally rounding up rents on her lease, Sally Ayers pocketed money due her sister Betsey's children, and during the 1820s a gaggle of Redheads—Jinney, Billy, John, and the Widow

Redhead herself—accepted a farmer's payments at one time or another.[30] These shared duties reinforced the bonds already established by activities—hunting, gathering, farming—in which families traditionally engaged.

The networks maintained throughout life were renewed as death approached and a Catawba had to decide what to do with this new species of property. Spouses and children were the usual beneficiaries, but there were many exceptions to this rule.[31] Billy Canty left his lease to his sister Harriet, Kitty Deloe specified that hers go to her uncle John Ayers, and the money due Billy Brown ended up in the hands of Gemmima Joe, a stepdaughter of Billy's wife. Canty, Deloe, and Brown were unusual because they went to the trouble to make a will, appearing before the state's agent and getting their wishes down in writing. More often, when someone died, a member of the family simply stepped in, and the only record of the arrangement relatives had worked out among themselves was a line through the owner's name in the Rent Book and the successor's written in beneath it.[32]

Catawbas acquiring leases, accepting rents, and leaving both to their heirs wove what appears to us an extraordinarily tangled web of kinship.[33] Their marriages complicated matters further. The Ayers clan, for example, overlapped with several other kin groups. Jacob Ayers's daughter Betsey married Jacob Scott's son John, and another of Jacob's daughters wed James Clinton and William Harris in turn. Meanwhile, Jacob's brother John married James Kegg's sister Betsey. And so it went, one family intertwining with another until, as one observer noted, "most of the Catawbas are . . . related."[34]

The result of the marriages and wills, the leases assigned and rents collected was to make all Catawbas feel a part of something larger than themselves. The Indians' terminology apparently extended this sense of kinship into the more remote branches of each family without losing the intimacy close relatives enjoyed. Thus the Catawba word for an aunt, stepmother, or mother-in-law meant "mother-resembling," the term for aunt's husband was "mother's husband," and that for a niece or granddaughter translated as "daughter-resembling."[35] The words, which suggest an intensity of feeling among what we might regard as distant relatives, point to far-reaching ties of acquaintance and affection.

As they extended across space, so kin relations also stretched across time to tie a person to the past. While the Scotts' claim of direct descent from Hagler might have outshone the rest, they had no monopoly on distinguished ancestors. The Ayers family took its name from one of Hagler's captains, an interpreter named "Ears" (Hixayoura), while Harrises looked to a 1739 Cheraw chief named John Harris and the Georges to a war captain by that name from Nassaw Town. Descendants of colonial traders, like Brown and Evans, could also boast a long and impressive pedigree.

Naming patterns strengthened the connections between past and present. Thomas Brown and John Harris bore the names of their famous ancestors, but many parents in the early nineteenth century named children after older living relatives. Jacob Ayers and Jacob Scott were especially remembered. One of Betsey Ayers-Scott's sons was called "Jacob Jr" to honor his grandfathers, and both men had nephews named Jacob. The women, too, followed tradition: in the George family were both a Nancey and a Little Nancy as well as Patsey George and her daughter Patsey Junior. The last public use of the older forms of personal names died out soon after 1800 when New River, Pine Tree George, and Sugar Jamey passed away. Nonetheless, many Catawbas answering to perfectly ordinary English names bore a special relationship with people who had come before.[36]

Living within the warm embrace of an extended family brought benefits that went beyond keeping one in touch with the past. Relatives offered instruction, comfort, and protection. This last privilege should not be underestimated: Catawbas settled their own differences well into the nineteenth century, and that meant relying on kinfolk. "For years," recalled one of the Nation's neighbors in 1870, "the law among themselves was their own, and no white officer of justice thought of interfering with them. What was between themselves, was among themselves." No one knew this better than Sam Scott, a Catawba who had killed a member of the Canty family in the mid-nineteenth century and fled to escape punishment. Years later, fully armed, he returned home, only to find everything quiet. With time Scott became less cautious, and soon his skull was crushed with a rock thrown by his victim's own daughter. That was the end of it: to the Catawba mind the power of kin obligations had been upheld and justice served.[37]

That a young woman and not a young man killed Sam Scott is a reminder that within the Nation's kinship system the sexual balance of power was more even than it was among whites. The few surviving clues suggest that the Indians continued to think in matrilineal terms. At marriage it was customary for a woman to keep her surname, which she passed on to her children. Thus Betsey Kegg remained a Kegg after wedding John Ayers, and Nancy Harris, the wife of Sam Evans, bore a child she named Allen Harris. Behind this symbolism lay substance. Women were involved in almost half of all the lease assignments and rent transactions, and when the time came, they appeared before the agent to dispose of their estates just as a man did.[38] At least some of these female entrepreneurs kept their property separate from their husbands'. When Peter Harris died in 1823 owing his wife Betsey Dudgeon thirty dollars, she went to the agent, Hugh White, to make sure that Peter's rents went to her until that debt was erased.[39]

White, who may have been uncomfortable talking business with women, did his best to convert Catawbas to ways more familiar to him. Refusing to listen to Betsey Dudgeon or tampering with Kitty Deloe's will would only cause trouble; so, consciously or unconsciously, he changed their last names. In White's records Betsey Dudgeon became Betsey Harris, and in 1816, shortly after Betsey Kegg wed John Ayers, she was "Betsey Kegg now Betsey Ayres." He went a step further and denoted Prissy Bullen's son David as a Harris and Sally Scott's daughter Jane an Allick. Whether the Indians went along with this—whether they even knew what White was doing—is unclear. Certainly Betsey "Ayres" and Jane "Allick" represented the ultimate victors in the tug-of-war between reckoning by the mother or the father. How much that victory was still confined to White and his Rent Book cannot be known.[40]

If Catawbas were indeed beginning to adopt the new nomenclature, they had a long way to go before they would depart from their matrilineal habit of mind. The Nation continued simply to assume that any Cherokee man who married a Catawba woman became a Catawba.[41] More important still as an index of Catawba feeling was the decision to deed the entire reservation to the Nation's women. In the 1780s the headmen had taken on the task of assigning leases in the name of the Nation, and they would continue to do so. But on April 6, 1796, three of those men—New River, John Ears, and John Brown—sat down with Hugh White, Thomas Spratt, and two other agents to draw up a document granting all fifteen miles square of Catawba territory to Sally New River and the "other women of the s[ai]d Nation." Why did they do it? The leaders said only that there were "Divers good causes unto them done by her the said Sally New River."[42] For the past twenty-five years Catawbas had been afraid that the reservation would somehow be wrenched from their hands, and this may have been a means of hiding ownership where whites were less likely to look while also removing temptation from the leading men, who could have been under enormous pressure to sell.[43] Perhaps it was designed to reflect the Catawba conviction that women, not men, controlled the land, that whatever decisions the headmen might make regarding its use, it belonged to someone else. At this remove it is impossible to say what was on their minds. If nothing else, however, the document speaks eloquently to the responsibility resting in the hands of Catawba women.

While women could still wield authority behind the scenes, it was men like New River, Brown, and Ears who strode onto the public stage as the Nation's leaders. Their performances bore a closer resemblance to those of earlier headmen than most whites realized. Hidden by all of the praise for the Indians' switch from a monarchy to a republic was the simple fact that authority underwent no drastic changes. Citizens of the new nation made much of the elections Catawbas held after 1776, forgetting that the Indians' council had routinely chosen the chief all along. Frow, for example, owed his position as eractasswa to a meeting of forty-two Catawba headmen in 1765, a meeting South Carolina officials had referred to as "the Election of a Catawba King."[44] When Catawbas later elected leaders, then, the event was hardly the republican revolution their neighbors liked to think it was.

A successful candidate's qualifications also remained much the same. To be considered, a man still had to be connected in some way to the family that had produced Frow, Hagler, and their pre-decessors.[45] General New River's own family background is un-known, but he was bound to Hagler at least by marriage to Sally, who was said to be the great eractasswa's granddaughter. Jacob Scott, who followed New River shortly after 1800, was also a grand-child of Hagler's, and James Kegg, another nineteenth-century Ca-tawba chief, "prided in [his] royal blood." So much for renouncing the principle of hereditary succession.[46]

As always, Catawbas demanded more of a prospective chief than the correct blood line. Those chosen after the Revolution also had to earn the respect of their people by proving themselves in com-bat. The Nation's first general was a consummate military man, having won his name at a victory over the Shawnees on the banks of the New River in western Virginia. "New River had no other name," one planter recalled; "he would have felt insulted at the idea of such a change[;] he gloried in that of N. River." Though Scott and his successor Jacob Ayers had more prosaic names, their credentials were also impeccable; both had served in the Revolu-tion, thereby either establishing or strengthening their status as warriors.[47]

A chief's basic duties changed as little as the method of his selec-tion did. Generals, like the kings before them, were expected to serve as mediators between the Nation and the outside world. Upon arrival visitors were directed to the chief's house, and it was his responsibility to entertain them.[48] Similarly, any message sent by the Nation carried the general's mark above all others, so that New River, Scott, and then Ayers laid claim to Hagler's pride of place on the page. As usual, though, none of these documents car-ried a chief's mark alone; generals no more thought of issuing orders on their own initiative than kings had. Like the 1796 deed, every decision carried the weight of collective endorsement, with the marks of three or more men bearing witness to that fact.

That leases were the documents headmen most commonly put their hands to after 1800 indicates that the Nation's leaders exer-cised their authority in ways unforeseen by Yanabe Yatengway or Hagler. On each lease, as on every paper issued in the Nation's name, the general's mark came first, followed by a handful of offi-cers from colonel on down to lieutenant. It was these men who, after consulting the Nation's wishes, sat down with the agents to assign plots, terms, and landlords. The meetings of the Indians gave new luster to Catawba leaders and breathed new life into the Catawba community. As the Nation's population declined and diplomatic relations broke off, there were fewer collective decisions to make and therefore less need for headmen to make them. Tradition alone could not sustain vestigial authority figures or keep alive that spark of common feeling. There had to be a reason to come together, to have someone speak for the Nation: renting land provided the reason. Regularly, perhaps even annually, Catawbas convened to discuss leases, resolve disputes, and instruct their leaders on the best way to proceed. How far these gatherings resembled earlier assemblies is unclear. At the very least, they offered headmen a forum in which to exercise their authority and served to counter the centrifugal forces spinning individuals or families off into their own little worlds.[49]

The authority Catawba leaders continued to wield may have rested on more than tradition and charisma. Their penchant for inhabiting King's Bottoms, a corner of the reservation on the east bank of the Catawba River, may indicate a spiritual sanction beneath the kin connections, character, and leases that were the more visible signs of their prestige. Whites looked at this spot and saw rich soil; it meant much more than that to the Indians, though exactly what is tantalizingly obscure.[50] King's Bottoms was a burial ground, and the name hints that the graves held the remains of eractasswas. Perhaps, too, its location in the Waxhaw Indians' old fields had special significance to Catawbas, who had not forgotten these extinct neighbors.[51] Whatever the source of its power, King's Bottoms was so important to the Nation that the Indians hung on to it tenaciously. It was there that both New River and his wife lived and died, as did Jacob Ayers and his brother John. Moreover, long after much poorer lands had been auctioned off, Catawbas refused to rent King's Bottoms, having "sense enough," as one observer knew (even if he did not suspect their reasons), "to reserve [it] for their children."[52] King's Bottoms was clearly sacred ground, and the intensity of the Indians' feeling for it contradicts Drayton's claim that their past was forgotten, their spiritual life "entirely lost."[53]

The most convincing testimony to the vitality of Catawba religion, and, indeed, of Catawba culture itself, was the failure of missionaries to wean Catawbas from it. Throughout these years there was talk of converting the Nation, or more precisely of "Civilizing and Christianizing" it, since the two endeavors invariably went hand in hand. Few proposals ever advanced beyond talk—schools were never built, preachers never showed up—and the few programs that led to a course of instruction soon met native indifference and disappeared.[54]

Of the many plans laid and projects launched, the most famous was undertaken by the College of William and Mary. The school had long been in the missionary business: for most of the eighteenth century, college officials, using funds left by the English scientist Robert Boyle, had brought young Indians to Williamsburg, instructed them in the art of being an Englishman, and sent them home to "improve [their] tribe." While the results had been disappointing, the college did not give up hope. When the first Catawba pupil (a lad named John Nettles) arrived in the late 1760s, there was every expectation that this, "the most promising boy in the Nation," would succeed. In the space of two or three years Nettles completed his course of study with high honors.[55]

The college was to be disappointed again. Shortly before he was to return home in 1771 or 1772, young John slipped off to a local tavern and was found, hours later, lying drunk in the street. Such youthful indiscretions were not unheard of among students at the college, but Nettles was not just any student. He carried the future of his people on his young shoulders, and passing out in the gutter seemed, to say the least, to jeopardize that future. The professors and trustees, deeply shaken, waited until he sobered up before calling him to account, "explaining in the most feeling terms," according to one who later heard the story, "the object in educating him." Then they sent him home and hoped for the best.

Accounts differ on whether Nettles reformed once he got back to the Nation. One acquaintance remembered him as "dissipated," but the weight of the evidence had him "a decent man, discreet and sensible," whose "[h]abits were peaceable, moral and temperate." Regardless of their views on his character, all concurred that once among his own people Nettles slipped easily back into Catawba ways. He married a woman from the Nation, fought along-side New River, Scott, and Ayers in the Revolution, and over the next thirty years rose slowly in the ranks until, as Major Nettles, he was signing reservation leases.[56] In 1786 Elkanah Watson found him "a perfect Indian in his appearance and habits," and a set-tler named David Hutchison, who knew him for twenty years, remarked that "he appeared to have lost his education almost entirely."[57]

Catawbas would have disagreed. Where others looked for, and found, the Indian in him, his own people were more likely to note his peculiarities. Despite his efforts to conform, Nettles was some-how tainted by his years in Williamsburg. He had been away from the Nation at just the point in the lives of young men when they learned the secrets of the hunt, listened to old men's stories, and in a host of ways prepared themselves to become full members of Catawba society. He came back with a Bible, a preference for breeches instead of breechclouts, and a flair for the dances favored in Williamsburg society.[58] Time never fully bleached out these stains of English civility, and to the end of his days he stood apart from his people as starkly as his signature on a lease stuck out from the marks made by other Catawba headmen. Indeed, the whites' very habit of singling Nettles out as "the educated Indian" indi-cated just how much an outsider he remained.[59] His uniqueness was proof that, however much his time at William and Mary had shaped his own life, he and his sponsors failed in the larger pur-pose of converting Catawbas.

Before dismissing Nettles as one more failed missionary, how-ever, it is wise to consider his story from the point of view of the Nation rather than the college. From this perspective his career takes on a more successful cast. Ironically, Catawbas may have sent Nettles to Williamsburg, not because they wanted to embrace an alien way of life, but because they hoped to avoid it. An educated Indian could strengthen rather than weaken the barrier between peoples, for he would have the tools to serve as a messenger across the cultural frontier. The Indians probably thought that young John Nettles had learned a lot of nonsense in Williamsburg, but they also knew the value of certain skills he brought home, and they wasted no time putting him to work. Within a year of his return he was at meetings with colonial officials, and the Nation was now insisting that it receive speeches in writing so "that the Interpreter (John Nettles) Might Read it to them and Explain it when they were by them Selves."[60] Over the years Nettles came to serve as a combination of goodwill ambassador and public relations director. Had a visitor arrived unannounced? Let John Nettles squire him around the village for a day. Was an amateur linguist and historian curious about the Nation? Have Nettles supply him with some Indian words and a story about Hagler. Did the local militia want a Catawba veteran on center stage at a muster? Tell Nettles to put on his uniform and saddle his horse. By teaching one Catawba so well, William and Mary had made it easier, not harder, for the rest to remain indifferent to the missionary message. They did not have to learn how to decipher all of the secrets of the alien world; John Nettles would handle that for them.[61]

Nowhere was this Catawba's importance to his people more evident than in a petition the Nation sent to South Carolina officials in 1801, which Nettles himself signed. "We ... [are] desirous to have two or three of our young boys taught to read and right," the petition said, "that the[y] might be an assistance to our Nation." The Indians' lack of enthusiasm for the full course of "Christianizing and Civilizing" was clear. They wanted no religious conversions, no fancy costumes, no silly dances, just basic knowledge needed to cope with the surrounding society. Moreover, only a handful of boys were to learn this trade, enough to ensure that Nettles (now getting on in years) would have a successor, not enough to fill every Catawba head with "a liberal and finished education."[62]

The petition's sentiments undermined the second major campaign to convert Catawbas before it even got under way. In 1803 a Baptist minister by the name of John Rooker settled near the Indians to begin "teaching and preaching."[63] As a veteran of the Revolutionary war and an avid hunter and fisherman, Rooker felt that he already had much in common with his Catawba charges. To strengthen his appeal, he enlisted the service of Robert Marsh, like Rooker a veteran of the war and a Baptist preacher. That Marsh was a Pamunkey Indian who had married a Catawba woman and lived in the Nation gave Rooker the entrée every missionary craved. Together with yet another minister, Rooker and Marsh hired a young teacher and built a school that doubled as a church. At first, Catawbas trooped in to hear what these men had to say, and Rooker, "a man of cheerful and happy disposition," dared think that his dreams would be fulfilled.[64]

Within a few short years the missionaries' "great hopes" had been destroyed, and Rooker, distinctly unhappy now, was convinced that "he left them worse than he found them." What had gone wrong? No one was quite sure: Catawbas went from "orderly" to "uneasy" to "disgusted," then they simply "Became unattentive" and drifted off. Most disappointing of all were the children, theoretically less steeped in Indian ways and therefore Rooker's principal targets. Until they were ten or eleven, Catawba youngsters were model students, obedient and easily taught, but the approach of adulthood changed them. "They would then take to travelling about with the older ones," Rooker noted, "and forget all they had learned." When the time came to acquire the ways of their own people, the young had retreated from the frontier between cultures and followed their elders down paths leading back into the Catawba world. In the end Rooker had accomplished nothing, and poor Marsh was not even able to convert his own wife.[65]

Apparently Rooker and John Nettles met at least once to compare notes on their progress. Here was a meeting that might indeed have fitted Benjamin Barton's description of "a melancholy task." Nettles had been reading the Bible to the Indians, including the tale of "dat Jonah who swallowed de whale." Rooker could tell a story of his own, about the catechism of an old warrior named Peter George who, when asked about the Resurrection, replied, "It was not so that dry bones rose again and put on flesh . . . [;] he saw their bones lays in the grave all the time."[66] In such garbled tales and commonsense retorts lay a life of frustration for anyone courageous enough or foolish enough to take on the Catawba mission. Yet in the same responses was the evidence to convict Drayton and the other heralds of Catawba collapse of hyperbole, if not outright falsehood.

With time some people gradually realized just how wrong the prophets of doom had been, how far Catawbas were from either extinction or civilization. "These wretched Indians," wrote an exas-

perated Robert Mills in 1826 in his compendium of South Carolina, "though they live in the midst of an industrious people, and in
an improved state of society, will be Indians still." Seventeen years
later the state's new agent, Joseph White, emphatically agreed that,
despite the "great efforts" made in recent decades to change them,
"they remain almost as Savage now as they were 50 years ago."
"Depend on it," he cautioned anyone still entertaining thoughts of
converting Catawbas, "they are a people who will not be forced into
measures."[67] The Catawba Nation was no paradise, and its inhabitants were no saints. They drank, often to excess. They fought, with
each other and with their tenants. They were illiterate and impov-
erished and, therefore, put upon by those who were neither. Yet
none of these facts warrants the common assumption that Catawba
culture was all but dead.

II

Like the ancestors with whom they were so often unfavorably
compared, Catawbas in the decades after the Revolution defied the
predictions of their demise. But even as the Indians were ignoring
Rooker and moving to the cadence set by calendar, kin, and headmen, events were shifting the ground beneath the Nation's feet.
The change stemmed from causes as various as Indian wars and
voting rights; in 1840 these forces came together to sweep away
the reservation and dump Catawbas into the ranks of the uprooted.

The decline of conflicts with traditional foes was the first shock
to the Nation. Until the late eighteenth century the old routine of
raid and reprisal, boasting and mourning, was largely intact. The
Revolutionary war dealt it a severe blow, however, leaving the
Shawnees and the rest of the Catawbas' enemies too weak and too
preoccupied with problems closer at hand to contemplate forays
southward. Add to this the large number of settlers now in the way
and the small number of Catawba scalps still available, and one
understands why the cycle of conflict wound down, until by 1810
the last war party had come and gone.[68]

Catawba men with no Indians to fight cast about desperately for
ways to carry on their craft. For a time, British troops and runaway
slaves made up for the dwindling stock of native foes, and militia

musters offered another place where a man's martial skills still commanded respect. Some Catawbas, "vagrant archers," headed for Camden or Charleston or Fayetteville in North Carolina to put on shows for the locals, hitting coins tossed in the air and pocketing the proceeds.[69] A handful of warriors went on still longer journeys. Shortly after the Revolution Peter Harris and three companions toured theaters in Great Britain, performing their songs and dances in front of packed houses.[70]

Most of these performances enjoyed only a short run. After 1783 the British were gone, and when they returned in 1812, South Carolina decided that it could do without Catawba assistance. Slaves still ran away, of course; but after the chaos of the Revolutionary war subsided, whites insisted on taking care of this problem themselves.[71] Eventually the militia muster was also closed to the warriors. Soon after the War of 1812, Governor David Williams, concluding that the Indians lacked proper military discipline, ordered them off the muster field, and they never returned.[72] By then, Peter Harris's stage career had come to an ignominious end. At the close of their tour the Indians' promoter had absconded, taking all of the profits and leaving them stranded in London. Though sympathetic Englishmen eventually paid the Catawbas' passage home, three of the despondent warriors jumped overboard en route, leaving Harris to make his way back to the Nation alone and dissuade others from repeating his folly. In the end only the "vagrant archers" remained, not to disappear until the early twentieth century.

More important than leaving Catawba warriors with nothing to do but entertain ignorant crowds was the impact peace had on the Nation as a whole. What happens when a people accustomed to choosing headmen from the ranks of its warriors finds that there are no more warriors? Catawbas faced this question in the 1830s as the last men who had seen action with Thomas Sumter or Nathanael Greene died; the Indians had no answer. After the death of General Jacob Ayers in 1837, the Nation was said to be "in a confused state," without a leader. "Acting chief" William Harris passed away shortly after Ayers, and the next in line, James Kegg, never won the wholehearted endorsement of his people. Kegg's claim to the position rested on seniority (at fifty-five, he was probably the oldest man in the Nation) and on the "royal blood" in which he took so much pride. They were not enough. Before long, Agent Joseph White sent word that many Indians "have no confidence in Kegg."[73] What was wrong with the man? Catawbas did not say, but one possibility is that Kegg had been born too late to be a warrior. To allow such a person to fill the place once held by Ayers, Scott, and New River may have been more than Catawbas could accept. Perhaps the Indians indirectly acknowledged their loss when, shortly after 1840, they stopped calling their leaders "General" or "Colonel." Chiefs there might still be; the military titles followed the warriors into oblivion.[74]

The thinning ranks of respected leaders could hardly have come at a worse time, for during these years Catawbas needed to marshal all of the resources at their disposal to fend off an attack on the Nation's land rights. As early as the 1780s the Nation's tenants were complaining about their situation, and they never stopped. Quite apart from any stigma attached to having an Indian landlord, the lessees argued, there was the rent itself. A farmer, after paying for the privilege of taking up the land, then faced annual rents with no prospect of owning what he had worked so hard to improve. As if a century's bondage were not enough, some had to hand over the rent more than once to satisfy Indians arguing over who had been assigned a particular tract. And all this, tenants groaned, for the right to be second-class citizens in their own state, to bear all of the burdens of citizenship and enjoy none of its blessings. They paid taxes on everything but their land, they served on juries, they trained with the militia; yet because they were not freeholders, they lacked the right to vote. To be subject to Indians and oppressed by the state as well was too much.[75]

By 1812, tenants had complained loudly enough that South Carolina gave them voting rights. Still they were not happy. Now that leaseholders had the vote, they wanted a new district of their own or, failing that, a polling place on the reservation.[76] The continual grumbling only masked the settlers' real fear, the insecurity of their tenure. If the Indians ever sold the reservation to outsiders, a lifetime of work could vanish, for there was no guarantee that the new owners would allow people to renew leases. In the late 1820s tenants panicked on hearing a rumor that unnamed "wealthy individuals" were planning to buy the reservation, wait for the current agreements to expire, and then take over the land.[77] There was only one solution: get title before somebody else did.

Around 1830 the Catawbas' tenants launched a campaign to acquire the land, and year after year they sent petitions to the state legislature. The campaign proceeded on two fronts. The first was to guarantee that title would go to the lessees if it went to anyone, a battle that was won with the passage of a law in 1838.[78] The second front, following naturally from the first, aimed at winning the reservation's title itself by persuading the Indians to give it up. As early as 1825 the South Carolina agent, Hugh White, was already thinking of the day when Catawbas would no longer have "the form . . . of a Nation" or at the very least "should think fit to sell and dispose of their lands and leases."[79] Now, with those ugly rumors of outside buyers floating about, it was time to act. In 1832 the state appointed commissioners to negotiate with the Catawba headmen, and the executive threw its weight behind the measure. Governor Robert Hayne paid the Nation a visit in its own village, and six years later one of Hayne's successors, Pierce Mason Butler, gave his blessing to the leaseholders' plans.[80]

Butler's speech laid out the reasons the state supported the tenants. Certainly he was concerned "that full justice should be secured to this last remnant of the official holders of the soil"; tradition, he proclaimed, demanded nothing less, for "the conduct of our State, towards the Indians, has, from the beginning been a pleasing feature in her history." At the same time, however, Butler could not help noticing that the lands in question were "among the most fertile in the State," that the Indians were "daily diminishing," and that "the State is deriving no revenue from a productive section of her territory." The course was clear: treat the Indians fairly, but get them out.

Catawbas were vulnerable to this mounting pressure, in part at least because they had reasons of their own to dislike the rent system. Trespassers sneaked onto the reservation, claimed that they had a legitimate lease granted sometime in the distant past, and demanded that Indians prove otherwise. A farmer with his papers in order could also make trouble. Some fell behind in their payments or pleaded with the headmen to "renew" the initial bargain without telling the Indians that this actually entailed an extension for another ninety-nine years.[81] To combat these abuses the Nation relied on its agents, heirs of the "good men" of an earlier era. The problem was that the agents were tenants themselves; like the fisherman cheating Catawbas or Hugh White looking toward the day when his Indian charges would be gone, they were sometimes more adversary than advocate. Further, after 1800 they answered, not to the Indians, but to the state. The governor had begun to appoint the agents, and he fended off Catawba efforts to reclaim that right.[82]

On top of the Nation's unhappiness and the tenants' offensive, the loss of traditional leaders seriously weakened the Catawbas' ability to resist the temptation to sell. As if to highlight the central role played by the Nation's elders, crucial setbacks in the Indians' defense of their homeland seemed to coincide with the death of certain revered people. It was shortly after General Jacob Scott and Sally New River died in late 1820 that the first crisis came. In February 1822, James Kegg, with no authority beyond his relationship to Sally New River (he would not sign a lease on the Nation's behalf or claim the title of General for another sixteen years), made a secret deal with one John Hutchison. In one stroke Kegg signed away rental rights to land in or near King's Bottoms and pledged that Turkey Hill, currently off limits to settlers, would also go to Hutchison if it ever went to anyone.[83] Little more than three years later—about the time two other important headmen, John Genet Brown and Thomas Brown, passed away—Catawbas made it official: for a bounty of one hundred dollars and a rent of ten dollars per year, much of King's Bottoms was gone.[84]

Tenaciously as the Catawbas held onto King's Bottoms, acquiring the right to lease that tract was easy compared to capturing ownership of the whole reservation. Some Catawbas, including James Kegg, were ready to sell out and join the Cherokees in North Carolina, where prospects seemed brighter. Against the would-be migrants of the Nation, "the aged among them" stood fast, and the elders' influence was so great that even those wishing to leave stayed on, "only waiting the death of their aged leaders." Toward the state the old headmen (probably including Lewis Canty, Jacob Ayers, and his brothers Jesse and John) took a stance equally unyielding. Year after year South Carolina appointed commissioners to negotiate with the Nation; year after year they got nowhere. At the Catawbas' meeting with Hayne the headmen "professed a readiness to treat, but never seemed ready."[85]

The waiting finally paid off. By 1838 Lewis Canty and the Ayers brothers were all dead, and under new leaders resistance quickly softened.[86] Jacob and John Ayers were hardly in the ground before acting chief William Harris and his wife Sally (Jacob's daughter) sold the lands in King's Bottoms where the two old men had lived. With every inch of the reservation now in other hands, Indians were reduced to "wandering through the Country, forming kind of camps." To escape this fate, some of the "leading ones" fell into the habit of traveling back and forth to the Cherokees in North Carolina, further loosening attachments to the Catawba River valley. At last, in late 1839 or early 1840, the Indians pronounced themselves ready to talk.[87]

Once Catawbas finally opened the door to negotiations, agreement was quickly reached. In March 1840 the two sides convened at Nation Ford, a crossroads on the west side of the river above the place where Thomas Brown's traders once had crossed. It took only two meetings to set the terms. Catawbas agreed to give up their lands; in return, the state pledged to spend five thousand dollars to purchase on the Nation's behalf a tract of land near the Cherokees "or in some other mountainous or thinly populated region" of the Indians' choosing. If no suitable site could be found, the Nation was to receive the five thousand dollars in cash. Whatever the outcome of the land search, the state would pay the Catawbas twenty-five hundred dollars when they left their current home and another fifteen hundred dollars every year for nine years. On March 3 the document was signed, and some of the Indians hurried back to North Carolina to look after the crops they had planted there.[88]

Compared to other southeastern Indians, Catawbas were fortunate. This was, after all, the Age of Indian Removal, and for most peoples removal did not mean wandering off to a Cherokee town or some other "thinly populated" area they fancied; it meant being uprooted at bayonet point and prodded a thousand miles west. No doubt more than one Cherokee, Creek, Choctaw, or Seminole would gladly have traded places. Still, celebrating the Nation's good fortune cannot obscure the significance of what happened at that crossroads overlooking the river. Three centuries after Europeans first saw the Catawba River, the descendants of the people Hernando de Soto met had signed away the last acre of land they could call home. With it went something impossible to define yet infinitely precious, so precious that Catawbas have been trying ever since to get it back.

III

The Treaty of Nation Ford was brief and succinct. Other land would be found and bought, Catawbas would move there, and the state would pay the balance of what it owed. With only three articles to observe, what could possibly go wrong? The answer, of course, was everything. In trying to carry out the agreement, South Carolina ran into a series of problems, and one wonders whether state officials ever looked longingly toward the bayonets as a way of felling the monster they had created.

The Catawba reservation was gone: the surveyors who moved in during the winter of 1841–1842 had made certain of that.[89] Still to be determined was what, if anything, would take its place. The treaty left the decision up to the Nation, and the Nation could not decide. The group headed by James Kegg had its heart set on joining the Cherokees who had escaped removal to the west by hiding out in the North Carolina mountains.[90] A smaller faction, looking farther afield for a new home, talked of joining the Choctaws or the Chickasaws who had been moved to Indian Territory beyond the Mississippi River.[91] Many Catawbas preferred to stay closer to home, though they could not decide where. Along the Saluda River, near Chester or Greenville, just across the North Carolina border—at one time or another all came under consideration, and emissaries were dispatched to look into the possibilities.[92] At least some Indians did not want to go anywhere. "The Catawbas are decidedly averse to removing to any considerable distance from their old boundary," the state's recently appointed agent Joseph White observed in January 1842, "and are, as far as I have been able to learn their wishes[,] inclined to Settle in the midst of the people with whom they have been born and raised."[93] Whether these natives were devoted to their neighbors or their ancestral lands is a matter for debate. What is beyond dispute is their reluctance to leave.

State authorities, presented with so many different choices, tried to carry out all of them and ended up succeeding in none. Plans to purchase land in some "mountainous or thinly populated" part of South Carolina never went beyond the emissaries' expeditions. Removal across the Mississippi generated more excitement but no results. When in 1848 the federal government committed five thousand dollars to help pay for the Catawbas' removal, the legislature in Columbia looked for ways to make up the difference in total cost and began discussing where to settle the Nation in the West. In their eagerness to see the plan work, the legislators dismissed Indian opposition: "a little steadiness" by the agent would take care of any Catawba reluctance, and Washington could deal with the western Indians who were to be the Nation's hosts. It was not to be so easy. Catawbas were doubtful, Chickasaws and Choctaws hostile. Though now and then a handful of Catawbas did head for Indian Territory in search of a better life, hopes for the Nation's removal to the West were dead.[94]

The biggest setback to the state's effort to oust Catawbas came, not from Chickasaws or Choctaws, but from the Cherokees and their white guardians. It was to the Cherokees that the treaty had pointed the Catawbas, and it was to the Cherokees that James Kegg, at least nominally the Nation's chief, was determined to lead them. But no one thought to ask the government of North Carolina about the idea. When Joseph White finally inquired in August 1841 "how far such a measure would be agreeable" to his sister state, he found Governor John M. Morehead "utterly opposed to this species of population being brought into our territories. . . . The same motives, which induce your State to get clear of such a population, induce us to keep clear of it, as far as we can," Morehead continued, "and the arguments which would readily occur to you, why our Cherokees should not be sent to your state to reside among, and amalgamate with your Catawbas, are equally strong, against your sending your Catawbas, to our State."[95] Morehead's logic was hard to fault, and South Carolina did not try. James Kegg did: the following spring he headed for Raleigh to lobby the governor, but he had no more success than White had.[96]

Kegg was not one to give up easily. Morehead might be able to block the purchase of a new reservation in North Carolina; he would have a harder time stopping Catawbas from simply moving in with Cherokees. The Cherokee council had already approved Kegg's idea, and throughout the early 1840s Catawbas drifted into the Cherokee embrace. From fifteen or twenty in 1842 the number of emigrants grew over the next few years until perhaps five times that many made their home in the North Carolina mountains.[97]

Even as the emigrants' population grew, their enthusiasm waned. The agent, and the treaty money, remained in South Carolina, and Catawbas who wanted a share of it had to make the long trek back. So many took this trip that one observer termed it "the system of traveling to So[uth] Carolina," and it left Indians with the sense that they were "running to and fro unsettled."[98] Moreover, people in North Carolina kept trying to meddle with them. In 1848 William Holland Thomas, the Cherokees' friend and protector, unveiled his proposal for an "Experiment . . . calculated to change their [Catawbas'] condition."[99] Catawbas probably could have handled Thomas as they once had dealt with Rooker and Nettles. The real obstacle was the Cherokees themselves. Perhaps Kegg was too optimistic when he expected the Nation to get along with Indians who still had men named "Catawba-Killer." Adding further insult, Cherokees thought that some of Kegg's people had "bad habits"; to break those habits the Cherokee council began to insist that the refugees give up their language and their identity. This threat was decisive. In September 1849 a visitor found that Catawbas were "not willing to remain with the Cherokees, nor remove with them."[100]

State officials, their more elaborate schemes crumbling, put their hopes in an "experiment" closer to home.[101] In November 1841, shortly after being rebuffed by North Carolina, agent White proposed to buy a small tract of land for the Indians and set them up as farmers. He selected 630 acres along the west side of the river, a choice Catawbas applauded because it was within the borders of the old reservation and included some of their settlements. White persuaded fifteen or twenty Indians to join an equal number who had stayed on there since the treaty, and in the spring of 1843, using tools he supplied, they were hard at work getting a crop in the ground. By the end of the year Governor James Henry Hammond was pleased to report that almost all of the Indians still in the state were now living on the new reservation.[102]

Hammond did not know it, but the high point of White's program had already passed. Even as the governor spoke, the settlement was falling apart, and the Indians were dispersing. No one asked them what went wrong, and the disappointed agent volunteered no explanation beyond their "want of continued and pursuing industry and management." White himself may have been the problem. Kegg and his followers in North Carolina complained that the agent was too far away; those still at home might well have felt him too close. White had begun his career as agent with every intention of paying "strict regard to the permanent interest of the Indians, and their wishes and convenience." He soon changed his mind. Catawbas, he observed in early 1842, were "thoughtless"; therefore, he would have to do their thinking for them.[103] The Indians who moved to White's experimental farm were accustomed to being left alone. Placing them in the hands of this man, who had become convinced that they were "individually and collectively taken the most lazy, dissipated, worthless people that could possibly exist," was to guarantee failure.[104] By fall, having harvested nothing, the farmers left, and for years the new reservation sat almost empty (at one point only an old Catawba woman and six children were there) while state officials debated the wisdom of putting it up for sale.[105]

The failure of one experiment after another left Catawbas living everywhere and nowhere, without lands and without homes.[106] Just how scattered Catawbas were did not become clear until 1849, when South Carolina attempted to assess its Indian problem by undertaking a census of the Nation. Governor Whitemarsh B. Seabrook assigned the job to Benjamin Massey, one of the state's representatives at the Treaty of Nation Ford and now, nine years later, again sitting on a commission to look into Catawba affairs. Massey soon learned that Catawbas were hard to find. His first stop was a small farm just over the North Carolina line, where he knew an Indian named Billy Ayers had moved in the early 1840s, but

Ayers was dead and his family gone. The commissioner had better luck when he retraced his steps to South Carolina; 14 Indians lived in their old neighborhood along the Catawba, and 13 more were just southwest of there. Then it was back to North Carolina to track down one living near Asheville and another 50-odd among the Cherokees. On a tip from these people Massey headed back into South Carolina looking for more. He was fortunate enough to meet Catawbas on the road at several points, some heading into North Carolina, others on their way to Spartanburg. From them the weary commissioner was able to compile a roster of 110 names to complete his task and confirm the Nation's dispersal.[107]

Catawbas had always left home at certain seasons to pursue game or enemies, to gather nuts or clay. The difference was that now they no longer returned home, in part because home was gone. In part, too, however, their dispersal stemmed from differences within the Nation that precluded living together even in some new place. In the autumn of 1842 the headmen informed Joseph White that they "were altogether averse to settling upon any lands whatever," for if they did, "disputings wrangling and quarreling would of a certainty ensue and consequently dispersion and confusion would take place with them."[108] So Catawbas went their separate ways, and the Nation fell apart. Toward the end of the decade the Indians still in the state were "totally disorganized," and those in North Carolina "acknowledge no Chief, and have no organization," surviving "as well as they can as men individuals and families." "As a Nation," Governor David Johnson concluded in 1847, "they are, in effect, dissolved."[109]

As it splintered Catawbas into fragments, the Treaty of Nation Ford also plunged them deeper into poverty.[110] No more rents were coming in, and the state was slow to make up the difference. Catawbas were never to see the five thousand dollars promised them if South Carolina failed to spend it on land, or the twenty-five hundred dollars to be paid "at or immediately after" their removal. In confirming the treaty the state legislature, apparently without consulting the Indians, had changed the terms so that these funds were earmarked *only* for the purchase of land and "the establishment and outfit" of the Indians on that land. Of the fifteen hundred dollars per year due them through the end of the decade, natives saw not a cent in 1841 or 1842. "It will be remembered," agent White answered dryly when the state assembly brought up money matters in early 1843, "that the Indians have not been the recipients of any appropriations heretofore made. Appropriations upon paper furnish too light a diet for Indians to subsist upon." White's sarcasm barely concealed his anger: he was supplying Catawbas out of his own pocket, and his neighbors felt besieged by beggars.[111]

Even after White did begin to receive the promised funds, the system remained less than ideal from the Indians' point of view.[112] The agent generally used the money to buy goods and then handed these items over to any Catawbas who approached him. The arrangement discriminated by distance. Those nearby, while they had their own problems, were able to knock at the agent's door whenever they needed something. Catawbas farther away had to make the long trip themselves or ask someone else to pick up a few things, trusting that the middleman would not keep the merchandise or sell it on the way back. It was, in a sense, state-subsidized begging; Catawbas had to come to White, hands outstretched, and accept what he decided to give them. After the cash transactions of the past, it seemed humiliating and unfair. "The great grandfathers of we the Catawbas come into the country without an angent," the Indians pointed out in 1844, and two years later they were "clamorous against the Agent, because he did not feel at liberty to give them the uncontrolled use of the funds."[113]

White eventually tired of the state's demands that he do more and the Indians' insistence that he do less. He had tried, but he considered these Indians hopeless. "They are but the fragment of a Tribe," he moaned in 1848, "without order, law, industry, sobriety, honesty, truth, or motion to action, utterly destitute [of] every quality that is requisite towards forming the character of a human being in the pale of civilization." What should South Carolina do, then? White was "clearly of the Opinion that [the] best Service the State can do for them, is to divide their funds and pay to the head of each family, . . . their proportion in money, and let them go to that State which the Savageness of their character so preeminently qualify them to fill." The Assembly, after sending Massey and other commissioners to investigate matters the following summer, was inclined to agree "that the plan heretofore pursued by the State . . . does not work well." Like White, most observers blamed Catawbas. The state, "fostering and parental, . . . was always defeated by the waywardness and Migratory habits of the Indians themselves," wrote Archibald S. Whyte, one of Massey's colleagues on the 1849 commission. Time and time again, South Carolina's "benevolent intentions have been thwarted by the vacillation and waywardness of the Indians. The fault," Whyte repeated, "was not with the Agent, but on the part of the Indians."[114]

Despite the frustration of the Nation's putative benefactors, they could not bring themselves to do what many must, in weaker moments, have longed to do: sell the new reservation and exile the Catawbas. Massey, Whyte, and the other commissioners appointed by Governor Seabrook in 1849 were asked whether it was "expedient to dispose of their Land" and whether "humanity require[d] that they should be forced to reside in their new settlement in North Carolina, or elsewhere beyond the limits of this State." To both questions the answer was no. The Catawbas' almost unblemished record of friendship, memories of their patriotism, and pity combined to stay the state's hand. Much later someone recalled that when "the poor Indians backed out [of removal], . . . nobody had the heart to use force, as they had used [it] in Georgia a few years before."[115]

The decision to do nothing gave the Indians a future. Even as Governor Johnson was pronouncing the Nation dissolved and Benjamin Massey was mapping that dissolution, Catawbas were turning toward home. Dispersal and internal disputes did not erase memories of living together on common ground. In 1844, Catawbas in North Carolina longed to "make our nation whole" again. "We have no home," they wrote, and "we feel lost without a home."[116] At the time, these petitioners were looking west toward a new land where they might make a fresh start. By decade's end the Nation's thoughts shifted back to the sliver of ancestral land that was still theirs. In late 1847 came the first hints that Catawbas were freeing themselves from the Cherokee orbit. A year later James Kegg and ten or eleven followers had returned from North Carolina, and over the next two years more kept straggling in until by the fall of

1850 one hundred Catawbas were back, leaving behind only a handful among the Cherokees. If talk of moving yet again never altogether ceased, it also never led to action. Catawbas were home for good.[117]

IV

One reason to let the Indians come together again along the Catawba was the expectation "that they would soon die out and disappear and settle the trouble that way." As they had done in the past, outsiders predicted that the Nation was "soon to be extinct" and that before long "the last sod will be thrown on . . . [its] grave."[118] Catawbas, announced one observer, "have lost the remarkable elasticity of character which peculiarly distinguished them among the aboriginal nations." With that loss went any chance of their surviving. In 1856 an amateur linguist was certain that the Catawba tongue was "not only a *dead language*, but a *language of the dead*."[119]

The news would have come as a surprise to the Indians. To them the future might have looked bleak; few would have suspected that they did not have one. Once again the miscalculations of the self-proclaimed experts can be traced to wishful thinking and sheer ignorance. Catawbas were no more willing to open their lives to an outsider in 1850 than they had been in 1800 or 1700, and upon their return home they were often seen but seldom heard. One Indian woman who lived for years near Fishing Creek was a mystery even to whites who saw her frequently. "There is so little poetry about Nancy that I can write neither fiction nor history of her," observed one. "Indeed she appears to me as apathetic as an icicle." Inhabitants of the reservation were also aloof toward prying strangers. The Nation's few visitors found the natives "proud and reticent, seldom speaking unless spoken to." Sometimes a bottle of whiskey made them more talkative; sometimes nothing worked.[120]

Information from a Catawba willing to talk could be as misleading as silence. For example, Patsey George and John Scott assured one inquisitor that they "were positive that the Catawbas never had, as far back as memory and tradition of their tribe go, any

Figure 8. Margaret (Wiley) Brown. 1906. *Courtesy of American Philosophical Society*

Figure 9. Sally (Brown) Gordon. 1938. *Courtesy of American Philosophical Society*

Indian names; but had always (as far as their knowledge and tradition extend) been know[n] by English names." Only later did others find out that Indians in the Nation—including George (*Yáwe'i*) and Scott (*Siman*)—often went by Catawba names until about 1900.[121] Students of Catawba affairs, repeating the mistakes of their predecessors, were blinded by incorrect assumptions and Indian obfuscations. When one A. McCullough begged funds for a Catawba who claimed that he had not received any of the state's money, agent White dismissed the request, scoffing that McCullough "has suffered himself to be made an Indian dupe." McCullough was not alone.[122]

Besides the undeniable fact of Catawba survival, the best proof of how wrong the chroniclers of collapse were lies in the Catawba children who grew up in the mid-nineteenth century. After 1900 a handful of these people, now among the Nation's elders, rehearsed their formative years at the prodding of Frank G. Speck and other anthropologists. The principal pools of Catawba memory tapped by this new breed of strangers were Susan (Harris) Owl (1847–1934), Robert Harris (1867–1954), Margaret Wiley Brown (1837–1922), and Mrs. Brown's children Sally (Brown) Gordon (1865–1952) and Samuel Blue (1873–1959). Their recollections help to map Catawba culture during the years after the Treaty of Nation Ford. Sketchy as it is, the map reveals that the Indians, again defying the experts, lived in a distinctive cultural landscape.[123]

In large part the distinctiveness was due to the abiding influence of older Catawbas. The deaths of aged leaders before 1840 had done nothing to diminish the Indians' customary respect for the elderly. Benjamin Massey discovered just how deep a child's devotion to these people could be when he agreed to take a Catawba named Allen Harris along with him during his 1849 peregrinations in search of Indians. To the commissioner's dismay, on the day of departure Harris showed up with a young girl in tow, explaining that "she was so anctious to see her grandmother that he was oblige[d] to take her with him."[124] The Catawbas Speck met formed similar attachments to people whose own lives stretched back toward the beginning of the nineteenth century. John Scott, born in 1826, was Margaret Brown's half-brother, and Patsey George, seven years older, was her aunt. Billy George, who signed

Figure 10. Samuel Blue. 1933. *Courtesy of American Philosophical Society*

Figure 11. Mrs. Samson (Susan Harris) Owl(?). 1927. *Courtesy of American Philosophical Society*

the treaty in 1840 at the age of twenty-four, was also related to Speck's informants and dispensed traditional lore until his death in the last decade of the century. Together these and other Catawbas helped link the eighteenth century to the twentieth.[125]

Young Catawbas learned from their elders in several ways. Samuel Blue picked up a lot simply by eavesdropping on adult conversations. His belief that it was best to hunt during a new moon came from what "he had heard the older people say," and he knew that the aurora borealis was an ill omen because he remembered "hearing the old people comment upon its meaning." Blue also satisfied his "great interest in the old men's affairs" by tagging along. "I followed them about," he recalled. "When they cleared off a place and had a pow wow or a dance I was always there." Blue's quest for knowledge of the old ways ultimately led him to live with a traditionalist named Tom Stevens so that the lessons could go on continuously.[126]

Even those who did not go to such lengths to get an education routinely copied their elders' example and paid attention to the tales they told. Robert Harris, for one, was well aware of the purpose served by the stories he had heard from his parents or grandparents. "It was understood by the Catawba of a generation ago," Harris told Speck, "that story-telling was intended to develop the mind, to make children think, to teach them the ways of life. It gave them . . . something to think about; otherwise they would lack the means of developing their minds through the experiences recounted of others concerning human beings and animals."[127] The voice of experience spoke with authority on the reservation after 1850, and children like Blue, Brown, and Harris listened carefully.

Those spinning tales and tutoring Blue spoke Catawba, not English. Margaret Brown and Robert Harris, who as children knew only Catawba, were the rule rather than the exception until after the Civil War.[128] This language barrier was a vital part of Catawba education. Language expresses a people's collective consciousness, its own special way of interpreting the world. By itself, then, language is both a vehicle for transmitting the essence of a culture and a powerful tool of socialization in that culture. It leads people to speak—and therefore also to think—according to established formulas. Indians brought up to think Catawba during the mid-nine-

Figure 12. Robert L. Harris and Wife (Nettie Owl Harris). About 1920. *Courtesy of American Philosophical Society*

teenth century were equipped to cross the threshold into the mental world of their ancestors.[129]

Entrance to that world came by way of a curriculum steeped in the past. Though whites asserted that Catawbas "forget the past" and "know nothing of their ancestors," it is clear that history was among the first subjects a child learned.[130] Indeed, Indians considered it so vital to keep the past alive that they apparently designated one person to serve as their historian. In 1849 the position was held by Nancey George, at seventy the oldest Catawba "and the one according to their costom that keeps the records of the nation." What Nancey George knew besides the name and age of every living Catawba is a mystery; Massey, the only person to take note of her role, was interested in nothing else.[131] But her own experience included Nettles, New River, Thomas Spratt, and John Rooker, and it is easy to envision Nancey telling Margaret Brown about these men as well as others of whom she had heard as a child.

Few Indians could match Nancey George's memory. All, however, grew up with an appreciation of their people's history. The ways of "the ancient people" were the topic of many a conversation, as were the battles these people had waged against their foes.[132] Tuscaroras, Shawnees, and Chickasaws probably peopled more than one Catawba child's dreams, and some of these dreams may have been nightmares, for the nineteenth-century storytellers stressed that other Indians were "wild people," "mean people," "not good," "very bad." Lest a child become too frightened, the tales usually had a happy ending. A Catawba war party caught the Shawnee raiders and tied their scalps to a pole beside the road; a Chickasaw ended up stuffed inside the belly of his own horse. "Whenever the Shawnee came they were killed," one story concluded with comforting finality.[133]

The greatest Catawba hero of all, Hagler, occupied a special place in the Nation's memory. Forty years after his death, the narrative of the Shawnee attack that ended his life—and the Catawbas' glorious revenge on his killers—circulated on the reservation, and four decades after that the Indians still recalled his exploits "with much feeling." Even the skeptic who in 1867 was positive that Catawbas had no recollection of their ancestors had to admit that they still referred to Hagler as "the great chief." What more children learned of Hagler has been lost in the silence that engulfs so much of the Nation's oral history. We know only that his star shone brighter than any other in the galaxy of Catawba heroes.[134]

A young person's passage into the past was made easier still by the nearby reminders of olden times. Children not only heard about the ways of the ancient people; they could visit the towns where these people had lived and the graveyards where they lay buried. Children not only listened to stories of bloody conflicts; they could return to the battleground and try to imagine for themselves what it had been like. Children not only sat through the narratives of Hagler's exploits; they could be taken to his secret resting place and pay homage. Connecting words to places must have deepened the Nation's attachment to its history, ensuring that past and present would coexist in the Catawba mind.[135]

Bringing the past to life gave people like Harris and Blue a clear sense of their identity as Indians—as quite unlike surrounding whites and blacks—and as Catawbas, not Shawnees or Cherokees. "The people who lived on the land outside were different," began the account of the unfortunate Chickasaw, making explicit the message in virtually every tale.[136] The Catawbas' penchant for drawing boundaries was so deeply ingrained that they even continued to insist some people on the land *inside* were different. In the 1840s the Nation's Cheraws were still distinguished from Catawbas by language, if nothing else. At least these two peoples "lived in great harmony"; Pamunkeys who joined the Nation were not so fortunate. Almost a century after Robert Marsh married a Catawba, the Nation looked down on his descendants because of their supposedly "sullen disposition." Perhaps Pamunkeys were sullen because, after several generations and many marriages into Catawba families, they were tired of trying to fit in.[137]

Anchoring Blue's generation firmly in history was essential, but it would do little to help that generation cope with the present. To do that, the young must learn how to understand their surroundings. Here, too, the ancient people had advice to offer. Many of the tales told to children on the reservation in the mid-nineteenth century explained the mysteries of the universe. How did the chipmunk acquire his stripes, the opossum his strange grin and tail, the blackbird his red wings, the robin his red breast? Where did storms come from, what made people sicken and die, why did water flow? Catawba elders had answers to all these questions and more, answers that helped render the world understandable to their young audience.[138]

While explaining these mysteries, storytellers also supplied the tools to deal with the powerful forces impinging on daily life. Throwing ashes out the door could clear up bad weather. If that failed, Margaret Brown and her daughter knew prayers the ancient people spoke to avert storms. Prayers or charms could also drive away the little wild people, mischief-makers said to inhabit the nearby woods, and there were formulas for silencing witchowls. Ghosts required a stouter defense, for Catawbas, like their forebears in colonial times, knew that "the shade, or shadow, of a dead person" or "evil spirits entering the body" caused disease.[139] Praying to be good sometimes helped, but careful treatment of the deceased was far more important. During the nineteenth century a death in the Nation triggered an elaborate ritual that involved fasting, wakefulness, a taboo on speaking the name of the deceased, and blowing ashes on the dead person to appease the spirit. If the spirit was satisfied, it would return after three days to drink from a pot of water placed at the head of the corpse; rippling water in the pot signaled that the deceased would not trouble the living.[140]

None of these efforts to propitiate ghosts guaranteed good health. But if illness did strike, Catawba elders had an arsenal of weapons ready. While living among the Cherokees in the 1840s, Catawbas had impressed their hosts with their medical skills. Upon their return home these Indians must have taught their craft to the young, for a century later Frank Speck collected almost one hundred curative items that could cope with everything from backache and boils to warts and worms. The secret to success lay in proper treatment as much as in strong medicine. Blowing an herbal remedy onto a patient, scratching a wound with fish teeth to speed the healing, plunging into the river in order to let its curative powers do their work—all of these arts of the healer, practiced by Margaret Brown on the advice of the ancient people, proved the enduring value of the traditional wisdom.[141]

During their short stay among the Cherokees, Catawbas gained renown not only as doctors but as "leaders of the dance," and the two skills may have been related. Dances remained a regular feature of reservation life until the late nineteenth century, and at least some of them, like funerals and medicines, were performed with the invisible world in mind.[142] The wild goose dance and the bear dance may have represented attempts to appease the spirits of animals killed, while another dance performed at harvest time, like its earlier incarnations, could have combined gratitude for the crops just in with a prayer for future success. The participants in these affairs made a point of wearing "native costumes," and a specific person, the "driver," directed each occasion, perhaps to ensure conformity to instructions handed down from an earlier day.[143]

Even armed with prayers and ceremonies, a Catawba could not hope to conquer the mysterious forces dominating the world. One could, however, be prepared by knowing the proper signs, and omens were an important part of the stories old passed along to

Figure 13. Medicine Blowing. *Courtesy of American Philosophical Society*

young. A falling star and a salamander "barking" meant death or some unforeseen trouble, the hoot of an owl good news. Certain birds predicted the weather, while "birds . . . talking" and a "red bird flying up" foretold a visit or some other unexpected event. By teaching children to decipher these signs, the ancient lore helped future generations interpret their surroundings.[144]

A bird's meaning, a river's healing power, a ghost's demands—such matters were more resistant to change than was the business of earning a living. In this more mundane sphere a Catawba boy found it harder to heed the advice of ancestors who had been warriors and hunters. Recollections of the bear dance only brought home more poignantly that the men of Sam Blue's generation had killed none of these animals and probably never would.[145] Bereft of many of their traditional tasks, Catawba men had to look for another source of income and perhaps, too, another way to earn respect, to be good at something that mattered. Many refused to undertake the search, and it was said that the Nation's men, "still too proud to work, live on in worthless dignity." Some hired themselves out to nearby planters or hauled wood to nearby towns, and eventually, entering a place where the wisdom of their elders had said they should not go, they made their way into the fields and took over farming from the women.[146]

Picking up a hoe or hitching up a plow did not divorce Catawba men from the past, however. In the hearts and minds of many, old skills mingled with new. Billy George, who worked on a nearby farm, never lost his dexterity with the bow and arrow. As a young man Robert Harris, a carpenter by trade, had followed his ancestor Peter Harris and signed on with a traveling show.[147] And most men still headed into the woods in search of game. The persistence of a hunting tradition, however attenuated from former days, gave substance to the ancient words about the chase. Tales of the man who fell asleep and missed a deer reminded listeners of the importance of staying alert, just as the fox who shared his kill with a raccoon taught the virtue of sharing, a message reinforced by the old rule about young hunters' giving away the fruits of their first success.[148] Robert Harris's life bore little resemblance to Peter's a century earlier; nonetheless, men like Peter Harris could still speak to their descendants.

Among Catawba women, past pursuits were more relevant, largely because of pottery's increasing importance to the Nation's economy.[149] The manufacture of pots was more than a business, however; it was central to both personal and collective identity. Each step in the process, from finding the right clay and molding it to firing and finishing it, had to be learned from a master, and a girl apprenticed herself to her mother or grandmother in order to gain acceptance into this prestigious guild. Her course of study was in its essence profoundly conservative. Year after year women returned to the same clay pits, some of these sites so secret that Catawbas left curious outsiders behind. While preparing a vessel they observed taboos against touching certain animals and obeyed the "old people's" strictures against decorating the finished piece with snakes or lizards. The debt to the past acquired tangible form when a girl inherited pipe molds and polishing stones from her tutors, precious relics that she would hand on to the future in due course.[150]

Pottery gave shape and meaning to life on the reservation during these years. Pots were everywhere—waiting to be fired, cooling nearby, already in use or for sale, lying broken and discarded in the corner—and everywhere were the scrapers, pebbles, pestles, and molds that went into their manufacture. Everywhere, too, were people heading off to dig clay or sell pots, to stoke the fire or check on the progress of the latest batch. At the center of it all were the Catawba women, artisans who, perpetuating an ancient craft, perpetuated the old ways.

Making pots and shooting arrows, reading signs and speaking Catawba, Samuel Blue and his sister, like their mother before them and her mother before her, grew up in a place where old taught young what it meant to be a Catawba, where the bearers of a distinctive cultural tradition owned a monopoly on a child's mind. Outsiders interested only in what Indians recall of ancient times have questioned how traditional this curriculum was, sighing when a white glove run across the shelf of nineteenth-century Catawba life picked up so few smudges of aboriginal dust. To these people, Catawbas were hopelessly tainted by centuries of contact with Europeans. Potters sometimes turned their hands to bookends, paperweights, and ashtrays, and hunters were lucky to bag a raccoon. Moreover, livestock were scattered through everything the Nation's elders told the young in the mid-nineteenth century. The Catawba word for *buffalo* was "cattle wild," and *groundhog* translated as "hog in ground." In the repertoire of the storyteller the tale of the fox sharing with the raccoon stood alongside one about a boy who was raised by hogs. The dance driver was as likely to organize a horse dance as a bear dance, and recipes for survival included methods of tanning cowhide. After finding a pig or a horse everywhere they look, aboriginalists have tended to conclude that Blue's generation learned little of the old ways after all, and most of what they did learn they forgot.[151]

Figure 14. Polishing Stone. *Courtesy of American Philosophical Society*

Figure 15. Catawba Cooking Pot. Probably early twentieth century. *Courtesy of McKissick Museum, University of South Carolina. Photograph by Gordon Brown*

Figure 16. Catawba Bowl Pipe. Before 1920. *Courtesy of McKissick Museum, University of South Carolina. Photograph by Gordon Brown*

Figure 17. Indian Head Vase. By Sara Ayers, 1979. *Courtesy of McKissick Museum, University of South Carolina. Photograph by Gordon Brown*

Far from proving Catawba culture bankrupt, such changes were crucial to the Nation's survival. The new words Speck jotted down testified to the continuing vitality of the Catawba language and suggest why the power of Catawba speech remained undiminished well into the nineteenth century. The same is true of the texts he recorded. The specific origin of these tales was of no importance to a child like Robert Harris. Whether they were about pigs or Shawnees, horses or bears, the stories were Catawba because they came from the Nation's elders rather than someone else. All had the sanction of tradition whether they were traditional by scholarly standards or not; they belonged to the ancient people even if those people never would have recognized them. Catawbas were no more able or willing to live in the past than were their white and black neighbors. These Indians neither held onto some fossilized aboriginal way nor abandoned their culture for another. Instead, they continued to do what they had always done: take ideas, customs, crafts, and objects from beyond their cultural frontier and then make those things their own. This creative response enabled Catawbas to adjust to changing conditions while keeping intact the core of their ancient culture.

V

Like aboriginalists, today the new peoples of the piedmont tend to look for natives who are not there, as if the only real Indians are dead Indians. It would be an exaggeration to say that Catawbas are forgotten but not gone while upcountry natives generally are gone but not forgotten—but not much of one. Visitors to the Catawba reservation are few compared to the crowds that flock to Carolina museums exhibiting reconstructions or remains of vanished Indian civilizations.[152] More popular still is the hobby of poking through the detritus left by societies long gone. For generations people have been plucking potsherds and arrowheads from the piedmont's surface to add to their personal collections or put on display in store windows. Abandoned Indian villages, which promise a rich harvest of these relics, have also served to pique curiosity and remind the living of the dead.[153]

Most intriguing of all have been the mounds. From the lands of

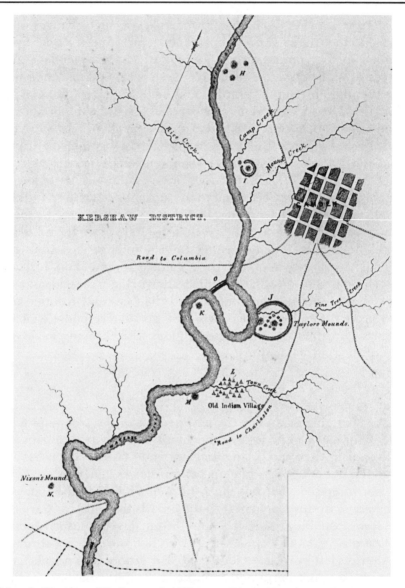

Map 8. "Ancient Works on the Wateree River, Kershaw District, South Carolina." *Drawn by William Blanding. In E. G. Squier and E. H. Davis,* Ancient Monuments of the Mississippi Valley: Comprising the Results of Extensive Original Surveys and Explorations, Smithsonian Contributions to Knowledge, *I (Washington, D.C., 1848), facing p. 105*

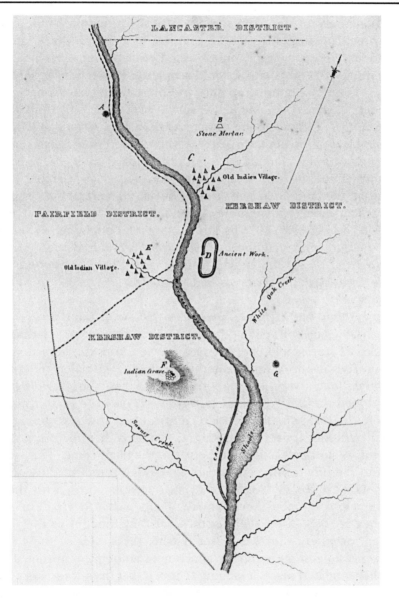

the Congarees to the haunts of the Monacans, mounds have cast their spell on the locals.[154] The largest of these, a cluster near Camden that was probably built by the Cofitachiques, even became something of a tourist attraction. During the Revolution American troops dined in a house atop one, and fifteen years later a party of Camden citizens paid the same site a visit. "You will think me *Mound Mad*," exclaimed one woman in 1849 after writing at length to her brother of her own trip to "those interesting relicks of a race passed away."[155] Many people were indeed a bit crazy about mounds. Coveting one of their very own, they proclaimed any bump on the land an ancient Indian burial site and all but begged it to reveal its secrets. Genuine or not, the Indian mounds, like the old villages, were silent. "Who knows what tales might be related of this" mound on a neighboring plantation, wondered the *Camden Gazette* in 1816, "if the Indian traditions had been preserved; or if the Catawbas and Waterees had produced an Herodotus or an Homer."[156]

Maybe they had. Apparently places that stood mute at the approach of whites still spoke clearly enough to the original piedmont peoples. If stories told over the past two centuries can be believed, certain sites in the Virginia interior retained a special significance to natives long after the last aboriginal inhabitants supposedly had abandoned the area. Thomas Jefferson was only the first of many to note the sudden appearance of unidentified Indians who, after making straight for a certain mound, lingered there before disappearing as suddenly and mysteriously as they had come. This went on into the nineteenth century, to the bewilderment of those who happened to see it. Neither they nor we can know who these "strange looking men" were, why they came, what they said to one another as they gazed at the spot, what they thought as they departed, or where they went. But if true, the stories of these pilgrimages suggest an enduring attachment among the uprooted to another time and place, a longing to touch that distant territory.[157]

Catawbas did not have to go on a pilgrimage to find the past; it was all around them, and not just in the broken pots or arrowheads that whites were so fond of. In the Nation the old villages were noisy places. One evening at dusk Margaret Brown's parents stood outside their house, and "from across the river, where the ancient people had lived, they could hear somebody beating a pot-drum very hard (and people dancing and singing). But there was nobody over there, where all the noise came from."[158] Other Indians also heard drumbeats echo across the Catawba and peered in vain through the fog or gathering darkness to see who was there. A few caught a glimpse of figures in the mist, and at least one got a closer look. Near one of the old towns, the anthropologist John Swanton was told during a visit to the Catawbas, "a man once saw a woman dressed in the ancient manner, with a bundle on her back and bows and arrows (!)."[159] Swanton's editorial exclamation speaks volumes for the void that still divided the Catawba world from his own. To the Indians such stories were far from quaint fables, just as villages were more than silent reminders of "a race passed away." The tales, like the towns, spoke to those who knew how to listen, helping them to be "Indians still."

Epilogue

I Have Been Incommoded:
George Washington's Journey

I have . . . been incommoded, at this place [Mount Vernon], by a visit of several days, from a party of a dozen Catawbas; and should wish while I am in this retreat, to avoid a repetition of such guests.

—George Washington

IN THE spring of 1791, President George Washington set out from Philadelphia on a tour of the southern states. His later assessment of the trip reveals its original purpose: "It has enabled me to see with my own eyes the situation of the country," he wrote after his return, "and to learn more accurately the disposition of the people ["towards the general government"] than I could have done by any information."[1] Like some monarch on a royal progress, the new president planned not only to see but to be seen; he would help unify the fragile nation by spreading his presence and his prestige widely among its citizens. With these aims in mind, Washington left the federal capital on March 21 in the company of an aide, a valet de chambre, a coachman, a postilion, and two footmen. A carriage bore the general; the others either rode one of the five saddlehorses or drove the supply wagon.[2]

Washington had prepared for the trip as he would for a military campaign. First he charted the route and estimated mileage; next he calculated how long he would pause at each stop; to this total he then added eight days for the "casualties" of bad weather, lame horses, or disabled wagons. What the old soldier called his "line of march" was plotted to carry him through the major population centers lying south of the Potomac River.³ After a short stay at Mount Vernon, the party proceeded along the coastal plain, pausing at Fredericksburg and Richmond before passing through the North Carolina settlements of Halifax, Tarboro, New Bern, and Wilmington. On April 27 Washington entered South Carolina, where he visited Georgetown and Charleston. The citizens of Georgia got a look at their new leader at Savannah and Augusta before he swung north again, stopping to see the new South Carolina capital at Columbia and pausing at Camden before heading up the Catawba-Wateree River valley into North Carolina. Not until June 12 did he finally make it back to Mount Vernon.

Throughout his long journey Washington paid close attention to the land and its prospects. Most of the time he traveled along the coastal plain and was unimpressed. The road from New Bern to Wilmington passed through "the most barren country I ever beheld," and farther south among the pine forests the country was much the same, if not worse. Not until the party made its way up the Wateree Valley were there signs of improvement. North of Camden "the Lands took quite a different complexion" and "began to assume a very rich look." Before then, the countryside had a dreary, "perfect sameness."⁴

Though the people Washington met along the way also displayed a certain sameness, they were anything but dreary. At every stop enthusiastic crowds greeted the president, crowds that had often been waiting for hours to catch a glimpse of him.⁵ The approach, the visit, and the departure quickly fell into a rut. Well before the famous traveler reached the outskirts of a community, a party of militia and local dignitaries would ride out to escort him into town. These welcoming committees were so persistent, and the dust their horses raised so annoying, that Washington tried to avoid them or, failing that, send them home. He rarely succeeded, and his arrival in each village or city took on the appearance of a noisy parade. The parade became even noisier when the inhabitants saluted their hero with artillery and conducted him through the streets to the public square. From that point on, the excited citizenry kept its honored guest busy with a round of ceremonies that would have overwhelmed a lesser man. One public dinner after another celebrated the visit. At each of these affairs, the addresses and replies, toasts and balls, fireworks and bonfires were so predictable that the celebrants might have been following the same script.

Local variations on the theme helped relieve the monotony. In Columbia, 150 people crowded into the still-unfinished capitol for the privilege of dining with the great Washington. The citizens of Camden had no statehouse to show off; they had lost that fight to Columbia a few years before. To compensate they made a point of mentioning Baron Johann de Kalb, the Revolutionary war hero killed there, and they later took the president to inspect the baron's tomb as well as the old British headquarters.[6] But it was in Charleston that he received the most extravagant hospitality. There the ladies outdid themselves in a lavish display of their feelings. At a gathering on May 4 "most of them wore ribbons with different inscriptions, expressive of their respect for the President, such as, 'long live the President,' etc. etc." Two days later "the homage of his feminine admirers was in their hairdress. Nearly all the coiffures included a bandeau or fillet on which was painted a sketch of Washington's head or some patriotic, sentimental reference to him."[7]

The inhabitants of Charleston, Camden, Columbia, and the other cities were not the only ones to see the new nation's leader. On Friday, May 27, when Washington stopped for the night at Robert Crawford's north of Waxhaw Creek on the road from Camden to Charlotte, several Catawba headmen came to see him. Washington did not say who was in the party, but we can guess. New River, an old man now but still an imposing figure, probably headed the delegation. At his elbow would be ranking officers like John Ears, John Brown, and Jacob Scott. Perhaps John Nettles was there, too, as their interpreter.[8] Everyone but Nettles would be wearing the scalp lock and facial tattoos that marked them as warriors, the clanking silver breastplates signifying that they were men of distinction, and the military uniforms bestowed upon true patriots. Nothing in their costume would have surprised Washington, whose acquaintance went back a long way with these people. In the 1750s he had recruited them or their fathers to fight the French, and as they shook hands, they may have reminded the president of those days. Still, their visit was more than a courtesy call; Catawbas were worried, and they looked to their old comrade-in-arms for help.

They "seemed to be under apprehension," he noted in his diary, "that some attempts were making or would be made to deprive them of part of the 40,000 Acres w[hi]ch was secured to them by Treaty and w[hi]ch is bounded by this Road." Neither Washington nor anyone else remarked further on the meeting; by four the following morning the traveler was on his way again, headed north toward home.[9]

Two months of listening to speeches and drinking toasts was enough for any man, and Washington was glad to return to Mount Vernon. Like a soldier at the end of a long campaign, he was proud that his meticulous planning had paid off. "I performed a journey of 1887 miles without meeting with any interruption by sickness, bad weather, or any untoward accident," he wrote. He was equally pleased with the "disposition" of the citizenry, affirming that "the country appears to be in a very improving state, and. . . . tranquility reigns among the people."[10]

Washington's progress through the South told him much about the new nation. For us, it offers a useful point of comparison with the travels of John Lawson nine decades earlier. On one level the two bear a close resemblance. Both men wanted to see for themselves the lay of the land and find out what the locals thought of a government recently established in a distant capital. To accomplish this, both followed trails that took them through the region's population centers. And, of course, in a general sense the two were seeing the same landscape: rivers followed the same channels, the pine barrens were just as bleak, and the contrast between lowlands and piedmont remained striking.

Encounters with the natives were also similar. Washington, like Lawson, was the guest of honor at a series of pageants—including dinners, dances, speeches, and sightseeing tours—put on to welcome, entertain, and impress him. The feast at the Waxhaw "State-House" even had echoes, sixty miles away and ninety years later, in the dinner put on for Washington at the "State House" in Columbia.[11] And to us the distinctive hairdos of the Indian trading girls who tempted Lawson seem no more bizarre than the coiffures adorning the Charleston ladies who curtsied before the president.

Ultimately, however, the differences between the two journeys outweighed the similarities, for in the years separating Lawson from Washington the Southeast had been transformed. Lawson had wandered through a land inhabited by "none but Savages"; Washington, making his way across the same region, never left his own society. Mounted militiamen stood in for Indian warriors, guiding the novice along thoroughfares that could accommodate a carriage, where, ninety years before, a traveler on foot risked his neck. Those broad highways now took the visitor into American cities, not the Indian towns where all roads once had led. On the outskirts of each community, mayors and committees, not chiefs and councillors, stood ready to greet the sojourner and lead him to a very different sort of statehouse. And when they sat down together, hosts would give their guest lessons in local history, making Kalb's tomb serve the same purpose as the piles of stones Lawson had seen near the Catawba towns.

Thus the resemblance, while clear enough, was no more than superficial. At one end of the century stood an Indian world where a man like Lawson was at best a welcome visitor, at worst an unwelcome intruder. At the other end natives, not newcomers, were the outsiders. As Lawson saw—and as we, too, have seen—the shift from one to the other was under way before 1701, and it would continue after 1791. Still, the eighteenth century was pivotal; it was then that the balance tipped irrevocably away from the Indians. By its close all that remained of the native presence that had threatened to overwhelm John Lawson were a few river names and a tiny band of Catawbas, a people living on the forgotten fringe of southern society.

Washington's meeting with those Catawbas helps give a more concrete sense of just how much the world had changed. During the Seven Years' War he, like James Glen and everyone else who served the crown, had courted these Indians despite his dislike of them.[12] Now, when he no longer needed them, he could afford to pay less attention. Indifference or absentmindedness—or, at the very least, confusion—marked his end of the conversation: they "seemed" upset that someone (who?) had tried (or was it would try?) to steal their lands, which consisted of 40,000 acres (he was off by 104,000). Five years later, when a dozen Catawbas made their way to Mount Vernon to pay their respects, the story was much the same: the president was "incommoded" and trying "to avoid a repetition of such guests."[13] Far from unusually cruel or callous, Washington was typical of the time. He and most of his fellow Americans had come to regard Catawbas as something of a nuisance, a ragged, insignificant people hardly worth a second thought, or even a first.

What did the Catawba headmen think of their meeting as they left Crawford's late that day? Certainly they were not ready to give up on the president. Within a few years they would be back again, this time camped on his doorstep. Moreover, their memory of Washington lingered on long after both he and the Catawbas who knew him were gone. In January 1851, as the Nation again coalesced along the Catawba River, Franklin Canty and Eliza Scott had a child that they named George Washington Canty. And shortly after this Indian died in the early 1890s, Billy George was asserting that the lands taken from Catawbas in 1840 had been granted them by Washington, not by that other George that America had overthrown in 1776.[14]

Quite apart from these ripples of the splash made in 1791, that brief conversation holds a larger significance. Simply intercepting Washington was further proof of the Catawbas' sophisticated understanding of the society that had surrounded and conquered them; the Indians learned of the president's progress, and they knew the potential benefits of an audience with him. Considered in its broadest terms, their visit to Crawford's plantation was one more link in the long chain of intercultural encounters, a chain stretching back to de Soto's day and forward to our own.

The Catawbas' ability to cross the cultural divide as they did that day in 1791 was one secret of their survival. The other was their refusal, throughout the centuries, to remain on the far side. As New River and his companions trudged home from Crawford's, they made their way back to a place where people lived out their lives in ways that, though by no means identical to those of a century or two before, were nonetheless their own. Washington's people rarely bothered to follow these Indians back to the banks of the river in order to learn about their world; New River's never failed to make that return trip.

Acknowledgments

As Debts of Gratitude ought most punctually to be
paid, so, where the Debtor is uncapable of Payment,
Acknowledgments ought, at least, to be made.
                                              —John Lawson

EXPLORING the Catawbas' world took longer than I thought.
It would have taken even longer—indeed, it might have taken forever—had I not received financial, intellectual, and emotional support from many different quarters. To all of these I owe much of
whatever is good in the story I have tried to tell; for the mistakes
that remain I have only myself to blame.

Funding from the Danforth Foundation, the Newberry Library,
the Institute of Early American History and Culture, and Vassar
College helped free me from worries about finances so that I could
worry more about Catawbas and their neighbors. These grants also
enabled me to visit many libraries and archives, each staffed by
people who were almost unfailingly generous in helping me ferret
out sources. I am especially grateful to the libraries at The John
Hopkins University, the College of William and Mary, and Vassar
College, and to: the Newberry Library; the William L. Clements
Library; the Library of Congress; the Colonial Williamsburg Archives; the Research Laboratories of Anthropology at the University of North Carolina, Chapel Hill (where H. Trawick Ward has
been particularly helpful in keeping me abreast of the rapidly
changing archeology); the York County Public Library in Rock
Hill, South Carolina; the Winthrop College Archives; the South
Caroliniana Library (whose librarian, Allen Stokes, went far be-

yond duty in assisting my researches); and the South Carolina Department of Archives and History.

Lest anyone get the impression that this book was written by some solitary figure haunting the archival halls with grant money stuffed in his pocket, I hasten to add that while institutional backing and kindly archivists are necessary for a project like this, they are hardly sufficient. No less important are the scholars who continually encouraged my work yet somehow never let on if their own interest in Catawbas flagged. Before taking my first halting steps in the direction of Catawba history, I was inspired by earlier students of the Catawbas—Douglas Summers Brown, Steven G. Baker, and Charles M. Hudson—whose writings persuaded me that Catawbas could (and should) be studied. I have never met Douglas Brown, and I crossed paths with Steven Baker only later, but at the very beginning Professor Hudson went out of his way to invite me in when I ventured to ask whether there might be room for one more in the small band of Catawba scholars. As I then embarked upon my research, I was lucky enough to latch onto William Sturtevant, who placed his vast knowledge of southeastern Indians at my disposal. I was even luckier to have Jack P. Greene as my adviser in the early going. While cheerfully accepting my enthusiasm for Indians (which I suspect he considered somewhat eccentric) and letting me plow ahead at full steam, Jack always managed to keep me from running aground, in part by reminding me that there were colonists as well as Catawbas in my story, in part by chairing a seminar that gave me a captive audience to try out my half-formulated (and sometimes half-baked) ideas. A regular participant in that seminar was Philip Morgan, who started out as my teacher, became my friend, and ended up as my editor. It is a tribute to his editorial and diplomatic skills that he has remained both teacher and friend while helping me improve the manuscript.

My beginner's luck has held as my explorations took me farther afield and a book struggled to emerge from a dissertation. Fellowships at the Newberry Library's Center for the History of the American Indian (now the D'Arcy McNickle Center for the History of the American Indian) and the Institute of Early American History and Culture earned me my stripes in both Indian history and colonial American history, even as they convinced me that the distinction between the two camps is largely illusory. Several people at the Library and the Institute were particularly helpful in teaching me what a fellowship truly means. During my stay at the Newberry, Michael McConnell gave me a different perspective on the Catawbas from his perch in the eighteenth-century Ohio country, and while I was at the Institute, Daniel Richter offered similar assistance from Iroquoia. At the Institute, too, I learned much about the historian's craft from Thad Tate and Michael McGiffert, who taught by the grace of their example and their patience with my prose. From my fellowship years at these two jewels in the crown of American research centers I carried away an appreciation of how a relaxed atmosphere and rigorous intellectual inquiry go hand in hand. More recently, my colleagues at Vassar have reinforced this lesson. They have also placed me forever in their debt because they were among the first to accept my argument that someone who happened to study Indians in early America did not forfeit his membership in the club of colonial historians.

Two debts of longer standing are less intimately connected with Catawbas and more difficult to acknowledge adequately, much less repay. I first met Douglas Greenberg when he was a young professor (and I was an even younger undergraduate) at Lawrence University, and the word *Catawba*, if I had heard it at all, meant a variety of grape. In the years since then he has taught me a lot about the calling of teacher and scholar, but perhaps his most valuable lesson has been that some things are more important than teaching or scholarship. To my wife Linda—whom I also met at Lawrence, long before Catawba Indian history entered (and sometimes took over) my life—I owe thanks for preparing the maps that grace the foregoing pages. These illustrations, impressive as they are, represent the least of her contributions. From beginning to end, she has never failed to remind me, in her own gentle way, that the Catawbas' world was not the only one I inhabited.

Abbreviations

BMP—Microfilm listed in Lester K. Born, ed., *British Manuscripts Project: A Checklist of the Microfilms Prepared in England and Wales for the American Council of Learned Societies* (Washington, D.C., 1955)

BPRO-SC—W. Noel Sainsbury, comp., Records in the British Public Record Office Relating to South Carolina, 1663–1782, 36 vols. (microfilm, Columbia, S.C., 1955)

BPRO-SC—A. S. Salley, indexer, *Records in the British Public Record Office Relating to South Carolina*, 5 vols. (Atlanta, Columbia, S.C., 1928–1947)

CO—Colonial Office

CRNC—William L. Saunders, ed., *The Colonial Records of North Carolina*, 10 vols. (New York, 1968 [orig. publ. 1886–1890])

CVSP—William P. Palmer *et al.*, eds., *Calendar of Virginia State Papers and Other Manuscripts . . . Preserved in the Capitol at Richmond*, 11 vols. (Richmond, Va., 1875–1893)

DRCNY—E. B. O'Callaghan and Berthold Fernow, eds., *Documents Relative to the Colonial History of the State of New-York . . .* , 15 vols. (Albany, N.Y., 1853–1887)

DRIA—William L. McDowell, Jr., ed., *Documents Relating to Indian Affairs, May 21, 1750–August 7, 1754,* and *Documents Relating to Indian Affairs, 1754–1765,* Colonial Records of South Carolina, 2d Ser. (Columbia, S.C., 1958, 1970)

EJCCV—H. R. McIlwaine *et al.*, eds., *Executive Journals of the Council of Colonial Virginia*, 6 vols. (Richmond, Va., 1925–1966)

JCHA—J. H. Easterby *et al.*, eds., *The Journal of the Commons House of Assembly*, Colonial Records of South Carolina, 13 vols. to date (Columbia, S.C., 1951–)

JCHA-SC—A. S. Salley, Jr., ed., *Journal of the Commons House of Assembly of South Carolina*, 21 vols. (Columbia, S.C., 1907–1949)

JCIT—W. L. McDowell, ed., *Journals of the Commissioners of the Indian Trade, September 20, 1710–August 29, 1718,* Colonial Records of South Carolina (Columbia, S.C., 1955)

JHBV—H. R. McIlwaine and John Pendleton Kennedy, eds., *Journals of the House of Burgesses of Virginia*, 13 vols. (Richmond, Va., 1905–1915)

LC—Library of Congress, Washington, D.C.

MPCP—[Samuel Hazard, ed.], *Minutes of the Provincial Council of Pennsylvania, from the Organization to the Termination of the Proprietary Government*, 10 vols. (Harrisburg, Pa., 1838–1852)

NCDAH—North Carolina State Department of Archives and History, Raleigh

NCHR—North Carolina Historical Review

Pa. Arch.—Samuel Hazard, ed., *Pennsylvania Archives* . . . , 1st Ser., 12 vols. (Philadelphia, 1852–1856)

PRO—Great Britain, Public Record Office

RSUS—William Sumner Jenkins, comp., Records of the States of the United States of America (microfilm, Washington, D.C., 1949), cited by reel/unit, page number

SCCHJ—South Carolina Commons House Journals

SCCJ—South Carolina Council Journals

SCDAH—South Carolina Department of Archives and History, Columbia

SCG—South-Carolina Gazette (Charleston)

SCHGM/SCHM—South Carolina Historical and Genealogical Magazine, later *South Carolina Historical Magazine*

SCUHJ—South Carolina Upper House of Assembly Journals

SPG MSS—Society for the Propagation of the Gospel in Foreign Parts, Manuscripts (microfilm, Library of Congress)

VCRP-CW—Virginia Colonial Records Project (microfilm), Colonial Williamsburg Archives, Williamsburg, Virginia

VMHB—Virginia Magazine of History and Biography

VSL—Virginia State Library, Richmond

WMQ—William and Mary Quarterly

YCPL—York County Public Library, Rock Hill, South Carolina

Notes

Prologue

1. John Lawson, *A New Voyage to Carolina*, ed. Hugh Talmage Lefler (Chapel Hill, N.C., 1967), 7–11, quotations on 7. Lawson may have been appointed by the Carolina government to explore the interior and learn more about its inhabitants; see xi, and *JCHA-SC, for the Session Beginning October 30, 1700 and Ending November 16, 1700*, 22–23. For the sake of consistency I have modernized the colonial spelling of South Carolina's capital—"Charles Town"—throughout.

2. Lawson, *New Voyage*, ed. Lefler, 51, 54. The most authoritative account of Lawson's route through South Carolina may be found in Steven G. Baker, "Cofitachique: Fair Province of Carolina" (master's thesis, University of South Carolina, 1974), app. II. For an excellent account of Lawson and his journey in the context of American exploration, see Henry Savage, Jr., *Discovering America, 1700–1875* (New York, 1979), 19–25.

3. Lawson, *New Voyage*, ed. Lefler, 14–15 (insects), 33 (beasts), 50–51 (ducks and pigeons).

4. *Ibid.*, 174–176. Lawson wrote about Indians in two sections of this work: "A Journal of a Thousand Miles Travel among the Indians, from South to North Carolina," and "An Account of the Indians of North Carolina." With the exception of his description of the natives' appearance and his reference to "new world" and "*European* world," all citations in this Prologue are to the "Journal."

Using Lawson as a source for Indians living in the interior poses some problems. Though acquainted with these peoples, he probably knew best the Tuscaroras and other groups near the North Carolina settlements where he later lived, and it is not always possible to tell which Indians he is discussing. My own reading of his account has led me to agree with one student of the question who has concluded: "There is reason to believe that most of it is applicable to the Siouan-speaking tribes [of the interior]. Evidence for this is seen in the fact that a great many of the traits mentioned in this section ["An Account of the Indians of North Carolina"] are also mentioned for specific Siouan tribes in his 'A Journal of a Thousand Miles Travel among the Indians from South to North Carolina.' Also, he tends to point out whether he is speaking of all the tribes of his knowledge, or only of the Tuscarora . . . —with whom he was most familiar—or other non-Siouan tribes." Ernest Lewis, "The Sara Indians, 1540–1768: An Ethno-Archaeological Study" (master's thesis, University of North Carolina, 1951), 60.

5. Lawson, *New Voyage*, ed. Lefler, 47, 50, 58–59.

6. *Ibid.*, 34, 43–45, 55.

7. *Ibid.*, 35 (Congarees), 39 (Waxhaws), 58 (Keyauwees), 63 (Lower Quarter).

8. *Ibid.*, 42, 46, 49, 53, 61.

9. *Ibid.*, 25, 29, 49–50, 60–61.

10. *Ibid.*, 17, 25–26, 34.

11. *Ibid.*, 23, 48–49.

12. *Ibid.*, 23, 34, 51, 56 (range); 34 (English); 51, 56 (stones); 51–52 (creeks); 52 (Yadkin); 57 (fruit). Others have noted Lawson's keen interest in the land's agricultural promise. See Thad W. Tate, "The Discovery and Development of the Southern Colonial Landscape: Six Commentators," American Antiquarian Society, *Proceedings*, XCIII (1983), 301–302.

13. Lawson, *New Voyage*, ed. Lefler, 34, 40, 45, 48, 52, 89, 91. For another example of this sort of device, see J. H. Elliott, *The Old World and the New, 1492–1650* (Cambridge, 1970), 19.

14. Lawson, *New Voyage*, ed. Lefler, 22 (see also 6), 61.

Chapter 1

1. See Charles Hudson *et al.*, "The Hernando De Soto Expedition: From Apalachee to Chiaha," *Southeastern Archaeology*, III (1984), 66. I am indebted to Professor Hudson for sending me a copy of this article. The history, culture, and identity of the Cofitachique Indians remain unclear. The word *Cofitachique* has been used to identify both the principal village of these Indians and the entire population; I use it here in the latter sense. The best introduction to the Cofitachiques is Steven G. Baker, "Cofitachique: Fair Province of Carolina" (master's thesis, University of South Carolina, 1974).

2. Garcilaso de la Vega, *The Florida of the Inca: A History of the Adelantado, Hernando de Soto, Governor and Captain General of the Kingdom of Florida, and of Other Heroic Spanish and Indian Cavaliers . . .*, trans. and ed. John Grier Varner and Jeannette Johnson Varner (Austin, Tex., 1951), 297–301. See also *True Relation of the Vicissitudes That Attended the Governor Don Hernando De Soto . . . Now Just Given by a Fidalgo of Elvas*, trans. Buckingham Smith, in Edward Gaylord Bourne, ed., *Narratives of the Career of Hernando De Soto in the Conquest of Florida . . .*, 2 vols. (New York, 1904), I, 64–65 (hereafter cited as *True Relation*); and Gonzalo Fernandez de Oviedo y Valdés, *A Narrative of De Soto's Expedition Based on the Diary of Rodrigo Ranjel, His Private Secretary*, trans. Bourne, in Bourne, ed., *Narratives of De Soto*, II, 98–99 (hereafter cited as Oviedo, *Narrative*).

De Soto's precise route remains unclear, but the most thorough studies place the Cofitachiques' main village on the east side of the Wateree River near present Camden. See Baker, "Cofitachique," app. 5; Hudson *et al.*, "De Soto Expedition," *Southeastern Arch.*, III (1984), fig. 1, p. 67, and 71–73.

3. For these and other terms colonists used to describe the piedmont region, see John Lawson, *A New Voyage to Carolina*, ed. Hugh Talmage Lefler (Chapel Hill, N.C., 1967), xxxi, 56, 89, 145–146; and William P. Cumming, ed., *The Discoveries of John Lederer* (Charlottesville, Va., 1958), 9–10.

For details on the piedmont environment and its role as a "culture area," see Alfred L. Kroeber, *Cultural and Natural Areas of Native North America* (Berkeley, Calif., 1939), 92–94; Charles M. Hudson, *The Catawba Nation*, University of Georgia Monographs, no. 18 (Athens, Ga., 1970), 9–11, 17–20; Jack Hubert Wilson, Jr., "A Study of the Late Prehistoric, Protohistoric, and Historic Indians of the Carolina and Virginia Piedmont: Structure, Process, and Ecology" (Ph.D. diss., University of North Carolina, 1983), chap. 2. I am grateful to Dr. Wilson for providing me with a copy of his dissertation.

The archeological record for the southern piedmont is extraordinarily thin. The Siouan Project conducted by the Research·Laboratories of Anthropology at the University of North Carolina at Chapel Hill promises to add much to our knowledge of cultural development in the region. As the title suggests, however, these archeologists do not expect to overturn the argument put forward by earlier scholars that the piedmont was characterized by cultural uniformity, though the character and extent of that uniformity are yet to be established. See James B. Griffin, "An Interpretation of Siouan Archaeology in the Piedmont of North Carolina and Virginia," *American Antiquity*, X (1944–1945), 321–330; Ernest Lewis, "The Sara Indians, 1540–1768: An Ethno-Archaeological Study" (master's thesis, University of North Carolina, 1951), 332–335; Joffre L. Coe, "The Cultural Sequence of the Carolina Piedmont," in James B. Griffin, ed., *Archeology of Eastern United States* (Chicago, 1952), 301–311; Coe, *The Formative Cultures of the Carolina Piedmont* (American Philosophical Society, *Transactions*, N.S., LIV, pt. 5 [Philadelphia, 1964]); Jack H. Wilson, "Feature Fill, Plant Utilization, and Disposal among the Historic Sara Indians" (master's thesis, University of North Carolina, 1977), 12; Paul S. Gardner, "An Analysis of Dan River Ceramics from Virginia and North Carolina" (master's thesis, University of North Carolina, 1980), 86–88. The best summary of the work done, past and present, is Roy S. Dickens, Jr., "Introduction," in Dickens *et al.*, eds., *The Siouan Project: Seasons I and II*, Research Laboratories of Anthropology, University of North Carolina Monograph Series, no. 1 (Chapel Hill, N.C., 1987), 1–17.

Historic Catawba pottery resembles some ceramic ware found farther north, suggesting that the Catawba area, all but unexplored archeologically, belongs in this collection of peoples. See Steven G. Baker, "Colono-Indian Pottery from Cambridge, South Carolina, with Comments on the Historic Catawba Pottery Trade," Institute of Archeology and Anthropology, University of South Carolina, *Notebook*, IV (1972), 10; Richard P. Gravely, Jr., "Prehistory in the Upper Dan River Drainage System," in J. Mark Wittkofski and Lyle E. Browning, eds., *Piedmont Archaeology: Recent Research and Results*, Archeological Society of Virginia, Special Publication no. 10 (n.p., n.d.), 121–122. Physical evidence collected from present and past piedmont populations also links Catawbas to their neighbors to the north. See William S. Pollitzer, "Physical Anthropology of Indians of the Old South," in Charles M. Hudson, ed., *Red, White, and Black: Symposium on Indians in the Old South, Athens, Ga., 1970*, Southern Anthropological Society, Proceedings, no. 5 (Athens, Ga., 1971), 33, 34–35, 38–39.

4. On descent, see Coe, "Cultural Sequence," in Griffin, ed., *Archeology*, 305–308. L. Daniel Mouer ("A Review of the Archeology and Ethnohistory of the Monacans," in Wittkofski and Browning, eds., *Piedmont Archaeology*, 34) posits a linguistic separation between Virginia Siouan-speakers and those to the west "within the last 1000 years of prehistory," but he has found no archeological evidence to confirm this migration.

On pottery and arrowheads, see Lewis, "Sara Indians," 289–291, 332–335; Coe, *Formative Cultures*, 49; Robert W. Keeler, "An Archaeological Survey of the Upper Catawba River Valley" (bachelor's honors thesis, University of North Carolina at Chapel Hill, 1971), 37–41; Griffin, "Interpretation of Siouan Archaeology," *Am. Antiq.*, X (1944–1945), 327–329.

On agriculture, see Hudson, *Catawba Nation*, 18. The balance between horticulture and hunting was indeed more even in the north, but no piedmont Indians fit the Powhatans' deprecating descriptions of them as people who relied exclusively on hunting and gathering (see below). Colonial records and modern studies alike reveal the piedmont natives' skill in settling near the richest soils. See William J. Hinke, trans. and ed., "Report of the Journey of Francis Louis Michel from Berne, Switzerland, to Virginia, October 2, 1701–December 1, 1702," *VMHB*, XXIV (1916), 29; William Byrd, "History of the Dividing Line betwixt Virginia and North Carolina Run in the Year of Our Lord 1728," in Louis B. Wright, ed., *The Prose Works of William Byrd of Westover: Narratives of a Colonial Virginian* (Cambridge, Mass., 1966), 251; C. G. Holland, "Albermarle County Settlements: A Piedmont Model?" Archeological Society of Virginia, *Quarterly Bulletin*, XXXIII (1978–1979), 34; Herbert G. Fisher, "The Virginia Piedmont—A Definition: A Review of the Physiologic Attributes and Historic Land Use of This Region," in Wittkofski and Browning, eds., *Piedmont Archaeology*, 2–8; Mouer, "Archeology and Ethnohistory of the Monacans," in Wittkofski and Browning, eds., *Piedmont Archaeology*, 28–29.

The linguistic pattern in the piedmont remains a matter of considerable dispute. Earlier scholars placed a large number of groups under the Siouan umbrella; many later ones have demanded firmer evidence. While agreeing that the first students of the problem may have been too eager to label a people Siouan and that nonlinguistic considerations cannot prove linguistic relationships, I am persuaded by William C. Sturtevant's argument ("Siouan Languages in the East," *American Anthropologist*, N.S., LX [1958], 741): "Where we lack linguistic evidence . . . we must use whatever data exist. Cultural resemblances, geographical proximity, political association, brief lists of proper names without meanings, and contemporary summary statements on linguistic resemblances . . . indicate possibilities or even probabilities of linguistic relationship." These data suggest that most, if not all, of the Indians in the piedmont at the time of English contact spoke some form of Siouan. Included among these are Catawbas, Cheraws, Saponis, Tutelos, Occaneechees, Monacans, and Mannahoacs, and probably also Waterees, Enos, Keyauwees, Sugarees, Esaws, Shuterees, and Shakoris.

The linguistic debate may be followed in James Mooney, *The Siouan Tribes of the East*, Smithsonian Institution, Bureau of American Ethnology, Bulletin no. 22 (Washington, D.C., 1894); Frank T. Siebert, Jr., "Linguistic Classification of Catawba," *International Journal of American Linguistics*, XI (1945), 100–104, 211–218; Carl F. Miller, "Revaluation of the Eastern Siouan Problem with Particular Emphasis on the Virginia Branches—the Occaneechi, the Saponi, and the Tutelo," Smithsonian Institution, Bureau of American Ethnology, Anthropological Papers, no. 52, *Bulletin*, no. 164 (Washington, D.C., 1957); Sturtevant, "Siouan Languages," 738–743; Lewis R. Binford, "Comments on the 'Siouan Problem,'" *Ethnohistory*, VI (1959), 28–41; Hudson, *Catawba Nation*, 5–9, 27–28; Richard T. Carter, "The Woccon Language of North Carolina: Its Genetic Affiliations and Historical Significance," *Int. Jour. Am. Ling.*, XLVI (1980), 170–182; L. G. Moses, *The Indian Man: A Biography of James Mooney* (Urbana, Ill., 1984), 81–82; Mouer, "Archeology and Ethnohistory of the Monacans," in Wittkofski and Browning, eds., *Piedmont Archaeology*, 21–23.

5. Cumming, ed., *Discoveries of Lederer*, 23; Douglas L. Rights, "Traces of the Indian in Piedmont North Carolina," *NCHR*, I (1924), 280; Joffre L. Coe, "Keyauwee—A Preliminary Statement," Archeological Society of North Carolina, *Bulletin*, IV (1937), 8; Lewis, "Sara Indians," 129–130; Joseph L. Benthall, *Archeological Investigation of the Shannon Site, Montgomery County, Virginia*, Virginia State Library Publications, no. 32 (Richmond, Va., 1969), 2, 20; Mouer, "Archeology and Ethnohistory of the Monacans," in Wittkofski and Browning, eds., *Piedmont Archaeology*, 27.

6. Philip L. Barbour, ed., *The Complete Works of Captain John Smith (1580–1631)*, 3 vols. (Chapel Hill, N.C., 1986), II, 176.

7. For accounts of these expeditions, see David B. Quinn, *North America from Earliest Discovery to First Settlements: The Norse Voyages to 1612* (New York, 1977), 206–222, 271–275, 332–333, 451–452; Charles M. Hudson, *The Southeastern Indians* (Knoxville, Tenn., 1976), 97–119; Hudson *et al.*, "De Soto Expedition," *Southeastern Arch.*, III (1984), 65–77; Chester B. DePratter *et al.*, "The Route of Juan Pardo's Explorations in the Interior Southeast, 1566–1568," *Florida Historical Quarterly*, LXII (1983–1984), 125–158; Philip L. Barbour, *The Three Worlds of Captain John Smith* (Boston, 1964), 222–225, 237–239. After this section was written, I had the opportunity to read a draft of the most thorough study of Pardo's journeys: Charles Hudson, *The Juan Pardo Expeditions: Exploration of the Carolinas and Tennessee, 1566–1568* (forthcoming). I am grateful to Professor Hudson for sending me a copy of his manuscript.

8. *True Relation*, in Bourne, ed., *Narratives of De Soto*, I, 69; "17 August 1585–18 June 1586: Ralph Lane's Discourse on the First Colony," in David Beers Quinn, ed., *The Roanoke Voyages, 1584–1590 . . .*, 2 vols., Hakluyt Society, 2d Ser., CIV–CV (London, 1955), I, 268. Mangoaks, long thought to be Tuscaroras, are now believed to be Siouans. See Raymond J. DeMallie, "The Tutelo and their Congeners," MS.

9. "Lane's Discourse," in Quinn, ed., *Roanoke Voyages*, I, 270.

10. On de Soto: in Bourne, ed., *Narratives of De Soto: True Relation*, I, 66, 68; *Relation of the Conquest of Florida Presented by Luys Hernandez De Biedma . . . ,* trans. Buckingham Smith, II, 14; Oviedo, *Narrative*, 100–102; and Garcilaso, *Florida*, ed. Varner and Varner, 311–314. On Pardo: Juan de la Vandera, "Proceeding of the account which Captain Juan Pardo gave of the entrance which he made into the land of the Floridas, Prepared for the Lieutenant Governor of Florida, Santo Domingo, April 1, 1569," A.I., 1569, 54-5-9, Vandera (typescript translation [by Herbert Ketcham?] of a photostatic copy in the Spanish Archives Collection, NCDAH), 25, 44–46 (hereafter cited as Vandera, "Proceeding"); DePratter *et al.*, "Pardo's Explorations," *Fla. Hist. Qtly.*, LXII (1983), 152–154. Lane: "Lane's Discourse," in Quinn, ed., *Roanoke Voyages*, I, 269–270. Newport and Smith: Smith, *Works*, ed. Barbour, I, 238, II, 175.

11. For de Soto, see in Bourne, ed., *Narratives of De Soto: True Relation*, I, 36–37, 39, 43, 45, 63, 67, 69–70; Oviedo, *Narrative*, II, 97. Pardo: Mary Ross, "With Pardo and Boyano on the Fringes of the Georgia Land," *Georgia Historical Quarterly*, XIV (1930), 277–278, 283; DePratter *et al.*, "Pardo's Explorations," *Fla. Hist. Qtly.*, LXII (1983), 131, 158. Lane: "Lane's Discourse," in Quinn, ed., *Roanoke Voyages*, 268, 270. Newport and Smith: Smith, *Works*, ed. Barbour, I, 238, II, 175–176.

12. *True Relation*, in Bourne, ed., *Narratives of De Soto*, I, 69–70; Smith, *Works*, ed. Barbour, I, 238, II, 72, 175–177.

13. Smith, *Works*, ed. Barbour, II, 177.

14. *True Relation*, in Bourne, ed., *Narratives of De Soto*, I, 55; Smith, *Works*, ed. Barbour, II, 176–177.

15. This point is made in Nancy Oestreich Lurie, "Indian Cultural Adjustment to European Civilization," in James Morton Smith, ed., *Seventeenth-Century America: Essays in Colonial History* (Chapel Hill, N.C., 1959), 33–60.

16. Coe, "Cultural Sequence," in Griffin, ed., *Archeology*, 308–309; Leland Greer Ferguson, "South Appalachian Mississippian" (Ph.D. diss., University of North Carolina, 1971), 116–118, 147–148, 177, 214–215, 218, chap. 5; George Edwin Stuart, "The Post-Archaic Occupation of Central South Carolina" (Ph.D. diss., University of North Carolina, 1975), abstract, and chap. 4; Baker, "Cofitachique," 153; Wilson, "Indians of the Piedmont," 483–485. I am conservative in charting the depth of this penetration into the piedmont; recent students of the Pardo expedi-

tion place the barrier west of Charlotte, North Carolina. See Hudson *et al.*, "De Soto Expedition," *Southeastern Arch.*, III (1984), 73. The boundary probably fluctuated, and only further archeological research can reveal its true location.

17. Edwin Randolph Turner III, "An Archaeological and Ethnohistorical Study on the Evolution of Rank Societies in the Virginia Coastal Plain" (Ph.D. diss., Pennsylvania State University, 1976); J. Frederick Fausz, "The Powhatan Uprising of 1622: A Historical Study of Ethnocentrism and Cultural Conflict" (Ph.D. diss., College of William and Mary, 1977), chap. 2.

18. The pioneering work on the Mississippian society in South Carolina was done by Baker ("Cofitachique"), and my understanding of these people owes a great debt to his work. For more general discussions, see Hudson, *Southeastern Indians*, 77–97; Chester Burton DePratter, "Late Prehistoric and Early Historic Chiefdoms in the Southeastern United States" (Ph.D. diss., University of Georgia, 1983). The Powhatans shared all of these traits except the temple mounds.

19. Smith, *Works*, ed. Barbour, I, 165; William Wallace Tooker, *The Algonquian Names of the Siouan Tribes of Virginia, with Historical and Ethnological Notes*, The Algonquian Series, V (New York, 1901), 44, 47, 65–66. It should be noted that Amoroleck also described his own Mannahoac people in similar terms (Smith, *Works*, ed. Barbour, II, 176).

20. For Mississippians, see Ferguson, "South Appalachian Mississippian," 216, 245–246; Stuart, "Post-Archaic Occupation," 153; Coe, "Cultural Sequence," in Griffin, ed., *Archeology*, 309.

For Powhatans, see "Relacion de Bartolomé Martínez," in Clifford M. Lewis and Albert J. Loomie, eds., *The Spanish Jesuit Mission in Virginia, 1570–1572* (Chapel Hill, N.C., 1953), 161; Smith, *Works*, ed. Barbour, I, 166–167, II, 119–120; C. G. Holland, "Archeology and Ethnohistory: An Illustration," Arch. Soc. of Va., *Qtly. Bull.*, XXI (1966–1967), 2–3, 6–7; Turner, "Evolution of Rank Societies," 198; A. H. Luckenbach *et al.*, "Movement of Prehistoric Soapstone in the James River Basin," Arch. Soc. of Va., *Qtly. Bull.*, XXIX (1974–1975), 202; L. Daniel Mouer, "Powhatan and Monacan Regional Settlement Hierarchies: A Model of Relationship between Social and Environmental Structure," Arch. Soc. of Va., *Qtly. Bull.*, XXXVI (1981–1982), 8, 17–18. Mouer ("Archeology and Ethnohistory of the Monacans," in Wittkofski and Browning, eds., *Piedmont Archaeology*, 29–30) dates the origins of this conflict much earlier, as early as the 10th century A.D., and argues that it was more "a 'cold war' or 'detente' situation" than continuous fighting. The evidence on which he bases this assertion is unclear.

21. For signs and symbols, see "Report of Francisco Fernández de Écija," in Philip L. Barbour, ed., *The Jamestown Voyages under the First Charter, 1606–1609*, 2 vols., Hakluyt Society, 2d Ser., CXXXVI–CXXXVII (Cambridge, 1969), II, 302, 319; Cumming, ed., *Discoveries of Lederer*, 13; John Banister, "Of the Natives: Their Habit, Customes and Manner of Living," in Joseph Ewan and Nesta Ewan, eds., *John Banister and His Natural History of Virginia, 1678–1692* (Urbana, Ill., 1970), 384; Lawson, *New Voyage*, ed. Lefler, 48–49, 213–214.

For interpreters, see Garcilaso, *Florida*, ed. Varner and Varner, 302, 310; Vandera, "Proceeding," 5, 8, 9–10, 19, 20, 47, 59; Écija, "Report," in Barbour, ed., *Jamestown Voyages*, II, 295, 298, 299, 302, 303, 314, 317–318; Smith, *Works*, ed. Barbour, II, 107, 120.

22. "Captain Juan Pardo's Account of His Expeditions into the Interior in 1565 and 1566," in David B. Quinn, ed., *New American World: A Documentary History of North America to 1612*, 5 vols. (New York, 1979), II, 542–544; Lawson, *New Voyage*, ed. Lefler, 48–49.

On at least one occasion the Indians may have been more receptive to these agents of conquest. The priest at Pardo's fort among the Guatari (Wateree, probably at that time along the Yadkin River) claimed considerable success in teaching the native headmen the rudiments of Christianity and the Spanish language. The sincerity of the Guataris' enthusiasm and the extent of their knowledge remain unclear; in any event, the priest's stay was very brief—six years at most, more likely less than two—and the long-term effects of his efforts must have been negligible. See Michael V. Gannon, "Sebastian Montero, Pioneer American Missionary, 1566–1572," *Catholic Historical Review*, LI (1965–1966), 335–353.

23. *True Relation*, in Bourne, ed., *Narratives of De Soto*, I, 70–71; Garcilaso, *Florida*, ed. Varner and Varner, 329–330; Vandera, "Proceeding," 8–16. For more general assessments of the limitations to authority, see Hudson, *Southeastern Indians*, 205–206; Bruce D. Smith, "Variation in Mississippian Settlement Patterns," in Smith, ed., *Mississippian Settlement Patterns*, Studies in Archeology (New York, 1978), 495. My views on the extent of the Cofitachiques' authority tend to be more conservative than those found in Baker ("Cofitachique," fig. 1) and DePratter ("Prehistoric and Historic Chiefdoms," esp. 22).

24. Hudson, *Southeastern Indians*, 80; Lawson, *New Voyage*, ed. Lefler, 24, 35, 115–116; Banister, "Of the Natives," in Ewan and Ewan, eds., *Banister and His Natural History*, 376; Wilson, "Feature Fill," 83, 115–116; Henry Trawick Ward, "The Spatial Analysis of the Plow Zone Artifact Distributions from Two Village Sites in North Carolina" (Ph.D. diss., University of North Carolina, 1980), 196, 198; Kristen Johnson Gremillion, "Plant Remains from the Fredricks, Wall, and Mitchum Sites," in Dickens *et al.*, eds., *The Siouan Project*, 269–270, 273.

25. Ferguson, "South Appalachian Mississippian," 259–260; James P. Ronda, "Frazer's Razor: The Ethnohistory of a Common Object," *We Proceeded On*, Aug. 1981, 13.

26. In Bourne, ed., *Narratives of De Soto: True Relation*, I, 69; *Relation of De Biedma*, II, 14; Oviedo, *Narrative*, II, 100. Letter of Juan Ragel to Francis Borgia, Aug. 28, 1572, in Lewis and Loomie, eds., *Spanish Jesuit Mission*, 111. The potsherd, from the Upper Saratown site (31sk1a), is in the Research Laboratories of Anthropology, University of North Carolina at Chapel Hill, Catalogue no. 2270p3466. Other Eastern Indians worshipped these new weapons. See James Axtell, *The Invasion Within: The Contest of Cultures in Colonial North America* (New York, 1985), 11. For other efforts to depict images of Spaniards, see Ross, "With Pardo and Boyano," *Ga. Hist. Qtly.*, XIV (1930), 281. For Mississippian influence, see Stuart, "Post-Archaic Occupation," 154.

27. Ferguson, "South Appalachian Mississippian," 228–238; Hudson, *Southeastern Indians*, 85; Wilson, "Indians of the Piedmont," 245, 296–297, 315, 351, 367, and chap. 18.

Colono-Indian ware requires more thorough analysis and more extensive investigation in the piedmont. It was produced primarily for an Anglo-American or Afro-American market. However, it has been found on Indian sites, suggesting that the decision to copy European forms was more than merely economic. And some has turned up within a generation of European intrusion. Ivor Noël Hume, "An Indian Ware of the Colonial Period," Arch. Soc. of Va., *Qtly. Bull.*, XVII (1962–1963), 4–5; Lewis R. Binford, "Colonial Period Ceramics of the Nottoway and Weanock Indians of Southeastern Virginia," Arch. Soc. of Va., *Qtly. Bull.*, XIX (1964–1965), 86–87; Baker, "Colono-Indian Pottery," Inst. Arch. and Anthro., *Notebook*, IV (1972), 9–10; Stephen R. Potter, "Ethnohistory and the Owings Site: A Re-Analysis," Arch. Soc. of Va., *Qtly. Bull.*, XXXI (1976–1977), 171; Gregory A.

Waselkov and R. Eli Paul, "Frontiers and Archaeology," *North American Archaeologist*, II (1980–1981), 321 (I thank Professor Waselkov for sending me a copy of this article); Mouer, "Archeology and Ethnohistory of the Monacans," in Wittkofski and Browning, eds., *Piedmont Archaeology*, 25.

28. Marshall D. Sahlins, *Tribesmen*, Foundations of Modern Anthropology Series (Englewood Cliffs, N.J., 1968), 45–46; Hudson, *Southeastern Indians*, 96; Smith, *Works*, ed. Barbour, I, 165–166, II, 119–120, 175–177; Wilson, "Indians of the Piedmont," 197–200, 573–575. For a discussion of Monacan political organization which posits the development of a "segmentary confederacy" (but without attributing its origins to a need for defense), see Mouer, "Regional Settlement Hierarchies," Arch. Soc. of Va., *Qtly. Bull.*, XXXVI (1981–1982), 1–21. Mouer suggests elsewhere that it was growing piedmont organization that led to Powhatan's rise, not vice versa (see "Archeology and Ethnohistory of the Monacans," in Wittkofski and Browning, eds., *Piedmont Archaeology*, 29), though he acknowledges the importance of "predatory expansion of neighboring groups" on Monacan political development (24).

29. Baker ("Cofitachique," 112, 169–172, 207–209) argues that the Catawba Nation is in fact a "recrystallization" of the Cofitachique polity, marked by a "dual tradition" of piedmont Siouans and Mississippians.

30. Smith, *Works*, ed. Barbour, II, 175. For the Under World, see Hudson, *Southeastern Indians*, 122–128. For other examples of Indians' equating Europeans with mythic beings from the natives' cosmology, see Christopher L. Miller and George R. Hamell, "A New Perspective on Indian-White Contact: Cultural Symbols and Colonial Trade," *Journal of American History*, LXXIII (1986–1987), 318–322.

31. *True Relation*, in Bourne, ed., *Narratives of De Soto*, I, 66. My understanding of disease has been immeasurably aided by Alfred W. Crosby, "Virgin Soil Epidemics as a Factor in the Aboriginal Depopulation in America," *WMQ*, 3d Ser., XXXIII (1976), 289–299.

32. Lawson, *New Voyage*, ed. Lefler, 34. Some idea of the diseases in the area during the 16th and 17th centuries may be found in Henry F. Dobyns, *Their Number Become Thinned: Native American Population Dynamics in Eastern North America* (Knoxville, Tenn., 1983), essay 1, though Dobyns's claims have come under heavy attack (David Henige, "Primary Source by Primary Source? On the Role of Epidemics in New World Depopulation," *Ethnohistory*, XXXIII [1986], 293–312). See also George R. Milner, "Epidemic Disease in the Postcontact Southeast: A Reappraisal," *Mid-Continental Journal of Archaeology*, V (1980), 39–56.

33. Lawson, *New Voyage*, ed. Lefler, 17, 232; Ward, "Spatial Analysis," 182.

34. Lawson, *New Voyage*, ed. Lefler, 17; Crosby, "Virgin Soil Epidemics," *WMQ*, 3d Ser., XXXIII (1976), 296; Milner, "Epidemic Disease," *Mid-Continental Jour. Arch.*, V (1980), 47.

35. Ross, "With Pardo and Boyano," *Ga. Hist. Qtly.*, XIV (1930), 285. For a general discussion of kinship, see Hudson, *Southeastern Indians*, 185–202.

36. Lawson, *New Voyage*, ed. Lefler, 189.

37. Francis Le Jau to the Secretary, June 13, 1710, in Frank J. Klingberg, ed., *The Carolina Chronicle of Dr. Francis Le Jau, 1706–1717*, University of California Publications in History, LIII (Berkeley, Calif., 1956), 78.

38. Lawson, *New Voyage*, ed. Lefler, 43, 45, 177–178, 210, 219, 239; Cumming, ed., *Discoveries of Lederer*, 14, 27, 41.

39. Lawson, *New Voyage*, ed. Lefler, 17–18, 49, 54, 232.

40. *Ibid.*, 18, 27, 30–31, 49, 222–228.

41. The evidence of Cheraw burial practices derives from Gravely, "Prehistory in the Upper Dan River," in Wittkofski and Browning, eds., *Piedmont Archaeology*, 122;

Liane Navey, "An Introduction to the Mortuary Practices of the Historic Sara" (master's thesis, University of North Carolina, 1982), esp. chaps. 5–6; Roy S. Dickens, Jr., *et al.*, *The Historic Occaneechi: An Archaeological Investigation of Culture Change: Preliminary Report of 1984 Investigations* (Chapel Hill, N.C., 1984), 53; H. Trawick Ward and Homes H. Wilson, "Mortuary Behavior, Human Skeletal Remains, and Culture Change in the North Carolina Piedmont," paper presented at the 51st Annual Meeting of the Society for American Archaeology, New Orleans, Apr. 1986. I am grateful to Dr. Ward for sending me copies of this and other papers presented at this meeting.

42. *True Relation*, in Bourne, ed., *Narratives of De Soto*, I, 66.

43. David I. Bushnell, Jr., *The Manahoac Tribes in Virginia, 1608*, Smithsonian Miscellaneous Collections, XCIV, no. 8 (Washington, D.C., 1935); Bushnell, *The Five Monacan Towns in Virginia, 1607*, Smith. Misc. Colls., LXXXII, no. 12 (Washington, D.C., 1930); Christian F. Feest, "Notes on Saponi Settlements in Virginia Prior to 1714," Arch. Soc. of Va., *Qtly. Bull.*, XXVIII (1973–1974), 152–155; Lawson, *New Voyage*, ed. Lefler, 53; "Map of Carolina: Showing the Route of the Forces Sent in the Years 1711, 1712, and 1713, from South Carolina to the Relief of North Carolina, and in 1715 of the Forces Sent from North Carolina to the Assistance of South Carolina, Also Showing the Contraverted Bounds between Virginia and Carolina . . . [1715] . . . ," PRO, CO Library, Carolina 4 (copy in Archer Butler Hulbert, comp., *The Crown Collection of Photographs of American Maps*, 3d Ser., I [Cleveland, Ohio, 1913], pls. 17–18); William Byrd, "A Journey to the Land of Eden, Anno 1733," in Wright, ed., *Prose Works*, 398.

44. Lawson, *New Voyage*, ed. Lefler, 46; Banister, "Of the Natives," in Ewan and Ewan, eds., *Banister and His History*, 379. See also Mouer, "Archeology and Ethnohistory of the Monacans," in Wittkofski and Browning, eds., *Piedmont Archaeology*, 23–24; Gary L. Petherick, "Architecture and Features at the Fredricks, Wall, and Mitchum Sites," in Dickens *et al.*, eds., *The Siouan Project*, 68.

45. Smith, *Works*, ed. Barbour, I, 154, 164. For these zones, see Steven G. Baker, "The Working Draft of: The Historic Catawba Peoples: Exploratory Perspectives in Ethnohistory and Archaeology" (MS, Department of History, University of South Carolina, Columbia, 1975), 25–36; E. Randolph Turner, "An Intertribal Deer Exploitation Buffer Zone for the Virginia Coastal Plain–Piedmont Regions," Arch. Soc. of Va., *Qtly. Bull.*, XXXII (1977–1978), 42–46; DePratter, "Prehistoric and Historic Chiefdoms," 33–39; Howard A. MacCord, Sr., "Indians of Piedmont Virginia: An Abbreviated Culture History," paper prepared for the Conference on Piedmont Archaeology, Yorktown, Va., May 1983, 9; Daniel L. Simpkins, "Some Spatial Configurations of the Late Archaeological Components in the Carolina-Virginia Piedmont," paper delivered at the annual meeting of the Society for Historical Archaeology, Williamsburg, Va., Jan. 1984.

On tales, see Robert Sandford, "A Relation of a Voyage on the Coast of the Province of Carolina" (1666), in Alexander S. Salley, Jr., ed., *Narratives of Early Carolina, 1650–1708*, Original Narratives of Early American History (New York, 1911), 106. See also William Owen to Lord Ashley, Sept. 15, 1670, in Langdon Cheves, ed., *The Shaftesbury Papers and Other Records Relating to Carolina and the First Settlement on Ashley River Prior to the Year 1676*, South Carolina Historical Society, *Collections*, V (Charleston, S.C., 1897), 201 (hereafter cited as *Shaftesbury Papers*).

46. Lawson, *New Voyage*, ed. Lefler, 130; Garcilaso, *Florida*, ed. Varner and Varner, 283–284, 331; *True Relation*, in Bourne, ed., *Narratives of De Soto*, I, 59–62.

47. "Pardo's Account," in Quinn, ed., *New American World*, II, 542–543. Francis Yeardley, "Narrative of Excursions into Carolina, 1654," in Salley, ed., *Narratives of Carolina*, 27–28; Cumming, ed., *Discoveries of Lederer*, 24, 27 ("mean Stature"), 28,

30; Lawson, *New Voyage*, ed. Lefler, 27, 43, 89 ("Gigantick"), 180 (games), 182 (snakes), 204 (headmen), 240 (months).

48. Lawson, *New Voyage*, ed. Lefler, 24, 184, 190, 212.

49. A short word list taken from the mixed population at Fort Christanna in 1716 reveals a combination of languages. Of the 32 identifiable terms, 16 were Siouan, 10 Algonquian, 4 used by both, and 2 used by Algonquian and Iroquoian. The significance of this is unclear, though it seems to represent a blend of forms as well as peoples. See Edward P. Alexander, "An Indian Vocabulary from Fort Christanna, 1716," *VMHB*, LXXIX (1971), 303–313; Ives Goddard, "Brief Mention," *Int. Jour. Am. Ling.*, XXXVIII (1972), 220.

50. Lawson, *New Voyage*, ed. Lefler, 193.

51. See Robert A. Levine and Donald T. Campbell, *Ethnocentrism: Theories of Conflict, Ethnic Attitudes, and Group Behavior* (New York, 1972), 108. For a discussion of the process of amalgamation in the piedmont, see Daniel L. Simpkins and Gary L. Petherick, "Settlement Pattern Changes in the Carolina Piedmont during the Contact Period," paper presented at the 51st Annual Meeting of the Society for American Archaeology, New Orleans, Apr. 1986.

52. *EJCCV*, III, 367, 376, 396, 407; Alexander Spotswood to the Bishop of London, Jan. 27, 1714[/15], in R. A. Brock, ed., *The Official Letters of Alexander Spotswood, Lieutenant-Governor of the Colony of Virginia, 1710–1722*, 2 vols. (Virginia Historical Society, *Collections*, N.S., I–II [Richmond, Va., 1882–1885]), II, 88.

53. Treaty of Peace between Virginia and the Saponis, Stuckanoes, Occoneechees, and Totteros, Feb. 27, 1713[/14], CO 5/1316 (LC transcripts, p. 622); Spotswood to Bishop of London, Jan. 27, 1714[/15], in Brock, ed., *Letters of Spotswood*, II, 88.

54. H. Trawick Ward, "The Spatial Dimension of Siouan Mortuary Ritual: Implications for Studies of Change," paper delivered at the Annual Meeting of the Society for Historical Archeology, Williamsburg, Va., Jan. 1984; Ward, "Mortuary Patterns at the Fredricks, Wall, and Mitchum Sites," in Dickens *et al.*, eds., *The Siouan Project*, fig. 4.31, p. 109. At some historic sites a common cemetery may have served to integrate different ethnic groups (Simpkins and Petherick, "Settlement Changes in the Carolina Piedmont").
For the endurance of these ethnic distinctions, see "Virginia in 1726," *VMHB*, XLVIII (1940), 142; Byrd, "History," in Wright, ed., *Prose Works*, 314; Horatio Hale, "The Tutelo Tribe and Language," APS, *Proceedings*, XXI (1883–1884), 10.

55. Feest, "Saponi Settlements," Arch. Soc. Va., *Qtly. Bull.*, XXVIII (1973–1974), 152–155; Griffin, "Interpretation of Siouan Archaeology," *Am. Antiq.*, X (1944–1945), 324–325; Coe, "Cultural Sequence," in Griffin, ed., *Archeology*, 307. Some Indians took the bones of their ancestors with them upon moving. See Lawson, *New Voyage*, ed. Lefler, 28–29, 188.

56. Cumming, ed., *Discoveries of Lederer*, 12, 19–20; Lawson, *New Voyage*, ed. Lefler, 29, 50; J. G. Rusmiselle, Jr., "Two Stone Heaps in Augusta County," Arch. Soc. Va., *Qtly. Bull.*, XX (1965–1966), 84; Edward Bland *et al.*, "The Discovery of New Brittaine" (1650), in Salley, ed., *Narratives of Carolina*, 13–14; Robert Beverley, *The History and Present State of Virginia*, ed. Louis B. Wright (Chapel Hill, N.C., 1947), 214.

57. Lawson, *New Voyage*, ed. Lefler, 63; Banister, "Of the Natives," in Ewan and Ewan, eds., *Banister and His History*, 377; Hinke, trans. and ed., "Report of Michel," *VMHB*, XXIV (1916), 29.

58. Lawson, *New Voyage*, ed. Lefler, 214.

59. Council Journals, Aug. 4, 1716, *CRNC*, II, 242–243; Byrd, "Land of Eden," in Wright, ed., *Prose Works*, 398; *EJCCV*, III, 440. For archeological evidence that

hints at a preference for older sites, see Simpkins and Petherick, "Settlement Pattern Changes in the Carolina Piedmont."

60. A useful summary of the southeastern trade's origins may be found in Paul Chrisler Phillips, *The Fur Trade* (Norman, Okla., 1961), I, chap. 9. For general discussions of intercultural exchange, see Wilcomb E. Washburn, *The Indian in America*, New American Nation Series (New York, 1975), 66–80; Preston Holder, "The Fur Trade as Seen from the Indian Point of View," in John Francis McDermott, ed., *The Frontier Re-examined* (Urbana, Ill., 1967), 129–139; Francis Jennings, *The Invasion of America: Indians, Colonialism, and the Cant of Conquest* (Chapel Hill, N.C., 1975), chap. 6; Toby Morantz, "The Fur Trade and the Cree of James Bay," in Carol M. Judd and Arthur J. Ray, eds., *Old Trails and New Directions: Papers of the Third North American Fur Trade Conference* (Toronto, 1980), 39–58; Neal Salisbury, *Manitou and Providence: Indians, Europeans, and the Making of New England, 1500–1643* (New York, 1982), chaps. 2, 5.

61. Developments in the Virginia colony may be followed in Edmund S. Morgan, *American Slavery, American Freedom: The Ordeal of Colonial Virginia* (New York, 1975), 134–135; Wesley Frank Craven, *The Southern Colonies in the Seventeenth Century, 1607–1689*, vol. I of *A History of the South* (Baton Rouge, La., 1949), 196–198. For the interest in exploration, see A. J. Morrison, "The Virginia Indian Trade to 1673," *WMQ*, 2d Ser., I (1921), 217–236; William Waller Hening, ed., *The Statutes at Large: Being A Collection of All the Laws of Virginia, from the First Session of the Legislature in the Year 1619*, 13 vols. (Richmond, Philadelphia, 1809–1823), I, 262, 315, 376–377, 381; E[dward] W[illiams], *Virginia, More Especially the South Part Thereof, Richly and Truly Valued . . .* , 2d ed. (London, 1650), 18, 34–37, I2[A]–I3.

The most detailed study of Virginia's exploration, Alan Vance Briceland's *Westward from Virginia: The Exploration of the Virginia-Carolina Frontier, 1650–1710* (Charlottesville, Va., 1987), appeared after this section was written. While I agree with many of Professor Briceland's conclusions, my reading of the sources is at variance with his main thesis. He argues that before about 1675 fear of the unknown combined with provincial trade regulations to limit Virginia's penetration of the interior; there were, he believes, only a handful of exploratory expeditions, one in 1650, the rest not until 1669–1674. I see less evidence of "the chains of fear that shackled Virginians to tidewater," which Briceland grants that "Virginians did not often express" (93, 94), and I am less convinced of their obedience to trade regulations. Nor do I agree that a lack of evidence for other journeys during the 1650s and 1660s means that none occurred. Briceland himself (28) believes that there may have been explorers active in the 1630s and 1640s who did not set down an account of their travels for posterity; the same may have been true after 1650.

62. Thomas Ludwell to [Lord Arlington], June 27, 1670, CO 1/25, 85 (VCRP-CW, M-304). See also Petition of Mathias Decost, n.d., CO 1/66, 170 (VCRP-CW, M-328); *A Perfect Description of Virginia . . .* (London, 1649), 8–9, 13, in Peter Force, ed., *Tracts and Other Papers, Relating Principally to the Origin, Settlement, and Progress of the Colonies in North America, from the Discovery of the Country to the Year 1776*, 4 vols. (Washington, D.C., 1836–1841), II.

63. Cumming, ed., *Discoveries of Lederer*, 25–26, 37–42. For William Byrd's background, see Pierre Marambaud, "William Byrd I: A Young Virginia Planter in the 1670s," *VMHB*, LXXXI (1973), 131–150. For the crystal, see Byrd to Perry and Lane, June 16, 1688, in Marion Tinling, ed., *The Correspondence of the Three William Byrds of Westover, Virginia, 1684–1776*, 2 vols. (Charlottesville, Va., 1977), I, 82, Byrd to the Hon. Charles Howard, June 16, 1688, I, 83, Byrd to [Perry and Lane], ultimo 1. 1688[/89], I, 94 (quotation on 94). The dream of riches never faded completely. See Thad W. Tate, "The Discovery and Development of the Southern

Colonial Landscape: Six Commentators," American Antiquarian Society, *Proceedings*, XCIII (1983), 301–302.

Lederer's route has long been a subject of controversy (see Briceland, *Westward from Virginia*, chap. 7; Baker, "Cofitachique," app. 3). Some scholars assert that Lederer reached the Catawba River valley, others place him in central North Carolina, and still others are convinced that he invented the entire journey from secondhand accounts. Lederer's vagueness leaves room for many plausible interpretations, but most modern scholars agree that he did indeed make a journey into the interior, and his travels brought him into contact with many of the piedmont peoples under consideration here.

64. Henrico County Records [Deeds and Wills], 1677–1692, part 1, 216, microfilm, VSL. For notches and initials, see Cumming, ed., *Discoveries of Lederer*, 39; "The Expedition of Batts and Fallam: John Clayton's Transcript of the Journal of Robert Fallam," in Clarence Walworth Alvord and Lee Bidgood, eds., *The First Explorations of the Trans-Allegheny Region by the Virginians, 1650–1674* (Cleveland, Ohio, 1912), 186, 188, 191–192 (hereafter cited as Fallam, "Journal"); Byrd, "Land of Eden," in Wright, ed., *Prose Works*, 400. For the rivers, see Byrd, "History," in Wright, ed., *Prose Works*, 308–309.

65. Nicholson to Board of Trade, Dec. 2, 1701, CO 5/1312, part I, doc. no. 20 (LC trans., 212–213). One merchant later put the figure at 100 before 1708 (Journals of the Board of Trade, May 17, 1716, CO 391/108 [VCRP-CW, M-523]). For the "tradeing Voyage," see Henrico County Records [Deeds and Wills], 1677–1692, part 1, 216. South Carolina had not yet made its presence felt in the lands north of the Santee River. See below, chap. 2.

66. Precontact exchange awaits further investigation. But see Hudson, *Southeastern Indians*, 316; Sharon Iowa Goad, "Exchange Networks in the Prehistoric Southeastern United States" (Ph.D. diss., University of Georgia, 1978); Gloria J. Wentowski, "Salt as an Ecological Factor in the Prehistory of the Southeastern United States" (master's thesis, University of North Carolina, 1970), 2, chaps. 4–5. The fullest discussion of yaupon's place in the native Southeast is Charles M. Hudson, ed., *Black Drink: A Native American Tea* (Athens, Ga., 1979).

67. Cumming, ed., *Discoveries of Lederer*, 31. For the Cheraws' early trade with Virginia, see Byrd, "Land of Eden," in Wright, ed., *Prose Works*, 400; Wilson, "Feature Fill," xiv. For trade in 1701, see Lawson, *New Voyage*, ed. Lefler, 44, 48, 232.

68. Banister, "Of the Natives," in Ewan and Ewan, eds., *Banister and His History*, 384; Cumming, ed., *Discoveries of Lederer*, 20, 30, 32, 38–39. The one time Lederer did follow "the Indians instruction" he traveled by "easie journeys" (24). For others traveling on native paths, see Bland *et al.*, "Discovery of New Brittaine," in Salley, ed., *Narratives of Carolina*, 8–9, 11, 13, 16–18; Fallam, "Journal," in Alvord and Bidgood, eds., *First Explorations*, 184, 185, 187, 189.

69. Lawson, *New Voyage*, ed. Lefler, 34; Byrd, "History," in Wright, ed., *Prose Works*, 310; Cumming, ed., *Discoveries of Lederer*, 41.

70. Cumming, ed., *Discoveries of Lederer*, 23; Lawson, *New Voyage*, ed. Lefler, 192.

71. Bland *et al.*, "Discovery of New Brittaine," in Salley, ed., *Narratives of Carolina*, 10, 11, 18; Oviedo, *Narrative*, in Bourne, ed., *Narratives of De Soto*, II, 105–106; Garcilaso, *Florida*, ed. Varner and Varner, 333–334; Écija, "Report," in Barbour, ed., *Jamestown Voyages*, II, 299–300, 315–316.

72. Byrd to Perry and Lane, Apr. 25, 1684, in Tinling, ed., *Correspondence of Byrds*, I, 14. For the importance of gifts, see Lawson, *New Voyage*, ed. Lefler, 240; Byrd, "History," in Wright, ed., *Prose Works*, 222.

73. Lawson, *New Voyage*, ed. Lefler, 203, 232–233. For another reference to Vir-

ginia Indians' measuring by arm's length, see Stanley Pargellis, ed., "An Account of the Indians in Virginia," *WMQ*, 3d Ser., XVI (1959), 231.

74. Lawson, *New Voyage*, ed. Lefler, 192, 210; Byrd to Thomas Grendon, Apr. 29, 1684, in Tinling, ed., *Correspondence of Byrds*, I, 16, Byrd to ———, May 10, 1686, I, 59. For an earlier killing, see Abraham Wood to John Richards, Aug. 22, 1674, in Alvord and Bidgood, eds., *First Explorations*, 215–217. For later deaths, see Inventory of Henry Kent, Henrico County Records [Deeds and Wills], 1677–1692, part 2, 388; Francis Nicholson to the Committee, Jan. 26, 1690/91, CO 5/1306, 43 (LC trans.); *EJCCV*, I, 254–255.

The specific causes of these deaths are unknown. It is possible, of course, that traders were killed by Iroquois raiders or by piedmont peoples for any number of reasons other than bad manners. But given the penchant of later traders for pushing their luck (see chap. 2), and given the sharp native responses to breaches of custom (see Prologue), it seems likely that at least some of these men died because they had in some way offended the Indians. At the very least, their deaths were educational in the sense that they could make others more cautious.

75. Cumming, ed., *Discoveries of Lederer*, 38, 41.

76. Lawson, *New Voyage*, ed. Lefler, 24, 39.

77. Byrd to Perry and Lane, Mar. 29, 1685, in Tinling, ed., *Correspondence of Byrds*, I, 30, Byrd to Arthur North, Mar. 29, 1685, I, 31, Byrd to [Arthur North], June 5, 1685, I, 41 (cloth). Byrd to Perry and Lane, July 8, 1686, I, 64, Byrd to Perry and Lane, Nov. 10, 1686, I, 66 (beads). Byrd to [Arthur North?], Mar. 8, 1685[/86], I, 57 (hoes).

For a more general discussion, see Arthur J. Ray, "Indians as Consumers in the Eighteenth Century," in Judd and Ray, eds., *Old Trails and New Directions*, 255–271.

78. Banister, "Of the Natives," in Ewan and Ewan, eds., *Banister and His History*, 385. Excavation of a site thought to be Lawson's Occaneechee Town revealed that 92% of the trade beads were white. Linda F. Carnes, "Euroamerican Artifacts from the Fredricks, Wall, and Mitchum Sites," in Dickens *et al.*, eds., *The Siouan Project*, 151–152.

79. Julia E. Hammett, "Shell Artifacts from the Carolina Piedmont," in Dickens *et al.*, eds., *The Siouan Project*, 169, and fig. 7.3, p. 171; Lawson, *New Voyage*, ed. Lefler, 44–45; Stuart, "Post-Archaic Occupation," 133, fig. 72, B; Navey, "Mortuary Practices of the Sara," chap. 4. See also Carnes, "Euroamerican Artifacts," in Dickens *et al.*, eds., *The Siouan Project*, 145, 148–149; Ward and Wilson, "Mortuary Behavior"; Ward, "Mortuary Patterns," in Dickens *et al.*, eds., *The Siouan Project*, 81–110.

80. Lawson, *New Voyage*, ed. Lefler, 33, 63. Hinke, trans. and ed., "Report of Michel," *VMHB*, XXIV (1916), 42. Archeologists have found glass arrowheads in South Carolina. See Tommy Charles, "Thoughts and Records from the Survey of Private Collections of Artifacts throughout South Carolina: A Second Report," Inst. Arch. and Anthro., *Notebook*, XV (1983), 31.

81. Lawson, *New Voyage*, ed. Lefler, 104, 107, 109; Hinke, trans. and ed., "Report of Michel," *VMHB*, XXIV (1916), 129; V. Ann Tippitt and I. Randolph Daniel, Jr., "Lithic Artifacts from the Fredricks, Wall, and Mitchum Sites," in Dickens *et al.*, eds., *The Siouan Project*, 217–236 (bows and arrows). Carnes ("Euroamerican Artifacts," in *The Siouan Project*, 162) also notes the continuing manufacture of arrows, but wonders whether the trade guns were very popular with Indian customers. Coe, "Cultural Sequence," in Griffin, ed., *Archeology*, 310 (clay pots). Lawson, *New Voyage*, ed. Lefler, 197, 200; Hinke, trans. and ed., "Report of Michel," *VMHB*, XXIV (1916), 130, 132 (clothing). Cadwallader Jones to Lord Baltimore, Feb. 6,

1681/82, PRO, CO 1/48, ff 115–116 (VCRP-CW, M-327); Byrd to Stephanus Van Cortlandt, Aug. 3, 1691, in Tinling, ed., *Correspondence of Byrds*, I, 163; Inventory of Giles Webb, Feb. 1713/14, Henrico County Records [Deeds, Wills], 1710–1714, part 1, 241 (shell beads). See also Edward Porter Alexander, ed., *The Journal of John Fontaine: An Irish Huguenot Son in Spain and Virginia, 1710–1722* (Williamsburg, Va., 1972), 97–98.

82. Byrd to Perry and Lane, July 21, 1690, in Tinling, ed., *Correspondence of Byrds*, I, 118, Byrd to Van Cortlandt, Aug. 3, 1691, I, 163 (by "those Indians" Byrd meant Tuscaroras in this instance); Jones to Lord Baltimore, Feb. 6, 1681/82, CO 1/48, f 115.

83. Banister, "Of the Natives," in Ewan and Ewan, eds., *Banister and His History*, 382, 384; Garcilaso, *Florida*, ed. Varner and Varner, 313, 315–316; Oviedo, *Narrative*, in Bourne, ed., *Narratives of De Soto*, II, 102, 104; W[illiams], *Virginia*, 35.

84. John Evans, who kept a record of his trading activities in the Carolina piedmont between 1702 and 1715, recorded 515 deerskins, 9 beaver pelts, 7 otters, and 12 foxes. See John Evans, "Journal of a Virginia[?] Indian Trader in North and South Carolina[?] . . . ," South Caroliniana Library, University of South Carolina, Columbia. A general list of peltries shipped from the upper James River between 1712 and 1715 totaled 7,137 deerskins, 291¼ pounds of beaver pelts, 27 otters, 3 foxes, 3 wolves, 1 "catt," 12 elk, and 1 raccoon. "Abstract of the Export of skins and Furrs from ye Upper District of James River in Virginia for the four Years last past," CO 5/1318, 60 (LC trans., 39).

85. Hudson, *Southeastern Indians*, 274–279; Bruce D. Smith, "Middle Mississippi Exploitation of Animal Populations: A Predictive Model," *Am. Antiq.*, XXXIX (1974), 287–290; Gregory A. Waselkov, "Prehistoric Dan River Hunting Strategies" (master's thesis, University of North Carolina, 1977), 100–102; Jeannette Runquist, "Analysis of the Flora and Faunal Remains from Proto-Historic North Carolina Cherokee Indian Sites" (Ph.D. diss., North Carolina State University, 1979), 263, 275–276; Michael B. Barber and John C. Baroody, "Analysis of Vertebrate Faunal Remains from the Shannon Site, Montgomery County, Virginia," Arch. Soc. Va., *Qtly. Bull.*, XXXI (1976–1977), 104.

86. Lawson, *New Voyage*, ed. Lefler, 40; Edmund Berkeley and Dorothy S. Berkeley, eds., "Another 'Account of Virginia,' by the Reverend John Clayton," *VMHB*, LXXVI (1968), 434; Bruce D. Smith, *Middle Mississippi Exploitation of Animal Populations*, Museum of Anthropology, University of Michigan, Anthropological Papers, no. 57 (Ann Arbor, 1975), 19.

87. On stalking, see Lawson, *New Voyage*, ed. Lefler, 17, 29, 31, 51, 215; John Banister to Robert Morison, Apr. 6, 1679, and Banister, "Of the Natives," in Ewan and Ewan, eds., *Banister and His History*, 42–43, 385–386; Hinke, trans. and ed., "Report of Michel," *VMHB*, XXIV (1916), 41–42. The archeological evidence that suggests stalking may have been more common than drives awaits confirmation (Barber and Baroody, "Vertebrate Faunal Remains," Arch. Soc. Va., *Qtly. Bull.*, XXXI [1976–1977], 104; Waselkov, "Dan River Hunting," 124–125).

On fire-hunting, see Stephen J. Pyne, *Fire in America: A Cultural History of Wildland and Rural Fire* (Princeton, N.J., 1982), 48–50, chap. 2, 143–144. Doubts are being raised about Indians' systematic use of fire in forest management, however. See Emily W. B. Russell, "Indian-Set Fires in the Forests of the Northeastern United States," *Ecology*, LXIV (1983), 78–88. I am grateful to Timothy Silver for this reference.

88. Peter Martyr d'Anghera, *De Orbe Novo: The Eight Decades of Peter Martyr D'Anghera*, trans. Francis Augustus MacNutt, II (New York, 1912), 259; Cumming, ed.,

Discoveries of Lederer, 10, 18, 34, 35; Fallam, "Journal," in Alvord and Bidgood, eds., *First Explorations*, 190; *True Relation*, in Bourne, ed., *Narratives of De Soto*, I, 57.

89. On meat: Barber and Baroody, "Vertebrate Faunal Remains," Arch. Soc. Va., *Qtly. Bull.*, XXXI (1976–1977), 102; Runquist, "Analysis of Flora and Faunal Remains," 267; Waselkov, "Dan River Hunting," 95. On hides: *True Relation*, in Bourne, ed., *Narratives of De Soto*, I, 66, and Oviedo, *Narrative*, II, 99, 101. Smith, *Works*, ed. Barbour, II, 215; "Testimonio del viaje que hizo el Capitan Francisco Fernández de Écija . . . ," in Gene Waddell, *Indians of the South Carolina Lowcountry, 1562–1751* (Spartanburg, S.C., 1980), 226.

90. Henry Fleet, "A Brief Journal of a Voyage Made in the Bark Virginia, to Virginia and Other Parts of the Continent of America," in Edward D. Neill, ed., *The Founders of Maryland as Portrayed in Manuscripts, Provincial Records, and Early Documents* (Albany, N.Y., 1876), 20, 24.

91. J. Leitch Wright, Jr., *The Only Land They Knew: The Tragic Story of the American Indians of the Old South* (New York, 1981), 94, 132–137. For Virginia laws, see Hening, *Statutes*, I, 481–482, II, 143, 283, 346, 404, 490–492.

92. Henrico County Records [Deeds and Wills], part 1, 134–135, 216; Henry Woodward, "A Faithful Relation of My Westoe Voiage" (1674), in Salley, ed., *Narratives of Carolina*, 133; Jones to Lord Baltimore, CO 1/48, f 115; Henrico Co. Order Book, 1678–1693 (transcript, p. 84).

93. Garcilaso, *Florida*, ed. Varner and Varner, 329–330; Smith, *Works*, ed. Barbour, II, 120; Theda Perdue, *Slavery and the Evolution of Cherokee Society, 1540–1866* (Knoxville, Tenn., 1979), chap. 1.

94. Garcilaso, *Florida*, ed. Varner and Varner, 488; Le Jau to the Secretary, Sept. 15, 1708, in Klingberg, ed., *Carolina Chronicle of Le Jau*, 41; Cumming, ed., *Discoveries of Lederer*, 30; Lawson, *New Voyage*, ed. Lefler, 30.

95. Lawson, *New Voyage*, ed. Lefler, 58, 177; for midwinter rituals, see 34, 39, 42–45, 177. Archeological evidence of subsistence continuity is just now coming to light. See Mary Ann Holm, "Faunal Remains from the Wall and Fredricks Sites," in Dickens *et al.*, eds., *The Siouan Project*, 237–258, and Gremillion, "Plant Remains," 259–277.

96. Lawson, *New Voyage*, ed. Lefler, 220.

97. See Greg Dening, *Islands and Beaches: Discourse on a Silent Land: Marquesas, 1774–1880* (Honolulu, 1980), 235–236, 287; Lewis Hyde, *The Gift: Imagination and the Erotic Life of Property* (New York, 1979), chaps. 1–5. I am grateful to Peter Wood for alerting me to the latter reference.

98. Garcilaso, *Florida*, ed. Varner and Varner, 306; Lewis, "Sara Indians," 310; Coe, *Formative Cultures*, 49–50; Michael Trinkley and S. Homes Hogue, "The Wachesaw Landing Site: The Last Gasp of the Coastal Waccamaw Indians," *Southern Indian Studies*, XXXI (1979), 11; Tippitt, "Lithic Assemblages," 14–15.

99. Lawson, *New Voyage*, ed. Lefler, 18, 63, 210, 211, 212; Beverley, *History*, ed. Wright, 182. Some Virginia Indians tried to contain alcohol's excesses by appointing one or two to stay sober "and take care of the rest" when everyone got drunk. See Pargellis, ed., "Indians in Virginia," *WMQ*, 3d Ser., XVI (1959), 231. For general discussions of native American drinking, see Jerrold E. Levy and Stephen J. Kunitz, *Indian Drinking: Navaho Practices and Anglo-American Theories* (New York, 1974); Craig MacAndrew and Robert B. Edgerton, *Drunken Comportment: A Social Explanation* (Chicago, 1969), esp. chap. 5.

100. Lawson, *New Voyage*, ed. Lefler, 18, 240; see also 184, 211.

101. Harold Hickerson, "Fur Trade Colonialism and the North American Indians," *Journal of Ethnic Studies*, I (Summer 1973), 18–22; Hyde, *The Gift*, chap. 4.

The redistributive exchange pattern in areas under the Cofitachiques' authority may have been somewhat different. Even here, however, since constituent peoples remained self-sufficient, it can be argued that tribute and redistribution were more for political, ceremonial, and symbolic purposes.

102. "Virginias Deploured Condition . . . ," in *The Aspinwall Papers*, pt. 1 (Massachusetts Historical Society, *Collections*, 4th Ser., IX [Boston, 1871]), 167; Wood to Richards, Aug. 22, 1674, in Alvord and Bidgood, eds., *First Explorations*, 211, 215–217, 223–225; Cumming, ed., *Discoveries of Lederer*, 25–26. For Bacon's attack, see Wilcomb E. Washburn, *The Governor and the Rebel: A History of Bacon's Rebellion in Virginia* (Chapel Hill, N.C., 1957), 42–46.

For earlier efforts to maintain a middleman's position, see Bland *et al.*, "Discovery of New Brittaine," in Salley, ed., *Narratives of Carolina*, 10–12.

103. Lawson, *New Voyage*, ed. Lefler, 64.

104. Coe, "Cultural Sequence," in Griffin, ed., *Archeology*, 308; Stuart, "Post-Archaic Occupation," abstract, and 158. Some scholars suggest that the Town Creek people's collapse predated European intrusion. See Baker, "Cofitachique," 151.

105. Stephen Bull to Lord Ashley, Sept. 12, 1670, in Cheves, ed., *Shaftesbury Papers*, 194. The best study of Westos is John T. Juricek, "The Westo Indians," *Ethnohistory*, XI (1964), 134–173.

106. Maurice Mathews to Lord Ashley, Aug. 30, 1671, in Cheves, ed., *Shaftesbury Papers*, 334; Cumming, ed., *Discoveries of Lederer*, 30.

107. See Verner W. Crane, *The Southern Frontier, 1670–1732* (New York, 1981 [orig. publ. 1928]), 16–21. Lords Proprietors to the Governor, Grand Council, and Parliament, Sept. 30, 1683, in *BPRO-SC, 1663–1684*, 255–258.

108. For fuller discussion of the conflict's origins, see James H. Merrell, "'Their Very Bones Shall Fight': The Catawba-Iroquois Wars," in Daniel K. Richter and James H. Merrell, eds., *Beyond the Covenant Chain: The Iroquois and Their Neighbors in Indian North America, 1600–1800* (Syracuse, N.Y., 1987).

109. Banister to Morison, Apr. 6, 1679, in Ewan and Ewan, eds., *Banister and His History*, 38–40; Lawrence H. Leder, ed., *The Livingston Indian Records, 1666–1723* (Gettysburg, Pa., 1956), 54–55, 61, 70–71, 85, 87; *JHBV, 1619–1658/59*, 147, 159; *EJCCV*, I, 253; "Virginia in 1681," *VMHB*, XXV (1917), 369; Jones to Lord Baltimore, Feb. 6, 1681/82, CO 1/48, f 115; "Queries Sent by the Lords of the Councell of trade and Plantations to be Answered by the Govern[o]r of Virginia," encl. no. 1, Edmund Andros to Board of Trade, Apr. 22, 1697, CO 5/1309, doc. no. 16 (LC trans.).

110. Lawson, *New Voyage*, ed. Lefler, 53.

111. Richard Aquila, "Down the Warrior's Path: The Causes of the Southern Wars of the Iroquois," *American Indian Quarterly*, IV (1978), 211–221; Daniel K. Richter, "War and Culture: The Iroquois Experience," *WMQ*, 3d Ser., XL (1983), 528–559; Anthony F. C. Wallace, *The Death and Rebirth of the Seneca* (New York, 1970), 41–48 (quotation on 47). Virginia was convinced that their principal goal was the destruction of the colony's neighboring Indians. See Nicholas Spencer to ———, Nov. 23, 1683, CO 1/53, 183 (VCRP-CW, M-327); Leder, ed., *Livingston Records*, 125.

112. *JHBV, 1619–1658/59*, 15; Leder, ed., *Livingston Records*, 85; "Notes from the Records of Stafford County, Virginia, Order Books," *VMHB*, XLV (1937), 378; "Observations of Wentworth Greenhalgh. In a Journey from Albany to the Indians, Westward; Begun May 20th, 1677, and Ended July the 14th Following," *DRCNY*, I, 13. See also "Virginia in 1681," *VMHB*, XXV (1917), 369.

113. Garcilaso, *Florida*, ed. Varner and Varner, 284, 330. Smith, *Works*, ed. Barbour, II, 119–120. But see also Garcilaso, *Florida*, ed. Varner and Varner, 488:

"Regardless of where they are found, [they] are always provided with arms, for in no place are they secure from enemies."

114. Lawson, *New Voyage*, ed. Lefler, 50, 53 (see also 29, 52, 55, 56); Cumming, ed., *Discoveries of Lederer*, 25. Jones to Lord Baltimore, Feb. 6, 1681/82, CO 1/48, f 115. For archeological evidence of increased storage, see Simpkins and Petherick, "Settlement Changes in the Piedmont."

115. Lawson, *New Voyage*, ed. Lefler, 59. Archeological evidence also suggests a growth in the number of traumatic injuries and violent deaths. It should be stressed, however, that the evidence is by no means conclusive. See Homes Hogue Wilson, "Human Skeletal Remains from the Wall and Fredricks Sites," in Dickens *et al.*, eds., *The Siouan Project*, 122–123, 127, 138–139.

116. Lawson, *New Voyage*, ed. Lefler, 61–66 (quotations on 61, 62).

117. *Ibid.*, 62.

118. Byrd, "Land of Eden," in Wright, ed., *Prose Works*, 382. Byrd called this 78-year-old Indian "Shacco-Will," an understandable mistake if the Enos and Shakoris had merged many years earlier. Will's age, his personality, and especially his familiarity with the Eno River and its tributaries all make it extremely likely that Byrd and Lawson met the same man. He probably moved to Virginia shortly after 1710, and some of his people may have accompanied him. See *EJCCV*, III, 240.

119. Lawson, *New Voyage*, ed. Lefler, 64–65. Virginia Indians had a similar attitude. See Pargellis, ed., "Indians in Virginia," *WMQ*, 3d Ser., XVI (1959), 236.

120. Lawson, *New Voyage*, ed. Lefler, 26. Lawson knew others, similarly struck by "the Pox," who saved themselves and went on to become medicine men as a result (229). This malady apparently was a form of venereal disease which, as Lawson pointed out, "had its first Rise . . . in this new World" (25). Thus the ailment can hardly be considered foreign to the Western Hemisphere. On the other hand, however, Lawson believed that the strain which struck the Santees was one "the *Indians* often get by the *English* Traders that use amongst them" (25), so Santees could well have considered it a new and alien illness. In any case, the point lies less in the origins of the disorder than in the priest's response to it.

121. *Ibid.*, 26–27.

122. Cumming, ed., *Discoveries of Lederer*, 4.

123. Banister to Morison, Apr. 6, 1679, in Ewan and Ewan, eds., *Banister and His History*, 41–42. Byrd to Daniel Horsmanden, Aug. 8, 1690, in Tinling, ed., *Correspondence of Byrds*, I, 136; Henrico Co. Recs., Order Book, 1678–1693 (transcript, p. 40); Evans, "Journal."

For Byrd's knowledge, see "Extract from a Letter of Mr. Clayton to the Royal Society, read to them October 24, 1688," in Alvord and Bidgood, eds., *First Explorations*, 194. For his ruthlessness, see Nicholas Spencer to ———, Mar. 18, 1679/80, CO 1/44, 131 (VCRP-CW, M-319); Hinke, trans. and ed., "Report of Michel," *VMHB*, XXIV (1916), 30.

124. Banister, "Of the Natives," in Ewan and Ewan, eds., *Banister and His History*, 382 (spoon); Lawson, *New Voyage*, ed. Lefler, 47 (trading girls), 62 (bird), 176 (fingernails).

125. Lawson, *New Voyage*, ed. Lefler, 184; Pargellis, ed., "Indians in Virginia," *WMQ*, 3d Ser., XVI (1959), 232.

126. Hinke, trans. and ed., "Report of Michel," *VMHB*, XXIV (1916), 131; Lawson, *New Voyage*, ed. Lefler, 44–45.

127. For "Northern," see Alexander S. Salley, Jr., ed., *Journal of the Grand Council of South Carolina, April 11, 1692–September 26, 1692* (Columbia, S.C., 1907), 53.

For "Esaws," see Maurice Mathews to Lord Ashley, Aug. 30, 1671, in Cheves, ed., *Shaftesbury Papers*, 334; A. S. Salley, Jr., *Journal of the Grand Council of South Carolina*,

August 25, 1671–June 24, 1680 (Columbia, S.C., 1907), 64; Instructions for Mr. And[re]w Percivall, Feb. 21, 1680/81, *BPRO-SC, 1663–1684*, 106; "A Plat of the Province of Carolina in North America The South part Actually Surveyed By Mr: Maurice Mathews. Joel Gascoyne fecit.," British Museum, Photostats of Maps, box 1, Newberry Library, Chicago. For the translation of *Esaw*, see Albert S. Gatschet, "Onomatology of the Catawba River Basin," *Am. Anthropologist*, N.S., IV (1902), 52.

For "Western," see Gov. Nicholson to the Board of Trade, Dec. 2, 1701, CO 5/1312, part I, doc. no. 20 (LC trans.); Spotswood to Council of Trade, July 26, 1712, *CVSP*, I, 171–172. For "Usherees," see Cumming, ed., *Discoveries of Lederer*, 30; Banister, "Of the Natives," in Ewan and Ewan, eds., *Banister and His History*, 384; Byrd, "History," in Wright, ed., *Prose Works*, 309.

128. Henry Woodward to Sir John Yeamans, Sept. 10, 1670, in Cheves, ed., *Shaftesbury Papers*, 186; see also Yeamans to Lords Proprietors, 1670, 218, Bull to Lord Ashley, Sept. 12, 1670, 194. Baker ("Cofitachique," xiii, 5, 111) suggests the lingering Spanish influence.

129. See Lord Ashley to William Owen, Apr. 10, 1671, in Cheves, ed., *Shaftesbury Papers*, 313, Maurice Mathews to Lord Ashley, Aug. 30, 1671, 334. For last references to the Cofitachiques, see Instructions for Percivall, Feb. 21, 1680/81, *BPRO-SC, 1663–1684*, 106. Baker ("Cofitachique," 34–38) is more willing to grant the Cofitachiques considerable power as late as 1670, based on his conviction that colonists did indeed have a clear idea about the political character of the societies they met.

130. See below, chap. 2.

131. Lawson, *New Voyage*, ed. Lefler, 239–240.

Chapter 2

1. John Lawson, *A New Voyage to Carolina*, ed. Hugh Talmage Lefler (Chapel Hill, N.C., 1967), 18–19.

2. *Ibid.*, 19.

3. *EJCCV*, III, 412.

4. Alexander S. Salley, Jr., ed., *Journal of the Grand Council of South Carolina, April 11, 1692–September 26, 1692* (Columbia, S.C., 1907), 53. South Carolina's early expansion may be followed in Verner W. Crane, *The Southern Frontier, 1670–1732* (New York, 1981 [orig. publ. 1928]), chaps. 1–3, pp. 109–110, 132–133.

For Charleston's fleeting contacts with peoples to the north, see H[enry] Woodward to Sir John Yeamans, Sept. 10, 1670, in Langdon Cheves, ed., *The Shaftesbury Papers and Other Records Relating to Carolina and the First Settlement on Ashley River Prior to the Year 1676*, South Carolina Historical Society, *Collections*, V (Charleston, S.C., 1897), 186–187, Carolina Council to the Lords Proprietors, Sept. 11, 1670, 191, Stephen Bull to Lord Ashley, Sept. 12, 1670, 194, William Owen to Lord Ashley, Sept. 15, 1670, 201; Maurice Mathews to Lord Ashley, Aug. 30, 1671, 334, John Locke's notes on a letter from Joseph West, 1671, 388; A. S. Salley, Jr., ed., *Journal of the Grand Council of South Carolina, August 25, 1671–June 24, 1680* (Columbia, S.C., 1907), 64, 66; Maurice Mathews, "A Contemporary View of Carolina in 1680," *SCHM*, LV (1954), 155; Instructions for Mr. And[re]w Percivall, Feb. 21, 1680/81, *BPRO-SC, 1663–1684*, 106.

For possible trade to the north, see Daniel W. Fagg, Jr., "St. Giles' Seigniory: The Earl of Shaftesbury's Carolina Plantation," *SCHM*, LXXI (1970), 117–123; Records of the Secretary of the Province, 1675–1695, 80, SCDAH; Thomas Cooper and D.

J. McCord, eds., *The Statutes at Large of South Carolina*, 10 vols. (Columbia, S.C., 1836–1841), I, 66; John Archdale, "A New Description of That Fertile and Pleasant Province of Carolina" (1707), in Alexander S. Salley, Jr., ed., *Narratives of Early Carolina, 1650–1708*, Original Narratives of Early American History (New York, 1911), 301–302.

5. *JCHA-SC for the Two Sessions of 1697*, 21; *JCHA-SC for the Two Sessions of 1698*, 25. See also Edmond Jenings, Deputy Secretary; Address of the Governor of Virginia to the House of Burgesses, Oct. 23, 1697, *CVSP*, I, 55; *JHBV, 1659/60–1693*, 105.

6. Lords Proprietors to the Governor and Council at Ashley River in Carolina, Mar. 7, 1680/81, *BPRO-SC, 1663–1684*, 116, 118.

7. *Ibid.*, 116.

8. *JCHA for 1698*, 25. See also Crane, *Southern Frontier*, 153–157; Paul Chrisler Phillips, *The Fur Trade* (Norman, Okla., 1961), I, 336–340; John Phillip Reid, *A Better Kind of Hatchet: Law, Trade, and Diplomacy in the Cherokee Nation during the Early Years of European Contact* (University Park, Pa., 1976), 40–41.

9. *JCHA for 1698*, 22.

10. Lawson, *New Voyage*, ed. Lefler, 48–49 (tribute); *JCHA-SC for the Session Beginning February 4, 1701 and Ending March 1, 1701*, 8; Cooper and McCord, eds., *Statutes at Large*, II, 164–165 (horses). See also *JCHA-SC, 1702*, 23.

11. Cooper and McCord, eds., *Statutes at Large*, II, 309–316 (quotation on 310). For the story of trade regulation, see Crane, *Southern Frontier*, chap. 6.

12. Jenings to the Board of Trade, June 24, 1708, CO 5/1316, f 7 (LC transcripts, 23), Jenings to Board of Trade, Oct. 8, 1709, and enclosures, f 41 (LC trans., 177–179, 183–193); *EJCCV*, III, 177–178, 191, 194, 197, 201, 203; Jenings to the Earl of Sunderland, June 24, 1708, *CVSP*, I, 124; Lords Commissioners of Trade and Plantations to the Lords Proprietors of Carolina, Nov. 10, 1708, in *BPRO-SC, 1701–1710*, 211, Lords Proprietors to the Lords Commissioners of Trade and Plantations, Dec. 9, 1708, 212, Lords Commissioners of Trade and Plantations to the Lords Proprietors, Feb. 2, 1708/9, 236, Lords Proprietors to the Lords Commissioners of Trade and Plantations, Aug. 8, 1709, 290–291. Crane (*Southern Frontier*, 155) follows the Carolina proprietors in arguing that the law Moore used was an older one requiring payment of an export duty on deerskins; the timing of the journey favors the more recent statute.

13. For Hix's efforts, see Jenings to Nathaniel Johnson, Apr. 22, 1708, encl. in Jenings to the Board of Trade, Oct. 8, 1709, CO 5/1316, ff 41 (LC trans., 183), Deposition of Robert Hix, encl. (LC trans., 189–190); *JCHA-SC, October 22, 1707–February 12, 1707/8*, 9.

14. Savannah attacks on the colony are noted in SCCHJ, Apr. 8, 1707, in Commons House Journals, March 6, 1706–April 24, 1707, box 1, 31–33, SCDAH; *JCHA-SC, June 5, 1707–July 19, 1707*, 26–27; Council Journal, July 22, 1707, *MPCP*, II, 404.

For attacks on Northern Indians, see *JCHA-SC, October 22, 1707–February 12, 1708*, 23, 38, 45.

15. *JCHA-SC, 1707–1708*, 62; see also 55; Francis Le Jau to the Secretary, Mar. 13, 1708, in Frank J. Klingberg, ed., *The Carolina Chronicle of Dr. Francis Le Jau, 1706–1717*, University of California Publications in History, LIII (Berkeley, Calif., 1956), 35.

16. Governor and Council to the Lords Commissioners of Trade and Plantations, Sept. 17, 1708, *BPRO-SC, 1701–1710*, 209; SCCHJ, Apr. 21, 23, 28, 30, 1709, RSUS, S.C. A.1b, 1/1, 142, 147–148, 153–155, 160; Joseph W. Barnwell, ed.,

"The Tuscarora Expedition: Letters of Colonel John Barnwell," *SCHGM*, IX (1908), 35. For the Tuscarora War, see Crane, *Southern Frontier*, 158–161; J. Leitch Wright, Jr., *The Only Land They Knew: The Tragic Story of the American Indians in the Old South* (New York, 1981), 117–121; Thomas C. Parramore, "The Tuscarora Ascendancy," *NCHR*, LIX (1982), 307–326.

17. Crane, *Southern Frontier*, app. A, table 1.

18. For Privy Council actions, see Copy of an Order of Council of the 26th, upon a Representation of the 6th of September, 1709, CO 5/1316, f 33 (LC trans., 159–160); PRO Privy Council, 2/84, 66 (Dec. 19, 1712), VCRP-CW, M-899. For the 1711 act, see Cooper and McCord, eds., *Statutes at Large*, II, 357–359. For confiscations, see Lt. Gov. Spotswood to the Council of Trade, Dec. 15, 1710, in R. A. Brock, ed., *The Official Letters of Alexander Spotswood, Lieutenant-Governor of the Colony of Virginia, 1710–1722*, 2 vols. (Virginia Historical Society, *Collections*, N.S., I–II [Richmond, Va., 1882–1885]), I, 42, Spotswood to the Council of Trade, Sept. 5, 1711, I, 112, Spotswood to the Council of Trade, July 26, 1712, I, 172; *JCIT*, 14, 33; SCCHJ, May 16, June 3, 7, 1712, RSUS, S.C. A.1b, 1/3, esp. 6, 11, May 16, 1712, 1/4, 31.

19. Spotswood to Col. Craven, Mar. 26, 1715, *CVSP*, I, 180. See also *EJCCV*, III, 194.

20. *EJCCV*, III, 201; Petition of the Visitors and Governors of the College of William and Mary to the President and Council of Virginia, Nov. 1708, encl. in Jenings to the Board of Trade, Nov. 27, 1708, CO 5/1316, f 16, encl. ii (LC trans., 102).

21. My views here have been shaped by John Phillip Reid, *A Law of Blood: The Primitive Law of the Cherokee Nation* (New York, 1970), esp. chap. 16.

22. Salley, ed., *Jour. Grand Coun., 1692*, 53; H. R. McIlwaine, ed., *Legislative Journals of the Council of Colonial Virginia*, 3 vols. (Richmond, Va., 1918–1919), I, 139.

23. William Byrd to [Perry and Lane], June 3, 1691, in Marion Tinling, ed., *The Correspondence of the Three William Byrds of Westover, Virginia, 1684–1776*, 2 vols. (Charlottesville, Va., 1977), I, 153; Cooper and McCord, eds., *Statutes at Large*, II, 64–68; Salley, ed., *Jour. Grand Coun., 1692*, 31.

24. Fagg, "St. Giles' Seigniory," *SCHM*, LXXI (1970), 117–123.

25. SCCHJ, Feb. 9, 23, 1710/11, RSUS, S.C. A.1b, 1/1, 272–274, 288; *EJCCV*, III, 200, 207, 214, 567.

26. Archdale, "Description," in Salley, ed., *Narratives of Carolina*, 285; Coun. Jour., July 27, 1739, *MPCP*, IV, 337–340.

27. Le Jau to the Secretary, Feb. 1, 1710, in Klingberg, ed., *Carolina Chronicle of Le Jau*, 68; SCCHJ, June 14, 1711, RSUS, S.C. A.1b, 1/1, 309.

28. SCCHJ, June 14, 1711, RSUS, S.C. A.1b, 1/1, 309.

29. *JCIT*, 14, 18, 19; A. S. Salley, Jr., *George Hunter's Map of the Cherokee Country and the Path Thereto in 1730*, Bulletin of the Historical Commission of South Carolina, no. 4 (Columbia, S.C., 1917). For the identity of the Indians on this map, see John R. Swanton, *The Indians of the Southeastern United States*, Smithsonian Institution, Bureau of American Ethnology, Bulletin, no. 137 (Washington, D.C., 1946), 177, 184; Part of a Creek Town and Population List, done by Charles. Glover, encl. in Francis Varnod to the Secretary, Mar. 21, 1725, SPG, MSS A, XIX, 93.

30. Christian F. Feest, "Notes on Saponi Settlements in Virginia Prior to 1714," Archeological Society of Virginia, *Quarterly Bulletin*, XXVIII (1973–1974), 152–155; Jenings to the Board of Trade, Sept. 20, 1708, CO 5/1316, no. 9 (LC trans., 55); *EJCCV*, III, 188–189, 196, 296, 310, 332, 366, 566.

31. Treaty of Peace between Virginia and the Saponis, Stuckanoes, Occonee-chees, and Totteros, Feb. 27, 1713[/14], CO 5/1316 (LC trans., 620–627). Spots-

wood to the Council and House of Burgesses, Nov. 1713, *CVSP*, I, 168–169; *EJCCV*, III, 363–368, 376, 396–397.

32. For the fort, see Edward P. Alexander, ed., *The Journal of John Fontaine: An Irish Huguenot Son in Spain and Virginia, 1710–1719* (Williamsburg, Va., 1972), 91, 93, 96–97; Richard Beresford to ——, July 4, 1716, CO 5/1265, 162–163 (VCRP-CW, M-2004); Mary C. Beaudry, "Colonizing the Virginia Frontier: Fort Christanna and Governor Spotswood's Indian Policy," in Stephen L. Dyson, ed., *Comparative Studies in the Archaeology of Colonialism*, B.A.R. International Series 233 (Oxford, 1985), 130–152. I am grateful to Professor Beaudry for sending me this essay.

33. Beresford to ——, July 4, 1716, CO 5/1265, 162 (VCRP-CW, M-2004); Alexander, ed., *Journal of Fontaine*, 93–94, 98; Deposition of Charles Griffin, Jan. 4, 1716[/17], encl. in Spotswood to the Board of Trade, Jan. 16, 1716/17, CO 5/1318, 181 (LC trans., 143).

34. Alexander, ed., *Journal of Fontaine*, 93; Treaty of Peace between Virginia and the Saponis, Feb. 27, 1713[/14], CO 5/1316 (LC trans., 621–625).

35. William P. Cumming, ed., *The Discoveries of John Lederer* (Charlottesville, Va., 1958), 41–42. Archeological evidence confirms the disparity. A town on the Dan River, tentatively identified as Cheraw and dated to the latter half of the 17th century, contained an abundance of beads, spoons, bracelets, and scissors, but scarcely a trace of arms and ammunition. See Henry Trawick Ward, "The Spatial Analysis of the Plow Zone Artifact Distributions from Two Village Sites in North Carolina" (Ph.D. diss., University of North Carolina, 1980), 180–182, 191; Liane Navey, "An Introduction to the Mortuary Practices of the Historic Sara" (master's thesis, University of North Carolina, 1982).

This transition period was even more complex than suggested here. Often the same observers—Lederer, Lawson, and others—who noted native control of the trade also included in their accounts glimpses of the future, when the situation was reversed. In dividing native from colonial dominance for analytical purposes, then, to some degree I simplify the process. I am grateful to Neal Salisbury for pointing this out to me.

36. John Banister, "Of the Natives: Their Habit, Customes and Manner of Living," in Joseph Ewan and Nesta Ewan, eds., *John Banister and His Natural History of Virginia, 1678–1692* (Urbana, Ill., 1970), 382; Lawson, *New Voyage*, ed. Lefler, 38.

37. Lawson, *New Voyage*, ed. Lefler, 107, 175. Linda F. Carnes, "Euroamerican Artifacts from the Fredricks, Wall, and Mitchum Sites," in Roy S. Dickens *et al.*, eds., *The Siouan Project: Seasons I and II* (Chapel Hill, N.C., 1987), 144.

38. Byrd, "The History of the Dividing Line betwixt Virginia and North Carolina Run in the Year of Our Lord 1728," in Louis B. Wright, ed., *The Prose Works of William Byrd of Westover: Narratives of a Colonial Virginian* (Cambridge, Mass., 1966), 228 (cures), 254 (horses), 253 (sky), "The Secret History of the Line," 94, 99 (cures), "A Journey to the Land of Eden Anno 1733," 395 (whistle).

Byrd's recorded travels with the traders took place in 1728 and 1733, well after the period under discussion here. There are, however, a number of good reasons for extending his portrait of the traders into an earlier era. First, Byrd knew about the trade and the traders from his father and from his own contacts with them since his father's death in 1704. Hence it is likely that he would have noted any deviation from earlier norms. Second, his companions were themselves longstanding members of the trading fraternity: men like Robert Hix and John Evans had been visiting the piedmont before the turn of the century. Finally, while there undoubtedly were changes in the details of the trading routine, it is more likely that the development traced here—that traders felt comfortable or at home in the piedmont—began before the Yamasee War, when many men entered the area annually, than after 1720, when the flow was reduced (see below).

39. Warmth: *ibid.*, "History," 266, "Secret History," 127. Bear: "History," 265, "Secret History," 126–127. Intoxicants: "History," 240, "Land of Eden," 401–402.

40. *Ibid.*, "History," 249, "Secret History," 126.

41. T. H. Breen, *Puritans and Adventurers: Change and Persistence in Early America* (New York, 1980), chaps. 6, 8; Byrd, "Land of Eden," in Wright, ed., *Prose Works*, 395, 397.

Byrd, in Wright, ed., *Prose Works*. Swamps: "History," 182–183, 185, 187–188, 201, "Secret History," 58–59, 60, 61–62, 71. Packs: "History," 189, "Secret History," 62, 71. Injuries: "Land of Eden," 395.

42. Byrd, in Wright, ed., *Prose Works*: "Secret History," 58, 115, "History," 241–242, "Land of Eden," 399.

43. *Ibid.*, "Secret History," 71, 99, 135–136, "History," 197.

44. Cumming, ed., *Discoveries of Lederer*, 41–42; Byrd to [Arthur North], June 5, 1685, in Tinling, ed., *Correspondence of Byrds*, I, 41, Byrd to [Arthur North?], Mar. 8, 1685[/86], I, 57.

45. Lawson, *New Voyage*, ed. Lefler, 232–233; Lords Proprietors to the Grand Council of South Carolina, May 13, 1691, in [William James Rivers], *A Sketch of the History of South Carolina to the Close of the Proprietary Government by the Revolution of 1719* (Charleston, S.C., 1856), 416.

46. Lawson, *New Voyage*, ed. Lefler, 65 (see also 57, 59, 63, 64); John Evans, "Journal of a Virginia[?] Indian Trader in North and South Carolina[?] . . . ," South Caroliniana Library, Columbia.

47. Evans, "Journal"; Hugh Jones, *The Present State of Virginia, from Whence Is Inferred a Short View of Maryland and North Carolina*, ed. Richard L. Morton (Chapel Hill, N.C., 1956), 57. For false steelyards, see William Waller Hening, ed., *The Statutes at Large: Being a Collection of All the Laws of Virginia, from the First Session of the Legislature in the Year 1619*, 13 vols. (Richmond, Philadelphia, 1809–1823), I, 391; Talk of Gov. Glen to the Cherokees, Nov. 20, 1751, *DRIA, May 21, 1750–August 7, 1754*, 186. See also Ludovic Grant to Glen, May 3, 1752, *DRIA, 1750–1754*, 262; Grant to Glen, Mar. 27, 1755, in *DRIA, 1754–1765*, 41.

48. Lawson, *New Voyage*, ed. Lefler, 49–50, 60–61. The evidence for this shift can be only impressionistic. William Byrd's letters from the 1680s suggest that the traders went out in early March and returned in May. After 1700, on the other hand, traders were among the Indians in July, August, October, and December. For pre-1700, see Byrd to Thomas Grendon, Apr. 29, 1684, in Tinling, ed., *Correspondence of Byrds*, I, 16, Byrd to [Arthur North?], Mar. 8, 1685[/86], I, 57; Byrd to Perry and Lane, Mar. 8, 1685[/86], I, 58; Byrd to ———, May 10, 1686, I, 59; Byrd, "Land of Eden," in Wright, ed., *Prose Works*, 400; Henrico County, Virginia, Record Book, No. 2, 1678–1693 [Deeds, Wills, Settlements of Estates, Etc.] (transcript of Henrico County Order Book, 1678–1693), 74, microfilm, VSL; Henrico County Records [Deeds and Wills], 1677–1692, part 2, 487, microfilm, VSL. For the years after 1700, see Depositions of Robert Hix, David Crawley, James Lundy, and Nathaniel Urven, encl. in Jenings to Board of Trade, Oct. 8, 1709, CO 5/1316, f 41 (LC trans., 189–193); Evans, "Journal"; Copy of a bond required of those authorized to trade with the Western Indians, and Copy of a passport given to traders with the Western Indians, July 1712, *CVSP*, I, 155–156; Louis B. Wright and Marion Tinling, eds., *The Secret Diary of William Byrd of Westover, 1709–1712* (Richmond, Va., 1941), 447–448.

49. Evans, "Journal."

50. Lawson, *New Voyage*, ed. Lefler, 35–36, 192.

51. *Ibid.*, 23, 24.

52. *EJCCV*, I, 254. See also Nicholson to the Committee, Jan. 26, 1690/91, CO 5/1306, f 37 (LC trans., 43); Representation of the Lieut. Governor and Council of Virginia, Jan.[?] 1691, CO 5/1306, f 41 (LC trans., 89–90).

53. David Crawley to Lords Commissioners of Trade and Plantations, July 30, 1715, BPRO-SC, VI, 110–111. The transcript has "minds" being debauched, which appears to be a copyist's error.

54. Besides the 1707 incident noted above, see SCCHJ, Feb. 17, 1715, RSUS, S.C. A.1b, 1/4, 359.

55. The only recorded Virginia abuses may be found in *EJCCV*, II, 351–352, 381–382, 390, 402, 405; Nathaniel Johnson to Jenings, July 22, 1708, encl. in Jenings to the Board of Trade, Oct. 8, 1709, CO 5/1316, f 41 (LC trans., 187). For examples of South Carolina's abuses, see Crane, *Southern Frontier*, 152–153, 162–166; Wright, *Only Land They Knew*, 121–122.

56. Lawson, *New Voyage*, ed. Lefler, 10.

57. *JCIT*, 9, 11. For Yamasees, see Crane, *Southern Frontier*, 25–26.

58. Crawley to Lords Commissioners of Trade and Plantations, July 30, 1715, BPRO-SC, VI, 111. For Wright and Nairne, see Crane, *Southern Frontier*, 150–152.

59. See Richard L. Haan, "The 'Trade Do's Not Flourish as Formerly': The Ecological Origins of the Yamasee War of 1715," *Ethnohistory*, XXVIII (1981), 341–358.

60. Reid, *Better Kind of Hatchet*, chaps. 5–6; *JCIT*, 65. This census may be found in Gov. Johnson to the Lords Commissioners of Trade and Plantations, Jan. 12, 1719/20, BPRO-SC, VII, 238–239.

61. See Crane, *Southern Frontier*, chap. 7. Le Jau to the Secretary, May 10, 1715, in Klingberg, ed., *Carolina Chronicle of Le Jau*, 152, Le Jau to the Secretary, May 14, 1715, 154, Le Jau to the Secretary, May 21, 1715, 158; Gov. Craven to Sec. Lord Townshend, May 23, 1716, *CRNC*, II, 177–178; Thomas Hasell to the Secretary, May 26, 1715, SPG MSS A, X, doc. no. 17, 97–98, William Tredwell Bull to the Secretary, Aug. 16, 1715, XI, 57–58, Nathaniel Osborne to the Secretary, May 29, 1715, X, doc. no. 18, 99–100.

62. Le Jau to the Secretary, May 10, 1715, in Klingberg, ed., *Carolina Chronicle of Le Jau*, 153; George Rodd, "Relation" (in French), CO 5/387, no. 1, quoted in Crane, *Southern Frontier*, 171.

63. SCCHJ, May 6–13, 1715, RSUS, S.C. A.1b, 1/4, 388–415, esp. 397 (quotation on 389).

64. *Ibid.*, May 8, 1715, 398–399; Le Jau to the Secretary, Aug. 23, 1715, in Klingberg, ed., *Carolina Chronicle of Le Jau*, 163; Rev. Claudius Philippe de Richebourg to the Secretary, Feb. 12, 1716, SPG MSS A, XI, 140. For another account of the Northern Indians' participation in the Yamasee War, see Douglas Summers Brown, *The Catawba Indians: The People of the River* (Columbia, S.C., 1966), 133–150.

65. Le Jau to the Secretary, May 10, 21, 1715, in Klingberg, ed., *Carolina Chronicle of Le Jau*, 152, 158.

66. Benjamin Dennis to the Secretary, May 28, 1715, SPG MSS A, X, doc. no. 20, 102; Le Jau to the Secretary, May 21, 1715, in Klingberg, ed., *Carolina Chronicle of Le Jau*, 159, 160.

67. See Le Jau to the Secretary, May 10, 1715, in Klingberg, ed., *Carolina Chronicle of Le Jau*, 153; Bull to the Secretary, Aug. 16, 1715, SPG MSS A, XI, 57–62; Testimony of several Carolina planters, merchants, and ship captains before the

Lords Commissioners of Trade and Plantations, July 16, 1715, BPRO-SC, VI, 137–138.

68. Only one complaint against South Carolina survives, and even that was apparently resolved without bloodshed. See *JCIT*, 33. For another (unsubstantiated) claim of Virginia abuses, see Phillips, *The Fur Trade*, I, 337.

69. Lawson, *New Voyage*, ed. Lefler, 210.

70. See Samuel Cole Williams, ed., *Adair's History of the American Indians* (New York, 1974 [orig. publ. 1930]), 167–168.

71. Crane, *Southern Frontier*, 158–159. The war's causes and course may be followed in Hugh T. Lefler and William S. Powell, *Colonial North Carolina: A History* (New York, 1973), 65–80.

72. Barnwell, ed., "Letters of Barnwell," *SCHGM*, IX (1908), 38, 42, 51, 52–53.

73. *EJCCV*, III, 304; see also 310–311, 324.

74. Spotswood to the Lords Commissioners of Trade, May 9, 1716, in Brock, ed., *Letters of Spotswood*, II, 147–148; Barnwell, ed., "Letters of Barnwell," *SCHGM*, IX (1908), 38.

75. Barnwell, ed., "Letters of Barnwell," *SCHGM*, IX (1908), 40–41.

76. Spotswood to the Lords Commissioners of Trade, June 4, 1715, in Brock, ed., *Letters of Spotswood*, II, 114.

77. Le Jau to the Secretary, Feb. 20, 1712, in Klingberg, ed., *Carolina Chronicle of Le Jau*, 109.

78. Spotswood to the Lords Commissioners of Trade, June 4, 1715, in Brock, ed., *Letters of Spotswood*, II, 114; Catawba Nation to the Creeks, 1751[?], George Clinton Papers, XIV, William L. Clements Library, Ann Arbor, Mich.

79. *EJCCV*, III, 412. Some scholars argue that the Yamasee War was a nativistic movement that united the remnants of the Cofitachiques. The list of participants does not match the Cofitachiques' domain very closely, however. See Steven G. Baker, "Cofitachique: Fair Province of Carolina" (master's thesis, University of South Carolina, 1974), 182; Wright, *Only Land They Knew*, 121.

80. Extracts of Letters from Carolina relating to the Indian War, *CRNC*, II, 251. See also *CRNC*, II, 252–253; *EJCCV*, III, 405–406; Robert Daniell and others to Spotswood, June 22, 1715, *CVSP*, I, 181–182; Memorial from Mr. Kettleby and several merchants trading to Carolina, Sept. 16, 1715, *CRNC*, II, 201–202.

81. Evans, "Journal." For other evidence that Indians may have stocked up on weapons and ammunition, see William Guy to the Secretary, May 25, 1715, SPG MSS A, X, doc. no. 19, 101.

82. Robert Beverley, *The History and Present State of Virginia*, ed. Louis B. Wright (Chapel Hill, N.C., 1947), 204; Spotswood to the Council of Trade, July 26, 1712, in Brock, ed., *Letters of Spotswood*, I, 167.

83. *EJCCV*, III, 405–406.

84. Letter from a Gentleman in Charleston (probably George Rodd) to the Carolina Agents in London, July 19, 1715, in Langdon Cheves, ed., *City of Charleston, Year Book—1894* (Charleston, S.C., 1895), 320.

85. Barnwell, ed., "Letters of Barnwell," *SCHGM*, IX (1908), 35; Spotswood to Hunter, Mar. 2, 1716, *CVSP*, I, 178; *EJCCV*, III, 412.

86. Richebourg to the Secretary, Feb. 12, 1716, SPG MSS A, XI, 140–141; Le Jau to the Secretary, May 21, 1715, in Klingberg, ed., *Carolina Chronicle of Le Jau*, 158–160; SCCHJ, May 7, 1715, RSUS, S.C. A.1b, 1/4, 392; Crane, *Southern Frontier*, map, frontispiece; Dennis to the Secretary, May 28, 1715, SPG MSS A, X, doc. no. 20, 102.

87. Le Jau to the Secretary, May 21, Aug. 23, 1715, in Klingberg, ed., *Carolina*

Chronicle of Le Jau, 158, 163, Le Jau to [?] John Chamberlain, Aug. 22, 1715, 161; Letter from a Gentleman, July 19, 1715, in Cheves, ed., *Year Book*, 319; SCCHJ, Aug. 20, 1715, RSUS, S.C. A.1b, 1/4, 442; Robert Mills, *Statistics of South Carolina, Including a View of Its Natural, Civil, and Military History, General and Particular* (Spartanburg, S.C., 1972 [orig. publ., 1826]), 487–488.

88. Le Jau to the Secretary, May 21, Aug. 23, 1715, in Klingberg, ed., *Carolina Chronicle of Le Jau*, 159, 163, Le Jau to [?]Chamberlain, Aug. 22, 1715, 160–161; Bull to the Secretary, Aug. 16, 1715, SPG MSS A, XI, 58; Mills, *Statistics of South Carolina*, 488.

89. SCCHJ, May 7, 1715, RSUS, S.C. A.1b, 1/4, 391; Le Jau to [?]Chamberlain, Aug. 22, 1715, in Klingberg, ed., *Carolina Chronicle of Le Jau*, 161, Le Jau to the Secretary, Aug. 23, 1715, 163–164; *Boston News-Letter*, July 11, 1715; Bull to the Secretary, Aug. 16, 1715, SPG MSS A, XI, 58; Letter from a Gentleman, July 19, 1715, in Cheves, ed., *Year Book*, 319–320.

90. *EJCCV*, III, 405–406.

91. Spotswood to the Lords Commissioners of Trade, Aug. 9, 1715, in Brock, ed., *Letters of Spotswood*, II, 128.

92. See *Boston News-Letter*, Aug. 26, 1715.

93. Letter from a Gentleman, July 19, 1715, in Cheves, ed., *Year Book*, 320. Henceforth Cherokees would be on the side of peace, using diplomacy or threats against South Carolina's northern enemies to bring them to give up the fight as well. See Commons House Committee to the South Carolina Agents in London [?], Aug. 6, 1716, BPRO-SC, VI, 241; *JCIT*, 221; [George Chicken], "Journal of the March of the Carolinians into the Cherokee Mountains, in the Yemassee Indian War, 1715–1716, from the Original Manuscript," in Cheves, ed., *Year Book*, 340–342; SCCHJ, Mar. 5–7, 1716, RSUS, S.C. A.1b, 2/1, 26.

94. Le Jau to [?]Chamberlain, Aug. 22, 1715, in Klingberg, ed., *Carolina Chronicle of Le Jau*, 161–162; Letter from a Gentleman, July 19, 1715, in Cheves, ed., *Year Book*, 321; Commissioners of the Commons House of Assembly to the South Carolina Agents, Aug. 25, 1715, BPRO-SC, VI, 133–134.

95. *EJCCV*, III, 405–406 (for shipments, see 402–404); Spotswood to the Lords Commissioners of Trade, July 15, 1715, in Brock, ed., *Letters of Spotswood*, II, 119–120; Letter from a Gentleman, July 19, 1715, in Cheves, ed., *Year Book*, 320.

96. *EJCCV*, III, 412.

97. William Guy to the Secretary, Sept. 20, 1715, SPG MSS A, XI, 68; *EJCCV*, III, 412.

98. Gov. Hunter to Sec. Popple, Oct. 10, 1715, *DRCNY*, V, 450; Le Jau to the Secretary, July 1, 1716, in Klingberg, ed., *Carolina Chronicle of Le Jau*, 180.

99. *JHBV, 1702/3–1705, 1705–1706, 1710–1712*, 80, 90, 116; W. Neil Franklin, ed., "Act for the Better Regulation of the Indian Trade: Virginia, 1714," *VMHB*, LXXII (1964), 141–151. Spotswood to the Bishop of London, Jan. 27, 1714[/15], in Brock, ed., *Letters of Spotswood*, II, 88–89, Spotswood to the Lords Commissioners of Trade, Jan. 27, 1714[/15], II, 95.

100. Memorial from Kettleby, Sept. 16, 1715, *CRNC*, II, 201–202, Extracts of Letters from Carolina, II, 252–253; Commons House Commissioners to the South Carolina Agents, Aug. 25, 1715, BPRO-SC, VI, 131–132; SCCHJ, June 28, 1716, RSUS, S.C. A.1b, 1/3; Extract of a Letter from South Carolina, Feb. 6, 1717, BPRO-SC, VII, 20–21; Coun. Jour., Aug. 23, 1716, *CRNC*, II, 246–247.

101. Bull to the Secretary, Aug. 16, 1715, SPG MSS A, XI, 58. See also Le Jau to the Secretary, Aug. 23, 1715, in Klingberg, ed., *Carolina Chronicle of Le Jau*, 164; *Boston News-Letter*, July 11, 1715.

102. Le Jau to [?]Chamberlain, Aug. 22, 1715, in Klingberg, ed., *Carolina Chronicle of Le Jau*, 162. See also Memorial from Kettleby, Sept. 16, 1715, *CRNC*, II, 201; *Boston News-Letter*, Oct. 31, 1715.

103. *EJCCV*, III, 406, 412, 422; Spotswood to Mr. Sec. Stanhope, Oct. 24, 1715, in Brock, ed., *Letters of Spotswood*, II, 131. See also *EJCCV*, III, 406, 412, 422, 447; Passport to the Southern Indians to come to Virginia to treat for peace and commerce, *CVSP*, I, 182.

104. Spotswood to the Lords Commissioners of Trade and Plantations, Feb. 7, 1715[/16], in Brock, ed., *Letters of Spotswood*, II, 209, Spotswood to Mr. Popple, Apr. 16, 1717, II, 237. See also Memorial of Indian Traders and Merchants to the Governor, Council, and Commons House of Assembly of South Carolina, July 4, 1735, BPRO-SC, XVII, 414.

105. For South Carolina, see Bull to the Secretary, May 16, 1716, SPG MSS A, XI, 148; SCCHJ, June 15, 1716, RSUS, S.C. A.1b, 1/3; Le Jau to the Secretary, July 1, 1716, in Klingberg, ed., *Carolina Chronicle of Le Jau*, 180.

For Virginia, see *EJCCV*, III, 442–443; Spotswood to Popple, Apr. 16, 1717, in Brock, ed., *Letters of Spotswood*, II, 236–237; "Journal of the Lieut. Governor's Travels and Expeditions Undertaken for the Public Service of Virginia," *WMQ*, 2d Ser., III (1923), 44–45.

106. Waxhaws: Commons House Committee to the South Carolina Agents [?], Aug. 6, 1716, BPRO-SC, VI, 241. Santees and Congarees: SCCHJ, Nov. 21, 28–30, Dec. 4, 7, 12, 13, 1716, Jan. 25, Dec. 5, 1717, RSUS, S.C. A.1b, 1/3; *JCIT*, 138. Cheraws: SCCHJ, June 28, Dec. 14, 1716, RSUS, S.C. A.1b, 1/3; Le Jau to the Secretary, July 1, 1716, in Klingberg, ed., *Carolina Chronicle of Le Jau*, 180–181; Extracts of Letters from Carolina, *CRNC*, II, 251–252; Coun. Jour., Aug. 4, 23, 1716, *CRNC*, II, 242–243, 246–247; *EJCCV*, III, 435–436; Extract of a Letter from South Carolina, Feb. 6, 1717, BPRO-SC, VII, 20–21; *JCIT*. Waccamaws: ——— to Joseph Boone, June 24, 1720, BPRO-SC, VIII, 26; SCCHJ, June 22, 1722, RSUS, S.C. A.1b, 2/3, 47; Commons House to Thomas Moore, [May 6, 1720], BPRO-SC, VII, 309. Yamasees: Thomas Hasell to the Secretary, Aug. 1, 1719, SPG MSS A, XIII, 239; Francis Yonge to the Lords Commissioners of Trade and Plantations, [Feb. 1723], BPRO-SC, X, 2; SCCHJ, Aug., Sept. 1727, RSUS, S.C. A.1b, 3/2.

107. SCCHJ, May 6, 1715, RSUS, S.C. A.1b, 1/4, 389: Hasell to the Secretary, Oct. 11, 1718, SPG MSS A, XIII, 191; Clergy of South Carolina to the Secretary, Oct. 13, 1715, in Frank J. Klingberg, ed., *Carolina Chronicle: The Papers of Commissary Gideon Johnston, 1707–1716*, University of California Publications in History, XXXV (Berkeley, Calif., 1946), 147; Report of the Lords Commissioners of Trade and Plantations, Sept. 8, 1721, BPRO-SC, IX, 72. See also Spotswood to the Lords Commissioners for Trade and Plantations, Apr. 5, 1717, in Brock, ed., *Letters of Spotswood*, II, 227. For earlier and similar assessments, see Lawson, *New Voyage*, ed. Lefler, 243–244; "De Graffenried's Manuscript, copied . . . from the Original Mss. in the Public Library at Yverdon, Switzerland . . . ," *CRNC*, I, 984. For an admission that trade was to blame, see SCCHJ, June 30, 1716, RSUS, S.C. A.1b, 1/3.

108. *JCIT*, 177, 179; *EJCCV*, III, 422.

109. Franklin, ed., "Act for the Indian Trade," *VMHB*, LXXII (1964), 144. For details on its operation, see the debate over the law's validity in CO 5/1317, 1318, CO 391/108, and Spotswood to the Lords Commissioners of Trade, May 9, 1716, in Brock, ed., *Letters of Spotswood*, II, 144–150.

110. Commons House Agents to the Lords Commissioners of Trade and Plantations, [Dec. 5, 1716], BPRO-SC, VI, 265. The story of the act's passage may be

followed in SCCHJ, May, June, 1716, RSUS, S.C. A.1b, 1/3. The act itself is reprinted in *JCIT*, 325–329. For the Catawbas' presence, see SCCHJ, June 30, 1716, RSUS, S.C. A.1b, 1/3. Further details about its operation may be found in *JCIT*. The best scholarly discussion of the public monopoly is in Reid, *Better Kind of Hatchet*, chaps. 8–12.

111. Francis Yonge to the Lords Commissioners of Trade and Plantations, Mar. 22, 1722/3, BPRO-SC, XXII, 348–349.

112. CO 5/1318, 144 (LC trans., 130). South Carolina received the news in Lords Proprietors to the Governor and Council, July 22, 1718, BPRO-SC, VII, 145. For the debates, see Reid, *Better Kind of Hatchet*, 123–125; Jack P. Greene, "The Opposition to Lieutenant Governor Alexander Spotswood, 1718," *VMHB*, LXX (1962), 35–42.

113. *JHBV, 1712–1714, 1715, 1718, 1720–1722, 1723–1726*, 212; Cooper and McCord, eds., *Statutes at Large*, III, 86–96, 141–145, 230–231. See Reid, *Better Kind of Hatchet*, chaps. 13–14, 16; and Crane, *Southern Frontier*, chap. 8.

114. See Reid, *Better Kind of Hatchet*, 88.

115. *JCIT*, 95, 144, 180, 211, 212; see also 156, 211.

116. *Ibid.*, 221. For the opening of trade, see *EJCCV*, III, 440; Memorial of the Virginia Indian Company in answer to the petition of persons styling themselves merchants trading to and inhabitants of Virginia and Maryland, Apr. 24, 1717, CO 5/1318, 88 (LC trans.). For Virginians among the Cheraws, see Extract of a Letter from South Carolina, Feb. 6, 1717, BPRO-SC, VII, 20–21; *JCIT*, 265, 276.

117. Byrd, "History," in Wright, ed., *Prose Works*, 310, 311; *JCIT*, 211, 221, 272; Rena Vassar, ed., "Some Short Remarkes on the Indian Trade in the Charikees and in Managment Thereof since the Year 1717," *Ethnohistory*, VIII (1961), 405–412.

118. *JCIT*, 207, 211–212; Deposition of George Rives, Sept. 8, 1719, Prince George County, Virginia, Deeds, Etc., 1713–1728, part II, 350, microfilm, VSL.

119. Spotswood to the Board of Trade, Feb. 1, 1719[1720], in Brock, ed., *Letters of Spotswood*, II, 331 (falling prices). *EJCCV*, IV, 1–2, 17–18. Richard West to the Lords Commissioners of Trade and Plantations, Oct. 25, 1722, BPRO-SC, XXII, 338–345; W. Neil Franklin, "Virginia and the Cherokee Indian Trade, 1673–1752," East Tennessee Historical Society, *Publications*, IV (1932), 14–15.

120. Byrd, "History," in Wright, ed., *Prose Works*, 308; Statement by [?John Savy], 1728, PRO, *Calendar of State Papers, Colonial Series, America and West Indies, 1728–1729* (London, 1937), no. 396, p. 210. For more on the Virginia traders, see SCCHJ, May 23, 1734, RSUS, S.C. A.1b, 4/3, 179; Gov. Robert Johnson to the Lords Commissioners of Trade and Plantations, Nov. 9, 1734, BPRO-SC, XVII, 190–191.

121. *JCIT*, 152, 153; Vassar, ed., "Some Short Remarkes," *Ethnohistory*, VIII (1961), 406; *JCHA, February 20, 1744–May 25, 1745*, 20–21; Thomas Brown Inventory, Charleston Inventories, MM, 1746–1748, 169, SCDAH; Alexander Kilpatrick Will, in Wills, Book LL, 1737–1740, 229–231, SCDAH.

122. *JCIT*, 119, 156, 177, 181; SCCHJ, Nov. 17, 1716, RSUS, S.C. A.1b, 1/3.

123. The story of the Congarees garrison may be followed in *JCIT*.

124. Vassar, ed., "Some Short Remarkes," *Ethnohistory*, VIII (1961), 416.

125. SCCJ, Dec. 2, 1735, RSUS, S.C. E.1p, 1/2, 25; *JCHA, September 12, 1739–March 26, 1741*, 114–115, *March 28, 1749–March 19, 1750*, 360.

126. *JCIT*, 110, 112–113, 163. The Northward factory was eventually placed where the Indians wanted it (*JCIT*, 74, 80, 111, 208, 210). Compare prices set for Settlement Indians with those at Savannah Town, the Cherokees, and the Creeks, in *JCIT*, 89, 104, 269, 281; for outsiders' visiting the lowcountry, see 259.

127. SCUHJ, Jan. 5, 1722, RSUS, S.C. A.1a, 1/1, 150; *SCG*, Dec. 19, 1743 (proclamations). Cooper and McCord, eds., *Statutes at Large*, III, 332, 371–372; SCCHJ, Sept. 14, 15, 1733, RSUS, S.C. A.1b, 4/1, 1127, 1129–1130; Petition of Thomas Brown, in SCUHJ, Nov. 28, 1733, RSUS, S.C. A.1a, 2/1, 668–669.

128. For Wigan, see *JCIT*; SCCHJ, Dec. 4, 8, 14, 15, 1716, RSUS, S.C. A.1b, 1/3. For John, see *JCIT*, 74, 76, 192, 265, 275–276; SCCHJ, June 20, Dec. 14, 1716, RSUS, S.C. A.1b, 1/3.

129. *JCIT*, 119, 132, 137, 144, 297; George Chicken, "Colonel Chicken's Journal to the Cherokees, 1725," in Newton D. Mereness, ed., *Travels in the American Colonies* (New York, 1916), 104, 132–133; SCUHJ, Jan. 18, 1738/39, RSUS, S.C. A.1a, 3/1, 140; *JCHA, November 10, 1736–June 7, 1739*, 595.

130. SCCHJ, May 24, 1734, RSUS, S.C. A.1b, 4/3, 186; *JCIT*, 202, 320. Public Treasurer's Accounts, Dec. 9, 1725, Ledger A, 1726, f 57, SCDAH; Evans to Glen, Dec. 16, 1755, *DRIA, 1754–1765*, 89; Evans to William Henry Lyttelton, Sept. 7, 1759, William Henry Lyttelton Papers, Clements Library.

131. One exception was Marr, accused of trade abuses in 1724. But Marr apparently assaulted fellow traders and colonists as often as he did Indians. In any case, he was more a holdover of past habits than a harbinger of future behavior. See *JCHA-SC, June 2, 1724–June 16, 1724*, 4, 11, 33, 45–46; Records of the South Carolina Court of Common Pleas, Judgment Rolls, 1723, no. 215, 1724, nos. 18A, 19A, SCDAH.

132. Williams, ed., *Adair's History*, 369 (Brown); Evans to Glen, Apr. 18, 1748, in SCCJ, Apr. 27, 1748, RSUS, S.C. E.1p, 3/4, 233 (Evans). For other examples, see Journal of John Evans, Oct. 1755, *DRIA, 1754–1765*, 87, Feb.–Mar. 1756, 107 (Lewis John). Public Treasurer's Accounts, Apr. 23–28, 1725, Ledger A, 1725; Jour. of Evans, Oct. 1755, *DRIA, 1754–1765*, 86 (James Bullen).

133. SCCJ, May 6, 1760, RSUS, S.C. E.1p, 8/3, 120.

134. Brown to Glen, July 23, 1744, *ibid.*, July 25, 1744, 2/3, 427; *JCHA, 1736–1739*, 488; *JCHA, September 14, 1742–January 27, 1744*, 194, 250–251, 257, 364, 377; Catawbas to Glen, Oct. 15, 1754, *DRIA, 1754–1765*, 14; Glen to Stephen Crell, Mar. 22, 1747/48, in SCCJ, Mar. 29, 1747/48, RSUS, S.C. E.1p, 3/4, 186.

135. Byrd, "History," in Wright, ed., *Prose Works*, 311.

136. *JCHA-SC for the Session Beginning February 23, 1724/5 and Ending June 1, 1725*, 113; A Treaty between North Carolina Commissioners and the Catawba Indians, Aug. 29, 1754, *CRNC*, V, 144a.

137. SCCJ, May 29, 1758, RSUS, S.C. E.1p, 8/1, 204.

138. SCCHJ, May 24, 29, 1717, RSUS, S.C. A.1b, 1/3 (no gift). *Ibid.*, Nov. 1, 1717; *JCIT*, 223 (Creeks). *EJCCV*, III, 507.

139. For this incident, see Jones, *Present State of Virginia*, ed. Morton, 57, 59; *EJCCV*, III, 442–443, 450; Spotswood to Mr. Sec. Methuen, May 30, 1717, in Brock, ed., *Letters of Spotswood*, II, 251–252, Spotswood to the Lords Commissioners for Trade and Plantations, Aug. 29, 1717, II, 257–259; Spotswood to Hunter, May 30, 1717, in Lawrence Leder, ed., *The Livingston Indian Records, 1666–1723* (Gettysburg, Pa., 1956), 222–223.

140. Jones, *Present State of Virginia*, ed. Morton, 59; Spotswood to Popple, Apr. 16, 1717, in Brock, ed., *Letters of Spotswood*, II, 236, 237; Spotswood to Hunter, Mar. 2, 1715, *CVSP*, I, 179.

141. *JHBV, 1712–1714, 1715, 1718, 1720–1722, 1723–1726*, 199; see also 201, 204–205, 207, 213–216, 335; *EJCCV*, III, 479.

142. "An Acco[un]t of Nathaniel Harrison's proceedings when he went out, by Order of Governm[en]t, to meet with the Cautaubau Indians . . . ," encl. in Gooch to Board of Trade, Sept. 21, 1727, CO 5/1321, 11 (LC trans., 13–14).

143. *JCHA, 1736–1739*, 488.

144. Byrd, "Land of Eden," in Wright, ed., *Prose Works*, 393.

145. Jones, *Present State of Virginia*, ed. Morton, 59.

Chapter 3

1. For Nicholson's arrival, see M. Eugene Sirmans, *Colonial South Carolina: A Political History, 1663–1763* (Chapel Hill, N.C., 1966), 131. For his career, see Stephen Saunders Webb, "The Strange Career of Francis Nicholson," *WMQ*, 3d Ser., XXIII (1966), 513–548; Bruce T. McCully, "Governor Francis Nicholson, Patron *Par Excellence* of Religion and Learning in Colonial America," *WMQ*, 3d Ser., XXXIX (1982), 310–333, esp. 330–331. The crown had taken control of the colony after a revolt against the proprietors in 1719.

2. "A Map Describing the Situation of the several Nations of Indians between South Carolina and the Massisipi River; was Copyed from a Draught Drawn and Painted upon a Deer Skin by an Indian Cacique: and Presented to Francis Nicholson Esqr. Governour of Carolina," PRO, CO Library, North Am. Colonies, General 6 (copies in LC and Archer Butler Hulbert, comp., *The Crown Collection of Photographs of American Maps*, 3d Ser., I [Cleveland, Ohio, 1913], pls. 7–8). This was one of two deerskin maps Nicholson received. See G. Malcolm Lewis, "Indian Maps," in Carol M. Judd and Arthur J. Ray, eds., *Old Trails and New Directions: Papers of the Third North American Fur Trade Conference* (Toronto, 1980), 9–23, esp. 14–15.

3. See Juan de la Vandera, "Proceeding of the account which Captain Juan Pardo gave of the entrance which he made into the land of the Floridas, Prepared for the Lieutenant Governor of Florida, Santo Domingo, Apr. 1, 1569," A. I., 1569, 54-5-9, Vandera (typescript translation [by Herbert Ketcham?] of a photostatic copy in the Spanish Archives Collection, NCDAH), 16; John Lawson, *A New Voyage to Carolina*, ed. Hugh Talmage Lefler (Chapel Hill, N.C., 1967), 49–50. For South Carolina's shift to *Catawba*, see *JCIT*, 14, 19; "An Exact Account of the number and Strength of all the Indian Nations that were Subject to the Governm[en]t of South Carolina and Solely Traded with them in the begining of the Year 1715 . . . ," encl. in Gov. Robert Johnson to the Commissioners of Trade and Plantations, Jan. 12, 1719/20, BPRO-SC, VII, 239. For Virginia's shift, see *EJCCV*, III, 405–406; William Byrd, "The History of the Dividing Line betwixt Virginia and North Carolina Run in the Year of Our Lord 1728," in Louis B. Wright, ed., *The Prose Works of William Byrd of Westover: Narratives of a Colonial Virginian* (Cambridge, Mass., 1966), 309. The confusion over names is summarized in James Mooney, *The Siouan Tribes of the East*, Smithsonian Institution, Bureau of American Ethnology, Bulletin, no. 22 (Washington, D.C., 1894), 67–68; Douglas Summers Brown, *The Catawba Indians: The People of the River* (Columbia, S.C., 1966), 18–24.

For the way in which an intruding society perceives and identifies indigenous peoples, see Robert A. Levine and Donald T. Campbell, *Ethnocentrism: Theories of Conflict, Ethnic Attitudes, and Group Behavior* (New York, 1972), 91.

4. Glen to Lords Commissioners of Trade and Plantations, Feb. 1751, BPRO-SC, XXIV, 285.

5. SCCHJ, Nov. 21, 28–30, Dec. 4, 7, 12, 13, 1716, Jan. 25, 1716/17, RSUS, S.C. A.1b, 1/3; ——— to Joseph Boone, June 24, 1720, BPRO-SC, VIII, 26; Johnson to the Lords Commissioners of Trade and Plantations, Jan. 12, 1719/20, BPRO-SC, VII, 236. According to the *Oxford English Dictionary* the term "extirpate" may have meant merely to remove or root out rather than exterminate. I am grateful to Wesley White for pointing this out to me.

6. Johnson to the Lords Commissioners of Trade and Plantations, Jan. 12, 1719/20, BPRO-SC, VII, 236.

7. Spotswood to the Board of Trade, Dec. 22, 1718, CO 5/1318, 590 (LC transcripts, 488). This may have been smallpox, which was reported in Charleston earlier that year. See *JCIT*, 266.

8. Account of the Indian nations in 1715, encl. in Johnson to the Lords Commissioners of Trade and Plantations, Jan. 12, 1719/20, BPRO-SC, VII, 239; for the 1720 estimates, see Johnson to the Lords Commissioners of Trade and Plantations, Jan. 12, 1719/20, VII, 236, Answers to Queries, 1720, VIII, 70.

Catawbas, for example, were said to have 570 men in 1715, but only 900 women and children. In 1720 all of the Northern Indians were said to have 1,000 warriors, but only 2,500 people. The figures here are well below the generally accepted minimal warrior-to-population ratio for native American groups of 1:4 or 1:5. In 1755, the Catawbas' ratio was said to be 1:5. See Gov. Arthur Dobbs to the Board of Trade, Aug. 24, 1755, *CRNC*, V, 359. For the generally accepted ratio, see Sherburne F. Cook, "Interracial Warfare and Population Decline among the New England Indians," *Ethnohistory*, XX (1973), 13; Henry F. Dobyns, *Their Number Become Thinned: Native American Population Dynamics in Eastern North America* (Knoxville, Tenn., 1983), essay 4, sect. 2.

9. *EJCCV*, III, 310.

10. *Ibid.*, III, 452, 499, 507–512, 514, 517–521, IV, 8, 126, 132–133, 139, 185–186; Lt. Gov. William Gooch to the Board of Trade, Mar. 26, 1729, CO 5/1321, 221 (LC trans.); Conference between Gov. Spotswood and the Five Nations, Aug.–Sept. 1722, *DRCNY*, V, 669–677. William Waller Hening, ed., *The Statutes at Large: Being a Collection of All the Laws of Virginia, from the First Session of the Legislature in the Year 1619*, 13 vols. (Richmond, Philadelphia, 1809–1823), IV, 103–106.

11. Conference between Gov. William Burnet and the Six Nations, Sept. 9, 13, 1726, *DRCNY*, V, 793, 796; W[illiam] Hatton to Gov. Nicholson, Nov. 14, 1724, BPRO-SC, XI, 277; George Chicken to Arthur Middleton, President of the Council, Aug. 30, 1725, SCUHJ, Nov. 1, 1725, RSUS, S.C. A.1a, 1/4, 124; Hugh Meredith, *An Account of the Cape Fear Country, 1731*, ed. Earl Gregg Swem (Perth Amboy, N.J., 1922), 28.

12. *EJCCV*, IV, 180. *JCHA, February 20, 1744–May 25, 1745*, 20–22, 131–132; SCCJ, June 8, 15, 1739, RSUS, S.C. E.1p, 1/6, 26–27.

13. *EJCCV*, IV, 76–77, 133; Byrd, "The Secret History of the Line," in Wright, ed., *Prose Works*, 146, "History," 315; SCCHJ, Dec. 15, 1732, RSUS, S.C. A.1b, 4/1, 888, SCUHJ, Dec. 15, 1732, Jan. 17, 1733, A.1a, 2/1, 258, 342, 344.

14. A few Saponis did join Tuscarora remnants in North Carolina during the 1730s. See below.

15. "The Examination of Antonio Eleanore a Spaniard belonging to St. Augustin ... taken Before The Governour and Council ... ," Nov. 10, 1719, BPRO-SC, VIII, 7 ("Cattapaws" and "Wahaws" living at Saint Augustine). For the Saponi peoples among the Iroquois, see below.

16. See *JCIT*, 110, 115–116, 119, 132, 140, 203 (deerskin traders); 280 (packhorsemen); 92–93, 202, 318 (boat); 187, 189 (tanning).

For Indians' serving as slavecatchers before the Yamasee War, see R[obert] F[erguson], *The Present State of Carolina, with Advice to the Settlers* (London, 1682), 5; *JCHA-SC for the Four Sessions of 1693*, 27; SCCHJ, May 20, 1712, RSUS, S.C. A.1b, 1/3, [12].

For the continuation of this role after the conflict, see *JCIT*, 80; *JCHA-SC for the Session Beginning February 23, 1724/5 and Ending June 1, 1725*, 25, 49; SCCHJ, May 8, 1728, Mar. 5, 1730/31, May 12, July 15, 1731, Jan. 19, 1732, RSUS, S.C. A.1b,

4/1, 506, 638, 686, 751, 896, SCCHJ, Feb. 4, 1733/34, 4/2, 94; *JCHA-SC, November 8, 1734–June 7, 1735,* 59.

For allies in the Yamasee War, see SCCHJ, Aug. 8, 9, 1715, RSUS, S.C. A.1b, 1/4, 429, 430, SCCHJ, June 30, Nov. 21, 28–30, Dec. 7, 12, 1716, Jan. 25, 1716/17, Apr. 17, 1717, 1/3. For later alliances and ranger service, see John Barnwell to Gov. Nicholson, Sept. 17, 1723, BPRO-SC, X, 148; SCCJ, Sept. 29, 1727, May 3, 1729, Feb. 8, 1730, WM 91, 104, 192–193, 250, microfilm, SCDAH; SCCHJ, May 3, 1728, RSUS, S.C. A.1b, 4/1, 502.

17. For examples, see Frank J. Klingberg, ed., *The Carolina Chronicle of Dr. Francis Le Jau, 1706–1717,* University of California Publications in History, LIII (Berkeley, Calif., 1956); Robert Maule to Mr. Chamberlaine, Aug. 2, 1711, SPG MSS A, VII, 363–365, Benjamin Dennis to the Secretary, Mar. 21, 1714, X, 83–84, Representation of the Inhabitants of St. James Santee in South Carolina to Gov. Nicholson, encl. in Nicholson to the SPG, Nov. 6, 1721, XV, 65, reports of Thomas Hasell, pastor of St. Thomas Parish, to the SPG, X, 98 (doc. no. 17), XIII, 241, XIV, 70, XV, 55, XVI, 63, 82, XVII, 79, 123, XVIII, 72, XIX, 53, Francis Varnod to David Humphreys, Apr. 1, 1724, Ser. B, IV, no. 173 (quoted in Frank J. Klingberg, *An Appraisal of the Negro in South Carolina: A Study in Americanization* [Washington, D.C., 1941], 56–57); W. Orr to the Secretary, St. Paul's Parish, Mar. 30, 1743, North Carolina Letterbook of the SPG, *CRNC,* IV, 622; Robert Beverley, *The History and Present State of Virginia,* ed. Louis B. Wright (Chapel Hill, N.C., 1947), 195–198, 200–201; Byrd, "Secret History," in Wright, ed., *Prose Works,* 118–120, "History," 246–248.

18. Ludlam to the Secretary, Mar. 22, 1725, SPG MSS A, XIX, 62.

19. Edward Porter Alexander, ed., *The Journal of John Fontaine: An Irish Huguenot Son in Spain and Virginia, 1710–1719* (Williamsburg, Va., 1972), 94–95; Byrd, "Secret History," in Wright, ed., *Prose Works,* 82 (see also Byrd, "History," 222). For other contacts with Indian women, see Byrd, "History," 218, 314.

20. SCCJ, June 8, 1739, RSUS, S.C. E.1p, 1/6, 26. For livestock, see *JCIT,* 137; SCCHJ, Apr. 18, 1717, RSUS, S.C. A.1b, 1/3. For fences, see SCUHJ, Sept. 13, 1727, CO 5/429, 177 (BMP D491, microfilm, SCDAH).

For instances of local Indians' killing innocent slaves, see SCCHJ, Jan. 26, 1721/22, RSUS, S.C. A.1b, 2/2, 5, SCCHJ, July 17, 1728, Mar. 17, 19, June 3, July 2, 15, 1731, Feb. 25, 1732, 4/1, 547, 641, 648, 716, 729–730, 750, 861–862, SCUHJ, Mar. 19, 1730/31, May 18, 1734, A.1a, 2/1, 61, 706.

21. *JCIT,* 208.

22. *EJCCV,* III, 365–366.

23. "Queries Sent by the Lords of the Councell of trade and plantations to be Answered by the Govern[o]r of Virginia," encl. no. 1, Andros to the Board of Trade, Apr. 22, 1697, CO 5/1309, doc. no. 16 (LC trans.), Andros to the Board of Trade, July 1, 1697, CO 5/1309, doc. no. 24 (LC trans., 108–109), Spotswood to the Board of Trade, Dec. 22, 1718, CO 5/1318, 590–591 (LC trans., 488).

24. SCCHJ, Feb. 23, 29, 1728, RSUS, S.C. A.1b, 4/1, 402–403, SCCHJ, Apr. 18, 1733, 4/1, 1018. Spotswood to the Earl of Dartmouth, Mar. 9, 1713, in R. A. Brock, ed., *The Official Letters of Alexander Spotswood, Lieutenant-Governor of the Colony of Virginia, 1710–1722,* 2 vols. (Virginia Historical Society, *Collections,* N.S., I–II [Richmond, Va., 1882–1885]), II, 53–54.

25. Gooch to the Board of Trade, Mar. 26, 1729, CO 5/1321, 221 (LC trans.); Byrd, "History," in Wright, ed., *Prose Works,* 315; Thomas Arent to ———, 1728, in *CVSP,* I, 215; Gooch to the Board of Trade, June 29, 1729, CO 5/1322, 19–20 (LC trans., 8–9).

26. Nor did Saponis forget. In the early 19th century, descendants of the

Christanna Indians still spoke of the "Wars they had with the Virginians, and many of them having been treacherously deceived, and lulled into security and then put to death." See John Norton, *The Journal of Major John Norton, 1816*, ed. Carl F. Klinck and James J. Talman (Toronto, 1970), 82.

27. Extracts of Letters from Carolina relating to the Indian War, *CRNC*, II, 251–252; *JCIT*, 160, 163, 209, 254, 264; *EJCCV*, III, 397; Coun. Jours., *CRNC*, II, 242 (Cheraws). [George Chicken], "Journal of the March of the Carolinians into the Cherokee Mountains, in the Yemassee Indian War, 1715–16, from the Original Manuscript," in Langdon Cheves, ed., *City of Charleston: Year Book—1894* (Charleston, S.C., 1895), 331 (Keyauwees).

28. *JCIT*, 208; SCCJ, Sept. 12, 1717, Green Copy, vol. I, 122, SCDAH; *EJCCV*, III, 411–412, 421–422; "Journal of the Lieut. Governor's Travels and Expeditions Undertaken for the Public Service of Virginia," *WMQ*, 2d Ser., III (1923), 44.

29. *EJCCV*, III, 406, 412, 421–422, 442; "Lieut. Gov.'s Travels," *WMQ*, 2d Ser., III (1923), 44.

30. Committee of the Commons House of Assembly to the South Carolina Agents [?], Aug. 6, 1716, BPRO-SC, VI, 241; *EJCCV*, III, 406.

31. Robert Mills, *Statistics of South Carolina, Including a View of Its Natural, Civil, and Military History, General and Particular* (Spartanburg, S.C., 1972 [orig. publ. 1826]), 600–601.

32. For the order, see SCCHJ, Nov. 29, Dec. 15, 1716, RSUS, S.C. A.1b, 1/3. For the sanctuary, see Samuel Cole Williams, ed., *Adair's History of the American Indians* (New York, 1974 [orig. publ. 1930]), 236; Catawba Indians to Gov. Lyttelton, June 16, 1757, William Henry Lyttelton Papers, William L. Clements Library, Ann Arbor, Mich.

33. *JCIT*, 177. Exactly what they meant by "belonging" is unclear. It could be taken to mean property, but it seems more likely, given the alliance then existing between Catawbas and Waterees, that they meant it in a political sense.

34. Extract of a letter from President Carter to Sir Richard Everard, 1727, *CVSP*, I, 214, Thomas Arent to ———, 1728, I, 215; *EJCCV*, III, 510, IV, 152–153; "An Acco[un]t of Nathaniel Harrison's proceedings when he went out, by Order of Governm[en]t, to meet with the Cautaubau Indians . . . ," encl. in Gooch to Board of Trade, Sept. 21, 1727, CO 5/1321 (LC trans., 7–17). For the Cheraws, see Hatton to Nicholson, Nov. 14, 1724, BPRO-SC, XI, 277–278.

35. Account of Harrison's proceedings, Sept. 1727, CO 5/1321 (LC trans., 9); *JCHA-SC, November 1, 1725–April 30, 1726*, 42–43; Gov. Glen to John Evans, Aug. 28, 1755, in SCCJ, Aug. 29, 1755, RSUS, S.C. E.1p, 7/2, 309–310; Lyttelton to Samuel Wyly, Oct. 1, 1757, in William Henry Lyttelton, Letters Sent, 1757–1759, 25–26 (photocopies, SCDAH); SCCJ, Apr. 24, 1759, RSUS, S.C. E.1p, 8/2, 89.

36. Precisely when and how each group made the decision cannot be determined. Williams, ed., *Adair's History*, 236 (Waterees among Catawbas); SCUHJ, Feb. 28, 1743/44, RSUS, S.C. A.1a, 4/1, 16; *JCHA, September 12, 1739–March 26, 1741*, 410, 486, 493, *May 18, 1741–July 10, 1742*, 315, 343, *1744–1745*, 20–22, 131–132 (Waterees still in their earlier location). The Public Accounts of John Hammerton, Esq., Secretary of the Province, in Inventories, LL, 1744–1746, 47, SCDAH (Pedees among Catawbas); for Pedees in the lowcountry, see below. SCUHJ, Sept. 13, 1727, CO 5/429 (BMP D491), 276–277 (Waccamaws among Catawbas); SCCHJ, July 17, 1728, Mar. 17, 19, 1731, Apr. 18, 1733, RSUS, S.C. A.1b, 4/1, 547, 641, 648, 1018, SCUHJ, Mar. 19, 1731, A.1a, 2/1, 61 (Waccamaws in lowcountry). Hatton to Nicholson, Nov. 14, 1724, BPRO-SC, XI, 277; SCUHJ, Sept. 13, 1727, CO 5/429 (BMP D491), 276–277 (Cheraws among Catawbas); SCCJ, June 8, 15, 1739, RSUS, S.C. E.1p, 1/6, 26–27 (Cheraws in their former homes along the Pee Dee).

For Cheraws, Pedees, and Waccamaws among the Catawbas, see Glen's speech to King Hagler, n.d., encl. no. 3 in Glen to the Lords Commissioners of Trade and Plantations, May 29, 1755, BPRO-SC, XXVI, 204.

37. SCCHJ, Feb. 29, 1728, RSUS, S.C. A.1b, 4/1, 402–403 (Winyaw); *JCHA, November 10, 1736–June 7, 1739*, 563–565 (Natchez); Mills, *Statistics of South Carolina*, 485 (Cape Fear). Some also lived with Waccamaws. SCCHJ, Apr. 18, 1733, RSUS, S.C. A.1b, 4/1, 1018; Journal of John Evans, Oct. 1755, *DRIA, 1754–1765*, 86.

38. SCCJ, May 26, 1749, RSUS, S.C. E.1p, 4/1, 419 (Cape Fear); *JCHA-SC, 1726*, 44–45; Hammerton, Public Accounts, 23, 51, 55; Glen to Clinton, May 24, 1751, George Clinton Papers, 85, Clements Library; Thomas Cooper and D. J. McCord, eds., *The Statutes at Large of South Carolina*, 10 vols. (Columbia, S.C., 1836–1841), III, 327, 371, 400, 517.

39. Williams, ed., *Adair's History*, 367, 369; Hasell to the Secretary, May 16, 1723, SPG MSS A, XVII, 79. See also Alan R. Calmes, "The Culture and Acculturation of the Cusabo Indians, 1520–1720" (master's thesis, University of South Carolina, 1964), 84–87.

40. *JCHA, 1736–1739*, 564–565, *1739–1741*, 105. For their service in the Stono revolt, see *JCHA, 1739–1741*, 65, 183, 209 (quotation on 209). For Coachman's later service as a mediator, see SCCJ, Apr. 11, July 5, 1744, RSUS, S.C. E.1p, 2/3, 187–188, 383–384.

41. SCCJ, July 6, 1750, RSUS, S.C. E.1p, 4/2.

42. Hasell to the Secretary, Oct. 20, 1722, SPG MSS A, XVI, 82; see also Hasell to Secretary, May 16, 1723, XVII, 79, Hasell to Secretary, Apr. 15, 1724, XVIII, 72, Brian Hunt to the Secretary, May 25, 1724, XVIII, 82.

43. John Brickell, *The Natural History of North-Carolina* . . . (Raleigh, N.C., 1911 [orig. publ. 1737]), 42; Wilbur R. Jacobs, ed., *Indians of the Southern Colonial Frontier: The Edmond Atkin Report and Plan of 1755* (Columbia, S.C., 1954), 45; Williams, ed., *Adair's History*, 370. For their earlier services, see F[erguson], *Present State of Carolina*, 16; J. Leitch Wright, Jr., *The Only Land They Knew: The Tragic Story of the American Indians in the Old South* (New York, 1981), 157–167.

44. Glen to Lords Commissioners of Trade and Plantations, Oct. 2, 1750, BPRO-SC, XXIV, 130. See also Glen to Gov. Hamilton, Oct. 3, 1753, *DRIA, May 21, 1750–August 7, 1754*, 463. My discussion of this educational process both here and in chap. 6 owes a debt to Peter L. Berger and Thomas Luckmann, *The Social Construction of Reality: A Treatise in the Sociology of Knowledge* (Garden City, N.Y., 1967), esp. 55–58, and the writings of Erving Goffman, esp. *The Presentation of Self in Everyday Life* (Garden City, N.Y., 1959), *Behavior in Public Places: Notes on the Social Organization of Gatherings* (London, 1963), and *Interaction Ritual: Essays in Face-to-Face Behavior* (Chicago, 1967).

45. Hunt to the Secretary, May 25, 1724, SPG MSS A, XVIII, 82; see also Richard Ludlam to the Secretary, Mar. 22, 1725, XIX, 62; "Copy of the Answers of Francis Fauquier, Esqr., Lieutenant Governor of Virginia to the Queries proposed by the Lords of Trade, 1763," British Library, King's 205, f 266 (VCRP-CW, M-276).

46. Williams, ed., *Adair's History*, 370. For language, see Hunt to the Secretary, May 25, 1724, SPG MSS A, XVIII, 82; Hening, ed., *Statutes at Large*, IV, 461; Glen to Evans, Aug. 28, 1755, in SCCJ, Aug. 29, 1755, RSUS, S.C. E.1p, 7/2, 309.

47. Mills, *Statistics of South Carolina*, 486; William Harlen Gilbert, Jr., "Surviving Indian Groups of the Eastern United States," Smithsonian Institution, *Annual Report . . . for . . . 1948* (Washington, D.C., 1948), fig. 1 (p. 408), 421–422; Brewton Berry, *Almost White* (New York, 1963); William C. Sturtevant and Samuel Stanley, "Indian Communities in the Eastern States," *Indian Historian*, I, no. 3 (June 1968),

15–19; B. Eugene Griessman, ed., "The American Isolates," *American Anthropologist*, N.S., LXXIV (1972), 693–734, 1276–1306.

48. *South-Carolina Gazette; and Country Journal* (Charleston), Nov. 4, 1766. The announcement ran through Apr. 14, 1767.

49. For tattoos, see John R. Swanton, *The Indians of the Southeastern United States*, Smithsonian Institution, Bureau of American Ethnology, Bulletin, no. 137 (Washington, D.C., 1946), 532–536; Charles Hudson, *The Southeastern Indians* (Knoxville, Tenn., 1976), 30, 203, 247, 380, and figs. 48, 56, 73, 79. For Catawba facial tattooing, see Figure 2, above. Wright (*Only Land They Knew*, 147 n. 65) argues that South Carolina planters also branded their slaves with powder.

50. For another example of this process in early America, see T. H. Breen and Stephen Innes, *"Myne Owne Ground": Race and Freedom on Virginia's Eastern Shore, 1640–1676* (New York, 1980).

51. See Byrd, "History," in Wright, ed., *Prose Works*, 309; Hammerton, Public Accounts, 29, 47; SCCJ, July 6, 1739, RSUS, S.C. E.1p, 1/6, 30; Ammunition delivered to the Catawbas, Jan. 21, 1755, *DRIA, 1754–1765*, 35; "Cuttahbaw Nation: men fit for warr 204 In the year 1756 [by John Evans]," Dalhousie Muniments, General John Forbes Papers, doc. no. 2/104, copy in SCDAH.

52. For "eractasswa," see SCCJ, Sept. 6, 1749, RSUS, S.C. E.1p, 4/1, 619; and "A Treaty between Virginia and the Catawbas and Cherokees, 1756," *VMHB*, XIII (1905–1906), 244. Another term used was "orata" (see Vandera, "Proceeding," 16, and Hammerton, Public Accounts, 29). For Weyaline as King's Town, see Journal of Evans, Feb.–Mar. 1756, *DRIA, 1754–1765*, 107. For head warrior, see Hammerton, Public Accounts, 47, and Catawbas to Glen, Apr. 26, 1750, in SCCJ, May 22, 1750, RSUS, S.C. E.1p, 4/2.

53. Council held at Conestogoe, July 19, 1717, *MPCP*, III, 12. Though the transcripts of this conference use the past tense, it is clear from the context of the headman's talk that he referred to "Catawbas" as he perceived them at that time.

54. Williams, ed., *Adair's History*, 235–236. The Coosah identification is from Gene Waddell, *Indians of the South Carolina Lowcountry, 1562–1751* (Spartanburg, S.C., 1980), 269–270. See also Brown, *The Catawba Indians*, 3; and the excellent work Steven G. Baker has done in piecing together the constituent elements of the Nation ("The Working Draft of: The Historic Catawba Peoples: Exploratory Perspectives in Ethnohistory and Archaeology" [MS, Department of History, University of South Carolina, 1975], chap. 3, and fig. 5, p. 70).

55. SCUHJ, Sept. 13, 1727, CO 5/429, 176–177 (BMP D491) (Waccamaw Town). Hammerton, Public Accounts, 29, 51; Ammunition delivered to the Catawbas, Jan. 21, 1755, *DRIA, 1754–1765*, 35; Lyttelton to Hagler, Dec. 12, 1757, in Lyttelton, Letters Sent, 57; Evans Map; William Richardson, "An Account of My Proceedings since I accepted the Indian Mission in October 2d 1758 . . . ," Wilberforce Eames Collection, New York Public Library (copy in YCPL), entry for Nov. 8, 1758 (Cheraw Town). Williams, ed., *Adair's History*, 236; *JCHA, 1744–1745*, 131 (Wateree Town). Ammunition delivered to the Catawbas, Jan. 21, 1755, *DRIA, 1754–1765*, 35 (Pedee Town).

Hammerton, Public Accounts, 47; Jour. of Evans, Oct. 1755, *DRIA, 1754–1765*, 87 (Pedee headmen). SCUHJ, Sept. 13, 1727, CO 5/429, 176–177 (BMP D491) (Waccamaw headmen). Hammerton, Public Accounts, 29, 51; *SCG*, June 2, 1746; Evans to Glen, Apr. 18, 1748, in SCCJ, Apr. 27, 1748, RSUS, S.C. E.1p, 3/4, 233; Wyly to Lyttelton, Apr. 26, 1759, Lyttelton Papers; SCCJ, May 30, 1759, RSUS, S.C. E.1p, 8/2, 93–94 (Cheraw headmen). Hammerton, Public Accounts, 44 (Wateree headmen).

Jour. of Evans, Oct. 1755, *DRIA, 1754–1765*, 87 (hunting camps). SCUHJ, Sept. 13, 1727, CO 5/429, 176–177 (BMP D491); SCCJ, May 30, 1759, RSUS, S.C. E.1p, 8/2, 93–94; *SCG*, June 2, 1759 (war parties).

56. Hammerton, Public Accounts, 44, 47; Williams, ed., *Adair's History*, 236. For the Cheraws, see Philip Edward Pearson, "Memoir of the Catawbas. Sent to Governor James Henry Hammond [1842?]," typescript in YCPL. For the possibility that Pedees retained their own language, see Jour. of Evans, Oct. 1755, Feb.–Mar. 1756, *DRIA, 1754–1765*, 87, 107.

57. Hammerton, Public Accounts, 29, 47, 53; SCCJ, July 6, 1739, RSUS, S.C. E.1p, 1/6, 29–30 (leaders). Ammunition delivered to the Catawbas, Jan. 21, 1755, *DRIA, 1754–1765*, 35; Dobbs to Lyttelton, May 27, 1757, Lyttelton Papers.

58. SCUHJ, Sept. 13, 1727, CO 5/429, 176–177 (BMP D491).

59. Weiser to Sec. Richard Peters, Feb. 10, 1744/45, *Pa. Arch.*, I, 671.

60. See SCCJ, July 6, 1739, RSUS, S.C. E.1p, 1/6, 29–30.

61. Hugh Jones, *The Present State of Virginia, from Whence Is Inferred a Short View of Maryland and North Carolina*, ed. Richard L. Morton (Chapel Hill, N.C., 1956), 57; *JHBV, 1712–1714, 1715, 1718, 1720–1722, 1723–1726*, 197; Coun. Jour., Mar. 3, 1719, *MPCP*, III, 77–78; Evans to Glen, Apr. 18, 1748, in SCCJ, Apr. 27, 1748, RSUS, S.C. E.1p, 3/4, 233. See also Williams, ed., *Adair's History*, 421–424.

62. SCCHJ, Mar. 17, 1730/31, RSUS, S.C. A.1b, 4/1, 643 (emphasis added); Glen's speech to Hagler, n.d., encl. no. 3 in Glen to the Lords Commissioners of Trade and Plantations, May 29, 1755, BPRO-SC, XXVI, 204, Glen to Lords Commissioners of Trade and Plantations, Dec. 1751, XXIV, 414.

63. *JCHA, 1736–1739*, 482, 487 (emphasis added). For another example, see SCCJ, May 12, July 6, 1739, RSUS, S.C. E.1p, 1/6, 22–23, 29–30; *SCG*, July 7, 1739; *Virginia Gazette* (Williamsburg), Oct. 5, 1739; *EJCCV*, IV, 443.

64. For analyses of the impact of Europeans on the formation of Indian "tribes" or "nations," see Morton H. Fried, *The Notion of Tribe* (Menlo Park, Calif., 1975), chap. 12; Fred Gearing, *Priests and Warriors: Social Structures for Cherokee Politics in the Eighteenth Century*, American Anthropological Association, Memoir, no. 93 (*American Anthropologist*, LXIV, no. 5, part 2 [Oct. 1962]).

65. *EJCCV*, IV, 269, 287, 290–291, 293–294; Coun. Jour., Aug. 6, 16, 1733, *MPCP*, III, 542–543, 550; A. G. Grinnan, "The Last Indians in Orange County, Virginia," *VMHB*, III (1895–1896), 189–190.

66. Coun. Jours., Apr. 3, 1733, *CRNC*, III, 537–538 (Tuscaroras). Wesley D. White, "Historical Overview of the [Saponi] Tribe: Second Essay . . . ," 65–69 (MS, Lumbee River Legal Services, Pembroke, N.C.) (Eaton). Grinnan, "Last Indians in Orange County," *VMHB*, III (1895–1896), 189–190 (Spotswood). A List of all the Indian names present at the Treaty held in Lancaster in June 1744, *Pa. Arch.*, I, 657; James Sullivan *et al.*, eds., *The Papers of Sir William Johnson*, 14 vols. (Albany, N.Y., 1921–1965), IX, 114, 118, 560–561; Horatio Hale, "The Tutelo Tribe and Language," American Philosophical Society, *Proceedings*, XXI (1883–1884), 1–47 (Iroquois). For another possible splinter group, see C. G. Holland, "A Saponi Note," Archeological Society of Virginia, *Quarterly Bulletin*, XXXVII (1982), 42.

67. Relations did not break off completely. See Evans to Glen, Apr. 18, 1748, in SCCJ, Apr. 27, 1748, RSUS, S.C. E.1p, 3/4, 233; Richardson, "Account," Nov. 8, 1758; North Carolina, Rowan County, Court of Pleas and Quarter Sessions, II, 72, NCDAH.

68. Byrd, "History," in Wright, ed., *Prose Works*, 315.

69. For the north-south division, see Swanton, *Indians of the Southeastern United States*, table 1. Baker ("Historic Catawba Peoples," chap. 3) comes to similar conclu-

sions about the Catawbas' ability to absorb outsiders, though we differ on the strength of the Cofitachique connection.

70. See below, chap. 7.

71. For population, see *JCIT*, 177; Byrd, "History," in Wright, ed., *Prose Works*, 309; William Bull to the Lords Commissioners of Trade and Plantations, June 15, 1742, BPRO-SC, XX, 570, Glen to the Lords Commissioners of Trade and Plantations, Feb. 3, 1747/8, XXIII, 74; Thomas Lee to the Board of Trade, Sept. 29, 1750, CO 5/1327, 244 (LC trans.); Glen to the Earl of Holdernesse, June 25, 1753, BPRO-SC, XXV, 302; Matthew Rowan to the Board of Trade, June 3, 1754, *CRNC*, V, 124; Jacobs, ed., *Atkin Report*, 42.

72. *JCHA, 1736–1739*, 74.

73. Jacobs, ed., *Atkin Report*, 47. See "Map . . . Drawn . . . by an Indian Cacique." For conflicts, see "A Copy of Mr. [William] Walis's Jou[r]nal to North Carolina begun 10th May 1731," encl. in Gov. Robert Johnson to the Lords Commissioners of Trade and Plantations, Dec. 15, 1732, BPRO-SC, XVI, 19. For contacts, see "A Conversation between . . . the Governor of South Carolina and Chuconunta a Headman of the Cherokees whose name formerly was Ouconecan," Jan. 12, 1756, encl. no. 5, in Glen to the Lords Commissioners of Trade and Plantations, Apr. 14, 1756, BPRO-SC, XXVII, 96, Glen to the Lords Commissioners of Trade and Plantations, Dec. 1751, XXIV, 408–409; SCCJ, July 18, 1748, RSUS, S.C. E.1p, 3/4, 366–367.

74. For an example of peacemaking that failed, see Thomas Brown to Glen, July 23, 1744, in SCCJ, July 25, 1744, RSUS, S.C. E.1p, 2/3, 426–427; Glen to the Lords Commissioners of Trade and Plantations, Sept. 22, 1744, BPRO-SC, XXI, 401–402.

75. "Walis's Jou[r]nal," encl. in Johnson to the Lords Commissioners of Trade and Plantations, Dec. 15, 1732, BPRO-SC, XVI, 16, 20.

76. In Wright, ed., *Prose Works*. Meherrins: Byrd, "Secret History," 79; see also "History," 213. Nottoway town: "History," 217 (for Catawba attacks on the Nottoways, see *EJCCV*, IV, 356). Tuscaroras: "History," 303, "A Journey to the Land of Eden, Anno 1733," 390 (see also 385, 387, 388).

77. *EJCCV*, III, 443, 446, 450; Coun. Jour., July 12, 19, 20, 1720, *MPCP*, III, 85–99.

78. Glen to the Lords Commissioners of Trade and Plantations, Feb. 3, 1747/8, BPRO-SC, XXIII, 74; Jacobs, ed., *Atkin Report*, 47; Williams, ed., *Adair's History*, 235; Weiser to Peters, Feb. 10, 1744/45, *Pa. Arch.*, I, 671; Hagler to Glen, Mar. 14, 1756, *DRIA, 1754–1765*, 107.

79. Jacobs, ed., *Atkin Report*, 49; John Phillip Reid, *A Law of Blood: The Primitive Law of the Cherokee Nation* (New York, 1970), 5.

80. Glen to the Lords Commissioners of Trade and Plantations, June 25, 1753, BPRO-SC, XXV, 324.

81. *SCG*, Aug. 20, 1753; Williams, ed., *Adair's History*, 133. Capt. John Fairchild to Glen, Feb. 27, 1752, *DRIA, 1750–1754*, 218.

82. A Treaty held at Lancaster with the Six Nations, July 4, 1744, *MPCP*, IV, 733.

83. Talk of the Nottowaga Indians, n.d., *DRIA, 1750–1754*, 47; Treaty at Lancaster, June 30, 1744, *MPCP*, IV, 721; Williams, ed., *Adair's History*, 143; Conrad Weiser's Journal of a trip to Onondaga, 1743, *MPCP*, IV, 668.

84. For the epithets, see James Logan to Gov. Clarke, Dec. 6, 1740, James Logan Papers, IV, 21, APS Library, Philadelphia; Weiser to Peters, Feb. 10, 1744/45, *Pa. Arch.*, I, 671–672; Coun. Jour., Aug. 16, 1749, *MPCP*, V, 402, Treaty at Lancaster, June 30, 1744, IV, 721. For examples, see Hunter to the Board of Trade, July 1717, *DRCNY*, V, 483; William Hand Browne *et al.*, eds., *Archives of Maryland . . . ,*

72 vols. (Baltimore, 1883–1972), XXV, 362, 367, 369; Treaty at Lancaster, June 30, 1744, *MPCP*, IV, 721.

85. Peter Wraxall, *An Abridgement of the Indian Affairs Contained in Four Folio Volumes, Transacted in the Colony of New York, from the Year 1678 to the Year 1751*, ed. Charles Howard McIlwain (Cambridge, Mass., 1915), 177–179; *EJCCV*, IV, 209; Capt. Civility to Gov. Patrick Gordon, 1729, *Pa. Arch.*, I, 238–239, 240–241, Gordon to Shekallamy, etc., 1729, I, 241–242 (incident). Weiser to Peters, Feb. 10, 1744/45, *Pa. Arch.*, I, 671; Journal of the proceedings of Conrad Weiser, *MPCP*, V, 473; William Bull to Glen, July 25, 1751, *DRIA, 1750–1754*, 95.

86. Williams, ed., *Adair's History*, 158–159. See Daniel K. Richter, "War and Culture: The Iroquois Experience," *WMQ*, 3d Ser., XL (1983), 529–558.

87. "Treaty between Virginia and the Catawbas and Cherokees, 1756," *VMHB*, XIII (1905–1906), 241; "A Coppy of a Paper from O Tassity, commonly called Judge Freind, to, Connecotte, called Old hop, May 26th, 1757," encl. in Raymond Demere to Lyttelton, July 4, 1757, Lyttelton Papers.

88. Byrd, "History," in Wright, ed., *Prose Works*, 248.

89. For mixed-bloods, see Williams, ed., *Adair's History*, 369–370; SCCJ, July 6, 1750, RSUS, S.C. E.1p, 4/2; Stephen Crell to Glen, May 2, 1751, *DRIA, 1750–1754*, 46 (William Brown). Evans to Glen, Apr. 18, 1748, in SCCJ, Apr. 27, 1748, RSUS, S.C. E.1p, 3/4, 233, SCCJ, May 5, 1760, 8/3, 119, SCCJ, May 15, 1762, 8/6, 498 (Evans). Jour. of Evans, Feb.–Mar. 1756, *DRIA, 1754–1765*, 107; Minutes of the Catawbas' Conference with Superintendent Atkin at Jamestown Ferry, May 18, 1757, HM 3992, Henry E. Huntington Library, San Marino, Calif.; Catawbas to Lyttelton, Aug. 23, 1759, [Oct. 1759], Lyttelton Papers (Lewis John). Jour. of Evans, Oct. 1755, *DRIA, 1754–1765*, 86; SCCJ, Nov. 6, 1755, RSUS, S.C. E.1p, 7/2, 440; George Washington to Dinwiddie, May 29, 30, 1757, in John C. Fitzpatrick, ed., *The Writings of George Washington, from the Original Manuscript Sources, 1745–1799*, 39 vols. (Washington, D.C., 1931–1944), II, 39, 41–42 (James Bullen).

90. SCUHJ, Sept. 13, 1727, CO 5/429, 176 (BMP D491). For later interpreters, see SCCJ, Oct. 5, 1744, RSUS, S.C. E.1p, 2/3, 488; Toole to Glen, Apr. 30, 1752, *DRIA, 1750–1754*, 213; SCCJ, Apr. 30, 1755, RSUS, S.C. E.1p, 7/2, 175; Jour. of Evans, Feb.–Mar. 1756, *DRIA, 1754–1765*, 107; Orders, Oct. 28, 1756, in Fitzpatrick, ed., *Writings of Washington*, I, 486; SCCJ, May 27, 1758, RSUS, S.C. E.1p, 8/1, 196.

91. Richardson, "Account," Nov. 8–11, 1758. SCCJ, Aug. 24, 1756, RSUS, S.C. E.1p, 7/3, 335.

92. Lawson, *New Voyage*, ed. Lefler, 49. SCCJ, Mar. 4, 1761, RSUS, S.C. E.1p, 8/5, 100 ("out towns"). For Nassaw or Catawba Town, see Byrd, "History," in Wright, ed., *Prose Works*, 309; "Sketch Map of the Rivers Santee, Congaree, Wateree, Saludee, etc., with the Road to the Cuttauboes [1750]," PRO, CO Library, Carolina 16 (copies in LC, and Hulbert, comp., *Crown Collection of American Maps*, 3d Ser., I, pls. 25–26); "Treaty between Virginia and the Catawbas and Cherokees, 1756," *VMHB*, XIII (1905–1906), 226.

93. For a useful summary of the Catawba towns, see Baker, "Historic Catawba Peoples," 111–115, esp. table 2, p. 111, and fig. 6, p. 114. For New Town, see James McCord to Glen, Mar. 28, 1749, in SCCJ, Apr. 6, 1749, RSUS, S.C. E.1p, 4/1, 277; Ammunition delivered to the Catawbas, Jan. 21, 1755, *DRIA, 1754–1765*, 35. The Shuteree link is conjectural, and is based on the disappearance of Shuteree, or "Soutry," Town from the records in the early 1740s, the same time "New Town" begins to appear. See Hammerton, Public Accounts, 29, 47. For the Sugaree move, see "Road to the Cuttauboes [1750]." This move was apparently temporary. By 1756, Sugarees were back on Sugar Creek (see Evans Map).

94. For the Waxhaw fields, see Williams, ed., *Adair's History*, 236. For the advantageous position in the trade, see "Sketch Map [1750]."

95. *JCIT*, 177; Brown to Glen, Apr. 1, 1746, in SCCJ, Apr. 11, 1746, RSUS, S.C. E.1p, 3/2, 82. For circular, see Richardson, "Account," Nov. 8, 1758; "Road to the Cuttauboes [1750]," which also depicts the square forts. According to this map, Nassaw Town was particularly impressive, with its two entrances and guard towers on each corner. Whether these towers were of aboriginal or colonial design is unclear. For Indian forts with towers, see Charles M. Hudson, *Elements of Southeastern Indian Religion* (Leiden, 1984), fasc. 1 of *North America*, sect. 10 of Th. P. van Baaren *et al.*, eds., *Iconography of Religions*, 8, pl. XVIII, a, b.

96. Alexander, ed., *Journal of Fontaine*, 96–97. For other "modern" designs, see Daniel L. Simpkins and Gary L. Petherick, "Settlement Pattern Changes in the North Carolina Piedmont during the Contact Period," paper presented at the 51st Annual Meeting of the Society for American Archaeology, New Orleans, Apr. 1986.

97. For the clothing, see Public Treasurer, Ledger A, 1725 (May 14), and Ledger A, F112, SCDAH; SCCJ, Sept. 15, 1744, RSUS, S.C. E.1p, 2/3, 471; *JCHA, 1744–1745*, 442–443, *January 19, 1748–June 29, 1748*, 294–295; *SCG*, July 10, 1736; SCCJ, Sept. 7, 1749, RSUS, S.C. E.1p, 4/1, 625–626. For the wig, see SCCHJ, Mar. 16, 1728, RSUS, S.C. A.1b, 4/1, 459, 473.

98. Brickell, *Natural History*, 280, 283–285; Alexander, ed., *Journal of Fontaine*, 94; Gregory A. Stiverson and Patrick H. Butler III, eds., "Virginia in 1732: The Travel Journal of William Hugh Grove," *VMHB*, LXXXV (1977), 30–31; SCCJ, Aug. 23, 1756, RSUS, S.C. E.1p, 7/3, 332; Lt. Col. George Mercer to Gen. John Stanwix, Aug. 12, 1759, in Donald H. Kent *et al.*, eds., *The Papers of Henry Bouquet*, III (Harrisburg, Pa., 1976), 545.

99. Alexander, ed., *Journal of Fontaine*, 93–94. For tattooing, see Brickell, *Natural History*, 284. For ornaments, see Figure 2, above.

100. See SCCJ, May 29, 1754, RSUS, S.C. E.1p, 6/2, 264, Apr. 30, 1755, 7/2, 175. For these and other names, see SCCJ, Sept. 6, 1749, RSUS, S.C. E.1p, 4/1, 619.

101. SCCJ, Nov. 6, 1755, RSUS, S.C. E.1p, 7/2, 439–440. See also Glen to the Catawbas, Dec. 18, 1754, *DRIA, 1754–1765*, 28, and Hagler, King of the Catawbas, to Glen, Oct. 21, 1755, 85; "Treaty between Virginia and the Catawbas and Cherokees, 1756," *VMHB*, XIII (1905–1906), 243; Richardson, "Account," Nov. 8, 1758.

102. The figure given here is based on occasional references to numbers in a hunting camp. See Thomas Cresap to Gov. Samuel Ogle, Mar. 17, 1750, in Browne *et al.*, eds., *Arch. Md.*, XLVI, 415–416; Hagler to Glen, Oct. 21, 1755, *DRIA, 1754–1765*, 85. For women and children's being left alone in camp, see Fairchild to Glen, n.d., in SCCJ, June 13, 1748, RSUS, S.C. E.1p, 3/4, 308; Cresap to Ogle, Mar. 17, 1750, in Browne *et al.*, eds., *Arch. Md.*, XLVI, 415–416.

103. Burrington to the Secretary, Nov. 2, 1732, *CRNC*, III, 369 (Cape Fear). Hagler to Glen, Oct. 21, 1755, *DRIA, 1754–1765*, 85, Evans to Glen, Feb. 2, 1756, 92, James Francis to Lyttelton, Dec. 23, 1757, 426 (Edisto and south side of Santee/Congaree drainage). "Observations in relation to His Majesty's Order of Council, dated the 19th of May 1737," encl. in Henry McCulloh to the Lords Commissioners of Trade and Plantations, July 27, 1744, *CRNC*, IV, 670; "Journal of the Proceedings of the Southern Congress at Augusta From the Arrival of the Several Governors at Charles Town, South Carolina, the 1.st October to their Return to the same Place etc. the 21.st November 1763," BPRO-SC, XXX, 84 (Pee Dee). "Journal of the Proceedings at Augusta," BPRO-SC, XXX, 84; North Carolina Land Grants, Anson no. 045, no. 856, Grant 352, book 2, p. 389; Grant no.

257, file no. 1285, book 18, p. 218, Land Grant Office, Secretary of State, Raleigh (Broad). Fairchild to Glen, n.d., in SCCJ, June 13, 1748, RSUS, S.C. E.1p, 3/4, 308 (Black). Evans to Glen, Feb. 2, 1756, *DRIA, 1754–1765*, 92 (Lynches Creek).

104. Settler quoted in Robert L. Meriwether, *The Expansion of South Carolina, 1729–1765* (Kingsport, Tenn., 1940), 79–80; Dobbs to Gov. Thomas Boone, Aug. 28, 1762, in Coun. Jours., *CRNC*, VI, 788.

105. Meriwether, *Expansion of South Carolina*, 61, 101; *JCHA, 1739–1741*, 114–115, *23 April 1750–31 August 1751*, 52.

106. William Owen to Lord Ashley, Sept. 15, 1670, in Langdon Cheves, ed., *The Shaftesbury Papers and Other Records Relating to Carolina and the First Settlement on Ashley River Prior to the Year 1676* (South Carolina Historical Society, *Collections*, V [Charleston, 1897]), 201.

107. Lawson, *New Voyage*, ed. Lefler, 44. In 1737 an Iroquois war party attacked the Catawbas and "killed three of their Nation and five of their horses as they were returning from hunting." James Logan (on behalf of the Pennsylvania Proprietor and Council) to the Six Nations, Sept. 27, 1737, Logan Papers, IV, 67.

108. Byrd, "History," in Wright, ed., *Prose Works*, 288; Alexander, ed., *Journal of Fontaine*, 99.

109. Byrd, "History," in Wright, ed., *Prose Works*, 316. Evidence for Indians on horseback comes principally from saddles given them as presents and accounts submitted for pasturage of a native delegation's horses in Charleston. See SCCHJ, Jan. 11, Feb. 7, 1733/34, RSUS, S.C. A.1b, 4/2, 61, 104; *JCHA, 1739–1741*, 488, *March 28, 1749–March 19, 1750*, 402; SCCJ, July 6, 1739, RSUS, S.C. E.1p, 1/6, 30, SCCJ, Feb. 12, 1745, 3/1, 72–73, SCCJ, Apr. 30, May 3, 1755, 7/2, 176, 178; Demere to Lyttelton, Aug. 21, 1756, *DRIA, 1754–1765*, 165; James Adamson to Lyttelton, June 12, 1759, Lyttelton Papers.

110. SCCJ, July 3, 1762, RSUS, S.C. E.1p, 8/6, 528. Paradoxically, the horse both enabled a hunter to cover more ground and compelled him to do so. Together with the animals brought by colonial traders and kept near Indian villages, the natives' horses competed with the deer population for food. Thomas Brown Inventory, Inventories, MM, 1746–1748, 169, SCDAH; Treaty between North Carolina Commissioners and the Catawbas, Aug. 29, 1754, *CRNC*, V, 143–144. And see below, chap. 5.

111. For Catawba references to "the Woods," see "Treaty between Virginia and the Catawbas and Cherokees, 1756," *VMHB*, XIII (1905–1906), 243; Mercer to Bouquet, Aug. 30, 1759, in Kent *et al.*, eds., *Papers of Bouquet*, III, 637. For planting time, see Logan to the Six Nations, Sept. 27, 1737, Logan Papers, IV, 67.

112. *EJCCV*, IV, 198, 303. For a similar reading, see Francis Jennings, *The Invasion of America: Indians, Colonialism, and the Cant of Conquest* (Chapel Hill, N.C., 1975), 63.

113. Byrd, "Secret History," in Wright, ed., *Prose Works*, 118–120, "History," 246–248. The two accounts differ in some details but not in their general picture of Bearskin's views. All quotations are from these pages.

114. Swanton (*Indians of the Southeastern United States*, 751) notes that while either Bearskin or Byrd may have embellished this tale, and the Fort Christanna missionaries "may have had some influence . . . the substructure is no doubt Indian nonetheless." See an earlier Carolina version in Lawson, *New Voyage*, ed. Lefler, 187, to which Bearskin's corresponds closely. For a general discussion of the afterlife among Southeastern Indians, see Chester Burton DePratter, "Late Prehistoric and Early Historic Chiefdoms in the Southeastern United States" (Ph.D. diss., University of Georgia, 1983), 79–83. The question of where aboriginal beliefs end and

Christian ones begin is discussed in Åke Hultkrantz, "The Problem of Christian Influence on Northern Algonkian Eschatology," *Sciences Religieuses / Studies in Religion,* IX (1980), 161–183.

115. Byrd, "History," in Wright, ed., *Prose Works,* 239, 243–244, 247, "Secret History," 116, 117.

116. Jones, *Present State of Virginia,* ed. Morton, 59–60; SCCJ, Aug. 24, 1756, RSUS, S.C. E.1p, 7/3, 335; Hagler to Glen, Oct. 21, 1756, *DRIA, 1754–1765,* 85.

117. Alexander, ed., *Journal of Fontaine,* 93–94, 97; Christofer French, Journals, I, Expedition to South Carolina, Dec. 22, 1760 to Nov. 14, 1761, 78, 89, 91, LC (copy in YCPL). See also Toole to Glen, Oct. 28, 1752, *DRIA, 1750–1754,* 358.

Chapter 4

1. Glen to Lords Commissioners of Trade and Plantations, Dec. 23, 1749, BPRO-SC, XXIII, 452; Toole to Glen, July 15, 1754, *DRIA, May 21, 1750–August 7, 1754,* 515; SCCJ, Nov. 6, 1755, RSUS, S.C. E.1p, 7/2, 440.

2. Glen to Lords Commissioners of Trade and Plantations, Dec. 1751, BPRO-SC, XXIV, 404. For Glen's interest in Indian affairs, see *JCHA, September 10, 1746–June 13, 1747,* 215, *January 19, 1748–June 29, 1748,* 14; Glen to Lords Commissioners of Trade and Plantations, Feb. 3, 1747/8, BPRO-SC, XXIII, 73–74, Answers to the Queries from the Lords Commissioners of Trade and Plantations, encl. in Glen to Lords Commissioners of Trade and Plantations, July 19, 1749, XXIII, 373; Glen to Gov. Dinwiddie, Mar. 13, 1754, *DRIA, 1750–1754,* 478, Glen to Lachlan McGillivray, Oct. 28, 1755, *DRIA, 1754–1765,* 83.

3. Wilbur R. Jacobs, ed., *Indians of the Southern Colonial Frontier: The Edmond Atkin Report and Plan of 1755* (Columbia, S.C., 1954), 47. It is possible that the greater number of recorded raids on Catawbas during these years is the result of improved sources. With European settlements spreading farther into the piedmont, there were more people to witness and report on the activities of war parties. But it also seems clear that there were more activities to report.

For the Savannah-Shawnees, see Council Journal, July 20, 1720, Aug. 10, 1737, July 27, 1739, *MPCP,* III, 96–98, IV, 234–235, 337. The Cherokee story is in John Richard Alden, *John Stuart and the Southern Colonial Frontier: A Study in Indian Relations, War, Trade, and Land Problems in the Southern Wilderness, 1754–1775* (Ann Arbor, Mich., 1944), 24; Peter Wraxall, *An Abridgement of the Indian Affairs Contained in Four Folio Volumes, Transacted in the Colony of New York, from the Year 1678 to the Year 1751,* ed. Charles Howard McIlwain (Cambridge, Mass., 1915), 225–226; Gov. George Clerke to Lt. Gov. William Bull, Sept. 15, 1742, in SCCJ, Jan. 12, 1743, RSUS, S.C. E.1p, 1/7, 603–604; Jacobs, ed., *Atkin Report,* 47; *SCG,* June 2, 16, 1746; Glen to Lords Commissioners of Trade and Plantations, July 26, 1748, BPRO-SC, XXIII, 171–172; Glen's Talk to the Cherokees, Nov. 13, 1751, *DRIA, 1750–1754,* 158–159. The French threat is chronicled in Jacobs, ed., *Atkin Report,* 4–7, 47; Glen to Newcastle [?], May 3, 1746, BPRO-SC, XXII, 151.

4. In 1750 Thomas Lee of Virginia believed that Catawbas "are generally Victors over the parties of the Six Nations sent to War with them." Lee to the Board of Trade, Sept. 29, 1750, PRO, CO 5/1327, 244 (LC transcripts). For examples of Catawbas holding their own, see Conrad Weiser to Sec. Richard Peters, Jan. 2, 1745, *Pa. Arch.,* I, 665–666; Thomas Cresap to Gov. Samuel Ogle, Mar. 17, 1750, in William Hand Browne *et al.,* eds., *Archives of Maryland . . . ,* 72 vols. (Baltimore, 1883–1972), XLVI, 415–416; Catawbas to Glen, Apr. 26, 1750, in SCCJ, May 22, 1750, RSUS, S.C. E.1p, 4/2; William Johnson to George Clinton, May 24, 1750, George Clinton Papers, William L. Clements Library, Ann Arbor, Mich.

5. For the forts, see Thomas Brown to Glen, Apr. 1, 1746, in SCCJ, Apr. 11, 1746, RSUS, S.C. E.1p, 3/2, 82. For the enemy's approach, see John McCord to Glen, Mar. 28, 1749, in SCCJ, Apr. 6, 1749, 4/1, 277 ("small mile"), SCCJ, May 16, 1751, 5/2, 88 (150 yards), Evans to Glen, Apr. 18, 1748, in SCCJ, Apr. 27, 1748, 3/4, 232 (70 yards); Glen's Speech to King Hagler, n.d., encl. no. 3 in Glen to the Lords Commissioners of Trade and Plantations, May 29, 1755, BPRO-SC, XXVI, 205 ("very Doors").

6. Evans to Glen, Apr. 18, 1748, in SCCJ, Apr. 27, 1748, RSUS, S.C. E.1p, 3/4, 232, Catawbas to Glen, Apr. 26, 1750, in SCCJ, May 22, 1750, 4/2.

7. See Robert L. Meriwether, *The Expansion of South Carolina, 1729–1765* (Kingsport, Tenn., 1940), chaps. 2, 5, and 9. See also below, chap. 5.

8. William Bragg to George Beely, July 29, 1769, Bragg Letterbook, 1768–1771, p. 34, William Bragg Papers, 1765–1781, Manuscript Department, Duke University Library, Durham, N.C. For the higher quality of piedmont skins, see John Lawson, *A New Voyage to Carolina*, ed. Hugh Talmage Lefler (Chapel Hill, N.C., 1967), 129. William Byrd found hunters busy along the Roanoke River in the late 1720s. See Byrd, "The Secret History of the Line," and "History of the Dividing Line betwixt Virginia and North Carolina Run in the Year of Our Lord 1728," in Louis B. Wright, ed., *The Prose Works of William Byrd of Westover: Narratives of a Colonial Virginian* (Cambridge, Mass., 1966), 100, 230. For the later presence of hunters, see Diary of Bishop Spangenburg, *CRNC*, V, 4, 6, 12; Matthew Rowan to the Earl of Holdernesse, Nov. 21, 1753, *CRNC*, V, 25; Dobbs to Board of Trade, Aug. 24, 1755, *CRNC*, V, 354; Richard J. Hooker, ed., *The Carolina Backcountry on the Eve of the Revolution: The Journal and Other Writings of Charles Woodmason, Anglican Itinerant* (Chapel Hill, N.C., 1953), 39; William Bull to the Earl of Hillsborough, Oct. 4, 1769, BPRO-SC, XXXII, 108–109; Antonio Pace, trans. and ed., *Luigi Castiglioni's Viaggio: Travels in the United States of North America, 1785–87* (Syracuse, N.Y., 1983), 148–150. For the relationship between hunters and planters, see Rachel N. Klein, "Ordering the Backcountry: The South Carolina Regulation," *WMQ*, 3d Ser., XXXVIII (1981), 668–677.

9. Affidavit of Alexander Rattray, May 24, 1751, *DRIA, 1750–1754*, 61. Rattray captained a militia company of 100 men (*ibid.*). Another planter in the area reported that the strength of his company had more than doubled in two years, from 35 to 83 (Roger Gibson to Glen, May 9, 1751, *ibid.*, 50). Figures for other militia companies suggest what the Catawbas confronted. In 1757 the Nation was encircled by South Carolina militias (to say nothing of those serving North Carolina), comprising 414 "Private Men" in seven companies—three west of the Wateree River, one east, two at the Waxhaws, and one above the Catawba towns. See SCCJ, May 4, 1757, RSUS, S.C. E.1p, 8/1, 85–86.

10. Glen to Lords Commissioners of Trade and Plantations, Dec. 23, 1749, BPRO-SC, XXIII, 452; see also *JCHA, November 21, 1752–September 6, 1754*, 215. *SCG*, May 4, 11, 25, June 29, Oct. 5, 1738. The Cherokee figures are in John Duffy, *Epidemics in Colonial America* (Baton Rouge, La., 1953), 82–83.

11. The absence of reports of illness before midcentury probably reflects the poverty of the extant records rather than the health of the Indians. *JCHA, 1748*, 292; Glen to Lords Commissioners of Trade and Plantations, Dec. 23, 1749, BPRO-SC, XXIII, 449–452; Glen to Gov. George Clinton, Oct. 15, 1751, Clinton Papers; Robert Stiell to Glen, July 23, 1753, *DRIA, 1750–1754*, 454; Catawbas to Gov. of Virginia, July 26, 1753, *CVSP*, I, 248; Catawbas to Glen, Oct. 15, 1754, *DRIA, 1754–1765*, 14; SCCJ, Apr. 30, 1755, RSUS, S.C. E.1p, 7/2, 176; Catawbas to Cherokees, [1757], William Henry Lyttelton Papers, Clements Library; Lyttelton to James Bullen, Nov. 5, 1757, in William Henry Lyttelton, Letters Sent, 1757–

1759, 40 (photocopies, SCDAH); Edmond Atkin's Instructions to Christopher Gist, Nov. 16, 1757, Loudoun Papers 4847, 4–5, Henry E. Huntington Library, San Marino, Calif. ("national Distemper"); Atkin to Hagler, Dec. 17, 1757, encl. in Atkin to Lyttelton, Jan. 6, 1758, Lyttelton Papers; William Richardson, "An Account of My Proceedings since I accepted the Indian Mission in October 2d 1758 . . . ," Wilberforce Eames Collection, New York Public Library (copy in YCPL), entry for Nov. 6, 1758. Five of the reports of sickness came in August, September, or October. The others were in June, July, and November. Doubtless the diseases often extended over a lengthy period of time, but it seems clear that late summer was the most dangerous season.

12. Stiell to Glen, July 23, 1753, *DRIA, 1750–1754*, 454; SCCJ, June 13, 1748, RSUS, S.C. E.1p, 3/4, 307–308; Cresap to Ogle, Mar. 17, 1750, in Browne *et al.*, eds., *Arch. Md.*, XLVI, 415–416; *SCG*, June 9, 1759 (attacks on hunting camps). Glen to Catawbas, Dec. 18, 1754, *DRIA, 1754–1765*, 28 (hunters called in).

13. SCCJ, Nov. 6, 1755, RSUS, S.C. E.1p, 7/2, 439–440. For more on the settlers' effect on hunting, see below, chap. 5.

14. W. Neil Franklin, "Virginia and the Cherokee Indian Trade, 1673–1752," East Tennessee Historical Society, *Publications*, IV (1932), 18; Meriwether, *Expansion of South Carolina*, 69; Samuel Cole Williams, ed., *Adair's History of the American Indians* (New York, 1974 [orig. publ. 1930]), ix, xxxv; Thomas Brown Inventory, in Inventories, MM, 1746–1748, 168, SCDAH.

15. SCCJ, Mar. 29, Apr. 21, 1748, RSUS, S.C. E.1p, 3/4, 183–185, 218–220; *SCG*, Mar. 28, 1748; Williams, ed., *Adair's History*, 368–370; Catawba King to Glen, Mar. 24, 1747[/48], in SCCJ, Apr. 27, 1748, RSUS, S.C. E.1p, 3/4, 230–231, Toole to Glen, May 18, 1750, in SCCJ, May 22, 1750, 4/2; Catawbas to Glen, Apr. 9, 1754, *DRIA, 1750–1754*, 487, Oct. 15, 1754, *DRIA, 1754–1765*, 14.

16. See Toole to Glen, n.d., *DRIA, 1750–1754*, 167–168, Glen to Catawba King, n.d., 372–373; Glen's speech to Hagler, n.d., encl. no. 3 in Glen to Lords Commissioners of Trade and Plantations, May 29, 1755, BPRO-SC, XXVI, 205. For the effects of disease on subsistence, see Marvin Thomas Hatley III, "The Dividing Path: The Direction of Cherokee Life in the Eighteenth Century" (master's thesis, University of North Carolina, 1977), 12–13; Alfred W. Crosby, "Virgin Soil Epidemics as a Factor in the Aboriginal Depopulation in America," *WMQ*, 3d Ser., XXXIII (1976), 294, 296.

17. Stiell to Glen, July 23, 1753, *DRIA, 1750–1754*, 454; see also Stiell to Glen, Mar. 11, 1753, 371, SCCJ, Aug. 23, 1756, RSUS, S.C. E.1p, 7/3, 333; for similar reports, see SCCJ, Nov. 5, 1755, 7/2, 438, SCCJ, Apr. 24, 1759, 8/2, 88, SCCHJ, Mar. 31, 1757, A.1b, 16/1, 83; Samuel Wyly to Glen and Council, Feb. 2, 1756, *DRIA, 1754–1765*, 97; Coun. Jours., Mar. 18, 1756, *CRNC*, V, 655; Hagler to Lyttelton, Jan. 3, 1759, *DRIA, 1754–1765*, 482.

18. SCCHJ, Nov. 25, 1755, RSUS, S.C. A.1b, 16/1, 9.

19. *JCHA, November 10, 1736–June 7, 1739*, 335. These may have been Sugarees, who moved to the Waxhaws area at about this time. See chap. 3.

20. Brown to Glen, Apr. 1, 1746, in SCCJ, Apr. 11, 1746, RSUS, S.C. E.1p, 3/2, 82; Glen to Lords Commissioners of Trade and Plantations, Dec. 1751, BPRO-SC, XXIV, 414; *SCG*, June 2, 1746.

21. SCCJ, Nov. 6, 1755, RSUS, S.C. E.1p, 7/2, 440; Dobbs to Board of Trade, Aug. 24, 1755, *CRNC*, V, 360–361. See also Journal of John Evans, Oct. 1755, *DRIA, 1754–1765*, 86.

22. Evans to Lyttelton, June 20, 1759, Lyttelton Papers.

23. See The Public Accounts of John Hammerton, Esq., Secretary of the Province, in Inventories, LL, 1744–1746, 29, 47, SCDAH.

24. SCCJ, Aug. 25, 1750, RSUS, S.C. E.1p, 4/2; Glen to Lords Commissioners of Trade and Plantations, Oct. 2, 1750, BPRO-SC, XXIV, 129. See also *JCHA, 1752–1754*, 215.

25. Evans to Glen, Apr. 18, 1748, in SCCJ, Apr. 27, 1748, RSUS, S.C. E.1p, 3/4, 233.

26. For infanticide, see below, chap. 7.

27. After reporting the drought's effect on Catawbas, one settler remarked that "the white people in them parts would be in as bad a plite were it not for their Crops of wheat" (Samuel Wyly to Lyttelton, Oct. 27, 1758, Lyttelton Papers).

28. John Brickell, *The Natural History of North-Carolina* . . . (Raleigh, N.C., 1911 [orig. publ. 1737]), 119–120; SCCJ, Nov. 6, 1755, RSUS, S.C. E.1p, 7/2, 440; Evans to Glen, Feb. 2, 1756, *DRIA, 1754–1765*, 92.

29. Glen to Lords Commissioners of Trade and Plantations, Dec. 1751, BPRO-SC, XXIV, 407 (I have reversed the clauses in Glen's sentence for the sake of clarity). SCCJ, Nov. 6, 1755, RSUS, S.C. E.1p, 7/2, 440, Catawba King to Glen, Mar. 24, 1747[/48], in SCCJ, Apr. 27, 1748, E.1p, 3/4, 231. See Douglas Summers Brown, *The Catawba Indians: The People of the River* (Columbia, S.C., 1966), chap. 10.

30. Catawba King to Glen, Mar. 24, 1747[/48], in SCCJ, Apr. 27, 1748, RSUS, S.C. E.1p, 3/4, 231; for calling together, see 230; and Jour. of Evans, Feb.–Mar. 1756, *DRIA, 1754–1765*, 107. Dobbs to Lyttelton, Oct. 24, 1757, Lyttelton Papers; see also Dobbs to Lyttelton, May 27, 1757.

31. Evans to Glen, Apr. 18, 1748, in SCCJ, Apr. 27, 1748, RSUS, S.C. E.1p, 3/4, 232; for an earlier rumor, see SCCJ, June 21, 1744, 2/3, 349.

32. Glen to Gov. Ogle, Dec. 13, 1749, in Browne *et al.*, eds., *Arch. Md.*, XXVIII, 496; Glen to Lords Commissioners of Trade and Plantations, Oct. 2, 1750, BPRO-SC, XXIV, 129.

33. Glen to Lords Commissioners of Trade and Plantations, Sept. 22, 1744, BPRO-SC, XXI, 402; and see Glen to Lords Commissioners of Trade and Plantations, Dec. 1751, XXIV, 395, 404. *JCHA, March 28, 1749–March 19, 1750*, 98; Williams, ed., *Adair's History*, 1, 140 (see also 34–35).

34. Glen to Lords Commissioners of Trade and Plantations, Mar. 1751, BPRO-SC, XXIV, 306; see also Jacobs, ed., *Atkin Report*, 3–4. Glen to Clinton, July 7, 1750, George Clinton Papers, Clements Library; Glen to Lords Commissioners of Trade and Plantations, Oct. 10, 1748, BPRO-SC, XXIII, 204, Dec. 23, 1749, XXIII, 452. For earlier sentiments, see *JCHA, 1736–1739*, 346.

35. Bull to Lords Commissioners of Trade and Plantations, Oct. 5, 1739, BPRO-SC, XX, 180, Charles Pinckney to Lords Commissioners of Trade and Plantations, June 29, 1754, XXVI, 78.

36. See James Crokatt[?] to Henry Fox, Jan. 31, 1749/50, *ibid.*, XXIV, 205; Glen to the President of the Coun. of N.C., Mar. 14, 1754, *DRIA, 1750–1754*, 479–480; Jacobs, ed., *Atkin Report*, 18, 39.

37. Address to the Assembly, 1750, James Glen Papers, South Caroliniana Library, Columbia.

38. Glen to N.C. Coun. Pres., Mar. 14, 1754, *DRIA, 1750–1754*, 479–480; Wyly to Lyttelton, Aug. 23, 1759, Lyttelton Papers.

39. Bull to Lords Commissioners of Trade and Plantations, May 25, 1738, BPRO-SC, XIX, 109. For similar sentiments by another member of the South Carolina Council, see Jacobs, ed., *Atkin Report*, 38.

40. Throughout eastern North America other Indians and other Europeans had been or were then groping toward a similar accommodation. See Francis Jennings, *The Ambiguous Iroquois Empire: The Covenant Chain Confederation of Indian Tribes with English Colonies from Its Beginnings to the Lancaster Treaty of 1744* (New York, 1984);

Jennings *et al.*, eds., *The History and Culture of Iroquois Diplomacy: An Interdisciplinary Guide to the Treaties of the Six Nations and Their League* (Syracuse, N.Y., 1985).

41. *JCHA, 1736–1739*, 716–717.

42. The figures here include all formal encounters between Indian headmen and representatives of English government. Most meetings occurred in Charleston, but some took place in other colonial capitals, at the Congarees, and at various other locales. For an example of uninvited guests and the colony's inability to turn them away, see SCCJ, Apr. 23, 24, 26, 1745, RSUS, S.C. E.1p, 3/1, 176–177, 179–183. The peaks are 14 in May and 11 in August, as opposed to lows of none in December, 2 in January, and 3 in both June and November.

43. SCUHJ, Sept. 13, 1727 (BMP D491), 176, SCDAH; SCCJ, July 6, 1739, RSUS, S.C. E.1p, 1/6, 29, Sept. 6, 1749, 4/1, 619.

44. SCCJ, Aug. 25, 1750, RSUS, S.C. E.1p, 4/2 (25 people); Aug. 23, 1756, 7/3, 331 (52); May 30, 1759, 8/2, 93 (45). For sickness, see *JCHA, September 12, 1739– March 26, 1741*, 149, *JCHA, 23 April 1750–31 August 1751*, 205.

45. Wyly to Lyttelton, May 5, 1759, Lyttelton Papers; SCCJ, May 7, 1752, RSUS, S.C. E.1p, 5/2, 214; Catawbas to Glen, n.d., *DRIA, 1754–1765*, 49; *EJCCV*, III, 421.

46. SCCJ, July 18, 1748, RSUS, S.C. E.1p, 3/4, 367; Glen to Lords Commissioners of Trade and Plantations, Dec. 1751, BPRO-SC, XXIV, 402. See also Jacobs, ed., *Atkin Report*, 30. For examples of Catawbas' becoming ill, see Glen to Lords Commissioners of Trade and Plantations, Dec. 23, 1749, BPRO-SC, XXIII, 450– 452; *JCHA, 1748*, 292; SCCJ, June 8, 1748, RSUS, S.C. E.1p, 3/4, 293. Catawbas mentioned their fear of the lowcountry environment in *JCHA, 1750–1751*, 382.

47. Glen to Lords Commissioners of Trade and Plantations, Dec. 23, 1749, BPRO-SC, XXIII, 449–450.

48. Glen to Lords Commissioners of Trade and Plantations, Dec. 1751, *ibid.*, XXIV, 408–409 (quotation on 409). See also *SCG*, May 6, 1745. For a similar reception, see Crokatt[?] to Fox, Jan. 31, 1749/50, BPRO-SC, XXIV, 207.

49. SCCJ, June 2, 1748, RSUS, S.C. E.1p, 3/4, 288; for other examples, see Aug. 23–24, 1756, 7/3, 331, 334, May 27, 1758, 8/1, 196, Apr. 20, 24, 1759, 8/2, 82, 86. For the handshake's antiquity, see Lawson, *New Voyage*, ed. Lefler, 210. For its significance in relations among Indians, see Treaty with the Six Nations, July 1751, *DRIA, 1750–1754*, 143; SCCJ, Aug. 23, 1756, RSUS, S.C. E.1p, 7/3, 332–333.

50. Minutes of the Catawbas' Conference with Superintendent Atkin at Jamestown Ferry, May 19, 1757, HM 3992, Huntington Library.

51. Lawson, *New Voyage*, ed. Lefler, 233; Edward Porter Alexander, ed., *The Journal of John Fontaine: An Irish Huguenot Son in Spain and Virginia, 1710–1719* (Williamsburg, Va., 1972), 93; SCCJ, Oct. 5, 1744, RSUS, S.C. E.1p, 2/3, 478. For Hagler's command of English, see Richardson, "Account," Nov. 11, 1758.

52. For a list of terms drawn from the Iroquois councils, see Jennings *et al.*, eds., *Iroquois Diplomacy*, 115–124.

53. Catawbas to Lyttelton, June 16, 1757, Lyttelton Papers; Jour. of Evans, Oct. 1755, *DRIA, 1754–1765*, 86 (South Carolina). Conference with the Catawbas, Salisbury, May 1756, *CRNC*, V, 584 (North Carolina). "A Treaty between Virginia and the Catawbas and Cherokees, 1756," *VMHB*, XIII (1905–1906), 241; Catawbas to Cherokees, [1757], Lyttelton Papers (Cherokees). Catawbas to Iroquois, Nov. 11, 1752, Clinton Papers (Six Nations, Hendrick). Glen to Thomas Brown[?], Apr. 10, 1746, James Glen Letterbook, 1–2, SCDAH; Glen to the Duke of Newcastle, Feb. 11, 1745/6, BPRO-SC, XXII, 137–138 (Glen as father). Lt. Col. George Mercer to Gen. John Stanwix, Aug. 12, 1759, in Donald H. Kent *et al.*, eds., *The Papers of Henry Bouquet*, III (Harrisburg, Pa., 1976), 544 (Gist).

54. Ears: Catawbas to Gov. of Virginia, July 26, 1753, *CVSP*, I, 248; A Treaty between North Carolina Commissioners and the Catawba Indians, Aug. 29, 1754, *CRNC*, V, 141; Catawbas to Iroquois, Nov. 11, 1752, Clinton Papers. Doors: Catawbas to Iroquois, Nov. 11, 1752; Catawbas to Creeks, n.d., *DRIA, 1754–1765*, 421. Hatchets: Catawbas to Gov. of Virginia, July 26, 1753, *CVSP*, I, 248; Catawbas to Creeks, n.d., *DRIA, 1754–1765*, 421.

55. One womb: Conference with the Catawbas, Salisbury, May 1756, *CRNC*, V, 582; Jamestown Ferry Conference, May 19, 1757; SCCJ, Apr. 30, 1755, RSUS, S.C. E.1p, 7/2, 175. One spoon: SCCJ, May 27, 1758, RSUS, S.C. E.1p, 8/1, 200. Pipe and fire: SCCJ, Mar. 4, 1761, RSUS, S.C. E.1p, 8/5, 100. For a discussion of the image of the path, see Hatley, "Dividing Path," 78–83.

56. SCCJ, July 6, 1739, RSUS, S.C. E.1p, 1/6, 30; Dobbs to Hagler, Dec. 26, 1756, *DRIA, 1754–1765*, 102. Dobbs arrived to take office on Oct. 31, 1754 (*CRNC*, V, iv).

57. *EJCCV*, VI, 32; *SCG*, June 2, 1746; SCCJ, May 6, 1760, RSUS, S.C. E.1p, 8/3, 121. This assessment is based on all of the available evidence on Catawba formal discourse. Other sources or other studies could refute these findings.

58. Conference with the Catawbas, Salisbury, May 1756, *CRNC*, V, 583; *SCG*, May 6, 1745. For Glen's use of the term "fire," see Glen to the Iroquois, Nov. 11, 1752, Clinton Papers. See also Glen to the Six Nations, n.d., *DRIA, 1750–1754*, 206. For its use by Catawbas, see Treaty with the Six Nations, July 1751, *DRIA, 1750–1754*, 144, Hagler to Glen, Oct. 21, 1755, *DRIA, 1754–1765*, 85; SCCJ, Mar. 4, 1761, RSUS, S.C. E.1p, 8/5, 100. See also Jennings *et al.*, eds., *Iroquois Diplomacy,* 118.

59. "Treaty between Virginia and the Catawbas and Cherokees," *VMHB*, XIII (1905–1906), 243; Raymond Demere to Lyttelton, Nov. 18, 1756, *DRIA, 1754–1765*, 249. See also John Phillip Reid, *A Better Kind of Hatchet: Law, Trade, and Diplomacy in the Cherokee Nation during the Early Years of European Contact* (University Park, Pa., 1976), 35; Charles M. Hudson, *The Southeastern Indians* (Knoxville, Tenn., 1976), 310.

60. Glen to Lords Commissioners of Trade and Plantations, July 15, 1750, BPRO-SC, XXIV, 74; George Chicken, "Colonel Chicken's Journal to the Cherokees, 1725," in Newton D. Mereness, ed., *Travels in the American Colonies* (New York, 1916), 153.

61. Catawba headmen used these commissions or other papers from colonial officials as proof of their loyalty as early as 1727. See "An Acco[un]t of Nathaniel Harrison's proceedings when he went out, by Order of Governm[en]t, to meet with the Cautaubau Indians . . . ," encl. in Gooch to Board of Trade, Sept. 21, 1727, CO 5/1321 (LC trans., 14). For requests, see SCCJ, Apr. 30, May 3, 1755, RSUS, S.C. E.1p, 7/2, 176, 178, 182, Aug. 23, 1756, 7/3, 333, May 5, 1760, 8/3, 119; Glen's speech to Hagler, n.d., encl. no. 3 in Glen to Lords Commissioners of Trade and Plantations, May 29, 1755, BPRO-SC, XXVI, 205.

62. Dobbs to Board of Trade, Aug. 24, 1755, *CRNC*, VI, 361.

63. SCCJ, Aug. 25, 1750, RSUS, S.C. E.1p, 4/2, Apr. 30, May 3, 1755, 7/2, 176, 182 (quotation on 182).

64. *Ibid.*, Apr. 28, 1748, 3/4, 242 (the request is in Evans to Glen, Apr. 18, 1748, in SCCJ, Apr. 27, 1748, 3/4, 233), May 27, 29, 1758, 8/1, 199, 202–203, Nov. 6, 1755, 7/2, 440.

65. Glen to Lords Commissioners of Trade and Plantations, Dec. 1751, BPRO-SC, XXIV, 408; Toole to Glen, July 15, 1754, *DRIA, 1750–1754*, 514; SCCJ, Aug. 7, 1760, RSUS, S.C. E.1p, 8/5, 15, Catawba King to Glen, Mar. 24, 1747[/48], in

SCCJ, Apr. 27, 1748, 3/4, 230, SCCJ, Aug. 24, 1756, 7/3, 335. *SCG*, June 9, 1746; Catawbas to Glen, Nov. 21, 1752, *DRIA*, *1750–1754*, 361; Hagler to Glen, Oct. 21, 1755, *DRIA*, *1754–1765*, 85, Jour. of Evans, Feb.–Mar. 1756, *1754–1765*, 107.

For possible aboriginal models, see Frank G. Speck, *Catawba Hunting, Trapping, and Fishing*, Joint Publications, Museum of the University of Pennsylvania and the Philadelphia Anthropological Society, no. 2 (Philadelphia, Pa., 1946), 22; F. G. Speck and C. E. Schaeffer, "Catawba Kinship and Social Organization with a Resume of Tutelo Kinship Terms," *American Anthropologist*, N.S., XLIV (1942), 566–567; Hudson, *Southeastern Indians*, 223. When making peace with South Carolina in 1716, Catawbas had sent a delegation "with a flag." Le Jau to the Secretary, July 1, 1716, in Frank J. Klingberg, ed., *The Carolina Chronicle of Dr. Francis Le Jau, 1706–1717*, University of California Publications in History, LIII (Berkeley, Calif., 1956), 180.

66. SCCJ, May 30, 1759, RSUS, S.C. E.1p, 8/2, 93, May 15, 1762, 8/6, 496; for another example by another headman, see July 3, 1762, 8/6, 528.

67. Report of Mercier, Crell, and Stiell, Feb. 14, 1752, *DRIA*, *1750–1754*, 217–218. The estimate of its worth is based on a partial price list from Thomas Brown's trading inventory (Inventories, MM, 1746–1748, 162–169).

68. The numbers that can be totaled give 1,972 pounds of powder, 4,016 pounds of bullets, and 2,750 flints. Catawbas also received 76 guns. All of these figures must be taken as an absolute minimum, since colonial officials did not always specify the amounts given. This was especially true of the weapons supplied to the Indians.

69. For the negotiations about food shipments, see SCCJ, Nov. 5, 22, 25, 27, 1755, RSUS, S.C. E.1p, 7/2, 438, 490–491, 502, 511–512, Jan. 13, 14, 19, 1756, 7/3, 48, 54, 72, Aug. 23, 1756, 7/3, 333; SCCHJ, Nov. 25, 1755, RSUS, S.C. A.1b, 16/1, 10, Mar. 31, Apr. 1, 1757, 16/1, 83, 87; Evans to Glen, Dec. 16, 1755, *DRIA*, *1754–1765*, 89, Evans to Glen, Feb. 2, 1756, 92, Wyly to Glen, Feb. 2, 1756, 97, Glen to Hagler, Feb. 12, 1756, 95; Commons House to Lyttelton, Apr. 1, 1757, Lyttelton Papers; Lyttelton to Hagler and Warriors, Jan. 11, 1759, Lyttelton, Letters Sent, 278; SCCJ, Apr. 24, 1759, RSUS, S.C. E.1p, 8/2, 88, Aug. 7, Oct. 8, 1760, 8/5, 15, 36. Steven G. Baker has noted the importance of this food to Catawba survival ("The Working Draft of: The Historic Catawba Peoples: Exploratory Perspectives in Ethnohistory and Archaeology" [MS, Department of History, University of South Carolina, Columbia, 1975], 104–105).

70. Wyly to Glen, Feb. 2, 1756, *DRIA*, *1754–1765*, 97.

71. For the Indians' complaints, see Hill to Toole, Mar. 2, 1751/52, *DRIA*, *1750–1754*, 377–378, Gordon to Stiell, May 11, 1752, 378, Catawbas to Glen, Nov. 21, 1752, 361, Glen to N.C. Coun. Pres., Mar. 14, 1754, 479–480, Matthew Rowan to Glen, Apr. 16, 1754, 489, Glen to Catawbas, May 9, 1754, 498–499; SCCJ, Apr. 29, May 3, 1755, RSUS, S.C. E.1p, 7/2, 175, 176, 178; Glen's speech to Hagler, n.d., encl. no. 3 in Glen to Lords Commissioners of Trade and Plantations, May 29, 1755, BPRO-SC, XXVI, 209–210; SCCJ, May 2, 6, 1760, RSUS, S.C. E.1p, 8/3, 119, 121. For colonial examples, see SCCJ, May 22, 1750, RSUS, S.C. E.1p, 4/2, Nov. 15, 1752, 6/1, 9–10; Treaty between N.C. and the Catawbas, Aug. 29, 1754, *CRNC*, V, 141–144b, N.C. Coun. Jours., May 21, 1754, 175–176; Waxhaw Inhabitants to Samuel Wyly, Apr. 16, 1759, encl. in Wyly to Lyttelton, Apr. 26, 1759, Lyttelton Papers. Relations with colonial settlers are further explored below, chap. 5.

72. Glen to Lords Commissioners of Trade and Plantations, Dec. 1751, BPRO-SC, XXIV, 414–415; *SCG*, June 2, 1746; Catawba King to Glen, Nov. 21, 1752, *DRIA*, *1750–1754*, 362.

73. *SCG*, June 9, 1746; Lee to Board of Trade, May 11, 1750, CO 5/1327, 179–180 (LC trans.). See also Dinwiddie to Catawbas, Nov. 3, 1752, *DRIA, 1750–1754*, 362; Glen to Lords Commissioners of Trade and Plantations, Dec. 16, 1752, BPRO-SC, XXV, 130, Dinwiddie to Glen, May 23, 1753, encl. no. 1 in Glen to the Earl of Holdernesse, June 25, 1753, XXV, 304; Dinwiddie to Catawbas, May 31, 1753, CO 5/1327, 653–654 (LC trans.); Catawbas to Gov. Virginia, July 26, 1753, *CVSP*, I, 248; Gov. Horatio Sharpe to Dinwiddie, Dec. 10, 1754, in Browne *et al.*, eds., *Arch. Md.*, VI, 141; *EJCCV*, V, 410, 415–417.

74. Glen to Lords Commissioners of Trade and Plantations, Dec. 1751, BPRO-SC, XXIV, 409–413, Glen to Lords Commissioners of Trade and Plantations, Sept. 22, 1744, XXI, 401–402; SCCJ, July 25, Oct. 5, 1744, Jan. 26, Feb. 12, Apr. 27, May 6, 1745, RSUS, S.C. E.1p, 2/3, 423–428, 477–478, 3/1, 53–55, 72–73, 75, 189, 214, Catawbas to Glen, Apr. 26, 1750, in SCCJ, May 22, 1750, 4/2; Col. Vanderdussen's Testimony to the Lords Commissioners of Trade and Plantations, May 25, 1748, BPRO-SC, XXIII, 12.

75. *SCG*, May 27, 1751; Glen to Lords Commissioners of Trade and Plantations, Dec. 1751, BPRO-SC, XXIV, 416.

76. Glen to Dinwiddie, June 1, 1754, *DRIA, 1750–1754*, 526; Jacobs, ed., *Atkin Report*, 47; SCCJ, Aug. 7, 1760, RSUS, S.C. E.1p, 8/5, 15; Wyly to Lyttelton, Apr. 26, 1759, Lyttelton Papers. See also Lyttelton to Wyly, Feb. 16, 1759, Lyttelton, Letters Sent, 288.

77. Meeting with Capt. Redhead, July 9, 1771, Joseph Brevard Kershaw Papers, South Caroliniana Library.

78. Catawbas to Glen, Apr. 26, 1750, in SCCJ, May 22, 1750, RSUS, S.C. E.1p, 4/2.

79. Glen's speech to Hagler, n.d., encl. no. 3 in Glen to Lords Commissioners of Trade and Plantations, May 29, 1755, BPRO-SC, XXVI, 205–206; *SCG*, May 6, 1745 (emphasis added). When Hagler became king, the Indians clearly made the choice, which Glen then confirmed. SCCJ, May 22, Aug. 25, 1750, RSUS, S.C. E.1p, 4/2; Glen's speech to Hagler, n.d., encl. no. 3 in Glen to Lords Commissioners of Trade and Plantations, May 29, 1755, BPRO-SC, XXVI, 205.

80. Glen to Catawbas, Mar. 14, 1752, *DRIA, 1750–1754*, 221; SCCJ, May 27, 29, 1758, RSUS, S.C. E.1p, 8/1, 200, 203; Treaty between N.C. and the Catawbas, Aug. 29, 1754, *CRNC*, V, 144.

81. Dobbs to Waddell and others, July 18, 1756, *CRNC*, V, 604; *SCG*, Aug. 12, 1756; SCCJ, May 6, 1760, RSUS, S.C. E.1p, 8/3, 121 (see also Aug. 24, 1756, 7/3, 336). Whether Dobbs ever made good on his promise (or threat) is unknown. Glen had earlier asked for similar "Satisfaction" when Catawbas robbed a colonist in 1752. See Glen to Catawbas, Mar. 14, 1752, *DRIA, 1750–1754*, 221.

82. SCCJ, Apr. 30, May 3, 1755, RSUS, S.C. E.1p, 7/2, 176, 178, May 2, 1760, 8/3, 119; Treaty between N.C. and the Catawbas, Aug. 29, 1754, *CRNC*, V, 142.

83. For the continuation of warfare after 1751, see Merrell, "'Their Very Bones Shall Fight': The Catawba-Iroquois Wars," in Daniel K. Richter and James H. Merrell, eds., *Beyond the Covenant Chain: The Iroquois and Their Neighbors in Indian North America, 1600–1800* (Syracuse, N.Y., 1987), 128–131.

84. Lyttelton to Lords Commissioners of Trade and Plantations, Apr. 14, 1759, BPRO-SC, XXVIII, 180; *SCG*, Mar. 24, 1759; Proceedings of the Coun. Concerning Indian Affairs, July 3, 1753, *DRIA, 1750–1754*, 432. See also Richard Coytmore to Lyttelton, Nov. 8, 11, 1759, Lyttelton Papers.

85. White Outerbridge to Lyttelton, Mar. 24, 1757, Lyttelton Papers. For other examples, see Evans to Glen, Apr. 18, 1748, in SCCJ, Apr. 27, 1748, RSUS, S.C. E.1p, 3/4, 232, Enos Dexter to Glen, Apr. 19, 1748, in SCCJ, Apr. 27, 1748, 3/4,

228, Chickilie's Talk, July 29, 1749, in SCCJ, Sept. 4, 1749, 4/1, 582–583; Catawba Nation to the Creeks, 1751[?], Clinton Papers, XIV; Catawbas to the Chickasaws, n.d., *DRIA, 1750–1754*, 502–503; Jour. of Evans, Oct. 1755, *DRIA, 1754–1765*, 86; Demere to Lyttelton, July 4, Oct. 11, 1757, McGillivray to Lyttelton, Oct. 17, 1758, Mar. 12, Apr. 2, 1759, Lyttelton Papers; *SCG*, Apr. 28, 1759.

86. See above, chap. 3.

87. Peacemaking also required a shift in the Anglo-American attitude toward Indian wars, a shift I discuss in "Their Very Bones Shall Fight," in Richter and Merrell, eds., *Beyond the Covenant Chain*, 125.

88. S.C. Coun. to Dinwiddie, Nov. 12, 1753, *DRIA, 1750–1754*, 467. In 1745, Catawbas had sent a message to Virginia "purporting that they could not listen to any Proposals of Peace with the Six Nations till they had received some Presents from them with the Marks of the head Men." See *EJCCV*, V, 188.

89. Wraxall, *Abridgement*, 199; Extract of Conrad Weiser's Report of his Journey to Onondaga, May 19, 1745, *MPCP*, IV, 779, 781; *EJCCV*, V, 188.

90. SCCJ, Aug. 25, 1750, RSUS, S.C. E.1p, 4/2. And see *JCHA, 1750–1751*, 382.

91. *JCHA, September 10, 1745–June 17, 1746*, 141. See also *ibid.*, 132; George Haig to Glen, Mar. 21, 1746, in SCCJ, Mar. 27, 1746, RSUS, S.C. E.1p, 3/2, 74–75.

92. Toole to Glen, July 15, 1754, *DRIA, 1750–1754*, 514–515. See also *EJCCV*, VI, 73.

93. SCCJ, May 22, 1750, RSUS, S.C. E.1p, 4/2.

94. Glen to Hagler, Feb. 12, 1756, *DRIA, 1754–1765*, 95; Dobbs to Lyttelton, May 27, 1757, Lyttelton Papers; *EJCCV*, VI, 32.

95. Washington to Dinwiddie, Dec. 19, 1756, in John C. Fitzpatrick, ed., *The Writings of George Washington, from the Original Manuscript Sources, 1745–1799*, 39 vols. (Washington, D.C., 1931–1944), I, 524, Washington to Gov. Fauquier, July 10, 1758, II, 234; Dinwiddie to Washington, Jan. 26, 1757, in R. A. Brock, ed., *The Official Records of Robert Dinwiddie, Lieutenant-Governor of the Colony of Virginia, 1751–1758*, 2 vols. (Virginia Historical Society, *Collections*, N.S., III–IV [Richmond, Va., 1883–1884]), II, 585. See also Gen. John Forbes to Atkin, Aug. 16, 1758, encl. in Atkin to Lyttelton, Oct. 15, 1758, Lyttelton Papers. For the Catawbas' service, see Brown, *Catawba Indians*, chap. 9.

96. Glen to Sec. of State, Aug. 15, 1754, BPRO-SC, XXVI, 93 (emphasis added); Evans to Lyttelton, May 11, 1757, Fran. Brown to Gov. Dobbs, May 26, 1757, encl. in Dobbs to Lyttelton, May 27, 1757, Lyttelton Papers.

97. Hagler to Glen, Oct. 21, 1755, *DRIA, 1754–1765*, 85. See also Catawbas to Glen, Apr. 9, 1754, *1750–1754*, 487, Catawbas to Glen, Oct. 15, 1754, *1754–1765*, 14; Catawbas to Lyttelton, Aug. 23, 1759, Lyttelton Papers.

98. SCCHJ, Oct. 5, 1759, RSUS, S.C. A.1b, 16/3, 34.

99. Atkin to Lyttelton, Nov. 23, 1757, Lyttelton Papers. For the continuing negotiations, see Hagler to Glen, Mar. 14, 1756, *DRIA, 1754–1765*, 108; Conference with Catawbas, Salisbury, May 1756, *CRNC*, V, 581, Dobbs to Waddell and others, July 18, 1756, V, 605; SCCJ, Aug. 24, 1756, RSUS, S.C. E.1p, 7/3, 335; Dobbs to Lyttelton, Oct. 26, Nov. 22, 1756, Lyttelton Papers; Dobbs to Board of Trade, Oct. 31, 1756, Jan. 20, 1757, *CRNC*, V, 639, 742; SCCJ, Jan. 27, 1757, RSUS, S.C. E.1p, 8/1, 13–14; Evans to Lyttelton, May 11, 1757, Lyttelton Papers; Leg. Jours., May 20, 1757, *CRNC*, V, 849; Dobbs to Lyttelton, May 27, 1757, and encl., Dobbs to Lyttelton, July 19, 1757, Lyttelton Papers; Dobbs to Board of Trade, Aug. 30, 1757, *CRNC*, V, 784; Lyttelton to Wyly, Oct. 1, 1757, Lyttelton, Letters Sent, 25; Dobbs to Lyttelton, Oct. 24, 1757, and encl., Lyttelton Papers; Lyttelton to Dobbs, Nov. 8, 1757, Lyttelton, Letters Sent, 41–42; Leg. Jours., Nov. 30, 1757, *CRNC*, V, 902; Atkin to Catawbas, Dec. 17, 1757, encl. in Atkin to Lyttelton, Jan. 8, 1758,

Lyttelton Papers; Leg. Jours., Nov. 24, 1758, *CRNC*, V, 1040; SCCJ, Apr. 24, 1759, RSUS, S.C. E.1p, 8/2, 87, 88; Adamson to Lyttelton, June 12, 1759, Lyttelton Papers. And see below, chap. 6.

100. SCCJ, Aug. 24, 1756, RSUS, S.C. E.1p, 7/3, 335; Catawbas to Glen, Oct. 15, 1754, *DRIA, 1754–1765*, 14. See also SCCJ, May 27, 1758, RSUS, S.C. E.1p, 8/1, 198.

101. SCCJ, Apr. 24, 1759, RSUS, S.C. E.1p, 8/2, 87; Jour. of Evans, Oct. 1755, *DRIA, 1754–1765*, 86.

102. Adamson to Lyttelton, June 12, 1759, Lyttelton Papers. Hagler reiterated this argument in a letter of his own. See Catawbas to Lyttelton, June 11, 1759, encl. *ibid.*

103. Catawbas to Dobbs, Oct. 5, 1757, encl. in Dobbs to Lyttelton, Oct. 24, 1757, *ibid.*

104. Richardson, "Account," Nov. 8, 11, 1758.

105. Catawbas to Dobbs, Oct. 5, 1757, encl. in Dobbs to Lyttelton, Oct. 24, 1757, Lyttelton Papers.

106. Treaty between N.C. and the Catawbas, Aug. 29, 1754, *CRNC*, V, 144a; Catawbas to Lyttelton, June 11, 1759, encl. in Adamson to Lyttelton, June 12, 1759, Lyttelton Papers.

Chapter 5

1. SCCJ, May 11, 1754, RSUS, S.C. E.1p, 6/2, 253. See also SCCJ, May 22, 1750, *ibid.*, 4/2; Samuel Cole Williams, ed., *Adair's History of the American Indians* (New York, 1974 [orig. publ. 1930]), 233.

2. The complaints are in Council Journals, Oct. 18, 1749, *CRNC*, IV, 971.

3. George Haig to Gov. Glen, Mar. 21, 1746, in SCCJ, Mar. 27, 1746, RSUS, S.C. E.1p, 3/2, 75.

4. *John Ellis* was a common name, and it is not easy to be certain of the connections linking son to father. A John Ellis was involved in a court case in Henrico County in 1678, for example, which has all the bluster of the events in 1749, but their kinship is unclear (Henrico County, Virginia, Order Book, 1678–1693, transcript [entitled "Henrico County, Virginia, Record Book, no. 2, 1678–1693 (Deeds, Wills, Settlements of Estates, Etc.)"], 13–14, microfilm, VSL). My attempt to trace the Ellis family's fortunes is from Henrico County, Deeds, Wills, Etc., 1688–1697, Original, 286, 605; Nell Marion Nugent, ed., *Cavaliers and Pioneers: Abstracts of Virginia Land Patents and Grants*, III (Richmond, Va., 1979), 31, 40, 98, 162, 269, 372; Henrico County Records [Deeds, Wills], 1706–1709, Original, 35; Benjamin B. Weisiger III, comp., *Prince George County, Virginia, Wills and Deeds, 1713–1728* (n.p., 1973), 61, 64, 98, 139; George Chicken, "Colonel Chicken's Journal to the Cherokees, 1725," in Newton D. Mereness, ed., *Travels in the American Colonies* (New York, 1916), 103; William Byrd, "The Secret History of the Line" and "History of the Dividing Line betwixt Virginia and North Carolina Run in the Year of Our Lord 1728," in Louis B. Wright, ed., *The Prose Works of William Byrd of Westover: Narratives of a Colonial Virginian* (Cambridge, Mass., 1966), 48, 61, 93, 97, 135–136, 141, 148, 150, 151n, 335.

5. Haig to Glen, Mar. 21, 1746, in SCCJ, Mar. 27, 1746, RSUS, S.C. E.1p, 3/2, 74–75. The trading camp on the Yadkin was patented in 1751. See Robert W. Ramsey, *Carolina Cradle: Settlement of the Northwest Carolina Frontier, 1747–1762* (Chapel Hill, N.C., 1964), 52, 106. The elder Ellis died in 1738. See Prince George County, Minute Book, 1737–1740, 109, 159–160, 167, microfilm, VSL.

6. For Brown, see SCCJ, Dec. 2, 1735, RSUS, S.C. E.1p, 1/2, 25. *JCHA, September 12, 1739–March 26, 1741*, 114–115. For Thompson, see *JCHA, November 10, 1736–June 7, 1739*, 430, 439, 552; SCCJ, June 8, 15, 1739, RSUS, S.C. E.1p, 1/6, 26–27.

7. Thomas Brown Inventory, Inventories, MM, 1746–1748, 166–168, SCDAH. For Ellis's later career, see James Beamer to Glen, Apr. 26, 1752, *DRIA, May 21, 1750–August 7, 1754*, 257; A Talk from Tistoe, and the Wolf, of Keowee to his Excellency the Governor of South Carolina, Mar. 5, 1759, encl. in Lachlan Mackintosh to William Henry Lyttelton, Mar. 4, 1759, William Henry Lyttelton Papers, William L. Clements Library, Ann Arbor, Mich. For another trader's activities in the 1750s, see Wesley D. White, "Historical Overview of the [Saponi] Tribe: Second Essay . . . ," 65–67, 104–109 (MS, Lumbee River Legal Services, Pembroke, N.C.).

8. This paragraph and the one following owe a great debt to Greg Dening, *Islands and Beaches: Discourse on a Silent Land, Marquesas, 1774–1880* (Honolulu, 1980), esp. 155.

9. Waxhaw Inhabitants to Samuel Wyly, Apr. 16, 1759, encl. in Wyly to Lyttelton, Apr. 26, 1759, Lyttelton Papers.

10. James Francis to Glen, May 2, 1748, in SCCJ, May 11, 1748, RSUS, S.C. E.1p, 3/4, 263. The men Francis referred to were probably colonial hunters, widely known as "very expert Woodsmen" although "litle more than white Indians" (George Cadogan to Glen, Mar. 27, 1751, *DRIA, 1750–1754*, 12).

11. Byrd, "History," in Wright, ed., *Prose Works*, 248. For the importance of "perceptual environment," see H. Roy Merrens, "The Physical Environment of Early America: Images and Image Makers in Colonial South Carolina," *Geographical Review*, LIX (1969), 530. In speaking of "settlers" here I am somewhat simplifying a very complex picture. Those who moved into Catawba Country during these years were divided into a number of different ethnic and religious groups, and each tended to remain together, excluding outsiders. From the Catawbas' perspective, however, it seems likely that the intruders seemed more similar than different, and I have adopted that perspective here.

12. A Talk Addressed to the Catawba King by Commissioners from North Carolina, n.d., in SCCJ, May 22, 1750, RSUS, S.C. E.1p, 4/2; Catawbas to Glen, Nov. 21, 1752, *DRIA, 1750–1754*, 361.

13. Wilbur R. Jacobs, ed., *Indians of the Southern Colonial Frontier: The Edmond Atkin Report and Plan of 1755* (Columbia, S.C., 1954), 46. The population estimate is from Matthew Rowan to the Board of Trade, June 6, 1754, *CRNC*, V, 124. For reports on the surveyors, see Jacobs, ed., *Atkin Report*, 46; Wyly to Clerk of the Council, Mar. 2, 1754, in SCCJ, Mar. 13, 1754, RSUS, S.C. E.1p, 6/1, 140; Glen to the President of the Council of N.C., Mar. 14, 1754, *DRIA, 1750–1754*, 479; Charles Pinckney to Lords Commissioners of Trade and Plantations, June 29, 1754, BPRO-SC, XXVI, 78.

14. Richard J. Hooker, ed., *The Carolina Backcountry on the Eve of the Revolution: The Journal and Other Writings of Charles Woodmason, Anglican Itinerant* (Chapel Hill, N.C., 1953), 14. Robert L. Meriwether, *The Expansion of South Carolina, 1729–1765* (Kingsport, Tenn., 1940), 259–260. Meriwether's figure is for South Carolina alone; others consider it too conservative. See Richard Maxwell Brown, *The South Carolina Regulators* (Cambridge, Mass., 1963), 3, 182. For the general pattern of migration, see Carl Bridenbaugh, *Myths and Realities: Societies of the Colonial South* (New York, 1972 [orig. publ. 1952]), 121–130.

15. My thinking in this section has been refined by William Cronon, *Changes in the Land: Indians, Colonists, and the Ecology of New England* (New York, 1983); Timothy Howard Silver, "A New Face on the Countryside: Indians and Colonists in the Southeastern Forest" (Ph.D. diss., College of William and Mary, 1985); Albert E.

Cowdrey, *This Land, This South: An Environmental History* (Lexington, Ky., 1983). For a view that early colonists had relatively little impact on the land, see Harry Roy Merrens, *Colonial North Carolina in the Eighteenth Century: A Study in Historical Geography* (Chapel Hill, N.C., 1964), 85.

16. Meriwether, *Expansion of South Carolina*, 58 (George Haig); Miscellaneous Records, KK, 484, SCDAH (John Evans).

17. Merrens, *Colonial North Carolina*, 25; Ramsey, *Carolina Cradle*, 108; Meriwether, *Expansion of South Carolina*, map 3, "The Congarees in 1759," p. 52. That Catawbas remained attached to their own means of dividing the land became clear when they began leasing acres to settlers. Within the reservation the lands were "generally bounded by water courses, or some natural division." *Correspondence Relative to the Catawba Indians, Embracing Gov. Seabrook's Letter to the Special Agent and Commissioners Appointed by Him* (Columbia, S.C., 1849), 9.

18. For the surveyor's craft I have relied on work done in Virginia. See Sarah S. Hughes, *Surveyors and Statesmen: Land Measuring in Colonial Virginia* (Richmond, Va., 1979), chap. 9, esp. 114–115. For initials, see North Carolina Land Grants, Anson County, file 010 (William Baird), file 080 (William Davis), Land Grant Office, Secretary of State, Raleigh; Anson, file 695, grant 163, book 10, p. 336 (George Cathey). For stakes, see Anson, file 219, grant 337, book 2, p. 67 (Christian Erwin); Anson, file 1637, grant 1017, book 15, p. 11 (Richard Graham); Anson, file 2126, grant 64, book 16, p. 6 (Samuel Neeley); Anson, file 226, grant 344, book 2, p. 68 (David Templeton); file 2538, grant 530, book 23, p. 305 (John Kimbro).

19. For fields, see S.C. Colonial Plats, IV, 241, 272, 400, 479, 508, V, 90, 108, SCDAH; N.C. Land Grants, Anson, file 080 (William Davis). For cabins, see N.C. Land Grants, Anson, file 856, grant 352, book 2, p. 389 (John Hitchcock), file 018, grant 677, warrant 585, entry 585 (John Barnet). For camps, see Anson, file 045 (Susanna Bole), file 1285, grant 257, book 18, p. 218 (John McKinney); "Grants to Earliest Settlers of Camden and Vicinity," in Thomas J. Kirkland and Robert M. Kennedy, *Historic Camden*, part 1, *Colonial and Revolutionary* (Columbia, S.C., 1905), diagram no. 9, 68. For the peach orchard, see N.C. Land Grants, file 018, grant 677, warrant 585, entry 585 (John Barnet). For the ditch and mound, see S.C. Colonial Plats, V, 51, 27.

20. [Robert Witherspoon], "Recollections of a Settler, 1780," in H. Roy Merrens, ed., *The Colonial South Carolina Scene: Contemporary Views, 1697–1774* (Columbia, S.C., 1977), 126, 127.

21. Quoted in Meriwether, *Expansion of South Carolina*, 141. For the huts, see [Witherspoon], "Recollections," in Merrens, ed., *Contemporary Views*, 126; Tarleton Brown, *Memoirs of Tarleton Brown, a Captain in the Revolutionary Army, Written by Himself* (Barnwell, S.C., 1894), 3; Samuel Eveleigh to George Morley, Provost Marshal of the Province (extract), May 1, 1735, BPRO-SC, XVII, 339; Meriwether, *Expansion of South Carolina*, 79, 165; Anne King Gregorie, *History of Sumter County, South Carolina* (Sumter, S.C., 1954), 15–16. For the log cabins and frame houses, see Hooker, ed., *Writings of Woodmason*, 7, 16, 18, 19, 33; Meriwether, *Expansion of South Carolina*, 49, 165; Gregorie, *Sumter County*, 16–17. At least one brick dwelling had been constructed in the vicinity before the Revolution. See S. L. Watson to Lyman C. Draper, Sept. 7, 1881, in the Draper Manuscripts Collection, Ser. VV, vol. XI, 206 (microfilm, original in Archives Division, State Historical Society of Wisconsin, Madison). For the three-stage building process, see Cary Carson *et al.*, "Impermanent Architecture in the Southern American Colonies," *Winterthur Portfolio: A Journal of American Material Culture*, XVI (1981), 139–141.

22. Hooker, ed., *Writings of Woodmason*, 16, 18, 33.

23. See Henry Glassie, *Folk Housing in Middle Virginia: A Structural Analysis of Historic Artifacts* (Knoxville, Tenn., 1975), esp. chaps. 2, 7.

24. For chimneys, see S.C. Colonial Plats, IV, 277; SCCJ, Aug. 24, 1756, RSUS, S.C. E.1p, 7/3, 335; Waxhaw Inhabitants to Wyly, Apr. 16, 1759, encl. in Wyly to Lyttelton, Apr. 26, 1759, Lyttelton Papers; Gregorie, *Sumter County*, 16. For floors, Meriwether, *Expansion of South Carolina*, 165. For locks, SCCJ, Aug. 24, 1756, RSUS, S.C. E.1p, 7/3, 335; Hooker, ed., *Writings of Woodmason*, 39, 47; Anson County, North Carolina, Record of Wills, 1751–1795, 92, 94, NCDAH. For glass, see Meriwether, *Expansion of South Carolina*, 165; Gregorie, *Sumter County*, 16; Account Book of Joseph Kershaw, 1774–1775, S.C. Mss. B (microfilm, State Historical Society of Wis., Madison), entry for Dec. 29, 1774. That southeastern Indians had square summer houses and council houses is well known; it does not appear that such shapes were common among the Siouan groups, however. See John R. Swanton, *Indians of the Southeastern United States*, Smithsonian Institution, Bureau of American Ethnology, Bulletin, no. 137 (Washington, D.C., 1946), 386, 389, fig. 5, p. 404, and 410–413.

25. Meriwether, *Expansion of South Carolina*, 46, 49, 50, 56. In 1753 a party of Catawba and "Northward" Indians raided a plantation in Amelia Township, plundering the "Negros' Houses." Moses Thompson to Glen, Mar. 30, 1753, *DRIA, 1750–1754*, 370.

26. Meriwether, *Expansion of South Carolina*, 50 (smokehouses). A Treaty between North Carolina Commissioners and the Catawba Indians, Aug. 29, 1754, *CRNC*, V, 141; Hooker, ed., *Writings of Woodmason*, 49; Meriwether, *Expansion of South Carolina*, 44, 56, 57, 63, 93, 100–101, 104–105, 109, 141, 143, 173; S.C. Colonial Plats, IV, 436, VII, 134, 145, 156, 379 (mills). Meriwether, *Expansion of South Carolina*, 105, 109 (vats). (For a description of these vats, see "Further Observations Intended for Improving the Culture and Curing of Indigo, etc. in South-Carolina," in Merrens, ed., *Contemporary Views*, 157–158.) James Adamson to Lyttelton, June 12, 1759, Lyttelton Papers; Anson County Wills, 1751–1795, 119; Meriwether, *Expansion of South Carolina*, 142–143 (stills).

27. Meriwether, *Expansion of South Carolina*, 50, 56, 165; Waxhaw Inhabitants to Wyly, Apr. 16, 1759, encl. in Wyly to Lyttelton, Apr. 26, 1759, Lyttelton Papers; Dobbs to Board of Trade, Aug. 24, 1755, *CRNC*, V, 354; Glen to N.C. Coun. Pres., Mar. 14, 1754, *DRIA, 1750–1754*, 479 (fences). Merrens, *Colonial North Carolina*, 140; Hugh T. Lefler and William S. Powell, *Colonial North Carolina: A History* (New York, 1973), 160; Meriwether, *Expansion of South Carolina*, 43, 82, 90; Gregorie, *Sumter County*, 9 (pens).

28. Glassie, *Folk Housing*, 12.

29. See Dobbs to Board of Trade, Aug. 24, 1755, *CRNC*, V, 355, 356; *SCG*, June 9, 1759; [George Milligen-Johnston], "A Short Description of the Province of South Carolina . . . Written in the Year 1763," in B. R. Carroll, comp., *Historical Collections of South Carolina: Embracing Many Rare and Valuable Pamphlets, and Other Documents Relating to the History of That State, from Its First Discovery to Its Independence, in the Year 1776*, 2 vols. (New York, 1836), II, 481; Hooker, ed., *Writings of Woodmason*, 22, 48; *South-Carolina Gazette; and Country Journal* (Charleston), July 15, 1766; Kershaw Account Book; Meriwether, *Expansion of South Carolina*, 44, 56, 62, 83, 94, 106, 139, 165–167; Merrens, *Colonial North Carolina*, 111–116.

30. For earlier techniques, see Meriwether, *Expansion of South Carolina*, 165–166; Merrens, *Colonial North Carolina*, 108; Lefler and Powell, *Colonial North Carolina*, 156–157. For plows, see Hooker, ed., *Writings of Woodmason*, 22; Anson County Wills, 1751–1795, 81, 91, 95, 159, 214, 270, 276, 303.

31. My thinking here owes a great debt to T. H. Breen, "Back to Sweat and Toil: Suggestions for the Study of Agricultural Work in Early America," *Pennsylvania History*, XLIX (1982), 249–253, and "The Culture of Agriculture: The Symbolic World of the Tidewater Planter, 1760–1790," in David D. Hall, John M. Murrin, and Thad W. Tate, eds., *Saints and Revolutionaries: Essays on Early American History* (New York, 1984), 247–284. For Indian planting time, see James Logan to the Six Nations, Sept. 27, 1737, James Logan Papers, IV, 67, American Philosophical Society Library, Philadelphia. For colonists' planting and plowing, see Anson County Wills, 1751–1795, 303.

32. See Affidavit of Charles Griffin, Jan. 4, 1716/17, in PRO, CO 5/1318, 181 (LC trans., 143); *JCIT*, 273, 319.

33. Thomas Brown had 43 head of cattle and 185 horses on his Congaree River plantation. Closer to the Nation's villages, one colonist along the Wateree River possessed 170 head of cattle, 28 horses, and 16 hogs in 1752. Robert and James McCorkle, denizens of the Waxhaws, owned 10 hogs, more than 40 head of cattle, and several horses, while Matthew Toole's plantation held a dozen horses and a herd of cattle more than twice that size at his death in 1757. Meriwether, *Expansion of South Carolina*, 58, 106, 143. For Toole, see Anson County Wills, 1751–1795, 281–282; for sheep, 81, 82, 83, 94.

34. Brown Inventory, Inventories, MM, 1746–1748, 169; John McCord to Glen, Mar. 28, 1749, in SCCJ, Apr. 6, 1749, RSUS, S.C. E.1p, 4/1, 277; Anson County Wills, 1751–1795, 315.

35. Edward Moseley, *A New and Correct Map of the Province of North Carolina, 1733*, copy in William P. Cumming, *The Southeast in Early Maps* (Princeton, N.J., 1958), pls. 51–54; Ramsey, *Carolina Cradle*, 7. For livestock range, see Diary of Bishop Spangenburg, *CRNC*, V, 4–9, 12; Meriwether, *Expansion of South Carolina*, 163. Coastal groups had undergone a similar experience some years before. See Richard L. Haan, "The 'Trade Do's Not Flourish as Formerly': The Ecological Origins of the Yamasee War of 1715," *Ethnohistory*, XXVIII (1981), 341–358. Before long the Cherokees would face a similar situation. See Marvin Thomas Hatley III, "The Dividing Path: The Direction of Cherokee Life in the Eighteenth Century" (master's thesis, University of North Carolina, 1977), chap. 2.

36. Dobbs to Board of Trade, Aug. 24, 1755, *CRNC*, V, 354, 356, 363. See Hatley, "Dividing Path," 32–36, for practices among the Cherokees, and Cowdrey, *This Land, This South*, 14–15, for the Southeast. For Catawba burning habits, see Interview with Joseph White, Aug. 1871, Draper Mss., 11 VV 295.

37. Merrens, *Colonial North Carolina*, 193. In 1762, one Harris allegedly set fire to the woods near the house of a settler named McFerran because McFerran had settled land that Harris claimed. Dobbs to Boone, July 5, 1762, *CRNC*, VI, 782–783.

38. Rowan County, N.C., Minutes of Court of Pleas and Quarter Sessions, II, 86, NCDAH. Traces of these roads are still visible. See Kenneth E. Lewis, *The American Frontier: An Archaeological Study of Settlement Pattern and Process*, Studies in Historical Archaeology (Orlando, Fla., 1984), fig. 6.8, p. 158. Bridenbaugh (*Myths and Realities*, 146) notes that some lower roads were 35 feet wide.

39. S.C. Colonial Plats, VI, 27, 70 (Cut); VI, 84, VII, 65, 184 (Wagon); VI, 218, VII, 224 (Broad); VII, 269, VIII, 451 (Great). For the Wateree road, see Hooker, ed., *Writings of Woodmason*, 34–35; Meriwether, *Expansion of South Carolina*, 106–107, 143 n. 19, 170–172.

40. Anson County Wills, 1751–1795, 303; Wyly to Lyttelton, Aug. 23, 1759, Lyttelton Papers. "Journal of an Officer, who travelled over a part of the West Indies,

and of North America, in the Course of 1764, and 1765," British Library, King's 213, ff 1–69, pp. 51–52 (VCRP-CW, M-276); Meriwether, *Expansion of South Carolina*, 50, 56, 63, 105, 143; *SCG*, June 9, 1759; Bridenbaugh, *Myths and Realities*, 147. For the campground, see John Rossen to Draper, Feb. 11, 1873, Draper Mss., 13 VV 4²–4³; see also Rossen to Draper, Apr. 19, 1873, 7². Rossen recalled that it had served in this capacity for 40 years when he first came to know it in 1819.

41. *JCHA, November 21, 1752–September 6, 1754,* 160; N.C. Land Grants, Anson, file 219, grant 337, book 2, p. 67 (Christian Erwin); Meriwether, *Expansion of South Carolina,* 44, 50–51, 63, 106–107; Ramsey, *Carolina Cradle,* 173; Hooker, ed., *Writings of Woodmason,* 63; *JCHA, March 28, 1749–March 19, 1750,* 399; Thomas Cooper and D. J. McCord, eds., *The Statutes at Large of South Carolina,* 10 vols. (Columbia, S.C., 1836–1841), IX, 213–216 (ferries). Meriwether, *Expansion of South Carolina,* 49, 84; Hooker, ed., *Writings of Woodmason,* 18, 63; S.C. Colonial Plats, V, 125, VI, 415 (bridges).

42. Cooper and McCord, eds., *Statutes at Large,* IX, 214, 253–255. In North Carolina, ferry operators refused Tuscarora Indians passage or overcharged them. See Coun. Jours., Mar. 22, 1735, *CRNC,* IV, 45.

43. S.C. Colonial Plats, V, 415, 430; Cooper and McCord, eds., *Statutes at Large,* VII, 504–506, and see IX, 253–254, for continuing efforts to clear the Wateree. See also Hooker, ed., *Writings of Woodmason,* 63; Wyly to Lyttelton, Apr. 26, 1759, Lyttelton Papers.

44. Meriwether, *Expansion of South Carolina,* 101, 104, 109; S.C. Colonial Plats, IV, 436, VII, 142, 145, 156, 379. Rice fields can be found in "The Congarees in 1759," in Meriwether, *Expansion of South Carolina,* map 3, p. 52. For later millponds in the Nation, see Douglas Summers Brown, "Catawba Land Records, 1795–1829," *SCHM,* LIX (1958), 69, 73, 171, 229.

45. For beavers, see "Fredricksburgh Township: Copied from old Plat in Office of Secretary of State, Columbia, S.C.," in Kirkland and Kennedy, *Historic Camden,* part 1, diagram no. 1, p. 11; N.C. Land Grants, Anson, file 1684, grant 1083, book 15, p. 24 (Matthew Toole). For fishtraps, see Brown, "Catawba Land Records," *SCHM,* LIX (1958), 71, 231, and *The Catawba Indians: The People of the River* (Columbia, S.C., 1966), photograph facing p. 33. For hunting camps, see Meriwether, *Expansion of South Carolina,* 101; "Grants to Earliest Settlers of Camden and Vicinity," in Kirkland and Kennedy, *Historic Camden,* part 1, diagram no. 9, p. 68.

46. [Witherspoon], "Recollections," in Merrens, ed., *Contemporary Views,* 126.

47. See also Ramsey, *Carolina Cradle,* 173.

48. For Catawba Path and its synonyms, see "Fredricksburgh Township," in Kirkland and Kennedy, *Historic Camden,* part 1, diagram no. 1, p. 11; S.C. Colonial Plats, IV, 424, V, 125, 290, 415, 420, VI, 159. For "Road to Upper Settlements," see "Cuttahbaw Nation: men fit for warr 204 In the year 1756 [by John Evans]," Dalhousie Muniments, General John Forbes Papers, document no. 2/104 (copy in SCDAH); S.C. Colonial Plats, VI, 317, 415, VII, 134; *JCHA, November 21, 1752–September 6, 1754,* 522–523; SCCHJ, May 10, 1754, May 21, 1762, RSUS, S.C. A.1b, 15/1, 384–385, 17/2, 114; Cooper and McCord, eds., *Statutes at Large,* IX, 199. This did not change overnight. See S.C. Colonial Plats, VIII, 288, 497, 605. Moreover, some travelers coming from the north still termed the road that swept across North Carolina to the Catawba River "the trading path." See Rowan County, Minutes of Court of Pleas and Quarter Sessions, II, 183, 472, 551; J.F.D. Smyth, *A Tour in the United States of America . . . ,* 2 vols. (London, 1784), I, 197.

49. Hooker, ed., *Writings of Woodmason,* 20, 33–36, 50; Smyth, *Tour,* I, 184, 196–197.

50. Meriwether, *Expansion of South Carolina*, 60, 140, 144, 171, and maps 1, 3, pp. 2, 52; "Sketch Map of the Rivers Santee, Congaree, Wateree, Saludee, etc. with the road to the Cuttauboes [1750]," PRO, CO Library, Carolina 16 (copy in Archer Butler Hulbert, comp., *The Crown Collection of Photographs of American Maps*, 3d Ser., I [Cleveland, Ohio, 1913], pls. 25–26).

51. S.C. Colonial Plats, VI, 22, 91, 311, VIII, 387, 636; Meriwether, *Expansion of South Carolina*, map 3, p. 58; Captain Collet, "A colored map of part of the southern part of North Carolina, from Newberne on the north to Cape Fear on the South, and westward to the Savannah River, in South Carolina," British Museum Photostats of Maps, box III, Newberry Library, Chicago.

52. Meriwether, *Expansion of South Carolina*, 144; for churches, see 47–48, 51, 57, 64–65, 96–97, 143–144. Lewis (*American Frontier*, fig. 3.18, p. 63) shows an increase from no churches in the region to nine between 1750 and 1760. S.C. Colonial Plats, VII, 339, VIII, 346.

53. Ramsey, *Carolina Cradle*, 157, 161; Rowan County, Minutes of Court of Pleas and Quarter Sessions, II, 56, 58, 60, 63, 64, 78, 86, 94, 96, 99, 100, 103, 130, 138.

54. Hooker, ed., *Writings of Woodmason*, 96–97; Meriwether, *Expansion of South Carolina*, 140.

55. Hooker, ed., *Writings of Woodmason*, 12, 13, 14, 30, 56, 98–99.

56. Brown, *Memoirs*, 4; Lewis Cecil Gray, *History of Agriculture in the Southern United States to 1860*, 2 vols. (Washington, D.C., 1933), I, 147, 149; Meriwether, *Expansion of South Carolina*, 12. For wagons, see Wyly to Lyttelton, Aug. 23, 1759, Lyttelton Papers; Catawbas to Glen, Oct. 15, 1754, *DRIA, 1754–1765*, 14; Hooker, ed., *Writings of Woodmason*, 49, 53. Some settlers in other parts of the interior may have made the trip at a different time. See *SCG*, June 9, 1759.

57. William Richardson, "An Account of My Proceedings since I accepted the Indian Mission in October 2d 1758 . . . ," Wilberforce Eames Collection, New York Public Library (copy in YCPL), entry for Nov. 8, 1758. See also Frank G. Speck, "Division of Time," MS in Frank Speck Papers, box 18, IV (Southeast), E (Catawba), 12, APS Library.

58. Brown, *Catawba Indians*, 30, 34. See Cronon, *Changes in the Land*, 65–66; Arthur J. Krim, "Acculturation of the New England Landscape: Native and English Toponymy of Eastern Massachusetts," in Peter Benes and Jane Montague Benes, eds., *New England Prospect: Maps, Place Names, and the Historical Landscape*, Dublin Seminar for New England Folklife, *Annual Proceedings*, V (1980), 69–88.

59. Dobbs to Board of Trade, Aug. 24, 1755, *CRNC*, V, 355; Hooker, ed., *Writings of Woodmason*, 39; and see Meriwether, *Expansion of South Carolina*, 164–165. N.C. Commissioners' Talk to the Catawba King, n.d., in SCCJ, May 22, 1750, RSUS, S.C. E.1p, 4/2; Letter from Bishop Spangenburg, Sept. 12, 1752, *CRNC*, IV, 1313. See also Treaty between N.C. and the Catawbas, Aug. 29, 1754, *CRNC*, V, 142; Waxhaw Inhabitants to Wyly, Apr. 16, 1759, encl. in Wyly to Lyttelton, Apr. 26, 1759, Lyttelton Papers.

60. James H. Merrell, "The Racial Education of the Catawba Indians," *Journal of Southern History*, L (1984), 363–384. The percentage of blacks is from Rachel Klein, "Ordering the Backcountry: The South Carolina Regulation," *WMQ*, 3d Ser., XXXVIII (1981), 665.

61. Hooker, ed., *Writings of Woodmason*, 63, 228.

62. For hunters, see *JCHA, 23 April 1750–31 August 1751*, 52, 253. For warriors, Rowan County, Minutes of Court of Pleas and Quarter Sessions, II, 125; Committee of Public Claims, May 1, 1760, in Walter Clark, ed., *The State Records of North Carolina*, XXII (Goldsboro, N.C., 1907), 819, 820, 822; *SCG*, Nov. 10, 1758. For

diplomats, see Rowan County, Minutes of Court of Pleas and Quarter Sessions, II, 72. For church attendance, see Hooker, ed., *Writings of Woodmason*, 20; Elam Potter, "An Account of Several Nations of Southern Indians: In a Letter from Rev. Elam Potter, to Rev. Dr. Stiles, A.D. 1768," Massachusetts Historical Society, *Collections*, 1st Ser., X (Boston, 1809), 120. For mills, see Treaty between N.C. and the Catawbas, Aug. 29, 1754, *CRNC*, V, 141. For stores, see n. 86 below, as well as Wyly to Lyttelton, Aug. 23, 1759, and Evans to Lyttelton, Sept. 7, 1759, Lyttelton Papers. For camping on farms, see *SCG*, June 9, 1759.

63. Conference with the Catawbas, Salisbury, May 1756, *CRNC*, V, 581 (Hagler). Journal of John Evans, Oct. 1755, *DRIA, 1754–1765*, 86 (Gent's Ford). SCCJ, May 5, 1760, RSUS, S.C. E.1p, 8/3, 119 (Waxhaws). "Journal of the Proceedings of the Southern Congress at Augusta From the Arrival of the Several Governors at Charles Town, South Carolina, the 1.st of October to their Return to the same Place etc. the 21.st November 1763," BPRO-SC, XXX, 84.

64. Glen to Lords Commissioners of Trade and Plantations, Oct. 2, 1750, BPRO-SC, XXIV, 129; Dobbs to Board of Trade, Jan. 19, 1760, *CRNC*, VI, 219. Neither of these discussions stemmed directly from the pressure of settlement; nonetheless, settlers contributed to the malaise that prompted both.

65. Robert Stiell to Glen, Mar. 11, 1753, *DRIA, 1750–1754*, 371; Waxhaw Inhabitants to Wyly, Apr. 16, 1759, encl. in Wyly to Lyttelton, Apr. 26, 1759, Lyttelton Papers. For Catawbas' driving out other planters, see Dobbs to Board of Trade, Sept. 11, 1759, *CRNC*, VI, 58. (Colonists sometimes took similar action against fences they did not like. See Gray, *History of Agriculture*, I, 146.)

66. SCCJ, Feb. 6, 1769, RSUS, S.C. E.1p, 10/3, 9; A meeting with the Catawbas, June 1771, Joseph Brevard Kershaw Papers, South Caroliniana Library, Columbia, S.C.; SCCJ, July 12, 1771, RSUS, S.C. E.1p, 10/5, 142; Misc. Records, OO, 622–623, SCDAH. See also Frow to the Governor, Mar. 15, 1770, in SCCJ, Mar. 27, 1770, RSUS, S.C. E.1p, 10/4, 56.

67. Conference with the Catawbas, Salisbury, May 1756, *CRNC*, V, 581 ("bad and quarrelsome"), Dobbs to Board of Trade, Aug. 30, 1757, V, 784 ("haughty"), Dobbs to Board of Trade, Aug. 24, 1755, V, 364 ("ill neighbours"); Henley to Dobbs, June 27, 1757, encl. in Dobbs to Lyttelton, July 19, 1757, Lyttelton Papers ("mere Wantonness"); Williams, ed., *Adair's History*, 234 ("mischief sake").

68. Jacobs, ed., *Atkin Report*, 47.

69. See "Journal of the Proceedings at Augusta," BPRO-SC, XXX, 84, for the dispute over timber. Peter A. Thomas ("Contrastive Subsistence Strategies and Land Use as Factors for Understanding Indian-White Relations in New England," *Ethnohistory*, XXIII [1976], 1–18) also stresses the competition for resources, though he emphasizes the different use to which those resources would be put by each culture.

70. Coun. Jours., Mar. 18, 1756, *CRNC*, V, 655; for the drought's impact on colonists, see Dobbs to Board of Trade, Aug. 24, 1755, V, 356; "Early History of the Moravians in North Carolina" ("Reprinted from Martin's History of North Carolina, v. I, App."), V, app., 1148.

71. The fullest account of the Indians' actions is in Treaty between N.C. and the Catawbas, Aug. 29, 1754, *CRNC*, V, 142–143 ("Churlish and ungreatfull" quotation on 142). Wyly to Lyttelton, Feb. 9, 1759, Lyttelton Papers ("plundering and beging"). See also Capt. Fairchild to Glen, Feb. 27, 1752, *DRIA, 1750–1754*, 218, Alexander Gordon to Col. LeJau, Mar. 4, 1752, 218–219, Glen to the Catawbas, encl. in Gordon to Toole, Mar. 14, 1752, 221, Catawbas to Glen, Nov. 21, 1752, 361; Dobbs to Board of Trade, Aug. 24, 1755, *CRNC*, V, 363–364.

72. Thomas Brown Inventory, Inventories, MM, 1746–1748, 169; Treaty be-

tween N.C. and the Catawbas, Aug. 29, 1754, *CRNC*, V, 143–144; N.C. Commissioners' Talk to the Catawba King, n.d., in SCCJ, May 22, 1750, RSUS, S.C. E.1p, 4/2; Stiell to Glen, Mar. 11, 1753, *DRIA, 1750–1754*, 371, Thompson to Glen, Mar. 30, 1753, 370; Dobbs to Board of Trade, Aug. 24, 1755, *CRNC*, V, 364.

73. Treaty between N.C. and the Catawbas, Aug. 29, 1754, *CRNC*, V, 143; Waxhaw Inhabitants to Wyly, Apr. 16, 1759, encl. in Wyly to Lyttelton, Apr. 26, 1759, Lyttelton Papers; *JHBV, 1758–1761*, 217; Charles Hill to Toole, Mar. 2, 1751/2, *DRIA, 1750–1754*, 377–378, Gordon to Stiell, May 11, 1752, 378, Catawbas to Glen, Nov. 21, 1752, 361; Treaty between N.C. and the Catawbas, Aug. 29, 1754, *CRNC*, V, 144–144a; SCCJ, Apr. 30, May 3, 1755, RSUS, S.C. E.1p, 7/2, 176, 178; Glen's Speech to King Hagler, n.d., encl. no. 3 in Glen to Lords Commissioners of Trade and Plantations, May 29, 1755, BPRO-SC, XXVI, 209; SCCJ, May 5, Oct. 8, 1760, RSUS, S.C. E.1p, 8/3, 119, 8/5, 37.

74. Lefler and Powell, *Colonial North Carolina*, 95–96. Though the survey of 1772 eventually ensured that Catawbas would be in South Carolina, two decades earlier inhabitants of that colony accused surveyors from North Carolina of running out land 30 miles *south* of the Nation (*JCHA, November 14, 1751–October 7, 1752*, 329). For the continuing boundary dispute and the problems it caused, see also Coun. Jours., May 10, 1753, *CRNC*, V, 33; Wyly to Clerk of Coun., Mar. 2, 1754, in SCCJ, Mar. 13, 1754, RSUS, S.C. E.1p, 6/1, 138–140; Glen to N.C. Coun. Pres., Mar. 14, 1754, *DRIA, 1750–1754*, 479; Dobbs to Board of Trade, Feb. 8, 1755, *CRNC*, V, 331; Adamson to Lyttelton, June 12, 1759, Lyttelton Papers; Dobbs to Gov. Boone, July 5, 1762, *CRNC*, VI, 780–786, Information of John Frohock and others, Dec. 10, 1762, VI, 793–796.

75. Hooker, ed., *Writings of Woodmason*, 45, 52, 61; Information of Frohock and others, Dec. 10, 1762, *CRNC*, VI, 794–795.

76. Treaty between N.C. and the Catawbas, Aug. 29, 1754, *CRNC*, V, 143; Catawbas to Glen, Nov. 21, 1752, *DRIA, 1750–1754*, 361.

77. Toole to Glen, Oct. 28, 1752, *DRIA, 1750–1754*, 358–359; Treaty between N.C. and the Catawbas, Aug. 29, 1754, *CRNC*, V, 143.

78. See SCUHJ, Jan. 18, 1738/9, RSUS, S.C. A.1a, 3/1, 140, SCCJ, Dec. 14–16, 1743, E.1p, 2/2, 437–438, 446–447, 449–451; *SCG*, Dec. 19, 1743; Toole to Glen, Oct. 28, 1752, *DRIA, 1750–1754*, 359; Glen to Catawbas and Glen to Kirkland, in SCCJ, Nov. 15, 1752, RSUS, S.C. E.1p, 6/1, 9–10; Treaty between N.C. and the Catawbas, Aug. 29, 1754, *CRNC*, V, 142, 143; SCCJ, Apr. 30, 1755, RSUS, S.C. E.1p, 7/2, 175; Conference with the Catawbas, Salisbury, May 1756, *CRNC*, V, 581, 583; Catawbas to Lyttelton, June 16, 1757, Lyttelton Papers, Catawbas to Dobbs, Oct. 5, 1757, encl. in Dobbs to Lyttelton, Oct. 24, 1757, Adamson to Lyttelton, June 12, 1759; Williams, ed., *Adair's History*, 234.

79. Hooker, ed., *Writings of Woodmason*, 7; see also 12, 30, 39, 53, 56, 97–99; and Ramsey, *Carolina Cradle*, 181. The importance of liquor is reflected in sales from Kershaw's store (see Kershaw Account Book).

80. Treaty between N.C. and the Catawbas, Aug. 29, 1754, *CRNC*, V, 143; SCCJ, May 5, 1760, RSUS, S.C. E.1p, 8/3, 119.

81. Rowan County, Minutes of Court of Pleas and Quarter Sessions, I, 21 ("Insults"); Coun. Jours., May 21, 1754, *CRNC*, V, 176 ("gross abuses"); Dobbs to Lyttelton, July 19, 1757, Lyttelton Papers ("increasing Insolence"); Catawbas to Lyttelton, June 11, 1759, encl. in Adamson to Lyttelton, June 12, 1759, Lyttelton Papers; SCCJ, May 5, 1760, RSUS, S.C. E.1p, 8/3, 119. See also SCCJ, Oct. 8, 1760, 8/5, 36.

82. Treaty between N.C. and the Catawbas, Aug. 29, 1754, *CRNC*, V, 141–143.

83. Conference with the Catawbas, Salisbury, May 1756, *ibid.*, 582, 583; Atkin to Hagler, Dec. 17, 1757, encl. in Atkin to Lyttelton, Jan. 6, 1758, Lyttelton Papers;

SCCJ, Apr. 24, 1759, RSUS, S.C. E.1p, 8/2, 87, 88; Wyly to Lyttelton, May 5, 1759, and Adamson to Lyttelton, June 12, 1759, Lyttelton Papers. For later log cabins, see Winslow C. Watson, ed., *Men and Times of the Revolution; or, Memoirs of Elkanah Watson, Including Journals of Travels in Europe and America, from 1777 to 1842 ...* (New York, 1856), 257; Journal of Lady Liston, 25–26, in Robert Liston Papers, MS 5697, National Library of Scotland, Edinburgh. I am indebted to Philip Morgan for providing me with this last reference.

84. Catawbas to Glen, Oct. 15, 1754, *DRIA, 1754–1765*, 14.

85. For examples of attacks on colonists near the Nation, see Affidavit of Alexander Rattray, May 24, 1751, *DRIA, 1750–1754*, 61–62, Francis to Glen, May 14, 1751, 63; Col. John Clark to Pres. Rowan, Sept. 25, 1754, and Rowan to Board of Trade, Oct. 22, 1754, *CRNC*, V, 140, 144d; Public Claims, Oct. 14, 1755, in Clark, ed., *State Records of N.C.*, XXII, 815; Catawbas to Glen, Oct. 15, 1754, *DRIA, 1754–1765*, 14. For alliances, see Conference with the Catawbas, Salisbury, May 1756, *CRNC*, V, 581, 583; Bethabara Diary, May 29, 1756, in Adelaide L. Fries *et al.*, eds., *Records of the Moravians in North Carolina*, 11 vols. (Raleigh, N.C., 1922–1969), I, 166; Wyly to Lyttelton, May 5, 1759, Lyttelton Papers; *SCG*, May 12, June 9, 1759; Catawbas to Lyttelton, June 11, 1759, encl. in Adamson to Lyttelton, June 12, 1759, Lyttelton Papers.

86. Catawbas to Lyttelton, June 16, 1757, Lyttelton Papers. SCCJ, May 29, 1758, RSUS, S.C. E.1p, 8/1, 202; Catawbas to Lyttelton, June 11, 1759, encl. in Adamson to Lyttelton, June 12, 1759, Wyly to Lyttelton, Nov. 5, 1759, Lyttelton Papers. Conference with the Catawbas, Salisbury, May 1756, *CRNC*, V, 581; Catawbas to Dobbs, Oct. 5, 1757, encl. in Dobbs to Lyttelton, Oct. 24, 1757, Lyttelton Papers, Adamson to Lyttelton, June 12, 1759; R. J. Hagins to Draper, Mar. 10, 1873, Draper Mss., 12 VV 365–366; Toole to Glen, Oct. 28, 1752, and Kirkland to Glen, Nov. 30, 1752, *DRIA, 1750–1754*, 359; Glen to Kirkland, in SCCJ, Nov. 15, 1752, RSUS, S.C. E.1p, 6/1, 10, SCCJ, Apr. 25, 1754, 6/2, 201–202.

87. Affidavit of John Evans, in SCCJ, Nov. 6, 1755, RSUS, S.C. E.1p, 7/2, 439. For McClanahan, see Meriwether, *Expansion of South Carolina*, 139, 140, 145. For a later example of this practice, see Affidavit of Liddy[?], Jan. 1784, Kershaw Papers.

88. Treaty between N.C. and the Catawbas, Aug. 29, 1754, *CRNC*, V, 142; see also Conference with the Catawbas, Salisbury, May 1756, V, 581; SCCJ, Oct. 8, 1760, RSUS, S.C. E.1p, 8/5, 36. *JCHA, 1749–1750*, 360, 415; Wyly to Lyttelton, May 5, 1759, Lyttelton Papers.

89. Jacobs, ed., *Atkin Report*, 47; Williams, ed., *Adair's History*, 235.

90. Treaty between N.C. and the Catawbas, Aug. 29, 1754, *CRNC*, V, 144a; SCCJ, Mar. 27, 1770, RSUS, S.C. E.1p, 10/4, 56, SCCJ, Aug. 17, 1769, 10/3, 102.

91. Wyly to Lyttelton, Apr. 26, 1759, and encl., Lyttelton Papers.

92. Adamson to Lyttelton, June 12, 1759, *ibid.*

93. Catawbas to Glen, Oct. 15, 1754, *DRIA, 1754–1765*, 14; Evans to Lyttelton, June 20, 1759, Lyttelton Papers.

Chapter 6

1. Catawbas to Lyttelton, Aug. 23, 1759, and Evans to Lyttelton, Sept. 7, 1759, William Henry Lyttelton Papers, William L. Clements Library, Ann Arbor, Mich.; Lt. Col. George Mercer to Gen. John Stanwix, Aug. 12, 1759, in Donald H. Kent *et al.*, eds., *The Papers of Henry Bouquet*, III (Harrisburg, Pa., 1976), 543–545, and Mercer to Bouquet, Aug. 30, 1759, III, 637–638.

2. Adamson to Lyttelton, Aug. 4, 1759, Wyly to Lyttelton and Catawbas to Lyttelton, Aug. 23, 1759, Evans to Lyttelton, Sept. 7, 1759, Lyttelton Papers; Lyttelton to Adamson, Aug. 8, 1759, William Henry Lyttelton, Letters Sent, 1757–1759, 381 (photocopies, SCDAH); *SCG*, Aug. 25, Sept. 15, 1759.

3. John Stuart to Lyttelton, Sept. 2, 1759, and Evans to Lyttelton, Sept. 7, 1759, Lyttelton Papers; Lyttelton to Catawbas and Lyttelton to Wyly, Sept. 11, 1759, Lyttelton, Letters Sent, 407–408, Lyttelton to Catawbas, Oct. 1, 1759, 432–433.

4. Dobbs to Board of Trade, Sept. 11, 1759, *CRNC*, VI, 58.

5. For the smallpox, see *EJCCV*, VI, 140; David B. Trimble, "Christopher Gist and the Indian Service in Virginia," *VMHB*, LXIV (1956), 164–165; Mercer to Stanwix, Aug. 12, 1759, in Kent *et al.*, eds., *Papers of Bouquet*, III, 544. Catawbas noted specifically that the disease came from this source, though one scholar has argued for a southern origin. Catawbas to Lyttelton, [Oct. 1759], Lyttelton Papers; Steven G. Baker, "The Working Draft of: The Historic Catawba Peoples: Exploratory Perspectives in Ethnohistory and Archaeology" (MS, Department of History, University of South Carolina, Columbia, 1975), 106–108.

6. Catawbas to Lyttelton, [Oct. 1759], Atkin to Lyttelton, Jan. 6, 1760, Richard Coytmore to Lyttelton, Nov. 11, 1759, Lyttelton Papers.

7. For the corpses, see Maurice A. Moore, "Reminiscences of York: By a Septuagenarian," *Yorkville Enquirer* (S.C.), Jan. 6, 13, 20, 1870, copy in Draper Manuscripts Collection, Ser. VV, vol. XIV, 139 (microfilm, original in Archives Division, State Historical Society of Wisconsin, Madison). This account is said to be of a smallpox epidemic that struck the Nation sometime during the American Revolution. Such an epidemic seems to be confirmed by other sources (see Interview with Maurice Moore, July 30–Aug. 2, 1871, Draper Mss., 11 VV 332; Philip Edward Pearson, Manuscript History of Fairfield District, S.C., in Logan Mss., Extracts, in Draper Mss., 16 VV 172–173; David Hutchison, "Catawba Indians: By Request," *Palmetto-State Banner* [Columbia, S.C.], Aug. 30, 1849, copy in Draper Mss., Ser. U, vol. X, doc. 100, column 2 [hereafter cited as Hutchison, "Catawba Indians," and column number]). However, there is no contemporary eyewitness account from either Indians or colonists of such an outbreak; the only sources date from the mid-19th century and are therefore suspect. Moreover, Catawba population levels showed no dramatic drop after 1759, again suggesting that this epidemic was the last to strike the Nation. See Baker, "Historic Catawba Peoples," table 1, p. 102; Douglas Summers Brown, *The Catawba Indians: The People of the River* (Columbia, S.C., 1966), 181. For the water cure, see *SCG*, Dec. 15, 1759; William Gerard De Brahm, *Philosophico-Historico-Hydrogeography of South Carolina, Georgia, and East Florida*, in Plowden Charles Jennett Weston, ed., *Documents Connected with the History of South Carolina* (London, 1856), 216–217; J.F.D. Smyth, *A Tour in the United States of America . . .*, 2 vols. (London, 1784), I, 186–187; Coytmore to Lyttelton, Nov. 11, 1759, Lyttelton Papers.

8. Henry R. Schoolcraft, *Historical and Statistical Information Respecting the History, Condition, and Prospects of the Indian Tribes of the United States . . .*, 6 vols. (Philadelphia, 1851–1857), III, 295. This evidence, too, dates from the Revolution, but in all likelihood refers to events in 1759 (see n. 7).

9. Catawbas to Lyttelton, [Oct. 1759], Wyly to Lyttelton, Nov. 5, 1759, Lyttelton Papers; Dobbs to Board of Trade, Jan. 19, 1760, *CRNC*, VI, 219; An Answer to the several Queries sent by the Lords Commissioners for Trade and Plantations, *CRNC*, VI, 616; Richard Richardson to Lyttelton, Feb. 26, 1760, Lyttelton Papers.

10. *SCG*, Dec. 15, 1759; Dobbs to the Secretary (of the SPG), Apr. 15, 1760, *CRNC*, VI, 235. More than a month earlier Dobbs and others put the figure even

lower—fewer than 60 warriors, even as low as 40—but these preliminary estimates carry less weight, for in those months the survivors were still scattered. Richardson to Lyttelton, Feb. 26, 1760, Lyttelton Papers; Dobbs to the Secretary (SPG), Jan. 22, 1760 (P.S. Mar. 12, 1760), *CRNC*, VI, 224. The total population figure is based on a 1:4 or 1:5 ratio of warriors to population (see chap. 3, n. 8). My estimate here matches Baker, who put the total loss at three-fourths ("Historic Catawba Peoples," 107).

11. Catawbas to the Iroquois, Nov. 11, 1752, George Clinton Papers, Clements Library. See also Catawba King to Glen, Mar. 11, 1753, *DRIA, May 21, 1750–August 7, 1754*, 371.

12. Dobbs to Board of Trade, Jan. 19, 1760, *CRNC*, VI, 219; Richardson to Lyttelton, Feb. 26, 1760, Lyttelton Papers. *SCG*, May 3, 1760; SCCJ, May 5–6, 1760, RSUS, S.C. E.1p, 8/3, 119, 121; Dobbs to the Secretary (SPG), Mar. 30, 1762, *CRNC*, VI, 710, Dobbs to Gov. Thomas Boone, July 5, 1762, VI, 787; "A Map of the Catawba Indians Surveyed agreeable to a Treaty Entered into with Them At Augusta in Georgia on the tenth Day of November 1763. . . . Executed, Certified and Signed by me the 22.nd Day of February Anno Domini 1764, Saml Wyli D[eputy] S[urveyo]r," Miscellaneous Records, H, 460, SCDAH; "Plan of the boundary line between the Provinces of South and North Carolina from the Corner Tree on Salisbury Road to the Cherokee Line," John McCrady Plats, no. 2120, SCDAH. The Wyly 1764 map suggests another settlement upstream between King Creek and Sugar Creek, in the area later known as King's Bottoms. For conflicting reports of the Catawbas' location during these years—some farther upstream, some on both sides of the river—see Answers to Queries, 1761, *CRNC*, VI, 616; Captain Collet, "A colored map of part of the southern part of North Carolina, from Newberne on the north to Cape Fear on the South, and Westward to the Savannah River, in South Carolina," British Museum Photostats of Maps, box III, Newberry Library, Chicago; Hutchison, "Catawba Indians," col. 1; Baker, "Historic Catawba Peoples," fig. 7, p. 135.

13. Baker, "Historic Catawba Peoples," 116, 132.

14. G. Hubert Matthews and Red Thunder Cloud, "Catawba Texts," *International Journal of American Linguistics*, XXXIII (1967), 19. For a similar reaction, this time allegedly to the first smallpox epidemic, see Bob Ward, *The Children of King Hagler* (Rock Hill, S.C., 1940), 1.

15. Dobbs to the Secretary (SPG), Jan. 22, 1760 (P.S. Mar. 12, 1760), *CRNC*, VI, 224; for similar sentiments see Dobbs to Boone, July 5, 1762, VI, 787.

16. John Stuart to Board of Trade, Dec. 2, 1766, *ibid.*, VII, 280. That the soil downstream was poorer is suggested by Hutchison, "Catawba Indians," col. 1.

17. Report of the Commissioners appointed to treat with the Catawba Indians, Apr. 3, 1840, in A[rchibald S.] Whyte, "Account of Catawba Indians, Prepared for the Indian Land Chronicle, Nov. 1858," Draper Mss., 10 U 96[6] ("harmless and friendly"); Waxhaw Inhabitants to Samuel Wyly, Apr. 16, 1759, encl. in Wyly to Lyttelton, Apr. 26, 1759, Lyttelton Papers ("proud and deveilish"); Smyth, *Tour*, I, 192 ("inoffensive"); Toole to Glen, Oct. 28, 1754, *DRIA, 1750–1754*, 358 ("unsufferable"); D. G. Stinson to Draper, July 4, 1873, Draper Mss., 9 VV 278–279 ("may beg, but . . . will not steal").

18. Pearson, History of Fairfield, Extracts, Draper Mss., 16 VV 172.

19. *SCG*, Aug. 9, 1760; SCCJ, May 2, 5, 6, 1760, RSUS, S.C. E.1p, 8/3, 117–121. For the other visits, see Aug. 7, 1760, 8/5, 14–15, Oct. 8, 1760, 8/5, 35–37, Mar. 2, 4, 1761, 8/5, 94–95, 97–100, Sept. 12, 1761, 8/5, 155–158, Nov. 17, 1761, 8/5, 177–178, May 15, 1762, 8/6, 496–498; SCCHJ, May 18, 19, 1762, RSUS, S.C. A.1b, 17/2, 108–109, SCCJ, July 3, 1762, E.1p, 8/6, 527–528.

20. SCCJ, May 5, 1760, RSUS, S.C. E.1p, 8/3, 118; see also Aug. 7, 1760, 8/5, 14–15, Oct. 8, 1760, 8/5, 36; *SCG*, Feb. 14, 1761; SCCJ, Mar. 2, 1761, RSUS, S.C. E.1p, 8/5, 95. For Catawba participation in this conflict, see *SCG*, Jan. 12, May 10, 31, June 14, 21, July 5, 1760, Feb. 14, May 30, June 20, 1761; SCCJ, May 5–6, Aug. 7, 1760, Sept. 12, 1761, RSUS, S.C. E.1p, 8/3, 118–121, 8/5, 14–15, 156; Bull to Lords Commissioners of Trade and Plantations, May 8, 1760, July 17, 1761, BPRO-SC, XXVIII, 335, XXIX, 126.

21. See *SCG*, Aug. 9, 1760; Bull to the Commons House of Assembly, in SCCHJ, Oct. 14, 1760, RSUS, S.C. A.1b, 16/3, 14–15. The Indians gave up the larger claim because it was based on a grant made by Gov. Glen years before that had never been accepted by North Carolina or approved by the crown. Indeed, Glen's action had since been repudiated by his successor, Lyttelton. By 1760 there was little, if any, hope that an Indian population so small could lay claim to an area so large, especially since much of the land contested already had been invaded by colonists clutching deeds. Catawbas, in agreeing to surrender these lands, were giving up what they no longer had and could never get back in exchange for the promise of more effective protection of what was left. They had made the best of a bad situation. For the earlier land dealings, see Matthew Rowan to Board of Trade, June 3, 1754, *CRNC*, V, 124, Dobbs to Board of Trade, Aug. 24, 1755, V, 358–360; SCCJ, Aug. 24, 1756, RSUS, S.C. E.1p, 7/3, 336; Dobbs to Lyttelton, Nov. 22, 1756, Lyttelton Papers; Lyttelton to Lords of Trade, Nov. 30, 1757, Lyttelton, Letters Sent, 51–52.

22. For the earlier negotiations on the fort, see chap. 4, n. 99. For an Indian's memories of it, see Spratt to Draper, Jan. 12, 1871, Draper Mss., 15 VV 100–101. For requests, see *SCG*, May 3, 1760; SCCJ, Aug. 7, Oct. 8, 1760, RSUS, S.C. E.1p, 8/5, 15, 37 (quotation). For the colony's action, see SCCJ, Oct. 15, 1760, Sept. 12, 1761, 8/5, 39, 157–159; *SCG*, Oct. 18, 1760; Public Treasurer of South Carolina, General Tax Receipts and Payments, 1761–1769 (1771), 29, SCDAH; Wyly, "Map of the Catawba Indians . . . 1764"; "Plat of Land of Catawba Indians, the Indian Land; Surveyed Feb. 22, 1764; pursuant to Treaty of Augusta. a fragment," map box 7, folder 4, SCDAH.

23. SCCJ, Sept. 12, 1761, Sept. 14, 1768, RSUS, S.C. E.1p, 8/5, 158–159, 10/1, 248. A 1772 map ("Plan of the boundary line . . . ," McCrady Plats 2120) depicts the fort intact, but whether occupied is unclear. It receives no further mention in the documents.

24. Catawbas to Lyttelton, June 16, 1757, Lyttelton Papers; SCCJ, May 15, July 23, 1762, RSUS, S.C. E.1p, 8/6, 497–498, 534–535; "Journal of the Proceedings of the Southern Congress at Augusta From the Arrival of the Several Governors at Charles Town, South Carolina, the 1.st October to their Return to the same Place etc. the 21.st November 1763," BPRO-SC, XXX, 84.

25. Bull to Lords Commissioners of Trade and Plantations, Dec. 10, 1764, BPRO-SC, XXX, 225–227; Bull to Thomas Gage, Apr. 9, 1765, Thomas Gage Papers, American Series, 1755–1775, XXXIII, Clements Library; Wyly, "Map of the Catawba Indians . . . 1764"; "Plat of Land of Catawba Indians, . . . a fragment."

26. SCCJ, May 15, 1762, RSUS, S.C. E.1p, 8/6, 497.

27. *Ibid.*, Feb. 12, 1765, 9/3, 443. That the Catawbas held the paper is clear from General Assembly, Petitions, 1792, no. 26, SCDAH.

28. John Wyly to Joseph Kershaw, Jan. 28[?], 1773, and enclosure ("A Copie of The Talk Deliver[e]d by Mr. Drayton to the Catawba Indians th8 January 1773. as nigh as I Can Recolect"), Joseph Brevard Kershaw Papers, South Caroliniana Library, Columbia; SCCJ, Dec. 1, 1772, RSUS, S.C. E.1p, 10/6, 247–248 (quotation on 248).

29. Wyly to Kershaw, Jan. 28[?], 1773, and encl., Kershaw Papers.

30. SCCJ, Dec. 1, 1772, RSUS, S.C. E.1p, 10/6, 247, Jan. 20, 1773, 11/1, 29. See also Stuart to the Catawbas, Feb. 18, 1773, Kershaw Papers. The Catawbas later reminded the South Carolina Council that rumors they had sold their land to Drayton were false, "for they would not part with their Land to any people whatsoever[,] that as long as any Indians remained the Land was to belong to them but if they were dead the Land should then belong to the King" (SCCJ, Oct. 30, 1773, RSUS, S.C. E.1p, 11/2, 2).

31. SCCJ, Sept. 12, 1761, RSUS, S.C. E.1p, 8/5, 156–157.

32. A brief meeting with Hagler, his grandson, and two other Catawbas in November had passed without incident and without the sort of rhetoric that was becoming common. See *ibid.*, Nov. 17, 1761, 177–178.

33. *Ibid.*, May 15, 1762, 8/6, 496, SCCHJ, May 18, 19, 1762, A.1b, 17/2, 108, SCCJ, July 3, 1762, E.1p, 8/6, 528.

34. Only occasional murmurs of dissatisfaction were heard earlier, and these arose, not because Catawbas came, but because so many more came than were expected. Even then, the tone was more polite and apologetic than hostile. In 1759 Governor Lyttelton told Catawbas that "as there are many of you, you must not expect so rich presents as you would otherwise have." SCCJ, Apr. 24, 1759, *ibid.*, 8/2, 88; see also Aug. 24, 1756, 7/3, 337, Apr. 30, 1759, 8/2, 94.

35. Glen to Lords Commissioners of Trade and Plantations, Sept. 22, 1744, BPRO-SC, XXI, 402; Lyttelton to John Pownall, Aug. 7, 1758, Lyttelton, Letters Sent, 168; "A Rough Sketch of a Plan for the management of Indians . . . ," encl. in Boone to the Secretary of State, Southern Department, Nov. 24, 1763, BPRO-SC, XXIX, 397.

36. SCCJ, Sept. 12, 1761, RSUS, S.C. E.1p, 8/5, 158.

37. For Hagler's death, see William Richardson and others to Col. Richardson, Aug. 31, 1763, *ibid.*, Sept. 5, 1763, 9/1, 90. For an analysis of Hagler's career, see James H. Merrell, "'Minding the Business of the Nation': Hagler as Catawba Leader," *Ethnohistory*, XXXIII (1986), 55–70.

38. "Journal of the Proceedings at Augusta," BPRO-SC, XXX, 63, 70–85, 90–105. Stuart to Amherst, Dec. 3, 1763, Jeffrey Amherst Papers, 1759–1764, VII, Clements Library.

39. SCCJ, Nov. 3, 1766, RSUS, S.C. E.1p, 9/3, 859–860; *SCG*, Nov. 10, 1766.

40. SCCJ, May 31, 1768, RSUS, S.C. E.1p, 10/1, 153.

41. *Ibid.*, Aug. 20, 1767, 9/4, 219, May 31, 1768, 10/1, 155, Aug. 17, 1769, 10/3, 103, Mar. 27, 1770, 10/4, 57; see also July 17, 1771, 10/5, 151, Jan. 25, 1772, 10/6, 14.

42. *Ibid.*, July 3, 1762, 8/6, 528, May 31, 1768, 10/1, 155, Aug. 17, 1769, 10/3, 102–103, Mar. 20, 1771, 10/5, 71 (emphasis added); see also Jan. 25, 1772, 10/6, 14.

43. *Ibid.*, May 31, 1768, 10/1, 154, Mar. 20, 1771, 10/5, 71.

44. Bull to Lords Commissioners of Trade and Plantations, Oct. 5, 1739, BPRO-SC, XX, 180, Charles Pinckney to Lords Commissioners of Trade and Plantations, June 29, 1754, XXVI, 78; SCCJ, Dec. 17, 25, 1765, Feb. 27, Mar. 1, 1766, RSUS, S.C. E.1p, 9/3, 680–681, 682–683, 727–728, 730–732, SCCHJ, Jan. 14, 15, Feb. 28, Mar. 15, Apr. 9, 1766, A.1b, 18/1, 34–36, 76, 77, 88–89, 92 (quotation on 34); Bull to Lords Commissioners of Trade and Plantations, Jan. 25, 1766, BPRO-SC, XXXI, 20–21; Bull to Kershaw, Mar. 1, 1766, Kershaw Papers; Report of the Council Committee on the Boundary Between North and South Carolina, encl. in Gov. Charles G. Montagu to the Earl of Hillsborough, Apr. 19, 1769, BPRO-SC, XXXII, 145–146.

45. SCCHJ, Mar. 18, 1774, RSUS, S.C. A.1b, 19/3, 140–141; for an example of their refusal, see SCCHJ, Feb. 14, 1775, 19/3, 201.

46. Speech to New River and the Headmen and Warriors of the Catawba Nation [c. 1781, misdated 1771], Kershaw Papers.

47. SCCJ, Aug. 17, 1769, RSUS, S.C. E.1p, 10/3, 102 (Georgia). Gov. Joseph Martin to the Earl of Hillsborough, Dec. 12, 1771, *CRNC*, IX, 69; Committee of Public Claims, Sept. 13, 1775, in Walter Clark, ed., *The State Records of North Carolina*, XXII (Goldsboro, N.C., 1907), 866 (North Carolina). Purdie and Dixon's *Virginia Gazette* (Williamsburg), Apr. 28, 1768; Rind's *Virginia Gazette* (Williamsburg), Jan. 5, Oct. 26, 1769; *EJCCV*, VI, 311; Wilmer L. Hall, ed., *Journals of the Council of the State of Virginia*, III (Richmond, Va., 1952), 143–144 (Virginia). There may have been a later formal visit to Richmond. See *North-Carolina Journal* (Halifax), Aug. 22, 1792. I am grateful to Wesley White for sending me this reference.

48. Benjamin Lincoln, Sec. of War, to President of Congress, Nov. 1, 1782, Papers of the Continental Congress, 1774–1789, National Archives Microfilm Publications (Washington, D.C., 1958), microfilm 247, roll 163, item 149, vol. II, 121; Report of Mr. Duane, Mr. Ramsay, and Mr. Wharton, Nov. 2, 1782, *ibid.*, roll 34, item 27, 199. For other possible approaches to the federal government or federal officials, see George Washington to Sec. of War, July 18, 1796, in John C. Fitzpatrick, ed., *The Writings of George Washington, from the Original Manuscript Sources, 1745–1799*, 39 vols. (Washington, D.C., 1931–1944), XXXV, 146–147; Benjamin Smith Barton, *New Views of the Origins of the Tribes and Nations of America* (Philadelphia, 1798), appendix, 22; John Stale to Governor, Apr. 12, 1798, *CVSP*, VIII, 476, James McHenry to John Dawson, encl. in Dawson to Governor, July 19, 1798, VIII, 503; [Anne Ritson], *A Poetical Picture of America, Being Observations Made, during a Residence of Several Years, at Alexandria, and Norfolk, in Virginia* . . . (London, 1809), 59–63. I am indebted to Philip Morgan for this last reference.

49. Boone to Lords Commissioners of Trade and Plantations, Oct. 9, 1762, BPRO-SC, XXIX, 245–246, quotation on 246; Richard J. Hooker, ed., *The Carolina Backcountry on the Eve of the Revolution: The Journal and Other Writings of Charles Woodmason, Anglican Itinerant* (Chapel Hill, N.C., 1953), 20.

50. For encroachments, see Catawbas to Lt. Gov. Bull, Jan. 29, 1765, in SCCJ, Feb. 12, 1765, RSUS, S.C. E.1p, 9/3, 443, Nov. 19, 1772, 10/6, 226. For hunting disputes, see Feb. 6, 1769, 10/3, 9, Catawbas to Governor, Mar. 15, 1770, in SCCJ, Mar. 27, 1770, 10/4, 56; A meeting with the Catawbas, June 1771, Kershaw Papers; SCCJ, July 12, 1771, RSUS, S.C. E.1p, 10/5, 142; Proclamation, July 12, 1771, Misc. Recs., OO, 622–623; SCCJ, Oct. 30, 1773, RSUS, S.C. E.1p, 11/2, 2–3 (reference to passes).

51. Thomas Dryden Spratt, "Recollections of His Family, July 1875," 47–51, typescript, South Caroliniana Library; Spratt, "Recollections of the Spratt Family by Thomas D. Spratt of Fort Mill, S.C., July 1876," typescript, copied from a manuscript in the possession of Miss Zoe White of Fort Mill, S.C., by Douglas Summers Brown, Rock Hill (1952), 13, David Hutchison Papers, box 1, folder 2, Winthrop College Archives, Rock Hill, S.C. (quotation "almost forced"); Spratt to Draper, Jan. 12, 1871, Draper Mss., 15 VV 101; W. B. Ardrey, "The Catawba Indians," *American Antiquarian*, XVI (1894), 266; Moore, "Reminiscences," in Draper Mss., 14 VV 140–141. In 1787 Spratt still had 4,700 acres left (Spratt, "Recollections, 1876," 13).

52. Hutchison, "Catawba Indians," col. 2. See also SCCJ, Nov. 19, 1772, RSUS, S.C. E.1p, 10/6, 226.

53. Hutchison, "Catawba Indians," col. 2; Ardrey, "Catawba Indians," *Am. Antiquarian*, XVI (1894), 267; Moore, "Reminiscences," Draper Mss., 14 VV 141;

Spratt, "Recollections, 1875," 53, "Recollections, 1876," 9, 13; Travel Diary of Marshal and Benzien from Salem to South Carolina, 1790, in Adelaide L. Fries *et al.*, eds., *Records of the Moravians in North Carolina*, 11 vols. (Raleigh, N.C., 1922–1969), V, 1997; Hutchison, "Catawba Indians," col. 2; A. Whyte, Commissioners' Report on the Catawba Indians, Oct. 2, 1849, copy in Whyte, "Catawba Indians," Draper Mss., 10 U 102[6–7]. For the details of this arrangement, see below, chap. 7.

54. Gen. Ass., Petitions, 1791, no. 44 (there were 350 families on the Indian land in 1795; see *ibid.*, 1795, no. 86); Senate Journals, Dec. 8, 1801, RSUS, S.C. A.1a, 21/2, 122.

55. Catawba Petition to the Legislature of South Carolina, Feb. 13, 1784, Kershaw Papers; Gen. Ass., Petitions, 1787, no. 1, 1792, no. 26.

56. For moccasins, see Edwin J. Scott, *Random Recollections of a Long Life, 1806 to 1876* (Columbia, S.C., 1884), 13. For baskets and mats, see Smyth, *Tour*, I, 193.

57. Smyth, *Tour*, I, 193, 194; [Lucius Verus Bierce], "The Piedmont Frontier, 1822–1823," in Thomas D. Clark, ed., *South Carolina: The Grand Tour, 1780–1865*, Tricentennial Edition, no. 5 (Columbia, S.C., 1973), 64; Scott, *Random Recollections*, 13; William Gilmore Simms, "Caloya; or, The Loves of the Driver," in *The Wigwam and the Cabin* (New York, 1856), 361–362.

58. Simms, "Caloya," in *Wigwam*, 361–364; Charles Fraser, *Reminiscences of Charleston, Lately Published in the Charleston Courier, and Now Revised and Enlarged by the Author* (Charleston, S.C., 1854), 16–17 (I am indebted to J. Ashley Sharpe for this reference); Scott, *Random Recollections*, 13; Anne King Gregorie, *Notes on Sewee Indians and Indian Remains of Christ Church Parish, Charleston County, South Carolina*, Contributions from the Charleston Museum, V (Charleston, S.C., 1925), 21.

For a general discussion of the pottery trade, see Baker, "Historic Catawba Peoples," 188–194, and "Colono-Indian Pottery from Cambridge, South Carolina, with Comments on the Historic Catawba Pottery Trade," Institute of Archeology and Anthropology, University of South Carolina, *Notebook*, IV (1972), 3–30. Since Baker wrote, other scholars have deemphasized the Indians' role in the manufacturing of this colono-Indian ware, arguing that most of it was probably made by Afro-Americans. See Leland Ferguson, "Looking for the 'Afro-' in Colono-Indian Pottery," in Stanley South, ed., *The Conference on Historic Site Archaeology Papers, 1977* (Columbia, S.C., 1978), 68–86; William B. Lees and Kathryn M. Kimery-Lees, "The Function of Colono-Indian Ceramics: Insights from Limerick Plantation, South Carolina," *Historical Archaeology*, XIII (1979), 1–13. This is not the place to enter the debate, and it need only be said that Catawbas were clearly heavily involved in production and exchange of these items, however much of this ware generally may turn out to have been made by non-Indian hands. I am grateful to Philip Morgan for introducing me to the Afro-American side of the subject.

59. Smyth, *Tour*, I, 194.

60. Catawba Petition to the Legislature, Feb. 13, 1784, Kershaw Papers; John Lawson, *A New Voyage to Carolina*, ed. Hugh Talmage Lefler (Chapel Hill, N.C., 1967), 210; SCCJ, Oct. 8, 1760, RSUS, S.C. E.1p, 8/5, 36, Nov. 19, 1772, 10/6, 226.

61. Ardrey, "Catawba Indians," *Am. Antiquarian*, XVI (1894), 268 (Spratt). Catawbas to the Governor, Mar. 15, 1770, in SCCJ, Mar. 27, 1770, RSUS, S.C. E.1p, 10/4, 57; Affidavit of Liddy[?], Jan. 1784, Kershaw Papers (Drinnon). Woodmason to John Chesnut, June 30, 1769, in Hooker, ed., *Writings of Woodmason*, 144; Account Book of Joseph Kershaw, 1774–1775, S.C. Mss. B (microfilm, State Historical Society of Wisconsin, Madison), 24, 44, 109, 130, 190, 225, and May 1775 (Kershaw). Catawba Petition to the Legislature, Feb. 13, 1784, Kershaw Papers (Patton). For Patton, see also Antonio Pace, trans. and ed., *Luigi Castiglioni's Viaggio: Travels in the United States of North America, 1785–87* (Syracuse, N.Y., 1983), 150–151.

62. Catawbas to the Governor, Mar. 15, 1770, in SCCJ, Mar. 27, 1770, RSUS, S.C. E.1p, 10/4, 57; Meeting with Catawbas, June 1771, Kershaw Papers. It is unclear when Catawbas gave this document to Kershaw. In 1792 they note only that it was in his possession. See Gen. Ass., Petitions, 1792, no. 26.

63. Catawba Petition to the Legislature, Feb. 13, 1784, Kershaw Papers; Lark Emerson Adams and Rosa Stoney Lumpkin, eds., *Journals of the House of Representatives, 1785–1786*, The State Records of South Carolina (Columbia, S.C., 1979), 549, 589, 591, 594 (quotation on 549); Spratt, "Recollections, 1875," 56–59.

64. J. F. White to Draper, n.d., Draper Mss., 15 VV 96; T. D. Spratt to Draper, Jan. 12, 1871, *ibid.*, 99–102 (quotation on 100); Comptroller General, Accounts Audited of Claims Growing out of the Revolution in South Carolina, roll 64, no. 3368-A, SCDAH. The tie here was also economic, since the Spratts were leaseholders of Sally New River. See Surveyors' Plat Book and Indian Commissioners' Rent Book, Part II, 171, and Part III, 3, copies in SCDAH and YCPL.

65. White to Draper, Dec. 14, 1870, Draper Mss., 15 VV 92 (grog shop). Spratt, "Recollections, 1876," 10; and Spratt to Draper, Jan. 12, 1871, Draper Mss., 15 VV 100 (New River). Spratt to Draper, Sept. 9, 1874, Draper Mss., 6 VV 291–292 (Canty). White to Draper, n.d., Draper Mss., 15 VV 96, Spratt to Draper, Jan. 12, 1871, 15 VV 101–102, Spratt to Draper, May 7, 1873, 15 VV 108; and Spratt, "Recollections, 1875," 67–69 (tales). Ezekiel Fewell to Draper, Mar. 30, 1875, and n.d., Draper Mss., 15 VV 239, 318, Stinson to Draper, July 27, Aug. 6, 1874, 5 VV 40, 7–8.

66. Frank W. Porter III, ed., *Strategies for Survival: American Indians in the Eastern United States*, Contributions in Ethnic Studies, no. 15 (Westport, Conn., 1986).

67. Fewell to Draper, Mar. 30, 1875, Draper Mss., 15 VV 239, White to Draper, Dec. 15, 1870, 15 VV 91; Hutchison, "Catawba Indians," col. 3.

68. Smyth, *Tour*, I, 192, 194; Winslow C. Watson, ed., *Men and Times of the Revolution; or, Memoirs of Elkanah Watson, Including Journals of Travels in Europe and America, from 1771 to 1842* . . . (New York, 1856), 258; Report of Commissioners, Apr. 3, 1840, in Whyte, "Catawba Indians," Draper Mss., 10 U 96^{5–6}.

69. For other Indians in the American Revolution, see James H. O'Donnell III, *Southern Indians in the American Revolution* (Knoxville, Tenn., 1973); Barbara Graymont, *The Iroquois in the American Revolution* (Syracuse, N.Y., 1972).

70. Stuart to Gage, Sept. 15, 1775, Papers of the Continental Cong., M-247, reel 65, item 51, vol. I, 56; Brown, *Catawba Indians*, 260–261. Thomas Spratt was also a patriot. See Spratt, "Recollections, 1876," 8–9; Notes from D. G. Stinson, Aug. 8–18, 1871, Draper Mss., 9 VV 26–27. The importance of a "man of influence" in determining allegiance in each upcountry locality has been stressed in Rachel N. Klein, "Frontier Planters and the American Revolution: The South Carolina Backcountry, 1775–1782," in Ronald Hoffman *et al.*, eds., *An Uncivil War: The Southern Backcountry during the American Revolution* (Charlottesville, Va., 1985), 44–47.

71. "Journal of the Council of Safety, for the Province of South-Carolina, 1775," South-Carolina Historical Society, *Collections*, II (1858), 31–34, 63. See also William Edwin Hemphill, ed., *Extracts from the Journals of the Provincial Congresses of South Carolina, 1775–1776* (Columbia, S.C., 1960), 56.

72. For a summary of Catawba actions, see Brown, *Catawba Indians*, 260–271.

73. Stuart to Gage, Sept. 15, 1775, Papers of the Continental Cong., M-247, reel 65, item 51, vol. I, 56. For references to an Indian Company of Rovers that may have included Catawbas, see "Journal of the Second Council of Safety, Appointed by the Provisional Congress, November, 1775," S.C. Hist. Soc., *Colls.*, III (1859), 87, 89, 90, 102, 103, 107; for specific references to Catawbas, see 253, 263–264. For the Cherokee campaign, see Transcription of the Laurens Mss. in the South

Carolina Historical Society, Draper Mss., 3 VV 155–158, "Journal of an Expedition, in 1776, Against the Cherokees, Under the Command of Captain Peter Clinton," 3 VV 167, Mss. in Papers of W. G. Sims [*sic*], 3 VV 183–184; Mary Elinor Lazenby, comp., *Catawba Frontier, 1775–1781: Memories of Pensioners* (Washington, D.C., 1950), 81.

74. Pay Bill, Catawba Indian Company, Accounts Audited of Claims Growing out of the Revolution, roll 77, no. 3931-A (a copy of this document is in Brown, *Catawba Indians*, 268–269). Sebastian Sumter Interview, July 12, 1871, Draper Mss., 11 VV 504, Samuel McCalla to Draper, Jan. 23, 1873, 14 VV 453 (Rocky Mount). Hutchison, "Catawba Indians," col. 1 (Ninety Six, Hanging Rock, Haw River, and Guilford). Spratt to Draper, May 7, 1873, Draper Mss., 15 VV 108 (Stono). U.S. Senate, 54th Congress, 2d session (1897), doc. 144, "The Catawba Tribe of Indians," 10; William Morrison Day Book, Augusta, Georgia, Mar. 24, 1778, Sol Feinstone Collection of the American Revolution (microfilm, M-1190.2, Colonial Williamsburg Archives, Williamsburg, Va.) (Georgia). I am indebted to Philip Morgan for this last reference. Deposition of William Vaughan, Sept. 24, 1832, copy in Draper Mss., 6 VV 66–67 (Cornwallis).

75. Brown, *Catawba Indians*, 266. "From the Records in the Pension Office," notes taken by Lyman C. Draper, Draper Mss., 11 VV 352, 373, 379, 385, 386, 399, 419, 443, 457, 468. "Fragment of a Manuscript reputedly in Major Joseph McJunkin's own handwriting, in possession of the Saye family, Rodman, S.C.," 6–7 (photostatic copy, YCPL), quoted in Brown, *Catawba Indians*, 266–267 (also in Draper Mss., 23 VV 208). British estimates of the number of men were higher. See Rawdon to Cornwallis, July 7, 1780, Cornwallis Papers, PRO, 30/11/2 (VCRP-CW, M-776), 252.

76. Col. Jas. Williams to Mrs. Williams, July 4, 1780, in *Gibbes Documentary History, 1776–1782*, 1367, copy in Draper Mss., 4 VV 161 ("Camp Catawba Old Nation"). For Cornwallis, see Intelligence Report [Sept. 1780], Cornwallis Papers, PRO 30/11/3 (VCRP-CW, M-775), 26 and verso, Memorandum, Sept. 12, 1780, 98 and verso, Arch[ibal]d McArthur to Cornwallis, Oct. 2, 7, 1780, 174, 199–200; Gen. Jethro Sumner to Maj. Gen. Gates, Sept. 24, 1780, in Walter Clark, ed., *The State Records of North Carolina*, XIV(Winston, N.C., 1896), 646–647.

77. McJunkin MS, quoted in Brown, *Catawba Indians*, 266; Samuel C. Williams, ed., "General Richard Winn's Notes—1780," *SCHGM*, XLIV (1943), 7. For Catawbas' supplying corn, see Hutchison, "Catawba Indians," col. 2.

78. For (Hastings-)Rawdon, see Rawdon to Cornwallis, June 11, 1780, Cornwallis Papers, PRO 30/11/2 (VCRP-CW, M-776), 123–124; White Interview, Aug. 18, 1871, Draper Mss., 11 VV 291. Williams, ed., "Winn's Notes," *SCHGM*, XLIV (1943), 7; Diary of the Congregation in Salem, 1781, in Fries *et al.*, eds., *Records of the Moravians*, IV, 1695–1696. Rumors place the Catawbas among the Pamunkeys during this sojourn, but there is no clear evidence to support this theory. See Brown, *Catawba Indians*, 270. For the Catawbas on their way homeward, see Joseph A. Waddell, ed., "Diary of Capt. John Davis, of the Pennsylvania Line," *VMHB*, I (1893–1894), 14.

79. William Feltman, "Diary of the Pennsylvania Line, May 26, 1781–April 25, 1782," *Pennsylvania Archives*, 2d Ser., XI (Harrisburg, Pa., 1896), 741, 742; Hutchison, "Catawba Indians," col. 2.

80. Charles M. Hudson, *The Catawba Nation*, University of Georgia Monographs, no. 18 (Athens, Ga., 1970), 51. The most recent study of the Carolina campaigns does not mention Catawbas. See John S. Pancake, *This Destructive War: The British Campaign in the Carolinas, 1780–1782* (University, Ala., 1985). A more general analysis of South Carolina during the Revolutionary era notes only the slave-

catching episodes of 1765 and 1787. See Jerome C. Nadelhaft, *The Disorders of War: The Revolution in South Carolina* (Orono, Maine, 1981), 5, 132.

81. A. S. Salley, Jr., ed., *Journal of the House of Representatives of South Carolina, January 8, 1782–February 26, 1782* (Columbia, S.C., 1916), 59–60, 65, 102. See also A. S. Salley, Jr., ed., *Journal of the Senate of South Carolina, January 8, 1782–February 26, 1782* (Columbia, S.C., 1941), 44, 50.

82. Theodora J. Thompson and Rosa S. Lumpkin, eds., *Journals of the House of Representatives, 1783–1784*, The State Records of South Carolina (Columbia, S.C., 1977), 472, 489, 491–492, 499; Sen. Jour., Feb. 24–25, 1784, RSUS, S.C. A.1a, 6/3, 141–142, 149–150; Adams and Lumpkin, eds., *JHR, 1785–1786*, 97, 133.

83. "During all this time," one settler later recalled of the decades after the Revolution, "the Indians were scarcely noticed by the Legislature" (Hutchison, "Catawba Indians," col. 3).

84. Speech to New River and the Catawba Nation, Kershaw Papers. Gen. Ass., Petitions, 1786, no. 32; see also 1792, no. 26.

85. Accounts Audited, roll 64, no. 3368-A; Sen. Jour., Dec. 6, 11, 12, 21, 1822, RSUS, S.C. A.1a, 26/1, 100, 138, 160, 161, 258, Dec. 8, 1801, 21/2, 122; Robert Mills, *Statistics of South Carolina, Including a View of Its Natural, Civil, and Military History, General and Particular* (Spartanburg, S.C., 1972 [orig. publ. 1826]), 114.

86. Madley to Draper, May 6, 1873, Draper Mss., 14 VV 255, Madley to Stinson, May 31, 1873, 260. This report went on to say that Catawbas fought well only when the enemy had no cannons: "They always ran from artillery."

87. Fewell to Draper, n.d., *ibid.*, 15 VV 319, Stinson to Draper, Aug. 6, 1874, 5 VV 8, Robert S. Leeper to Draper, May 18, 1874, 11 VV 147. For other examples, see White Interview, Aug. 18, 1871, 11 VV 292, Narrative Copied from Logan Mss., 16 VV 318–319, Samuel McCalla to Draper, Sept. 29, 1873, 14 VV 471.

88. Thomas C. McCarkin to Draper, n.d., *ibid.*, 16 VV 56. For other positive remarks, see John Rossen to Draper, Feb. 11, 1873, 13 VV 46, Stinson to Draper, July 4, 1873, 9 VV 279.

89. Fewell to Draper, n.d., *ibid.*, 15 VV 318, Stinson to Draper, July 27, 1874, 5 VV 40, Spratt to Draper, May 7, 1873, 15 VV 108, Interview with White, Aug. 18, 1871, 11 VV 291–292, White to Draper, n.d., 15 VV 96.

90. Spratt to Draper, May 7, 1873, *ibid.*, 15 VV 108. In an earlier interview with Draper (11 VV 289) Spratt said that Harris got the weapon from Thomas Spratt. The letter, however, seems to me to carry more weight than Draper's interview notes, where the chances of a misunderstanding were greater. On the coat, see Journal of Lady Liston, p. 28, Robert Liston Papers, MS 5697, National Library of Scotland, Edinburgh. Whether this coat was a gift from patriots or captured from the enemy is unclear. Some soldiers on both sides wore green coats in the Carolina campaigns. See Pancake, *This Destructive War*, 49. For another example of the symbolic weight of a uniform, see Alfred F. Young, "George Robert Twelves Hewes (1742–1840): A Boston Shoemaker and the Memory of the American Revolution," *WMQ*, 3d Ser., XXXVIII (1981), 615–616.

91. Thomas Coke, *Extracts of the Journals of the Rev. Dr. Coke's Five Visits to America* (London, 1793), 149.

92. Hutchison, "Catawba Indians," col. 3; R. Craighead to "Cousin Thomas," Jan. 7, 1874, encl. in C. Craighead to Draper, Jan. 6, 1874[?], Draper Mss., 15 VV 41, R. C. McRee to Draper, Apr. 27, 1874, 42–43, R. Craighead to Draper, Dec. 4, 1873, 47–49, R. Craighead to Draper, Jan. 6, 1874, 53. The captain left the state in 1789.

93. James Kershaw, Diary, vol. IV, entry for Dec. 3, 1801, South Caroliniana

Library; From Mrs. Louisa Murrell [Sumter's granddaughter], n.d., Draper Mss., 11 VV 514; Kate Furman, "General Sumter and His Neighbors," Southern History Association, *Publications*, VI (1902), 382.

94. For musters, see John Belton O'Neall, "The Last of the Catawbas," *Historical Magazine*, Feb. 1861, 46, copy in Draper Mss., 20 VV 226. For Nettles, see Stinson to Draper, Aug. 6, 1874, Draper Mss., 5 VV 8. Another possible reference to the muster is in Gen. Ass., Governors' Messages, 1795–1802, no. 818-01-2.

95. Fewell to Draper, n.d., Draper Mss., 15 VV 318.

96. White Interview, Aug. 18, 1871, *ibid.*, 11 VV 291; *Charleston City-Gazette*, Aug. 14, 1794, quoted in Thomas J. Kirkland and Robert M. Kennedy, *Historic Camden*, part 1, *Colonial and Revolutionary* (Columbia, S.C., 1905), 320 (abdicated); Hutchison, "Catawba Indians," cols. 2–3 (died); Liston Journal, 25; Williams, ed., "Winn's Notes," *SCHGM*, XLIV (1943), 6–7; Hutchison, "Catawba Indians," cols. 2–3.

97. See below, chap. 7.

98. Quoted in Kirkland and Kennedy, *Historic Camden*, part 1, 319, 320.

99. Hutchison, "Catawba Indians," cols. 2–3; Report of Commissioners, Apr. 3, 1840, in Whyte, "Catawba Indians," Draper Mss., 10 U 114, Spratt to Draper, Jan. 12, 1871, 15 VV 99, Moore, "Reminiscences," 14 VV 139, 140; Ward, *Children of Hagler*, 9; Brown, *Catawba Indians*, 245.

100. Robert L. Meriwether, *The Expansion of South Carolina, 1729–1765* (Kingsport, Tenn., 1940), 70–71; Wilbur R. Jacobs, ed., *Indians of the Southern Colonial Frontier: The Edmond Atkin Report and Plan of 1755* (Columbia, S.C., 1954), 145–146. For the details of the Chickasaws' early years on the Savannah River, see *JCIT*, 215; SCCHJ, June 21, Aug. 4, 1722, RSUS, S.C. A.1b, 2/3, 36, and 3/1; George Chicken, "Colonel Chicken's Journal to the Cherokees, 1725," in Newton D. Mereness, ed., *Travels in the American Colonies* (New York, 1916), 168–172; Mark Catesby, *The Natural History of Carolina, Florida, and the Bahama Islands . . . ,* 3d ed., 2 vols. (London, 1771), I, 13–14; Glen to Lords Commissioners of Trade and Plantations, Sept. 29, 1746, BPRO-SC, XXII, 201.

101. Their numbers were also comparable after 1759. The Chickasaws, with 70 warriors reported in 1748 and again in 1757, had an estimated 57 men in 1760. See Enos Dexter to Glen, Mar. 19, 1748, in SCCJ, Mar. 29, 1748, RSUS, S.C. E.1p, 3/4, 189; Daniel Pepper to Lyttelton, Mar. 30, 1757, *DRIA, 1754–1765*, 356; SCCJ, Sept. 3, 1760, RSUS, S.C. E.1p, 8/5, 21.

102. *JCHA, November 10, 1736–June 7, 1739*, 369; Daniel Pepper to Lt. Gov. Bull, Aug. 14, 1742, in SCCJ, Aug. 27, 1742, RSUS, S.C. E.1p, 1/7, 226 (Spanish). Lyttelton to the Commons House of Assembly, SCCHJ, Oct. 5, 1759, RSUS, S.C. A.1b, 16/3, 32; White Outerbridge to Lyttelton, Nov. 7, 1759, Lyttelton Papers; *SCG*, Nov. 17, 1759; SCCHJ, Apr. 19, 1760, RSUS, S.C. A.1b, 16/3, 127, SCCJ, Aug. 7, Sept. 3, 1760, E.1p, 8/5, 15, 20–23; *SCG*, May 30, June 20, July 11, 1761; SCCHJ, June 6, 1761, RSUS, S.C. A.1b, 17/1, 141; Bull to Lords Commissioners of Trade and Plantations, July 17, 1761, BPRO-SC, XXIX, 126 (Cherokees). Bull to Lords Commissioners of Trade and Plantations, Oct. 5, 1739, BPRO-SC, XX, 180 (slaves). On land, see Glen to Lords Commissioners of Trade and Plantations, Sept. 29, 1746, BPRO-SC, XXII, 201; Jacobs, ed., *Atkin Report*, 45; SCCHJ, Mar. 27, 1765, RSUS, S.C. A.1b, 18/1, 70.

103. Jacobs, ed., *Atkin Report*, 45. SCCJ, Mar. 26, 28, 1765, RSUS, S.C. E.1p, 9/3, 487–488, SCCHJ, Mar. 27, 1765, A.1b, 18/1, 70, 72. On gifts, see, for example, SCCHJ, July 25–26, 1764, RSUS, S.C. A.1b, 17/2, 152, 153–154, SCCJ, Oct. 29, 1766, E.1p, 9/3, 855–856.

104. For Catawba contacts with Chickasaws, see Outerbridge to Lyttelton, Nov. 7, 1759, Lyttelton Papers; *SCG*, May 30, July 11, 1761, Oct. 9, 1762; Bull to Lords

Commissioners of Trade and Plantations, July 17, 1761, BPRO-SC, XXIX, 126. Relations had not always been cordial. See SCCJ, Apr. 11, 17, 1746, RSUS, S.C. E.1p, 3/2, 82–83, 93; *JCHA, September 10, 1745–June 17, 1746,* 188, 190, *January 19, 1748–June 29, 1748,* 292, 394.

105. SCCHJ, Mar. 27, 1765, RSUS, S.C. A.1b, 18/1, 70. Jacobs, ed., *Atkin Report,* 45 (selling). Conference between William Bull and the Chickasaw Indians, *DRIA, 1754–1765,* 475–476; Lachlan McGillivray to Lyttelton, Oct. 17, 1758, Lyttelton Papers (exchanges). That these exchanges were halted can be deduced from SCCHJ, Mar. 27, 1765, RSUS, S.C. A.1b, 18/1, 70, 72; for Chickasaw forgetfulness, see SCCJ, Mar. 26, 1765, E.1p, 9/3, 487–488.

106. Journal of the House of Representatives, Dec. 16, 17, 19, 20, 1791, Dec. 12, 21, 1792, RSUS, S.C. A.1b, 22/3, 122, 130–131, 143–144, 172, 23/1, 159–160, 300–303. In 1796 a few of them turned up in Camden, but the reasons for their visit are unknown. Were they on their way to or from the Catawba Nation? See James Kershaw, Diary, vol. III, entries for June 20, 22, 26, 1796. There was a "Chickisaw Jemmy" living with Catawbas in these years. See Pay Bill, Catawba Indian Company, Accounts Audited, roll 77, no. 3931-A; Gen. Ass., Petitions, 1792, no. 26.

107. Papers of the Continental Cong., Nov. 2, 1782, M-247, roll 34, item 27, 199. See also Smyth, *Tour,* I, 194–195; Donald Jackson and Dorothy Twohig, eds., *The Diaries of George Washington,* 6 vols. (Charlottesville, Va., 1976–1979), VI, 149. The process whereby South Carolina took this land and made it a state reservation has been lost, if it was ever done officially. After the war, observers simply noted that Indians lived "on a stretch of land ceded to them by the State of South Carolina" (Pace, trans. and ed., *Castiglioni's Viaggio,* 151).

108. Pace, trans. and ed., *Castiglioni's Viaggio,* 151; Jackson and Twohig, eds., *Diaries of Washington,* VI, 149 (40,000 acres). Johann David Schoepf, *Travels in the Confederation [1783–1784],* trans. and ed. Alfred J. Morrison, 2 vols. (Philadelphia, 1911), II, 155 (12 square miles). See also Elmer E. Clark, ed., *The Journal and Letters of Francis Asbury,* 3 vols. (London, 1958), I, 595 (12 miles square). On restriction, see Schoepf, *Travels,* trans. and ed. Morrison, II, 155; Gen. Ass., Petitions, 1786, no. 32, 1.

109. Gen. Ass., Petitions, 1792, no. 26; Gen. Ass., Governors' Messages, 1795–1802, no. 818:7. For examples of a lease's changing hands many times (in these cases, five), see York County (S.C.), Plat Book G, p. 197, no. 214, SCDAH; Secretary of State, Papers Pertaining to State Grants of Catawba Indian Lands, bundle 164, p. 3, SCDAH.

110. Sen. Jour., Feb. 1, 1787, RSUS, S.C. A.1a, 7/3, 18–19 (this petition is also in Gen. Ass., Petitions, 1787, no. 1); Gen. Ass., Petitions, 1792, no. 26.

111. Catawba Petition to Thomas Jefferson, Oct. 26, 1805, in Petitions, Daniel Parker Papers, Historical Society of Pennsylvania, Philadelphia. I am indebted to Maurice Bric for this reference.

112. Watson, *Memoirs of Watson,* 257.

113. Coke, *Journals,* 150.

114. For infanticide, see Charles M. Hudson, *The Southeastern Indians* (Knoxville, Tenn., 1976), 231. It may be that this is only another variation on a standard theme in the Indian captivity narratives, in which Indians did the same to colonists' children. See Leslie A. Fiedler, *The Return of the Vanishing American* (New York, 1968), 91–92.

115. Spratt, "Recollections, 1876," 14. The full story is in Spratt, "Recollections, 1875," 62.

Chapter 7

1. J.F.D. Smyth, *A Tour in the United States of America* . . . , 2 vols. (London, 1784), I, 193; Robert Mills, *Statistics of South Carolina, Including a View of Its Natural, Civil, and Military History, General and Particular* (Spartanburg, S.C., 1972 [orig. publ. 1826]), 115, 113.

2. Samuel Cole Williams, ed., *Adair's History of the American Indians* (New York, 1974 [orig. publ. 1930]), 234; Mills, *Statistics of South Carolina*, 115. For begging, see also Antonio Pace, trans. and ed., *Luigi Castiglioni's Viaggio: Travels in the United States of North America, 1785–87* (Syracuse, N.Y., 1983), 151; [Lucius Verus Bierce], "The Piedmont Frontier, 1822–1823," in Thomas D. Clark, ed., *South Carolina: The Grand Tour, 1780–1865*, Tricentennial Edition, no. 5 (Columbia, S.C., 1973), 64.

3. Smyth, *Tour*, I, 192, 194; Winslow C. Watson, ed., *Men and Times of the Revolution; or, Memoirs of Elkanah Watson, Including Journals of Travels in Europe and America, from 1777 to 1842* . . . (New York, 1856), 258; John Drayton, *A View of South-Carolina, as Respects Her Natural and Civil Concerns* (Spartanburg, S.C., 1972 [orig. publ. 1802]), 94; John Drayton to Dr. Benjamin Smith Barton, Sept. 9, 1803, Correspondence and Papers of Benjamin Smith Barton, Historical Society of Pennsylvania, Philadelphia (I am indebted to Maurice Bric for this last reference). For more on alcohol, see Smyth, *Tour*, I, 187–189; Williams, ed., *Adair's History*, 234; Pace, trans. and ed., *Castiglioni's Viaggio*, 151; Charles Fraser, *Reminiscences of Charleston, Lately Published in the Charleston Courier, and Now Revised and Enlarged by the Author* (Charleston, S.C., 1854), 16; David Hutchison, "Catawba Indians: By Request," *Palmetto-State Banner* (Columbia, S.C.), Aug. 30, 1849, copy in Draper Manuscripts Collection, Ser. U, vol. X, doc. 100, col. 2 (microfilm, original in Archives Division, State Historical Society of Wisconsin, Madison). For those blaming Indians, see Mills, *Statistics of South Carolina*, 115.

4. Mills, *Statistics of South Carolina*, 114; Watson, *Memoirs*, 258 (see also Smyth, *Tour*, I, 186); Fraser, *Reminiscences*, 16. For the negative views, see Watson, *Memoirs*, 258; Mills, *Statistics of South Carolina*, 113.

5. Drayton to Barton, Sept. 9, 1803, Corresp. of Barton. Frank G. Speck called these years a "crack-up" for the Catawbas. See Speck, *Catawba Hunting, Trapping, and Fishing*, Joint Publications, Museum of the University of Pennsylvania and the Philadelphia Anthropological Society, no. 2 (Philadelphia, 1946), 4. Speck was unsure how serious this "crack-up" was, however. For his occasional more positive assessments, see p. 21, and his *Catawba Texts*, Columbia University Contributions to Anthropology, XXIV (New York, 1934), xiii. Most scholars tend to follow the contemporary observers in positing a loss of traditional culture during this era. See Douglas Summers Brown, *The Catawba Indians: The People of the River* (Columbia, S.C., 1966), chap. 12, esp. 279, 286–287, 298, 301; Charles M. Hudson, *The Catawba Nation*, University of Georgia Monographs, no. 18 (Athens, Ga., 1970), 59; Steven G. Baker, "The Working Draft of: The Historic Catawba Peoples: Exploratory Perspectives in Ethnohistory and Archaeology" (MS, Department of History, University of South Carolina, Columbia, 1975), 101, 121, 146. However, Baker does note continuity and recognizes that Catawbas were also building something new in these years (see 193–194).

6. Mills had probably never been to the Nation. Drayton relied on an unknown "Gentleman" who lived near the Indians, and Adair, who gives no evidence of having been among Catawbas since about 1743, heard updated information from "several respectable inhabitants in their neighbourhood" (Drayton to Barton, Sept. 9, 1803, Corresp. of Barton; Williams, ed., *Adair's History*, 234).

7. For an excellent discussion of this pluralistic structure, see Hudson, *Catawba Nation*, 52–53.

8. Watson, *Memoirs*, 257; Smyth, *Tour*, I, 185–186, 193. Only later, after visiting several Indian settlements in Kentucky, did Smyth discover that the Catawba village was the rule, not the exception. The disillusioned traveler spared the reader a lengthy discourse on the Western Indians, explaining: "I found there was scarcely any variety in the manner of living and customs of the different Indian nations or tribes; for seeing one nation will enable a person to form a very just and exact judgement of all the rest. So that the description already given, of the Catawba Towns, reduced and enervated as they are, is an exact representation of the Shawnese, Miniamis, etc." See *Tour*, I, 339–340.

9. Drayton, *View of South-Carolina*, 94.

10. Benjamin Smith Barton, *New Views of the Origin of the Tribes and Nations of America* (Philadelphia, 1797), li. See John Lawson, *A New Voyage to Carolina*, ed. Hugh Talmage Lefler (Chapel Hill, N.C., 1967), 45.

11. William Feltman, "Diary of the Pennsylvania Line, May 26, 1781–April 25, 1782," *Pennsylvania Archives*, 2d Ser., XI (Harrisburg, Pa., 1896), 742. See also Journal of Lady Liston, p. 25, Robert Liston Papers, MS 5697, National Library of Scotland, Edinburgh.

12. Liston Journal, 27; Drayton to Barton, Sept. 9, 1803, Corresp. of Barton. The Indians could also convey different impressions to different people. Smyth came away in 1772 convinced that "they all spoke English very intelligibly," while a visitor 20 years later left the Nation certain that "the generality of them understand nothing of the *English* language." See Smyth, *Tour*, I, 185; Thomas Coke, *Extracts of the Journals of the Rev. Dr. Coke's Five Visits to America* (London, 1793), 149.

13. The best estimates to 1800 are in Gov. Joseph Martin to the Earl of Hillsborough, Dec. 12, 1771, *CRNC*, IX, 69 (600); Williams, ed., *Adair's History*, 235 (slightly more than 100 warriors); Speech to New River and the Headmen and Warriors of the Catawba Nation [c. 1781, misdated 1771], Joseph Brevard Kershaw Papers, South Caroliniana Library, Columbia (100 warriors); Liston Journal, 25 (300 people); J. F. White to Draper, n.d., Draper Mss., 15 VV 96 (300–400 in the early 19th century). The 1826 estimate is from Mills, *Statistics of South Carolina*, 773, which includes totals of 30 warriors and 110 people in all. The estimate was probably low, since Catawbas were living on both sides of the Catawba River at this time, and those familiar with one group were not always conversant with the other. See Mills, *Statistics of South Carolina*, 115, 773; Spratt to Draper, Sept. 3, 1874, Draper Mss., 6 VV 291, 292.

14. Liston Journal, 26; Watson, *Memoirs*, 257; Coke, *Journals*, 149. Coke claimed that "in general they dressed like the white people" before going on to describe the many features that contradicted his first impression.

15. Liston Journal, 25–26; Watson, *Memoirs*, 257–258; Coke, *Journals*, 149.

16. Watson, *Memoirs*, 258; Liston Journal, 27. For claims, see Williams, ed., *Adair's History*, 234; Hutchison, "Catawba Indians," col. 2; Mills, *Statistics of South Carolina*, 773. For agriculture, see Pace, trans. and ed., *Castiglioni's Viaggio*, 151; Coke, *Journals*, 148–149; Liston Journal, 27; General Assembly, Petitions, 1821, no. 8, SCDAH. In 1842 their agent, attempting to downplay Catawba agriculture, estimated that they had grown 300 bushels of grain in the past two decades. J. F. White to Gov. J. P. Richardson, Oct. 26, 1842, Legislative Papers, Indian Affairs, Governors' Correspondence, SCDAH.

17. Watson, *Memoirs*, 257; Liston Journal, 27; Travel Diary of Marshal and Benzien from Salem to South Carolina, 1790, in Adelaide L. Fries *et al.*, eds., *Records of*

the Moravians in North Carolina, 11 vols. (Raleigh, N.C., 1922–1969), V, 1996–1997. For the Catawbas in Charleston, see William Gilmore Simms, "Caloya; or, The Loves of the Driver," in *The Wigwam and the Cabin* (New York, 1856), 361. For a possible merchant record of Catawbas' trading at a Statesburg store, see William Murrell Letterbook, 1795–1812, in William Murrell Papers, Manuscript Department, Duke University Library, Durham, N.C. Murrell does not record whether the deer and otter skins he received came from Indian or white hunters. However, the Catawbas were often in the area digging clay or visiting Thomas Sumter, who may have sent them on to Murrell.

18. *Correspondence Relative to the Catawba Indians, Embracing Gov. Seabrook's Letter to the Special Agent and Commissioners Appointed by Him* (Columbia, S.C., 1849), 9–10. See also Hutchison, "Catawba Indians," col. 2. The figures, derived from the land leases in the South Carolina Department of Archives and History (Secretary of State, Papers Pertaining to State Grants of Catawba Indian Lands, hereafter cited as Land Leases), are 28 leases for $10 or more out of a total of 392 leases extant (7%). This includes subleases, which may account for the lower totals; however, the settlers' "any land" would seem to include these. The variation in the average is due to the variable rates set for the life of the lease—often substantially lower for the first decade or so after the agreement was made. Thus the lower average is based on this reduced rental rate, and the higher represents the later, more substantial rent. The $.12½ is in Land Leases, bundle 281, 9–10. Catawbas themselves set the range at between $2 and $10. See Gen. Ass., Petitions, 1810, no. 6.

19. This held true on 82 of 392 leases (21%). David Hutchison ("Catawba Indians," col. 3) claimed that this practice began only in the 1830s. It began much earlier. See, for example, Land Leases, 11:5, 32:7, 42:5, 53:5–6.

20. Gen. Ass., Petitions, 1810, no. 6; see also 1811, no. 28.

21. The merchandise exchanged can be found in the Surveyors' Plat Book and Indian Commissioners' Rent Book, copies in SCDAH and YCPL. Scattered payments are also noted in the Land Leases. The Rent Book records transactions made between approximately 1810 and 1830 and may not include the entire reservation or every transaction. It does, however, give considerable insight into the Catawbas' land system. See Douglas Summers Brown, "Catawba Land Records, 1795–1829," *SCHM*, LIX (1958), 64–77, 171–176, 226–233. From these sources it appears that Catawbas received a total of 34 horses. They received credit at a store 14 times. One lease (Land Leases, 76:9–10) set the rate at 50 bushels of corn; this may have been an advance.

22. See Land Leases, 101:7–8. For the extremes, see Rent Book, II, 72, 62.

23. See Rent Book, II, 143, III, 1–4. Sally New River had eight leases (three shared), and Jesse Ayers nine. Another Catawba named "W. Redhead" (Widow Redhead?) also had eight. The precise number of individuals assigned leases is difficult to pinpoint because of confusion in the names—W. and Widow Redhead, or Billy and B. Ayers—plus two granted to "Stephens Children," two to "Sally Jinney's daughter," one to "Stephens Daughter," and one to "Nation all."

24. These totals are compiled from the payments in the Rent Book and do not include sums she received on behalf of someone else.

25. These figures are based on 725 rent transactions recorded in the Rent Book, exclusive of any payments made at the time of formally signing the lease (when only headmen might be present) and payment "at sundry times." I have defined winter as December 1–April 1, when a total of 15.1% of the payments were made. The summer figure is 48.8%, the July total 19.4%.

26. For the annual cycle, see Fraser, *Reminiscences*, 16; Edwin J. Scott, *Random Recollections of a Long Life, 1806 to 1876* (Columbia, S.C., 1884), 13; White to Rich-

ardson, Oct. 26, 1842, Leg. Papers, Indian Affairs, Gov. Corresp.; D. G. Stinson to Draper, May 7, 1873, Draper Mss., 9 VV 212; Thomas D. Spratt, "Recollections of the Spratt Family by Thomas D. Spratt of Fort Mill, S.C., July 1876," typescript, copied from a manuscript in the possession of Miss Zoe White of Fort Mill, S.C., by Douglas Summers Brown, Rock Hill (1952), 14, David Hutchison Papers, box 1, folder 2, Winthrop College Archives, Rock Hill, S.C. Fraser, Stinson, and Spratt described the Indians' journeys only as "regular" or "yearly." Others placed Catawba potters near Camden in spring and fall (see William Blanding, quoted in E. G. Squier and E. H. Davis, *Ancient Monuments of the Mississippi Valley: Comprising the Results of Extensive Original Surveys and Explorations, Smithsonian Contributions to Knowledge*, I [Washington, D.C., 1848], 108). Simms ("Caloya," in *Wigwam*, 363) said they headed for the lowcountry in spring, which does not conform to the reports of more informed sources.

27. Report of the Commissioners appointed to treat with the Catawba Indians, Apr. 3, 1840, in A[rchibald S.] Whyte, "Account of Catawba Indians, Prepared for the Indian Land Chronicle, Nov. 1858," Draper Mss., 10 U 96[7] (I have rearranged the wording in this quotation for the sake of clarity).

28. Liston Journal, 26. See above, chap. 1.

29. For family, see Rent Book, II, 142; for husband and wife, 29; for sisters, 139; for mother and daughter, 125.

30. *Ibid.*, 96, 125, 128.

31. There were 7 bequests from husband to wife, 10 from father to daughter. These figures can be only guesses, as it is often impossible to tell what relationship the individuals involved bore to one another. Names are not a sure guide, for reasons outlined below.

32. Rent Book, II, 119, III, between pp. 50 and 51; Land Leases, 228:8. For examples of informal arrangements, see Rent Book, II, 91, 114, 131, 132, 133.

33. See F. G. Speck and C. E. Schaeffer, "Catawba Kinship and Social Organization with a Resume of Tutelo Kinship Terms," *American Anthropologist*, N.S., XLIV (1942), 555–563.

34. William Holland Thomas to Gov. Johnson, Jan. 22, 1848, Leg. Papers, Indian Affairs, Gov. Corresp.

35. Speck and Schaeffer, "Catawba Kinship," *Am. Anthro.*, N.S., XLIV (1942), 556–557. Speck and Schaeffer took these terms from Catawbas born between 1835 and 1875. They suspect (555) that the ubiquity of terms such as "like" and "resembling" is "a catch-basket for terms not known or understood" by their informants rather than a sign of closer affinity. While there may be some truth to their argument, I am less inclined to assume Catawba amnesia (see below).

36. Rent Book, II, 78 (Jacob, Jr.), II, 49, 77. For the women, see *Correspondence Relative to Catawbas*, 19; U.S. Senate, 54th Congress, 2d session (1897), doc. 144, "The Catawba Tribe of Indians," 8. For the private Catawba names, see below.

37. Maurice A. Moore, "Reminiscences of York: By a Septuagenarian," *Yorkville Enquirer* (S.C.), Jan. 6, 1870, copy in Draper Mss., 14 VV 140. My estimate of when this event took place is conjecture based on the fact that Scott was one of the leaders at the 1840 treaty with South Carolina and was included in a census of the Nation (including those in North Carolina) taken nine years later. See *Correspondence Relative to Catawbas*, 18.

38. Spratt to Draper, Sept. 3, 1874, Draper Mss., 6 VV 291; Land Leases, 228:6. For other examples of naming, see Rent Book, III, 40; Land Leases, 108:5–6. For assignments the figure is 42% (46% if W. Redhead was Widow Redhead), and for collection, 44%. Of the 114 Indians who collected rent, 59 were women. For wills, see Rent Book, III, between pp. 50 and 51, and 65.

39. Rent Book, III, 40, 47.

40. For Dudgeon, *ibid.*, [64]; for Kegg, 21. For other examples, see II, 81, 82; Land Leases, 228:10. For the children, see Rent Book, II, 91, 125; see also 133.

41. Report of Commissioners, Apr. 3, 1840, Whyte, "Catawba Indians," Draper Mss., 10 U 96[8].

42. Lancaster County (S.C.), Deed Book G, 166, Lancaster County Courthouse. I am indebted to Louise Pettus for sending me a copy of this document.

43. See chap. 6 and Epilogue.

44. SCCHJ, RSUS, S.C. A.1b, 18/1, 265; for the selection process, see SCCJ, Feb. 20, Nov. 9, 1764, Jan. 3, 29, Feb. 12, 1765, S.C. E.1p, 9/2, 40–41, 354, 9/3, 395, 442–444; *SCG*, May 4, 1765. Drayton (*View of South-Carolina*, 98) was aware of the continuity here.

45. Frow may have been Hagler's cousin. See SCCJ, Feb. 20, 1764, RSUS, S.C. E.1p, 41. Baker ("Historic Catawba Peoples," 146) has stressed the continuing importance of kin connections after the Revolution.

46. For New River, see Spratt to Draper, Jan. 12, 1871, Draper Mss., 15 VV 99–100. For Scott, see Drayton, *View of South-Carolina*, 98; Mills, *Statistics of South Carolina*, 124. New River may have been a Scott, since Watson (*Memoirs*, 257) called him "New River, *alias* Genl. Scott." For Kegg, see Spratt to Draper, Jan. 12, 1871, Draper Mss., 15 VV 100; Mills, *Statistics of South Carolina*, 112.

47. White to Draper, n.d., Draper Mss., 15 VV 96; for the origins of the name, see Spratt to Draper, Jan. 12, 1871, 100. For their service in the Revolution, see Pay Bill, Catawba Indian Company, Accounts Audited of Claims Growing out of the Revolution in South Carolina, roll 77, no. 3931-A, SCDAH.

48. Watson, *Memoirs*, 257–258; Liston Journal, 25–26, 28.

49. For these meetings, see Hutchison, "Catawba Indians," cols. 3, 7; Spratt to Draper, Sept. 3, 1874, Draper Mss., 6 VV 292, Spratt to Draper, Jan. 12, 1871, 15 VV 100. The lease signings, and the assemblies that assented to them, may have followed the old calendar of general meetings in late summer. Almost two-thirds (63%) of the leases were signed in July, August, or September.

50. Mills (*Statistics of South Carolina*, 115) termed it "a very rich tract of land." One South Carolinian buying land in Natchez, Mississippi, still could not get this place out of his mind, boasting that his purchase in the West was "better Land than any in York [District] Not excepting Kings bottom." James Moore to David Hutchison, Nov. 10, 1816, Hutchison Papers, box 1, folder 7, Winthrop Coll. Arch.

51. The site was designated "Old Indian Town and Graves" on an 1841 plat. See York District (S.C.), Plat Book G, Plat no. 91, p. 90, SCDAH. It may also have been this burying ground that North Carolina surveyors tramped across in 1762 (see Baker, "Historic Catawba Peoples," 145). It is first mentioned by this name in the 1796 lease to the Nation's women. For the Waxhaw connection, see Baker, "Historic Catawba Peoples," 134, 136, 144–145; Mills, *Statistics of South Carolina*, 600–601.

52. White to Draper, Dec. 15, 1870, Draper Mss., 15 VV 90; Land Leases, 8:5; Mills, *Statistics of South Carolina*, 115. That this was an explicit policy may be surmised from an agreement dated Feb. 7, 1822 stating that "if the land Called the Turkey Hill Could be rented to any white man John Hutchison should have the preference." Turkey Hill was either in King's Bottoms or adjacent to it. The King's Bottoms village was called Turkeyhead (Mills, *Statistics of South Carolina*, 115, and Baker, "Historic Catawba Peoples," fig. 7, 135), and the same Indian, Betsey Ayers, claimed title to both Turkey Hill and King's Bottoms. See Rent Book, III, between pp. 50 and 51; Land Leases, 70:9–11.

53. Drayton to Barton, Sept. 9, 1803, Corresp. of Barton.

54. The quotation is from Stinson to Draper, July 4, 1873, Draper Mss., 9 VV

276. For the plans after 1760, see Dobbs to the Secretary (of the SPG), Mar. 30, 1762, Mar. 29, 1764, *CRNC*, VI, 710, 1040; John Richard Alden, *John Stuart and the Southern Colonial Frontier: A Study of Indian Relations, War, Trade, and Land Problems in the Southern Wilderness, 1754–1775* (Ann Arbor, Mich., 1944), 304, 353; Lark Emerson Adams and Rosa Stoney Lumpkin, eds., *Journals of the House of Representatives, 1785–1786* (Columbia, S.C., 1979), 97; Elmer E. Clark, ed., *The Journal and Letters of Francis Asbury*, 3 vols. (London, 1958), I, 595; Coke, *Journals*, 149; Mills, *Statistics of South Carolina*, 114, 115, 120, 773. For short-lived efforts, see Brown, *Catawba Indians*, 288 n. 28, 289 n. 30; Hutchison, "Catawba Indians," col. 7. The Indians occasionally seemed to express an interest in going along. See Elam Potter, "An Account of Several Nations of Southern Indians: In a Letter from Rev. Elam Potter, to Rev. Dr. Stiles, A.D. 1768," Massachusetts Historical Society, *Collections*, 1st Ser., X (Boston, 1809), 120; Martin to Hillsborough, Dec. 12, 1771, *CRNC*, IX, 69; Alden, *John Stuart*, 304.

55. For a summary of William and Mary's missionary enterprise, see James Axtell, *The Invasion Within: The Contest of Cultures in Colonial North America* (New York, 1985), 193–196. The quotations here and in the next paragraph are from Hutchison, "Catawba Indians," col. 7.

56. Stinson to Draper, Aug. 6, 1874, Draper Mss., 5 VV 8. The positive assessments are in Drayton to Barton, Sept. 9, 1803, Corresp. of Barton; Hutchison, "Catawba Indians," col. 7; Watson, *Memoirs*, 257. For his marriage, see Hutchison, "Catawba Indians," col. 7. For service, see Pay Bill, Catawba Indian Company, Accounts Audited, roll 77, no. 3931-A. For his position in the Nation, see Gen. Ass., Petitions, 1792, no. 26; Gen. Ass., Governors' Messages, 1795–1802, no. 818:5, 7. For Nettles, see White to Draper, Dec. 14, 1870, Draper Mss., 15 VV 93. For leases, see Land Leases, 1810–1812. Judging from the leases, Nettles died about 1812. Hutchison's claim that he "ranked among the lowest" and that Indians shunned him are belied by the evidence from other sources on Nettles's later career.

57. Watson, *Memoirs*, 257; Hutchison, "Catawba Indians," col. 7.

58. For breeches and Bible, see Hutchison, "Catawba Indians," col. 7. His dancing skills are praised in Stinson to Draper, Aug. 6, 1874, Draper Mss., 5 VV 8.

59. Watson, *Memoirs*, 257.

60. "A Copie of The Talk Deliver[e]d by Mr. Drayton to the Catawba Indians th8 January 1773. as nigh as I Can Recolect," encl. in John Wyly to Joseph Kershaw, Jan. 28[?], 1773, Kershaw Papers.

61. Watson, *Memoirs*, 257; Drayton to Barton, Sept. 9, 1803, Corresp. of Barton. It was from Nettles that Drayton learned what he could about Catawba religion. Whether religious beliefs were indeed so vague and hollow, Nettles was keeping quiet about them, or Nettles—because of his own background and special position in the Nation—knew little about them is unclear, though as noted above I incline toward the latter two possibilities. For the muster, see chap. 6.

62. Gen. Ass., Governors' Messages, 1795–1802, no. 818:7. Hutchison, "Catawba Indians," col. 7. The petition went to South Carolina rather than to William and Mary because Boyle's money had been diverted to the West Indies and the Indian school closed in 1793. See "Brafferton Manor," *WMQ*, 1st Ser., XIX (1910–1911), 43.

The Indians may have gotten their wish. In 1810 two other Catawbas—Henry White and James Brown—were signing their names to petitions. See Gen. Ass., Petitions, 1810, no. 6. A few other Catawbas also showed signs of literacy during this period. See Spratt to Draper, Sept. 3, 1874, Draper Mss., 6 VV 292; Land Leases, 76:7 (James Patterson), and 51:3 (James Kegg).

63. Rooker's story is told in Hutchison, "Catawba Indians," col. 7, and Stinson to

Draper, July 4, 1873, Draper Mss., 9 VV 274–277 (quotation from Hutchison). Stinson called him Jacob Rooker, but Brown (*Catawba Indians,* 272 n. 79), citing other sources, asserts that it is John, and I follow her here.

64. Hutchison, "Catawba Indians," col. 7. For Marsh, see *ibid.*; Stinson to Draper, July 4, 1873, Draper Mss., 9 VV 274–277, Stinson to Draper, Sept. 24, 1873, 9 VV 322–323, A. Q. Madley to Draper, May 6, 31, 1873, 14 VV 255, 260–261. Rooker may also have married into the Nation. In the 1820s there was a Catawba named John Rooker Redhead, son of Molly Redhead. Whether this was Rooker's son or just a child named after him is unknown. See Rent Book, II, 36, 43, 48.

65. Stinson to Draper, July 4, 1873, Draper Mss., 9 VV 276, 277; Hutchison, "Catawba Indians," col. 7.

66. White to Draper, Dec. 15, 1870, Draper Mss., 15 VV 93. White does not mention Rooker by name, but his description of an "old man who settled near the Indians as a preacher of the gospel" fits this Baptist minister, who was 51 in 1803 (see Brown, *Catawba Indians,* 272 n. 79). Whether White is here suggesting that it was Nettles or his audience that still followed Catawba grammatical rules in English speech is unclear; in either case the slip boded ill for Nettles's missionary endeavors.

67. Mills, *Statistics of South Carolina,* 773; White to Thomas, Feb. 4, 1843, William Holland Thomas Papers, Manuscript Department, Duke University Library; White to Richardson, Oct. 26, 1842, Leg. Papers, Indian Affairs, Gov. Corresp.

68. See James H. Merrell, "'Their Very Bones Shall Fight': The Catawba-Iroquois Wars," in Daniel K. Richter and James H. Merrell, eds., *Beyond the Covenant Chain: The Iroquois and Their Neighbors in Indian North America, 1600–1800* (Syracuse, N.Y., 1987), 131–133.

69. See Speck, *Catawba Hunting,* 10 (quotation); Fraser, *Reminiscences,* 16; F. J. Kron, "Antiquities of Stanley and Montgomery Counties, North Carolina," *Annual Report of the Board of Regents of the Smithsonian Institution . . . for the Year 1874* (Washington, D.C., 1875), 389–390; Thomas J. Kirkland and Robert M. Kennedy, *Historic Camden,* part 1, *Colonial and Revolutionary* (Columbia, S.C., 1905), 59; Douglas L. Rights, "Traces of the Indian in Piedmont North Carolina," *NCHR,* I (1924), 288.

70. Thomas Dryden Spratt, "Recollections of His Family, July 1875," 67–69, typescript, South Caroliniana Library. Moore, "Reminiscences," Draper Mss., 14 VV 140, Moore Interview, Aug. 1871, 11 VV 311–312. These may have been the two Catawba "chiefs" who performed at Sadler's Wells. See "Songs, etc. In the Catawba Travellers: Or, Kiew Neika's Return. A Musical Entertainment. With Indian Scenery, Spectacle, etc. Performed at Sadler's Wells. 1797" (program of a play), copy in YCPL.

71. The Indians were furious at their exclusion from the War of 1812. See Journal of the House of Representatives, Nov. 23, 1812, RSUS, S.C. A.1b, 26/4, 4; [Bierce,] "Piedmont Frontier," in Clark, ed., *Grand Tour,* 64. I have found no evidence of Catawbas' being recruited as slavecatchers between the 1780s and the Civil War. See Hutchison, "Catawba Indians," col. 2; Stinson to Draper, July 4, 1873, Draper Mss., 9 VV 278.

72. John Belton O'Neall, "The Last of the Catawbas," *Historical Magazine,* Feb. 1861, 46, copy in Draper Mss., 20 VV 226.

73. Hutchison, "Catawba Indians," col. 3; White to Richardson, Sept. 18, 1841, Leg. Papers, Indian Affairs, Gov. Corresp. See also Report of Commissioners, Apr. 3, 1840, in Whyte, "Catawba Indians," Draper Mss., 10 U 96⁸. Some did give Kegg their confidence. See White to Richardson, Oct. 26, 1842, Leg. Papers, Indian Affairs, Gov. Corresp. For Harris, see Land Leases, 108:5, 272:12.

74. Brown, *Catawba Indians*, 321. (Another possible reason for resistance to Kegg was his decision in the early 1820s to cede King's Bottoms.) Hutchison noted that after the death of Jacob and John Ayers the Indians tried unsuccessfully to elect other chiefs. One young man (probably William Harris) died soon after his election, and since the candidate had to come from those on the reservation, the Indians "found that the materials" were not suitable, "the most promising and industrious class" having already migrated to the Cherokees (Hutchison, "Catawba Indians," col. 3). Whether the Indians chose men whites deemed best is unclear, but there can be little doubt about the confusion in the Nation at this time. For legends about the young man chosen, see Brown, *Catawba Indians*, 298–299.

75. *Correspondence Relative to Catawbas*, 9. The leaseholders summarized their complaints *ibid.*, 9–10; "Memorial from the Citizens of the Indian Land, to the . . . Legislature of South Carolina," Sept. 1840, in Whyte, "Catawba Indians," Draper Mss., 10 U 97[2-4]; Hutchison, "Catawba Indians," cols. 2–4. Their grievances first reached state officials in petitions. See Senate Journal, Feb. 1, 1787, RSUS, S.C. A.1a, 7/3, 18, Jour. HR, Feb. 5, 13, 1787, A.1b, 21/3, 65, 115; Gen. Ass., Petitions, 1791, no. 44, 1795, no. 86.

76. Thomas Cooper and D. J. McCord, eds., *The Statutes at Large of South Carolina*, 10 vols. (Columbia, S.C., 1836–1841), V, 678–679; Sen. Jour., Dec. 13, 14, 1815, RSUS, S.C. A.1a, 24/4, 140, 152, Nov. 29, 1824, 26/3, 42.

77. Whyte, "Catawba Indians," Draper Mss., 10 U 95[5].

78. For the petitions, see *ibid.* For the bill, Cooper and McCord, eds., *Statutes at Large*, VI, 602.

79. Rent Book, III, 54. Significantly, White crossed out "to the State" at the end of this sentence. Though the Indians eventually did sell to South Carolina, he may have been hoping for a direct bargain with each tenant to eliminate the chance (later taken care of by the 1838 act) that the state, upon acquiring title, might then choose to sell the land to someone else.

80. For the commissioners, see Sen. Jour., Dec. 19, 1832, RSUS, S.C. A.1a, 27/6, 139–140. For Hayne's visit, see Whyte, "Catawba Indians," Draper Mss., 10 U 95[5]. Butler's speech in support is in *Journal of the Proceedings . . . of the General Assembly . . . of 1838* (Columbia, S.C., 1839), 16, copy in RSUS, S.C. A.1a:b, 28/1.

81. Gen. Ass., Petitions, 1815, no. 5; Cooper and McCord, eds., *Statutes at Large*, VI, 18–19; Gen. Ass., Petitions, 1821, no. 9. That tenants fell behind in their payments is clear from the land leases and Rent Book, this despite the settlers' claim that very few were in arrears because "the Indians did not indulge much in that way" (Whyte, "Catawba Indians," Draper Mss., 10 U 98[4]). For examples of arrears, see Land Leases, 247:5 (11 years); Rent Book, II, 39 (15 years), 70 (14 years).

82. Gen. Ass., Governors' Messages, 1795–1802, no. 818:7; Records of the Gen. Ass., Reports, 1801, no. 42, SCDAH; Records of the Gen. Ass., Resolutions, 1802, no. 1, SCDAH; Gen. Ass., Petitions, 1805, nos. 5–6.

83. The death dates that follow are only estimates, based on an individual's disappearance from the lease signings or rent collections. For Scott, see Land Leases, 70:5–6, 88:5–6, 184:3–4, 290:3–4, 292:3. For New River, Rent Book, II, 72. Kegg's bargain is in Rent Book, III, between pp. 50 and 51.

84. Land Leases, 70:9–11; Rent Book, III, 54.

85. Hutchison, "Catawba Indians," cols. 2–3; Whyte, "Catawba Indians," Draper Mss., 10 U 95[5], and see also Report of Commissioners, Apr. 3, 1840, 10 U 96[4]. For renewing appointments, see Journal of the General Assembly of the State of South Carolina, Dec. 4, 1833, RSUS, S.C. A.1a:b, 28/1, 25, Dec. 17, 1834, 81, Dec. 19, 1835, 84, Dec. 19, 1836, 72, Dec. 6, 7, 9, 11, 1837, 35–37, 46, 52 (pagination is by

session for each year in this unit); *Journal of the Proceedings of . . . the General Assembly of South Carolina . . . of 1839* (Columbia, S.C., 1839), 91–92, 94, 108, 118, 121, 130, copy *ibid.*

86. This was clearly a changing of the guard. Of the seven men who signed the treaty in 1840, only two had been signing leases during the tenure of the Ayers brothers—John Joe from 1827 to 1829 and Sam Scott from 1834 on. The others began in 1837–1838. Moreover, many were quite young in 1840. Kegg was in his 50s and Scott 41, but David Harris was only 31, Allen Harris 26, and Billy George 24. The ages of the others are unknown. See *Correspondence Relative to Catawbas*, 17–18.

87. Land Leases, 108:3, 5–6; Report of Commissioners, Apr. 3, 1840, in Whyte, "Catawba Indians," Draper Mss., 10 U 96[4]. The land leases confirm that signings were climbing from a low of 4 in 1833 to 14 in 1836 and 19 in 1839. See also Hutchison, "Catawba Indians," cols. 2–3. Hutchison later revealed that there may have been an effort to get around Catawba intransigence by decreeing that "when the tribe became reduced to a certain number"—an unspecified figure, but one that Hutchison claimed the Indians had already reached in the 1830s—"they . . . would cease to have claim to the original boundary." Whether this was wishful thinking is unclear; Hutchison said that the documents supporting his contention had been misplaced. See Hutchison to Gov. John Morehead, Apr. 26, 1842, in John Motley Morehead Papers, January–April 1842, Governors' Papers, box 100, NCDAH.

88. Brown, *Catawba Indians*, 305; for a copy of the treaty, see 306. For the meeting, see Hutchison, "Catawba Indians," cols. 4–5.

89. For the surveys, see York District, Plat Book G.

90. White to Richardson, Sept. 18, 1841, Leg. Papers, Indian Affairs, Gov. Corresp.; Hutchison to Morehead, Apr. 26, 1842, Morehead Papers, Gov. Papers, box 100; Thomas to Hutchison, Dec. 31, 1842, Hutchison Papers, box 2, folder 11; White to Johnson, Nov. 29, 1848, Leg. Papers, Indian Affairs, Gov. Corresp. For these Cherokees, see John R. Finger, *The Eastern Band of Cherokees, 1819–1900* (Knoxville, Tenn., 1984).

91. White to Johnson, Nov. 29, 1848, Leg. Papers, Indian Affairs, Gov. Corresp. The size of this group and the intensity of its desire to move west are unclear. Some were among the Catawbas living in North Carolina. Whites may have exaggerated Catawba enthusiasm for this course since it was what many whites hoped and expected would happen. For Catawbas in North Carolina favoring removal, see Thomas to Hutchison, Dec. 31, 1842, Hutchison Papers, box 2, folder 11; Gen. Ass., Petitions, 1844, no. 24. For white hopes, see White to Thomas, Feb. 4, 1843, Thomas Papers; Message of Gov. Hammond, Nov. 28, 1843, in *Journal of the Senate of the State of South-Carolina Being Its Annual Session of 1843* (Columbia, S.C., 1843), 15, copy in RSUS, S.C. A.1a, 28/2. For other talk of removal among Catawbas, see White to Gov. Seabrook, May 26, 1849, Leg. Papers, Indian Affairs, Gov. Corresp.; Message of Seabrook, Nov. 27, 1849, in Whyte, "Catawba Indians," Draper Mss., 10 U 103[6], Message from the governor [John Means], Nov. 25, 1851, in Whyte, "Catawba Indians," 10 U 104[2].

92. White to Richardson, Sept. 18, 1841, Leg. Papers, Indian Affairs, Gov. Corresp.; *Report of the Indian Agent, to His Excellency the Governor* (Nov. 23, 1841), *ibid.* Hutchison claimed that these Indians were being duped by unscrupulous whites who wanted Catawbas to stay and spend the state's money there ("Catawba Indians," cols. 4–5). For the search, see White to Johnson, Nov. 29, 1848, Leg. Papers, Indian Affairs, Gov. Corresp. (Chester and the Saluda); White to Seabrook, Oct. 18, 1850, Leg. Papers, Indian Affairs, Gov. Corresp., and Extract of Message of

Gov. Seabrook, Nov. 26, 1850, in Whyte, "Catawba Indians," Draper Mss., 10 U 104 (Greenville); White to Richardson, Sept. 18, 1841, Leg. Papers, Indian Affairs, Gov. Corresp. (King's Mountain in North Carolina).

93. White to Richardson, Jan. 15, 1842, Leg. Papers, Indian Affairs, Gov. Corresp.

94. Report of the Committee on Ways and Means, Dec. 1849, in Whyte, "Catawba Indians," Draper Mss., 10 U 1037–12, quotation on 1039. For general discussions of the plans for Catawba removal, see James W. Covington, "Proposed Catawba Indian Removal, 1848," *SCHM*, LV (1954), 42–47; Brown, *Catawba Indians*, 322–329.

95. White to Morehead, Aug. 10, 1841, and Morehead to White, Sept. 8, 1841, Morehead Letter Book, 1841–1842, Governors' Letter Books, 33, 165–166, NCDAH. The original White letter is in Morehead Papers, July–Sept. 1841, Gov. Papers, box 98. Morehead's reply was printed in South Carolina, and I have followed the capitalization and spelling of the printed version: *Report of the Indian Agent* (Nov. 23, 1841), Leg. Papers, Indian Affairs, Gov. Corresp.

96. Hutchison to Morehead, Apr. 26, 1842, Morehead Papers, Jan.–Apr. 1842, Gov. Papers, box 100.

97. For the council's blessing, see Thomas to Hutchison, June 16, 1841, Hutchison Papers, box 2, folder 11, and Extract from Gov. Johnson's Message, no. 7, Dec. 14, 1847, in Whyte, "Catawba Indians," Draper Mss., 10 U 1012. For the Catawba migration, see Hutchison to Morehead, Apr. 26, 1842, Morehead Papers, Jan.– Apr. 1842, Gov. Papers, box 100; Thomas to Hutchison, Dec. 31, 1842, Hutchison Papers, box 2, folder 11; Seabrook to Gov. Charles Manley, Aug. 2, 1849, Manley Papers, 1848–1849, Gov. Papers, box 123.

98. Thomas to Johnson, Jan. 22, 1848, Leg. Papers, Indian Affairs, Gov. Corresp. Gen. Ass., Petitions, 1844, no. 24. For other references to this trip, see White to Johnson, Nov. 29, 1848, Leg. Papers, Indian Affairs, Gov. Corresp.; *Correspondence Relative to Catawbas*, 13; Report of Ways and Means Committee, Dec. 1849, in Whyte, "Catawba Indians," Draper Mss., 10 U 1037.

99. Thomas to Johnson, Jan. 28, 1848, Leg. Papers, Indian Affairs, Gov. Corresp. Methodists at the Echota Mission also worked with the Catawbas. See *Correspondence Relative to Catawbas*, 16.

100. James Mooney, "Myths of the Cherokee," in J. W. Powell, *Nineteenth Annual Report of the Bureau of American Ethnology to the Secretary of the Smithsonian Institution, 1897–1898*, part 1 (Washington, D.C., 1900), 237; Report of Ways and Means Committee, Dec. 1849, in Whyte, "Catawba Indians," Draper Mss., 10 U 1038; *Correspondence Relative to Catawbas*, 4. For earlier hints of disillusionment, see Extract from Johnson's Message, no. 7, Dec. 14, 1847, in Whyte, "Catawba Indians," Draper Mss., 10 U 1012–3.

101. For the term's use in this context, see Annual Message from Gov. Hammond, Nov. 28, 1843, in *Sen. Jour. of 1843*, 15, in RSUS, S.C. A.1a, 28/2.

102. The story can be followed in *Report of the Indian Agent* (Nov. 23, 1841), Leg. Papers, Indian Affairs, Gov. Corresp.; *Journal of the Proceedings of the . . . General Assembly of South Carolina, at Its Regular Session of 1841* (Columbia, S.C., 1841), 19, copy in RSUS, S.C. A.1a:b, 28/1; Report of the House Judiciary Committee, Dec. 6, 1841, in Whyte, "Catawba Indians," Draper Mss., 10 U 992; White to Richardson, Jan. 15, 1842, Leg. Papers, Indian Affairs, Gov. Corresp.; White to Thomas, Feb. 4, 1843, Thomas Papers; *Sen. Jour. for 1843*, 15, in RSUS, S.C. A.1a, 28/2; White to Johnson, Nov. 29, 1848, Leg. Papers, Indian Affairs, Gov. Corresp.

103. White to Johnson, Nov. 29, 1848, Leg. Papers, Indian Affairs, Gov. Corresp.; *Report of the Indian Agent* (Nov. 23, 1841), Leg. Papers, Indian Affairs, Gov.

Corresp., White to Richardson, Jan. 15, 1842.

104. This was his view as he launched the experiment. White to Thomas, Feb. 4, 1843, Thomas Papers. See also Whyte, "Catawba Indians," Draper Mss., 10 U 98[6].

105. For the land, see York District, Plat Book G, Plat no. 322, p. 316. The Indians living there are noted in White to Johnson, Nov. 29, 1848, Leg. Papers, Indian Affairs, Gov. Corresp. See also Whyte, "Catawba Indians," Draper Mss., 10 U 101[6]; for talk of selling, see 101[1]; *Correspondence Relative to Catawbas*, 5.

106. *Report of the Indian Agent* (Nov. 23, 1841), Leg. Papers, Indian Affairs, Gov. Corresp.; Richardson Message, Nov. 23, 1841, *Jour. of Gen. Ass. . . . 1841*, 19, in RSUS, S.C. A.1a:b, 28/1; Gov. Johnson, Message no. 3, Dec. 1848, in Whyte, "Catawba Indians," Draper Mss., 10 U 101[4]; Brown, *Catawba Indians*, chap. 14.

107. Massey to Seabrook, Sept. 29, 1849, Leg. Papers, Indian Affairs, Gov. Corresp. For the census, see *Correspondence Relative to Catawbas*, 17–19. For the commission, see Whyte, "Catawba Indians," Draper Mss., 10 U 101[8]. With Catawbas so widely scattered, this figure should be considered a minimum.

108. White to Richardson, Oct. 26, 1842, Leg. Papers, Indian Affairs, Gov. Corresp.

109. Report of Ways and Means Committee, Dec. 20, 1848, in Whyte, "Catawba Indians," Draper Mss., 10 U 101[4–5], Extract from Johnson's Message, no. 7, Dec. 14, 1847, 101[3].

110. For agents' reports on their condition, see *Report of the Indian Agent* (Nov. 23, 1841), Leg. Papers, Indian Affairs, Gov. Corresp., White to Richardson, Jan. 15, 1842; *Correspondence Relative to Catawbas*, 4.

111. "An Act to Carry into Effect the late Agreement Between the Catawba Indians and the Commissioners on the Part of the State, and for other purposes," copy in Whyte, "Catawba Indians," Draper Mss., 10 U 98[1–2]; White to Hammond, Feb. 22, 1843, in Whyte, "Catawba Indians," Draper Mss., 10 U 99[7]. For the resolution, see 10 U 99[6]. See also 10 U 99[3]; White to Richardson, Oct. 26, 1842, Leg. Papers, Indian Affairs, Gov. Corresp. For begging, Hutchison, "Catawba Indians," cols. 5–6.

112. This may have begun as early as 1843. See Annual Message from Gov. Hammond, Nov. 1843, in Whyte, "Catawba Indians," Draper Mss., 10 U 99[8], and Comptroller General's report, 101[3]. For a sample of the goods distributed, see *Correspondence Relative to Catawbas*, 13–14.

113. Gen. Ass., Petitions, 1844, no. 24; Whyte, "Catawba Indians," Draper Mss., 10 U 101[1]. For the system, see Gen. Ass., Petitions, 1844, no. 24; Extract from Johnson's Message, no. 7, Dec. 14, 1848, in Whyte, "Catawba Indians," Draper Mss., 10 U 101[3]; White to Johnson, Nov. 29, 1848, Leg. Papers, Indian Affairs, Gov. Corresp.; Report of Ways and Means Committee, Dec. 20, 1848, in Whyte, "Catawba Indians," Draper Mss., 10 U 101[5]. On one occasion White noted that he gave Indians from North Carolina credit at a nearby store if he did not have something they wanted (*Correspondence Relative to Catawbas*, 13). In another letter he said he was "supplying all the Catawba Indians with such articles as they want, as they apply for them" (White to Seabrook, May 26, 1849, Leg. Papers, Indian Affairs, Gov. Corresp.). However, those in South Carolina apparently had to be content with "provisions and articles of cloathing in such quantities as I thought their necessities required" (White to Johnson, Nov. 29, 1848, Leg. Papers, Indian Affairs, Gov. Corresp.).

114. White to Johnson, Nov. 29, 1848, Leg. Papers, Indian Affairs, Gov. Corresp.; Report of Ways and Means Committee, Dec. 1849, in Whyte, "Catawba Indians," Draper Mss., 10 U 103[8]; Whyte, "Catawba Indians," Draper Mss., 10 U 98[6], 101[6–7].

115. *Correspondence Relative to Catawbas*, 5–6. [A. S. White], "Indians Who Were Once Powerful: A Fort Mill Man Writes Interestingly of the Catawbas," written for the *News and Courier* (Charleston), reprinted in *Rock Hill Record*, Oct. 31, 1905.

116. Gen. Ass., Petitions, 1844, no. 24.

117. Extract from Gov. Seabrook's Message, Nov. 27, 1849, in Whyte, "Catawba Indians," Draper Mss., 10 U 103⁵; White to Johnson, Nov. 29, 1848, Leg. Papers, Indian Affairs, Gov. Corresp.; *Correspondence Relative to Catawbas*, 14; White to Seabrook, May 18, June 3, July 2, Oct. 18, 1850, Leg. Papers, Indian Affairs, Gov. Corresp.; Extract from Message of Seabrook, Nov. 26, 1850, in Whyte, "Catawba Indians," Draper Mss., 10 U 104–104². See also Mooney, "Myths of the Cherokee," *Nineteenth Annual Report of the Bureau of American Ethnology*, part 1, 105.

118. [White], "Indians Who Were Powerful," *Rock Hill Record*, Oct. 31, 1905; O'Neall, "Last of the Catawbas," Draper Mss., 20 VV 226, Message of Seabrook, Nov. 27, 1849, in Whyte, "Catawba Indians," 10 U 103⁵.

119. Simms, "Caloya," in *Wigwam*, 362; see also Whyte, "Catawba Indians," Draper Mss., 10 U 104⁷. Oscar M. Lieber, "Vocabulary of the Catawba Language, with Some Remarks on Its Grammar, Construction, and Pronunciation," South Carolina Historical Society, *Collections*, II (Charleston, S.C., 1858), 342. Once again, scholars have gone along. See Brown, *Catawba Indians*, 321–322.

120. James H. Saye to Draper, Oct. 21, 1870, Draper Mss., 22 VV 33–34; J. H. Edwards, "The Last of the Catawbas," *Rock Hill Herald*, July 20, 1882. For the infrequency of visits, see W. B. Ardrey, "The Catawba Indians," *American Antiquarian*, XVI (1894), 268. The reference to liquor is in Frank Vivian, "Letter from the Country: Land's Ford, South Carolina, September 6, 1867," *Daily Courier* (Charleston), Sept. 12, 1867.

121. Stinson to Draper, Oct. 12, 1874, Draper Mss., 8 VV 29. See also Vivian, "Letter from the Country," *Daily Courier*, Sept. 12, 1867. For the names, see Speck and Schaeffer, "Catawba Kinship," *Am. Anthro.*, N.S., XLIV (1942), 572. See also Excerpt of a letter from James Mooney to Albert Gatschet, Sept. 20, 1887, Bureau of American Ethnology Archives, copy in Catawba Indian File, no. 30, part 2, YCPL; H. Lewis Scaife, *History and Condition of the Catawba Indians of South Carolina* (Philadelphia, 1896), 20.

122. McCullough to Seabrook, Apr. 24, 1850, White to Seabrook, June 3, 1850, Leg. Papers, Indian Affairs, Gov. Corresp.

123. Much of this section is derived from work already published (James H. Merrell, "Reading 'An almost erased page': A Reassessment of Frank G. Speck's Catawba Studies," American Philosophical Society, *Proceedings*, CXXVII [1983], 248–262). I am indebted to Frank T. Siebert for setting me straight on a number of points, including Sally Gordon's date of death. My thinking here also owes a debt to Peter L. Berger and Thomas Luckmann, *The Social Construction of Reality: A Treatise in the Sociology of Knowledge* (Garden City, N.Y., 1967). For a view that dissents from mine on the character of 19th-century Catawba culture, see George L. Hicks, "Cultural Persistence versus Local Adaptation: Frank G. Speck's Catawba Indians," *Ethnohistory*, XII (1965), 343–354.

124. Massey to Seabrook, Sept. 29, 1849, Leg. Papers, Indian Affairs, Gov. Corresp. More evidence on the close connection between young and old can be gathered from Archibald Whyte to R.F.W. Allston, July 17, 1860, R.F.W. Allston Papers, South Carolina Historical Society, Charleston.

125. For a general list of these people, see Speck, *Catawba Texts*, xi; Speck, "Catawba Religious Beliefs, Mortuary Customs, and Dances," *Primitive Man*, XII (1939), 21 (for John Scott, see 55). Brown, *Catawba Indians*, 330, 349; Stinson to Draper, July 4, 1873, Draper Mss., 9 VV 280; Speck and Schaeffer, "Catawba

Kinship," *Am. Anthro.*, N.S., XLIV (1942), 572. For Patsey George, see "Catawba Kinship," 572; Stinson to Draper, July 4, 1873, Draper Mss., 9 VV 280–283, Oct. 12, 1874, 8 VV 29. For Billy George, see Speck, *Catawba Hunting*, 21; "Catawba Kinship," 572; Scaife, *Catawba Indians*, 18, 20–21. Siebert (personal communication) argues that Patsey George was Margaret Brown's grandmother rather than her aunt.

I have revised the dates of birth substantially (Merrell, "Reassessment of Speck," APS, *Procs.*, CXXVII [1983], 251), to conform to the 1849 census by Massey, which reveals that these people were younger than they or others claimed. For the census, see *Correspondence Relative to Catawbas*, 17–19. I am grateful to Wesley White for pointing out the discrepancy to me.

126. Speck, *Catawba Hunting*, 14; and "Catawba Religious Beliefs," *Primitive Man*, XII (1939), 30–31. Bob Ward, *The Children of King Hagler* (Rock Hill, S.C., 1940), 9. For Tom Stevens, see Speck, "Catawba Religious Beliefs," 53–54; Speck, *Catawba Hunting*, 7; Speck and Schaeffer, "Catawba Kinship," *Am. Anthro.*, N.S., XLIV (1942), 565; Brown, *Catawba Indians*, 347. Robert Harris did much the same. See Ward, *Children of Hagler*, 9.

127. Speck, *Catawba Texts*, xv. See also Ward, *Children of Hagler*, 5.

128. Ward, *Children of Hagler*, 9. See also Speck, *Catawba Texts*, xiii; Frank G. Speck, "The Question of Matrilineal Descent in the Southeastern Siouan Area," *Am. Anthro.*, N.S., XL (1938), 5 n. 16; Speck, "Catawba Text," *International Journal of American Linguistics*, XII (1946), 64.

For other evidence of Catawba's being spoken, see Porcher Collection: Frederick A. Porcher Notes on the Catawba Language, file 11/316/3, Porcher Family Papers, S.C. Hist. Soc.; Lieber, "Vocabulary of Catawba," S.C. Hist. Soc., *Colls.*, II (1858), 342; Vivian, "Letter from the Country," *Daily Courier*, Sept. 12, 1867; Edwards, "Last of the Catawbas," *Rock Hill Herald*, July 20, 1882. For its decline, see McDonald Furman, "Indians in South Carolina: In the Home of the Red Man," *Mountaineer* (Greenville, S.C.), June 5, 1894, copy in "Photostats of News Articles and Clippings found in the rear of the note book of Albert Gatschet. Archives of the Smithsonian Insitution, Bureau of American Ethnology," Catawba Indian File, no. 30, part 1, YCPL; "Catawba Indians at Gastonia," *Rock Hill Herald*, Aug. 15, 1905; Leola Blue to Speck, Oct. 27, 1919, box 18, IV (Southeast), E (Catawba), 2 (Correspondence with other Informants), Frank G. Speck Papers, APS Library, Philadelphia.

129. See Berger and Luckmann, *Social Construction of Reality*, esp. chap. 1, part 3, and pp. 64, 133; T. J. Brasser, "Persistence and Disappearance of Aboriginal Languages," *Mens en Maatschappij*, XXXIX (1964), 280.

130. White to Seabrook, May 26, 1849, Leg. Papers, Indian Affairs, Gov. Corresp.; Vivian, "Letter from the Country," *Daily Courier*, Sept. 12, 1867. See also "Excerpt from Note Book of Albert S. Gatschet [1881], Bureau of American Ethnology Archives, Smithsonian Institute, Copied August 1954 by Douglas Summers Brown," Catawba Indian File, folder no. 30, part 2.

131. Massey to Seabrook, Sept. 29, 1849, Leg. Papers, Indian Affairs, Gov. Corresp. Nancey George's age is in *Correspondence Relative to Catawbas*, 19; I am assuming here that she is the elder Nancey George. Another woman by that name was 44 years old at the time of the census (17).

132. See Speck, *Catawba Texts*, 39, 42, 43, 51, 67, 91. Reciting the succession of Catawba leaders as far back as the 18th century gave concrete reality to these notions of ancient people. See Speck, "Matrilineal Descent," *Am. Anthro.*, N.S., XL (1938), 8 n. 23; Speck and Schaeffer, "Catawba Kinship," *Am. Anthro.*, N.S., XLIV (1942), 564–565.

133. Speck, *Catawba Texts*, 6–7, 28, 29–30; Ward, *Children of Hagler*, 6.

134. Drayton, *View of South-Carolina*, 97–98; Henry R. Schoolcraft, *Historical and Statistical Information Respecting the History, Condition, and Prospects of the Indian Tribes of the United States . . .* , 6 vols. (Philadelphia, 1851–1857), III, 295; Vivian, "Letter from the Country," *Daily Courier*, Sept. 12, 1867. See also Brown, *Catawba Indians*, 248. It is possible that at least some of the sentiment was manufactured for white audiences that knew of no other chiefs.

135. For the towns and burial grounds, see A. S. Gatschet to McDonald Furman, Dec. 16, 1888, Charles James McDonald Furman Papers, South Caroliniana Library; Furman, "Indians of South Carolina," *Mountaineer* (Greenville), June 5, 1894, in Gatschet Photostats, Catawba Indian File, no. 30, part 1. For the battleground, see Scaife, *Catawba Indians*, 20. For Hagler's grave, see Mrs. D. E. Dunlap to Furman, Apr. 2, 1897, McDonald Furman Papers, Manuscript Department, Duke University Library; Brown, *Catawba Indians*, 248.

136. Speck, *Catawba Texts*, 30.

137. Philip Edward Pearson, "Memoir of the Catawbas. Sent to Governor James Henry Hammond [1842?]," typescript in YCPL; Mooney to Gatschet, Sept. 20, 1887, in Gatschet Photostats, Catawba Indian File, no. 30, part 2.

138. Speck, *Catawba Texts*, 4–11, 17, 27, 42, 47, 87–88; Speck, "Catawba Religious Beliefs," *Primitive Man*, XII (1939), 32–33; Speck, "Catawba Medicines and Curative Practices," in D. S. Davidson, ed., *Twenty-fifth Anniversary Studies*, Philadelphia Anthropological Society, *Publications*, I (Philadelphia, 1937), 180–181.

139. Speck, *Catawba Texts*, 27, 37–38, 42, 43, 47; Speck, "Catawba Medicines," in Davidson, ed., *Twenty-fifth Anniversary Studies*, 180–181. For the earlier view, see Lawson, *New Voyage*, ed. Lefler, 222.

140. Speck, *Catawba Texts*, 44–45, 67–68; Speck, "Catawba Religious Beliefs," *Primitive Man*, XII (1939), 42–46.

141. Mooney, "Myths of the Cherokee," *Nineteenth Annual Report of the Bureau of American Ethnology*, 165; Speck, "Catawba Medicines," in Davidson, ed., *Twenty-fifth Anniversary Studies*, 179–197; Speck, "Catawba Herbals and Curative Practices," *Journal of American Folklore*, LVII (1944), 37–50.

For medicine blowing, see Speck, "Catawba Medicines," in Davidson, ed., *Twenty-fifth Anniversary Studies*, 183–184. For scratching, see Speck, *Catawba Texts*, 50–51; "Catawba Medicines," 184–185; Lawson, *New Voyage*, ed. Lefler, 48–49, 210, 223, 232. For the water cure, see Speck, "Catawba Medicines," 186–187; Lawson, *New Voyage*, ed. Lefler, 226, 232.

142. Mooney, "Myths of the Cherokee," *Nineteenth Annual Report of the Bureau of American Ethnology*, 165; Speck, "Catawba Religious Beliefs," *Primitive Man*, XII (1939), 46–47.

143. See John R. Swanton, "Catawba Notes," *Journal of the Washington Academy of Sciences*, VIII (1918), 629; Speck, *Catawba Texts*, 64–66; Speck, "Catawba Religious Beliefs," *Primitive Man*, XII (1939), 47–57; Ward, *Children of Hagler*, 9.

144. Speck, *Catawba Texts*, 34, 35–36, 37, 39.

145. See Speck, *Catawba Hunting*, for an analysis of what was hunted.

146. Moore, "Reminiscences," in Draper Mss., 14 VV 139. For hiring out, see White to Seabrook, May 18, 1850, Leg. Papers, Indian Affairs, Gov. Corresp.; Spratt to Draper, May 7, 1873, Draper Mss., 15 VV 107; Excerpt from Gatschet Notebook [1881], Catawba Indian File, no. 30, part 2; Scaife, *Catawba Indians*, 20; "Catawba Indians at Gastonia," *Rock Hill Herald*, Aug. 15, 1905. For hauling, see Dunlap to Furman, Jan. 10, Nov. 2, 1900, Furman Papers, Duke University. For agriculture, see Furman, "The Catawba Tribe," *Rock Hill Herald*, July 20, 1895; Scaife, *Catawba Indians*, 18; Dunlap to Furman, Nov. 13, 1900, Furman Papers,

Duke University; "A Day with the Catawba Indians," *Rock Hill Herald*, May 1, 1909.

147. Spratt to Draper, May 7, 1873, Draper Mss., 15 VV 107; Scaife, *Catawba Indians*, 21; Ward, *Children of Hagler*, 9.

148. Speck, *Catawba Texts*, 18–19; Speck, "Catawba Religious Beliefs," *Primitive Man*, XII (1939), 35–36.

149. For general analyses of the trade, see Hudson, *Catawba Nation*, 72, 75–76, 90–91; Baker, "Historic Catawba Peoples," 188–196; Baker, "Colono-Indian Pottery from Cambridge, South Carolina, with Comments on the Historic Catawba Pottery Trade," Institute of Archeology and Anthropology, University of South Carolina, *Notebook*, IV (1972), 3–30. Simms predicted its imminent demise ("Caloya," in *Wigwam*, 362–363). For contemporary accounts of its survival, see Moore, "Reminiscences," in Draper Mss., 14 VV 139; Edwards, "Last of the Catawbas," *Rock Hill Herald*, July 20, 1882; Furman, "South Carolina Indians," draft of a newspaper article (1895), Furman Papers, South Caroliniana Library; Scaife, *Catawba Indians*, 19; Dunlap to Furman, Apr. 2, 1897, Oct. 20, 1898, Aug. 31, 1899, Furman Papers, Duke University; "Catawba Indians at Gastonia," *Rock Hill Herald*, Aug. 15, 1905; M. R. Harrington, "Catawba Potters and Their Work," *Am. Anthro.*, N.S., X (1908), 399–407; "A Day with the Catawbas," *Rock Hill Herald*, May 1, 1909; S. W. Pennypacker, "A Note on Catawba Ceramics," *Pennsylvania Archaeologist*, VII (1937), 55–56; Vladimir J. Fewkes, "Catawba Pottery-Making, with Notes on Pamunkey Pottery-Making, Cherokee Pottery-Making, and Coiling," APS, *Procs.*, LXXXVIII (1944), 69–124.

150. For the sites, see Ward, *Children of Hagler*, 4; Fewkes, "Catawba Pottery-Making," APS, *Procs.*, LXXXVIII (1944), 73 n. 7. For taboos, see Pennypacker, "Catawba Ceramics," *Pa. Archaeologist*, VII (1937), 55. For the molds and stones, see Fewkes, "Catawba Pottery-Making," APS, *Procs.*, LXXXVIII (1944), 81, 87, and figs. 1, 8, 25, 29 (my assessment of the potter's craft and its conservatism relies heavily on this work, 71–97, 107–110).

151. Fewkes, "Catawba Pottery-Making," APS, *Procs.*, LXXXVIII (1944), 83, 84, and figs. 20, 21; Speck, *Catawba Hunting*, 5, 9; Speck, *Catawba Texts*, 21–22 (tale), 64–65 (dance), 61 (cure), 73 (tanning). The term "aboriginalist" is Speck's (*Catawba Hunting*, 5). For his disappointment, see Merrell, "Reassessment of Speck," APS, *Procs.*, CXXVII (1983), 248–249; Speck, "Catawba Religious Beliefs," *Primitive Man*, XII (1939), 21–23, 41–42. Frank Siebert (personal communication) disputes Speck's translation of "buffalo," arguing that it is a precontact term.

152. For another view that argues for the attention paid Catawbas in recent times, see Hudson, *Catawba Nation*, chap. 6.

The most prominent displays of villages are at the Town Creek site and in the Schiele Museum of Natural History in Gastonia, North Carolina. At the latter there is a clear effort to show changes over time, from precontact to the mid-19th century.

153. For the profusion of relics, see Jethro Rumple, *A History of Rowan County, North Carolina, Containing Sketches of Prominent Families and Distinguished Men* (Salisbury, N.C., 1881), 35–36, 38; Rights, "Traces of the Indian," *NCHR*, I (1924), 277–288; Ardrey, "Catawba Indians," *Am. Antiquarian*, XVI (1894), 269. For the store display, see *Camden Journal*, Dec. 14, 1850, quoted in George Edwin Stuart, "The Post-Archaic Occupation of Central South Carolina" (Ph.D. diss., University of North Carolina, 1975), 64. For towns, see Smyth, *Tour*, I, 253; Pace, trans. and ed., *Castiglioni's Viaggio*, 151; Squier and Davis, *Ancient Monuments*, pl. 37, facing p. 105; maps of Catawba lands drawn by D. G. Stinson, 1874, in Draper Mss., 5 VV 45–46.

154. For Virginia mounds, see David I. Bushnell, Jr., "'The Indian Grave'—A

Monacan Site in Albermarle County, Virginia," *WMQ,* 1st Ser., XXIII (1914–1915), 106–112. For North Carolina, see Rumple, *History of Rowan County,* 35–36. For mounds in the Catawba area, see Mills, *Statistics of South Carolina,* 600–601; Edwards, "Last of the Catawbas," *Rock Hill Herald,* July 20, 1882; Squier and Davis, *Ancient Monuments,* 105–108. For an Indian burial ground near the Catawbas, see S. E. Belk to Draper, Feb. 13, 1874, Draper Mss., 15 VV 27, and map, p. 28.

155. Feltman, "Diary," *Pa. Arch.,* 2d Ser., XI, 743; James Kershaw, Diary, vol. III, entry for Jan. 18, 1796, South Caroliniana Library. Lucy Carpenter to William Blanding, Apr. 12, 1849, William Blanding Papers, Correspondence, South Caroliniana Library; for her eagerness to visit them, see also her letters of Jan. 23, Feb. 8, 23, Mar. 19, 1849. Blanding was "Mound Mad" himself; his map and letter on them had just been published in Squier and Davis, *Ancient Monuments,* pl. 37, 105–108.

156. Louise Moody and C. G. Holland, "Archeological Folklore in Piedmont Virginia," Archeological Society of Virginia, *Quarterly Bulletin,* XXIII (1968), 31–35; *Camden Gazette,* June 6, 1816. Some people asked Catawbas to tell them about the secrets of the mounds. See Squier and Davis, *Ancient Monuments,* 106; Scaife, *Catawba Indians,* 20.

157. Bushnell, "Indian Grave," *WMQ,* 1st Ser., XXIII (1914–1915), 110–112, quotation on 112. Moody and Holland cast doubt on these visits, but they fail to distinguish carefully stories that clearly have no basis in fact from others with at least some plausibility. They prove that some "burial mounds" contain no burials, though this does not preclude these from being sacred sites of some sort. They rely on 19th-century studies to argue that no piedmont peoples such as the Saponis or Tutelos remained in the region, but modern studies suggest remnants of detribalized groups are scattered through the area even today. For all the obvious embellishments in some accounts, they may contain a kernel of truth about Indians in the 19th century visiting piedmont sites, as Indians had in Jefferson's day. For more recent studies, see J. K. Dane and B. Eugene Griessman, "The Collective Identity of Marginal Peoples: The North Carolina Experience," *Am. Anthro.,* N.S., LXXIV (1972), 694–704; Brewton Berry, *Almost White* (New York, 1963), esp. map following p. 52.

158. Speck, *Catawba Texts,* 91. The quotation here combines Speck's "Free Translation" with his specific translations of the Catawba words Margaret Brown spoke.

159. Swanton, "Catawba Notes," *Jour. Wash. Acad. of Sci.,* VIII (1918), 628. See also Ward, *Children of Hagler,* 6. For an analysis of the current Catawba view, see Thomas J. Blumer, "Wild Indians and the Devil: The Contemporary Catawba Indian Spirit World," *American Indian Quarterly,* IX (1985), 149–168.

Epilogue

1. Washington to David Humphreys, July 20, 1791, quoted in Douglas Southall Freeman, *George Washington: A Biography,* VI, *Patriot and President* (New York, 1954), 321. He had already made a similar journey through the northern states (see 240–245, and map inside front cover).

2. Donald Jackson and Dorothy Twohig, eds., *The Diaries of George Washington,* 6 vols. (Charlottesville, Va., 1976–1979), VI, 99. The best accounts of this journey are from this volume of Washington's diary, pp. 96–163, and Archibald Henderson, *Washington's Southern Tour, 1791* (Boston, 1923).

3. Freeman, *Washington*, VI, 307, and map inside back cover; Jackson and Two-hig, eds., *Diaries of Washington*, VI, 96–98.

4. Jackson and Twohig, eds., *Diaries of Washington*, VI, 118, 127, 150; see also 127, 145, 147.

5. For the crowds in central Carolina, see Henderson, *Southern Tour*, 260, 284–285, 287–288. The editors of the *Diaries* also note the receptions, which were less than lavish only when the citizenry had little warning. See Jackson and Twohig, eds., *Diaries of Washington*, VI, 107, 114, 115.

6. Jackson and Twohig, eds., *Diaries of Washington*, VI, 146, 148. Henderson, *Southern Tour*, 262, 268, 269. Washington replied in kind (Henderson, *Southern Tour*, 265).

7. *Maryland Journal* (Baltimore), May 24, 1791, quoted in Jackson and Twohig, eds., *Diaries of Washington*, VI, 130; Freeman, *Washington*, VI, 315. Similar "hair-dress" was worn elsewhere; see Jackson and Twohig, eds., *Diaries of Washington*, VI, 125, 126, 138. For a vivid memory of these objects and of Washington's visit, see Charles Fraser, *Reminiscences of Charleston, Lately Published in the Charleston Courier, and Now Revised and Enlarged by the Author* (Charleston, S.C., 1854), 18–19.

8. The roster is derived from General Assembly, Petitions, 1792, no. 26, SCDAH. For New River as an imposing figure, see Winslow C. Watson, ed., *Men and Times of the Revolution; or, Memoirs of Elkanah Watson, Including Journals of Travels in Europe and America, from 1777 to 1842 . . .* (New York, 1856), 258.

9. Jackson and Twohig, eds., *Diaries of Washington*, VI, 149.

10. Washington to Humphreys, July 20, 1791, quoted in Freeman, *Washington*, VI, 321.

11. The term "State House" is Washington's. See Jackson and Twohig, eds., *Diaries of Washington*, VI, 146.

12. For examples of his earlier impressions, see above, chap. 4.

13. Washington to the Secretary of War, July 18, 1796, in John C. Fitzpatrick, ed., *The Writings of George Washington, from the Original Manuscript Sources, 1745–1799*, 39 vols. (Washington, D.C., 1931–1944), XXXV, 146–147.

14. Book of Remembrance, Samuel Thunderbird Blue Papers, box 1, Winthrop College Archives, Rock Hill, S.C.; H. Lewis Scaife, *History and Condition of the Catawba Indians of South Carolina* (Philadelphia, 1896), 21.

Index

Abortion, 140
Adair, James, 110, 119–121, 137, 189
Adamson, James, 190, 192
Adoption, 36–37, 140–141
Agents, Indian, 66, 190–191, 211–212, 223–224, 234, 236, 237, 244, 247, 248, 250–256
Agriculture: among coastal Indians, 14; among piedmont Indians, 16, 37; importance of, 130, 131; sexual roles in, 130, 267; crisis in, 138, 141; Indian and colonial, compared, 174, 175; on Catawba reservation, 230, 252–253
Alcohol: among piedmont Indians, 5, 39–40; and punishment, 39, 102, 158; and violence, 98, 185–186; control of supply of, 101, 186; and settlers, 179, 186; and Catawba decline, 227
Alliances: of Catawbas, 160–162, 208, 215–216. *See also other Indian groups*
American Revolution: and Catawbas, 215–217; effects of, 217–222
Amoroleck: 10, 12, 13, 18
Andros, Gov. Edmund, 101
Apalachees, 67, 72
Armstrong, James, 187
Atkin, Edmond: and Catawbas, 119, 135, 156, 197; on Indian-colonial relations, 162, 183, 189
Attitudes: of Europeans toward Indians, 11–12, 46–48, 80, 99–102, 143, 169–170, 183, 204, 214, 226–229, 247; of Indians toward Europeans, 13, 46, 143, 183
Augusta Indian Conference, 204–205
Ayers (family), 235
Ayers, Betsy, 234
Ayers, Billy, 253–254

Ayers, Captain, 204
Ayers, Colonel, 139, 182
Ayers, Jacob, 234, 235, 238, 239, 245, 248–249
Ayers, Jesse, 231, 248–249
Ayers, John, 234, 239, 248–249
Ayers, Sally, 233

Bacon, Nathaniel, 40
Banister, John, 46, 91
Barker, Thomas, 76
Barker's Savannah, 76
Barnwell, John, 54, 69, 70
Barton, Benjamin Smith, 228
Baskets, 34, 210
Beale, Othniel, 203
Bearskin, Ned, 131–133
Blue, Samuel, 259–261
Boone, Gov. Thomas, 152, 203, 204
Bows and arrows, 33, 34, 38–39, 245, 267
Brown, Billy (Catawba), 234
Brown, Billy (mixed-blood), 123
Brown, John, 237
Brown, John Genet, 248
Brown, Margaret Wiley, 258–259, 261, 264, 265, 274
Brown, Patrick, 137
Brown, Thomas (headman), 248
Brown, Thomas (trader), 86–87, 137, 148, 154; and trade, 85, 104, 122, 129, 137, 168
Bull, Lt. Gov. William, 145, 148–149
Bull, Lt. Gov. William, II, 198, 205–207
Bullen, James (Spanau), 123, 139, 151
Burial mounds. *See* Mounds, Indian
Burial practices: among piedmont Indians, 16–17, 22–23, 25, 33, 42,

373